Destiny's Landfall

Destiny's

Landfall

A HISTORY OF GUAM

ROBERT F. ROGERS

 UNIVERSITY OF HAWAI'I PRESS, HONOLULU

13 12 11 10 09 08   11 10 9 8 7 6

Library of Congress Cataloging-in-Publication Data
Rogers, Robert F.
   Destiny's landfall: a history of Guam / Robert F. Rogers.
   p.   cm.
   Includes bibliographical references (p.) and index.
   ISBN 978-0-8248-1678-0 (pbk. : alk. paper)
   1.Guam—History.   I.Title.
DU647.R63   1995
996.7—dc20   94–25845
                                                            CIP

University of Hawai'i Press books are printed on acid-free
paper and meet the guidelines for permanence and
durability of the Council on Library Resources

Designed by Kenneth Miyamoto

www.uhpress.hawaii.edu

Contents

Maps and Tables

Illustrations

Acknowledgments

This book is intended primarily for students in undergraduate college courses in the history and governments of the Pacific region. The book was researched, written, and published independently of any Guam governmental, foundation, or business involvement, and at no cost to any Guam taxpayer through grants or funding other than the author's salary as a full-time teacher at the University of Guam. The following experts and friends graciously reviewed chapters or contributed material and insights to improve the book's accuracy; their help was invaluable:

Dirk A. Ballendorf
Paul J. Bordallo
Omaira Brunel-Perry
Oscar L. Calvo
Bruce Campbell
Curt Coe
Ulla-Katrina Craig
Theodore M. Critchfield
Lawrence J. Cunningham
Marjorie G. Driver
Don A. Farrell
Harry A. Gailey
Catherine S. Gault
John N. Holbrook
Francis X. Hezel
Rosalind L. Hunter-Anderson
Bruce G. Karolle

Frank H. Kilmer
Frank P. King
Hiro Kurashina
Juan M. H. Ledesma
Arnold H. Leibowitz
Rodrique Lévesque
Thomas B. McGrath
Gail S. Mullen
Joe Murphy
Kathleen R. Owings
Antonio M. Palomo
Florentino Rodao
Carlos P. Taitano
Charles H. Troutman
William L. Wuerch
Richard H. Wyttenbach

I am deeply grateful to Lois Perez for word processing the text of the book innumerable times, to Pramila Sullivan for deciphering the nerdish intricacies of the DOS computer system for me, and to the following staff of the Micronesian Area Research Center for their unfailing courtesy and help: Emilie G. Johnston, John P. Sablan, Elaine Concepcion, Rosita A. Hatfield, Rose Tosco, La Vonne Guerrero-Meno, Cecilia L. Salvatore, and Douglas E. Haynes. The maps, unless otherwise noted, were crafted by Philip A. Noble of Talisai Studio & Gallery, Guam.

The past is never dead.
It is not even past.

WILLIAM FAULKNER

Time out of mind is time nevertheless,
cumulative, informing the present.

ANNIE DILLARD

Prologue

Center of the First Province

Guam became the first inhabited island in the Pacific Ocean known to Europeans when Ferdinand Magellan stepped ashore there in the year 1521. Magellan's fateful landfall not only opened the age of European exploration of the Pacific; it also led inexorably to foreign domination of every traditional island society throughout that immense third of the earth's surface now called Oceania. During the historical transformation of the Pacific world in the centuries since Magellan, little Guam—only thirty miles long and 214 square miles in area—has played a strategic role far more significant than islands much larger, much less isolated, and much better known.

The significance of Guam for the rest of the world is due to its topography and the importance of its location to major maritime powers in the Pacific. In other words, Guam is important because of the enduring imperatives of geopolitics, an enormous and underestimated force in the histories of small, strategically located islands, straits, and canals.

The island of Guam is the largest and most heavily populated of the Mariana Islands. The Marianas are fifteen high volcanic islands that form a north-south archipelago nearly 500 miles long that lies mostly in the tropics about 1,500 miles east of the Philippine Islands. The main islands—Guam, Rota, Tinian, and Saipan—lie in the southern end of the chain and have two climatic seasons: one dry from January to about June, the other wet from June to January. Guam receives nearly 100 inches of rain annually. The wet season produces a high incidence of tropical cyclonic storms, the most powerful of which are typhoons with sustained winds higher than 74 miles per hour.

As the southernmost island, Guam sits almost dead center in the huge expanse of the western Pacific north of the equator. About half that area is considered the ethnographically distinct region of Micronesia, for which Guam serves as the commercial and military hub. Micronesia is one of the three great cultural regions—along with Polynesia and Melanesia—of Oceania, which in the past Europeans often referred to as the "South Seas" or the "South Pacific." In 1817, the Russian explorer Otto von Kotzebue appropriately called Micronesia the "First Province of the Great Ocean."

Within that province on the great circle axis that crosses 5,000 miles of the Pacific between Hawai'i and the Philippines, Guam is not only the largest but also the only high island with a protected major harbor and sufficient land for several airports. Similarly, on the nearly 3,000-mile north-south axis from Japan to Papua New Guinea, Guam again is the largest and most useful landfall for communications, shipping, and military bases. In fact, Guam alone constitutes 20 percent of the entire dry land area of the 1,045 square miles of all the islands of Micronesia together.

The Marianas also lie astride the northeast trade winds and the north equatorial ocean current that flows westward across the Pacific above the doldrums of the intertropical convergence zone along the equator. It was Magellan's genius to find the northeast trades when they blow strongest from January through March. The winds and the current carried him straight to the Marianas. Ever since then, ships have used the same winds, the same current, and the same islands to cross the Pacific from east to west above the equator.

Although Guam has served commercial maritime interests as a valuable communications and supply point, the postcontact history of the island has been—and continues to be—determined primarily by strategic political and military factors beyond the control or even the significant influence of the local people. Guam, in short, was destined after Magellan to be a pawn in the realpolitik of foreign powers. As a consequence, outside military forces have occupied the island uninterruptedly for the incredible span of over 320 years.

Moreover, Guam's postcontact history has not been one of successive and merging phases like waves falling on coral-ringed shores, as have the histories of many other Pacific islands. Rather, the island's development was shaped by sporadic and violent invasions by alien forces. These intrusions were largely indifferent to the complex adaptations evolved by humans and other living beings for survival in the Pacific island environments in the centuries prior to European contact. The indigenous Chamorro people of Guam, small in numbers and vulnerable geographically, adapted to the harsh new conditions imposed by each wave of conquerors and, in a remarkable feat of cultural endurance, managed to maintain their language, their identity, and their pride under the colonial domination of three of history's most powerful nation-states: Spain, Japan, and the United States of America.

Now, in the late twentieth century, American-ized, modern, and multiethnic, and still one of the world's last colonies, Guam continues to fulfill the geopolitical role imposed on it by outsiders over four centuries ago. In place of Spanish galleons, Guam now serves international airlines, nuclear-powered submarines, space satellites, and all the other creations of modern humans that follow for good or bad in Magellan's momentous wake.

All this, however, was in the future as Magellan approached Guam in the month of March in the year 1521. This resourceful Portuguese captain, frustrated in service to his own king, had been sent in 1519 by Charles V, emperor of the Holy Roman Empire and king of Spain (as Charles I), to find the five Spice Islands of the Moluccas by sailing south around and then westward beyond the still-mysterious New World found by Columbus only twenty-seven years earlier. Charles V wanted the sources of precious cloves and other spices for Spain before Portugal could claim them in the two kingdoms' violent rivalry for empire. By 1519, the Portuguese had already pushed around Africa and across the Indian Ocean and were penetrating the Moluccas by sailing eastward.

Magellan successfully dodged Portuguese fleets hunting him in the Atlantic, and, in late 1520, he threaded the dangerous straits that would bear his name on the southern tip of the New World. Then he struck out boldly into the unknown Pacific Ocean with three sun-cracked and poorly provisioned ships: the *Trinidad* (or *Trinidada*), the *Concepción,* and the *Victoria* (or *Vittoria*). The flotilla sailed northwest into the Pacific from the Straits of Magellan. Magellan knew from experience in the Atlantic Ocean that trade winds blow steadily in a band above the 12°N latitude. He may have sought similar winds above the equator in the Pacific in order to traverse above the southern latitudes, where he knew the hostile Portuguese lurked in the East Indies. When the Spanish vessels were above the equator and into the northeast trade winds, Magellan turned west. By 5 March, they had been sailing for over three months since departing South America. No inhabited islands were found, only a

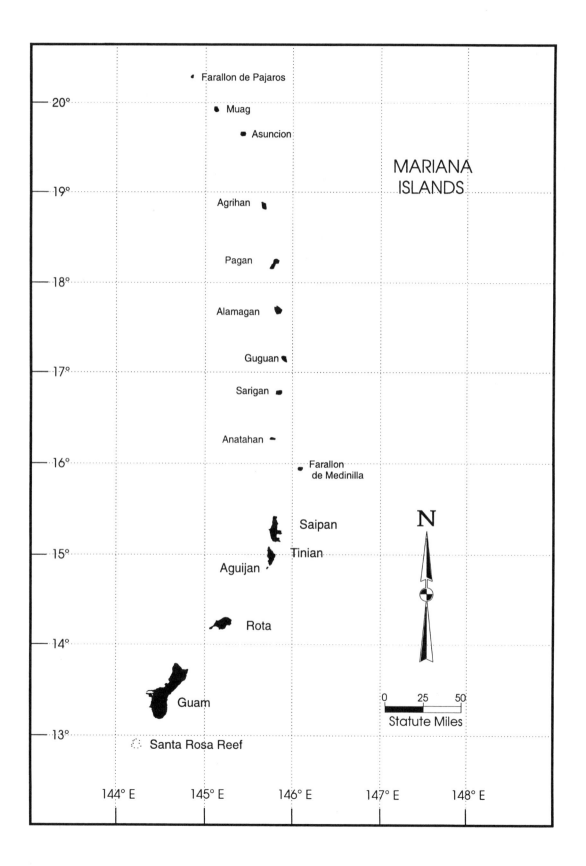

Farallon de Pajaros

Muag

Asuncion

MARIANA
ISLANDS

Agrihan

Pagan

Alamagan

Guguan

Sarigan

Anatahan

Farallon
de Medinilla

Saipan

N

Tinian

Aguijan

Rota

Guam

0   25   50

Statute Miles

Santa Rosa Reef

20°
19°
18°
17°
16°
15°
14°
13°

144° E   145° E   146° E   147° E   148° E

few silent palm-covered islets in an otherwise empty and endless ocean.

It was the dry season in the tropics, and rain rarely fell to replenish the near-empty water casks. The crews had not yet learned to troll for the easily-caught dolphin fish (*dorado* in Spanish, *mahimahi* in Hawaiian, and *Coryphaena hippurus* to marine biologists). These delicious gilded fish are plentiful in the Pacific in that season. Instead, Magellan and his crews ate rats, sawdust, and ox-hide rigging. Men began to sicken and die from a combination of thirst, semistarvation, and scurvy.

Nevertheless, the tattered little flotilla groped resolutely on across the great mother ocean of the world into longitudes beyond any known to Europeans at the time. These longitudes would soon unveil to them the Philippines. Before reaching the Philippines, however, Magellan's flotilla would first land on Guam. If fate is preordained but destiny is not, then much of humankind's loss of innocence on this island called earth is mirrored in the often tragic history of the island of Guam since Magellan's landfall. This is the story of that special island, a small green oasis in the vast blue reaches of the Pacific Ocean. The purpose in telling this story is to reconcile human culture with historical event in an account of a specific colonial experience, an experience not yet ended.

1

Aliens
1521–1638

First Intrusion

On Wednesday, 6 March 1521, as the sun began to rise over the western Pacific Ocean, a tired and hungry seaman on the dawn watch of Magellan's flagship *Trinidad* saw a broad, bluish hump slowly materialize out of the dark haze on the northwestern horizon off the ship's starboard bow. Then a smaller dark bump loomed above the rim of the sea just to the south of the first shape. The seaman, who was in the ship's crow's nest nearly sixty feet above water level, waited anxiously, staring hard to make sure that the shapes were not clouds. Convinced the humps were land, the lookout finally raised the cry that would reverberate down through history, "¡Tierra! ¡Tierra!"

Below him on the main deck, the mixed crew of Spaniards, Basques, Italians, Portuguese, Frenchmen, Greeks, and even an Englishman scrambled to the starboard rail, some thanking God, others laughing through gums swollen and cracked by scurvy. Aft on the high poop deck, Captain General Ferdinand Magellan, a lame, heavily bearded, and implacably determined man, limped to the rail and squinted at the horizon to the northwest. Quickly several men gathered beside him; they were his officers and pilots and one extroverted young Italian nobleman, Antonio Pigafetta, who was personal gentleman-in-waiting to Magellan and unofficial chronicler of the voyage. The men on the decks of the ships could see two mesa-like shapes, one small, the other quite large, approximately twenty miles off their starboard bows, but the low peninsula that connected the shapes remained hidden below the horizon, so the land to the northwest looked like two islands to everyone on the decks.

Suddenly, the *Trinidad's* lookout yelled again and pointed to the southwest. There an oblong shoreline of cliffs glistened low on the sunlit horizon about twenty miles off the port bow of the *Trinidad*. Although not as high as the first land sighted, the island to the southwest was broader.

Magellan studied the islands with the sharp eyes of an experienced master seaman as the trade winds rose briskly behind his ships in the tropical sun's heat. The daytime winds pushed his three small square-rigged *naos* (which would evolve into galleons; *naos* derived from carracks used in Mediterranean trade) up to eight knots per hour in the heavy white-capped swells of the Pacific Ocean. Sails had not been reset for weeks because of the reliable winds out of the northeast, *brisas* to the Spaniards, and because of the weak state of the crews. The *brisas* and the north equatorial current had kept the flotilla steady on a westward course along the 14°N latitude. After sighting land, Magellan did not immediately alter course; the flotilla sailed on for

5

another hour or two until the ships were between the islands.

The larger island to the southwest was downwind. Magellan could see that it would be safer to land on its leeward, protected side than on the taller island to the northwest. One of the *Victoria's* pilots, a Greek from Rhodes named Francisco Albo, later wrote in his log, probably after talking to his ship's lookout, as was customary, "And on this day we saw land and we went to it, and there were two islands, which were not very large, and when we came between them we headed to the southwest, and we left one to the northwest." Although unknown to Magellan and his men, the island first sighted was Rota, which initially appears as two islands when seen from the southeast. The larger island to the southwest toward which they turned was Guam.

Years later in Europe, when Pigafetta wrote his vivid chronicle of Magellan's voyage, he recalled only the two peaks of Rota and the one island of Guam. He thus described that historic first landfall as three islands, not two, as Albo and other pilots recorded. Pigafetta also confused the directions of the islands in his text. These errors by Pigafetta, or by the scribes who copied and translated various versions of his chronicle, puzzled explorers and historians for centuries. They conjectured several alternative landfalls in the Marianas, such as Saipan, Tinian, and Rota, in order to conform to Pigafetta's account. Albo's log and the sparse accounts of Magellan's other pilots, notably that of an anonymous Genoese pilot confirming Albo's, give a more accurate nautical picture of the landfall on Guam than does Pigafetta's.

As Magellan's three ships sailed toward Guam, Albo wrote, "We saw many small sails which were coming to us." These were the remarkable Micronesian outrigger canoes called proas, each with a single triangular lateen sail. The proas nimbly darted around Magellan's clumsy ships as they neared Ritidian Point, Guam's northernmost tip. Pigafetta wrote that the proas were "like dolphins jumping from wave to wave."

The islanders in the proas were darkly tawny, stalwart men, according to Pigafetta. They stood taller than the Spaniards, had straight black hair, and were completely naked. Because the Spaniards were searching for the Indies in the early period of their explorations, they referred to all brown-skinned people by the term *indios* (Indians) when first encountered in the New World and in the Pacific and Asia. By the time Spain claimed Guam in 1565, the indigenous people of the Marianas would be called *Chamurres,* the Spanish version of the local term, *chamorri,* which is what the islanders called members of their high caste. The early Spanish sailors also interpreted *chamurre* to mean "friend." Eventually, the local people would be known variously as Marianos, Chamorris, and finally Chamorros after Father Diego Luís de San Vitores arrived to establish a Jesuit mission on Guam in 1668. The word *Chamorro* to describe the island's people is, therefore, apparently indigenous in origin as well as perhaps an adaptation of the old Spanish word *chamorro* for "bald" or "shorn" ("beardless" in Portuguese), which described some island men who wore only a topknot on an otherwise shaved head. No known records of Magellan's stay at Guam reported an indigenous name of the island, a curious omission for one of the most significant landfalls in human history.

About noon, as Magellan's flotilla passed Ritidian Point, the ships slowed to just a few knots speed when the wind dropped in the lee of the high cliffs along the island's northwest shore. From Ritidian, Magellan cruised cautiously in safe deep water outside low reefs marked by moderate surf. Inside the reefs along the entire coast lie shallow lagoons, each from about fifty to several hundred yards across and lined on shore by narrow, palm-fringed beaches. Behind the beaches are a series of flat enclaves a mile to several miles in width and up to a half mile deep. Each enclave ends against steep, jungle-clad slopes or rocky, reddish-grey cliffs that lead up to a limestone plateau. This broad, flat plateau forms the northern half of Guam.

Every enclave contains lush green coconut groves and freshwater springs or small streams that flow out of the limestone plateau above. Each enclave also held villages with numerous Chamorros in Magellan's time. Ahead, down Guam's northwest coast, Magellan could see a number of rocky points between more enclaves, and, in the distance about fifteen miles away, a large point of land—now Orote Peninsula—juts out nearly five miles due west. Mountains, green with grass-covered summits and heavy jungle on their lower slopes, rise in the south beyond Orote Peninsula.

Hungry, thirsty, and surrounded by proas with Chamorros full of curiosity beginning to clamber up the sides of the ships, Magellan and his crews were without doubt eager to anchor as quickly as possible to take on water and provisions. It is unlikely that they would have wandered on for another six to eight hours around Orote Peninsula to reach the bay of Umatac on the southwestern coast after nightfall. Later oral tradition among the Chamorros claimed that Magellan landed at Umatac, but this tradition may have derived from the next landing by Europeans, that of Miguel López de Legazpi forty-four years later in 1565 at Umatac, when he stayed for thirteen days, and from the subsequent numerous stops of the Acapulco galleons at Umatac. By late afternoon on 6 March, Magellan's flotilla was probably off Tumon Bay or Agana Bay, which present calm water and low reefs. Large villages on these bays indicated to the thirsty Spaniards that fresh water was available and that they need not go farther. By this time, Chamorros were swarming over the ships and carrying away anything loose. Magellan ordered his men to clear the boarders from the ships. The Europeans, too weak to manhandle the sturdy Chamorros, started firing crossbows.

The Chamorros had never seen ordinary bows and arrows, much less the metal-backed crossbows. The cultural shock was deadly. Pigafetta relates that, when struck in the body by an arrow, the Chamorros "drew it forth with much astonishment, and immediately afterwards they died." The crossbows were sufficient to chase off the boarders. Some later historical accounts of the fighting say firearms were used, but neither Pigafetta nor other eyewitnesses report their use, so it appears that the Spaniards did not fire their arquebuses or muskets in this initial encounter.

In the fighting, the Chamorros deftly made off with the small rowboat towed behind the *Trinidad.* This skiff was important. The crew used it to sound depths with a weighted line ahead of the ship in unknown shallow waters. Angry at the theft and apprehensive of the numerous islanders as the sun began to set, Magellan had the ships tack offshore for the night without anchoring.

The next morning, according to the Genoese pilot's account, the ships returned and anchored just off the reef where the skiff had been taken. Each of Magellan's ships carried a *fragate,* a kind of launch or pinnance, on deck along with a skiff. A *fragate* held up to twenty armed men who could easily row the launch through the surf over the reef of Tumon or Agana in a medium or high tide in March. The crews lowered two *fragates* for Magellan and a party of about forty men in armor to go ashore and recover the skiff.

So it was that the first Europeans to land on an inhabited island in the Pacific Ocean stepped ashore on a beach along Guam's northwest coast on Thursday morning, 7 March 1521. The newcomers were hostile and intent on imposing their will on the local people. Magellan's men proceeded to burn forty to fifty huts and several proas. They killed eight Chamorros who resisted, and retrieved the skiff. The Spaniards suffered no casualties.

Despite the violence of that first encounter, some Chamorros apparently continued the next day to exchange food for Spanish goods, particularly for anything of iron. Magellan's flotilla remained on Guam three days. During that time, Pigafetta and others visited the villages, judging by the brief but detailed description of the Chamorros in Pigafetta's chronicle. The Chamorros impressed Pigafetta as "ingenious and great thieves." Communication was only by sign language; none of the eyewitnesses indicate that the expedition's interpreter, Enrique (a Malay from Malacca or perhaps a Cebuan who was Magellan's slave), or anyone else in the crews could speak the Chamorro language.

The Europeans were unaware of a traditional

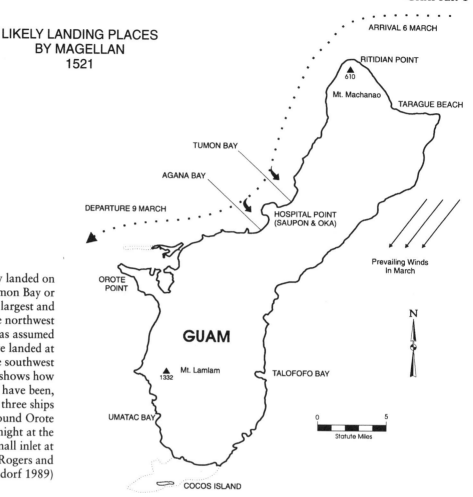

LIKELY LANDING PLACES
BY MAGELLAN
1521

ARRIVAL 6 MARCH

RITIDIAN POINT

610

Mt. Machanao

TARAGUE BEACH

TUMON BAY

AGANA BAY

DEPARTURE 9 MARCH

HOSPITAL POINT
(SAUPON & OKA)

Prevailing Winds
In March

OROTE
POINT

N

GUAM

Mt. Lamlam
1332

TALOFOFO BAY

UMATAC BAY

0   5

Statute Miles

COCOS ISLAND

Magellan probably landed on Guam at either Tumon Bay or Agana Bay, the two largest and calmest inlets on the northwest coast. For years, it was assumed Magellan may have landed at Umatac Bay on the southwest coast, but the map shows how unlikely that would have been, requiring Magellan's three ships to sail all the way around Orote Point to land at night at the unknown (to him) small inlet at Umatac. (Rogers and Ballendorf 1989)

custom among many Pacific islanders whereby new arrivals on an island present gifts to their hosts, who can take whatever they wish from the newcomers. The Chamorros, a communal people, also did not share the European's concept of individual items as private possessions not to be taken without the permission of the owner. Pigafetta noted that the Chamorros "have no lord or superior" and were not awed by the Europeans, perhaps because the latter appeared weak and bedraggled after their harrowing trans-Pacific voyage.

One result of the episode of the stolen skiff was that Magellan named the islands the Islas de los Ladrones (Islands of the Thieves). This misnomer clung to the archipelago for three centuries despite the later name change to the Mariana Islands by Father Diego Luís de San Vitores in 1668, in honor of Mariana of Austria, the Spanish queen regent who funded a Catholic mission in the islands. To add to the confusion over names, the islands were also initially called the Islands of Lateen Sails by Magellan and continued to be so titled by some later voyagers and mapmakers.

On Saturday morning, 9 March, according to Albo, Magellan's ships set sail west by southwest

The first map of the Mariana Islands. The original was drawn in Europe between 1523 and 1527 for the chronicle written by Antonio Pigafetta about the Magellan voyage. This version was drawn for a copy of the chronicle in French. North is at the bottom, as was the custom of the time. The large island on top entitled *Isles des Larrons* (Islands of the Thieves) is Guam. The two islands at the bottom are actually one island, Rota, of which Pigafetta saw only two peaks beyond the horizon. This is also the first picture of a Chamorro proa. Note the crow's nest on the proa and the two crewmen in typically European clothes, inaccuracies that indicate the drawing was by a European artist from Pigafetta's descriptions. (From the collection of the Micronesian Area Research Center, Mangilao, Guam)

away from Guam. No other islands were seen until the flotilla reached the Philippines. Pigafetta noted that a hundred or more proas followed the Spanish flotilla for miles out to sea and the Chamorros held up fish as if to trade, hurling stones when the ships did not halt. With that bad omen, the first European contact with Pacific islanders ended.

The encounter set a precedent that became a tragic pattern in later Spanish-Chamorro relations. The great cultural differences in the values and behavior of the two sides led repeatedly to hostility and armed conflict. The Spaniards invariably won these clashes because of their disciplined military organization and their more advanced technology in metal, arms, and ships.

*　　　*　　　*

Magellan's expedition sailed away to the Philippines and to the captain general's death in battle at Mactan on 26 April 1521. Subsequently, the *Concepción* was burned at Bohol Island because of insufficient men to crew all three ships. The remaining two ships wandered southward to reach Tidore, one of the five Spice Islands, in November 1521, where cargos of cloves were obtained. The *Trinidad* by then was leaking so badly it had to have a major overhaul. The sturdy little *Victoria* would continue westward under Captain Juan Sebastián de Elcano with Pigafetta and Albo still aboard. It departed Tidore in December 1521 and arrived in San Lúcar de Barrameda, Seville's ocean port at the mouth of the Guadalquivir River, on 8 September 1522, after an agonizing voyage across the Indian Ocean and around Africa. Only eighteen men survived, including Enrique, Magellan's slave, but the globe finally encompassed became a globe reduced forever after that epic first circumnavigation of planet Earth.

Back on Tidore, the *Trinidad* took until April 1522 to be repaired. Captain Gonzalo Gómez de Espinosa, with a small cargo of cloves, then attempted to return eastward back across the Pacific with the *Trinidad* to reach Darien in Panama, where Vasco Núñez de Balboa earlier had established Spanish settlements. This course meant that the *Trinidad* sailed against the *brisas* of the northeast trade winds, which proved impossible. The ship struggled against the northeast winds up to the northern arc of the Mariana Islands, reaching on 11 June an island at 18°44′N latitude. The Spaniards named the island Cyco or La Griega, now known as Agrihan. The Chamorros on Agrihan behaved so aggressively that Espinosa could not anchor, but, in a normal European tactic, he kidnapped one of them to augment his crew and provide information.

Beating on against the wind, the *Trinidad* reached approximately 42°N in the temperate zone, where a storm battered the ship for five days. With the *Trinidad*'s sails in tatters, the Spaniards were forced to turn back and soon anchored inside a ring of three small islands at about 20°N latitude. The Chamorro captive called the largest island, which

had only twenty Chamorro inhabitants, Mao or Pamo, according to the Genoese pilot who was aboard. From its description, the island was present-day Maug. The captive also apparently provided the Spaniards for the first time the Chamorro names for each of the Marianas, including Guahan for Guam. These names appeared on a Portuguese map in 1545, but the map was filed away or kept secret and forgotten until the twentieth century.

At Maug, the Chamorro captive was released, but three European crewmen deserted the jinxed *Trinidad*. One of these men was Gonzalo (Gregorio in some Spanish accounts) Alvarez de Vigo. Two of the deserters were killed by the Chamorros, but Gonzalo survived, the first of many Europeans to jump ship and become a beachcomber on the lovely isles of Micronesia. The Spaniards would later learn much about the Marianas when Gonzalo was retrieved on Guam in September 1526 by the next expedition to the Pacific, that of General Juan García Jofre de Loaysa.

Espinosa's information and Gonzalo de Vigo's later elaboration revealed the significance of the Marianas for the navigation of the eastward passage across the north Pacific. Pushed by the southwest monsoon in June and July, a ship on an eastnortheast course from the Philippines passes near the northern islands of the Marianas. Espinosa showed that these islands could serve as landfalls to take on provisions or as landmarks for voyages back to Mexico.

The *Trinidad* barely limped back to the Moluccas, where it was driven ashore and destroyed by a sudden squall at Ternate in the Spice Islands in October 1522. Eventually, only four of the *Trinidad*'s brave crew, including Espinosa and the pilot Ginés de Mafra, returned to Spain with information about their voyages. That information would be crucial in future Spanish probes into the Pacific.

Stepping Stone to the Philippines

After the *Victoria* with its meager but precious cargo of thirty tons of cloves and other spices docked at Seville in September 1522, the Spanish and the Portuguese kings immediately fell to arguing over which of them owned the spices and the right of access to the Moluccas. The Spaniards parried Portuguese claims based on the Treaty of Tordesillas of 1494, which divided Columbus' New World in the Americas between the two kingdoms on a line drawn by Pope Alexander VI in a papal bull in 1493. The problem was that it was unclear from the treaty where the pope's line of demarcation, the forty-sixth meridian, fell on the other side of the globe among the Molucca Islands in an area that today is part of Indonesia. Within the Moluccas lie the five small Spice Islands so avidly sought by the Europeans in the sixteenth century.

Both kingdoms secretly prepared new expeditions to seize the Moluccas while they negotiated. The Portuguese approach was eastward from bases in Africa across the Indian Ocean to a forward base in Malacca on the Malay Peninsula and then to the Spice Islands. The initial Spanish approach was westward across the Atlantic and south around South America and then westward again across the Pacific to the Moluccas on the route opened by Magellan.

In July 1525, Emperor Charles V sent out a fleet of seven ships from Spain under Juan García Jofre de Loaysa bound for the Moluccas with two charts of Magellan's route. Elcano was second in command. Both men died on the voyage in the mid-Pacific, and Toribio Alonso de Salazar became captain in the passage through Micronesia. Only Loaysa's flagship, the *Santa María de la Victoria*, reached Guam on 4 September 1526, after a terrible journey during which forty men on the ship died.

The *Victoria* approached the eastern, windward side of the island. Because of the rough surf and wind on that side, it took the Spaniards two days to anchor in exceedingly deep water, probably off one of Guam's small windward inlets now known as Pago, Ylig, and Talofofo. As the Spaniards sought to anchor, Chamorros approached in proas. One man in a proa astounded the Spaniards by welcoming them in fluent Spanish. It was Gonzalo de Vigo, who had deserted the *Trinidad* at Maug in the northern Marianas four years earlier. He had made

his way south to Guam and now joined the crew of the *Victoria*. Apparently pardoned for his desertion, he provided the information about the Marianas that later appeared on the 1544 map of Sebastián Cabot. The map showed the southernmost island—Guam—as Baham.

The *Victoria* departed Guam on 10 September. Before departing, Alonso de Salazar kidnapped eleven Chamorro men to work the water pumps on his leaky ship. The expedition next touched at Mindanao before reaching Tidore in the Spice Islands in October 1526. There they were attacked by the Portuguese. The *Victoria* was burned, and the survivors holed up in a fort at Tidore to await rescue by a new Spanish expedition.

In the meantime, the politics of empire building had changed substantially after Hernán Cortés crushed the Aztecs in 1521 and established New Spain in Mexico. By 1522, Cortés was constructing ships on Mexico's west coast at the village of Zacatula and was proposing expeditions north and south along the Pacific Coast. In 1526, however, Charles V ordered Cortés to send a third Spanish probe into the Pacific to search for Magellan's lost *Trinidad* and for the missing Loaysa, this time from Mexico's west coast to the Moluccas via Guam. Three ships constructed at Zacatula left the nearby harbor of Zihuatanejo on All Soul's Day in 1527 under the command of Álvaro de Saavedra Cerón in the leaky flagship *Florida*. They sailed for Guam but drifted south of Magellan's route. Only the *Florida* reached Guam. The other ships disappeared, probably wrecked on the dangerous atolls of what would later be called the Marshall Islands.

Saavedra, like Loaysa, approached the Marianas further south than Magellan and sighted the eastern side of Guam on 29 December 1527. He could not anchor and laid off the island to take on provisions from Chamorros in proas. Saavedra then went on to land temporarily on Mindanao before finally making the Spice Islands, where he died in 1529. The ship and crew were eventually seized by the Portuguese, who by then were consolidating their control over all the Moluccas.

Neither the Loaysa expedition nor that of Saavedra accomplished its mission. The Spanish goals were to trade for spices, spread the faith, rescue survivors of the preceding Spanish probes, and establish, if possible, Spanish authority in the Spice Islands. Instead, by 1528 the Portuguese dominated the Moluccan spice trade and held prisoners from all three initial Spanish expeditions into the Pacific.

These earliest European seafarers in the far Pacific and those who followed them in the next century were tough and courageous men who served their nations well in the face of incredible hardships and constant danger. Usually poor and trained as warriors, they came "to serve God and the King, and also to get rich," in the blunt words of Bernal Díaz del Castillo, who fought under Cortés in Mexico. If they survived, they would go home wealthy and powerful. Should they die, they had the firm consolation of dying in the faith with hope of salvation.

Not all Spaniards at the time accepted this ruthless culture of conquest. The most famous critic, Father Bartolomé de Las Casas, a Spanish Dominican, preached and wrote for many years until his death in 1566 in protest against Spain's treatment of Indians. Another Dominican, Francisco de Vitoria (1486–1546), a well-known professor of theology at the University of Salamanca in Spain whose work represented an early formulation of what would become international law, wrote that *indios* had rights under "the rules of international law...[and] they who violate these international rules, whether in peace or in war, commit a mortal sin."

The king of Spain, however, was more concerned with geopolitics than with the state of his soul. Frustrated by the failure of his Pacific efforts, and preoccupied with European imperial politics, Charles V signed the Treaty of Zaragoza in 1529 with King John III of Portugal. The agreement defined the pope's line of demarcation in the Moluccas in favor of Portugal. Charles V renounced all Spanish claims to the Spice Islands and to most of the remainder of Indonesia. In return, he received from the Portuguese 350,000 gold ducats and, as it would turn out, enough of

the western Pacific for Spain later to claim the Philippines and the islands of Micronesia, including Guam.

There was a pause in Spanish efforts in the Pacific between the Treaty of Zaragoza in 1529 and the next official probe westward in 1542 by Ruy López de Villalobos on a large expedition of six ships constructed in Mexico. Instead of stopping on Guam, he stumbled across several more southerly island groups in Micronesia, probably the Marshalls, Fais, and Yap. The expedition disintegrated in the Philippines and the Moluccas, and the remnants of the crews were captured in 1545 by the alert Portuguese in Tidore. López de Villalobos died in Ambon in 1546.

Villalobos, however, accomplished one thing of note: he named the Philippine Islands (they were formerly called the Islands of the West by the Spaniards). Villalobos formally named them Filipinas in honor of the royal heir who would become Felipe (Philip) II, king from 1556 to 1598 during the high tide of Spain's imperial power. Members of the Villalobos expedition who made it back to Spain reported the name, which appeared on a map by Abraham Ortelius of Antwerp in 1589. After Villalobos' failure, the Spanish authorities waited two decades before trying again to cross the Pacific. During that time, the prices of cloves and other spices, particularly pepper, rose to new heights. The supply of spices was still short of demand in Europe, and the Portuguese still controlled the sources in the Moluccas. So, when Philip II became king, he decided to open his own source of spices in the Philippines. The Spaniards mistakenly thought cloves grew there. In fact, only a limited supply of cinnamon grew in Mindanao.

In 1559, Philip II ordered the second viceroy of New Spain to colonize the islands that bore the king's name and to establish a spice trade there. It took five years to construct the ships in Mexico and prepare the expedition. In November 1564, a little fleet of four square-rigged *naos* sailed from Puerto de la Navidad north of Acapulco under the command of Miguel López de Legazpi, a prosperous middle-aged landowner from Mexico City. With him on the flagship *San Pedro* as adviser-navigator was his friend and Basque kinsman, and by then a friar *(fray* in Spanish, sometimes translated as "brother") in the Augustinian Recollect religious order, Andrés de Urdaneta, who had sailed with Loaysa nearly forty years earlier. The other ships were the *San Pablo,* the *San Juan,* and the *San Lucas.*

The king's lengthy instructions to Legazpi with respect to the Mariana Islands specifically charged him to "select sites and locations for colonization . . . [but] not occupy or take possession of any private property of the Indians." The expedition was essentially New World in composition (i.e., mostly *criollos*—Spaniards born outside Spain), the first of many with little direct participation by Spaniards born in Spain *(peninsulares* or *gachupines)*. Mestizos (people of Spanish and Indian blood) and mulattoes (people of Negro and Spanish or other blood) were recruited, but pure-blooded New World Indians were not because they were considered by the Spaniards as unreliable at that time. Unlike earlier Spanish expeditions in the Pacific, Legazpi's fleet was well provisioned and had little trouble in crossing the Pacific.

During the passage to Guam, one ship—the *San Lucas*—under the command of Alonso de Arellano, deserted the fleet, although he later claimed to have been lost. The *San Lucas* missed Guam but stopped at Truk and Pulap in the Caroline Islands before reaching the Philippines. Arellano then turned back, sailed north of the Marianas, and crossed the northern Pacific to land at Mexico in August 1565 ahead of Legazpi's return ship. The *San Lucas* was therefore the first ship to complete the round trip the galleons would later follow between Mexico and the Philippines.

While the *San Lucas* was off on its own, Legazpi's main contingent reached Guam on 21 January 1565. The three ships approached Guam from a more southeasterly direction than had Magellan and sailed around the tiny island of Cocos, "full of palm trees," on Guam's southwestern tip after sunset. The ships tacked off the strange shore during the night and prepared to anchor the next morning, 22 January 1565.

No one on board was quite sure if the island was Guam or one of the Philippines. Urdaneta and Legazpi's chief pilot, Esteban Rodríguez, in all likelihood knew of Umatac Bay from information furnished by Gonzalo de Vigo. Urdaneta believed the landfall to be Guam. Sunrise revealed to the Spaniards a lovely little bay, free of barrier reefs and nestled between high grassy ridges along a small river that leads back several miles into a deep jungle-filled valley. They could see a large canoe house and some huts near the rocky little estuary of the river outlet. Umatac Bay is only a quarter of a mile wide at the entrance and a third of a mile deep, so Legazpi's larger two ships, and later Spanish galleons, anchored just outside the bay.

Meanwhile, over 400 Chamorro proas collected about the alien ships, according to the accounts of the voyage. From one of the proas an old man called out, "Gonzalo, Gonzalo." The Chamorro remembered the name of Gonzalo de Vigo, which confirmed to Urdaneta that they were on Guam. Hernando de Riquel, the expedition's official notary, described in his account of the voyage how the Chamorros began to trade briskly with the Spaniards, who soon learned to be wary. After a deal was struck by sign language, the wily Chamorros would ask that the agreed payment in the form of iron items, mainly nails, be lowered down from the ships. Then they sent up baskets and large calabashes with some rice and many fruits.

The Spaniards soon found that, below the first layer of produce, the bottoms of the baskets were filled with sand and stones. The Chamorros also offered gourds filled with coconut oil, but below the oil, which floated on the surface, was seawater. The Chamorros merely laughed when caught; their view was that of "buyer beware" in trading. They clearly were in no more awe of Legazpi's men than they had been of Magellan's.

As with Magellan, the Chamorros made off with a ship's skiff, but this time the theft did not provoke a fight. Over the next few days skirmishes broke out repeatedly between Spanish soldiers and Chamorro warriors but were settled quickly as the Spaniards filled water casks and obtained provisions. Legazpi himself went ashore six days after his ships had anchored. Riquel described how Legazpi took a sword and cut branches of trees and "caused some crosses to be placed on treés, that is some coconut palms." An open-air mass was celebrated on the shore. Legazpi then formally claimed the islands in the name of Philip II of Spain. Riquel wrote out and notarized the official affirmation that Legazpi "occupied and took possession" of the island on 26 January 1565. In actuality, the Spaniards would neither "occupy" the islands nor take "possession" of them for another century, although all the European nations recognized Spain's claim to the islands. There was no consultation with the Chamorros, who were probably unaware of the meaning of the Spaniards' strange ceremonies.

The fights with Chamorro warriors became serious on 1 February, when a Spanish cabin boy was inadvertently left behind by a shore party. When the Spaniards heard shouts from shore and soldiers went back for the boy, they found him dead on the beach. He had been tied to a cross, stripped, killed by spears, his face skinned, and a stake driven into his mouth. Nearby a group of Chamorro warriors jeered at the angry Spaniards and waved the boy's clothes before being scattered by the soldiers. Meanwhile other Chamorros in proas continued trading with the Spaniards as if nothing was occurring. Calm indifference by some islanders alongside violent actions by others would be observed repeatedly in later years by visitors to Guam. This paradox may have been due to separate clans being involved simultaneously with the Spaniards, with each clan concerned only with its own affairs.

In retaliation for the cabin boy's death Legazpi sent his tough military commander, Captain Mateo de Saz, ashore the next day with soldiers to punish the Chamorros. Mateo set up an ambush near the deserted village and then set fire to the Chamorros' prized proas before simulating a return to the ships. When some Chamorro men hastily returned to put out the fires in their canoes, three were wounded

and one was captured unharmed by the soldiers hidden in ambush. Mateo promptly hanged the three wounded men from a tree near where the cabin boy was killed. As the soldiers were about to hang the fourth Chamorro, Spanish friars interceded and stopped the execution. In later years, Chamorros would often experience what was to them this curious contradiction in Spanish behavior: the vindictive cruelty of soldiers alongside the merciful forgiveness of the priests.

Following this tragic repetition of Magellan's scenario on Guam, Legazpi's ships weighed anchor the next morning, 3 February 1565, and departed to the west-southwest. Ten days later, they reached the Philippines, where Legazpi would succeed in establishing the first Spanish colony in Asia and the Pacific.

One of Legazpi's legacies in the Marianas was the first recorded use of names that were antecedents of what would evolve into the word *Guam*. Documents of the Legazpi expedition refer variously to *Goaam*, *Goam*, and *Guan* as the name of the island in the language of the Chamorros. By the early eighteenth century, the name had evolved into *Guana* and *Guahan*. In his authoritative 1806 history of early voyages in the Pacific, James Burney consistently used *Guahan* as the island's name. In the 1870s and 1880s, the Spanish governors used the similiar title *Guajan*. Finally, the Americans would officially designate the island as *Guam* in 1908, over 300 years after Legazpi's landfall.

Having set up a base at Cebú, one of Legazpi's most urgent tasks was to establish a return route to Mexico. On 1 June 1565, Legazpi sent the *San Pedro*, his fastest ship, back to Mexico from the Philippines with his seventeen-year-old grandson Felipe de Salcedo as captain, Urdaneta as adviser-pilot, and Esteban Rodríguez as pilot. Under Urdaneta's guidance, the *San Pedro* sailed on a northeast track until well above the Marianas at 39°N latitude. Then Urdaneta had the ship turn east across the north Pacific on about a Tokyo–San Francisco latitude, sailing 200 miles or more above the Hawaiian Islands.

Finally, on 18 September, over three months after departing Cebú, the *San Pedro* reached California and sailed south to arrive at Acapulco on 8 October 1565. Sixteen of the forty-four-man crew died en route, including Esteban Rodríguez, and four more died after arrival. One of these was a Chamorro, the first to reach the New World, sent by Legazpi with three Filipinos from Cebú. The Chamorro had apparently been abducted when Legazpi had claimed the Marianas nine months earlier. Urdaneta, however, had succeeded where Espinosa, Loaysa, Saavedra, Villalobos, and others had failed. The *San Pedro* delivered the first cargo of Asian products to Mexico by way of the Pacific.

Urdaneta returned to Spain to report to King Philip II on the Philippines venture and, collecting all the new navigational data on winds, courses, currents, and landmarks, put all such information on a map of the Pacific. This map, held secret for decades by the Spanish and updated periodically, standardized the galleon route as a great circular loop around the Pacific north of the equator. Urdaneta fixed the Marianas as a sure and useful landmark and stopover on the trans-Pacific trade route. The Hawaiian Islands, on the other hand, lie isolated by hundreds of empty miles near the center of the galleon loop around the Pacific and therefore remained unseen by Europeans for over 200 more years until the English explorer Captain James Cook found them in 1778.

The Chamorros' next experience with aliens was with the return ship from Mexico to resupply Legazpi's new Philippine outpost. The viceroy of New Spain in Mexico sent the *San Gerónimo* (or *San Jerónimo* in some accounts) under Pedro Sánchez Pericón on 1 May 1566 from Acapulco to carry soldiers, supplies, and ammunition to Legazpi, who was under attack by the Portuguese. Salcedo remained in Mexico to await Urdaneta's return from Spain and to prepare the *San Pedro* and *San Lucas* for return to the Philippines in 1567. The voyage of the *San Gerónimo* to the Philippines turned into a deadly melodrama of several murders, including that of Pericón, and the marooning of mutinous crew members in the Marshalls before

the ship reached Rota on 4 August 1566. On Rota, the undisciplined Spanish soldiers killed a number of Chamorros and burned numerous houses before the ship hastily departed to reach Cebú in October.

In August of the next year, Salcedo returned to the Philippines from Acapulco with the *San Pedro* and the *San Lucas* loaded with supplies, artillery, and soldiers to reinforce Legazpi at Cebú against the Portuguese. It is not known if Salcedo stopped at the Marianas on his way to Cebú from Acapulco. A year later, in June 1568, Legazpi dispatched back to Acapulco the *San Pablo* loaded with Chinese silk and porcelain and twenty tons of cinnamon, again under the command of Salcedo. Legazpi ordered the *San Pablo* to stop first at Guam to see if cloves or pepper grew on the island (they did not; only wild ginger was plentiful). At Guam, the *San Pablo* dragged anchor when a storm rose at night. The ship was smashed against a reef on 15 August 1568 at an unknown location. It was the first of many Spanish ships to be splintered on the coral reefs of the Mariana Islands.

Chamorros attacked the survivors but later treated them with kindness. The survivors saved a ship's launch and constructed a bark from the remains of the wrecked *San Pablo*. They then managed the remarkable feat of sailing with all the survivors, numbering 132 people, over 1,500 miles of open ocean back to the Philippines in the makeshift bark.

The persistent Salcedo set out again from the Philippines in July 1569 on the *San Lucas* and finally reached Mexico late that year. Thereafter, the trans-Pacific route for the galleons was an established fact in the empire of Spain. From the viewpoint of European colonial politics, the Pacific Ocean, except for the East Indies region, became a gigantic Spanish lake.

Galleons, Pirates, and Priests

By the time Legazpi died in 1572, the Spanish conquest of the Philippines was nearly complete. Legazpi made Manila the entrepôt of Spain's colony in Asia. Manila's role was to trade the New

World's silver, carried by the galleons from Acapulco, for luxuries brought to Manila by merchants from China and other exotic lands of the Orient. Few products of the Philippines themselves were shipped to Spain in the early decades of the galleon trade. More and more Chinese merchant fleets arrived by May each year in Manila with goods for the galleons. By 1596, there were 12,000 Chinese, called *Sangleyes* by the Spaniards, living in Manila. They became so intrusive that the Spaniards expelled them all that year. They would nonetheless drift back to become again a sizable minority in the Philippines.

Each year, in May or June, the accumulated oriental luxuries in the warehouses of Manila were crammed aboard the great fat galleons in Manila Bay for shipment over the long northern Pacific route to Acapulco and then across Mexico and the Atlantic to Spain. In the geopolitics of European colonialism, the safer alternative route from Manila to Spain southward through the Straits of Malacca, across the Indian Ocean, and around Africa was blocked to the Spaniards by Portuguese rights under the Treaties of Tordesillas and Zaragoza and then by the Dutch, who displaced the Portuguese.

The eastbound galleons, usually called *Naos de Manila* by the Spaniards, normally set sail from Cavite in Manila Bay with formal prayers and ceremony in June or July with the monsoon winds out of the southwest. The ponderous *naos* wallowed for five or more tedious but dangerous months across the chilly northern Pacific. At Acapulco, much of the cargo was sold through a trade fair timed for the galleons' arrival. The ships were then loaded with silver (usually Mexican pesos or *reales* coins, eight of which were cut from a peso, creating the term "pieces of eight") and Spanish and New World products to pay for the trade accounts in Manila. They also took on soldiers, merchants, missionaries, and government officials along with mail and supplies. These *Naos de Acapulco* usually departed in March to catch the northeast trade winds back across the Pacific.

In the Spanish galleon crossings, and in the Portuguese spice trade with the Moluccas, the Euro-

peans avoided Melanesia and Polynesia after the disappointing results of several expeditions into those areas. Of these, only the indomitable Pedro Fernandez de Quirós, pilot of the tragic second Álvaro de Mendaña expedition of 1596 under the command of Mendaña's widow, touched at Guam and Saipan. At Guam, his crew killed Chamorros "by an arquebus, owing to a matter of a piece of cask hoop." Iron was still worth dying for among Pacific islanders seventy-five years after Magellan's crossing.

The Spaniards also bypassed the islands of Micronesia outside the Marianas. Mostly atolls surrounded by dangerous reefs, these southerly island groups of Micronesia had few natural resources to merit conquest, and their populations were too small to attract sustained Spanish missionary efforts. Therefore, all the traditional Micronesian societies except that of the Chamorros in the Marianas escaped the full brunt of European civilization for nearly 300 more years until the nineteenth century, when whalers, traders, and missionaries would invade the region.

Even the Chamorros were largely spared for another century and a half after the intrusions of Magellan and Legazpi on Guam. The eastbound *Naos de Manila*, still well provisioned the first weeks out of the Philippines, swung north and avoided the Marianas. The westbound *Naos de Acapulco* usually passed through the Rota channel (called by the Spanish *la Bocana*, or "mouth," because it leads to the Philippines) between Guam and Rota just as did Magellan. The galleons often did not anchor, just slowed with furled sails near one of the two islands, not inside the bays where maneuver room was limited. The yearly passings of the galleons became so routine by the seventeenth century that Rota (*Luta* in Chamorro) began to appear on early maps and in accounts as *La Sarpana, Çarpana, Zarpana,* or *Harpana,* names derived from the Spanish verb *zapar* (to lift anchor). They took on provisions from Chamorros who flocked in proas to trade for iron.

The presence of Spanish galleons laden with treasures on isolated sea-lanes inevitably aroused

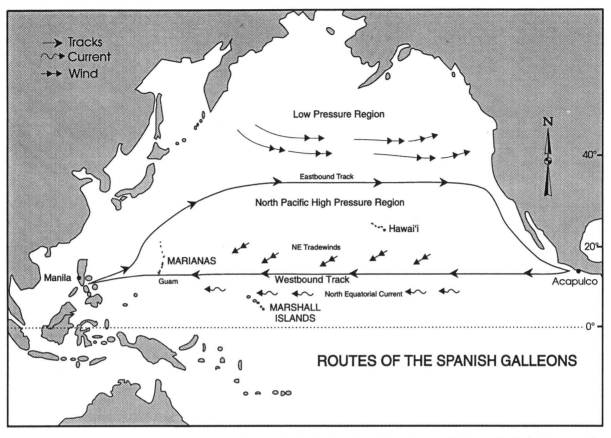

Routes of the Spanish galleons. The Manila galleons—loaded with oriental luxuries—sailed from Cavite in June or July with the monsoon winds out of the southwest, following a northeastern track to the north of the Marianas. They then turned eastward with the north Pacific current to reach California, where they turned south to arrive in Acapulco in November or December after a journey of nearly 3,000 miles. From Acapulco the cargos went to Mexico City, Havana, and Spain. The same ships, now called the Acapulco galleons, and loaded with passengers, mail, supplies, and silver for the Manila and Guam accounts, normally departed westward in March or April to catch the northeast trade winds along the fourteen-degree north latitude. The Acapulco galleons usually touched at Guam or Rota in May or June before reaching Cavite a week or two later. As a consequence of Spain's colonies and the great circular route of the galleons, the Pacific Ocean came to be considered an exclusive "Spanish lake" for over 200 years.

the attention of Spain's enemies, and it was not long before privateers arrived in the Pacific. Privateers were ships privately owned but commissioned to attack enemy merchantmen. The first English privateer, Thomas Cavendish, reached Guam in January 1588 on his appropriately named ship, *Desire*. Cavendish did not anchor but "passed near the Island of Guahan" and took on food and water from the proas that surrounded the *Desire*. When the persistent islanders followed the ship as it departed, Cavendish peevishly raked the proas with muskets but could not tell if he killed any Chamorros because the islanders were so nimble in falling backward off the proas and hiding under water when shots were fired at them. He sailed on to the Philippines and Java on the way to present his plunder to Elizabeth I in 1588, the landmark year of the defeat of the Spanish Armada by England and the

Chamorros trading with a Spanish galleon, 1590. The ship is probably the *San Pedro* as seen from the flagship *Santiago* on the stopover in the Marianas in May 1590 of Gómez Pérez Dasmariñas, governor-general of the Philippines, 1590–1593. The drawing was likely made in Manila by a Chinese artist employed by the Spaniards to illustrate a chronicle attributed to Gómez Pérez, *Relación de las yslas de los Ladrones* (now called the Boxer Codex), about the 1590 crossing. The Spaniards did not allow Chamorro men to board their ships but sent down barter items, usually bundles of nails, on lines to the Chamorros in proas. In return, the Chamorros sent up fruit, fish, and gourds filled with coconut oil. (Boxer Codex by permission of Professor C. R. Boxer)

beginning of Spain's long, slow decline in imperial power.

Meanwhile, the priests of Spain, with the deep religious zeal of the sixteenth century, became interested in the pagan Chamorros. Catholic missionary interest in the Marianas was an outgrowth of the church's rapid conversion of the Philippines. With able leaders and sound politics, Catholicism prospered in the Philippines even when Spanish trans-Pacific trade declined in the late eighteenth century. Manila became known as the Almacén de Fe (the warehouse of the faith) for conversion of infidels in the surrounding regions.

It was Franciscan Discalced (shoeless; they wore sandals) friars who impulsively and without permission undertook the initial missionary efforts in the Marianas. The first was Friar Antonio de los

Angeles, who in 1596 was aboard the *San Pablo* with twenty-two other Franciscans en route to assignments in the Philippines. When the galleon came to a halt in the Marianas, probably off Rota, Friar Antonio asked permission of his superior on board to stay in the islands, and the superior casually agreed, thinking the friar was joking. Soon afterward, Antonio dropped into a proa alongside and signaled the Chamorros to take him ashore. He had only his crucifix and breviary. As he sailed away in the proa, two Spanish crewmen jumped into another proa to bring him back. All three Spaniards were marooned when the galleon had to depart.

Fortunately, the three Spaniards were picked up the following year by the next galleon and taken to the Philippines. There, Antonio de los Angeles wrote a short account for King Philip II of his year-long stay in the Marianas. Friar Antonio was the first missionary in Micronesia. Others would follow him with even greater zeal.

Meanwhile, other European intrusions on Guam were not by Spaniards or the English but by the Dutch. Having gained their independence from Spain in 1579, by the turn of the century the Dutch were replacing the Portuguese in the Spice Islands and challenging Spain for trade. The first Dutch ships to reach the central Pacific came in 1600 from around South America and would proceed on around the world to the Netherlands in 1601. Under the command of Oliver van der Noort in his flagship *Mauritius,* the Dutch flotilla of four ships spent 15 and 16 September 1600 at Guam, bartering iron nails for provisions before sailing off to do battle against the Spaniards under Antonio de Morga in the Philippines.

Later, Dutch visitors to Guam included Joris Spilbergen, from 23 to 26 January 1616, and the "Nassau Fleet," which stopped for seventeen days in January and February 1625. They careened their ships at Umatac Bay, according to the Spanish Jesuit historian Francisco García. The Chamorros sold rice to the Dutchmen in bales of seventy to eighty pounds each but invariably included sand and rocks in the bottoms of the bales. The Nassau Fleet, with over 1,200 men on eleven ships, was the most formidable alien presence yet to appear in the Marianas. It was an intimidating omen of the future for the Chamorro people.

In the meantime, the Spaniards had continued to make landfalls in the Marianas in between the Dutch expeditions. In July 1601, after being disabled by a typhoon, the Manila galleon *Santa Margarita* sank off a northwest reef of Rota. Only a few dozen of the 300 people aboard survived, and some were rescued in March 1602 when a fleet of five Spanish ships arrived at Rota from Acapulco. Aboard one of the Acapulco ships was an energetic and perhaps overly zealous Capuchin friar, Juan Pobre de Zamora, who was leading a group of

thirty Franciscan missionaries whom he had recruited in Spain.

While the ships were surrounded by Chamorro proas, Juan Pobre and another friar, Pedro de Talavera, jumped into proas alongside their ship. They signaled that they wanted to be taken to shore, and the obliging Chamorros complied. The new governor-general of the Philippines, Don Pedro Bravo de Acuña, was with the fleet. He later wrote of the incident to King Philip II, saying that the Chamorro proas were too swift to be caught by the Spaniards and there was "nothing to do but entrust him [Juan Pobre] to some of the leaders among the *indios.*"

The two friars remained on Rota for seven months until October 1602, when the Manila galleon *Jesus María,* which had sailed from Cavite too late in the season and had to put into Rota in distress, took Juan Pobre aboard. In gratitude that the friar was safe and sound, the Spanish officers presented gifts to the Chamorro headman who had been the friar's protector. They gave him "a monkey, in addition to iron hoops, knives, and scissors." The headman, whom Juan Pobre referred to as his "master," was the first Chamorro to have his name recorded in Spanish accounts. He was Sunama, from the village of Tazga on Rota. This village is assumed to have been on the beach, now uninhabited, called Tatgua on the northwest coast of Rota.

While this reunion was taking place, the wind shifted, and the ship had to depart immediately for the Philippines. The captain kept the zealous Juan Pobre aboard, but in the hasty departure the other friar, Pedro de Talavera, was left behind along with another unfortunate Franciscan who earlier had wandered off from the *Jesus María* to find Juan Pobre and become lost. The two stranded friars were picked up by the next galleon on 18 March 1603, along with a soldier remaining from the *Santa Margarita* survivors.

Juan Pobre wrote a detailed and sympathetic account of Chamorro customs. His description showed that, as of 1602, eighty-one years after Magellan's landfall on Guam, the Chamorros had not yet been drastically changed by European contact. For the next sixty-six years, the galleons from Acapulco continued to pause about once a year off Guam or Rota. This calm pattern was disturbed in September 1638, when a mutiny occurred on the huge, 2,000-ton, heavily laden Manila galleon *Nuestra Señora de la Concepción* as it approached the Marianas. As several factions among the crew fought each other, the unattended galleon broached, and the masts broke, carrying the sails off into the sea. Helpless, the great ship smashed into the reef at Agingan Bay on the southwest tip of Saipan, probably on 20 September. Many of the 400 or so crew and passengers were likely drowned in the wreck. Chamorros then killed most of the remaining people aboard and looted the galleon, this time keeping gold jewelry as well as any object of iron. Some twenty-eight Spaniards and an unknown number of non-Spaniards survived, according to a report of the disaster: "Those who escaped went from island to island to those of *Uan* [Guam] and *Harpana* [Rota] . . . where they have been well treated."

Six of the survivors, led by Juan de Montoya, the ship's captain, sailed in two proas to the Philippines with two Chamorros provided by a young headman named Quipuha (Kepuha or Kipuhá in Chamorro) on Guam. The voyagers arrived in the Philippines on 24 July 1639, almost dead from the arduous 1,500-mile voyage. Another small group led by Francisco Ramos, a boatswain, made a boat and sailed to the Philippines in 1640, while a few other Spaniards, including the pilot, Esteban Ramos, were apparently picked up by galleons in the early 1640s.

Some of the shipwrecked *Concepción* Filipinos and Spaniards never left the Marianas; marooned for life, they married Chamorros and raised families. Spanish historians wrote that the Tinian headman Taga was baptized by one of the *Concepción's* Spaniards, identified as Marcos Fernandez, after a miraculous appearance before Taga of the Virgin Mary on Tinian. According to some accounts, Taga then protected the Spaniards and may have arranged for Quipuha on Guam to send the six survivors by proa to the Philippines. The wreck of the *Concepción* also released cats and dogs in the Marianas for the first time, and the animals soon multiplied. Rats had apparently come ashore already from earlier European visits. Chickens were brought later after the galleon trade was established. Chamorros later told Spaniards that the European ships even brought flies and mosquitos to the islands.

As a result of Chamorro aggressiveness, the Spaniards kept largely to their galleons when they paused briefly in the Marianas. The traditional way of life for the Chamorros in their villages therefore continued with only minor, gradual changes as a consequence of Spanish stopovers. The precontact culture of the Chamorros and the natural ecosystem of the Mariana Islands—called *tano' tasi* (land of the sea) by the Chamorros—prior to invasion by the Spaniards in 1668 are worth examining in their own right, for after that year Guam and the other Mariana Islands would be transformed forever. Nevertheless, the cultural roots and the genes of the Chamorro people would prove to be remarkably durable.

2

The Place of Before Time Ancestors
1638–1662

Tanoʻ Tasi: Land of the Sea

The islands of Palau, Yap, and the Marianas are the tips of an immense submerged mountain range along the eastern rim of the Philippine Sea. This range stretches over 1,400 miles in a great bend from Halmahera Island in the Moluccas of Indonesia northeastward to the Marianas. From the Marianas, the range turns north and disappears before reappearing above the ocean as the tiny Volcano and Bonin islands. Within this mountain range, the Marianas are high islands of comparatively recent volcanic origin in the long span of earth's geological time. They are not located over a volcanic hot spot, as is Hawaiʻi, but are on the eastern edge of the Pacific northwest tectonic plate in a subduction zone along the rim of the Philippine Sea.

The slow, grinding subduction of the Pacific tectonic plate under the smaller Philippine plate to the west causes volcanism from the Marianas north through the Bonins to Japan. Owing to this subduction, Guam and the other Marianas emerged from the ocean, subsided, and reemerged an unknown number of times, beginning in the early Cenozoic era. This makes Guam fairly young geologically, dating from about 60 million years ago. The interaction of the tectonic plates causes many earthquakes on Guam, with a severely destructive one about once a century over the past 300 years. The

first life on the islands undoubtedly came from the sea, such as calcareous algae, coral, polyps, mollusks, and crustaceans, which created layers of limestone and reef shelves over millions of years. Subsequently, beginning at least in the Pleistocene epoch over 10,000 years before the present (B.P.), living organisms other than sea life appeared in the Marianas.

During June and July into August of each of those thousands of years, birds, insects, and other wind-borne organisms—which had started to evolve in Southeast Asia when Indonesia and the Philippines were still part of the Asian mainland—were occasionally carried away by the southwest monsoons and swept across the Philippine Sea in a northeasterly direction. Among the common Pacific seabirds that made the Marianas their permanent home are the brown booby or gannet, the dark noddy tern, and the beautiful, pure white fairy tern. These all still fly from Guam's shores to fish miles out to sea, with the tiny fairy terns, usually in pairs, sure signals of fish when the birds wheel and dive from on high as if in aerial dances of delight. Migratory birds from Australia and other land masses followed flight patterns over the Marianas to the northern Pacific regions. Birds in turn carried seeds they had consumed, depositing some in their droppings on islands in Micronesia. Tiny seeds, pollen, and spores in the Indonesia-Philippines nexus may also have been carried by convection wind currents and storms up to higher altitudes. There the anti-trade winds wafted the living organic particles along with dust eastward in the upper atmosphere of the western Pacific, and some drifted down and landed on the islands of Micronesia.

Oceanic currents out of Indonesia flow at times toward the north and northeast, carrying waterborne life, notably seeds and swimming animals such as turtles, into western Micronesia. Another oceanic current flows from the northern Philippines generally northward and then eastward into the northern Marianas, occasionally carrying coconuts, logs, and vegetation rafts with small reptiles and terrestrial invertebrates, mangrove seedlings and other plants, insects, and tiny rodents such as shrews and bats. Combined, the June–July–August southwest monsoon and the oceanic currents dispersed life forms northeastward and eastward out of the Indonesia-Philippines nexus each year for thousands on thousands of years.

Most of those ancient animal and plant travelers perished, but enough—just a few were sufficient out of millions—landed in Palau, Yap, and the Marianas to initiate living communities. Thus, no island was ever a unique biosphere separate from other ecosystems; all were linked despite vast distances between them. Today, among the most plentiful descendants of the early arrivals out of Southeast Asia are geckos. These small, harmless, tan or brown lizards are found in practically every building in the Marianas and sometimes startle newcomers with chirping calls that are surprisingly loud for a creature only a few inches long.

The first humans to enter Micronesia also came out of Southeast Asia; they were proto-Austronesians. By the time they moved beyond Indonesia and the Philippines, they may have already been organized into a variety of kinship clans and ethnolinguistic groups of overlapping cultures, not just a single, proto-Micronesian or proto-Oceanic people. In hand-carved log canoes, and probably with some form of outriggers and square or lateen sails woven of natural fibers, these "boat people" began to sail deliberately or accidentally eastward and northeastward, probably during the June–July–August monsoons, with the oceanic currents. The voyages began perhaps 1,500 or more years prior to the Christian era, that is, at least 3500 B.P. The seafarers likely carried with them food plants and seeds, such as bananas, taro, breadfruit, yams, betel nut, and coconuts. They had knowledge of fire and pottery, were probably expert fishermen, and navigated by the stars, winds, and currents.

These earliest human probes by boat people into western Micronesia, whether by accident or purposeful, must have been of small numbers, sporadic over long periods of time, and exceedingly hazardous. There was probably no original, single wave of migration to any one island group but many small efforts, most of which did not become permanent. Nonetheless, some probes succeeded, and they were the geneses of the cultures of the Palauans, the Yapese, and the Chamorros, as these peoples are known today.

Evidence for human migration out of Southeast Asia lies in the languages of the Palauans, Yapese, and Chamorros. These people all speak tongues different in linguistic origin from the rest of Micronesia. The Chamorro and Palauan languages are separate subfamilies of the generic Austronesian family (formerly called Malayo-Polynesian). They show linguistic affiliations with Indonesian languages in north Sulawesi and with Ilocano and Tagalog in the Philippines, which in turn have links to Taiwan (once part of the Asian mainland). Yapese, on the other hand, is an anomaly, a seemingly independent language, although also of Austronesian roots. None of these three western Micronesian languages is a dialect of any other known language, and none was written prior to arrival of the Europeans.

The remainder of Micronesia to the east is of different geological and linguistic origins than Palau, Yap, and the Marianas. The eastern and much of the central parts of Micronesia are composed of numerous tiny atolls that make up today's Federated States of Micronesia (FSM) and the Marshall

Islands. Languages there appear closer to Polynesian languages in origin.

The distinctiveness of the Chamorro, Palauan, and Yapese languages from each other and from the rest of Micronesia indicates separate evolution over a very long time. The northeasterly human migration out of Southeast Asia halted in the Marianas. Once the islands of the Marianas had been settled, migrations eastward to the distant Hawaiian Islands or the Marshalls were impractical in the face of the implacable trade winds. Beyond the Marianas to the northeast lie only cold, empty seas for thousands of miles until the coast of North America. Furthermore, the southwest monsoon winds generally die out about the time they reach the Marianas, limiting sailing voyages beyond those islands.

Interisland trade by canoes developed throughout Micronesia, but such trade was conducted principally by low islanders, the atoll dwellers of the central and eastern Carolines. Their small, resource-poor environments tended to impel continuing trade and population shifts with other islands, but the Chamorros, the Palauans, and the Yapese nonetheless became separated culturally over time from their Southeast Asian roots and from whatever sociopolitical connections they may have originally had with each other. Once firmly rooted, each of the western Micronesian island groups evolved on its own path until the Europeans invaded the islands. The cultures of western Micronesia thus span some 3,500 years and could be older, although earlier dates, particularly for Palau's settlers, have not been substantiated.

As a consequence of separate development, in the words of one anthropologist, the Chamorros are not a "mixture of Caucasoid and Mongoloid elements—they are simply what they are, from past evolution and drift among local groups." This view holds that the Chamorro culture and the flora and fauna of the Marianas were adaptive; life and human culture evolved to fit the specific local conditions of the Mariana Islands within the oceanic environment that dominates these islands. The Chamorro language expresses the idea cogently: the

Mariana Islands are *tano' tasi,* land of the sea. All life in the islands responded to the vibrations of the winds, waters, and tides that embraced the Marianas.

A corollary of this view is that Micronesia and certainly the Mariana Islands were not stepping stones in the human colonization of Polynesia, neither to Hawai'i in the east nor to islands in the southern Pacific. The Marianas became a small world of their own in which the Chamorros were a self-sustaining people, living in a stateless society and in relative harmony with the land and with the sea around them well prior to the human settlement of Polynesia. Because the Chamorro population was probably derived from a small number of progenitors, the precontact islanders were likely to have been a highly interrelated group with a small pool of genes (in comparison to larger continental populations) as a result of inbreeding. One consequence of this genetic similarity was to make the Chamorros highly susceptible to infectious disease introduced by Europeans.

While the people, and much of the early flora and fauna, of western Micronesia had ancestors independent of eastern Micronesia, Melanesia, or Polynesia, some flora and fauna also came from the east. The oceanic currents generally flow westward in central Micronesia and likely dispersed coconuts and other water-borne seeds, insects, vegetation, larval creatures, and some small animals on vegetation rafts from out of eastern Micronesia and Polynesia to the Marianas.

After Polynesia and eastern Micronesia had been settled by humans, these islanders sailed with the westward currents and with the northeast trade winds into western Micronesia for a variety of reasons: by accident, for adventure, as exiles, because of population pressures, or in trade and war. These intrusions produced some mixtures in the cultures and ecosystems already established, but without obliterating their core elements, such as language. As a consequence, all surviving ecosystems and ethnolinguistic groups throughout Micronesia show likenesses with counterparts in the Polynesian, Indonesian-Philippines, and Melanesian regions.

Nonetheless, once introduced to the Micronesian islands, life evolved some unique biological species in the flora and fauna as well as independent languages and cultural attributes among the human societies. In this regard, microevolution through natural selection on isolated island ecosystems can be quite swift, shaping new forms in just a few generations. An example is the small Guam reef damsel fish, native only to Guam's reefs. Several plants are indigenous (native or—if they evolved wholly on Guam—endemic) only to the Marianas. Among these are the palm-like federico nut plant, the wild piper shrub, and the magnificent serianthes tree.

Unique indigenous birds include the *koko* (the flightless Guam rail), the Marianas crow, the Marianas fruit dove with its iridescent green body and rose-crowned head, and the little black and white Micronesian kingfisher. Only one snake is indigenous, but it is tiny, blind, and more like a worm than a serpent. There were no crocodiles and only a few indigenous land mammals other than humans in the Marianas when the Europeans arrived: two species of fruit bat similar to species in Southeast Asia and Melanesia and a small insectivorous bat. The small bat is now extinct; the fruit bats, called *fanihi* in Chamorro, have become rare, as have many other indigenous species, owing to loss of habitat to the island's rapidly expanding human population in the late twentieth century.

Although conjectural, the theory presented above of the precontact development of Guam is confirmed to some degree by artifacts and settlement remains with respect to human cultural linkages. A form of early pottery, called *Marianas red ware* by archaeologists, was fairly common on Guam by about 3000 B.P. This type of pottery appears to be similar to a widespread style of early Malaysian red pottery and is related to Lapita clay vessels found in an arc from northern Melanesia through parts of Indonesia into the Philippines. Lapita pottery is distinctive; it was made without a potter's wheel. By about A.D. 800–900, plain pottery was abundant in the Marianas. The linkages in shapes and styles between the Lapita-like pottery of the Marianas and the Lapita pottery in the Indonesia-Philippines nexus indicate either parallel human development or contact among the early boat peoples of those areas.

Among all the central Pacific islanders, only the Chamorros apparently cultivated rice, as was common in Southeast Asia well prior to European contact. On the other hand, the Chamorros never invented the wheel or the plough, neither of which was particularly useful in a small island precontact environment. Because of the near absence of mammals in the Marianas, the Chamorros never fabricated leather until after cattle were introduced by the Spaniards. In the absence of leather, the islanders developed to a high degree the use of plant fibers for a variety of purposes.

The absence of readily available ore deposits on the islands prevented metalworking, and none of the precontact Micronesians fabricated tools or weapons in bronze, iron, or other metals. One of the most useful Chamorro tools was the short-handled adze with an oval blade made of stone or from the *Tridacna gigas* clamshell. The form of the adze—called *shouldered* by archaeologists—in the Marianas was similar to those in the Indonesia-Philippines nexus. Despite assertions by some European writers that the Chamorros did not know of fire, the islanders could make fire long before the European arrival, as evinced by the firing of island pottery centuries before the Christian era.

The anthropological evidence to date on the origins of the Pacific islanders shows that Micronesia was a highly diverse biological and cultural region centuries before Magellan arrived in 1521. Within that diversity, the islanders of the Marianas, or *tao-tao tano'* (people of this land), as they called themselves in Chamorro, were organized into a stable, unilingual society based on the use of stone and shell tools by the time the Romans were conquering the Iberian tribes on the peninsula in Europe that would eventually become Spain. These Chamorros, who would in a future time confront the descendants of the Iberian tribesmen, had created a culture similar in many respects to other traditional

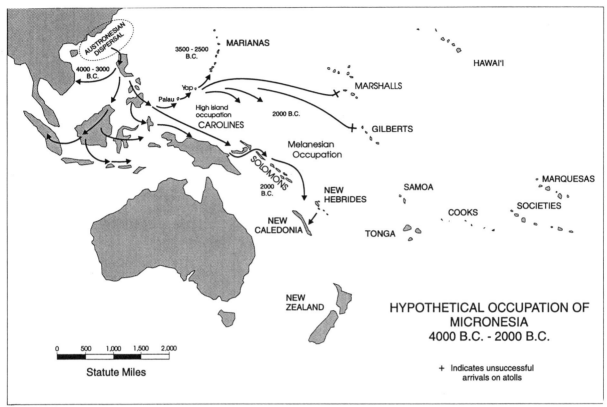

Hypothetical occupation of Micronesia, 4000–2000 B.C. Dispersal of people with Austronesian languages begins about 4000 B.C. from an unknown region in or adjacent to South China and spreads through the Philippines and Indonesia. Movements out of Indonesia and the Philippines reach Palau, Yap, and the Marianas from 3500 to 2500 B.C. Voyages to Micronesia succeed in settling on the high islands by 2000 B.C. but fail to establish on atolls in the Western Caroline Islands. (Adapted from Howells 1973)

Pacific island societies, but with their own highly distinctive and durable attributes.

Taotao Tano': People of This Land

Most of the original myths and oral traditions of Chamorro precontact culture were lost or substantially altered after the Spanish conquest. From early Spanish accounts, the Chamorros, like many other traditional cultures, apparently thought that they were the original humans. They referred to their precontact forefathers as "Before Time Ancestors." In one of the earliest references to Chamorro myths, Friar Antonio de los Angeles reported disap-

provingly in 1596 that the Chamorros "believe they were born of a rock—whence they go each year for a fiesta." The rock gave "birth to two men and that one of them had become a woman." This site has been identified as Lalas Rock at Fouha Bay on Guam's southwestern coast.

In reality, the first permanent villages on Guam were most likely established by small, separate bands of Austronesian people in the many leeward coastal enclaves where freshwater springs and streams flow out of the higher ground inland. The largest enclaves along the west coast of the island are now called Tumon, Agana, Asan-Piti, Agat, Sella, Cetti, Fouha, Umatac, and Merizo. Fouha

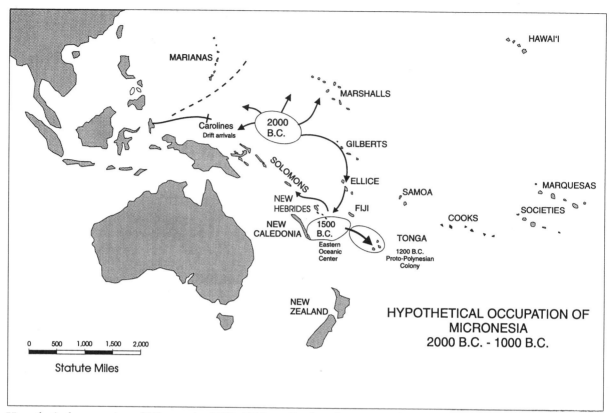

Hypothetical occupation of Micronesia, 2000–1000 B.C. Further chance arrivals from Indonesia on atolls in the Western Carolines fail to establish permanent settlements, but in Eastern Micronesia adaptation to atolls begins about 2000 B.C. By 1500 B.C., atoll dwellers with Eastern Oceanic languages from Eastern Micronesia reach points in Eastern Melanesia. (Adapted from Howells 1973)

Bay just north of Umatac may therefore have been one of the earliest settlements, although the coastline has been altered by typhoons and earthquakes since the earliest arrivals of humans. Fishing and reef gleaning are easiest from these coastal terraces, where the land and sea interface in protected enclaves.

As elsewhere in Oceania, coconut palms (*niyok* in Chamorro) and other trees provided fruit and oil for food in addition to fiber and leaves for sennit ropes, plaited mats, and many other uses by the precontact Chamorros. The fruit of the breadfruit tree was a major source of starch, along with taro, yams, and bananas, balancing the high protein content of seafood in the Chamorro diet. The seedless

and most readily edible variety of breadfruit is infertile and must be cultivated. Since this variety of breadfruit was present on Guam before the Spaniards arrived, it is probable that young seedling plants were brought to the island by early settlers. The inner bark of the breadfruit tree was made into a soft fiber cloth, and the sap provided glue, paint, and caulking for Chamorro canoes. The tall, straight trunks of the breadfruit trees of the seeded variety, called *dukduk* in Chamorro, were chiseled with adzes by the islanders into hulls for canoes.

As the human population of the Marianas grew, so did subsistence sedentary farming. Food plants included rice, taro, sugar cane, and yams, but not tapioca (also called manioc or cassava). This staple

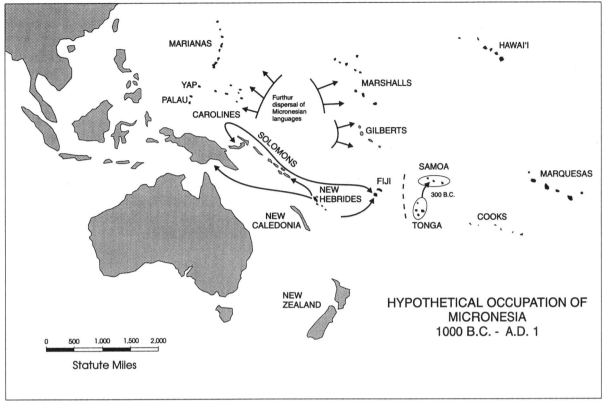

Hypothetical occupation of Micronesia, 1000 B.C.–A.D. 1. Peoples on high islands in Palau, Yap, and the Marianas in Western Micronesia develop separate languages and cultures. Atoll occupation proceeds westward in Eastern Micronesia and into the Gilberts and Marshalls by Eastern Oceanic speakers. Samoa is settled from Tonga. (Adapted from Howells 1973)

was one of more than 100 plant species introduced to Guam by the Spaniards from the Americas and the Philippines, as were papayas and various hot peppers, which are now eaten at practically every meal by modern Chamorros.

Friar Juan Pobre reported that, in 1602, nearly all Chamorros chewed wads made of betel nut of the *areca* palm wrapped in pepper leaf and powdered with lime obtained by burning coral. This mildly narcotic and astringent mixture originated in India and spread throughout Southeast Asia. Chewing betel nut, *pugua* in Chamorro, is still popular on Guam, but without the pepper leaf and lime, which stain lips and gums bright red and teeth black.

The Chamorros produced no intoxicating drinks

until *tuba* (a fermented drink made from coconut palm sap) as well as more powerful alcoholic drinks called *aguardiente* ("burning water" in Spanish, also called *aguayente,* or *agi* for short), usually a liquor distilled from coconut flowers or *tuba,* and *arak* (a wine made from coconut juice or rice) were brought to the Marianas from the Philippines. The Spaniards had not known of *tuba* until it was served to Magellan in the Visayan Islands in 1521. Once the Chamorros learned after 1668 from the Spanish and Filipino soldiers with Father San Vitores how to ferment *tuba* and distill *aguardiente,* these drinks became permanently popular in the Marianas.

Fishing complemented agriculture as the foundation of the precontact Chamorro economy. Juan

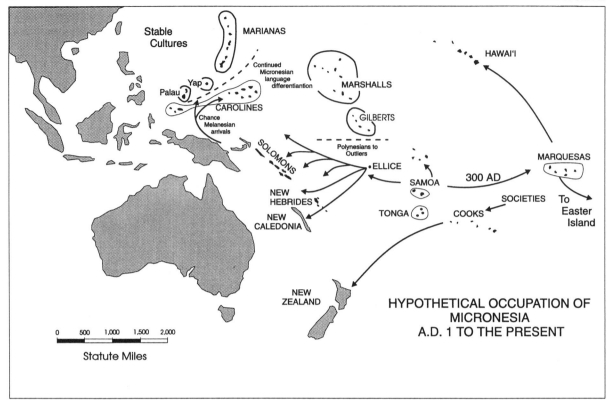

Hypothetical occupation of Micronesia, A.D. 1 to the present. Westward movement of atoll-dwellers in Micronesia continues but does not seriously affect the established cultures in Yap, Palau or the Marianas. The *Latte* period begins in the Marianas, A.D. 800–1000, and ends with the Spanish conquest, A.D. 1668–1698. All Polynesia is occupied by movements out of Samoa, and by dispersals out of the Marquesas to Tahiti, New Zealand, Hawai'i, etc. (Adapted from Howells 1973)

Pobre wrote admiringly, "No better seamen or divers have ever been known to exist." Van der Noort's pilot, Captain Melis, noted in his diary of the 1600 Dutch visit to Guam that Chamorro women "swam as well as the men." At the age of four or five, Chamorro boys in the coastal villages were taken beyond the reef to fish in small-size proas made by their fathers. By age eighteen, they were fishing alone far out to sea in proas of their own construction. They trolled for dolphin fish, wahoo, tuna, and marlin, using bone and shell hooks and natural fiber lines. The Pacific blue marlin grows to over 1,000 pounds in the waters of the Mariana Islands. To catch and boat one of these of even moderate size in a sailing canoe requires con-

siderable skill, stamina, and courage. Juan Pobre relates how his Chamorro protector, Sunama, handled a large marlin in his proa off Rota in 1602:

After having eaten the first flying fish, and after having baited his hook with the second . . . a very large blue marlin took the hook. . . . [Sunama's] line was very thin and . . . he very cautiously began playing and tiring it. This took a long time. Meanwhile, a large shark appeared and attacked the blue marlin in the mid-section of its back. In order not to let go of his line, the *indio* allowed his boat to capsize. Then he tied the line to the capsized proa, followed the line through the water to the shark, and diverted him from his catch. Then he brought the blue marlin back to his boat, righted the craft, and sailed home, flying a woven mat as a banner from the masthead.

As a consequence of healthy diet and constant exercise, the Chamorros had strong physiques and a pleasing appearance in the eyes of numerous European visitors. The Jesuit historian Francisco García, not always a kind commentator, writing in Spain in 1681 from Jesuit reports from Guam for his history of Father San Vitores published in 1683, described Chamorros as "a somewhat lighter shade than Filipinos, larger in stature, more corpulent and robust than Europeans, pleasant and with agreeable faces. They are so fat they appear swollen. . . . They remain in good health to an advanced age and it is very usual to live ninety or one hundred years."

Some early Spanish visitors described the Chamorro men as giants who could lift two Spaniards, each by a foot, as if they were children. It should be noted that Europeans of the sixteenth and seventeenth centuries were fairly small in stature compared with sizes today. While some Chamorros were undoubtedly large and powerful, there is no evidence from precontact burial remains that the people were huge, just larger than Spaniards. A picture of precolonial Chamorros was given by Gómez Pérez Dasmariñas when he stopped at Guam in 1590 on the galleon *Santiago* with its consort *San Pedro* on his way to become the governor-general of the Philippines. He wrote of the Chamorros, "They are men with well-built bodies, especially their legs. . . . Their faces are wide and flat, . . . their mouths are very large, and they sculpture their teeth, sharpening them like those of a dog—even more so."

The only Chamorro disease observed by the early Spaniards on Guam was dropsy, or edema, in which fluids beneath the skin and in the lungs caused swelling and other disorders. Modern archaeological analyses of precontact Chamorro remains also indicate high incidence of yaws. One customary Chamorro remedy for illness, according to Juan Pobre, was a kind of intense massage with feet, called *ugot* in Chamorro: "Someone will stand on the afflicted area and, lifting one foot and then the other, will pound on it with his feet. Now and then, one sees a sick person with one *indio* standing on one thigh, someone else on the other, and a third person standing on his back."

Women worked in the house, on the reefs, and in the gardens. Men fished, helped with the gardening, and went to war. The men also participated in long and lively public debates over social matters among large groups from several villages. In these debates, which Juan Pobre stated could lead to armed skirmishes, men practiced rhetorical skills that the Jesuit historian García called "fabulous poetry." They also made up satirical ballads to mock opponents and to poke fun at people from other villages.

The Chamorros did not tattoo their bodies, a practice prevalent nearly everywhere else in the Pacific. Early visitors to the Marianas noted that the Chamorros took pride in their unadorned bodies and disdained clothing.

Men and women smeared their bodies with coconut oil, and Chamorro hair and teeth styles varied. On his stopover at Guam in 1588, the privateer Cavendish noted (in Elizabethan English) that the Chamorros had "haire marveilous long; yet some have it made up and tyed with a knot on the crowne and some with two knots." A hundred years later, the San Vitores mission reported that the men no longer wore their hair long but gathered it into a single small knot about the length of a finger on top of an otherwise shorn scalp. Women often bleached their hair blonde or flaxen, probably by using lime as women did elsewhere in Oceania.

The character of the Chamorros during the period of early European contacts was described by most observers as sociable, proud, and deceptive. Those Spaniards who lived alone among them, like friars Antonio de los Angeles and Juan Pobre de Zamora, considered the islanders to be "loving" and of a "peaceful nature." Those visitors who traded with them or fought them thought the Chamorros deceitful and vengeful. Captain Melis with van der Noort in 1600 called Chamorros "subtle deceivers" who cheerfully cheated the

Earliest known picture of a Chamorro of Guam. Original in the Boxer Codex chronicle attributed to Gómez Pérez Dasmariñas and probably drawn around 1590 or 1591 by a Chinese artist in Manila from descriptions by the Dasmariñas party. The Chamorro is a typical robust warrior who wears no clothing, jewelry, or other adornment and is not tattooed. He carries a wooden spear tipped with a sharpened human shinbone. (Boxer Codex by permission of Professor C. R. Boxer)

Dutch visitors in the same manner that they had Legazpi thirty-five years earlier. A high Spanish official in Manila, Antonio de Morga, called them in 1609 "a very burly and barbarous race."

Juan Pobre pointed out that they were not an idle people living in a carefree paradise: "Sometimes when they return from fishing, or when they do not go fishing at all, they go to the hillside or jungle to see to their farm plots where every able-bodied person goes to work. . . . The men and women are hardworkers, not lazy, and have little regard for those who do not work. While their sons and daughters are very young, they make them work and teach them to perform their tasks." Juan Pobre goes on to say, "They are happy people and mockers," and they like to "brag before the leading citizens." The friar was particularly impressed by how gently Chamorro parents raised their children:

"They never spank them, and they even scold them with loving words." This reflected the powerful family and communal ties of the Chamorros. Families provided bountiful food to sick relatives and neighbors and constructed and repaired houses as communal efforts.

The Chamorros, however, had a different sense of privacy and of personal ownership of possessions or property than did the Europeans. They shared food, labor, and their own possessions freely and consequently expected the Europeans to do the same. Juan Pobre commented, "Some ties are so close that when one goes to a friend's house, whether he is at home or not, the visitor will take whatever he wants from there, as if it were his own." This kind of behavior may be one reason the Spaniards judged the Chamorros to be thieves.

Public gatherings by Chamorros for debates,

feasts, marriages, and funerals could be enormous. Juan Pobre states: "These gatherings included not just the people of a particular village but those of others as well, and they reciprocate with festivities and banquets, saving their salted fish for such occasions. Two or three thousand people gather for some of these feasts, though usually not more than one or two hundred, possibly a thousand, depending upon the resources of the fiesta's host."

The characteristics and customs of the Chamorros as described by early European visitors were not strikingly different from those of many other traditional cultures of island peoples of the Pacific. In fact, most attributes—fishing and sailing prowess, headmen of clans, subsistence agriculture, and large feasts with conspicuous displays for prestige purposes—were quite similar to those in other island cultures. But two developments of precontact Chamorro culture were distinctive among the island societies of the Pacific: first, the sophistication of their outrigger canoes and, second, the use of large, uniquely shaped stone pillars, called *latte* in Chamorro, as foundations for their most prominent buildings.

The distinctiveness of the Chamorro proa was not in its function; beautiful and highly practical canoes were constructed by other island peoples throughout the Pacific. What made the outrigger canoe of the Marianas special was its refinement of form. The asymmetrical shape and weight of the hull and the dimensions, balance, and placement of the single outrigger and the one lateen sail were among the most sophisticated technically of all sailing canoes. Swift, light, and graceful, the proa of the Chamorros was one of the highest state-of-the-art expressions of that most essential instrument of all traditional Pacific islanders, the ocean-going sailing canoe.

The first Europeans to describe the Chamorro outrigger canoe were Pigafetta and Albo with Magellan. The Genoese pilot with Magellan called it a *parão,* a Portuguese word that came to be *proa* in English. The Spaniards knew of outrigger boats from Portuguese accounts of the Moluccas and

Malaysia, where the Malay word for boats was *prahu.* All Spanish observers admired the proas as marvelously nimble. Later European voyagers familiar with canoes in the Pacific held that the Chamorro proa was the swiftest of all such craft, so fast that they were often called "flying proas." The English master mariner William Dampier, who observed flying proas on Guam in 1686, wrote, "I do believe they sail the best of any boats in the world."

As with most Pacific outriggers with lateen sails (called sprit sails by Europeans), to change direction the sail could be shunted on a movable yard (which held the sail) to either end of the canoe, both of which were pointed. This placement allowed the outrigger to remain to windward when tacking, and thus no rudder was needed on small proas, only a paddle; removable rudders were used on larger canoes. The triangular sails were quite large and were made by women from the native pandanus palm's tough, slender leaves, "so delicately woven that they appear of linen," according to Esteban Rodríguez with Legazpi at Guam in 1565. Chamorros normally painted the hulls and outriggers of their proas red with white or black trim from natural earth pigments mixed with lime and coconut oil. Vulnerable as well as valuable, the proas were never left in the water if not in use. All were stored carefully in canoe houses or sheds on the shore or were covered with palm fronds.

The Chamorros used different-sized canoes for specific functions. Close to the reef and inside bays they used shallow-draft paddling canoes. For fishing and coastal sailing they utilized a standard proa twenty-one to twenty-four feet long with a narrow hull that could hold up to twelve persons. These standard proas were much admired by the English privateer Woodes Rogers when he saw them in 1710: "I verily believe they may run 20 miles or more in the time [per hour], for when they viewed our ships, they passed by us like a Bird flying." For interisland trade or war, or perhaps as headman proas, the Chamorros built larger versions called *sakman* similar to those still in use in the Caroline Islands today. Commodore Anson (later

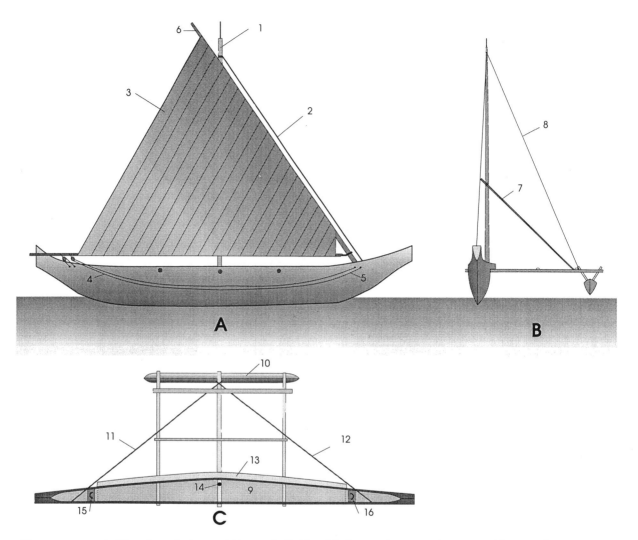

Chamorro proa. A: View from the leeward (downwind) side with the wooden mast, 1, supported by one of two coconut fiber sennit stays, 2 (the other stay is hidden by the sail); the lateen sail, 3, of finely woven pandanus matting; running sennit rope stays, 4 and 5, to adjust and steady the sail; the movable wooden yard, 6, to which the sail was attached. B: Head view, outrigger to windward with bamboo mast brace, 7, and sennit rope shroud line, 8. C: View from above with wooden hull, 9 (32 feet long and 2 feet deep in this version) made from a breadfruit tree trunk; a 16-foot wooden outrigger, 10; bamboo braces, 11 and 12, for the outrigger frame; a thin wooden plank, 13, to slow shipping of water and for carrying items; a carved wooden base, 14, in which the mast is fixed on the middle outrigger boom; and carved wooden sockets, 15 and 16, in one of which the movable yard is mounted, according to tack. (Adapted from Anson 1789)

Lord Anson) and his men captured one of the larger proas on their visit to Tinian in 1742. By that date, nearly fifty years after the Spanish occupation, the proa that Anson captured was no longer purely indigenous and showed Filipino influence.

When the Spaniards were subjugating the people of the Marianas, they compelled all Chamorros to live on Guam and Rota. Interisland trips, or even sailing beyond the reef, were prohibited without permission of the Spanish authorities. These restrictions were intended to prevent the islanders from fleeing to the northern Marianas or to the Carolines. As a consequence, the original Chamorro flying proa disappeared by the 1780s. By then, most canoes on Guam reflected Filipino designs such as the *agaraide,* or *galaide',* which were dugouts, often without sails, with arched booms that connected outriggers to hulls. The Chamorros themselves were by then no longer a people of the open sea, only beach-bound throwers of *talaya* cast nets to catch tiny reef fish or leisurely gatherers of non-pelagic fish with various seine nets.

Chamorro *latte* stones, on the other hand, would last on after the Spanish conquest, even though only as ruins in lonely jungle glades throughout the Marianas. The *latte* were so prominent in the Chamorro culture that archaeologists have divided all precontact history of the Marianas into a pre-*latte* period, which lasted up until between A.D. 800 and A.D. 1000, and a *latte* period thereafter, when the Chamorros began to erect the great stone pillars as foundations for their main buildings. The *latte* period ended abruptly after the arrival of Father San Vitores in 1668.

Social evolution and the creation of the *latte* among the Chamorros could have been impelled by population growth. With Guam's limited coastal areas, land with access to fishing rights was occupied by the earliest families. Coastal settlements spread into valleys and the interior of the island. This brought about an economy based on a barter of food products. Juan Pobre noted, for example, "The people living along the shore have an abundance of fish; those who live inland have an abundance of agricultural produce. Consequently, they arrange exchanges, trading fish for rice, for tubers, and for other varieties of fruit that the land produces."

As the island-wide society grew and became more interdependent, social stratification became more permanent, perhaps rooted in inheritance of land and fishing areas. Families whose lineages granted them the wealthier coastal areas and knowledge of oceanic skills such as pelagic fishing and canoe building evolved into the high-ranking clans who erected the *latte* buildings. Inland people who depended on subsistence farming may have become the lower-ranking families, at least on Guam. Money was created in the form of polished turtle shell pieces and disks of various sizes strung on long cords. Trade grew among the Mariana Islands and with the Carolines, and there may also have been sporadic foreign contacts by boats blown to the Marianas from Japan, China, and the Philippines. The arrival of the Chinaman Choco from the Philippines during a storm in 1648 is documented in the accounts of the San Vitores mission.

The *latte* type of construction may thus have been an expression of increased social complexity in the Chamorro culture. These stone pillars became the foundations of dwellings for high-ranking families and for large communal buildings such as men's houses and canoe sheds. Spanish accounts said that the Chamorros called these buildings "big houses." The pillars raised high-ranking families above the dwellings of lower-ranked people. *Latte* buildings were never described by Spanish observers as religious temples, but they may have symbolized intervillage social integration. When buildings were abandoned because of war, typhoons, or earthquakes (all of which are not infrequent in the Marianas), the *latte* were apparently left in place.

Latte were upright slabs, called in Chamorro *haligi,* from three to sixteen feet high (a few found still in quarries on Rota but never erected would be twenty-five feet in length with capstones). They were hewn out of solid limestone or basalt, and each was fixed securely in its own separate foundation in a hole with stone supports. Each slab had a hemispheric capstone of limestone called a *tasa* (cup) mounted on top with its curved side down, flat side up, so that it resembled a tall, bulky mushroom with an inverted top. The *latte* for each building were usually aligned in two rows of paired sets. Most buildings had eight or ten *latte* in four or five sets.

The buildings on *latte* pillars were in central or favored locations in villages. Wood beams and floors and high-pitched palm frond roofs were constructed on the pillars. The wood was usually from either the *daok* tree (palomaría to the Spaniards), which is hard and of good quality, or the *ifil* (also called *ifid* or *ifet* in Chamorro) tree, which has an extremely dense wood and is termite resistant. Heavy coconut fiber ropes lashed around the beams and the *latte* caps held the structure together. The sizes and shapes of *latte* evolved gradually from crude, small early forms, sometimes with a coral head as a *tasa,* to smooth, large symmetrical columns by the time the Spaniards arrived. These pillars weathered into distinctive, mottled grey megaliths found nowhere else on earth.

Members of the Legazpi expedition in 1565 were the first Europeans to describe chamorro *latte* structures: "Their houses are high, well kept and well made . . . atop large stone pillars, upon which they lay the flooring and have a living room with bedrooms and quarters on each side of the living room. . . . They have other low houses on the ground where they cook and roast food." The large communal canoe house built on *latte* at Umatac impressed the Spaniards as a "beautiful structure with four transept naves," so spacious it could accommodate 200 people along with large canoes.

Thirty-seven years later, Juan Pobre corroborated that description of *latte* for Rota: "These are the best natives' houses I have ever seen because they are all built on stone pillars, which others do not have." The friar had traveled widely in the Philippines, Japan, and Mexico prior to his stay on Guam and had seen many traditional dwellings. The largest *latte* structures in the Marianas were in Rota and Tinian, with the "House of Taga" on Tinian built on *latte* sixteen feet high, a truly massive megalithic monument whose ruins remain today. Despite the *latte* form of construction, however, most buildings of the precontact Chamorros were of wood. These ordinary structures, along with most of the utensils, weapons, tools, and proas carved from wood, ended as food for termites, those ubiquitous terminators of all artifacts not made of stone, shell, or metal in the tropics.

The *latte,* like the flying proa, would cease being constructed or used by the Chamorros after the Spanish conquest. Today, the unique form of these pillars remains a motif everywhere on Guam in architecture, logos, and entranceways.

In their own way, the *latte* symbolized the separation of clans and the diffusion of authority among villages in Chamorro society. Each stone pillar was sound unto itself, like the clans, but linked to others by temporary bindings, not by a unified, solid foundation. The absence of political solidarity was a reflection of Chamorro kinship relations, which stressed clan and family autonomy. Kinship ties within clans and families, not tribal affinities, were the heartbeats of Chamorro culture.

A Parable of the Tribes

By the time the *latte* period of Chamorro development was fully under way several hundred years before Magellan's arrival, the island's social stratification was already fixed into hereditary clans in each village in control of land and resource rights and with specialized responsibilities. There was probably no unclaimed land. As a consequence, competition in the form of limited warfare increased between villages, as demonstrated by the much larger quantities of sling-stones and bone spear points in middens of *latte* sites as compared with the pre-*latte* periods.

As in many traditional societies, the basic social unit was the extended family, which could be quite large. The extended family lived in the same village or area, and kinship of relatives was determined through women. The Chamorro mother's lineage (matrilineage) determined ownership of property and land rights. Property rights extended beyond the shore and included portions of the fringe reefs,

House of Taga with *latte*. A reconstructed perspective of the ruins on Tinian with 16-foot-high *latte* stone columns and capstones supporting a wood frame "big house," as the Spaniards called the residences, canoe sheds, and men's houses (*uritao* in Chamorro) of precontact high-caste Chamorro clans in the Mariana Islands. These unique *latte* megalithic structures of the Chamorro culture were destroyed or fell into disuse during the Spanish conquest of the Marianas in 1668–1698. (Drawing from Morgan 1988)

offshore submerged reefs, and fishing rights out to sea. How far out is not known, but in Palau such rights extended as far as seabirds fly, or seventy-five to over 100 miles. The resources of the ocean were not free for all to take in traditional Pacific societies, although transit rights were usually open to everyone. Furthermore, any outsider who exploited a family's property, including the ocean, owed compensation to the owners, although the Spaniards and later the Americans were unaware of or indifferent to this custom.

Another Chamorro concept not shared by Europeans was that knowledge was private property of the clan or family and was not to be given away freely in the public domain or to strangers. Some knowledge, such as that concerned with medicine and magic, was held even more secret by a select few. Juan Pobre was offended by Chamorro evasions or lack of response when asked about customs: "Such is the foolishness with which they answer our questions, but they often say we are foolish to ask." This reticence may account for the Chamorro reputation among Spaniards of being deceitful. Pacific islanders today are still often evasive or reply with an answer they assume will be pleasing, not necessarily accurate, to interrogators on customary matters.

Land, reef, and water rights were not exclusive to individuals but were shared by family members. This use constituted a form of "managed commons" of resources rather than primitive communism, in which no one person owns land and which is managed for the common good by a political authority. Extended families made up the hereditary clans, each usually with its own village, whose members were hierarchically ranked by status. Clans were composed of two kinds of family castes (ascribed groupings into which people were born): one of low status called *manachang*, or commoners, and a high-ranking one called *chamorri* who had rights to property. The high and low castes did not normally intermarry and so were not related. There were different rankings among families within clans and between clans, depending on village location, wealth of property, genealogy, and so forth.

The *chamorri* high caste was composed of two classes (differing from castes in that a person's status could be changed): the *matua* (or *matao*), who were the highest class and from whom the headman *(maga'lahi)* and his wife *(maga'haga)* came, and the *acha'ot* (or *achoti*) class, members of whom were sometimes related to the *matua* but had been banished to be *acha'ot* because of some serious infraction of custom.

The *matua* and *acha'ot* were the fishermen and sailors, and the *manachang* were primarily farmers. The *manachang* did not own property, but they were not slaves to be bought or sold. They were free to seek land-use privileges and so had to be treated well by the *chamorri*. Juan Pobre described the relationship succinctly: "They do not use slaves to farm the land, instead they have *criados* whom they treat very well. They consider the people who live in the jungles and hills to be of lower status, and they call them *magachanes*. These, in turn, have great respect for the *principales* who live on the beaches, so much so that, without permission, they will not go near their houses, nor their *funeas*, nor their boats."

The Spanish word *criado* that Juan Pobre used can mean a servant or valet raised in a family, and *principales*—a term the Spaniards applied to all high-ranking Chamorros—refers to the *chamorri* (*funeas* were small, inshore proas). The traditional Chamorro social rankings would initially be respected, and exploited, by the Spaniards, but eventually they would be replaced by rankings determined primarily by race.

When a precontact Chamorro couple married, they lived with or in the village of the groom's maternal uncle (i.e., his mother's brother) on land of his clan, not with the parents of either spouse. Men kept the succession of clan *maga'lahi* and control of villages in their hands by having that title go to the *maga'lahi*'s brothers or, if none, to his nephews or cousins, not to his son by a wife, who was always from a different clan.

These relationships made marriage a form of political alliance between clans or families of different villages, but within the same caste stratifications. Bride's gifts were paid by the groom to the bride's father, and a large celebration was held at the marriage to legitimize the alliance. A husband was bound to his wife by the bride's gifts, which could be substantial and required help from his mother's clan to attain. If a man lost a wife (and thereby the bride's gifts) and wanted to marry again, he needed to get help once more from his matrilineage. Owing to property considerations, therefore, a man was under substantial pressure to make a marriage work, but the same pressure was not on a woman.

In this kind of society, male genealogy did not serve to perpetuate dynasties. Consequently, Chamorro politics involved constant realignments of kinship ties and endless shifts in the centers of male authority. Such realignments and shifts explain why there was neither political unity nor formal governmental institutions among the Chamorro clans. Another consequence of a communal matrilineal culture without a central political hierarchy was that no individual, including the village headman, assumed or was held to personal responsibility for the failure of any clan or family endeavor. The matrilineal core of their culture may also be a reason why the Chamorros—once they had been militarily defeated—so thoroughly embraced Spanish Catholicism with its focus on the cult of Mary.

Many visitors commented on the freedom of women in Chamorro society. García reports, rather disapprovingly, "In the home it is the mother who rules, and her husband does not dare give an order contrary to her wishes, nor punish the children, for she will turn upon him and beat him." Juan Pobre similarly noted the pecking order: "If the husband is unfaithful to his wife . . . she will leave the house, taking the children and all the household effects. . . . If the wife is unfaithful to the husband . . . this sin is considered less serious for the women than for the men."

While marriage was a commitment that involved control over wealth, premarital relations in which no property was involved were very liberal. A *chamorri* girl remained with her parents until mar-

riage, but a boy at puberty moved to live in the men's "big" house (*uritao* in Chamorro) in the village of his maternal uncle. In the men's house he was free to have sexual relations with unmarried women, usually from other villages. Illegitimate children were readily accepted into the mother's family. Chamorros were, however, exogamous; they permitted no sexual relations or marriages on the clan side within families.

In the *uritao,* a teenage *chamorri* boy was initiated into his uncle's clan (i.e., his mother's clan) and learned to fish, to navigate, and to use tools and weapons, particularly lances and slings for throwing stones. When adult, the young man married; he left the *uritao,* and he and his bride moved into a house built by their families in the village of his *uritao* and maternal uncle. Thus, uncles, not fathers, were the dominant males in Chamorro society. It was also important in property matters, as well as for family solidarity, to keep close ties among cousins, nieces, and nephews, a custom still strong on Guam today.

The freedom of unmarried people to have sex was promiscuous and immoral in the eyes of the Spanish priests. European soldiers and sailors, on the other hand, happily took advantage of the custom, but with disastrous results for the islanders. An Austrian who visited Guam on a Dutch ship in the 1620s described what happened when Chamorro women came aboard European ships: "They are well-shaped but very wanton because they showed us that we should do prostitution with them, which some of us actually did, but they had to suffer for it and to pay with their deaths." The suffering and deaths were caused by venereal and other diseases that European men transmitted to the Chamorros even before the Spaniards formally occupied the Marianas.

The complex kinship patterns of the Chamorros were related to their religious beliefs. They venerated their ancestors, who had bequeathed them their land and lineage. The spirit of one's own ancestor, called *anti,* was considered benign if due respect was shown to it. On the other hand, the spirit of an ancestor other than one's own, called *aniti* (sometimes spelled *anite;* pl., *maganiti* or *manganiti*), was feared as potentially dangerous.

Chamorros expressed veneration mainly by preserving an ancestor's skull as a talisman and by the practice of burying ancestors under *lattes* or in front of their houses. Fables and myths about ancestors were also sung at celebrations. Because of the practice of skull veneration, skulls separate from bodies and headless skeletons have been found by archaeologists in precontact Chamorro burial sites. The Chamorros, however, were neither headhunters nor cannibals, as were some other Pacific islanders.

After San Vitores arrived, some Spaniards thought that skull worship had been introduced by the Chinaman Choco, who opposed the missionaries. But Juan Pobre, writing much earlier, made it clear the Chamorros had long venerated their *anti*'s skulls: "Apparently, the one thing for which they have high regard are the skulls of their ancestors, especially those of their parents and grandparents. Many of these are kept in a high place inside their houses and, toward them, they make a kind of bowing gesture, thereby showing them a degree of respect."

Also associated with religion, as in most traditional cultures, was the ominous presence of the shaman-sorcerer in the society. The Chamorros called them *makahnas.* Juan Pobre described them: "These *macanas* have many skulls in their houses. . . . When the people of the village need water for their farmlands, they beseech the *macanas* to make rain." Chamorro society, however, was not theocratic; the *makahnas* did not wield formal political power, and Chamorro ancestor spirits apparently were never universalized; they remained local clan guardians. Thus, religious rituals of precontact Chamorros appear to have been meant to placate spirits rather than to worship deities. Before the Spanish priests arrived, the Chamorros had neither a unifying theology nor a formal philosophy in the European sense with an epistemology on the nature of knowledge and an ontology on the nature of being.

Casters of spells and healers of the sick, the *makahnas* interceded with dangerous *aniti,* who hid in large trees to guard ancestral lands. Later, under Spanish and American rule, *manganiti* would still be feared by the superstitious Catholic Chamorros as *taotaomo'na,* "people of before," hiding in banyan *(nunu)* trees. The Chamorro spiritual landscape was also peopled by mischievous elves, later called *duendes* in Spanish, who lurked in enchanted glades. The *makahnas* became enemies of the Catholic missionaries in the bloody confrontations over religion after the arrival of Father San Vitores, and the Spaniards suppressed them ruthlessly. Vestiges of *makahnas,* however, continued under the Spaniards and into the early American period as *kakahnas,* sorcerers of black magic who practiced in secret, and as *suruhanus* (men) or *suruhanas* (women), folk herb healers who appeared after the Spanish conquest.

The close family and clan linkages of the precontact Chamorro kinship structure were supplemented by a pervasive custom of mandatory obligations between unrelated individuals. The principal expression of such obligations was *chenchule',* the giving of gifts or services that obligates the recipient to reciprocate to the giver. *Chenchule'* could be a gift as small as sharing betel nut or as large as massive strings of precious turtle shell money. Important gifts had to be rewarded either by repayment in kind or by forming a kinship bond with the giver. Wealthy *chamorri* could therefore build a network of kinship bonds by giving gifts as well as by arranging marriages. A man's prestige was measured by the number of people who would come to his aid to reciprocate *chenchule'* when he was in need. Conversely, a man who shirked obligations would not receive aid when he needed it.

This giving of gifts for prestige existed in other oceanic traditional societies and was made possible by an economy that one anthropologist aptly described as "subsistence affluence." A man gained prestige, not by working hard and selling what he produced in order to attain a higher material standard of living, but by giving away what his skill produced. That ethos was diametrically opposite the European outlook, particularly the entrepreneurial aggressiveness of Americans, who delight in individual material acquisition and conspicuous personal consumption. *Chenchule'* among Chamorros survives today on Guam as a gift, usually money, and also in the form of *ayuda,* a Spanish term for reciprocal assistance, at weddings, fiestas, and wakes and in political loyalty and donations to charities.

Anyone to whom no reciprocal obligations were owed was a potential enemy to precontact Chamorros. A person who had obligations to another but did not fulfill them, or caused an injury, incurred the enmity of the entire clan of the injured person. Thus, most hostility among the islanders was caused by feuds between clans, usually one village fighting another located some distance away, over injuries to individuals. An implication of this was that Spaniards or other foreigners were potential prospects for mutual obligations, but when the aliens refused such obligations, either deliberately or through ignorance of the custom, they then became potential enemies of the Chamorros.

Competition and rivalry, as well as the potential for the eruption of warfare, were normal between Chamorros of unrelated villages and with anyone outside the culture. Sports for male youths focused on preparation for warfare, and weapons were carried for use by Chamorro men among strangers. Actual combat, however, was usually ritualistic. The chief weapons—sling-stones and lances—although dangerous, kept combatants at a healthy distance from each other.

Chamorro warfare was therefore mainly a cultural means to satisfy vengeance and perhaps to test manhood and the strength of alliances among clans, particularly as to land and resource rights. García observed, "When they arrive at the moment of battle, peace is quickly arranged, for one side, having lost two or three warriors, gives up the fight." Combat was usually between individuals or small groups, not masses of disciplined warriors.

When the Jesuit missionaries arrived in 1668, Guam's two largest villages were Agaña (*Hagatña*

in Chamorro, pronounced as *Agaña* in English as well as Spanish) and Tumon (*Tomhom* in Chamorro). Using information from the San Vitores mission reports, García stated that there were over 1,500 people in the area of Agaña, with fifty-three houses of the *chamorri* and 150 houses of the *manachang* when San Vitores arrived. Despite the authority of the *chamorri* in these two villages, neither village dominated the island of Guam, and there was no overall island chief or a tribal government in the Marianas as a whole. Father Martín Ignacio de Loyola, who stopped in the Ladrones on an Acapulco galleon in 1581, reported, "None of these islands has a king or recognized ruler, to whom the rest are subject." The authority of headmen rarely extended beyond their village's "immediate vicinity," according to García.

The political autonomy of Chamorro clans from each other did not lend itself to unified political or military efforts to maximize power. If a Chamorro was killed by Spaniards, only the members of that Chamorro's clan were obligated to redress the wrong; other clans would go on dealing with the Spaniards as if nothing had occurred. In other words, the Chamorro people were holistic culturally but not politically. The Chamorros were never a unified tribe. They held no concepts of the need for economic or political development in European terms or for religious conversion of other peoples even though their culture appeared to be evolving toward a larger and more complex societal organization that was blocked by the overwhelming intrusion of the Spaniards. The Chamorro ethos certainly fostered intellectual development, as evinced by their remarkable proas and *latte* structures.

Like many traditional island cultures, the precontact Chamorros lived in fragile symbiosis with nature, not in a balance, but in an interdependence that imposed an acceptance of limits on the part of humans. In contrast, the Spanish empire, unlike the precontact Chamorro society, was a power-maximizing system with a national mission stoked by spiritual fervor. Spain was the protector of the Catholic Church, itself a power-maximizing system for universal religious ends. And, in the Spanish empire, religion, government, and the military were fused into a massive collective singular under the Patronato Real—central control under the Spanish crown—in the unlimited pursuit of power to conquer nature, not compromise with it.

A central irony of the struggles of the Chamorro people against Europeans is that, in order to mount a successful defense, the islanders had to become like the outsiders. The Spaniards would impose on the politically decentralized Chamorro clans the need for governmental centralization to defend themselves. This paradox has been called the parable of the tribes: that is, political power under whatever guise is like a contaminant, a disease, that once introduced among peoples will inexorably become universal in a system of competing societies. Anthropologists have described the parable of the tribes as a division between "resilient societies" (which adapt by maintaining population and resource needs below the environmental carrying capacity) and "power-based societies" (which adapt by acquiring more territory, resources, and people). The resilient, non-power-based society is found more often among small traditional cultures, while the power-based kind is found mainly among "Western" (meaning European) nation-state societies.

One consequence of a power-based society is a growth economy, an ever-expanding materialistic system in competition with its neighbors, with its natural environment, and with its own past. It was this aggressive power system that the Europeans imposed worldwide in their colonial expansion after Columbus, Magellan, and other *conquistadores* opened up the pathways to lands beyond Europe. Peoples who do not become power maximizing are subsumed by such men and by their predatory system.

The need to centralize authority and maximize power would be imposed on the Chamorros by the arrival on Guam of the Jesuit missionary Diego Luís de San Vitores, a quintessential Spanish hero-saint, the conqueror and savior of the Mariana Islands. How the islanders responded to the parable of the tribes as posed by Father San Vitores backed by the power of the Spanish crown and the church of Rome would determine the destiny of the Chamorros as a people.

3 Father San Vitores
1662–1672

Soldier of an Alien God

On a sunlit day in May 1662, the Spanish ship *San Damián* furled sails and slowed in crystal blue tropical waters as it approached a high, dark green island in the western Pacific. The island was one of the Islas de los Ladrones, as they were still called by Europeans in that period. Which specific island was not recorded, but it was most likely either Guam or Rota, where such stopovers were by then routine. The ship, a two-masted brigantine (*patache* in Spanish) faster and smaller than a galleon and used to carry supplies, had left Acapulco in April en route to Manila with a contingent of fifteen Jesuit priests bound for assignments in the Philippines.

No Spanish settlement existed in the Ladrones at the time, so the ship did not anchor but as usual stood offshore from an inlet for a day or so to obtain water and fresh food from the islanders who sailed out in their proas. Dozens of these graceful canoes filled with naked Chamorros surrounded the *San Damián*. The islanders eagerly passed up baskets filled with glistening fish, colorful fruits, and other fresh produce in barter for iron and European goods lowered on ropes by the ship's crew. Chamorro men were still not allowed on board Spanish ships because they continued to steal things even after decades of contact with Europeans. This once-a-year arrival of Spanish ships had been going on for nearly three generations of

Chamorros by 1662. It was important for them as the only way to obtain barrel hoops of iron (*hiero* to the Chamorros, who apparently adopted the word from the Spanish *hierro*, "iron") and nails (*lulok* in Chamorro), on which they now depended to replenish their knife blades, adzes, and fishhooks.

On deck among the black-robed priests who watched the Chamorros clamor for the *hiero* and *lulok* stood the Jesuit superior, a slim thirty-four-year-old Spanish aristocrat, Father Diego Luís de San Vitores. He had the delicate white skin, light reddish-brown hair, and bright blue eyes of a Castilian from the city of Burgos in the north of Spain. His eyes were weak from long study of poorly printed religious texts in the dim light of Jesuit classrooms, so he wore eyeglasses. These were still clumsy, large-framed devices in the seventeenth century.

The glasses gave San Vitores an owlish look below his high forehead and over his long curved nose and small dark mustache. He disliked the glasses and later preferred not to wear them on treks through humid jungles. This meant he often had to be led by hand or rope by guides on trails in the Philippines and the Marianas. Without the glasses, he was a handsome man in a somber way, usually unsmiling and intense.

The vivid scene with the eager Chamorros in the Ladrones made a deep impression on Father San Vitores. To him, Chamorros were free, untamed pagans, like innocent children, living in an unenlightened state of nature. Like friars Antonio de los Angeles and Juan Pobre de Zamora before him, San Vitores felt an overwhelming responsibility to save these foresaken souls despite—or perhaps because of—their neglect by the Spanish authorities.

Acapulco was too distant to support a Spanish settlement in the Ladrones, so the authorities in Manila had been authorized several times by Madrid over the years to establish a mission on Guam, but they had not done so. Manila's priority was on the Philippines, where commerce and the demand to convert and serve a population much larger than that of the Ladrones already strained available manpower and other resources. It was also difficult most of the year to sail from the Philippines to the Ladrones against the northeast trade winds. With no mission in the islands, San Vitores, unlike the Franciscans earlier, as a dutiful Jesuit sailed on to the Philippines when the *San Damián* departed the Ladrones. However, he never forgot that first soul-stirring sight of pagan Pacific islanders, whose salvation he came to identify with his calling as a missionary.

Before departure, the crew of the *San Damián* took aboard for transport to Manila an old illiterate Visayan Filipino named Esteban who had been aboard the galleon *Concepción* wrecked at Saipan in 1638. In his long residence on Guam since the shipwreck, Esteban had become fluent in Chamorro. This shadowy old man would become San Vitores' Chamorro language interpreter.

San Vitores appears to have been destined from childhood to be a missionary in the Society of Jesus, that most disciplined and educated of all religious orders. Born in Burgos on 12 November 1627, he was baptized Diego Jerónimo de San Vitores y Alonso de Maluendo. His father, Jerónimo de San Vitores de la Portilla, was a prominent knight of the Order of Saint James. San Vitores' mother, the severe and haughty Doña María Alonso de Malu-

endo y Salamanca, was also from one of Burgos' oldest noble families. She claimed descent from El Cid Campeador, born Rodrigo Díaz de Vivar, the great hero-liberator of northern Spain in the eleventh century. Through his parents and relatives, San Vitores had access to the highest court and church circles in the reigns of Philip IV and his widow, Queen Regent Mariana of Austria. These connections to sources of power would be invaluable to San Vitores later in persuading reluctant Spanish officials to establish a mission in the Ladrones.

After early schooling by Jesuits, and despite family objections, San Vitores was admitted in 1640 at age thirteen as a Jesuit novitiate. He completed the arduous Jesuit studies in 1650 with distinction and in 1651 was ordained a priest in the Compañía de Jesús, as the Jesuit order was called in Spain. Following several more years of study and teaching, he was assigned in 1655 to the faculty of the prestigious university at Alcalá de Henares, normally a lifetime position.

Nonetheless, after recovering from several severe illnesses, he used all the influence he could muster, again overcoming family objections, to be sent abroad as a missionary and fulfill his apostolic vocation. Ordered to the Philippines, he sailed from Cádiz in May 1660 for Vera Cruz. In Mexico, where nearly a century and a half of harsh Spanish rule had tamed most Indians to docile acceptance of Christianity, the impatient San Vitores was held up for two years before sailing at last in 1662 on the *San Damián* for the Philippines by way of the Ladrones.

In the Philippines, San Vitores learned the Tagalog language so quickly he was preaching in it three months after his arrival. Innovative and energetic, he breathed new life into Tagalog parishes through "popular missions" in which he and other priests walked the streets, carrying a large crucifix while crying out the Act of Contrition in Tagalog in a loud voice. This was followed by fervent sermons as a crowd gathered, and led to emotional baptisms. These techniques had great response at the grass-roots level.

Although effective, most of this labor involved

parishes where conversions had already been made by earlier missionaries. This kind of service was not San Vitores' goal. He wanted to be at the vanguard of evangelical work among true infidels, not lapsed Christians. A complex but unswerving man, San Vitores aimed from an early age at conversion of the poor, symbolized in the biblical Latin phrase *Evangelizare pauperibus misi te* (I have sent you to evangelize the poor), to which he often referred in his letters. And, in his view, the poorest people, both spiritually and materially, whom he encountered were the Chamorros. In order to return to them, he launched a persistant campaign in the Philippines to open a mission in the Ladrones.

Establishment of a mission on Guam would entail not only a contingent of Jesuit priests to christianize the Chamorros but also Spanish soldiers to protect the missionaries. The Spaniards called such an effort a *reducción* to subdue, convert, and gather pagans into Christian congregations. The spiritual *reducción* of Indians, and the accompanying spread of Spanish secular authority by the military, also served Spanish trade. In other words, the cross of the church and the sword of the state supported each other in the complex relationship of the Patronato Real under the Spanish crown.

Through the Council of the Indies and the viceroys, governors, and *audiencias* (the highest council/court) in the colonies, the crown provided material support and security to the church's missionary efforts. This mutually reinforcing combination of spiritual and temporal powers gave Spain the greatest colonial empire on earth in the sixteenth and seventeenth centuries. Therefore, what San Vitores was requesting in the 1660s was not just a minor evangelical effort but a commitment by church and state to a modest but strategically significant extension of the Spanish empire into the Pacific Ocean.

The Jesuit superiors of San Vitores were reluctant to endorse his request but also hesitated to rebuff a person with court connections. So they sent him to the archbishop in Manila, Manuel Poblete, and to the governor-general, Diego Salcedo.

Archbishop Poblete supported the request, but Salcedo, backed by the members of the Audiencia in Manila, refused. They argued that, no matter how laudable spiritually, a mission in the Ladrones was impractical. The civil authorities were content to let the Ladrones remain as they were, a free reprovision point for the Acapulco galleons without need for expensive soldiers and supplies.

By 1664, San Vitores' quest for a mission among the Chamorros had become an obsession with him. Frustrated by the rebuffs of civil authorities in Manila, he decided to go over their heads and address his plea directly to the court in Spain. In July 1664, he posted a letter to his father, asking him to present an "enclosed letter" to King Philip IV. The letter was an extraordinary memorandum, entitled a *Memorial* in Spanish, written partially in the words of the long-dead Jesuit Saint Francis Xavier and partly in San Vitores' own words. The *Memorial,* using the words of Saint Xavier, prophetically warned the king he would soon die and be called to account by God (Philip IV was a notorious libertine, fathering thirty illegitimate children, but he was also famous for bouts of religious repentance out of fear of God's vengeance). Emerging with his own voice in the *Memorial,* San Vitores pointed out to King Philip that his ministers in the Indies were neglecting evangelization of infidels and allowing mistreatment of converted *indios* and that a mission should be established in the Ladrones.

San Vitores then followed up the *Memorial* by persuading Archbishop Poblete to write a letter in June 1665 directly to Philip in support of the mission. Two documents were enclosed with the archbishop's letter: a certificate by the Spanish admiral in Manila, Esteban Ramos (who had been the pilot on the *Concepción* and spent several years in the Marianas after the 1638 wreck), on the need for a mission in the Ladrones, and a long paper with the title *Papel de Motivos* that presented the "motives for not delaying further the conquest and instruction of the Islands of the Thieves."

Not content with these messages, San Vitores

added insurance to his quest by also writing in 1665 to the Austrian Father Juan Everardo Nithard, who was Queen Mariana's Jesuit confessor and thus in a position of great influence. San Vitores had met Nithard in Spain and knew that a message to him would reach the queen, which it did. San Vitores also knew that Mariana was a deeply religious woman who took personal interest in missionary work, particularly the baptism of infidel children. This queen was not timid; when younger, she was known as Coto Doñana because she loved to hunt on horseback in the Coto area of southern Spain. Through Nithard, San Vitores asked that the queen direct "all her energies towards the conversion and reduction of these Islands [the Ladrones] to the faith of Jesus Christ," and he stressed the need to save the Chamorro children.

As audacious as San Vitores' maneuverings may appear, his methods proved correct to circumvent the massive bureaucracy of the Spanish colonial system and to succeed in the murky politics of the court. According to one historian, the last years of Philip IV's reign found Spain "a shattered Monarchy, itself no more than a pallid relic of the great imperial past." Direct intervention at any governmental level by the sovereigns or their ministers in response to personal appeals by church officials and court favorites was normal. The king and queen received San Vitores' messages favorably, and, on 24 June 1665, Philip issued two *cédulas* (royal edicts), one to the governor-general in Manila that a ship be provided San Vitores and another to San Vitores to establish a mission at Guam. In eerie fulfillment of San Vitores' prediction, the king died in September 1665, leaving Mariana regent for their four-year-old heir, the feebleminded Charles II, for the next eleven years.

The *cédulas* took until June 1666 to reach Manila. Annoyed at San Vitores' pulling strings in Spain, Governor-General Salcedo and the Manila Audiencia nonetheless complied with the royal decrees and ordered that an auxiliary galleon of 300 tons be constructed in Cavite for the now-elated San Vitores. Salcedo commanded that the ship be named *San Diego* in honor of both himself and San Vitores.

The zealous Jesuit's troubles were still not over, however. There was no money authorized for the Ladrones mission, apparently an oversight by the king. Therefore, the *San Diego* was ordered by the governor-general to go first all the way to Mexico, where San Vitores was somehow to obtain funds before going to the Ladrones. This order greatly pleased the powerful Spanish merchants of Manila, who foresaw commercial profits from San Vitores' trip. They had earlier proposed that the ship go to Peru first, where even more profits could be had, but objections by San Vitores made them drop that project.

In August 1667, San Vitores and his fellow Jesuit Tomás de Cardenoso sailed in the brand-new *San Diego* from Cavite, arriving five months later in Acapulco. The Jesuits hurried to Mexico City and requested money of the viceroy, the Marqués de Mancera, and of the Audiencia of Mexico, which at that time had jurisdiction over the Philippines. The reply was a flat no: the treasury lacked funds, and in any case Mexico's viceroy had received no official instructions to give money to Father San Vitores.

It was during a subsequent conversation of San Vitores' with the viceroy and his wife that a coincidence occurred that was interpreted as divine intervention in favor of the priest. The viceroy was refusing impassioned pleas by both his wife and San Vitores to fund the Guam mission when a powerful earthquake struck Mexico City. The intimidated viceroy met hastily the next day with the Audiencia even though it was Sunday, and they all immediately pledged money to Father San Vitores. Other citizens of the city then donated even more funds, as well as jewels, clothing for the Chamorros, and furnishings for the churches to be built in the Ladrones.

Three months later, the *San Diego* departed Acapulco with San Vitores and Cardenoso aboard along with other Jesuits, some Filipino catechists, and a complement of soldiers. Just before departure, San Vitores wrote another letter to Queen

Mariana in which he asked for more money and supplies. The small missionary group also included Esteban, the Filipino survivor of the *Concepción* wreck who had been retrieved by the *San Damián* in 1662 on Guam. He had been hired by San Vitores in the Philippines to teach him the Chamorro language and was brought along as an interpreter for the Marianas mission. San Vitores had started studying Chamorro in the Philippines, where he translated some hymns and prayers. It was during the voyage from Acapulco that he completed in Latin the first rough grammar of the Chamorro language and translated the catechism into Chamorro with the help of Esteban.

On the morning of 15 June 1668, eighty-nine days out of Acapulco, the welcome cry, "Tierra, Tierra," rang out from a crewman as mass was being said aboard the ship. The flat mesa mountain of Rota showed above the horizon. Soon Guam was sighted, and in the afternoon dozens of proas filled with Chamorros surrounded the *San Diego*. The islanders busily commenced the usual barter alongside the ship, happily yelling, "Mauleg, mauleg" (good, good) at the black-robed priests on deck. A Jesuit scholastic (student priest), Brother Marcelo Ansaldo, who would continue on to the Philippines with the ship, later described the bartering in a letter to Queen Mariana: "Thirty years ago a ship which carried many little gold chains and many ivory crucifixes and other statuettes was wrecked here and many of these statuettes and chains were salvaged. To this day the natives barter those little gold chains or ivory images for iron." The ship to which Brother Ansaldo referred was the *Concepción*, wrecked on Saipan in 1638.

By nightfall, the *San Diego* was close to Guam near the village of Hagåtña, which the Spaniards at first called Agania or Agadna, and then Agaña, and which would become modern-day Agana (the Americans dropped the diacritic over the *n* but still pronounce it as "Agaña"). The *San Diego* first dropped anchor in a spot with a sandy bottom and slowly dragged anchor during the night. While this was going on, the Chamorros warily remained in their proas despite the priests' appeals for them to come aboard the ship, which from the Chamorros' experience was abnormal behavior for the Spaniards.

Only after the priests chanted the Litany of Our Lady, ending with words prophetic for the future of the Chamorros, "Sancta Maria: Ora pro nobis" (Holy Mary: Pray for us), did the islanders begin to climb aboard the *San Diego*. There they were greeted in strangely accented Chamorro phrases and embraced by a gaunt forty-year-old Jesuit who wore a well-worn black cassock and large-framed eyeglasses. The ship would not anchor firmly until the next day, 16 June 1668, but Father Diego Luís de San Vitores knew he was at last back in the Ladrones after six long years of dedicated effort to return.

A Mission of Martyrs

The landing the next day was described by Brother Ansaldo:

> It was God's will that all was fine, so on Saturday, June 16 at 4:00 P.M. we dropped anchor in front of what seemed to be a bay across from a coconut grove.... That afternoon the Pilot, Father Luís de Medina, Superior of the Philippine Mission, and his interpreter, who knew the language well, went ashore. More than 200 men, with spears made out of human shinbones, awaited their arrival. They wanted to know about the ship which had just sailed in. Father Medina and his interpreter told them that the priests had come to stay and would teach them the way to heaven.

The first Chamorro headman whom Medina's party met on the beach among the 200 warriors was a man called Fatahurno, to whom the Spaniards gave presents of iron. The presents were well received, and Medina returned to the *San Diego* for more barrel hoops, nails, and trinkets before once more landing on the beach. The party was then led across a stream to the village of Agaña, whose elderly headman was Kipuhá (at times spelled Kepuha and transliterated to Quipuha by the Jesuit historian García), one of the ranking high-caste *cha-*

Mariana of Austria. The queen regent of Spain from 1665 to 1677 in whose honor Father San Vitores in 1668 changed the islands' name bestowed by Magellan in 1521 from "The Islands of Thieves" to "The Mariana Islands." She is shown in a nun's habit she wore after the death of her husband, King Philip IV, in 1665. Mariana provided substantial funds and other assistance to the Jesuit mission on Guam. She was imprisoned in 1677 by her son Charles II so that he could become king; she died in 1696. (Seventeenth-century oil portrait attributed to Claudio Coello, Prado Museum, Madrid)

morri nobles on Guam. This headman may have been the same Quipuha who had helped the six Spaniards from the *Concepción* wreck sail to the Philippines in 1639. Medina gave Quipuha gifts of iron and a velvet hat, "with which he was very much pleased," wrote García. By then it was nearly sunset, so Medina and his companions spent the night as Quipuha's guests in a large, stuffy hut in Agaña.

While Medina's party spent the night on shore with the Chamorros, on board the *San Diego*

Father San Vitores was surprised when a Christian Visayan Filipino, Pedro Calonsor (or Casor, and sometimes Calangsor in different accounts), came aboard from Guam. He was a survivor of the wreck of the galleon *Concepción* on Saipan thirty years earlier. Pedro brought aboard his two-year-old half-Chamorro daughter. She was promptly baptized and given the baptismal name Mariana. The little girl was apparently the first person on Guam documented to be baptized a Christian. Pedro Calonsor became a catechist and trusted companion of San

Vitores. Another *Concepción* survivor, a Malabar native called Lorenzo de Morales, also joined the mission as a catechist.

It was after the baptism of Mariana that Father San Vitores named the archipelago Las Islas Marianas in honor of the queen regent. From then on the Spaniards often called Chamorros Marianos as well as *indios* and *nativos*. No formal ceremony was noted by García, and in fact, in earlier letters to Spain written in Mexico, San Vitores had called the islands the Marianas in place of Islas de los Ladrones. The new name would be used thereafter by the Spaniards in official references, but the old name Ladrones lingered because it was on numerous maps.

San Vitores went ashore for the first time the next day after Medina returned with news that all appeared peaceful. San Vitores was received with much dancing and celebration by the Chamorros. He said his first mass ashore at an altar erected on the beach near some small Chamorro huts that Medina had named the Pueblo de los Mártires in honor of the saints' day. This location must have been near present-day East Agaña, but the prescient title, like many of the new place names that the Spaniards bestowed everywhere in the islands, would later disappear as the old Chamorro names reasserted themselves in modified forms. Remarkably, San Vitores preached his initial sermon on Guam completely in Chamorro at this first mass. During the unloading of supplies from the ship, Brother Ansaldo recorded one historic little scene: "A moment of intense surprise and interest was when our sailors brought ashore rams, sheep, a little bull, a cow and three parrots which are to stay here. The *indios* had never seen any of these animals before so they greatly marvelled at seeing them."

On Tuesday, the *San Diego* departed for the Philippines, leaving the little mission of approximately fifty men on their own for a year until the next galleon would arrive. As the father superior, San Vitores was both the spiritual leader and the secular chief executive with control of the soldiers through the military commander, Captain Juan de Santa Cruz. The captain is sometimes erroneously listed as the first governor in history books, but the title governor would not be used until 1676. The mission consisted of five Jesuit priests, one scholastic brother (Lorenzo Bustillo), three Spanish officers, and about forty or forty-one non-Spaniards. These latter were mostly Filipinos but included some Mexican mestizos of Spanish and Indian descent. Thirty-one of the non-Spaniards were soldiers and the remainder either catechists or servants.

This small band of aliens was left to face a population of perhaps 12,000 Chamorros on the island of Guam and about 12,000–18,000 more throughout the Marianas, a total of between 24,000 and 30,000 Chamorros in the year 1668. The population may already have been in decline because of diseases introduced by aliens as far back as Legazpi in 1565.

In order to convert this many people with only five priests, San Vitores baptized infants, particularly those in danger of death, and the elderly in groups without catechizing them and with (or without, if necessary) the parents' concurrence for children. Adults other than the elderly were baptized after being catechized, often in mass groups. Instruction in religious doctrine was accomplished by the Chamorros singing in unison after the priests. In accord with the Jesuit practice of *Cuius regio, eius religio* (As the king, so the religion), the priests endeavored to convert the headmen and other *chamorri* of each village first as examples for the populace. At the first mass in Agaña, San Vitores baptized twenty-three children in one group, and 1,500 adults were "converted" (i.e., they indicated they wished to become Christians) to be baptized later after receiving doctrinal instruction.

Within a few days, San Vitores and a companion set out on an initial reconnaissance of Guam but were soon obliged to return to Agaña at the request of the *chamorri* there, who were worried that San Vitores might settle in some other village. The Chamorros in Agaña called San Vitores Padre Magas, or Father Superior. They jealously kept him a virtual prisoner in the village for almost two months. Word about the arrival of the foreigners had spread quickly among the Chamorros throughout the islands. It became a matter of prestige for a village to possess one of these novel new *makahnas* who handed out iron and other gifts in return for participation in their strange rituals. Rota sent a delegation to Agaña to ask that a priest be sent to that island.

To satisfy this initial wave of enthusiasm by the Chamorros, San Vitores spread his staff throughout the main islands. He and Lorenzo Bustillo remained in Agaña—named San Ignacio de Agaña by San Vitores—as the capital of the mission. Father Luís de Medina traveled to the other villages on Guam; Father Pedro de Casanova went to Rota; and Fathers Tomás de Cardenoso and Luís de Morales sailed by proas to Tinian and later to Saipan. Each priest usually had a Filipino catechist assistant, but the soldiers were stationed at Agaña.

All went exceedingly well for the missionaries the first few weeks. Quipuha made land available for a church and a residence. These shed-like buildings (called *camarins* by the Spaniards) were constructed of local palomaría and coconut logs with thatched palm roofs. The buildings of the first little Spanish mission were probably near the present-day Chief Quipuha Park. This area was later designated the Barrio de San Antonio and may have included the original Chamorro village of Hagåtña. The missionaries planted maize, the seeds for which they brought from Mexico, the first corn grown on Guam.

On his arrival on Rota, Father Casanova baptized more than 300 children. In his first three months on Guam, Father Luís de Medina reported he baptized over 3,000 people. The missionaries placed great value on these spiritual body counts, which were reported with pride to church officials and to the queen regent in Spain. It would take a later missionary in the Marianas—Father Francisco Salgado—to explain in a letter written in 1683 the exaggerated baptismal figures of the early priests. He wrote, "The explanation is that the natives

thoroughly enjoyed the ceremony, and, being delighted with the rosaries which they were given to wear around their necks, presented themselves again and again for baptism, unrecognized by the Padres until long after."

The very success of the new faith, however, led to the first negative reaction by the Chamorros. Because conversion was at first prestigious for the islanders, the *chamorri* nobles in Agaña demanded that baptism be restricted to them alone and not be accorded the *manachang* commoners. San Vitores insisted on equality of treatment. The *chamorri* (presumably Quipuha and his clan in Agaña) were adamant, and San Vitores experienced for the first time some disrespect and even danger from the *chamorri*, wrote García.

San Vitores held firm and refused to baptize anyone unless he could baptize all. The *chamorri* gave in, and Quipuha was the first adult baptized. With much solemnity, he was given the title and name Don Juan Quipuha. The Jesuits had been instructed to bestow the titles *don* and *doña* before Christian names on converted *chamorri* in recognition of their service to the church.

Victory for San Vitores in this first showdown was due not just to his strength of character. It was due also to indifference on the part of Europeans toward the values and customs of *indios* in general. For example, writing in 1681 of the Chamorros, García stated contemptuously, "They have no laws whatever." The Chamorros of course had numerous traditional laws. Their culture may have viewed the creed of the foreigners as powerful new knowledge and therefore a form of property. In their perceptions, such knowledge was not public property to be dispensed freely. Rather, the knowledge of the new religion was to be restricted to the highest clans, particularly the clan that was the protector of the missionaries.

Thus, in this first encounter over access to the new knowledge of the imported religion, the Jesuits indirectly started the erosion of the traditional rights of the governing *chamorri*. Perhaps still in awe of the aliens, for the time being the *chamorri* accepted this restriction on their rights, but their tolerance would fade rapidly in the face of further uncompromising demands by the missionaries.

Before baptizing Quipuha, San Vitores had already initiated the destruction of ancestor skulls and carved idols over the vehement objections of the Chamorros. This missionary zeal led to a confrontation with the Chinaman Choco. García states that Choco "began to circulate a report that the Padres...had been banished to Guam...that they would kill anyone they baptized, especially children, and that if one who was especially strong was able to resist that poisoned water, it would at least cause him to have dropsy, declaring he had seen it thus in Manila."

When some newborn infants died soon after baptism, the Chamorros began to fear that the baptismal water was poisonous, as Choco warned. Since the missionaries took care, in accord with Christian doctrine, to baptize infants who appeared to be near death in order to save their souls, the death rate was higher among baptized than non-baptized infants, thereby increasing Chamorro suspicions of the priests. By August 1668, only six weeks after the Jesuits arrived, the Chamorros began to turn hostile. On 16 August, Father Luís de Morales was wounded in the leg on Saipan. About the same time, Luís de Medina was wounded in the face on Guam. And, on 19 August, the Chamorros killed a Spanish soldier, Sergeant Lorenzo Castellanos, along with his Tagalog servant, Gabriel de la Cruz, in a proa on the ocean near Tinian.

San Vitores met the rising threat head-on; he sailed to Choco's village of Paa on Guam's southern coast in order to convert him. Prudently, he took along the Spanish military commander, Captain Juan de Santa Cruz, as well as three armed Filipinos. The confrontation with Choco amid a crowd of curious Chamorros lasted for three days of public debate. It reached a climax when the captain saved San Vitores from an inexplicable assassination attempt by one of his Filipino retainers just as the priest was about to baptize Choco. The captain was wounded, and the assailant fled to the hills above Malesso, a village that was later called Merizo by the Spaniards and the Americans. San Vitores showed great coolness and proceeded to christen the cowed Choco with the name Ignacio.

After San Vitores returned to Agaña, the Chinaman's conversion did not stick, and Ignacio reverted to Choco. The Chinaman may have harbored a grudge against Spanish priests from his days in the Philippines, where the Spaniards discriminated against Chinese merchants. Choco renewed his agitation against the Christians. From then on, the fieldwork of the missionaries throughout the Marianas became hazardous. It took considerable courage on the part of the Spaniards and Filipinos to continue to go forth among the now-sullen Chamorros.

Go forth they did, however. San Vitores and Luís de Morales sailed to the northern Marianas, in those days a hazardous voyage over hundreds of miles of open ocean in proas manned by converted Chamorros. Father Morales traveled all the way to Pagan in the far north, while San Vitores crisscrossed Saipan, Tinian, and Rota before returning to Guam in early 1669. Everywhere San Vitores pressed converted islanders to cover their nakedness in palm shirts and skirts (the original cloth brought from Mexico having been used up early on Guam). By this time San Vitores himself presented a rather strange sight, and he appeared to be seeking martyrdom. García describes him:

> His cassock, which he invented in Agadna, was a sack woven of palm leaves, to which he added a hat and a bonnet of the same material...he often went barefoot....In his hand he had a long staff with a Cross at its head, which with a handkerchief or similar object, served as a banner...in some places he was badly received by the villagers and treated as an enemy who had come to take the lives of their children; and sometimes while he was in the act of preaching they threatened to run him through with their lances.

In this kind of hostile environment, San Vitores must have been under great stress. To toughen his body and maintain his spiritual integrity, he wore under his cassock a cilice, a penitent's jacket or belt with wire points protruding inward. He also practiced *disciplina* nightly, according to García, wherein he beat himself about the neck and back with a cord in the customary Spanish flagellation for penitence. Both as an example and as befitted his own modest lifestyle, he lived an ascetic life, eating mainly yams, shredded coconut, and some fish, all foods that he found easier to eat as he had no teeth. He fasted often, and he entered trance-like states of religious ecstasy "outside himself," in García's words, in which he saw visions.

On his return to Agaña in early 1669, San Vitores initiated construction (out of coconut tree trunks and other wood) of a seminary, the Colegio de San Juan de Letrán (*colegio* in Spanish was then equivalent to a religious elementary school and not to a college of higher education). The school was to train carefully selected Chamorro boys to be interpreters and catechists for the priests. It would not be in full operation until 1673 and would later be rebuilt of coral masonry called *mampostería*. This school, the first European academic institution in Oceania, would last for over two centuries as Guam's main school until the last remnants were demolished in 1893–1895.

On 2 February 1669, a small wooden church named Dulce Nombre de María was dedicated. Soon after the dedication, Quipuha died of natural causes, depriving the missionaries of a powerful *chamorri* protector. San Vitores insisted Quipuha be buried in the Agaña church, the first Chamorro to be so honored. The headman's family, however, wanted him interred under "what they called big houses," according to a Jesuit report on the incident. San Vitores would not yield, and Quipuha was buried in the church with a mass. This dismissal of an important custom of the *chamorri* (that is, to have the spirit of the dead Quipuha under the family residence, where it could protect the living) provoked Chamorro resentment of the Jesuits in Agaña for the first time, resentment that would swell into warfare within two years.

*   *   *

In June 1669, to the immense relief of the beleaguered mission, the Acapulco galleon *San José* dropped anchor off Agaña with Manuel de León aboard, the new governor-general of the Philippines. The previous governor-general, Diego Salcedo, had been arrested by the Inquisition (one of the hazards of Spanish public office at the time), and Manuel de Léon was en route to replace him. The galleon remained several days and unloaded badly needed supplies. The new governor-general also left six soldiers, firearms, and ammunition for the defense of the mission. San Vitores sent off a batch of letters and reports, including another letter to Queen Mariana. He proudly reported that 13,000 Chamorros had been baptized in the Marianas, or over 1,000 per month during the first year of the mission, figures he later lowered.

The *San José* had sailed all around Guam before finding the Agaña anchorage. To avoid such navigational problems, and to assist the missionaries, a royal *cédula* had been issued in June 1668 that required the Acapulco galleon to put in at Guam. To prevent a galleon from missing the islands at night, the *cédula* ordered the mission to maintain all-night fires throughout May and June each year on Mount Machanao on north Guam and on the highest point on Rota, thereby bracketing the channel between the islands through which the galleons normally passed. Thus, over a century after Legazpi claimed it for Spain, Guam finally became an official port of call for the Acapulco galleons on the old Urdaneta route. Some galleons nonetheless would still sail through the Marianas without stopping, and sometimes several years went by without the appearance of any galleons, owing to wrecks or failure to sail from Cavite.

After the *San José*'s departure, Father San Vitores traveled back to Tinian and Saipan in July by proa with the Malabar catechist Lorenzo de Morales. On Saipan, the Chamorros held San Vitores and Lorenzo prisoners awhile, threatening at first to execute San Vitores, then placing him in the hands of *uritao* young men who, after ridiculing him, let him go as a harmless fool. He and Lorenzo traveled on by proa as far as Maug in the far northern Marianas before returning by way of Anatahan Island in August 1669. There he split up with Lorenzo, each going alone to villages to administer baptisms. In one village where a newborn child had recently died, the Chamorros accused Lorenzo of being a child killer. They killed him and cut out his eyes. He was the first religious martyr of the mission in the Marianas, and his body was never recovered.

While San Vitores was coping with the hostile Chamorros and trying to locate Lorenzo's body, a volcano erupted on Anatahan, frightening the islanders into letting the alien *makahna* go unharmed. He went on to Tinian, where Medina and Casanova were caught in a full-scale war between the two main *chamorri* clans on the island. One clan in the village of Marpo was struggling with another in Sungharon village for dominance of Tinian. The Jesuits tried to mediate but became embroiled in the fight. Unable to calm hostilities, San Vitores left the other two fathers to hold the little church they had constructed while he returned to Guam for reinforcements.

By now it was November 1669, a year and a half since his arrival in the Marianas, and San Vitores realized that his mission could no longer rely on the goodwill of some Chamorros to protect the priests. Jesuit historians such as García depict San Vitores as a man of peace. That he was, but, when it appeared necessary, he did not hesitate to use force to impose his will on the Chamorros. His actions showed he was not a pacifist. On Guam, he organized a military force of eight Filipino soldiers and two Spaniards, one of whom was the indispensable Captain Juan de Santa Cruz. San Vitores called his little band of priests and soldiers his Escuadrón Mariano (Marianas squadron), in military allusion to defending the faith.

The squadron sailed by proas to Tinian and set up an armed camp between the warring villages. The Chamorros in Marpo promptly mounted a surprise night assault on the Spaniards, but failed against the defenses erected by Captain Santa Cruz. This was the first armed clash of what would become the Spanish-Chamorro Wars and also the

first time one of the two small artillery pieces of the Spaniards was used with grapeshot against Chamorro warriors. Intimidated by the Spanish muskets and the thunderous little artillery piece, the Chamorros of both villages agreed to a settlement. On 24 January 1670, the two clans exchanged huge conch shells in the customary Chamorro sign of peace, but both villages remained sullenly hostile, particularly toward the meddlesome Spaniards.

Father Medina then left for the neglected parish of Saipan with two Visayan brothers, Hipólito and Agustín de la Cruz. The Chamorros on Saipan had been aroused by Choco. On 29 January 1670, almost as soon as the three missionaries arrived, they were attacked by *uritao* warriors, and Medina and Hipólito were killed by spears. Agustín escaped to report the murders. Captain Santa Cruz was unable to retrieve the remains of the dead men until April; he wanted to raze the villages responsible for the murders, but San Vitores refused to allow any retribution. The two martyrs were eventually buried in the church in Agaña.

In March, the fighting flared again in Tinian. The Marpo warriors attacked the Spanish camp, which now had more fortifications around it. Two warriors were killed, and the attack fizzled in face of the Spanish firearms. It was clear now that only the fear of Spanish arms kept the Chamorros in check. San Vitores later wrote sternly, "The natives of this and other Islands were afraid of our arms, and the rumor was soon heard that they [the arms] were much more than noise, and that infraction of the Law of God or of the good customs that we taught them, would not go unpunished."

With Tinian temporarily subdued, San Vitores returned in May 1670 to Guam, where more troubles awaited him. First the Acapulco galleon failed to appear; then the dry season turned into a drought. Converted Chamorros began to seek help from *makahnas* to invoke ancestral spirits to make rain. San Vitores found himself struggling on Guam and Rota against a resurgence of traditional Chamorro beliefs. A number of his Filipino soldiers temporarily deserted to live with women in apostate Chamorro villages before being persuaded to return to the fold.

Rain finally fell, which was attributed by the Christians to San Vitores' prayers and by pagan Chamorros to the *makahnas*. Among the Chamorros, it was no longer prestigious to be converted to Christianity, and the Jesuits were busy keeping those already converted from relapsing to the old beliefs.

On 9 June 1671, the galleon *Buen Socorro* arrived from Acapulco with supplies, letters, a few more soldiers, and arms. It also brought four new Jesuit priests for the mission: Francisco Solano, Alonso López, Diego de Noriega, and Francisco Ezquerra. The increased strength, however, was counterbalanced by the departure on the galleon a few days later of three of the veteran missionaries—Casanova, Morales, and Bustillo—on reassignment. Morales and Bustillo would later return to the Marianas. With them on the *Buen Socorro* San Vitores sent three baptized *chamorri* young men, Don Ignacio Osi, Don Pedro Guiran, and Don Matías Yay. They were sent abroad as examples of the mission's success, to broaden their education, and to help generate support for the Marianas mission. Guiran would die at sea; Osi and Yay would return to Guam in 1675 after having visited Manila, Acapulco, and Mexico City.

When the new priests arrived on the *Buen Socorro* in June 1671, they found the Marianas mission under a near siege. The *makahnas* threatened drought and misfortune if all the Christian missionaries were not removed from the islands. A ranking *chamorri* headman of Agaña named Hurao was on the side of the *makahnas*. After the galleon with its cannons and soldiers departed, Hurao's followers killed a young Mexican servant of San Vitores out gathering wood. In retaliation, some Spanish soldiers seized several Chamorros as hostages and killed by chance a man nicknamed Guafac, according to García's history (sometimes called Chafae in later accounts). This man turned out to be a high-ranking *chamorri*, thereby invoking his entire clan to seek revenge.

Hurao gathered warriors for war against the Spaniards, but took his time in the customary Chamorro manner. Gifts had to be exchanged, *chenchule'* obligations talked over, and food laid out by Hurao at feasts to motivate other villages to support him. In the history of San Vitores written in Europe in 1700 by the Jesuit Charles Le Gobien (who was against imperialism), he "quotes" verbatim an eloquent speech by Hurao to rally his followers against colonialism. The Spaniards in Hurao's time had no direct access to Chamorro war gatherings, so Hurao's speech was made up by Le Gobien, based perhaps on a similar speech attributed in García's history (parts of which Le Gobien copied) to the Chamorro headman Aguarin before a battle in 1676–1677.

A converted Chamorro from Agaña named Antonio Ayhi alerted the Spaniards of Hurao's preparations. The Spanish soldiers then quickly transformed the Agaña church and mission residence into a crude wooden fort composed of a stockade and two towers, all constructed of coconut tree logs. Each tower held a small brass cannon. With their fort in order, the Spanish soldiers seized the initiative in a foray against the nearby Chamorro big *latte* houses of Agaña, where they took Hurao prisoner. As a peace gesture, San Vitores wanted to release the headman, but the Spanish soldiers refused to let him go. San Vitores then made peace overtures to Hurao but was rebuffed.

The Chamorros attacked on 11 September 1671 with approximately 2,000 warriors. Using tactics of sudden separate assaults with sling-stones as their main weapons interspersed with attempts to burn down the buildings with flaming spears, the warriors kept up the attacks day and night for eight days. Meanwhile, the Chamorros dug siege trenches around the stockade beyond musket range and lined them with human skulls facing the Spaniards in a long string of skeletal grins.

By this time, the Chamorros had learned not to fear the loud noise of the small Spanish cannons, whose spasmodic firing caused little damage as long as the warriors kept moving. The islanders also constructed movable platforms with "heart-shaped shields" behind which they could deflect musket fire while they closed on the stockade, García noted, "to throw lances, stones and fire balls." This medieval platform apparatus was an invention of Choco, who was present, according to one account of the battle.

On 18 September, when it seemed the Chamorros would overwhelm the fort, providence once more intervened in favor of San Vitores, as it had before at key moments in his life. A mammoth typhoon smashed into Guam, destroying in one day almost all the Chamorro houses and wiping out most of the breadfruit and coconut trees on the island. The Spanish church and mission residence were also in ruins, but the stockade (miraculously, according to the Jesuit accounts, with some justification) was relatively undamaged. The two towers, each with its small cannon still in place, remained standing. The Spaniards quickly repaired the stockade walls and prepared for more fighting.

The Chamorros mistakenly thought the stockade was badly damaged. They mounted a final desperate assault, but the Spaniards repulsed them, wounding "many" and killing "some," according to García. The next day, the islanders, now exhausted and without food, sought peace, asking only that Hurao be released. The Spanish officers did not want to release him, but San Vitores insisted that the release of the *maga'lahi* would bring peace. Hurao was freed.

San Vitores was wrong. Hurao promptly rallied his people and again laid siege to the fort. This time the battle continued for thirteen days until the Spanish soldiers took the initiative and sallied out against the Chamorro trenches in a bold raid. They scattered the surprised islanders and smashed the skulls along the trenches. Disheartened, the Chamorros once more asked for peace, this time under a new leader, a second Quipuha who was a relative of the late Don Juan Quipuha. The Spaniards demanded that the Chamorros attend mass every Sunday and send their children to the church school and that they help repair the church. Quipuha accepted, and everyone set about repairing the damage caused by the typhoon and the war, but Chamorro resentment of the Spaniards festered below the temporary calm.

The second Quipuha would later take up arms again to fight the Spaniards, as would the persistent Hurao, who would be killed in battle. Choco, however, never reappeared in the Spanish accounts; his fate is unknown. The furious series of battles in 1671 had a great impact on the Chamorros of Guam, according to García: "There had never been such destruction of their houses and fields as there was in this war which had been waged. . . . They said it was easy to see that their demons were powerless. . . . They said their *Macajnas* were imposters who promised things they could not give."

A Crystal Tomb for a Saint

Thus, the parable of the tribes was brutally introduced to the Chamorro people. San Vitores took advantage of his increased power to expand his authority throughout the islands. He sent Francisco Ezquerra to Rota and Alonso López to Aguijan, Tinian, and Saipan. López founded a school on Tinian. He also gathered cartographic data, including names for all the Mariana Islands, and drew maps of Guam and the other islands. A copy of the Guam map appeared in Le Gobien's 1700 history of San Vitores. One of the new Jesuits, Father Diego de Noriega, became ill in Agaña; he died in San Vitores' arms in January 1672.

Meanwhile, powerful support for the isolated little mission was gaining momentum in distant palaces in Madrid and Mexico. The letters San Vitores had sent to Queen Mariana over the previous four years had started men, money, and provisions moving over the long Spanish colonial pipeline to the Marianas. Between June 1671 and June 1672, Queen Mariana issued no fewer than nine separate *cédulas* in which she ordered her viceroy in Mexico, the same Marqués de Mancera who had initially refused money to San Vitores, to supply the Marianas mission with whatever it needed, including the construction of a boat in the Philippines for interisland voyages in the Marianas by San Vitores. These *cédulas* were mostly in response to personal requests to her by Father San Vitores. This much personal attention by the monarch to one small outpost in the vast structure of the Spanish empire was unusual.

Mancera dutifully complied with the queen's decrees, although the long distances over which communications and supplies flowed usually caused two or more years slippage before anything tangible reached Guam. The civil authorities in Manila, still opposed to the unprofitable Marianas venture, managed to prevent San Vitores' boat from ever reaching Guam. As a consequence, much of the assistance the queen ordered for the Marianas mission would not reach Guam until after San Vitores' death on 2 April 1672. Despite his death, Queen Mariana continued to provide money, soldiers, and supplies to the Marianas, including an endowment called an *obra pía* (pious work) for the School of San Juan de Letrán. This endowment provided 3,000 pesos a year to the school for the next century and a half.

As part of the *reduccíon* of the Chamorros, in early 1672 San Vitores ordered churches to be constructed in the villages of Merizo in the south, at Pagat and Nisihan in the east just below the area now called Sasajyan south of Marbo Cave, and at Pigpug near Talofofo Bay. San Vitores took charge of the Nisihan church. Parishes were organized around each church as the center of new communities where Christian Chamorros would live and from which the priests would convert pagan *indios*. The problem was that the Chamorros did not cooperate, or at least the majority did not. There were, of course, many islanders who did compromise with the foreigners, as can be expected in any society. Similarly, there were also those who welcomed change in the status quo. People in the latter group appear to have included many of the *manachang* lower caste, attracted by the elevation in status they gained as Christians.

Opposition came from those who would lose their privileges under the new Christian system, primarily the *chamorri* and particularly the women, who were accustomed to considerable freedom and did not wish to lose it in the macho world of the Spaniards. This female opposition irritated the priests, who laid down the law that, in order for Chamorro women to become Christians, as García wrote, "It was necessary for them to subject themselves and renounce their mistaken rights of freedom and independence."

Renewed Chamorro resistance started with a headman among the *chamorri* of Agaña whom García called "one of the greatest *principales* of Agaña." This was the second Quipuha, who had been forced to accept peace with the Spaniards the previous year. He still wanted revenge for that humiliation; vengeance was a strong trait of the Chamorros, according to Spanish accounts. Since the peace settlement, Quipuha had also been rebuked several times in public by San Vitores for keeping a concubine, wrote García. Fed up with the Spaniards, Quipuha arranged to have two *uritao* young men kill Diego Barzán, the favorite catechist of San Vitores, whom he had recruited in Mexico City. Barzán was killed on 31 March 1672, near the village of Chuchugu (now an area known as Chochogo) at the narrow neck of central Guam while he was delivering a message from Agaña to Nisihan. That night Chamorros attempted to burn a Spanish sentry box at Agaña but were foiled when a sentry fired his musket.

Two Filipino soldiers were sent the next morning from Agaña to warn San Vitores at Nisihan of the sentry box incident. On the way they learned of Barzan's murder (then, as now, news spread rapidly on the island by word of mouth). On learning this news, San Vitores ordered all mission personnel to return to Agaña for safety. The two Filipino soldiers and an unarmed Spaniard who joined them returned by way of Chuchugu and were ambushed by about twenty Chamorro warriors, who killed the Spaniard and wounded the Filipinos. The Filipinos managed to kill the *chamorri* leader of the warriors, and, "in order to frighten the others, they chopped him into bits with their cutlasses." The two soldiers then fled but were later caught by

Chamorros and killed. Unconverted Chamorros all over the island began to stalk and kill Spaniards and Filipinos.

While these skirmishes were going on, San Vitores had remained at Nisihan with the catechist Pedro Calonsor in order to find San Vitores' old Chamorro language interpreter, the Visayan Esteban, who had been with him the past ten years. The old man, tired of Jesuit discipline, had run off a few days earlier, much to San Vitores' dismay. With Calonsor, San Vitores spent 1 April searching along the cliff line north of Nisihan, where they thought Esteban might be hiding in caves. Failing to find him (Esteban would disappear among the Chamorros for five years, reappearing in 1679 to be forgiven by the missionaries), San Vitores and Pedro hiked around the north side of Mount Barrigada and spent the night with converted *manachang* Chamorros in the inland hamlet of Facfac. The two missionaries may have wished to avoid the central trail to Agaña back through the dangerous Chuchugu area.

Early the next morning, they headed for Agaña by way of the lovely palm-lined beach along Tumon Bay. At Tumon, San Vitores learned from the villagers that a girl had just been born to the wife of Mata'pang, a *chamorri* of the village. San Vitores knew this headman; he had baptized him earlier and helped nurse him when Mata'pang was wounded by a lance in a fight. San Vitores went to him at his house in that portion of Tumon later called Naton Beach and asked permission to baptize the baby.

Like many other *chamorri* by that time, Mata'pang detested the *guirragos* (or *gilagos,* meaning "men from the north," as the Chamorros called white men). A Spanish report after the incident stated Mata'pang may also have feared that the Jesuit's baptismal water was poisoned. Mata'pang angrily refused the priest's request and threatened to kill him.

To give the headman time to calm down, San Vitores gathered some children and started them singing the catechism. In the meantime, Mata'pang turned to a Tumon warrior named Hirao (or Irao in some accounts), who had earlier casually tagged along with San Vitores and Calonsor as they walked into the village. After some argument, in which Mata'pang accused the reluctant Hirao of cowardice, the other man agreed to help kill the missionaries. The two Chamorros hurried off to a nearby hut for weapons.

Seeing Mata'pang depart, Father San Vitores stepped into the headman's house and proceeded to baptize the newborn infant. Calonsor remained outside to watch for Mata'pang.

Mata'pang and Hirao soon returned with lances and short heavy machetes called *cantanas* in hand. Enraged by the arrogance of San Vitores in going ahead and baptizing the child, Mata'pang hurled lances at Calonsor, who dodged several until one pierced his body. Hirao then split the catechist's head with a *cantana*. The Chamorros turned on San Vitores as he came out of the house and killed him in the same swift, brutal manner, spearing him in the body and slashing his head.

They removed the clothing and crucifixes of the dead men and spread burning coals to consume the pools of blood from the bodies. Mata'pang smashed a small cross that San Vitores wore, but he kept a large ivory crucifix of the priest's. Next they dragged the naked bodies down to the shore, placed them in a proa, and tied stones to the feet. After paddling over the Tumon reef in the proa, they tossed the bodies overboard. According to some accounts, San Vitores surfaced twice to grasp the proa's outrigger but was pried off each time by Mata'pang.

When San Vitores rose a third time and grasped the boat's stern, Mata'pang smashed the priest's head with a paddle. Father Diego Luís de San Vitores then sank for the last time into the crystalline waters of Tumon not far from where Magellan had first dropped anchor in the Pacific a century and a half earlier.

The details of the deaths of San Vitores and Calonsor are contained in the first history of San Vitores' life (*Vida y Martyrio de el Venerable Padre Luís de Sanvitores,* etc.) written in Spain around 1681 by

The martyrdom of Father San Vitores. The Jesuit founder of the Catholic mission on Guam in 1668 is shown being killed on 2 April 1672 in Tumon. The Chamorro headman Mata'pang is spearing San Vitores, while Hirao wields the machete; both Chamorros are shown in loincloths but actually were naked. This engraving was made in Europe to illustrate Father Francisco García's 1683 hagiographic history of San Vitores. The Chamorros were drawn with primitive features in order to enhance the innocence of the slain priest. The first engraving for the Spanish edition of García's history showed San Vitores wearing clumsy eyeglasses. This version was in a later Italian edition and the glasses had disappeared. (Francisco García, *Istoria della conversione alla nostra Santa Fede dell'Isole Mariane,* Naples, 1686, pl. XV)

his fellow Jesuit, Father Francisco García, and published in Madrid in 1683, only eleven years after San Vitores' martyrdom. García based his history on the various reports and letters written by the Jesuits in Guam. The Jesuit accounts (which differ somewhat in particulars) are based on statements attributed to Mata'pang in bragging to other Chamorros about his deed and on one eyewitness account by a Chamorro. These Chamorros told the story to the Jesuits on Guam, who in turn reported it to the Philippines, Mexico, and Spain.

The Catholic Church conducted four formal investigations, called Processes by the Spaniards, into San Vitores' death: one on Guam in 1673, a second in Manila in 1676–1677, the third in Mexico in 1676–1679, and the fourth at Toledo in 1688–1689. These investigations confirmed the main facts of the murders despite inconsistencies in the details. It was at the Manila Process in 1676 that the Society of Jesus initiated the request for beatification (which leads to canonization as a saint) of Father San Vitores. Beatification is a complicated procedure that in San Vitores' case would not be completed until over 300 years later on 6 October 1985, when he was officially beatified as the Blessed Diego of the Marianas, Apostle of Micronesia, by Pope John Paul II in Rome.

Father García and other Jesuits wrote that San Vitores expected to be killed in the Marianas, implying that he welcomed martyrdom when confronted by Mata'pang. All accounts agree that San Vitores held up his large ivory crucifix to Mata-'pang, exclaiming in Chamorro, "Si Yu'us ma'ase', Mata'pang" (May God have mercy on thee, Mata-'pang), as he was struck down. In a biblical allusion to Judas, some later reports claimed that Mata-'pang sold the ivory crucifix for thirty bags of rice. Even granting understandable exaggerations by Catholic writers in describing the tragedy, Father San Vitores surely died as he lived, courageously and absolutely firm in his faith.

A man of overwhelming intensity, Diego Luís de San Vitores made his life and his death into a metaphor of religious passion to reveal his God's love for the poor of the world. In the Marianas, the goal of San Vitores, which would eventually be accomplished after his death, was the transformation of the consciousness of the Chamorro people. This is the aim of a hero as well as a saint. A function of the hero in the European ethos is the conquest of instinct-driven nature and the establishment of civilization. Politically, this role meant not only the elimination of the traditional cultures of the Indians but also the establishment of a new government over them in accord with the parable of the tribes.

Father San Vitores therefore was both a hero and a saint for the Spanish empire and for the Catholic Church. The success of his extraordinary service to those two authorities shows the transforming power of illusion in which, at least in Guam's case, the decisions and actions of one individual can turn history around.

From the point of view of the Chamorros, however, San Vitores brought to them a bewildering and lethal psychodrama of the forgiving church and the intolerable military. His martyrdom would bring enduring benefits in the conversion of the people to Christianity, but it would also bring them massive tragedy through wars and epidemics. While San Vitores was alive, the islanders could refuse conversion without retaliation by the Spaniards. After San Vitores' death, the Chamorros no longer had a choice: either they accepted Christianity, or they were killed by the Spanish military, whose presence and authority expanded as a consequence of his martyrdom.

To the Chamorros, therefore, San Vitores was a savior and a conqueror, and their attitudes toward him have all the ambivalence this paradox implies. Even today in the late twentieth century, there are devout Catholic Chamorros who are still undecided whether San Vitores was a villain, one of the horsemen of their apocalypse, or a hero, the man who brought them God's grace.

4 The Spanish Conquest 1672–1698

A Mission of Soldiers

Guam's history might have been quite different if Father San Vitores had been an ordinary missionary whose martyrdom would have been duly celebrated but eventually forgotten among the thousands of other martyrs in the Catholic Church's long history. However, he was not ordinary. He was a member of the church's most militant order and the son of a high official in the Spanish government. Furthermore, Christianity had been challenged, and the Spaniards considered it a point of honor to defend the faith. For these reasons, the Spaniards reacted with force to retrieve a failing religious effort, particularly one in which their queen had a personal commitment. A key element in the Spanish response was the prompt initiative taken by the Society of Jesus to beatify San Vitores by Processes, books, and commemorations, all of which focused attention on the Mariana mission.

The news of San Vitores' murder reached Manila quickly because the *San Diego,* the same ship that had carried San Vitores to Guam, arrived at Umatac on 2 May 1672, just one month after his death. The galleon departed five days later, leaving some soldiers, firearms, and supplies for the mission, now surrounded by thousands of unfriendly Chamorros. The Chamorros, however, were not united in their opposition to the aliens. In the period right after San Vitores' death, the clans on

Guam were divided into two main factions. In García's words, "The villages in the southern part were friendly towards Padres and Spaniards, not to defend them, but merely to tolerate them, while those of the north were declared enemies."

Within days after the *San Diego*'s departure, Spanish soldiers began retaliation for San Vitores' death. On 11 May, they caught and killed Hurao in a skirmish and then shot an innocent Chamorro woman and wounded her male companion when the two fled in panic from a Spanish patrol. This incident upset the Jesuits, and the new superior, Francisco Solano, called the troops together and asked that they refrain from violence against the Chamorros.

The soldiers then busied themselves in the manufacture of adobe bricks from the red laterite soil in the hills behind Agaña to convert their wooden fort into one made of bricks. However, a work party was waylaid by Chamorros, and the project had to be abandoned. Angered, twenty-one Spanish soldiers (of whom only thirteen were armed with muskets) under Captain Juan de Santiago set out for Tumon on 17 May to punish Mata'pang.

The troops avoided an ambush on the way and proceeded to the largely deserted village, where they burned a dozen or so houses and destroyed all the proas they found. They captured one *chamorri* man and wife. On the way back, the soldiers burned more houses along the beach at Ypao. Mata-'pang appeared, sailing a proa parallel to the beach in full view of the soldiers. He taunted them until a lucky musket shot wounded him and he fled. Mata'pang and Hirao subsequently sought refuge on Rota.

After wounding Mata'pang, the soldiers marched around the inland side of Ypao, Saupon, and Oka points (now collectively called Hospital Point) to Agaña Bay. They were ambushed near the water's edge south of Oka Point by two Chamorro forces, one from land and one in a fleet of proas from the sea. The Spaniards formed a square and fought their way along the shore to safety in Agaña, suffering four wounded by lances. Three of the wounded men died later in agonizing convulsions from what the Spaniards believed to be poison on the bone tips of the lances but that may have been tetanus or peritonitis caused by infection. The Spaniards reported one Chamorro killed and a number wounded.

In the following months, the Chamorros used hit-and-run tactics by small bands of warriors, each band probably from separate *uritaos* more in competition with each other than in any coordinated plan against the aliens. In early June, two Filipino catechists were slaughtered on Rota and their bodies tossed into the sea. The Spaniards then constructed a large diamond-shaped wooden enclosure near the beach in Agaña. This compound became the first *presidio* (a military garrison, comprising troops and buildings), with residential buildings and a church inside the walls.

Hostilities persisted, and in May 1673 Father Alonso López and his catechists abandoned Tinian and returned to Guam for safety. Because southern Guam was still friendly or neutral, the Spaniards constructed a church for López at Fuuna (or Funa), which was probably a village on Fouha Bay just north of Umatac. The village of Umatac still had no Spanish settlement at this time despite galleons occasionally anchoring outside the bay there.

On 22 May 1673, the galleon *San Antonio* dropped anchor off Agaña with many of the sup-plies ordered by Queen Mariana for the mission. Among the items disembarked was the first horse, "whose beauty and speed delighted the *Marianos,* for they had never seen such an animal." The remainder of 1673 passed in a peace that was deceptive. The calm was broken on 2 February 1674, when Father Ezquerra and six Filipino cate-chists were massacred near the southern village of Ati (or Hati, now Cetti). The remaining missionaries and soldiers kept to the Agaña *presidio* until the galleon *Buen Socorro* arrived off Agaña in June 1674, but it was blown out to sea by strong winds after only one load of supplies and passengers had been lightered to shore. In the one launch that reached Agaña were Father Sebastián de Monroy and a Peruvian-born Spanish army officer named Damián de Esplana, along with three soldiers from Mexico, two of whom were Cholula Indians and the other a mestizo. Nearly every complement of soldiers arriving on Guam from this time on included Spanish-Indian mestizos from Mexico as well as Filipinos, usually Pampangos.

Esplana was a veteran army captain on his way to an assignment in the Philippines and had come ashore on Guam only to visit. Now stranded on the island, and as the senior military officer, he was made the mission's first *sargento mayor* (a Spanish military title, not a rank; it meant commander of soldiers at a *presidio* garrison and was not the same as a sergeant major in English).

Of benefit to the Spaniards at this time was the fighting still going on between unconverted Chamorro clans in northern Guam over old animosities unrelated to the menace of the Spaniards. Through divide-and-conquer tactics, the Spaniards were able to manipulate to their own advantage such divisions among the Chamorros, exploiting lingering traditional animosities between villages to foster commitment to the Christians as the price of alliance. Soon the missionaries were able to establish churches at Ritidian and at Tarague in the formerly hostile north.

In the meantime, Esplana vigorously pursued anti-Christian islanders. In November 1674, he attacked Tumon, killing a Chamorro who had murdered a Spaniard two years earlier. García noted grimly, "The dead native was quartered and hung on two poles as a warning to other villagers." Esplana then burned "all the settlement." Tumon never regained its former prominence as a village. About this time, Esplana had his soldiers erect a small chapel of coral masonry and a cross at the place in Tumon where San Vitores was killed in 1672. In later years, an annual red tide (actually rust brown) of unialgal blooms in Tumon in April was thought to be a miraculous appearance of the blood of San Vitores. The chapel and cross would also become the site of miracles for Christians, but the original buildings deteriorated into ruins.

In January 1675, Esplana made a sweep through the southern areas of Guam, which had turned rebellious. On these forays, Esplana began employing a force of friendly Chamorros led by the convert Antonio Ayhi, who by now was called Don Antonio Ayhi. One expedition burned Choco's old village of Paa and the nearby village of Hadian, where San Vitores' ivory crucifix and bloodstained cassock were recovered. As *sargento mayor,* Esplana rode the Spaniards' one horse, which gave him an advantage over surprised Chamorro warriors, who feared the strange new animal that they had never seen before.

In June 1675, the galleon *San Telmo* left another horse plus twenty soldiers, firearms and other supplies, and two Jesuits—Lorenzo Bustillo and Gerardo Bouwens—who had previously served on Guam. About this time, two Spanish soldiers encountered Mata'pang on northern Guam and wounded him once more, but he managed to flee again to Rota. In July, Esplana followed with his enlarged force to catch Mata'pang and punish the people of Rota for harboring renegades from Guam. People were scattered and houses burned as usual, but Mata'pang escaped again.

Calm returned for the next five months but was unexpectedly broken in a northern village. On 8 December 1675, Chamorros in the supposedly converted village of Ritidian killed Brother Pedro Díaz and his assistant when they tried to suppress *uritao* activities. The Chamorros then burned the church

and the priests' residence, and all the villagers took off in proas for Rota to escape the reprisal that they knew would come. The reprisal came from converted Chamorros in the nearby village of Tarague, who took advantage of the situation to settle an old clan revenge against their neighbors, burning the Ritidian houses and cutting down all fruit trees.

The next flare-up came at Upi village in the north, where villagers led by the *chamorri* Quenano killed the acting superior, a Sicilian Jesuit named Antonio María de San Basilio. The priest—a tall, lanky man—had written prophetically in a letter, "The *indios,* being practical in throwing lances, want my arms and legs because they are long, in order to make lances from my long bones." The Chamorros in fact did just that; Spanish soldiers recovered Basilio's body minus the arms and legs.

In June 1676, the galleon *San Antonio* arrived on schedule with more priests, fourteen soldiers, and—for the first time—two Spanish families, including children. It is not known if they were *peninsulares* (people born in Spain) or *criollos* (born in the colonies). The Spaniards maintained social distinctions between *peninsulares, criollos,* mestizos, Filipinos, and *indios* (Chamorros, also called *nativos*), in that rank order. At first, Filipinos were also often referred to as *indios* in Spanish records. In the 1670s, Spanish, Filipino, and mestizo soldiers began to marry Chamorro women in church ceremonies and set up permanent households. The first church marriage between a Spanish soldier and a Chamorro was in 1674, when Juan Zubiar married Margarita Loyola (doubtlessly her baptismal name).

Esplana departed on the 1676 galleon after he persuaded the commander on board, a Spanish general, to order a passenger, an army captain by the name of Francisco de Irisarri y Vivar, to take over command as *sargento mayor* on Guam. Irisarri was on his way to an assignment in the Philippines and had no idea of staying on Guam, but he followed orders and remained. To make the unexpected duty more acceptable to Irissari, the general gave him the title *governor,* the first man to be so named, although the title was honorary at the time.

The Jesuits, unhappy with Esplana, requested the governor-general in Manila to separate the military and the church chains of command on Guam. The request was granted by the Council of the Indies in Spain (the highest governmental authority in the Spanish empire below the monarch), and the separation of authority began in 1680.

Irisarri started off by making church attendance obligatory for all converted islanders. He compelled them to send their children to the church schools to learn, in García's words, "duties necessary to the formation of a Christian and political republic, banishing barbarism little by little." Also like his predecessors, Sargento Mayor Irisarri attacked rebel Chamorros, this time in the mountain village of Talisay inland from Agat. His forces killed five Chamorros, burned the *uritao* house, and scattered the villagers into the southern mountains. About this time, the Spaniards began to take away small Chamorro children who were orphaned or temporarily abandoned during Spanish attacks on villages. The children were given to the priests to be raised in mission schools.

In the same month of August 1676, an angry non-Christian Chamorro attacked Father Monroy at the Orote church where the man's converted daughter (called Dikiki, "small" in Chamorro, in the folk tale of the event) was being married to a Spanish soldier. Monroy was unhurt, but Irisarri quickly captured the Chamorro father and had him hanged in Agaña. The governor compelled all Chamorros in the vicinity to observe the hanging. To intimidate the islanders even more, the governor allowed converted Chamorro children to drag the body to the beach, shouting, "Let the dog die who has not wanted to become a Christian."

Not intimidated but extremely angered, a dynamic *chamorri* of Agaña named Aguarin (or Aguanin in some accounts) secretly began to organize an alliance of anti-Spanish clans in the vicinity of Agaña and the villages around what is now Apra Harbor. García attributes to Aguarin, whom he calls "an eloquent Indian in his savagery," a fiery speech to his followers in which the Chamorro declared, "I shall lead you with my lance, which

has killed many Spaniards and will kill them all; then we shall be able to reestablish the freedom our fathers and grandfathers enjoyed, which we have allowed to be lost because of our cowardice." In late August, Irisarri sent a detachment of eight soldiers headed by his second in command, Sergeant Nicolás Rodríguez Carvajal, with Father Monroy to the rebellious peninsular village of Orote in order to forestall an attack against the church there.

Threatened by belligerent Chamorros at Orote, the detachment retreated to what would later be Sumay village, where they were attacked by a large force of warriors but repulsed them with musket fire. A baptized *chamorri* called Cheref lured the Spaniards into fleeing with him by sea in a proa to reach safety in Agaña. When Cheref had the proa away from shore but still in shallow water, he treacherously capsized the canoe. With their gunpowder wet, the soldiers could not repulse the screaming Chamorro warriors who swarmed out from shore. All nine foreigners, including Monroy and Rodríguez, were killed. The Chamorros then burned the Orote church to the ground.

Throughout the next few months, Aguarin expanded the Chamorro alliance, handing out many turtle shells as gifts. His efforts were monitored by the Spanish intelligence system now operating through converted Chamorros such as Ayhi. The Spaniards prepared for battle by strengthening the *presidio* stockade and gathering the mission personnel as well as many converted Chamorros inside its walls. Sentry boxes were added to the stockade walls, which were still mostly of coconut logs. On 15 October 1676, Aguarin gathered his warriors and mounted some unsuccessful attacks before settling down to blockade the *presidio*. As supplies dwindled, the Spaniards cultivated yams and other quick-growing tubers in gardens inside the *presidio* grounds while occasionally charging out to skirmish with the Chamorros.

After a number of false starts, Aguarin set in motion a massive assault on the *presidio* in January 1677. The Chamorros approached the *presidio* in two forces with hundreds of warriors in each force.

One group came by sea in proas, the second group by land. With both groups "occupying all the beach and the hills back of town," García wrote, Irisarri took a gamble: he first rushed his troops out of the stockade in a feint against the Chamorros on the inland side, forestalling an attack from that direction. Then the Spaniards retreated into the *presidio*, where they had placed loaded but unmanned crossbows and (according to Le Gobien) fake muskets along the top of the stockade to give the impression of a prepared defense.

This tactic held the Chamorros in check on the inland side while Irisarri led his soldiers out in a charge on the beach side, where they fired muskets at the warriors in the proas. The Chamorros took cover behind their proa hulls and moved out of musket range. The Spaniards set up a small artillery piece on the beach and bombarded the proas, scattering the Chamorros into retreat.

Twelve days later, the persistent Aguarin massed his followers again in even greater numbers. Most of the warriors now carried shields of bark and wood for some protection against musket fire. It was to be a supreme effort by the Chamorros to eradicate the hated alien invaders.

Faced with impending defeat, Irisarri resorted to trickery. He knew each Chamorro warrior loved to show his individual prowess in battle. So the Spanish commander placed a flag within musket range at a clear spot on the ocean side of the stockade, where he could mass the musket fire of his soldiers along the top. The governor, García wrote, gambled that "some of the barbarians would want to capture it [the flag] in order to gain fame among their own people."

The Chamorros took the bait: twenty or more proas in the approaching sea force sprinted ahead to the beach, where dozens of warriors jumped out with their weapons and raced in a yelling mass to grab the Spanish flag. Just as the warriors reached the fluttering flag, the Spanish soldiers unleashed a withering musket barrage, mowing down the swiftest Chamorros in a bloody swath. The Spaniards then directed all their fire with muskets and cannons on the other warriors landing behind. Stunned

and disheartened, the Chamorros fled the battlefield.

Peace did not follow, only a deadly period during late 1677 and early 1678 of what is today called guerrilla warfare of sporadic hit-and-run raids by the Chamorros and reprisals by the Spaniards. Aguarin and his warriors retreated into fortified villages in northern Guam, principally Haputo, Tarague, and Janum. In June 1678, the *San Telmo* arrived at Umatac with a new governor-general for Manila, Juan de Vargas y Hurtado. He assigned a new honorary governor and troop commander, Captain Juan Antonio de Salas, and thirty more soldiers to Guam. Irisarri, who had not been popular with the Jesuits, departed for Manila.

The remainder of 1678 into 1679 saw the Spaniards mount scorched-earth sweeps into hostile areas throughout Guam, tearing down big *latte* houses, burning food stores, killing any hostiles they caught, and carrying off children to be baptized. On one raid they captured over forty children, who were turned over to the priests who always accompanied the troops. A growing force of converted Chamorros assisted the Spanish troops in hunting down hostile Chamorros. The friendly Chamorros were led by Antonio Ayhi of Agaña, Ignacio Hineti of Sinajana, and Alonso Soon of Agat, all of whom were rewarded with increased authority by the Spaniards.

The Spaniards encouraged Chamorros to kill known "troublemakers" and present their heads to avoid drastic reprisals by the Spanish soldiers. This brutal tactic was effective. Many heads were taken and brought to the Spanish, according to García's history. In January 1679, the people of Merizo killed and presented to the Spaniards the bodies of the warriors who killed Monroy and Ezquerra, including the Chamorro leader of the band. García states that Governor Salas "ordered that the man's head be cut off and taken to Agadna." There it was displayed to the public. Despite the measures to intimidate the Chamorros, much of Guam remained unsafe for the missionaries unless escorted by armed soldiers.

On 17 June 1679, the galleon *San Antonio*

arrived in blustery winds that again prevented a full unloading of supplies. Several new Jesuits, a new *sargento mayor* named Joseph (sometimes referred to as José) de Quiroga y Losada (Lozado or Lossado in some accounts), and a few soldiers landed by launch. Soon afterward, a Spanish patrol encountered by chance the fugitive *chamorri* headmen Cheref and Aguarin as they landed a proa near Tarague. The patrol killed Cheref, but Aguarin escaped to Rota.

In late August 1679, troops under Governor Salas attacked Janum, the most isolated of the remaining rebel stongholds. Janum is a hauntingly beautiful little cove beneath huge cliffs on the northeast coast of Guam. Using friendly Chamorros from Nisihan, who attacked Janum in proas from the sea while Spanish and Filipino soldiers descended the cliffs, the Christian forces overcame the defenders of the village after a battle García described as "the fiercest which had taken place in the Marianas." All *latte* houses and other buildings were burned, and Janum was never again to be a village.

In late 1679 and early 1680, hundreds of desperate Chamorros on Guam fled their villages to hide in caves or to sail to other islands for safety from the Spaniards. Many Chamorros gave up in embittered resignation. Of these once fiercely proud islanders who surrendered, García wrote, "They were received with much pleasure and were given to understand that the arms of his Majesty are not meant to do harm, but to oblige them not to try to shake off the gentle yoke of Christ . . . the vain custom or solemnity with which they celebrated the deeds of their departed has fallen into disuse."

Agaña was becoming a small colonial capital with three *barrios* or sections to which converted Chamorros flocked, "leaving their villages abandoned and even destroyed," according to García's history. Discipline among the mission soldiers declined during Governor Salas' tenure. According to Jesuit complaints, some of the soldiers from Mexico were convicts conscripted into the army and shipped off to be rid of at home. *Tuba* and *arak* rice wine, initially brewed by Spanish and Filipino soldiers despite Jesuit disapproval, were now fermented by Chamorros. The soldiers were also distilling the even more powerful *aguardiente*. Alcoholism among soldiers and Chamorros increased. The islanders were also becoming addicted to tobacco, which the Spaniards imported from the New World and the Philippines and then started growing on Guam.

In June 1680, the galleon *Santa Rosa* arrived on schedule. Twenty Filipino soldiers plus a number of Mexican-Indian troops disembarked. Juan Antonio de Salas, who had resigned as governor a few months earlier (probably at the instigation of the Jesuits, who felt that most of the military commanders had "little intellect and ability"), embarked for the Philippines. He was temporarily replaced as governor for the next year by Captain Joseph de Quiroga, who had arrived the previous year.

Don Joseph de Quiroga

Quiroga was a veteran Galician officer and aristocrat respected by the Jesuits. He had fought in Flanders for Spain. With the appointment of this stern and pious man as interim governor (the Jesuits called him the "Hermit" because of his lack of interest in women), the Spanish subjugation of the Mariana Islands entered its most severe phase. He received explicit orders (originally issued to Salas by Governor-General Juan de Vargas y Hurtado) to end all Chamorro resistance. Vargas instructed Quiroga to "be particularly solicitous about the pursuit and chastisement of murderers, rebels, and traitors who might impede the spread of the Christian religion." The implacable Quiroga would fulfill those orders to the letter.

With more troops available to him, Quiroga established a base camp in a central location on Guam at Machaute Hill, now called Macheche. From the camp he sent out squadrons in every direction to hunt down recalcitrant Chamorros. He increased pressure on all villages on Guam and Rota to turn in anti-Spanish ringleaders, most of whom he summarily executed in public. He soon earned a reputation as a ruthless and resourceful leader. Out of fear of Quiroga, the Chamorros on Rota captured Mata'pang. Lying bound in a proa and finally helpless after eight years of flight since he killed Father San Vitores, Mata'pang died of his wounds while being transported to Guam. His body was presented to Quiroga by the Rota Chamorros.

The trophy did not placate Quiroga. Still distrustful of Rota, where many people from Guam found refuge, the governor invaded the island in the latter half of 1680 with a large force. There he captured Aguarin (called the "War Chief" by the Jesuits) as well as other renegades. As usual, the rebel villages were burned. Quiroga ordered the people of Rota not to harbor any more Chamorro refugees from Guam. He rounded up 190 such fugitives and took them back to Guam, where they were resettled

in the new Christian communities. Aguarin was brought back to Agaña and executed. This courageous defender of the traditional Chamorro way of life died without tribute from either his enemies or his own people.

With the Chamorros largely compliant on Guam, the Spaniards constructed a network of roads, actually wide dirt tracks, throughout the island. In this period, they divided the island into five ecclesiastical districts called *partidos*, each around a *pueblo*, or main village, centered on a church. Each district constituted a parish. Chamorros were compelled to move to the *pueblos*. A priest and a soldier were assigned to each parish, and converted Chamorro leaders, *principales*, were given civil duties in each district. The families of the *principales* gradually formed a new upper class, called *principalía*, that replaced the *chamorri*. Schools for boys and girls

López map of Guam, 1700. This map was copied in Europe, and printed in Le Gobien's history—in French—of the San Vitores mission, from a map drawn on Guam about 1672 by Father Alonso López, a member of the mission. The parish churches that existed at the time on Guam are shown as tiny circles with a cross on top. The title *L'Isle de St. Jean* is French for the Spanish name bestowed in 1668 by San Vitores, *Isla de San Juan,* which was already changing to *Guahan* or *Guan* by this period, as indicated by the other titles of the map. (Le Gobien, 1700)

were created in each *pueblo,* with the priest as teacher. The villagers provided the upkeep of the churches and schools, but the Chamorros paid no tithes or taxes. By 1680, there were nine priests and three lay brothers on the island. The village priests and soldiers received from Agaña a small annual subsidy of supplies called a *socorro* and money, the *situado* or *subsidio real,* brought to Guam by the galleons from Mexico.

In late 1680, a settlement was started at Umatac for the first time in order to serve the galleons that were beginning to anchor regularly outside the bay. The church of San Dionisio, constructed of wood with a palm thatch roof, was dedicated in Umatac on 11 February 1681, nearly 116 years after Legazpi landed at Umatac Bay and claimed the islands for Spain. This church was burned by Chamorros in 1684, rebuilt again of wood, and destroyed again by a typhoon in 1693. It was rebuilt in 1694 of coral masonry and lasted until the great earthquake of 1849. Small forts were eventually constructed on hills on each side of the bay's entrance, and Umatac was designated as a *villa*—a town granted a charter with special privileges. Churches were also established in late 1680 at Agat and Inarajan. An inquisition was held in this period in which skulls used by *makahnas,* as well as lances tipped with bones, were gathered up all over the island and burned. On 11 November 1680, a typhoon swept across Guam. The *presidio* at Agaña escaped major damage, but Chamorro dwellings all over the island were blown away. García notes, "This storm served a useful purpose in destroying the houses of the *indios,* thus facilitating the matter of gathering them into the larger villages. The Padres at this time persuaded them that rather than repair their old houses they should build new ones in locations assigned to them. And thus they did."

Late in 1680, a magnificent shower of meteors fell over the western Pacific, portending major events in the eyes of the Jesuits and perhaps of the Chamorros. Forebodings by the Spaniards were confirmed in February 1681, when the new church at Inapsan (now Jinapsan) in the north was burned by supposedly converted Chamorros. All the people of the village immediately sailed off to Rota in fear of Spanish reprisals. They obstinately refused to return. Angered, Quiroga went after them in April, burned their new village, and made them all return to Guam.

It is with this incident that Father Francisco García ended his history of San Vitores and the mission in the Marianas. Over the previous five or six years, soldiers had replaced priests as the principal agents of the Spaniards to bring the Chamorros to heel, but the Chamorros would nevertheless continue to resist. Unaware of the battles yet to come, García concluded with unintended irony that "it was necessary for this land to be showered with the blood of martyrs in order that the church might reap her just harvest."

On 15 June 1681, the galleon *San Telmo* furled sails off Agaña and halted without anchoring. There disembarked one Antonio Saravia, who had the formal titles captain-general, governor, and commander in chief (in Spanish, *maestre de campo*) of Guahan. Quiroga departed on the *San Telmo* for Manila. As Quiroga's successor, Saravia (whose army rank was captain) had been given authority by King Charles II to act "independently of the Viceroy of New Spain and the Governor of the Philippines . . . to conquer, explore, and govern" the Marianas "and the adjacent and southern lands." Saravia's appointment as the first official governor of Guam (and of the rest of what would be known as Micronesia) was the result of a royal *cédula* dated 6 August 1679, in which King Charles II stated that he wished to retain the Marianas.

The new governor initiated construction of a fort in Agaña on the inland side of the Agaña River near the beach to protect the mission. This fort, named Santa María de Guadalupe and not completed until 1683, was of volcanic basalt stones and the standard coral masonry in a slightly elevated one-story quadrangular shape that could hold 400 soldiers. Bastions on each corner contained artillery, and the fort had one large catapult to hurl stones at attackers. More conciliatory toward the

Chamorros than earlier governors, Saravia made the reliable Antonio Ayhi a "lieutenant general" (despite Ayhi's scandalous relapse into sin with a concubine) and also appointed other *principales* to command Chamorro warriors allied with the Spaniards.

On 8 September 1681, Saravia gathered all the Chamorro appointees at the *presidio* to take an oath of allegiance in the Chamorro language to the Spanish king. In the oath, they promised to "abide by any law which His Majesty might be pleased to impose upon us." After they had all signed their names, "albeit crudely," cannons and muskets were fired, loud blasts were blown on triton trumpet shells, and everyone threw his hat into the air, shouting, "Long live the King Don Carlos Segundo." This ceremony marked the implementation of full Spanish rule over Guam. Henceforth, until 1898, the people of the Marianas were citizens as well as subjects of Spain.

How much the Chamorro world on Guam had been altered can be measured by the change in the value of *hiero* and *lulok,* formerly worth a Chamorro's life. In a letter to Manila in June 1682, Governor Saravia wrote, "Hachets, cutlasses and the like are very much on the market, and there is not an *indio* who wants them." By this stage in the conquest, the Spanish authorities were assuming ownership in the name of the Spanish crown of land abandoned by rebel Chamorros and redistributing it to loyal Christian Chamorros and Filipinos.

For a number of years, the missionaries on Guam had been pressing Manila and Mexico to assign a supply ship to make an annual round-trip between Cavite and Guam to supplement the Acapulco galleon stopover. The Manila authorities finally sent a small ship in April 1681. The timing, however, was too early to catch the southwest monsoon, and the ship was blown back by the northeast trade winds. In 1683, a second attempt was made. A single-masted sloop, the *San Francisco Xavier,* sailed under the command of Damián de Esplana, who was returning to Guam after seven years of duty in the Philippines. Also aboard was Joseph de Quiroga, returning after an assignment of two years in the Philippines. The *Xavier* caught the southwest monsoon this time and arrived successfully at Guam on 23 August 1683.

The arrival was important as the Acapulco galleon of 1683 failed to appear. Because of storms, the galleon had never left Manila. After being destroyed by a typhoon and rebuilt, the *Xavier* later returned to Cavite. From then on, until the 1740s, Cavite supply ships made the trip to Umatac almost annually with the annual *socorro* of necessities such as soap, flour, tools, metal, animals, seeds, and so forth. The Acapulco galleon continued to bring some specialty supplies, but its main cargo for Guam was the *situado* to pay the garrison and mission personnel.

The payroll money was in the form of silver, usually Mexican peso coins. Before Saravia's arrival, the Jesuit superiors handled distribution of both the *socorro* and the *situado.* Beginning with Saravia, the governors took over the *situado* and most of the *socorro* except for the priests' allotments. This control by the governor gave him a monopoly over trade as the annual Cavite ship and Acapulco galleon provided the only commerce with the Marianas until the nineteenth century. The official monopoly would allow future governors to profit tremendously from trade.

Pressed by the ever-zealous priests, Saravia decided to reestablish the Spanish presence in Saipan in October 1682. He headed off for the north with thirty soldiers in two Spanish-built boats. The Chamorros on Saipan, "where the people are cruel and the most churlish of the lot," according to Father Emmanuel de Solórzano, who was serving in Agaña at the time, were so threatening that Savaria retreated hastily back to Guam. In 1683, Saravia relocated the Agaña *presidio* buildings inland a few hundred yards around a new main square called the Plaza Principal. The governor's quarters, however, remained safely within Fort Guadalupe.

An official governor's residence, called a *palacio* in Spanish (sometimes *casa real* and *casa de gobierno,* and not equivalent to the English *palace*), would not be constructed until around 1700 in Agaña on the southwestern side of the main square. About 1683, Saravia also requested an increase in the size of the Guam garrison to 130 Spanish soldiers in order to complete the subjugation of the Chamorros. King Charles II eventually approved this increase in a royal *cédula* dated 29 September 1685, but it took several more years for the additional troops to reach Guam.

On 3 November 1683, the ailing Saravia died. Esplana succeeded him as interim governor, much to the displeasure of the Jesuits, while Quiroga took over command of the troops as *sargento mayor*. In March 1684, Quiroga once more invaded Saipan with the mission's two boats, this time with a force of seventy-six soldiers that included friendly Chamorros from Guam and two priests. On the way, they reestablished control over Aguijan and Tinian.

Approaching Saipan, the invaders were challenged by a large Chamorro force in proas, a favorite tactic of the islanders. Quiroga, firing small cannons mounted on his boats, dispersed the proas and landed. After sharp and bloody fighting, Saipan was secured by the Spaniards by the end of April 1684. This kind of fighting, in which the Spaniards had all the firepower plus sizable manpower, must have been discouraging to the Chamorros, who were still using sling-stones and lances plus some machetes. Nonetheless, the islanders threw themselves into battle. In an eyewitness account of the fighting, Father Peter de Coomans praised the Chamorro *maga'lahi* Punni, who led the Saipan warriors, as "a brave man who met death boldly, hurling his last spear at us, but uselessly."

With the island conquered, Quiroga sent off a detachment of twenty-nine soldiers with Father Coomans to subjugate the far northern islands (called Gani by the Spaniards) while Quiroga constructed a church and fort on the western, lee side of Saipan on the coast for quick escape by sea. Quiroga's men also salvaged more cannons and swivel guns from the ever-productive wreck of the *Concepción*. Since these weapons were of sound bronze that resisted seawater corrosion, many of them could still be used nearly fifty years after submersion.

In the meantime, on supposedly pacified Guam, disaffected Chamorros launched a totally unexpected assault on the Spaniards in mid-1684. Taking advantage of Quiroga's absence with the main body of Spanish troops, a lapsed Christian *chamorri* named Antonio Yura from Apurguan village on Agaña Bay organized a conspiracy among some forty to sixty apostate Chamorros. On Sunday, 23 July 1684, as Governor Esplana was walking unarmed and unattended down an Agaña street after mass, four Chamorro warriors attacked him with knives. Aroused by the screams of a boy, soldiers drove off the assailants and saved the nearly dead governor. One of the Chamorros was killed. An account of the attack by Father Luís de Morales, who was in Agaña at the time, says the dead man was Yura.

While the attack on Esplana was going on, other armed Chamorros fell on Jesuits inside the church and in the priests' residence inside the stockade. Wielding machetes, the warriors hacked two priests to death, one of whom was the father superior, Emmanuel de Solórzano. The Chamorros wounded four other priests, including Gerardo Bouwens. In the fighting, a number of Spanish soldiers were also killed, and several buildings of the *presidio* were burned.

With Chamorro warriors running amok in Agaña, disaster for the Spaniards was averted when Ignacio Hineti led a force of fifty friendly Chamorro warriors down from the hills of Sinajana to drive off the attackers and reestablish security around the outside of the fort's walls. According to Father Morales, these friendly Chamorros were "men who had been reared in the mountains and therefore not accustomed to sail and had no knowledge of seamanship." This indicates that Hineti's warriors were mostly *manachang* lower-caste people from the interior.

By a stroke of luck for the Spaniards, all the

priests on Guam earlier had been summoned to a meeting in Agaña that Sunday. All reached the fort in Agaña that day and night, except for one. Father Teófilo de los Angeles at the Ritidian church attempted to sail to the northern islands to alert Quiroga of the Guam uprising. He was caught by Chamorros and hanged from the mast of the proa in which he was about to sail.

Over the next few days, hostile Chamorros gathered at Apurguan to organize an attack. They sent out messengers and called for a general uprising against the *guirragos*. The Apurguan Chamorros were probably *chamorri* because of their village's prime location on one of Guam's best beaches and fishing sites.

The delay by the Chamorros in following up their first surprise attack was an error. Just as in the two earlier Chamorro sieges of Agaña, the inability of the Chamorros to act swiftly and decisively gave the Spaniards time to prepare a defense. With the governor out of action, a Filipino adjutant—Francisco Masongsong—and the Chamorro Hineti took charge at first, organizing the mixed force of friendly Chamorros, the seminary boys, and the mostly Filipino troops left by Quiroga to guard the *presidio*. By the time the Apurguan Chamorros mounted their first assault on the fort on 27 July, the defenders were ready and repulsed them.

On 19 August, according to Father Morales, who was inside the fort at the time, "The whole island came upon us on all four sides." Although gravely wounded, Governor Esplana resumed command. As the masses of screaming Chamorros moved forward, they were attacked outside the fort's walls by the friendly Chamorros led by Hineti under the cover of supporting musket and artillery fire from the fort. The hostiles could not surmount the stone walls and had to retreat. A few days later, the hostiles again attacked and again failed to breach the fort's walls. Father Morales and the Jesuit historian Le Gobien both make clear that, without the help of Hineti's warriors, the fort would have fallen.

It is one of the ironies of Guam's history that the Agaña mission was saved in this decisive battle of 1684 by Chamorros of interior clans, probably low-caste *manachang*, fighting against fellow Chamorros from coastal clans, most likely high-caste *chamorri*. For a brief period in these battles, the Chamorros held their destiny in their own hands, but they failed to meet the challenge of the parable of the tribes. Firearms undoubtedly gave the Spaniards a powerful advantage, but that advantage might well have been overcome by a united Chamorro army against the weak Spanish forces in Agaña in 1684. A Chamorro victory in Agaña would have left Quiroga and his small force stranded in Saipan. In the end, the Spanish tactics of divide and conquer gave the Spaniards victory over the Chamorro clans, who could not unite as one people against a common enemy, even in a life-or-death struggle.

The fighting in Agaña settled into a Chamorro siege of Fort Guadalupe. Sixty proas full of warriors came from Rota to help the men of Apurguan. The hostiles attempted to lure Hineti and several Filipinos married to Chamorros to desert the Spanish cause. Hineti remained loyal, and the wavering Filipinos were kept in line by Francisco Masongsong. In the meantime, all attempts by the Agaña garrison to communicate with Quiroga on Saipan failed. A priest on Rota, the Bohemian Jesuit August Strobach, attempted to sail to Saipan, but he was killed on Tinian when he stopped there en route. The Chamorros then killed the remaining Jesuit on Rota, the Austrian Karl Boranga.

On Saipan in the meantime, the unsuspecting Quiroga had sent south in early August a detachment in two Spanish boats to carry back to Guam ten of the cannons salvaged from the *Concepción*. On the way, a storm forced the boats to land on Tinian, where the entire detachment of seventeen men was massacred by Chamorros. The Spanish boats were sunk and the cannons dumped into the ocean. Following this Chamorro victory, warriors from Rota, Aguijan, and Tinian sailed to Saipan to join forces with the Saipanese against the still unsuspecting Quiroga and his force of thirty-six soldiers. The hostile force of about 800 men assembled secretly on Saipan to prepare a surprise attack.

Alerted by a Chamorro informer, Quiroga mounted a series of raids against the camps of the Chamorros, followed by retreats into the fort, keeping his enemy off balance. A tough commander, he led his small force in combat and did not hesitate to execute one of his own Spanish soldiers who disobeyed orders.

In mid-November, Quiroga finally managed to exchange messages with Governor Esplana, who ordered the *sargento mayor* to return immediately to lift the Agaña siege, now in its fourth month. Quiroga gathered his men in eight captured proas and slipped away at night on the ocean side of the fort after faking an attack on the inland side. Three of his boats with fifteen men were swept away by currents when they passed too close to Tinian, but in order not to lose the rest Quiroga disregarded their cries for help. The fifteen men later made their way back to Guam with the help of friendly Chamorros. Quiroga and his men landed at the Agaña shore on 23 November.

With the siege lifted, Quiroga was within days raiding rebel villages on Guam, striking fear into the weary Chamorros. According to Father Morales, "Large groups of them left this island of Guahan taking refuge in the neighboring islands." About this time, Father Coomans and three soldiers reappeared in Agaña, the only survivors of the detachment sent by Quiroga to the northern Marianas from Saipan. By early 1685, all organized Chamorro resistance on Guam against the Spaniards ended.

On 15 March 1685, the English privateer John Eaton anchored his ship, the *Nicolas,* on the west side of Guam near Umatac. No Spaniards appeared at first, and the Chamorros were friendly, but two days later some of Eaton's men were attacked by islanders on Cocos Island. The English sailors "killed and wounded some," according to the chronicle of the voyage written by Ambrose Cowley. Esplana contacted Eaton and gave him permission to kill as many Chamorros as he wished. The Englishmen then apparently went hunting for Chamorros as sport and killed three of four men they managed to capture. After a friendly exchange of gifts with Esplana (thirty hogs plus rice and vegetables for six small English guns), the Englishmen sailed away to the west.

In mid-June of the same year, the Acapulco galleon *Santo Niño* arrived at Umatac with forty-four soldiers as replacements along with supplies. Esplana, still recovering from his stab wounds, sent a personal request that he be relieved of his duties in order to recover in Manila. To placate the Jesuits during the interim, he allowed Father Coomans to venture back to Saipan to explore the possibility of the Spaniards returning there. The brave but perhaps overzealous Coomans was promptly killed by the Saipanese.

The next year during the month of May, Esplana was waiting anxiously in Umatac for the Acapulco galleon when a ship appeared on the horizon. It turned out to be another English buccaneer ship, the *Cygnet* under Captain Swan, with the English writer William Dampier aboard. They had been raiding the west coast of New Spain and arrived at Guam nearly starved after crossing the Pacific. When a Spanish priest and three Chamorros came out to the *Cygnet,* thinking it a Spanish ship, Swan took them hostage and sent back a Chamorro to demand provisions from the governor. Esplana quickly complied and sent out hogs and melons. Chamorros meanwhile visited the ship and asked Swan to help them attack the Spaniards, but the Englishman refused. Dampier noted that many of the Chamorros were "troubled with a kind of Leprosie." After releasing the priest with an exchange of gifts (Swan sent Esplana a gift of a "delicate large English Dog"), the Englishmen sailed away happily.

While Swan was on Guam, Esplana sent a boat out to meet the incoming galleon *Santa Rosa* to warn her of the English pirates. Alarmed, the captain of the great galleon swung away from Guam toward the southwest and ran smack into a large area of shallow shoals, now called the Santa Rosa Reef as a consequence of the incident. The galleon was floated off with its rudder damaged and on the way to Cavite discovered one of the islands east of

Yap, perhaps Faraulep, called Santo Barnabas at first and then La Carolina by the *Santa Rosa*'s commander, Lorenzo Lazcano, in honor of King Charles (Carlos) II. This designation would lead to all islands south of the Marianas in Micronesia being called collectively Las Islas Carolinas, the Caroline Islands.

In addition to the *Santa Rosa*'s failure to stop at Guam in 1686, the Cavite supply ship failed to arrive in 1687. By early 1688, the need for provisions was acute on Guam. Relations between Esplana and the missionaries were worse than ever because of his failure to act against the Chamorros on the northern islands. In February 1688, Esplana took the extraordinary step of sailing off for Manila in a large proa with four servants, seven Spanish crewmen, and six Pampangos. He left Quiroga in charge as acting governor. On arrival in Cavite, Esplana was arrested for desertion. Following several months of judicial hearings in Manila, he was acquitted and again appointed governor of Guam, but remained in the Philippines until 1689 while he set up business arrangements, both private and official, related to trade with Guam.

Obliterations

In 1688, the brigantine *San Francisco* from Acapulco and the Cavite supply ship *San Gabriel* both reached Guam with long-awaited supplies, but the *San Francisco* turned out to be a ship of death for the Chamorros. The crew or passengers infected the islanders with what the Jesuit historian Le Gobien called a bloody *rheum* with fever, perhaps influenza or smallpox. With no natural immunity to European diseases, Chamorros died in unknown numbers from what is today called a virgin soil epidemic.

The galleon that arrived the next year brought yet another unknown disease to strike down the Chamorros. Eighty people died within three months. This modest figure actually was nearly 5 percent of the population on Guam at the time. Writing a year later, Father José Hernández of the Umatac church stated that the entire population of

the island, including Spaniards and Filipinos, was only 1,800 people. Of the seven previous parishes, only five remained: Agaña, Pago, Agat, Fina, and Umatac, which by 1690 was the largest, with 700 souls.

The decline in population from the estimated 12,000 on Guam in 1668 when Father San Vitores arrived to fewer than 2,000 people twenty-two years later was disastrous. Numerous Chamorros born on Guam were still living in 1690, but not on Guam. They were the ones who fled to the neighboring islands and to the Carolines to the south. Father Hernández estimated the total population in all the Marianas other than Guam to be roughly 7,000 in 1690. Nonetheless, the loss of Chamorros during the Spanish-Chamorro Wars was enormous. What happened to them?

Obviously, warfare was one cause of the population decline. Beginning in 1671 and lasting until early 1685, numerous small-scale clashes between Chamorros and Spanish soldiers took place each year, causing hundreds of Chamorro deaths. Those not killed outright but wounded invariably died from infection. Larger numbers of deaths occurred in the major battles during the same period. These large-scale clashes revolved around the three lengthy and unsuccessful sieges of the Agaña forts: the first in 1671–1672 (Hurao's attacks with 2,000 warriors); the second in 1676–1677 (Aguarin's "hundreds" of warriors); the last in 1684 (the Apurguan uprising). Contrary to earlier Spanish descriptions of Chamorro warriors giving up after a few casualties, the accounts of the later battles show that the Chamorros attacked repeatedly and courageously in the face of fire from Spanish cannons and muskets. Furthermore, Chamorros in general, particularly the very old and the very young, probably died in higher than normal rates owing to disease, food shortages, stress, and other deprivation caused by the many punitive sweeps by Spanish troops all over Guam.

Another cause of the decline in the Chamorro population was the societal demoralization that occurs among people subjected to massive disruptive change. Disintegration of traditional life patterns leads to increased numbers of suicides and to declines in marriages and in the birthrate, declines accelerated by large shifts in population (such as whole Chamorro villages fleeing to other islands). Spanish histories and the accounts of later visitors stated that, in the Spanish-Chamorro Wars, "the women likewise, purposely sterilize themselves; or if they conceive, they find ways to abort, and some kill their children after birth in order to save them from the subjugation of the Spaniards." Disease-induced infertility among Chamorros caused by venereal and other infections introduced earlier by the Spaniards was also a cause of depopulation in the Marianas by the 1680s. Therefore, by the time the first major epidemic struck Guam in 1688, the birthrate must have already fallen precipitously.

The near decimation of the Chamorros thus came from a combination of causes—war, deprivation, diseases, disease-induced infertility, societal demoralization, and, finally, epidemics, all caused by the Spanish invasion. Although Spanish soldiers rarely wantonly killed Chamorros except in combat and the missionaries certainly tried to protect the islanders from harm as much as they could under harsh circumstances, the Spanish colonial system as a whole, including the church as well as the military, was responsible for the decimation of the very people it sought to save.

In a fundamental sense, the Spanish-Chamorro Wars resulted from the vast incompatibility between the character of the islanders and that of Europeans. In 1604, a Spanish writer, Miguel Agia, described that incompatibility with respect to Spaniards and the Indians of Peru in words that applied equally to the Chamorros: "The Spaniard and the Indian are diametrically opposed. The Indian is by nature without greed and the Spaniard is extremely greedy, the Indian phlegmatic and the Spaniard excitable, the Indian humble and the Spaniard arrogant, the Indian deliberate in all he does and the Spaniard quick in all he wants, the one liking to order and the other hating to serve."

The Spanish-Chamorro Wars cost the Spanish side a total of between 118 and 128 men killed, according to later Spanish accounts. Of these dead, twelve were Jesuit priests, six catechists or secular helpers, and the remainder soldiers, mostly Filipinos. Thus, for each Christian killed, 100 or more Chamorros died in the Spanish conquest of the Marianas.

As a consequence of their policies, the Spaniards found themselves in a paradox by 1689. The majority of Chamorros still alive in 1689 resided in Rota, Tinian, and Saipan, and—astoundingly—they were still not converted to Christianity despite the heroic efforts of the Jesuits over the previous twenty years. Guam was by this time underpopulated. It was thus imperative for the Spaniards to move all the remaining Chamorros in the northern islands back to Guam, not only to cultivate crops and livestock to supply the galleons and the Spanish garrison, but—most important of all—to complete the religious conversion of the islanders, which was a basic purpose of the Spanish presence in the Marianas from the beginning.

With this formidable task facing them, the Jesuits were disappointed when Damián de Esplana stepped off the Cavite supply ship as governor when it arrived at Umatac in September 1689. He immediately began to squabble with the priests and Quiroga. Esplana was by then interested only in making money before his retirement. Annoyed at the Jesuit demands for action against Chamorros in the northern islands, he peevishly removed Quiroga from command of the troops for several months, relenting only after pressure from his confessor.

Esplana solved his feud with Quiroga by simply moving to Umatac, where he constructed a *palacio* surrounded by a *presidio* compound. He divided the garrison between Umatac and Agaña and left Quiroga in charge of the Agaña *presidio*. This was the situation on 2 June 1690, when two galleons from Acapulco approached Guam from the southeast. The flagship was the *Santo Niño,* and its consort was the *Nuestra Señora del Pilar de Zaragoza.* The *Pilar* was a big ship of 1,200 tons with 300 people aboard, including twenty Franciscan missionaries and 100 soldiers and convicts from Mexico.

The galleons had to tack into an unusual west wind as they neared Cocos Island just after sunset. The west wind pushed the *Pilar*, which had sailed ahead of the *Santo Niño*, into the southwest corner of the Cocos reef, where she crunched up on the coral in shallow water. No one was seriously hurt, and everyone was safely evacuated to Umatac, along with much of the cargo. The other galleon held off shore to take on the high-ranking survivors and some immediately retrievable cargo and three days later sailed away to Cavite. The *Pilar*'s cargo, timbers, ship's boats, and parts of the superstructure were salvaged and used to construct a frigate and a schooner at Umatac. Soon the hull of the *Pilar* was pounded across the reef by the surf and slid into deep water on the northwest side of Cocos with whatever cargo may still have been aboard, including perhaps illegal silver (it was standard practice to carry illegal silver and goods deep in the galleon holds to avoid taxes).

Esplana put the marooned soldiers and convicts from the *Pilar* to work on crops and in hunting wild pigs. The Franciscans helped the Jesuits in the churches until they sailed to the Philippines in December 1690 on the Cavite supply ship. In February and March of the next year, a rumor went around that Esplana was planning to send the soldiers and convicts of the *Pilar* to the northern Marianas to fight Chamorros. Alarmed at this news, eighty of the soldiers and convicts planned to escape by seizing the Cavite supply ship when it next arrived. Esplana learned of the plot and had twenty of the men shot on the beach at Agaña and another three shot at Umatac. The convicts and soldiers then settled down until Esplana sent them to Manila in December 1691 on the frigate built from the *Pilar*.

Over the next few years, Guam remained tranquil while Esplana monopolized the lucrative sale of tobacco and sugar, which had become staples for the islanders and mission personnel. Tired of war, he would not move against the Chamorros in the northern islands. The tranquility was shattered in 1693 when another virgin soil epidemic, probably smallpox, killed Chamorros throughout the Marianas. The epidemic was followed by a super-typhoon that battered Guam on 23 November 1693. Churches all along the west coast were destroyed. Even Fort Guadalupe in Agaña was "knocked down" and inundated, according to Le Gobien. Le Gobien states that the converted *chamorri* Antonio Ayhi rebuilt the Agaña church while Alonso Soon rebuilt the one in Agat. Both these old Chamorro warriors were by then prosperous *principales* as a consequence of their loyal service to the Spaniards over the years.

Nine months later, on 16 August 1694, Damián de Esplana, by then a lieutenant general and governor and captain general of the Mariana Islands, died at age fifty-seven in Umatac. Quiroga succeeded Esplana as acting governor and processed the probate of the dead governor's estate. Quiroga discovered that Esplana had misappropriated 56,066 out of the 108,991 pesos sent in the annual *situados* over the previous three years. This theft amounted to over half the governmental payroll entrusted to the governor for the Guam garrison for those years. Esplana had also amassed a tidy fortune through profits on trade passing in and out of Guam. Some future governors would not only continue these practices but refine them to even greater personal profit.

Quiroga buried Esplana in the Agat church and then set off in September 1694 with fifty soldiers to subdue the Chamorros in the islands north of Guam. He went first to Rota to consolidate control, build roads, and intimidate any remaining rebel Chamorros before returning to Guam. On Rota, he left Father Johann Tilpe, who would serve the Rota mission until 1702. With Rota secure, Quiroga set sail again in July 1695 to the north with a strong force in a fleet of twenty proas and the frigate constructed on Guam from the remains of the *Pilar* wreck. When the Chamorros of Tinian saw the Spanish fleet, they sent their women and children to the small rugged island of Aguijan (sometimes spelled as Aguigan, and now known as Goat Island for its only inhabitants).

The Spaniards, however, bypassed Tinian and landed on Saipan, where the remaining Chamorros quickly capitulated. By this time, Joseph de Quiroga had a fearsome reputation as a hard man to oppose. He put Father Bouwens in charge of the Saipan mission, where the Flemish priest would serve until 1705, when he returned to Guam. Quiroga backtracked to Tinian only to find the island empty; the warriors had fled to join their families on Aguijan. Sailing on to Aguijan a few miles south of Tinian, Quiroga tried to negotiate with the Chamorros there. They defiantly rejected all peace offers.

The Island of Aguijan has no beaches. It rises directly out of the sea, with steep high cliffs crowned by a flat top. Quiroga's men landed and started up two narrow paths that led to the crown. One path was blocked, and the Chamorros tenaciously defended the other by rolling boulders down on the invaders. The Spaniards and their Chamorro allies led by a converted *chamorri* named Antonio Inoc pressed bravely up the cliff to rush the hostile Chamorros in trenches at the top. The defenders were finally overwhelmed after several of their men were killed. Some defiant Chamorros committed suicide by jumping from the cliffs. The valor shown in this last stand symbolized the destiny of the Chamorros as a people: they had to resist in order to be governed. The surviving Chamorros were taken to Guam for resettlement.

In 1698, the new governor, José Madrazo, dispatched a final expedition of 400 Spanish and Chamorro troops to the far northern islands of the Marianas. There the last Chamorro refugees, about a thousand people, were rounded up and sent to Guam. Many died en route when some of the boats were swamped by a typhoon. Thereafter, the Spaniards required all Chamorros to reside only on Guam, Saipan, or Rota. A tiny mission remained on Saipan until 1730, but from then on Aguijan, Tinian, Saipan, and the far northern islands would remain uninhabited until the nineteenth century, except for occasional fishermen and parties of hunters of cattle and hogs for meat to supply the garrison on Guam.

So ended the *reducción* of the Chamorros, thirty blood-drenched years after Father San Vitores stepped ashore at Agaña. During those years, which spanned an entire generation of Chamorros, the destiny of Guam was fixed as a small outpost in the worldwide empire of faraway masters. The parable of the tribes was fulfilled for the Chamorro people. The Mariana Islands now entered a twilight period of 200 years of solitude until the next invasion, when new conquerors would make Guam part of a different empire.

Oasis in the Ocean
1698–1800

The New Order

With the depopulation of the northern islands in 1698, Spanish government in the Marianas settled into a benevolent but heavy-handed despotism on the southern islands. The governor's title was *gobernador político-militar,* wherein he combined all civil and military responsibilities in direct authoritarian rule. He issued orders by edicts *(bandos)* and also acted as judge and chief of police. The legal system of the Marianas, like the Philippines, came under the church's ecclesiastical law as well as the Spanish civil and criminal code of 1680 called the Law of the Indies, which had been created originally for the Spanish colonies in the Americas but was amended to apply to the Philippines as well. Spanish justice in the colonies employed retributive punishment, often severe, including fines, confiscation of property, forced labor, lashing, and executions (the latter carried out only in Manila for Guam convictions).

The highest authority in each district (comprising a parish with a village center) in the Marianas was an *alcalde.* He was appointed by the governor from among active or retired Spanish or mestizo officers. His main duties were to maintain order in his district and to manage farming and cattle raising on *estancias* (large ranches) on crown lands. In the early 1700s parishes grew to six: Agaña, Agat, Umatac, Merizo, Inarajan, and Pago. Rota was a separate parish under Guam but was administered by the church at times together with Umatac, resulting in close ties between Chamorros in those two parishes.

Owing to the meagerness of natural resources in the Marianas, large numbers of Spaniards were never attracted to settle in the islands. Consequently, the system in the early Spanish colonial period of awarding *encomiendas* to Spaniards as in the Philippines and other colonies was not followed in the Marianas. Under that system, a Spanish colonist was awarded control of a population through a land grant in a conquered area (the *encomienda*), and all the adult males in the area paid a yearly tribute to the Spaniard from their crops and products or by labor. The absence of private *encomiendas* on Guam protected the remaining Chamorros from massive land alienation, as happened elsewhere to indigenous peoples in the Spanish empire. In addition to retaining much of their ancestral land, Chamorros remained largely free of tribute, taxes, and church tithes under Spanish rule.

Chamorro land tenure, however, changed under the Spaniards. The Spaniards introduced the concepts of land ownership by government for defense and other official needs and by individuals and institutions for private use. Communal ownership by Chamorro families of ancestral properties gradually devolved under Spanish rule into the hands of the new *principalía* class that replaced the old *chamorri* families as the clan structure disintegrated and Spanish male primogeniture inheritance replaced the traditional Chamorro matrilineal system.

Control of land, however, remained communal for families through the concept of "our land" instead of "my land." Baptismal Hispanicized family names slowly replaced most indigenous Chamorro names. A small elite class of families called "high people" *(manak'kilo* or *mantak'kilo)* evolved out of the *principalía* class. This privileged group lived in the center of Agaña, and their houses were normally of coral masonry. They adopted Spanish and Filipino manners and clothing and were educated in the Spanish language, but they continued to speak Chamorro in the home.

This small Agaña elite, a kind of local "city" gentry of about twelve families, tended to marry Spaniards and become mestizos. They remained socially aloof from the ordinary "low people" *(manak'papa)* of predominantly Chamorro blood, who lived mainly in peripheral parts of Agaña and in rural areas. The *manak'kilo* families within the *principalía* class gradually came to own the largest portions of private land on Guam. The Catholic Church also became a major landholder as land was bequeathed to it by parishioners.

Many ordinary Chamorros never owned property under the Spaniards. These landless *manak-'papa* leased or worked as hired laborers the lands of the *principalía* or the crown ranches. *Manak-'papa* who leased land, or who managed to retain their ancestral properties, worked on small ranch-farms called *lanchos,* where families raised pigs, chickens, cattle, fruit trees, and some crops on a subsistence level and for barter. All Chamorros, however, still had to attend compulsory religious services. As a result, most Chamorros lived in two residences under the Spaniards: a formal one in a village where they attended church on the weekends and an informal one on *lanchos* where they lived and worked most of the week.

While life in the smaller villages plodded along

in accord with the religious calendar, life in Agaña and Umatac revolved around the yearly arrivals of the Acapulco galleon, usually in May or June, and the Cavite supply ship, normally in August or September. Until the 1740s, both ships normally halted off Umatac. The supply ship often "wintered" over at Umatac or Merizo until the trade winds were steady enough to carry it back to Cavite, normally around February. The landings of the two ships became so important that the governor transferred his residence from Agaña to Umatac when the ships were expected.

After the ships unloaded, the supplies were transported by boat the twenty miles or so from Umatac around Orote Point to Agaña since no road existed between the two towns and Apra Harbor was not yet a regular anchorage. Agaña had been designated back in 1687 as a *ciudad,* or city, but it was actually just a small town. In fact, it was the first "town" in the European sense to be established in Oceania. It remained the seat of government for the province of the Marianas, one of the smallest provinces under the Spanish administration in the Philippine Islands, which in turn was under the viceroy and the Audiencia of Mexico. Although Umatac also had a governor's residence and was the main port until the 1740s, it was never the capital of Guam.

By 1700, the center of Agaña, by then several hundred yards inland from where San Vitores' original mission stood, was the large unpaved and irregular Plaza Principal, which would later be named the Plaza de Magallanes around 1846, then renamed the Plaza de España by the Americans after 1898. The main streets of Agaña stretched westward from the plaza toward Anigua since the Agaña River swamp blocked extension to the east. The town was divided into several precincts called *barrios,* which in turn were subdivided into *barangays.* Each *barangay* contained up to fifty families, usually related to each other, with mostly Spaniards, Filipinos, and mestizos in the central *barrios* near the plaza. All vestiges and even the exact location of the original Chamorro village of Hagatña disappeared as the Spanish town grew.

By the early 1700s, the main means of land transportation on Guam were two-wheeled wooden "bull carts," pulled leisurely by carabaos (water buffalo introduced from the Philippines), steer, or oxen, the latter introduced from Mexico. These animals were also used for plowing. Ordinary Chamorros and Filipinos lived in thatched wooden frame houses that lined the narrow dirt streets of Agaña and the rural villages. These houses stood several feet above ground on termite-resistant *ifil* posts, with the space below reserved for chickens and animals. There was no running water and no sewer systems. Kitchens were outside under a shed-like roof sometimes attached to the rear or side of the house. These Filipino-style houses would be used for nearly two and a half centuries until Agaña was bombed out by American forces in 1944.

The arrival in June 1700 of the first Acapulco galleon of the new century brought a devastating epidemic, probably influenza. Over 650 deaths occurred that year, leaving memories for generations on the island of "corpses . . . left unburied as there was no one to fulfill that general need," according to a Spanish historical account. In light of the deplorable conditions on Guam, the interim governor, Sargento Mayor Francisco Medrano y Asiain sent a letter to the king in 1701 with the startling proposal that Spain withdraw totally from the Marianas. He recommended that the few thousand surviving Chamorros be transported a few dozen at a time on the annual galleons to the Philippines for resettlement. As might be expected, the Jesuits on Guam objected to such an ignominious retreat. The Jesuit superior at the time, Lorenzo Bustillo, who had come to the Marianas as a student priest back in San Vitores' time, fired off a strong rebuttal to Manila.

While the Spaniards argued over the future of the Marianas, the Chamorros continued to wither away. The Jesuits kept records of all baptisms and deaths of Christians and reported that, for the years 1698–1702, the deathrate of Christianized Chamorros in the Marianas continued to outpace the birthrate. By the early 1700s, the old generation of

traditional Chamorros from the time of San Vitores was dying off. One such was Captain-General and Master of the Camp Don Antonio Ayhi, one of the most reliable and valuable—to the Spaniards—*chamorri* converts to Christianity. He died on 15 April 1702 and was eulogized by Father Bustillo in a letter to Manila as well as at his burial in the Agaña church.

Meanwhile, the Spanish authorities in Manila and Mexico became apprehensive over the threat of English privateers when the War of the Spanish Succession broke out in 1702 on the death of Charles II. Because of the threat of privateers, the Spanish authorities did not agree with Medrano's proposal that Spain withdraw from the Marianas. Troop strength on Guam remained at 130 men in three *compañías de dotación:* two of these companies were made up of men listed as Spaniards (who probably included many mestizos) and one company of Filipino Pampangos. The latter also provided carpenters and stonemasons for the garrison and mission.

These three companies, however, hardly constituted a crack security force. Spanish soldiers came from the poor and unemployed in Spain and Mexico and included convicts conscripted into the ranks. Soldiers often had to go barefoot and without uniforms while on duty. The troops proved useless when the English privateer William Dampier returned to the Marianas in 1705. Dampier had unsuccessfully attacked Spanish shipping off Central America before sailing his leaking twenty-six-gun ship, the *St. George,* badly mauled in losing a fight with a galleon off the Mexican coast, across the Pacific to drop anchor at Rota in 1705. There the crew leisurely reprovisioned before sailing off to the Far East without being threatened in the slightest by the Spaniards in the Marianas.

Sargento Mayor Manuel Argüelles y Valdés, who served from 1706 until 1709, took an informal census in 1708 and found the total population of the Marianas down to 5,532 people. Another epidemic in 1709, apparently diphtheria and typhus together, further reduced the Marianas population to barely 5,000 souls, according to a letter to

Manila by Juan Antonio Pimentel, who replaced Argüelles that year.

These early Spanish governors in the Marianas, all army officers of modest background and stuck for years in boring but potentially profitable colonial service, apparently formed an "old boy" network of mutual support. Argüelles, for example, was Pimentel's son-in-law. Pimentel was a friend of his fellow Peruvian *criollo* Damián de Esplana and like him would enrich himself as governor.

Among these officers, crusty old Joseph de Quiroga was an annoying anachronism. The "Hermit" continued to take the side of the Jesuits in the recurring squabbles between the missionaries and the military governors. To remove this thorn in his side, Governor Pimentel reported to Manila in 1709 that Quiroga had used Chamorros for forced labor (the same charge would later be made against Pimentel by Quiroga). The governor asked Manila to assign an *encomienda* in the Philippines to Quiroga to get him off Guam. The authorities in Manila took no action on Pimentel's request.

Governor Pimentel's tenure started off badly with the epidemic of 1709. That disaster was followed by the appearance the next year of more of the dreaded English privateers, this time under the command of the tough and skillful Captain Woodes Rogers. On 1 March 1710, Rogers hove to off Umatac in four ships of war. The combined English crews numbered over 200 battle-experienced freebooters. One of Rogers' pilots was William Dampier, who knew the Marianas well from his previous two visits.

Faced with this formidable fleet, whose guns and crew outnumbered his own cannons and ragtag troops, Pimentel prudently agreed to provide the privateers with whatever provisions they wanted as long as they put ashore Spanish prisoners, a condition Rogers agreed to. Over the next few weeks, the English and Spanish officers entertained each other and exchanged gifts. Finally, the freebooters sailed away to Mindanao on 21 March with their ships bulging with bullocks, cows and calves, hogs, chickens, and dozens of baskets of corn, rice, and yams as well as 800 coconuts. Rogers obligingly paid for the provisions with pieces of eight that he had earlier looted from the Spaniards in the New World.

Pimentel's—and Guam's—troubles were not over with Rogers' departure. The same year, 1710, a huge typhoon sent mammoth waves against the island's western shores, inundating Fort Guadalupe at Agaña and wiping away whatever remained of it from the 1693 typhoon. Nature's fury, however, was mild compared to the anger of Pimentel's superiors when they learned of his generosity to Spain's enemies. A magistrate was sent to carry Pimentel back to Manila in chains to answer to a special *residencia* (the highest judicial review of the conduct of Spanish officials) for aiding Woodes Rogers. The judges found Pimentel guilty in 1712. He had to forfeit the bond that governors put up when appointed; he was also removed as governor of the Marianas and sent to prison for a time while another *residencia* undertook an investigation of corruption under his administration.

Like many other *residencias,* which all governors underwent at the end of their appointments, evidence of wrongdoing was uncovered in Pimentel's case, but punishment did not inhibit subsequent governors from undertaking similar shady practices. Spanish colonial officials were grossly underpaid; consequently, some resorted to illegal means for compensation.

Government by Neglect

While the Spaniards were embroiled in fruitless bureaucratic housecleaning, economic conditions in the Marianas deteriorated. Although the Acapulco galleons were supposed to stop at Guam, for half the years from 1710 to 1720 they failed to halt, and in the four years 1723–1726 not one galleon stopped in the islands.

The Cavite ship also sometimes failed to arrive. In addition to problems caused by the unreliability of the galleons and the Cavite ships, venal exploitation of the *situados* and *socorros* by some governors continued to cause hardships for nearly everyone but the governors in the Mariana Islands. The governors were able to pocket much of the cash of the *situado* and to profit enormously from the *socorro* by their control of the government storehouse in Agaña, where everyone had to buy supplies at prices set by the governor. Some governors marked up imported food items (sugar, tobacco, chocolate, wine, etc.) as well as uniforms and cloth by as much as 500 percent over the prices in Mexico, pocketing the profits. The governors as well as the *manak'kilo* families readily extended loans to Chamorros and soldiers short of cash, but at usurious interest rates.

By 1710, the Chamorros found themselves being drafted regularly by the *alcaldes* to work two days or more a week on crown lands for wages as low as two or three leaves of poor-grade local tobacco for a day's work—that is, from sunrise to sunset. This labor was a variation of the *repartimiento* system (provisional allotments of *indio* laborers to Spanish landowners) that gradually replaced the *encomienda* system in other parts of the Spanish empire. On Guam, without *encomiendas*, a local variation of *repartimiento* emerged that required Chamorros to work (called *polo*) on communal projects in lieu of taxes. This forced labor of Chamorros amounted to a form of peonage and provoked angry outcries from the Jesuits during Pimentel's administration. He banished the two most outspoken Agaña priests —Father Ignacio Ibargüen and Father Juan Antonio Cantova—to rural churches until Pimentel himself was hauled off to Manila to answer for the Woodes Rogers episode.

During Pimentel's tenure, an unknown number of Chamorros on Guam still rejected Spanish authority, according to a French visitor, Le Gentil de la Barbinais. He was on Guam a week in June 1716 when four French ships reprovisioned on their way around the world. Barbinais wrote that unconverted Chamorros still lived in the hills and went naked in the traditional manner. The Chamorros, he wrote, suffered from leprosy in "epidemic" proportions.

As a consequence of Pimentel's *residencia,* Captain Luís Antonio Sánchez de Tagle replaced Pimentel as governor of the Marianas. Sánchez de Tagle received an unpleasant surprise when English privateers in the ship *Success* under Captain John Clipperton showed up at Guam in March 1721. They were there as a consequence of a brief war that had broken out between Spain and England in 1719 over dynastic politics in Europe. At Umatac, Clipperton sent ashore a Spanish nobleman whom he had captured earlier, the Marqués de Villa, who was to be exchanged for a ransom. After several days of reprovisioning the *Success* in exchange for powder and other military items, but without paying the ransom, Sánchez sent a letter to Clipperton "wherein the governor demands the marquis' jewels, some consecrated plate, and two Negroes, being Christians and subjects to the King of Spain," all still held by Clipperton. Sánchez also kept hostage two of Clipperton's officers who had escorted the marqués ashore.

Angered and drinking rum heavily, Clipperton decided to capture the Cavite supply ship *San Andrés,* which was anchored temptingly in the narrow Mamoan Channel at Merizo. As the *Success* maneuvered, it ran up on the coral reef of the Cocos Island lagoon that borders the channel. The Spaniards positioned some batteries on a high point above Merizo and began bombarding the stuck English ship.

In a desperate situation, with cannonballs smashing the ship's rigging, the frantic English sailors—with Clipperton stone drunk in his bunk—returned the Spanish fire until the next day, when, after freeing the ship and then grounding it again, they managed to haul the *Success* off the reef after fifty hours of fighting. They sailed away to the west with two dead and six wounded, abandoning their two officers held hostage by Governor Sánchez. The fate of the two Englishmen is unknown.

In the meantime, Governor Sánchez had settled down to the routine exploitation of his fiefdom in the Marianas. Because of Jesuit complaints about the blatant misuse of the governor's authority, Sánchez had been given strict instructions by his superiors to clean up the islands' administration. These instructions had no effect whatsoever. In a pathetic petition to King Philip V in March 1722—

written and forwarded by the Jesuit procurator general of the Philippines—*indios* in the Marianas and Mindanao asked the king to "preclude the coming [as governors] of corrupt men, who blinded with greed, enslave the *indios* and soldiers . . . and that the governor not keep them occupied every day." The king once more ordered that the abuses be corrected, but with little effect.

Exploitation of the garrison and the mission by the governors was also opposed by Quiroga, who was still *sargento mayor* in Agaña. The "Hermit" remained as stiffly moralistic as ever after over forty years of steadfast service to Spain and to the church in the Marianas. In 1720, Quiroga wrote a denunciation of Pimentel's corrupt tenure on Guam. Sánchez got rid of Quiroga by retiring him in May 1723. Soon thereafter, the old soldier died and was buried in the Agaña church. In the long sweep of Guam's history, Joseph de Quiroga ranks second only to Father San Vitores among the individuals who had the most direct personal impact on the tragic destiny of the Chamorro people.

Sánchez de Tagle got into hot water with his superiors in December 1724 when he recklessly ordered his soldiers to fire on the Cavite brigantine *San Francisco Xavier* at Merizo when the captain refused some of Sánchez's orders. The brigantine escaped to the Philippines. Fearing arrest by officials in Manila, and pleading sickness as an excuse, Sánchez fled to the Philippines with his family on one of Guam's boats and hid in a monastery. He ended this melodrama appropriately by dying of natural causes before a *residencia* could prosecute him.

While the colonial Spanish authorities bumbled along in comic-opera fashion on Guam, the number of pure-blooded Chamorros continued to decline. *Indios,* as they were still called, fell from 3,539 people in 1710 (the year of the first official Spanish census) to only 1,576 in 1742, according to Jesuit records. By 1742, Rota had only 248 Chamorros, whose main job was to cultivate rice for Guam. Concerned with the decline, King Philip V issued a

cédula on 28 May 1741 that exempted Chamorro women from work "not appropriate to their sex." Until then, the women had been compelled to weave thatch items such as mats and baskets for sale to the galleons.

Because the Chamorros appeared to be dying out, a proposal was first made in 1722 and repeated afterward in various forms over the years to transport Filipino families for voluntary resettlement in the Marianas to revitalize the economy. Finally, in 1748, a ship with Filipino migrants sailed for Guam, but en route it sank, and all on board drowned, ending efforts for mass migration. Filipinos would nevertheless continue to be the main migrants to Guam through individuals and small groups assigned as soldiers and mission personnel. A Spanish census of 1727, for example, reported more than 400 families of Spanish and Filipino soldiers and retirees, most of whom had Chamorro wives and children of mixed ethnicity. Filipino migration to Guam has been a recurring social phenomenon with major social impact throughout the postcontact history of the island, and it remains so today.

Frustrated with the many problems of the Marianas, in 1726 Manuel Argüelles, who was serving a second term as governor, proposed to his superiors an amended version of Governor Medrano's suggestion of 1701 that Spain withdraw from the Marianas. Instead of total withdrawal, Argüelles recommended leaving a custodial force of three priests in the mission and twenty-five soldiers under a corporal for security. The Chamorros, he said, should all be gathered into Agaña and Umatac.

In Madrid, the Council of the Indies did not agree with these proposals. The council feared that, if Spain gave up Guam or reduced its defenses, other imperial powers could occupy the Marianas and threaten the Pacific galleon trade, which was Spain's lifeline to the Philippines. If the lifeline was cut, Madrid believed that not only would trade be threatened but the Christian missions might also be jeopardized. The sustenance that kept this long and vulnerable artery alive was Mexican silver. Spain's colonies in the Pacific received about one-third of

Mexico's silver production from the sixteenth into the eighteenth centuries.

This Spanish view of the new geopolitics of the Pacific was not unrealistic. Great Britain was increasing its Pacific activities, and France was becoming a competitor for trade. The first French ship to cross the north Pacific and visit Guam en route to the Far East was the *Saint Antoine de Pade* under Captain Nicholas de Frondat in June 1708. By 1717, seventeen French ships had crossed the Pacific and touched at Guam, including the four merchantmen in 1716 with Barbinais. Concerned that their closed mercantile system was being pierced, the Spaniards mounted a naval expedition in the New World in 1716–1717 that captured six illegal French merchant ships and put a stop to the French trade for decades. Nonetheless, Great Britain and Holland remained threats. Thus, Madrid believed the Marianas had to be held to deny them to rival powers, even if the islands cost more than they produced. This "denial concept" became a fixed geopolitical assumption of the Spaniards and later of the Americans in Micronesia.

Instead of reducing Spain's presence in the Marianas as Argüelles proposed, Madrid issued orders to improve Guam's defenses to prevent incidents like Clipperton's attack. Sometime in the 1720s or 1730s, Fort Santiago, a small emplacement with cannons, was erected on top of Orote Peninsula overlooking Apra Harbor. Then, in 1734, a new anchorage for ships was opened in Apra Harbor that offered better protection from storms and was more easily defended than Umatac. And, in 1737, Fort San Luís with six muzzle-loading cannons was completed on the northern shoreline of Orote (near what is today Gab Gab Beach) to defend the anchorage. The harbor was thereafter called the Port of San Luís of Apra, with the shallow inner part, which was the most protected, called *la caldera chica* because of its crater-like topography, and the larger outer part called *la caldera grande* bordered on the north by the Calalan Bank, Luminao Reef, and Cabras Island (originally Apapas in Chamorro).

After 1740 most ships began to anchor in Apra Harbor when the wind was favorable. Cargo was transferred to small boats, which crossed shallow flats to unload at a pier near the village of Piti. From there, the goods were carried to the government store in Agaña by two-wheeled carts pulled by steer or oxen. The lumbering old Acapulco galleons continued to make their stops—usually for only one day and without anchoring—off Umatac. Supplies from the galleons were still transported by boat from Umatac to Agaña, as no road was ever built by the Spaniards over the steep mountain ridges south of Agat, only short segments in the bays between the ridges.

Argüelles left in early 1730 and was replaced by Diego Félix de Balboa, who served until 1734. He was the first naval officer posted as governor to the Marianas. He was followed by another naval officer, General of the Fleet Francisco Cárdenas Pacheco, who died on Guam of natural causes in 1740. Thereafter, the Spanish government occasionally assigned navy officers (who tended to be more liberal than army officers) to Guam. Subsequently, Spanish treatment of the Chamorros mellowed into an indolent paternalism, although it was never a model of social responsibility.

The next notable intrusion in the Marianas was the two-month-long visit of British Commodore George Anson at Tinian in 1742 on the big sixty-gun, 1,005-ton man-of-war *Centurion*. Spain was once more at war with Great Britain (the War of Jenkins' Ear, 1739–1741, which led into the War of the Austrian Succession, 1740–1748). Anson was sent to attack the Spaniards in the Pacific and to seize a galleon. At the small harbor on the leeward southwest coast of Tinian, the Englishmen captured a large proa (which was described admiringly in the several accounts of the voyage) with a Spanish sergeant and four Chamorros. These men were part of the detachment sent regularly from Guam to Tinian to slaughter cattle and hogs and to dry the beef into jerky and the pork into salted spareribs to supply Guam's garrison.

The English sailors found Tinian to be paradise after the hardships of their Pacific passage. The

Spaniards on Guam, without a warship, left the intruders undisturbed. With his crew restored to health, and after a near disaster with a typhoon, Commodore Anson departed Tinian on 22 October 1742.

The poetic descriptions of Tinian later published in England by Anson's crew members and the excellent drawings by Lieutenant Peircy Brett—including the first accurate diagram of a Chamorro proa—were part of European literature in the eighteenth century that romanticized Pacific islanders as "noble savages." Influential European readers of noble savage accounts in this period included the French encyclopedist Denis Diderot and Jean-Jacques Rousseau, the philosophical godfather of the American and French revolutions. In their writings, Diderot and Rousseau pictured Pacific islanders as "children of nature" who were all free and equal through inalienable "natural rights" under a universal natural law. They held up this ideal—however invalid it was in reality in the Pacific—of popular sovereignty as the source of governmental authority in place of hereditary kings and religions. Eventually, in the late twentieth century, Chamorro activists would cite the European concept of the natural right of all peoples to self-determination as justification for the independence of Guam from American sovereignty.

While the roots of revolution grew in America and Europe during the mid-eighteenth century, the Spaniards on Guam occupied themselves with the construction of a new *palacio* in Agaña for the governor. This building was probably started under Governor Cárdenas Pacheco and was completed under Governor Miguel Fernandez de Cárdenas in 1744. The new *palacio* was constructed of thick coral masonry on the site of the previous and much smaller residence of the governor built around 1700 on the southwestern corner of the plaza. The French visitor Barbinais in 1716 described the old Agaña *palacio* as a "modest" one-story building of only three rooms with a roof of palm leaves. The new building of 1744 was much grander, with two stories, a balcony facing the plaza, and a tile roof. The 1744 *palacio* would last—with many renovations—until 1884, when it was torn down and rebuilt by 1889.

Ship arrivals at Guam continued to be sparse and erratic from 1743 to 1753, and the number of troops on the island was reduced. Spanish neglect of the Marianas was exemplified in the celebrations on Guam of the funeral of King Philip V and the coronation in 1746 of his successor Ferdinand VI. In July 1747, two galleons from Acapulco paused at Umatac with the news of these important events that had to be commemorated throughout the Spanish empire.

The problem for the governor at the time, Domingo Gómez de la Sierra, was, in the words of his secretary Jorge Eduardo del Castillo, that "neither His Majesty nor this Infantry has in their Royal Account [on Guam] a single existing *real* because of not having received a *situado* for four years." In this situation, Governor Gómez de la Sierra "considered himself obliged to appear a faithful vassal" who should carry on the celebration with his own money. From 26 July to 6 August 1747, all of Guam celebrated the succession of the Spanish Bourbon kings with what pomp the little outpost could muster with the cash provided by the governor. According to the governor's secretary, the celebrations included

> the illumination of all the City, those of the Balcony of the *palacio,* Houses and Streets being a brilliance multiplied by the lights of the pleasant inventions which were presented on the Plaza. . . . The Governor. . . commanded in the name of their Majesties . . . a general pardon to fugitives and deserters . . . and there came eight lepers and twelve widows, to whom the Governor distributed one hundred pesos . . . the natives presented a lighted *magiganga* [slapstick-type festivities] with many ponies and a variety of animals . . . calling a great many times "Long live the King!"

Unfortunately, Gómez tried to recoup his money spent for the 1747 celebrations by expropriating some crown property. His *residencia* in 1749 found him guilty of selling effects of the *presidio* and cutting down coconut trees for his personal profit.

By the 1750s, more non-Spanish ships were appearing in the Pacific, particulary English men-of-war, which replaced the privateers of earlier years. During the Seven Years' War (1754–1763), Manila itself fell in 1762 to the English, who held the city for indemnity until 1763. When the Cavite ship brought the news of the war to Guam, Governor José de Soroa (a naval officer who served from 1759 to 1768) mobilized all able-bodied men for defense in case Great Britain invaded the island. In addition to the complement of sixty soldiers then assigned to the *presidio*, the records show ten lists of men by village and by race: there were sixty-seven Spaniards, fifty-seven mestizos, one hundred Filipinos, and several hundred Chamorros. The English, however, ignored Guam.

By the mid-eighteenth century, Portugal had become part of the Spanish empire, and the Dutch had declined as a maritime power. As a consequence, in 1765 Madrid authorized Spanish ships to sail between the Philippines and Spain by way of the Straits of Malacca, across the Indian Ocean, and around Africa's Cape of Good Hope. The impact on Guam of these developments was that even fewer Spanish vessels stopped at the island. For the eight years between 1760 and 1768, no Cavite supply ships came to Guam, according to the account of a French visitor, Vicompte Pierre Marie François de Pages, who crossed the Pacific on the 1768 Acapulco galleon. Despite this isolation, however, one of the most dramatic events in Guam's history was about to take place.

In the previous two centuries, the Jesuits had been the shock troops of Christianity, viewing themselves as the special soldiers of the pope since the founding of their society in 1540 by Saint Ignatius of Loyola. They formed an elite force to counter the erosion of Catholicism by the Protestant Reformation and to strengthen the church worldwide through conversion and education of non-Christians in the new colonial empires of Europe. The mission of Father San Vitores to the Marianas in

1668 was one small element in the dynamic global commitment of the Jesuits to those goals.

By the early eighteenth century, the Society of Jesus had become a formidable success. Wealthy, relatively independent of governmental administrators, and politically influential everywhere, the Jesuits came to be feared by the Catholic kings of Europe as a threat. A central issue was nationalism—that is, national control over the Catholic Church within each nation—versus the dominance of the church by the foreign ecclesiastical authority of the pope. The Jesuits were seen by the kings as siding with the pope and therefore posing a challenge to national autonomy.

In 1759 the Jesuits were expelled from Portugal and its colonies; France suppressed the society in 1764; and in 1765 Charles III reasserted his authority over the church by forbidding the establishment of any new monasteries, schools, churches, etc. in the Spanish empire without his approval. And, on 27 February 1767, he issued a chilling *cédula* signed imperiously, as were all royal edicts, *Yo, el Rey* (I, the King): "... have decided to expel from all my dominions of Spain and the Indies, the Philippine Islands and other adjacent territories, the religious of the Society of Jesus ... and to confiscate all the properties of the Society in my dominions."

The orders to carry out the edict were sent throughout the Spanish empire in double envelopes under three seals with the intimidating message, "Under pain of death this package is not to be opened until April 2, 1767, at the setting sun."

News of the impending expulsion did not reach Guam until June 1768, when a frigate from Acapulco, the *San Carlos*, arrived with the new governor and departed with José de Soroa. The new man, Henrique de Olavide y Michelena, was on his second assignment to the Marianas as governor (1768–1771) after a twelve-year interval. He had the singular duty of carrying out the harsh *cédula* of Charles III.

The formal orders of expulsion arrived on Guam on 25 August 1769, on the Cavite ship *Nuestra Señora de Guadalupe*, which also brought five

Augustinian Recollect friars to replace the three Jesuit priests and one brother at the mission. The next day, Olavide imprisoned the Jesuits in the School of San Juan de Letrán. Within a few days, all property of the mission was confiscated, inventoried, and handed over to the Augustinians under Friar Andrés Blázquez de San José as vice provincial and new rector of San Juan de Letrán. Two months later, on 2 November, the Jesuits were shipped off with a few personal belongings to the Philippines aboard the *Guadalupe* on the first leg of their long voyage back to Spain with all the other Jesuits from the Philippine missions.

The banishment of the Jesuits occurred 101 years after Father San Vitores had stepped ashore on Guam to create the Marianas mission. During that period, seventy-five Jesuit priests served in the Marianas, of whom thirty-seven, or nearly half, died in the islands. Of those who died, twelve met violent deaths as martyrs in the early years of the mission. In addition, six catechists were martyred by Chamorros. A Jesuit historian later wrote with sad pride, "The Marianas remained for many years one of the most dangerous mission fields in the annals of the Society of Jesus."

The impact on the Chamorros of the expulsion was negative after so many decades of Jesuit effort. The Jesuits had a large, successful ranch at Tachogna on a plateau in the central area of the island. This and other Jesuit farms were abandoned and the livestock turned wild. More important, education was disrupted by the change. The School of San Juan de Letrán, for example, was moved by the Augustinians to a different building in Agaña, and educational standards declined over the coming decades.

The entire Society of Jesus was dissolved in 1773 by Pope Clement XIV and would not be restored until 1814 under Pius VII. In 1829, sixty years after the expulsion, in an official historical review, the Spanish government would belatedly acknowledge that the Jesuits occupied the Marianas "in other times to the great advantage and glory of the church and state."

The Good Governor Tobías

After the dramatic but brief turbulence caused by the departure of the Jesuits in 1769, the people of Guam and Rota settled back into their old routines of life, but they found the Augustinian Recollects more casual about the rituals and disciplines of the church than the Jesuits. The aftermath of the expulsion of the Jesuits was softened by the arrival in September 1771 on the Cavite ship of a new governor, Sargento Mayor Mariano Tobías (also spelled Tovías). This energetic and capable army officer served on Guam for fewer than three years—until June 1774—but during that time he improved the government and the material well-being of the people more than had all the twenty-six previous governors combined.

The new governor moved quickly to improve agriculture, which had declined after the expulsion of the Jesuits. Tobías encouraged production of cotton, sugarcane, mangos, pineapples, and vegetables. The seeds and seedlings for these mostly introduced plants were brought in from Mexico and the Philippines. Many of the ingredients and methods of food preparation on Guam by that time were a blend of Chamorro, Mexican, and Filipino cooking, particularly the use of spicy Mexican peppers.

Tobías established small cotton gins and hand looms to make cloth and promoted the production of salt. He brought in a herd of deer from the Philippines and set them free. Called *benadu* or *binadu* in Chamorro (from the Spanish word *venado*), the deer survived down through the centuries and are still hunted on Guam. As *sargento mayor,* Tobías created a 200-man volunteer militia under Spanish officers and Filipino noncommissioned officers as backup to the regular troops. He paid the militia a small but regular salary (he stole no funds while on Guam) and had them raise crops on crown lands in place of the forced labor by Chamorros. The militia also worked on roads and other public works projects.

By the time of Tobías' tenure on Guam, European nations were dispatching numerous expeditions to explore the islands of the Pacific Ocean. On 27 September 1772, a French expedition—referred to as Crozet's Voyage—anchored in Apra Harbor with two small ships, the 140-ton *Mascarin* and the 100-ton *Marquis de Castries*. The expedition had initially been commanded by Captain Marc-Joseph Marion du Fresne. When the ships stopped at the Bay of Islands in northern New Zealand, Maori cannibals massacred Marion du Fresne and fifteen of his men and ate them all.

The survivors sailed to the Marianas with Chevalier du Clesmeur as captain of the *Castries* and in overall command and Lieutenant Julien Crozet as captain of the *Mascarin*. France was an ally of Spain at the time, and the Mariana Islands had by then a reputation as an oasis for recuperation in the Pacific. The expedition—with 200 cases of scurvy—remained at Guam nearly two months while the sick recovered with the kind assistance of Tobías.

Crozet took notes in which he praised Tobías as a "worthy and honorable" man and described Guam as a "really delightful abode . . . studded with picturesque and delicious scenes." Crozet noted that Chamorro men were "slightly given to drunkenness . . . and are passionately fond of cockfighting."

On Crozet's return to France, an antimonarchist former priest in Paris, the Abbé Guillaume Raynal, read Crozet's notes. Raynal promptly incorporated some of Crozet's statements into an anticolonial history that Raynal had written about imperialism in the West and East Indies. Raynal sharply criticized the Spaniards for decimating the Chamorro people, but he praised Governor Tobías as a model exception to what Raynal described as the normal greedy and exploitive officials of the Spanish empire. The edition of Raynal's history with Crozet's notes was published in 1778 and became a best-seller in France. The authorized, less inflammatory version of Crozet's notes edited by one of the expedition's members, the Abbé Alexis Marie de Rochon, would be published in 1783, but by then it was too late to calm Spanish outrage at Raynal's allegations.

While all this was occurring in Europe, the unsuspecting Tobías had been posted routinely from Guam to Manila. When Raynal's history became known in Manila in 1785, the Spanish authorities there removed Tobías from his regimental command and gave his salary to his wife, who left him when he fell out of favor. According to the French explorer La Pérouse, who saw Tobías in Manila in 1786, the ex-governor of Guam was "reduced to despair." Too progressive for his time and government and the hapless victim of unwanted exploitive publicity, Mariano Tobías returned to Spain to undeserved obscurity. His fate confirms the view that no good deed goes unpunished.

While that unfortunate scenario was unfolding, a disaster had occurred on Guam when a chicken pox epidemic enveloped the island in 1779, killing Chamorros but few Spaniards, mestizos, or Filipinos. As a consequence, the Spanish census in the year 1783 showed the population of non-Chamorros (1,623 people, which included Spaniards, mestizos, and Filipinos and their descendants, with many of the latter Chamorro mixtures) had overtaken by a slight majority the pure-blooded Chamorro population (1,608) for the first time in the Marianas.

After 1783, Spanish censuses showed pure-blooded Chamorros (called "Natural Indians" in the records) about equal in numbers with non-Chamorros in the censuses until 1816. After that year, pure-blooded Chamorros were a dwindling minority until finally absorbed by the end of the nineteenth century into a hybrid neo-Chamorro mixture. The years from 1783 to 1816 were therefore a demographic transition period in the Marianas. After 1816, the tide of genetic history would run inexorably and permanently against the remaining pure-blooded Chamorro *taotao tano'*, the once-free people of the sea.

Explorers and the Geopolitics of the Pacific

The year 1783 witnessed the conclusion of the American War of Independence, in which Spain was one of the victors for a change. With peace,

Britain and France resumed their expeditions of exploration into the Pacific. Spanish reaction to the British and French incursions into what the Spaniards considered to be their lake was to scold London and Paris in diplomatic notes that claimed Spain had exclusive rights as the only nation legally permitted to navigate the southern Atlantic and the entire Pacific. Spain based this grandiose claim on the old papal bulls of the 1490s, which divided the known world between Spain and Portugal, and on subsequent usage of those areas and treaties that confirmed the status quo in Spanish America.

France and Britain, as might be expected, considered Spain's claim preposterous, as did another contender, Russia, which was expanding into Alaska and down the coast of Canada into Spanish California. Alarmed at these threats to Spain's interests in the Pacific region, the viceroy of Mexico reported to Madrid in 1788 that "the Russian projects and those which the English may make . . . already menace us."

As a consequence, the Spanish court approved a proposal in 1788 by one of Spain's brightest naval officers, thirty-four-year-old Alessandro Malaspina, to mount a major expedition into the Pacific to reassert Spain's presence there while adding to Spanish scientific knowledge and prestige. Malaspina was handsome, well educated, and—what would later prove fatal to his career—politically ambitious. He assembled an impressive crew of 204 men and the latest scientific equipment aboard his new twin 306-ton corvettes and departed Cádiz in July 1789.

Malaspina's ships rounded Cape Horn in 1790 and explored various places on the coasts of both South and North America as far as Alaska (where a glacier was named after Malaspina). Two botanists accompanied the expedition, the French-born naturalized Spaniard Luis Née and the Bohemian Thaddeus Haenke, along with a Spanish geologist, Antonio de Pineda y Ramírez. By October 1791, the expedition was in Acapulco, where Malaspina prepared his ships to cross the Pacific, with the first stop to be Guam.

In the meantime, economic conditions on Guam were improving under a conscientious governor,

Joseph Arleguí y Leóz, who served from 1786 to 1794. In early 1791, Arleguí reported he was implementing a royal *cédula* of 1787 (the delay indicates the infrequency of ships with mail in that period) that ordered that *gobernadorcillos* be selected annually to assist the appointed Spanish *alcaldes* (who became *alcaldes administradores*) in the administration of parishes. Parishes by then were called *municipios*. Chamorros proposed the names of three *principales* to the governor, who selected one as *gobernadorcillo* of the *municipio* for the year. This official was given the title *don* and his wife made a *doña*. The new system was the beginning of village-level indigenous government under the Spaniards in the Marianas, but from 1793 on public offices could be held only by men who spoke Spanish.

Under Arleguí in 1788, a large group of islanders from Lamotrek in the Carolines arrived in canoes at Talofofo Bay on a trading mission to obtain iron. This was the first such expedition since the Spanish-Chamorro Wars halted trade between the islanders. A young Guam-born *sargento mayor,* Luís de Torres, befriended the Carolinians, and with his assistance they departed several months later for Lamotrek with iron and trade goods and a promise to return in 1789. The voyagers never reached Lamotrek. The people there assumed that the voyagers were killed by the still-feared Spaniards and so did not attempt to sail to Guam again. On Guam, Luís de Torres was puzzled by the failure of the Lamotrekese to return in 1789 as promised. He would not get an answer for fifteen years, until 1804, when he visited Woleai, but in the interim the matter remained a mystery.

While Torres was waiting for the Lamotrekese to return to Guam, the two ships of the Malaspina expedition anchored off Umatac in 1792. Unfortunately, the crew brought disease (unnamed in the accounts) from Acapulco, where an epidemic had caused many deaths. Despite the disease, Malaspina's botanists made the first thorough collection of plants in the Marianas, with Née covering the south and Haenke the north of Guam, while Pineda mapped for the first time the geology and zoology of the island. Pineda noted in his diary, "There are no roads other than narrow trails and the footpaths of horses and riding oxen." The only real road connected the pier at Piti in Apra Harbor with Agaña and was composed of crushed limestone *cascajo.*

On 24 February, after twelve days on Guam with a side trip to Tinian, the Malaspina expedition departed, returning eventually to Cádiz in September 1794. Initially on Malaspina's return he was acclaimed and promoted. Soon, however, he was caught up in court intrigues and romantically involved with Italian-born Queen María Luísa de Parma (wife of Charles IV, and called La Parmesana after the sharp Italian cheese because of her voracious sexual appetite). The queen and the chief minister, the adroit and unscrupulous Manuel de Godoy, were lovers, and Malaspina maneuvered to replace Godoy as the queen's favorite. Godoy reacted by having his rival arrested in late 1795 for

"reasons of state." In this corrupt and deceitful atmosphere Malaspina was convicted in 1796, stripped of his rank, and imprisoned for nearly seven years, followed by banishment and an obscure death in Italy in 1810.

Of perhaps greater tragedy than the shabby treatment of Malaspina, Godoy also impounded all the expedition's 4,000 or so documents and over 800 drawings. Furthermore, Godoy prevented publication of the scientific materials. Malaspina's trip diary was not published until 1885. One result of the Spanish government's suppression of information from the Malaspina voyage in the context of Spain's long history of a closed colonial system was that the European public remained ignorant of the many accomplishments of Spanish explorations in the Pacific. In contrast, Britain and France widely publicized the endeavors of their explorers. Thus, Tahiti, Hawai'i, and Polynesia in general became

Man of the island of Guam *(Hombre de la ysla de Guham).* A drawing from life by artist Juan Ravenet on the Malaspina expedition, 1789–1794. The man's features reflect the emergence of a neo-Chamorro racial mixture of Chamorro, Filipino, and possibly some Spanish blood after a century of Spanish rule in the Marianas. (From the collection of the Micronesian Area Research Center, Mangilao, Guam)

imprinted on European and American public perceptions as exemplifying the Pacific island world, while the Spanish Marianas and the rest of Micronesia, cut off from open commerce and described mainly in closed Spanish official documents, remained generally unknown.

As Malaspina's fate was being played out in Spain, disastrous events were occurring on Guam. On 2 March 1793, a huge fire swept through the buildings of Agaña, nearly destroying the town. Just as the inhabitants were getting back to normal conditions, a monstrous typhoon struck the island in December, destroying all crops and most fruit trees. Soon the islanders had slaughtered most of their domestic animals and began killing off the deer, wild pigs, and wild cattle for food.

Then another disaster struck in September 1794, this time a flu epidemic that caused convulsive coughing and killed its victims within a week. The flu was brought to the island by the ship on which the new governor, Lieutenant Colonel Manuel Muro, and his wife, María Agueda del Camino, arrived and on which Arleguí happily departed. The epidemic lasted three months. Fortunately, the ship had also brought a cargo of rice, without which many more people might have died.

With Guam nearly devastated, Governor Muro —a veteran *peninsular* who was forty-two years old, fat, and in poor health owing to dropsy—took vigorous action. With his own money, he bought rice as well as clothes from the ship's cargo and distributed them free to the people. To protect the island's deer and wild cattle from being wiped out, he prohibited further hunting. He laid out a new town plan for Agaña and put everyone to work on reconstruction. He required the men to work only half a day on public projects so that in the other half they could work on their own gardens and property. For the half-day labor he paid them a double ration of food so that the men could feed their families. In all this he was stern and demanding.

Because Spain was at war again in this period (first against revolutionary France in 1792–1795, then against Britain in 1796–1802; Spain lost both wars), all Spanish governors received orders to strengthen defenses in the empire. Muro used these orders to construct a new fort, San Rafael, to guard the Agaña channel in place of old Fort San Fernando, which had been allowed to deteriorate since its construction decades earlier in place of Fort Guadalupe. Then Muro rebuilt the main Agaña warehouse *(almacén)* of coral masonry near the *palacio* with a large enclosing wall. These projects were completed in 1799. Three main arches of the *almacén* wall still stand as of the 1990s.

Next, Muro built the stone bridge of San Antonio (named after Saint Anthony of Padua and called in Chamorro Tolai Acho') across a branch of the Agaña River, and Fort Santa Agueda (named after his wife) on Apugan Hill overlooking Agaña, completing both in the year 1800. The hill fort, now called Fort Apugan, still stands. The San Antonio Bridge remains in place also. It is now a historical monument in a small park (the river channel has been diverted) along with a statue erected in the 1970s of Sirena, a mermaid in a local legend. At the turn of the century, Muro was constructing in Apra Harbor a new fort with stone walls over sixteen feet thick and embrasures for eleven cannons. Named Fort Santa Cruz, this massive structure was completed in 1801 on the south side of the harbor to replace old Fort San Luís, which was in ruins by then.

While these various projects were under way, Governor Muro ordered, as usual every year, a Te Deum mass to be given at the Agaña church on 4 November 1798, in honor of the king's name day. This mass also marked another anniversary in that it was held almost exactly 100 years after the end of the Spanish-Chamorro Wars when the last rebellious Chamorros were forcibly resettled from the northern Marianas to Guam in 1698. In that century, the traditional Chamorro culture had changed greatly, but the core elements—the Chamorro language and maternal control of family life—endured as Guam entered a new century.

Twilight of Pax Hispanica
1800–1898

Americans, Alien Islanders, and Stagnation

The last century of Spanish rule in the Marianas began with minor but bad omens for the Spaniards. In 1798, Governor Muro's wife became sick and lingered near death for a long time. The governor fell into a severe depression owing to "melancholia" over his wife's illness, according to Spanish records, and in November 1799 sent a letter of resignation to Manila. In 1800, Governor-General Rafael María de Aguilar accepted Muro's resignation and named as his replacement Vicente Blanco. This routine administrative event—the leisurely replacement of a worn-out governor with a new man—would be repeated twenty-six more times before Spanish rule in the Marianas would stumble to an end like a slow death after a long sickness.

As of 1800, Guam had been without supplies for three years. So in 1801 the new governor resorted to chartering an American ship—the bark *Lydia* from Boston, trading out of Manila under Captain Moses Barnard—to take him and his party from Manila to Guam "for 5000 Spanish dollars." With the rise in Pacific trade, the term *Spanish dollars* gained use, usually in reference to the Mexican *duro* silver peso coin. There was no paper currency in the Spanish Pacific at the time.

The *Lydia* dropped anchor in Apra Harbor on 6 January 1802. Governor Muro's wife meanwhile had died and was preserved in a special coffin while waiting to be shipped back to Manila aboard the *Lydia*. The Chamorros described Muro to the Spanish-speaking first officer of the *Lydia*, William Haswell, as a "great Tyrant" who ran the island for his own profit in the time-honored Spanish colonial way. Grievances against Muro were raised at his *residencia,* but the investigation ended by commending him.

Of the ordinary people of Guam in 1802 Haswell wrote (in early nineteenth-century American prose),

> I frequently went into Indian Inland Villages, and always found them hard at work with the Tobacco, which all belongs to the King and as soon dry'd must be carried to the Governor, and he sells it at a Enormous Price as is everything else. . . . Their food is chiefly shell fish and Plaintains, cocoa Nuts and a kind of Sweet Potatoes which they dry and make flouer off, and it makes good bread when new. . . . They are generally healthy and strong, but the Venereal had made sad Ravages amongst them. . . . In the Inland places the Men and Women go Naked, but they have Cloathes and on the Appearance of a European they run and put them on and are proud of being dressed; but they cannot buy Clothes to wear in Common they are so dear, as the governor gains 8 hundred per Cent on all he sells them, and no other person is allow'd to

trade. They are very Obedient to the government and it is seldom that there is any Disturbance.

The ship *Lydia*—heavily loaded with oxen, hogs, poultry, deer, and the preserved remains of Governor Muro's wife—departed Guam on 16 February 1802 for Manila. Muro, who argued with Captain Barnard over the return fare, remained on Guam until a later ship took him to Manila. Many other American ships would halt at Guam in the coming years as the whaling and seal fur industries expanded in the Pacific along with the China trade. Guam's modest share in this commerce in the early nineteenth century included the provisioning of ships with fresh produce and livestock, just as in the old galleon days, but with the sale of trepang (also called *bêche de mer* and *balate*) now added.

Trepang refers to any of several large, slow-moving sea slugs—also called sea cucumbers—that are plentiful in the shallow waters of tropical Pacific islands. Easily caught, cleaned, and smoked, the rubbery shrunken trepang skins were sacked up by the thousands and shipped from all over the Pacific to China, where they sold for "15 Spanish dollars the Hundred pounds," according to Haswell. In China, trepang were used mainly in soup and were thought to be an aphrodisiac. On Guam, the Spanish governor held a monopoly on the trepang trade.

A more exotic product of Guam at the time was pearls. Haswell was shown two Guam pearls, each half an inch in diameter. By the late nineteenth century, pearl diving in the Marianas disappeared, perhaps because of overharvesting on the islands' fragile reef systems.

It was under Governor Blanco in 1804 that Captain Luís de Torres took passage on the American ship *Maria* under Captain Samuel William Boll when the *Maria* was passing through Guam on the way to the Caroline Islands in search of trepang. Luís de Torres wanted to discover why the Lamotrekese had never returned to Guam in 1789, as they had promised. When the *Maria* reached Woleai, Torres

and the Carolinians agreed that a storm in 1788 must have wiped out the voyagers on their way back from Guam. With the mystery cleared up, Torres then invited the Carolinians to reestablish trade between the Carolines and Waghal, as the Carolinians called Guam. The trading voyages resumed in 1805 and involved flotillas of up to eighteen ocean-going proas from the islands of Woleai, Lamotrek, and Satawal.

The interest of Luís de Torres in the Carolinian islanders was just one facet of a remarkable personality in a remarkable family. His grandfather, Joseph Miguel de Torres, had been assigned to Guam as an army officer in the late 1750s and brought his wife and children to the island. One son, Juan Francisco Regis (sometimes spelled Rexis) de Torres, remained on Guam and became an army officer, marrying a Chamorro woman and serving until his death in 1803. Juan Regis de Torres in turn was the father of Luís, who, like his father and grandfather, became an army officer (as a mestizo he could do so; men without Spanish blood were not given officer commissions). Luís de Torres was extolled by foreign visitors as an informed observer and protector of the Chamorro and Carolinian cultures. His career shows that life on Guam could be both personally rewarding and socially useful for the inquiring mind despite the remoteness and small size of the island. The Torres family remained on Guam as prominent *manak'kilo,* and the descendants of Joseph Miguel de Torres are still active in civic affairs on the island.

Except for the resumption of the Carolinian trade and the completion of a new fort—San José—on a hill north of Umatac Bay, Governor Blanco's administration was generally uneventful. He was replaced in 1806 by Alexandro Parreño, who served until 1812. Spain in 1806 was again stumbling into a disastrous war, this time against France. As a consequence, all Spanish colonies were neglected even more than previously, leading to revolutions against Spain throughout Latin America from 1808 until 1824.

These enormous events left distant Guam once more with little oversight by Manila, Mexico, or

Madrid. With a completely free hand, Governor Parreño turned out to be "a tyrant, whom they [the *Marianos*] never approached without trembling," wrote the Russian visitor Otto von Kotzebue. The rapacious Parreño earned a reputation for "insatiable cupidity," according to Kotzebue, owing to his "excesses, disorders, crimes, licentiousness, adultery, seduction and betrayal of girls."

About the only accomplishments of Parreño's were to build a stone bridge just south of Agat over Muja Creek (now called Ascola Sito, or Taleyfac Creek) and to complete Fort Nuestra Señora de la Soledad. This fort with a battery of six cannons was perched on the south side of Umatac Bay on an imposing bluff called Chalan Aniti in Chamorro, the Path of the Ancestors. The fort was poorly constructed and maintenance neglected, so by 1826 it was already in ruins. Maintenance has always been both a climatic and a human problem in Guam's postcontact history.

A new governor, José de Medinilla y Pineda, a dapper bachelor army lieutenant, replaced Parreño in 1812. Medinilla would serve until 1822 and then return to Guam to serve again from 1826 to 1831, a total of fifteen years, the longest service as governor in Guam's history. During that time, Spanish commerce and power were declining in the Pacific, but that decline was the least of Madrid's worries. The rising tide of revolution throughout Latin America was sweeping away the very heart of Spain's overseas empire. In late 1811, Mexican rebels in Acapulco seized the silver ready to be embarked on the galleon for Guam and Manila, leaving the Pacific colonies without *situados*. The lifeline of Spanish silver across the Pacific was finally cut, not by European enemies, but by one of Spain's own rebellious colonies.

In these conditions, the Manila governor-general discontinued the Manila to Acapulco voyages after the last two galleons from Manila departed Cavite in late 1811. By a *cédula* on 25 September 1813, King Ferdinand VII ordered the Spanish galleon trade in the Pacific to cease. The appropriately named *Magallanes* departed Acapulco for Cavite in 1815, the last of the famed Spanish galleons to cross the Pacific. From then on, all Spanish commercial ships out of Cavite with goods bound for Spain sailed across the Indian Ocean and around Africa to Cádiz.

It was in Governor Medinilla's first term that another major shipwreck occurred at Guam. On 19 February 1814, the *Infante Don Carlos,* a frigate of the Royal Company and popularly known as the *Santiago,* sailing from Callao, Peru, to Cavite by way of Guam, struck some coral heads of the Calalan Bank at the entrance to Apra Harbor. Thereafter, the coral heads that the frigate struck were called the Rocks of the Spanish Frigate, also known as the Spanish Rocks. No one was injured in the wreck, and most of the valuable part of the cargo—500,000 Mexican silver pesos—was promptly salvaged. For salvage divers, the Spaniards employed Carolinians and Hawaiians who could free dive to considerable depths despite the absence of masks and fins at the time.

By 1814, the Marianos of Guam had lost all the swimming skills of the old Chamorros. In the account of his 1817 visit to Guam on the Kotzebue expedition soon after the wreck, the naturalist Adelbert von Chamisso noted that "the present inhabitants no longer know the sea, are not sailors, not swimmers anymore, and they have ceased to build boats." When the Spaniards needed ocean-going canoes for interisland travel in the Marianas, they now purchased or chartered them from Carolinians, some of whom were remaining on Guam in between their annual trading voyages.

Guam at this time needed all the trade it could attract since no *situados* or *socorros* had arrived between 1810 and 1816 as a result of the revolution in Mexico. The Augustinian Order had let its presence dwindle to just two friars on Guam. Owing to the shortage of priests, regular church services were held in only four villages: Agaña, Pago, Agat, and Umatac. The Rota church had been abandoned but would be revived by mid-century.

As bad as the financial situation was, it became worse. On 29 September 1817, King Ferdinand VII ordered the annual *situado* for the Marianas reduced to only 8,000 pesos a year. The official *socorro* appears to have been discontinued about the same time. The same year, governmental supervision of the Philippines and the Marianas was removed from Mexico, by then no longer under Spanish control, and placed completely under Manila. The drastic shrinkage of the *situado* was caused principally by Spain's loss of Mexico's silver and by the enormous Spanish war debt. The result was an oversized and underfinanced government on Guam, a condition that became near permanent.

Scientists, Whalers, and Distant Revolutions

The end of the Napoleonic Wars in Europe in 1816 brought about a surge in Russian and French scientific expeditions into the Pacific. The first of these to visit Guam was in late 1817 by a Russian Navy brig, the 180-ton *Rurik,* on an around-the-world voyage from 1815 to 1818 commanded by Otto August von Kotzebue. Aboard was the famous naturalist and author Count Adelbert von Chamisso. On Guam less than a week on his 1817 visit, Kotzebue would return to Guam in 1825 for a second short stop on the sloop *Predpriatie* on another circumnavigation in 1823–1826. Kotzebue added much to Europe's hydrographic knowledge of the Pacific (he located over 400 small islands, many in Micronesia, previously unknown to outsiders), but he caused confusion with regard to Chamorro demographics. In his account of his 1817 visit to Guam he wrote, "There is only a man and his wife on the whole island, of the original branch [of Chamorros]. With the death of these two people the race of the old Ladrones will be entirely extinguished."

Kotzebue did not know Spanish and depended on the multilingual Chamisso as interpreter, so perhaps he misunderstood what the Spaniards told him of the Chamorros. In any case, his statement was wrong. Chamisso gave a different picture of the couple whom Kotzebue thought were the last Chamorros: "In Agaña when we were there, a robust old man aged 86 and four months was living still with his equally aged wife. Around them were no less than 135 descendants, down to the sixth generation."

Elsewhere in his accounts, Kotzebue provided figures of the official Spanish census for 1816 that showed 2,559 Chamorro *indios* on Guam, Rota, and Tinian, or nearly half the total population of 5,389 people. A significant number of these *indios* were likely to have still been of pure Chamorro blood. In particular, the 451 *indios* on Rota, an island Kotzebue did not visit, were mostly pure Chamorros as of 1816 because of minuscule immigration to Rota by non-Chamorros. On his 1819 visit to the Marianas, Captain Louis Claude Desaulses de Freycinet noted that the indigenous Chamorro race "has maintained itself best on Rota, where, until our time, are still found true examples of the ancient types."

In the mid-1850s, Governor Felipe de la Corte would report that Chamorros of "pure race," in his words, still numbered 600 persons in the Marianas. In 1889, the French visitor Antoine-Alfred Marche, who spent the years 1887–1889 in the Marianas, noted that there were still "pure blooded indigenes on Guam. . . . It is perhaps possible to find a few in Rota. There, only about fifteen families may represent what is left of pure blooded indigenes." As late as 1900, on an American military inspection of Guam, Major General Joseph Wheeler observed, "I saw a few people who I was informed were pure Chamorros, and they impressed me very favorably." Kotzebue's false assumption in 1817 that the Chamorros would soon be "completely extinguished," a conclusion given credence in Europe and America through the popular accounts of his voyages, did a disservice to the Chamorros. They have been a far more durable people than Kotzebue and other visitors imagined.

Kotzebue's 1817 visit to Guam was soon followed by two more Russian visits of short duration: the first under Vasilii Mikhailovich Golovnin in late November 1818, the second by Leontii Adrianovich von Hagemeister two months later in January

1819. Golovnin found that the old antiforeign attitudes of the Spaniards were changing with the more frequent arrivals of non-Spanish ships. He wrote, "For several years now, foreign shipping has been increasing in quest of fresh water and victuals; and when a foreign ship appears, the natives have a festival, for they get a good payment, in money or in kind, for their products."

After the Russians, the next significant visitors to the Marianas were members of the French expedition under Louis de Freycinet on the 350-ton corvette *Uranie*. This government-sponsored expedition around the world, like all others from this time forward, was not for exploration to discover islands (most had already been located by the Europeans) but to gather scientific data. The Freycinet expedition had already visited Australia and Timor prior to reaching Guam. In Timor, the crew suffered from malaria and dysentary, so Guam once more served as a recuperative oasis for sailors sick and battered from crossing great stretches of the Pacific Ocean. The *Uranie* anchored on 17 March 1819 off Umatac Bay and remained until 5 July 1819, or nearly three months.

Because of the long duration of the visit, and owing to the usual French intellectual curiosity, members of the Freycinet expedition compiled one of the most thorough scientific and historical descriptions of Guam of any visitors in the eighteenth and nineteenth centuries. Some of this information was based on the histories by García and Le Gobien, but it was greatly amplified by data from interviews with Chamorros and Spaniards on Guam, particularly Luís de Torres.

The first thing that struck the French visitors about Guam in 1819 in comparison with other Pacific islands that they had visited was the great poverty of the Chamorros. Rose Pinon de Freycinet, wife of the commander, was poignant in her description of Chamorros at Ypao village on Tumon Bay when Governor Medinilla took the French party to visit the site of San Vitores' martyrdom: "The strangeness, and above all the miserable conditions of the inhabitants astonished us, in view of the richness of the vegetation and the ease with which healthy food can be obtained with little work."

Despite the poverty of the people, one of the expedition's artists, Jacques Arago, noted, "Music is one of the most agreeable amusements of the inhabitants of the Mariannes; they sing the moment they awake, they sing during the hours of rest, and they fall asleep singing."

The amorous Arago found the girls of Guam to be among the most attractive of all Pacific island women. He also found them readily available for sex, and he claimed several seductions. Arago attributed the loose sexual behavior of the Chamorros, both men and women alike, to the casual attitudes of the Augustinians: "Nowhere, perhaps, is there so much and so little religion as at Guam. . . . I am convinced that as long as such pastors as Friar Ciriaco are sent to the Marianne islands religion will be little honoured there, and the morals of the people will not be in the slightest degree improved."

Despite Arago's verdict, Ciriaco del Espiritu Santo, a Tagalog secular priest, would go on to serve for thirty more years in Agaña, Agat, and Rota until his death on Guam in 1849. In that time, he fathered six children by his housekeeper, Juana Chrisostomo, known as "Juanan Chano."

The Frenchmen noted that the Chamorros continued much of the indigenous folklore and many traditional Chamorro customs but mixed them with those of the Spaniards and Filipinos. An example was the Chamorro practice of breathing, or simulating a kiss, called *mangnigni* (or *mannginge'*), on the cheek or the back of the hand of an older person as a sign of respect.

Louis de Freycinet provided the first written account of a popular legend on Guam of two lovers who committed suicide by jumping from a towering seaside cliff—Puntan de los dos Amantes, or Two Lovers Point—on the north side of Tumon Bay. According to Freycinet's informants, the tragedy took place before the arrival of the Spaniards. The young man was a high-caste *chamorri matua* who fell in love with a lovely but low-caste *manachang* maiden. Refused permission to marry by their families because of their caste difference, they were exiled from their villages. In despair, the lovers jumped together to their deaths from the great cliff. Since Freycinet's time the tale has changed: in the most popular later version, the Chamorro girl was betrothed by her family to a Spanish captain, who became enraged when he learned that she loved a Chamorro youth. In despair, the two Chamorros tied the locks of their long black hair together and leaped to their deaths in each other's arms from the cliff.

At the time of Freycinet's visit in 1819, the Spanish mission and garrison were in a deep economic depression as a consequence of the drastic reduction of the *situado*. Freycinet wrote that Guam's economy was "stagnating" in a "state of torpor." According to his account, packs of destructive semiwild dogs roamed the island. Descendants of these animals still roam free by the hundreds on Guam today, quite impervious to the feeble attempts of the Spanish, the American, and now the Guamanian governments to eradicate them.

One accomplishment of the Freycinet expedition was the first hydrographic survey of all the Marianas. This was published in 1826 with a folio atlas by Lieutenant Louis Isadore Duperrey of Freycinet's staff. The survey was the basis of later Spanish maps and a publication, *Derrotero de las Islas Marianas* (Navigational data for the Mariana Islands),

Women of Umatac, 1828 *(Femmes d'Umata).* Lithograph printed in 1833 in Paris by A. Belin from original by Louis de Sainson on the expedition of Jules S. C. Dumont d'Urville on Guam, 2–20 May 1828. (From the collection of the Micronesian Area Research Center, Mangilao, Guam)

Mayor, peasant, and hunter of Umatac, 1828 *(Alcade, Paysan et Chasseur d'Umata)*. Lithograph printed in 1833 in Paris by A. Belin from original by the artist Sainson on the expedition of Jules S. C. Dumont d'Urville on Guam, 2–30 May 1828. (From the collection of the Micronesian Area Research Center, Mangilao, Guam)

by the Spanish Hydrographic Office in 1863, which in turn was the basis of American maps in the early twentieth century.

By the 1820s, whalers were beginning to stop often in the Mariana Islands. The first recorded American whaler in the Marianas had been the New England ship *Ann & Hope* at Tinian in 1798. She was followed by the *Resource* in 1799, which stopped at Guam, where the thirsty whalers (called *bayuneros* in Chamorro, from the Spanish *balleneros*) were welcomed by the Spaniards and the impoverished Marianos. Captains of whaling ships

came to Guam for wood, water, and provisions; the crews came for women, *tuba*, and *aguardiente*. The results were predictable: drunken brawls, desertions by disgruntled crewmen, and the spread of the "pox" (venereal diseases, not smallpox) among the Chamorros until whaling declined after the American Civil War.

Local authorities and whalers were surprised in early March 1825 when a Spanish squadron of three men-of-war and a supply ship anchored off Umatac Bay on their way from Peru to the Philippines. Aboard were *peninsular* officers who had been released by South American insurgents after the defeat of the Spanish armies at the battle of Ayacucho, Peru, on 9 December 1824. That decisive battle resulted in the final loss of all Spain's colonies in South America. As a consequence, many *peninsular* officers were being transferred to Spain's remaining colonies. These *peninsulares,* all born in Spain, took precedence over local officers so that, for instance, a lieutenant from Spain ranked above a *criollo* or mestizo major born in the colonies. The same racial privileges applied among priests.

This discriminatory ranking caused much resentment against the *peninsulares* and in Manila sparked a brief but bloody revolt in June 1823 led by a *criollo* captain, Andrés Novales. Although the authorities suppressed the rebellion and executed Novales, the incident created fears among the Spanish *peninsulares* of conspiracies by *criollos* and locals against loyalist authorities. Spain itself was in political turmoil between conservative loyalists, who supported the despotic King Ferdinand VII, and liberals, who had forced the king to accept a liberal constitution in 1820.

It was in this climate of suspicion that the naval squadron from Peru arrived at Umatac in 1825. The crews and soldiers aboard the vessels were mostly *criollos* and mestizos from South America. They planned to take advantage of the stop at Umatac to seize the ships before they reached the still loyalist Philippines.

On the night of 10–11 March, the crews and soldiers on the warships rose in mutiny and after some scuffles arrested all the officers. The supply ship was burned and sank. The governor at the time, José Ganga Herrero, although a liberal, was unable to talk the rebels out of the mutiny and was afraid of attempting to retake the ships with his feeble local forces. The ships' officers and other *peninsulares* were taken ashore and subsequently departed on two whaling vessels to Manila. The victorious mutineers sailed two of the men-of-war to Mexico, while the other ended up in Chile.

The people of Guam were passive onlookers to these events since the Marianos were so isolated from outside news that they had not yet been infected by liberal politics. When the news of the mutiny finally reached Manila, the authorities there removed Governor Ganga. The busy Ganga was popular with the people of Guam. He had allowed free trade with non-Spanish ships and had made legitimate his children born out of wedlock on Guam. Spaniards often fathered children by island mistresses, but few officials bothered to make these children legitimate under Spanish law by formally giving them the man's family name in official records.

In July 1826, Ganga's replacement arrived. He turned out to be José de Medinilla, the former governor and staunch loyalist, who had been reappointed after King Ferdinand VII revoked the liberal constitution in Spain in 1823. Medinilla, a conservative of the old order who had squeezed the Chamorros, had not been popular on Guam. So at the change-of-command ceremony in Agaña on Sunday, 30 July 1826, Medinilla prudently canceled all tuba debts owed by the people and allowed *aguardiente* to be distilled without payment of a license fee. These gestures defused the discontent, but only temporarily.

Into this less than tranquil scene in the Marianas sailed another foreign scientific expedition, that of the Russian Ferdinand Petrovich von Lütke with two ships. They anchored at Apra on 15 February 1828 and would depart three weeks later on 8 March. Lütke had been with Golovnin on Guam back in 1818 and happily renewed his acquaintance with Governor Medinilla and Luís de Torres. The ever-gracious Torres provided his farm on Orote Peninsula for the Russian scientists to set up an astronomical observatory.

Members of the Russian party, like the French visitors, deplored the impact of Spanish rule on the islanders; the visitors compared the submissive Chamorros unfavorably with the still traditional and free Carolinians. Lütke also deplored the many white "tramps" whom he observed roaming around Guam. These were mostly runaway whalers.

Lütke was followed to Guam by yet another scientific expedition, this one from France under the command of Jules Sébastien César Dumont d'Urville in the corvette *Astrolabe*. The *Astrolabe* anchored at Umatac for four weeks from 2 to 30 May 1828, while thirty-six seriously sick sailors recovered ashore. D'Urville, like Lütke earlier, found a sizable expatriate community on Guam, but not just whaler runaways. The port pilot was by then a Scot, John Anderson, who had come with Freycinet and stayed, marrying María de Castro and raising twelve children. A Frenchman, Juan Roberto, was the pilot of the governor's schooner and had married a Chamorrita (*chamorrita* or *chamorita* originally meant a love song, and *kantan chamorrita* are improvised folk songs in Chamorro in rhyming couplets still sung on Guam; in the 1800s the word *Chamorrita* came to mean a young woman of Chamorro origin).

As in the past, Luís de Torres briefed Dumont d'Urville on local history and Micronesian customs. This fine Spanish officer would be elderly ten years later when on New Year's Day 1839 Dumont d'Urville again halted at Guam in the *Astrolabe,* this time with an escort, the 300-ton corvette *Zelée,* on another circumnavigation that would penetrate to the continent of Antarctica. In his accounts of his voyages, Dumont d'Urville was the first to popularize the division of the Pacific world into three major ethnographic regions—Micronesia, Melanesia, and Polynesia—a division that oversimplified the cultural complexities of Oceania but one that has nonetheless endured.

The final voyage by Dumont d'Urville in 1837–1840 was among the last of the nineteenth-century scientific expeditions into the Pacific that paused in the Marianas. By then, the Spaniards had attempted a number of reforms in the Marianas under an energetic Spanish officer whose good intentions were similar to those of Mariano Tobías of the century before but whose efforts to help the Chamorros would be just as ineffective.

Captain Villalobos

After the loss of most of the Spanish colonies in Latin America, and following the return of Ferdinand VII to the throne in 1823, the Spanish loyal-

ists became more attentive to the need to improve the defenses and governments of the remaining colonies of Cuba, Puerto Rico, and the Philippines. As before, the small Marianas figured in these concerns because of their strategic location as a link to the Philippines. In 1828, Madrid ordered Manila to improve security and administration on Guam. Several plans were debated before one proposed by Ganga Herrero, then assigned to the military staff in Manila, was approved by Governor-General Mariano Ricafort Palacín y Abarca.

Ganga's plan was approved because it was the cheapest. Under it, the Marianas were to cost the crown only 6,424 pesos a year in place of the 8,000 pesos then budgeted. On 17 December 1828, Ricafort promulgated Ganga's plan as an edict *(Bando de Ricafort)* with thirteen orders to Governor Medinilla on Guam. The most significant orders were (1) the creation of an "urban militia"; (2) the redistribution of unused crown lands to Marianos; (3) the elimination of the governor's monopoly over commerce; (4) the opening of the Marianas to trade and of Apra and Umatac as free ports; and (5) the creation of a new position, administrator of the royal treasury, who would handle finances of the *situado* to be sent every two years from Manila.

While these steps were being planned in Manila, Madrid also decided to look carefully at Guam for the first time at the Council of the Indies level. By a royal order of 14 December 1828, the Spanish government initiated an in-depth study of the Marianas. This resulted in a special report entitled *Memoria sobre las Yslas Marianas,* also called *Memoria de 1828,* which was distributed in 1829 as a set of thirteen recommendations, some of which duplicated the measures already implemented by Ricafort in 1828 (it is unclear if Madrid had already received a copy of Ricafort's *bando*). The *Memoria de 1828* was the first of an endless line of studies by the Spanish, the American, and the Guamanian governments that proposed much and produced little for the people of the Mariana Islands.

While the *Memoria* was being prepared, the Spanish government requested the Society of Jesus, restored in 1814 by Pope Pius VII, to send ten to twelve Jesuits to Guam to replace the Augustinians, who at the time had only one Spanish Recollect and one Filipino secular priest on the island. The Jesuits refused because of a shortage of priests. Madrid then made the same request of the Franciscans, but they too declined for the same reason. Ironically, the two religious orders that had brought about the conversion of the Chamorros were unable to return to reinvigorate the Christian faith in the people whose destiny they had once been so determined to shape.

Spanish insecurity about Guam was rudely confirmed on 17 May 1829, when a coup was attempted in Agaña against Governor Medinilla. This small rebellion was apparently initiated by expatriates and did not spark a general uprising by the Marianos. The disturbance was quickly suppressed, evidently without bloodshed, but left Spanish authorities in Agaña and Manila highly nervous. In reaction to the coup attempt on Guam, in June 1829 Ricafort appointed a young bachelor captain of artillery, Francisco Ramón de Villalobos, to head a mission to improve Guam's defenses against external and internal threats.

It took two ships to transport Villalobos and a large amount of supplies and armaments to Guam. The ships arrived at Apra in August 1829, where Governor Medinilla, now middle aged and a lieutenant colonel, received the Villalobos mission with proper protocol. By January 1830, Villalobos had sent several long reports to Manila full of proposals to improve the defenses and the economy of the Marianas. The outcome was that, on 26 September 1831, Villalobos replaced Medinilla as governor by order of Ricafort. To create an urban militia, Villalobos reorganized the three *compañías de dotación* into one *dotación* company (called a *battalion*) of approximately sixty men and officers. It became the guard unit in Agaña, and its ranks were filled over time by Chamorros, as were the ranks of the small artillery company also stationed in Agaña.

Villalobos also was the first to make a proposal later advocated by several governors but never approved: move the capital from Agaña to a location close to the port at Apra. Villalobos wanted the capital at Agat, which could be connected to the port by a short canal across the low-lying mangrove swamp area at the neck of the Orote Peninsula. The energetic young governor constructed kilns at Agat to make tiles, upgraded roads and bridges, and introduced the first vaccinations for smallpox.

Manila, however, sent no new funds, so additional forts for defense were never built; supplies still only trickled into Guam; the *colegio* was closed (it would reopen later); and education and religious observances remained inadequate since only a handful of new priests came to the island. Some reforms did help the Chamorros; for example, a number of families received land grants from the limited breakup of excess crown lands. But, in general, the locals reacted to Villalobos the way poor working people all over the world have to reform proposals by outsiders: *No te apures* (Take it easy).

The reduction of the island's subsidy in consequence of the Ricafort reforms had an impact on demographics in the Marianas. As the *situado* shrunk, any payments that had to be made in cash became a burden to the increasingly cashless residents. Spaniards, mestizos, and foreigners still had to pay taxes (such as a 10 percent tax called *diezmos prediales* on all farm produce) and license fees in cash as in the past. Equally burdensome, they had to pay cash for the obligatory church tithes and other ecclesiastical charges for marriages, baptisms, and so forth.

Payment of these charges, except for some church fees, applied to everyone except Chamorros. Therefore, mestizos, Filipinos, and others in Guam's multiethnic community began to list their newborn children, and themselves where possible, as *indios* in church and official records to avoid payment of cash charges. One unintended outcome of these claims to be *indios* (a categorization previously despised by non-Chamorros) was to resurrect the long dormant issue of a Chamorro identity, that is, the idea of a distinctive Chamorro grassroots presence as something of value. This dangerous idea would return to haunt governmental authorities.

On 1 October 1837, the administration of the good Captain Villalobos ended, and he was transferred back to Manila to continue his military career. Nearly every one of the thirteen reforms ordered in the 1828 *Bando de Ricafort* fell short of its intended effect. In 1839, on his return visit to Guam, Dumont d'Urville sadly commented in what could be an epitaph to Villalobos and other well-intentioned Spanish governors who tried to fulfill their duties in the Marianas but failed: "It was noticeable that Guam had gone downhill for ten years . . . the island was poverty stricken. The inhabitants, ravaged by leprosy, lived in filthy huts among beautiful orange groves. The school which had had pupils ten years before was now used by the curé to raise fighting cocks."

Earthquakes, Consuls, and Convicts

The governors who followed Villalobos over the next ten years were José Casillas Salazar (1837–1843), an alcoholic; Gregorio Santa María, (1843–1848), kindly and popular, and who died of an "apoplexy" stroke on Guam; and Félix Calvo y Noriega, elected by local officials to serve as interim governor from April to September 1848. Calvo was the administrator of the treasury. A *peninsular,* he founded one of Guam's most prominent *manak'kilo* families.

In his brief tenure as governor, Félix Calvo entertained another French visit from 26 June to 9 August 1848, that of Jean Edmund Jurien de la Gravière on the ship *Bayonnaise.* The French captain took refuge on Guam with his ship to avoid British warships (Britain was hostile owing to the 1848 French Revolution). Like Freycinet and d'Urville, Jurien de la Gravière was sharply critical of the Spanish administration and its destructive impact on the Chamorros. He wrote, "It is astonishing to see the swift ravages that primitive peoples suffer upon contact with our civilization. . . . Perhaps a day will come when they are called to a more noble destiny without violating the designs of

Providence. But today let us not carelessly bring them new suffering; let us not try their naive faith; let us respect their calm bliss."

With little oversight by Madrid and Manila in this period, the governors and the administrators of the treasury on Guam once more worked out ways to squeeze personal profits from the system. The governor prevented anyone other than himself from importing goods on the government-chartered Cavite ship, thus blocking competition. Goods were sold at huge markups in the government store (reopened despite the *Bando de Ricafort*), as in the old days, but now under the administrator's control. The governor and the administrator then shared the profits.

A prime source of income and trade goods for the locals on Guam in the 1840s was still from the sales of provisions, *aquardiente,* entertainment, and sex to the whalers who called at Apra Harbor. Up to sixty whaling ships a year stopped at Apra, often remaining several weeks. In trading with the whalers, many Chamorros learned English, which became the third main language on the island. The former Torres farm at Sume, by the 1840s a *barrio* of Agat, grew into the thriving little port town of Sumay. The Spanish authorities were strict with the whalers. The log of the *Emily Morgan,* an American whaler that visited Guam many times, described Spanish control: "By the laws of the island, every white man or foreigner must have a boarding-house, and be within doors at eight P.M. . . . If any are absent from their respective houses they are found and marched home; and should they be saucy, or show belligerent spirits, off they go to the calaboose."

Whaling was beginning to decline when a new governor, Pablo Pérez, arrived on Guam in 1848. Pérez's job was made more difficult than usual because of natural disasters: Guam and the Carolines had been battered by three typhoons in 1847; another struck in June 1848; and yet another swept through Micronesia, this time a supertyphoon, 10–12 August the same year. The August storm resulted in three boatloads of Carolinian refugees sailing to the Marianas, where Pérez allowed them to settle. As if these calamities were not enough, in January 1849 a whaling ship from Hawai'i brought an influenza epidemic that killed over 200 persons on Guam, mostly young women.

The influenza was followed on 25 January by a severe earthquake on Guam with two days of aftershocks. Massive rock slides crashed off the cliffs all around the island; big cracks opened and then closed in the ground, and most roofs fell in. The new tower on the church in Agaña collapsed, and the old *colegio* nearly crumbled. In Umatac, the *palacio,* the San Dionisio Church, and the *convento* (the priests' residence) were practically demolished. Only the church was rebuilt, and of wood, not coral masonry.

The earthquake of 1849 also caused disastrous tidal waves that swept over the atolls of Satawal, Lamotrek, and other Carolinian islands. In April, several canoes arrived at Guam from those islands with emaciated Carolinians who told of widespread death and destruction from the tidal waves. Pablo Pérez again permitted the Carolinians to settle, this time mostly on Saipan. Conditions worsened on Guam when a fire burned a half dozen houses in Agaña in May 1849 and a plague of worms consumed most crops in the July–September rainy season. Pérez appealed to Manila for help, and funds and supplies were quickly dispatched by Governor-General Narciso Clavería y Zalda, by the church, and also by many private citizens in the Philippines.

With conditions back to normal after a few years, Governor Pérez was surprised in November 1854 by the unexpected arrival of a foreign consul and his secretary, the first to be assigned to Guam. Samuel J. Masters was an itinerant American who had been a U.S. consul in British Guyana, a ship captain, and a police magistrate in the whaling port of Lahaina on Maui in the Hawaiian Islands. He obtained authorization from the U.S. secretary of state to be the official American merchant consul on Guam. He persuaded fellow American Josiah S. Van Ingen to join him as secretary. Masters and Van Ingen obtained permission in Manila to travel to Guam, but the Spanish officials, suspicious of American agents, never granted formal approval

for Master's consular authority. Masters and Van Ingen nonetheless headed off to Agaña anyway and presented themselves to the surprised Pablo Pérez.

On Guam, Masters showed the newcomer syndrome commonly found in Pacific islands whereby the recent arrival has immediate insight on how to solve all local problems, if people would only listen. As a consequence, he was soon in a dispute with Pérez over his consular authority and with American ship captains over crew matters. He even fought with Van Ingen, who sued him for unpaid expenses. A major concern in his sixteen-month stay on Guam was the case of the American merchant ship *Sarah Mooers.* This bark ran aground on Ngatik Atoll in the Carolines in late 1853. Twenty-nine survivors were kept almost as prisoners by Governor Pérez on Guam for several months. Masters interceded vigorously in Manila on behalf of his countrymen and helped obtain the release of a few still remaining on Guam when he arrived.

The governor-general in Manila solved the squabbles between Pablo Pérez and Masters by replacing Pérez with a new governor, Felipe María de la Corte y Ruano Calderón, who arrived on Guam on 16 May 1855. The new governor received a shock when the U.S.S. *Vandalia,* the first American warship to visit Guam, sailed unexpectedly into Apra Harbor on 6 July 1855. Its mission was to reprimand the Spaniards for holding the survivors of the *Sarah Mooers.* After negotiations with Masters and Commander John Pope of the *Vandalia* under the guns of the warship, Governor de la Corte apologized on behalf of the Spanish government.

The appearance of the *Vandalia* was evidence of new geopolitical conditions in the rimlands around the Pacific Ocean that would dramatically affect insular areas in Oceania. In 1848, California had become a territory of the United States as a result of the Mexican-American War (1846–1848). Discovery of gold in California the same year spurred a massive shift in American interest toward the Pacific. Japan began to emerge from its feudal *samurai* cocoon when Commodore Matthew Perry, backed by four U.S. warships, concluded the first Japanese-American trade treaty with the Tokugawa Shogunate in 1854.

Micronesia itself was being penetrated by non-Spanish traders and non-Catholic missionaries. In the 1840s, the English trader Andrew Cheyne set up the first trading stations in Palau. In 1852, evangelical Protestants from the United States established the first permanent missions on Kosrae and Pohnpei, and, in 1857, the American ship *Morning Star* brought a Protestant mission to Ebon in the Marshall Islands. German copra traders soon followed in the Marshalls.

While more nations encroached on the former Spanish lake of the Pacific, Spain was economically depressed and preoccupied with domestic power struggles. The lack of funds finally forced Manila to halt the Guam *situado* in 1855. The end of a regular subsidy plunged Guam's budgets into a deficit that would continue under the remainder of Spanish rule despite the temporary reinstitution of the *situado* later. Governor de la Corte wrote prophetically, "We beg our readers to never lose sight of this deficit, which will grow . . . and never drop."

All these misfortunes faded into insignificance, however, in the face of one of the greatest disasters in Guam's postcontact history: the massive smallpox epidemic of 1856.

Smallpox and Deportados

In late February 1856, when the American merchant schooner *Edward L. Frost* arrived at Apra from Manila, it was quarantined only three days before releasing passengers despite a man aboard having died of smallpox and been buried at sea just before the *Frost* reached Guam. Moreover, two passengers from influential Guam families—Silvestre Francisco Palomo and Francisco Tudela—were permitted to go ashore immediately when the ship anchored. Palomo and Tudela both soon sickened and died in May. The disease spread despite frantic efforts by the Spaniards to isolate the infected and to vaccinate the people. Father Aniceto Ibáñez del Carmen described the epidemic: "In the beginning

the victims were from Agaña only. By the end of August it had spread with the speed of lightning—like an electric spark—to all the villages of the island. The picture the island presented in September was horrible, sad, deplorable, and heartbreaking."

By November 1856, the smallpox had disappeared, but so had 5,534 people of all ages, or over 60 percent of the entire population of 8,775 on Guam before the dreadful epidemic. Since the majority of the dead were of Chamorro ancestry, the 1856 epidemic affected generations of Chamorros. One notable example was in consequence of the death of Silvestre Palomo (whose wife was the daughter of Luís de Torres), which convinced his son, José Bernardo Palomo y Torres, to enter the priesthood. He was ordained a secular priest by the bishop at Cebú in 1859, the first padre with Chamorro blood (the original Palomo on Guam was a Mexican *criollo*). Padre Palomo would serve throughout the Marianas into the twentieth century.

In 1857, political and social conditions on Guam began to change when the governor-general in Manila received a royal order to establish a prison in the Marianas for civilian convicts *(confinados)*. Governor de la Corte transformed the old barracks of the Agaña *presidio* into a prison, and in 1858 sixty-three Chinese civilian convicts from the Philippines arrived, all of whom were sent back to Manila when they turned out to be "vicious, extremely weak, and sick," in the words of Governor de la Corte. The governor disapproved of Madrid's efforts to make Guam into a penal colony. Despite his objections, a royal order in 1860 set up a new prison system, and Manila would dump convicts of all kinds in the Marianas and elsewhere in Micronesia in the coming decades.

Felipe de la Corte, a lieutenant colonel in the army engineers, was a perceptive man, and in 1865 he authored one of the most thorough descriptions of the Marianas written by any Spanish official. The book, *Memoria descriptiva é histórica de las Islas Marianas,* was published by the Spanish government in 1875 and contained numerous recommendations. None of his proposals were put into effect except one that urged the establishment of Spanish missions and government posts in Yap (created in 1886) and Pohnpei (set up in 1887).

One suggestion by de la Corte was that the Chamorros be dissuaded from eating federico nuts. Called *fadang* in Chamorro and *Cycas circinalis* by scientists, federico is a cycad, a kind of primitive palm that looks like a fern tree and bears large nutlike seeds that are poisonous. The people of Guam detoxify the nuts by soaking and boiling them. They then grind them into flour to make tortillas, which have an excellent taste distinctive from corn flour tortillas.

De la Corte recommended that federico nuts not be eaten because he believed that they cause "endemic illnesses which have become hereditary and produce the elephanteasis illness, often causing premature aging and short life." The Spaniards later called the illness *paralytico,* or *lytico* for short, and Chamorros called it *bodig,* which came from the Spanish word *bodega* (store), where people bought medicine for the illness. No one followed de la Corte's advice since no one could prove that *fadang* caused *lytico-bodig.* A later governor, Luís de Ibáñez y García (1871–1873), did not mention *lytico-bodig* in his book, *Historia de las Islas Marianas,* published in Spain in 1886. It was during Ibáñez y García's tenure that the historic Tribunal y Cárcel (the Agaña town hall and jail), a two-story coral masonry building on the ocean side of the plaza, was completed in 1873. It would stand until 1944 when it was destroyed by the American bombardment in World War II.

By the 1870s, Madrid was again convulsed by serious internal political troubles. With each change in Spain's government, supporters of the previous regime were arrested and deported as political convicts—*deportados*—to the colonies. Governmental upheavals in turn provoked reform movements in the colonies by mestizos, *criollos,* and locals against the privileges of the Spanish *peninsular* officials and priests. In the Philippines, reformists sparked the small but symbolically important Cavite Mutiny of

January 1872 led by Filipino priests. The Spaniards brutally crushed the mutiny and executed three priests (one was eighty-three years old). Numerous Filipinos were tried in secret and sentenced to be *deportados.*

Consequently, some 1,200 political exiles from Spain and the Philippines, as well additional ordinary convicts (called *presidiarios* because they were imprisoned in the Agaña *presidio*), ended up in the Marianas from 1872 to 1877. In 1872 the Spaniards demolished Fort San Rafael and used its basalt stones to expand the *presidio* prison. The *deportados* were often not imprisoned since it was difficult to escape from the island, and they worked and lived among the island people. There were so many convicts and *deportados* on Guam that the notorious American blackbirder (he kidnapped islanders for labor gangs) and sometimes pirate William Henry (Bully) Hayes went into business to smuggle them off Guam at $24.00 per head in his schooner *Arabia.* Hayes was arrested in April 1875 and sent off to prison in Manila. By mid-1875, Guam was so full of convicts that, when the steamer *Patino* arrived with 473 *deportados,* they were all sent to Saipan.

In June 1876, King Alfonzo XII freed all *deportados,* and most were repatriated, leaving mainly ordinary civilian and military convicts in the Marianas. Most of these ordinary convicts, with little money for ship fares, stayed on Guam when they completed their sentences and were freed. Many married local women and raised families. On the other hand, the *deportados,* particularly educated Filipinos with radical political ideas of "native rights," had a subversive impact on the Chamorros among whom they lived. One historian wrote of the Filipinos, "There never ceased to exist a secret revolutionary agitation which culminated in the events of 1898."

Spanish officials on Guam appear to have underestimated the dangerous influence of the new political ideas among the heretofore docile Chamorros. On the evening of 2 August 1884, as Governor Angel de Pazos y Vela-Hidalgo entered the *palacio* on his way to dinner, the guard at the entrance saluted and then shot him in the back as he passed, killing him almost instantly.

The guard was a twenty-year-old Chamorro soldier named José de Salas in the *dotación* company. He fled to hide behind the *colegio* while the *sargento mayor,* Captain Antonio Borredá y Arlares, immediately called out the company, coolly inspected the men, secured all their ammunition, and relieved them from duty. All the Spaniards and *manak'kilo* men then armed themselves and gathered their families in the *palacio,* but a feared uprising by the Chamorros did not take place. The next day the assassin turned himself in, and Pazos was buried in the Agaña cemetery.

The authorities at first thought that the killing was out of personal resentment at the unpopular Pazos, but a preliminary investigation revealed a conspiracy among the *dotación* soldiers, nearly all Chamorros, to overthrow the government. Father Francisco Resano del Corazon de Jesus, who administered the last rites to de Pazos, wrote, "Their plans had been to kill the governor first, then all the Spaniards, and some of the *principales* of Agaña—and then they would do whatever seemed best."

News of the event did not reach Manila for weeks until a boat sailed from Guam to Yap to inform the Spanish trading post there, and the Yap-based schooner *Bartola* arrived at Cavite on 20 October. The governor-general dispatched to Guam troops under Lieutenant Colonel Francisco Olive y García, who was made the new governor. The investigation lasted into 1885, when in January forty-seven suspects, all local soldiers in the *dotación* company, were sent to Manila for trial. Since the company totaled only fifty to sixty troops, almost all the soldiers who guarded the *palacio* and the Agaña *presidio* buildings were implicated. The new governor disbanded the *dotación* company and replaced it with a regular infantry company *(compañia de guarnición)* of Filipino soldiers under Spanish and mestizo officers.

In Manila at a military trial, twelve of the suspects were found innocent, thirty-one were found guilty and sentenced to prison terms, and four were found guilty and sentenced to death. All were then returned to Guam. On 10 April 1885, the four sentenced to death—José de Salas, Manuel Mendiola, Vicente Acosta, and Manuel Aguon—were shot to death on the beach at Agaña by a firing squad.

The Spanish authorities treated the murder of Pazos as a political crime, that is, "a conspiracy for rebellion." Years later, Father José Palomo made a different judgment from the local viewpoint when he wrote, "Don Antonio Borredá, who became Governor ad interim, endeavored to profit by this murder, trying to win promotion by making it appear a private act of an individual was the result of an insurrection, and to accomplish this he had several people imprisoned who, under torture, were made to testify."

The Spanish End Game

Regardless of where the truth was in the motivation for Pazos' murder, Guam was never again secure for Spain. As late as 1894, the Spanish naval officer Luís Cadarso y Rey, who was governor of the Caroline Islands, noted on a visit to Guam that Spaniards had to be on guard against Chamorros. This distinctive Chamorro identity was demonstrated most clearly by the fact that all Marianos still spoke the Chamorro language among themselves. The perseverance of the indigenous language was remarkable. By the 1890s, the people of the Marianas had lost much of their precontact culture, but the soft and musical Chamorro language was, and remains today, true to its roots. An American linguist later noted, "While Spanish may have left a lasting mark on Chamorro vocabulary, as it did on many Philippine and South American languages, it had virtually no effect on Chamorro grammar."

The Chamorro language was maintained through maternal control of family life (*si nana,* meaning Chamorro motherhood in local terms), an arrangement with precontact roots compatible with Catholicism's veneration of Mary as the mediatrix of all graces. Most racial admixtures of outsiders with Chamorros originated by foreign men fathering children with local women of Chamorro ances-

Padre Palomo. Photograph taken in the early 1900s. Born José Bernardo Palomo y Torres in 1836 to a prominent Agaña Chamorro-Spanish mestizo family, he was ordained in 1859 at Cebu, the first diocesan priest of Chamorro ancestry. He served as a stalwart pillar of the church and of the Chamorro people under the Spanish and the early American naval regimes until his death in 1919 on Guam. (From the collection of the Micronesian Area Research Center, Mangilao, Guam)

try. In a process of religious genius the Catholic Church transformed the Chamorros from children of women used by aliens to children of the Christian Virgin. This powerful integrative religious impulse served not only to reconcile the Chamorros with the outsiders, it also helped to preserve the Chamorro identity. Even though fathers were the heads of families and bilingualism was often practiced, the Mariano mothers invariably raised the children to speak Chamorro in the home, regardless of the father's language, and thereby passed on the Chamorro heritage by word of mouth.

The family in Chamorro society under the Spaniards was strengthened by local acceptance of Spanish Catholic marriage rites and godparent observances (in Chamorro *compare,* or *kumpaile,* for godfather and *comare/kumaile* for godmother). By the nineteenth century, a church marriage was an indissoluble bond quite unlike precontact marriage practices. The roles and obligations of godparents were also formalized as kinship ties, through the rite of baptism, thereby extending families and making them and the church the centers of social loyalty rather than civic attachment to a distant and alien Spain. This *pare* system based on strong familial ties would be carried into politics after World War II, resulting often in factionalism and rivalries between families in electoral politics.

The absorption of introduced customs shows that Chamorros were not just passive victims of foreigners, as many European visitors thought, but agents of their own transformation. The Chamorros, particularly the women, quietly manipulated alien systems for their own purposes, adopting new concepts and practices to meet local needs while stubbornly holding to the core of their language and control of family. Largely by means of this language-family linkage, and because Guam was a poor and isolated island, the Chamorros were neither totally Hispanicized nor replaced by a hybrid nonindigenous population, as occurred in Cuba and Puerto Rico. Instead, the Chamorros absorbed immigrants into a neo-Chamorro society with new attributes but still permeated by a distinctive univocal Chamorro consciousness at the grassroots level.

By the end of the nineteenth century, neo-Chamorro social organization had become in appearance closer to that of lowland Filipinos than to any traditional Oceanic society. Yet, despite many similarities, neo-Chamorros and Filipinos remained separate peoples, and each perceived themselves to be distinct ethnically and culturally. The neo-Chamorros never lost their roots.

The people of the Marianas developed a taste for irony and indeterminism manifested, for example, in a general indifference to planning and financial accounting or to the accumulation of cash. Also on Guam, as elsewhere in the Spanish empire, laws and regulations imposed by distant authorities were often ignored or evaded. This attitude, stated in Spanish, was "La ley se obedece pero no se cumple," that is, "The law is obeyed, but not fulfilled." This "live for now" attitude, often demonstrated as a calm fatalism (which was not laziness or a *mañana*

outlook, as some visitors mistakenly thought), may have derived from Guam's long, involuntary legacy of devastating typhoons, earthquakes, epidemics, and the imposition of alien values. The neo-Chamorros, however, never lost their sense of humor and of play. Jokes—often ribald—and mocking plays on words, along with frequent fiestas with free food and warm hospitality for visitors, lightened the conservative world of the neo-Chamorros on Guam in the nineteenth century.

The Chamorro attitude of chastened rebelliousness is illustrated in the many humorous stories about the legendary Juan Malo (lit., John the Mischievous) and his carabao companion under Spanish rule. In these folktales, the lowly Chamorro youth Juan Malo, a trickster and the people's hero, gets back at the all-powerful Spanish officials through his wit. The confrontation between the poor but clever Juan Malo on his stolid carabao and the rich but dumb Spanish governor on his haughty horse became an enduring symbol in local folklore of the Spanish era on Guam.

In real life, Governor Olive y García was a smart, hard-working army officer. In 1884, he started demolition of the old Agaña *palacio* and construction on the site of a more spacious residence that would take until 1889 to complete. Olive wrote a *Memoria* on the Marianas for an exhibition in Madrid in 1887 on the ethnology of the Philippines and Micronesia. He published the *Memoria* as *Islas Marianas: Lijeros Apuntes* (The Mariana Islands: Random notes) in Manila in 1887. In his book, Olive gave the population for the Marianas as of 31 December 1886 as 9,770, of whom 8,618 were listed as "Chamorros." Most locals, regardless of ancestry, were lumped into the Chamorro category, which by then was mostly of mixed ethnicity. Guam's population was 8,199, with 6,255 (76 percent) in Agaña alone. Olive grumbled that everyone on Guam had become "Chamorrized" to avoid taxes.

According to Olive, Guam's schools were so poor that students "wrote with little sticks on banana leaves." Nearly 90 percent of the population was partially or completely illiterate. The governor complained that Castilian Spanish "has been in the process of disappearing and continues to do so in the Marianas."

Only a few whalers a year stopped at Guam by the 1880s, and there was practically no commerce with the island. Traditional trade between the Carolines and Guam had quietly ceased. All adult local males, except the *principales*, still had to perform *polo* communal labor for forty days a year or pay for exemption. Land tenure on Guam had evolved to become a *hacienda* system in the nineteenth century whereby the *manak'kilo* families and the church had acquired large estates, the *haciendas*. A difference in the *hacienda* system on Guam from other Spanish colonies was that on Guam the major landowners resided mostly in Agaña (the *manggi Hagatña* in Chamorro) instead of on country *haciendas* as elsewhere in Spain's empire. In addition to the *polo* obligation, many ordinary Chamorros also fell into deep personal debt to the government store, to the church, and to *manak'kilo* families as a result of loans, leases of *lanchos*, and so forth. Debts were normally paid off by labor, resulting in peonage for many of the poorest people from one generation to the next, both for *polo* and on private *haciendas*. Peonage in turn increased Chamorro aversion to manual labor because such work benefited only the Spaniards and *principalía* families.

Consequently, many Chamorro men left the islands to work at jobs abroad, with nearly 800 Chamorros working in Honolulu alone in the 1880s. Olive wrote in puzzlement that on Guam Chamorros "are lazy, indolent, ignorant," but once abroad they became "good workers.... There is a common saying that the Chamorro away from his island is a lamp brightening a stranger's door." One positive note on Guam in the last decades of the nineteenth century was the emergence of limited democracy at the village level and free use of crown lands by Chamorros. By a royal order of 29 May 1885, *gobernadorcillos* and other local officials were elected for two-year terms from among the *principalía* class in the villages in place of appointed Spanish *alcaldes administradores*. The

gobernadorcillos and other officials were paid small salaries and formed the *patrones,* or bosses, of the villages and *barrios,* dispensing patronage among their families and friends. Further limited democratization at the local level in the Philippine provinces was ordered by a royal decree in May 1893, but by then dissatisfaction with Spanish rule was too widespread to halt.

Religion, not political reform, was the refuge of the poor on the island, and all Chamorros remained devout. In October 1894, the Cavite ship brought back to Guam the statue of Our Lady of Camarin (Santa Marian Kamalen/Santa Marian Camalin in Chamorro) from Manila, where it had been sent to be restored. The procession from Anigua to the Agaña cathedral behind the small, elaborately robed statue numbered some 7,000 people. Like similar statues in the Philippines, it was an object of deep veneration and remains so in the late twentieth century in its place of honor above the altar of the Agaña Cathedral-Basilica.

In August 1896, insurrection against the Spaniards erupted into bloody warfare in the Philippines. Spanish reaction was ruthless, and large numbers of Filipino rebels were rounded up and once more banished as *deportados* to the Marianas and the Carolines. No one on Guam was prepared for the sudden influx of prisoners, so the governor, Lieutenant Colonel Jacobo Marina, crammed many of them, men and women, into the dilapidated old *presidio* barracks in Agaña.

Among the *deportados* were many who had previously been exiled to Guam and knew the weaknesses of the old *presidio* barracks. On the night of 19 December, they attempted to escape through the thatched roof but were captured, with one killed and five wounded. The next night, the prisoners made another attempt, this time en masse through the roof and by battering on the doors. The guards—Chamorros from the artillery company— panicked. They blasted volley after volley of rifle fire into the mass of *deportados*.

Father Francisco Resano described the scene the next morning: "The *cuartel-prisión* doors were opened, and there before our eyes was a horrible sight: sprawled on the floor and bathed in their own blood were eighty dead and forty-five wounded."

The massacre of Filipino *deportados* at Agaña in 1896 brought to the surface the main themes in Guam's history under the long, fallible rule of Spain, themes that endured like tough threads in a well-worn old coat about to be discarded. The first theme was the close ties between Guam and the Philippines. From the first day of San Vitores' mission, Filipinos played a major role in Guam's evolution under the Spaniards. Tagalogs, Ilocanos, Visayans, and others repeatedly infused new blood, customs, commerce, and vitality into the Mariana Islands, sometimes as enemies, sometimes as allies, and sometimes as victims of the Chamorros.

A second underlying theme in Guam's history was the geopolitical role of the island in support of imperial interests in the western Pacific. Guam both linked the Philippines with and shielded them from the eastern Pacific and was the anchor of Spain's claims in Micronesia. By the 1890s, not only was Guam a central coaling station for trade in the region, but it was increasingly important as a naval crossroads. Nevertheless, by 1890 the whole region was openly or latently hostile to Spain owing to inept Spanish policies, and it needed only a shove to break away from Madrid's tired arms.

Even geopolitics, however, was not as prominent a factor in Guam's postcontact history as was Christianity. At first a scourge, then a refuge against natural calamities and the follies of alien humans, the fierce embrace of suffering and fate that is Roman Catholicism became an abiding spiritual heritage of the people of the Marianas. Of all the legacies of Spain—which included the *patrón* system with its privileges and elitism, the *pare* system with its bedrock reliance on family ties, and macho enthusiasm for military service—the Christian religion would be the most enduring for the Chamorros.

A fourth historical theme in the Mariana Islands almost as durable as Catholicism was the inadequacy—at times sheer incompetence—of government. Military government almost destroyed the indigenous people and was consistently inadequate in providing for the needs of the society that Spain sought to create in its own image on Guam. The government in Agaña—top-heavy and under-financed—failed to protect the interests of Spain herself despite the efforts of good governors such as Tobías, Villalobos, and de la Corte.

Colonial military government shaped a fifth theme in Guam's postcontact history: the Chamorros became peripheral to the political and economic development of their island. Nearly all efforts for improvement or reform aimed at satisfying the interests of the colonial power, not at improving the conditions of the indigenous people. In order for any government to be successful, its subjects must accept the legitimacy of the officials who wield power. The Spaniards were able to establish legitimacy in the Marianas with respect to religion but failed to do so with respect to political authority. The Spanish government remained authoritarian and alien to the Chamorros throughout Spain's rule over them.

Finally, the most hidden historical thread of all was the remarkable resiliency of the Chamorro identity beneath the seemingly heavy veneer of foreign acculturation. This identity was maintained through language and family ties that managed to adapt to conditions imposed by overwhelming alien forces. The neo-Chamorro culture of 1898 was therefore a synthesis of foreign and local customs, and it was considerably changed from the precontact culture. Yet the Chamorro core identity persevered, at least in the perceptions of the local people themselves.

Later, to the annoyance of American officials, Chamorro consciousness under the banner of indigenous self-determination would reemerge in the 1970s despite an even more thorough acculturization of the people of Guam under the rule of the United States than under the Spaniards. In fact, none of these themes would end with the coming of the North Americans; all reappeared in some form in the fabric of the new coat that Guam donned after 1898.

*   *   *

It is doubtful any of these matters were on the minds of officials on Guam when, on the morning of 20 June 1898, Governor Juan Marina (who had replaced his brother Jacobo in 1897) was brought information that four unidentified foreign vessels, one of them a warship, were steaming past Agaña en route to Apra Harbor. No news had reached Guam from the outside since 9 April, when the last mail boat from Manila arrived.

The governor issued instructions for the strange ships to be received as customary for friendly visitors. He would soon learn to his astonishment that they were hostile American vessels and that Spain had been at war with the United States since 25 April. The parable of the tribes was once more about to manifest itself. After two centuries of domination by the island's first alien intruders, the people of Guam would soon experience the second major invasion in their history, and this time the Spaniards would be the victims.

The Anglo-Saxon Way
1898–1903

The New Imperialists

Guam had nothing to do with the causes and little to do with the conduct of the Spanish-American War. Nonetheless, the war was an epochal turning point in the history of the Mariana Islands. The American clash with Spain grew largely out of the expansionist ambitions of highly aggressive, often paranoid, and mostly Republican party leaders in the United States. Men such as the hyperenergetic Theodore (Teddy) Roosevelt, the ultrareactionary Senator Henry Cabot Lodge, and the influential naval strategist Alfred Thayer Mahan wanted to make the United States a world naval power.

Mahan, a rare example of a precise military mind with intellectual vision, preached the gospel of geopolitics and nationalism, that the United States to become a great nation must extend its sea power beyond the North American continent to strategic locations in the Pacific and in the Caribbean. For Mahan, maritime geography was the bones of strategy, and trade followed the flag.

By 1898, the United States had already tiptoed into Oceania as a hesitant colonial power with claims of sovereignty over several tiny unclaimed islands: Jarvis, Baker, and Howland in 1856 and Midway in 1867. Mining of fertilizer (guano) from bird droppings was the main reason for acquisition. The Americans then took a giant imperial step with the purchase of Alaska from Russia in 1867. Next,

the United States, along with Germany and Great Britain, became a member of a protectorate over Samoa. This awkward but rewarding colonial initiative led in 1899 to U.S. acquisition of American Samoa with its strategic Pago Pago Harbor.

These steps paralleled American involvment in Hawai'i where in 1887 the United States obtained exclusive use of Pearl Harbor for a naval station in return for which the Kingdom of Hawaii could export sugar duty free to the United States. In 1893, American businessmen in Honolulu, eager to have Hawai'i a part of the United States, overthrew the last of the Hawaiian monarchs, Queen Liliuokalani. But the new "Republic of Hawaii" was kept waiting by the Democratic administration of Grover Cleveland, 1893–1897, and was not acquired until President William McKinley, a Republican elected in 1896, signed a treaty of annexation in July 1898 while the Spanish-American War was under way. With dubious logic, President McKinley remarked, "We need Hawaii just as much and a good deal more than we did California. It is manifest destiny."

Cuba, however, not the Pacific, was the focus of American colonialist paranoia in the late 1890s. American disapproval of the autocratic military rule of Spain in Cuba was fanned by the jingoistic U.S. "yellow press," such as William Randolph

Hearst's newspaper the *New York Journal*. Cuban rebels received U.S. support, and when the American battleship *Maine* mysteriously blew up on a visit to Havana on 15 February 1898, Hearst's headlines blared, "THE WHOLE COUNTRY THRILLS WITH WAR FEVER." Teddy Roosevelt, by then assistant secretary of the navy, wrote, "The *Maine* was sunk by an act of dirty treachery on the part of the Spaniards." In reality, no one yet knows who blew up the *Maine*.

Roosevelt had already dispatched the U.S. Asiatic Squadron of five new steam-powered cruisers and several gunboats, all under the command of Roosevelt's protégé Commodore George Dewey, to Hong Kong in order to blockade Spanish Manila should war break out. On 25 April 1898, the U.S. Congress declared war on Spain. Dewey immediately steamed for Manila, but he did not just blockade the bay. In seven hours of fighting, his squadron blew out of the water a collection of antique Spanish warships in the Battle of Manila Bay on 1 May. Dewey became an instant hero and was promoted to rear admiral.

The new rear admiral, however, faced an unanticipated problem: he could not capture Manila from the Spanish army because he was short of ground troops. Instead of American soldiers, Filipino rebels under Emilio Aguinaldo proceeded to lay seige to the city. Dewey feared the Spanish home fleet and sizable German and Japanese fleets in the area might attempt to relieve Manila. He cabled the Navy Department to send American ground troops and naval reinforcements urgently so that he could take Manila and Luzon.

It took three weeks before the first reinforcements in the form of the cruiser USS *Charleston* with a contingent of U.S. Marines left San Francisco under the command of Captain Henry Glass bound for Manila via Honolulu. Glass, an 1863 Annapolis graduate, was a conservative, fifty-four-year-old line officer who had fought in the American Civil War as a teenage ensign. The *Charleston* waited in Hawai'i until joined by three troop transports—the *City of Pekin*, the *City of Sydney*, and the *Australia*—all fully loaded with

U.S. Army units hastily mobilized on the U.S. West Coast.

On 4 June, the convoy of four ships under Glass put to sea from Honolulu. Anxious to join the fighting in the Philippines, Glass opened his sealed orders from Secretary of the Navy John D. Long as soon as he was clear of land. Instead of going directly to Manila, he was ordered "to capture the port of Guam, and to make prisoners of the governor and other officials and any armed forces that may be there." He was to take no more than "one or two days" to accomplish this chore, and only then was he to proceed to the Philippines. Earlier, on 8 May, the U.S. Naval War Board, which included Mahan and which advised on naval strategy, had recommended to Long the capture of Guam as a coaling station to support the campaign in the Philippines. On 10 May, Long sent Glass, by then in Honolulu, orders by telegram sealed for secrecy until after departure. Glass set course for the Marianas.

Early on the morning of 20 June, the ships entered la Bocana, the channel between Rota and Guam, and turned southwest on the same track Magellan had followed nearly four centuries earlier. Sailing past Ritidian Point and then by Tumon Bay, the *Charleston* swung close to shore off Agaña in an unsuccessful hunt for Spanish ships. Glass mistakenly thought Agaña was a port. The Americans had little information about Guam, and most of what they knew came from Thomas A. Hallet, a third officer on the *Australia,* who had years earlier visited Guam as a whaler captain and who now acted as pilot for the convoy.

Leaving the transports outside Apra, the *Charleston* entered the harbor through thick tropical rain squalls that made it difficult for Hallet to navigate the entrance. He steered close to Orote on the starboard to avoid the coral heads of the dangerous Rocks of the Spanish Frigate on the port side. "With all hands at general quarters and guns loaded we steamed in under Point Orote," according to Robert E. Coontz, a lieutenant aboard who would return to Guam fourteen years later as governor.

Little Fort Santiago on the top of Orote Peninsula remained silent as the cruiser passed by it to within range of old Fort Santa Cruz. Only a Japanese brigantine was anchored in the harbor. Glass fired shells from his three-inch guns at Fort Santa Cruz to draw fire, but no shots were returned. The only reaction was by a couple of startled fishermen at the fort, who paddled away frantically in dugout canoes. The Americans did not know that both of Apra's forts had been abandoned as fortifications years before. Disappointed at the lack of action, Glass had the *Charleston* anchor and prepared to land an armed force.

In the meantime, a group of Spanish officials and civilians had gathered leisurely at the Piti landing on the opposite side of the harbor to conduct customs and health inspections of the foreign ships in the usual manner. They assumed that the shelling was a salute and sent for two of the six little antique brass cannons in Agaña to be brought to the port to return the courtesy. Among the Spaniards was an American citizen, Francisco (Frank) Portusach. A Chamorro mestizo who spoke English, Portusach had once worked for the *San Francisco Chronicle* as an elevator operator. Naturalized in Chicago in 1888, he married an American woman, and they returned to Guam, where the family owned a store and some boats to service ships in Apra Harbor. The Spaniards and Frank Portusach sailed nonchalantly out to the American cruiser in separate boats. There, to their monumental surprise, they learned from Glass of the state of war between the United States and Spain and that the Spanish military officers were all now prisoners of war. Captain Glass then dispatched two of the Spaniards ashore on parole with a letter to Governor Juan Marina in which Glass demanded that the governor report immediately to the *Charleston* for the "surrender of the defenses of the Island of Guam."

While the two Spanish officers went off to Agaña to deliver the American ultimatum to Marina (and halt the salute cannons, which they met en route), Frank Portusach offered his boats to Glass to lighter coal from the transports to the cruiser and to provide supplies to the American ships. There was no coal on Guam at the time, so Glass accepted Portusach's offer. One of the U.S. soldiers later wrote that Portusach's boatmen sold fresh fruit at astoundingly low prices. For one penny they could purchase three bananas, or two mangos, or one pineapple, but a "live monkey" cost two American dollars.

When Governor Marina in Agaña got over his shock at receiving the ultimatum to surrender, he replied by letter that he could not board a hostile foreign warship. He agreed, however, to meet Glass on shore at Piti. By the time Glass received Marina's letter, it was evening, so the meeting was planned for the next morning.

Early the next day, Glass sent two naval officers, Lieutenant William Braunersreuther and Ensign Waldo Evans, ashore to Piti in a whaleboat with a small party of sailors under a white flag of truce. A backup force of two infantry companies of the Oregon Regiment of Volunteers on the *Australia,* along with thirty marines from the *Charleston* under the command of Lieutenant John T. Myers, followed in boats, but they remained offshore in view of the landing site. After a delay for the sake of Spanish pride, the governor wrote out and gave to Braunersreuther a letter in Spanish for Glass in which Marina stated, "I am under the sad necessity of being unable to resist such superior forces and I respectfully accede to your demands."

Following some arguments over procedure when Braunersreuther opened and read the letter on the spot, all the Spanish military officers were taken as prisoners to the *City of Sydney*. With no need to land, the U.S. backup force returned to the ships. One Spanish official, José Sixto (sometimes spelled Sisto) Rodríguez, was not made prisoner, apparently because he was a civilian. He returned to Agaña. Failure to arrest Sixto, who was the administrator of the treasury, would prove to be a mistake by the Americans.

Glass himself then inspected Fort Santa Cruz with a party that included three war correspondents. There the American flag was raised at 2:45 P.M. on 21 June 1898 for the first time in sovereign

Captain Henry Glass, U.S.N. In command of the cruiser USS *Charleston*, he captured Guam for the United States on 20–22 June 1898. By explicitly following his orders only "to capture the port of Guam," he missed the opportunity to take possession of the other islands of the Marianas or of Micronesia. As a consequence, the Germans and later the Japanese occupied all of Micronesia other than Guam, and the Marianas remain incongruously divided into two political entities today. (From the collection of the Micronesian Area Research Center, Mangilao, Guam)

authority over Guam, as a twenty-one-gun salute boomed out from the *Charleston* and the "Star Spangled Banner" was played by bands on the troop ships. The flag was lowered that afternoon and taken back to the *Charleston* since Glass did not know whether the United States intended to retain Guam permanently or not.

Later in the day, all the Spanish troops on Guam assembled at Piti to surrender to the busy Lieutenant Braunersreuther and a detachment of fifteen sailors and thirty-eight marines under Lieutenant Myers. Fifty-four regular Spanish marine infantry and two officers were disarmed. Fifty-two Chamorro militiamen and one officer of the local artillery company were released after turning over their weapons.

All the Spanish troops and officers and their small arms, along with four Spanish flags, were taken aboard the *City of Sydney*, but Glass did not bother with the arms, supplies, and munitions stored in Agaña. An American correspondent reported the "native soldiers joyfully relinquished their arms to the Americans." On the other hand, Spanish priests on Guam reported that the "population became alarmed. . . . Entire families, overwhelmed by fear and anguish, left their homes and fled into the bush."

According to Frank Portusach, whose boats were loading coal onto the *Charleston*, Captain Glass asked Portusach to "take care of the island until some other officers or man-of-war might reach Guam." This casual request was not put in writing, if it was actually made; the U.S. navy never confirmed it. According to Portusach, he accepted the offer and said that there would be no need for "aid, meaning soldiers for the island."

With the bloodless, almost comical seizure of "the port of Guam" completed, the convoy departed the next morning without American troops ever having entered Agaña. Glass, impatient to get to Manila, left no U.S. officers or enlisted men on Guam to oversee America's newest possession. Spanish authority, however, still remained present in the person of José Sixto, who was not a man to submit meekly to American rule.

The departure of Juan Marina left Guam without a colonial chief executive for the first time since 1668. This inadvertent interregnum, a period of confusion for everyone on Guam, would last nearly fourteen months, until the arrival of the first U.S naval governor on 7 August 1899.

A Colonial Interregnum

Elsewhere on 22 June, the day the American convoy departed Guam, an American army of 17,000 ill-trained but enthusiastic soldiers was invading Cuba. By 12 August, fighting in Cuba and Puerto Rico ceased under an armistice, as it did the next day in the Philippines after the "Battle of Manila," in which the Spanish forces surrendered after a mock show of resistance. The fighting had lasted less than four months, indeed a splendid little war from Teddy Roosevelt's viewpoint. A protocol signed on 12 August ended the fighting and outlined the terms of peace. Spain agreed to relinquish Cuba, to cede Puerto Rico and Guam to the United States, and to permit the United States to occupy "the city, bay, and harbor at Manila," pending a peace treaty to "determine the control, disposition and government of the Philippines."

While the victorious Americans organized a commission to negotiate a peace treaty in Paris with the Spaniards, Germany and Japan moved into the western Pacific as Spain withdrew. The Germans wanted a division of the Philippines and Micronesia with the Americans but were rebuffed. Germany then negotiated secretly with Spain, and, on 10 September 1898, the two countries concluded a secret agreement whereby Germany would purchase the Marshalls and Carolines, including Palau, and all the Marianas except Guam. The two countries agreed that the islands would remain under Spanish control until the Spanish treaty with the United States was concluded. The Japanese were left out of the agreement.

Meeting in late August 1898 to review the outcome of the war, the U.S. Naval War Board recommended that the United States obtain a Philippine base as the ultimate position in a chain of military stations across the Pacific in order to support American commercial and missionary interests in China. Owing to the distances involved—San Francisco is about 7,000 sailing miles from Manila—coaling stations were needed en route. Otherwise, steamships had to be accompanied by special coal-carrying ships called colliers to be recoaled within 2,000–4,000 miles. The Naval War Board suggested three stations west of Hawai'i: a transit station in the Marianas at Guam; a base at Cavite in Manila Bay; and a station at Pago Pago, Samoa, which was between the potential Panama Canal and Australia–New Zealand.

In September 1898, the *Literary Digest* confirmed public support of American expansionism in a poll (a new technique at the time) of 192 newspaper editors. The majority of editors favored U.S. annexation of the conquered Spanish areas for U.S. naval bases. By October, President McKinley was in a quandary over the pros and cons of annexing the Philippines. A religious man educated in a seminary, he later wrote, "The truth is I didn't want the Philippines and when they came to us as a gift from the gods, I did not know what to do about them. . . . I thought at first we would take only Manila; then Luzon; then other islands, perhaps, also. And then I went to bed, and went to sleep and slept soundly."

So, when the U.S. peace commissioners in Paris cabled for instructions, McKinley replied that the United States was to offer $20 million to Spain for all the Philippines, including Guam. Spain reluctantly accepted what amounted to an American ultimatum. Guam's destiny under the Americans, just as under the Spaniards, was tied to the Philippines.

In the treaty negotiations, the United States still had the opportunity to acquire the Carolines, or at least all the Marianas. In an article in October 1898, a perceptive American commentator, not knowing of the German efforts, had pointed out the strategic value of the Micronesian islands that surround Guam, and he noted the possibility of their falling into hands stronger than those of the Spaniards and thereby posing a threat to Guam. He wrote, "Guam is either too much or too little." Some American naval officers also favored U.S. control of the Carolines. One wrote, "In the hands of an enemy they would offer a serious menace to the line of communication between the Pacific Coast and the Philippines." Nonetheless, officials in Washington let the opportunity pass, and Guam would soon be surrounded by German islands.

The Treaty of Paris between Her Majesty María Cristina, queen regent of Spain, and the United States of America was signed on 10 December 1898, ratified in early 1899 by both governments, and proclaimed as law on 11 April 1899, when American sovereignty officially began. Most of the provisions of the 12 August 1898 protocol were implemented by the treaty. This treaty would be accepted by the international community, including eventually the League of Nations after World War I and the United Nations after World War II, as establishing U.S. sovereignty over Guam under international law.

The debate over the treaty was historic in that it made the United States a colonial nation and a major Pacific power. After initially opposing the treaty, the Democratic senators finally supported it under the erroneous assumption that the Philippines would be granted independence. Contrary to that expectation, the United States ended up fighting the Filipino independence movement in a bitter guerrilla war that did not end until 1901. With respect to Guam, the Treaty of Paris stated:

> Article II. Spain cedes to the United States the island of Porto Rico [sic] and other islands now under Spanish sovereignty in the West Indies, and the island of Guam in the Marianas or Ladrones.

> Article V. . . . Spain will . . . proceed to evacuate the Philippines, as well as the island of Guam. . . . Stands of colors, uncaptured war vessels, small arms, guns of all calibres, with their carriages and accessories, powder, live ammunition, live stock, and materials and supplies of all kinds, belonging to the land and naval forces of Spain in the Philippines and Guam, remain the property of Spain.

> Article VIII. . . . Spain . . . cedes . . . in the island of Guam . . . all the buildings, wharves, barracks, forts, structures, public highways and other immovable property which, in conformity with law, belong to the public domain, and as such belong to the Crown of Spain.

> Article IX. The civil rights and political status of the native inhabitants of the territories hereby ceded to the United States shall be determined by the Congress.

At no time in the transfer of sovereignty did American or Spanish officials consult with the inhabitants of Guam. And nowhere in the treaty did the United States explicitly obligate itself to bring the people of Guam to self-government or to improve their political, social, or economic well-being. There is no stipulation in the treaty that sovereignty remain in the hands of the indigenous people, and there is no acknowledgment of indigenous rights in the treaty other than what the U.S. Congress decides them to be.

With the conclusion of the Paris treaty, Germany signed its own treaty with Spain to take possession of the Marshall and Caroline Islands, including Palau, and all the Marianas other than Guam. The price for the islands was 18 million German marks (equivalent to 25 million Spanish pesetas or 4.2 million American dollars at the time), a bargain for Germany.

Meanwhile, the U.S. Navy was preparing to occupy Guam even before the Paris peace treaty was signed. On 9 December, the navy ordered a gunboat at Pearl Harbor, the *Bennington,* to visit Guam and conduct a hydrographic survey of Apra Harbor for the purpose of establishing a naval coaling and watering station. A naval collier, the

Brutus, was also ordered to Guam to recoal the *Bennington.* On 12 December, the Navy Bureau of Navigation—at the time in charge of all U.S. naval operations—recommended to President McKinley that Guam be placed under naval administration. McKinley obligingly issued Executive Order 108-A on 23 December 1898: "The Island of Guam in the Ladrones is hereby placed under the control of the Department of Navy. The Secretary of the Navy will take such steps as may be necessary to establish the authority of the United States and to give it the necessary protection and government."

On 12 January 1899, Navy Secretary Long selected Captain Richard Phillips Leary to be the first U.S. naval governor of Guam. Leary received his instructions the same date by letter, which stated ominously:

> Within the absolute domain of naval authority, which necessarily is and must remain supreme in the ceded territory until the legislation of the U.S. shall otherwise provide, the municipal [i.e., Spanish] laws of the territory... are to be considered as continuing in force... the mission of the United States is one of benevolent assimilation, substituting the mild sway of justice and right for arbitrary rule. In fulfillment of this high mission... there must be sedulously maintained the strong arm of authority, to repress disturbance and to overcome all obstacles to the bestowal of the blessings of good government upon the people of the Island of Guam under the green flag of the United States.

The instructions were clear on one point: the needs and desires of the military on Guam took precedence over all other matters in the administration of the island. The island government was designated as the "naval government of Guam." The chief executive was given two hats: one strictly military hat by appointment from the secretary of the navy as "Commandant, United States Naval Station, Guam," and a second hat by presidential commission as "Governor of Guam" with jurisdiction over all nonmilitary matters. Thus, despite the rhetoric about "the mild sway of justice and right," the American naval governor was given the same

supreme politico-military powers over the people and the Island of Guam as the "arbitrary rule" of the Spanish governors.

While decisions were being taken in Europe and Washington, events back on Guam had taken bizarre turns in the absence of American officials. After the departure of Glass, José Sixto assumed charge of the government of the Marianas, including the treasury, which still contained cash, mostly Mexican silver dollars. Sixto was the only man with a key to the treasury safe with the cash. In a report to the Spanish government delivered by a trading schooner to the Spanish consul in Yokohama, Sixto argued that U.S. sovereignty over Guam was "null" because of the Berlin treaty of 1885. In Sixto's view, that treaty established international law whereby possession of territory is only by "physical and true occupation by a military detachment or armed force," and Guam had been "abandoned by the enemy."

In the absence of American military authority, Sixto proceeded to pay himself a salary as acting governor from the cash on hand and to gather about him a pro-Spanish group, which included all the priests except Father Palomo. Sixto also paid the Chamorro militiamen salaries from the same cash in order to assure their loyalty to him and to Spain. Meanwhile, Frank Portusach, Father Palomo, and several other prominent Chamorros formed a pro-American group but did not attempt to occupy the governor's residence or take control away from Sixto.

On 17 September 1898, the transport USS *Pennsylvania* arrived from Manila en route to the U.S. West Coast. Aboard was Dr. José Romero, one of the *Charleston's* prisoners of war, who had returned for his family and possessions. He brought the news of the Spanish capitulation after the Battle of Manila in August. The *Pennsylvania* apparently also brought whooping cough to Guam, and an epidemic of the disease killed some 100 Chamorro children in the following months.

In December, the Spanish steamship *Uranus* arrived from Pohnpei. Aboard was Lieutenant

Commander Francisco García Gutiérrez, who had also been a prisoner on the *Charleston*. On Guam, he collected his family and that of Juan Marina, along with two Spanish priests, and they all departed in early December on the same ship for Iloilo and then Spain. Dr. Romero remained on Guam with his family since there was no room for them on the *Uranus*.

By Christmas 1898, Sixto had about emptied the Agaña treasury, mostly into his own pockets. Law and order were breaking down. A small riot with knife fights between Filipinos and Chamorros erupted at cockfights in December at the Sumay village fiesta. Filipinos on Guam who were former convicts were heartily disliked by the Chamorros, and the antipathy was mutual. Portusach, wielding a pistol, broke up the fighting at Sumay and arrested about twenty Filipinos, whom he packed off to jail in Agaña. The public disorder and the news of the American victory in Manila convinced the pro-American group that it was time to depose Sixto.

On New Year's Day 1899, Frank Portusach, Father Palomo, and several other pro-American leaders gathered at the Agaña Tribunal y Cárcel building and signed a document to dismiss Sixto and appoint Venancio Roberto in his place as acting governor. They then started across the plaza toward the governor's *palacio* to confront Sixto but halted at the sudden tolling of the signal bells of the old ammunition magazine on the hill behind Agaña. An American naval vessel was arriving. Everyone immediately postponed all action until the next day to present their cases to the American captain of the ship.

The ship was the collier *Brutus,* sent to recoal the *Bennington*, which was scheduled to arrive later in the month to survey Apra Harbor for a coaling and water station. The captain of the *Brutus,* Lieutenant Vincendon L. Cottman, was surprised the next day when the two local factions came aboard his ship at Apra Harbor. Cottman at the time had no information on the outcome of the Paris peace talks, so he let Sixto, now endorsed by Dr. Romero, continue as acting governor until word

was received on the political status of Guam under the Paris treaty.

Cottman and his officers then undertook reconnaissances of the Agaña and Apra areas to locate a coaling site. The twenty-eight-page handwritten report that Cottman prepared on 20 February 1899 for the secretary of the navy (who received it in March) was the first detailed and current information about Guam that Washington had received until then. Like many Spanish officers before him, Cottman made a number of recommendations to his superiors to improve conditions on Guam with respect to land matters, taxes, Apra Harbor, and so forth. Further, he proposed that all the Catholic priests be expelled; that lepers be sent to the leprosarium at Moloka'i, Hawai'i; that Filipino convicts be sent to Manila; that education be compulsory under a public school system; and that "American" English be made the official language. The Department of the Navy gave Cottman's report to Captain Leary, who was then preparing to depart the U.S. East Coast for Guam. Leary later implemented a number of Cottman's recommendations.

On 23 January 1899, the *Brutus* was joined on Guam by the *Bennington* under the command of Captain Edward D. Taussig, who brought news that the Paris treaty had been signed and that Guam was now U.S. territory. After being briefed by Cottman on the local situation, Taussig issued the first two general orders by an American official on Guam. The first order, proclaimed on 28 January, continued Spanish laws in force and instructed the *Bennington*'s assistant paymaster, Barren P. Dubois, to audit the treasury books. The second order on 30 January took possession of "all public lands, recently the property of the Spanish Government, bordering on the port of San Luís d'Apra." The land was needed as a coaling site and navy yard, and its seizure was the first of a long series of controversial steps whereby United States governmental agencies acquired large portions of land on Guam.

In going through the Spanish financial records, Dubois discovered that Sixto had paid himself and other employees eighteen months' advance pay.

Dubois recovered some of the funds, but Sixto's debts remained unsettled for the time being, leaving the treasury nearly empty for local governmental needs. Taussig stripped Sixto of his position and appointed Joaquín Pérez y Cruz as acting governor, Vicente Pérez as secretary, and Vicente Herrero in charge of finances. Taussig also approved of an advisory council, or junta, of six prominent Chamorros, including Pérez as chair, but without Frank Portusach. Pérez, from a *manak'kilo* family, was the *gobernadorcillo* of Agaña and thus respected locally.

On 1 February 1899, the Americans once more raised the U.S. flag over Fort Santa Cruz, but this time they simultaneously raised a flag over the governor's residence in Agaña before a detachment of U.S. Marines and the *Bennington* band. The *Brutus* departed later the same day for San Francisco, where Cottman would send his report, plus reports by Taussig, on to Washington, D.C. Back on Guam, the *Yorktown* arrived with mail and orders for the *Bennington* to report to Manila. The two ships sailed away on 15 February with Dr. Romero and his family as guests on the *Bennington*. Taussig, like Glass, felt no need to leave officers or troops on Guam.

With a new government, but still no American officials, the Chamorros settled down uneasily to await the next appearance of their casual new masters. While waiting, Joaquín Pérez arrested José Sixto for misappropriation of funds, which Sixto was ordered to repay. The Spaniard was allowed freedom as long as he did not leave the island. On 10–11 March, an American battleship, the *Oregon*, anchored in Apra and was recoaled by its collier the *Iris*, but no one stayed ashore.

Not until after 24 March 1899, when the American-chartered collier *Nanshan* arrived, did another U.S. official spend time ashore. He was Lieutenant Louis A. Kaiser, the only naval officer aboard the *Nanshan*. Of Hong Kong registry with an American civilian captain and a Chinese crew, the collier's mission was to recoal U.S. warships. Kaiser had few duties on the anchored *Nanshan*, so he rented a

house in Agaña and spent much of his time hunting with the pro-American group. Soon he was entangled in local politics even though he spoke no Spanish or Chamorro.

On 9 May, the old Spanish steamer *Elcano* arrived at Apra en route to Saipan with Colonel Eugenio Blanco, the new temporary Spanish governor of the northern Marianas. The *Elcano* was "frightfully overcrowded" with about 700 refugees from the Philippines, according to Kaiser. The passengers included nearly 300 "Macabebes," Pampango soldiers still loyal to Spain. Blanco requested that all Spanish arms, munitions, and medical supplies still on Guam be handed over to him in accord with Article V of the Paris treaty.

Kaiser refused Blanco's request on the grounds that he did not have a copy of the Paris treaty to confirm that provision. The *Elcano* departed 11 May without the arms and supplies but with a number of Filipino malcontents, to the relief of the Chamorros on Guam. Later in May, the *Elcano* returned to Guam from Saipan en route eventually to Spain and this time took away the troublesome José Sixto. He had repaid 1,875 Mexican dollars on his debt to the Guam treasury with money borrowed in part from Father Palomo. One unfortunate residue from the *Elcano*'s visit was a disease thought to be poliomyelitis that caused several deaths at Sumay village.

In June, the Spanish schooner *Esmeralda,* which had carried supplies to the Micronesian islands since 1888, arrived with a Spanish officer from Manila with another request for the Spanish arms and supplies on Guam. This time he had a letter from General Elwell S. Otis, the U.S. commander of all the Philippines, authorizing the turnover. Again Kaiser refused, stating that the army general had no authority on Guam. The *Esmeralda* sailed away empty-handed to Yap to retrieve Spaniards. By this time, Joaquín Pérez and the junta were fed up with Kaiser. He had become a sort of Lord Jim, as in Joseph Conrad's novel, assuming authority in his little tropical kingdom when it suited him, but without taking responsibility for the consequences.

For the first July Fourth celebration on Guam,

Lieutenant Kaiser took it on himself to organize a parade in Agaña with a twenty-one-gun salute by four old Spanish mortars and readings in English and Spanish of the American Declaration of Independence, followed by a dance and fireworks. The festivities did not go well, according to Kaiser's diary: "There seemed to be a kind of wet blanket thrown over the affair by a latent Spanish sympathy."

On 10 July, the *Esmeralda* returned to Guam, and this time Pérez allowed the Spaniards to take their arms and supplies. Kaiser—angry and insisting that he was the "senior officer" in charge on Guam—removed Pérez as acting governor the next day and appointed William (Willie) Pritchard Coe to the position. This was the first of innumerable later confrontations between island officials, who acted on the knowledge of complex, sometimes hidden local histories, and American officials, who demanded immediate solutions to problems on the basis of superficial information. Coe, a friend of Kaiser's, was a personable Samoan-American who had been on Guam only a short while. To get around Kaiser and Coe, on 23 July the Chamorros created a bicameral legislature. Three men, including Father Palomo, were elected to the upper house, and six were chosen for the lower house. Kaiser immediately disbanded what would have been the first legislature in Guam's history.

Willie Coe's two-week tenure as unofficial acting governor, and Kaiser's role as U.S. proconsul, ended on the morning of 7 August 1899. On that date, the USS *Yosemite* steamed into Apra Harbor with the stern Captain Richard Phillips Leary aboard, and Guam officially became a "U.S. Naval Station." From then on, there was no doubt in anyone's mind who was the real governor of Guam.

The First U.S. Naval Administration

Richard Leary was of the same conservative military mold as Henry Glass: an Annapolis graduate, a Civil War veteran, and a Protestant with long service as a line officer. Single, he spoke no Spanish and had little experience in civil governmental affairs. After he received his commission as the governor of Guam from McKinley in January 1899, Leary spent four months elaborately outfitting the *Yosemite,* an auxiliary cruiser of about 6,000 tons, as station ship for Guam. He also purchased considerable supplies and equipment to set up the governor's residence and offices out of an ample budget.

On 11 May 1899, the *Yosemite,* with a bright coat of white paint and after a visit by President McKinley himself, departed New York with a complement of about eighty sailors and a 120-man U.S. Marine battalion of two companies under Major Allen C. Kelton. The leisurely voyage of three months took the cruiser across the Atlantic and the Mediterranean, through the Suez Canal to Ceylon and then Singapore, and on to Manila. Leary purchased much equipment en route, such as a telephone system in Singapore.

On 10 August, just three days after his arrival, the new governor issued his first proclamation to the people of Guam. In it he stressed separation of church and state and submission to American authority: "All political rights heretofore exercized by the Clergy in dominating the people of the Island, are hereby abolished, and everyone is guaranteed absolute freedom of worship and full protection in the lawful pursuits of life, as long as that protection is deserved by actual submission to and compliance with the requirements of the Government of the United States."

Leary lived on the anchored *Yosemite* for the next three months during the renovation of the ten-year-old governor's residence in Agana (the Americans in this period dropped the diacritic over the written letter *n* but continued to pronounce the word as Agaña, as in Spanish). On 13 August, he was joined by his aide, Lieutenant William Edwin Safford, a thirty-nine-year-old bachelor who arrived on the *Brutus* along with his Japanese man-servant, Miyamoto, and three Jersey cows and one bull. The *Brutus,* with Lieutenant Cottman still captain, had come from the U.S. West Coast by way of Samoa to relieve the *Nanshan* of its collier duties. The *Nanshan* would depart from Guam three weeks later for Manila with the meddlesome Lieutenant Kaiser aboard as well as fifteen Filipino ex-convicts, two Spanish priests, and several Spanish citizens.

Safford in the meantime was ordered by Leary to move to Agana, where on 15 August the lieutenant took over José Sixto's old apartment in the treasury building on the Plaza de Magallanes, which the Americans began to call the Plaza de España. Safford relieved Willie Coe and assumed duties as the trial judge for local cases, recorder of deeds and titles, and auditor of the treasury. These duties in effect, but not in formal title, made him the lieutenant governor of Guam.

Although an Annapolis graduate, Safford was not a line officer like Leary or Glass. A former Catholic (but agnostic by 1899), he had served in Latin America and was fluent in German and Spanish. This unassuming, intelligent man studied Chamorro, built a plant nursery, began a catalog of local plants, acquired a house and two *lanchos* to raise his own food, and in his spare time taught classes in English at night to Chamorros.

He discovered the Spanish archives in Agana "eaten in places by termites, and edges mildewed . . . the writing for the most part beautiful." Subsequently, he sent all the Spanish documents except for land records back to the Library of Congress. For advice on local customs, he relied on Father Palomo, and the two men became close friends. Palomo brought Safford into contact with the *manak'kilo* of Agana, among whom he soon became liked and respected. He found this local elite well educated, highly Hispanicized, and rather

Lt. William Edwin Safford, U.S.N. Photograph taken about 1898. As aide from August 1899 to August 1990 to the first U.S. naval governor of Guam, Captain Richard Leary, Safford was in effect the first American lieutenant governor of the island. He wrote the first English-language textbook on the Chamorro language and authored the first two books in English on the plants and history of Guam. (From the Collection of the Micronesian Area Research Center, Mangiloa, Guam)

disdainful of the Americans as less sophisticated than the Spaniards. The first formal request of the Chamorros to Safford was a petition to have the Filipino ex-convicts remaining on Guam deported because they were a "menace to peace." Leary concurred, but Safford excepted two men because their Chamorro wives and children would be left destitute without their husbands (families were not deported). The deportees were the fifteen ex-convicts that departed on the *Nanshan* on 7 September with Lieutenant Kaiser.

While Safford was reorganizing civil authority in Agana, Leary was busy setting up a permanent American military presence on the island. He hired Chamorros as workers at twenty-four cents per day, but they turned out to be unwilling to do manual labor, so Leary put the marines to work on civil projects as well as military construction. In the meantime, more U.S. naval vessels were stopping at Apra Harbor, where a navy yard was created on the former Spanish crown property at Piti. One visitor was the USS *Nero,* whose mission was to survey the ocean floor for a trans-Pacific submarine telegraph cable. The *Nero* discovered the deepest canyon on earth, the Marianas Trench. This canyon begins approximately 200 miles east of Saipan and curves south to its deepest point 36,198 feet below sea level some 210 miles southwest of Guam beyond the Santa Rosa Reef.

On 16 August 1899, Leary issued his first two executive general orders on Guam. Order 1 prohibited the sale "of any intoxicating spirituous liquors . . . to any person who was not a resident of this island" under penalty of a stiff fine of 100 Mexican dollars. The second order prohibited the importation of any liquors without a license. Like the prohibition of alcohol elsewhere, these orders were impossible to enforce, and alcoholic beverages continued to be mysteriously available. Leary subsequently had to issue another order forbidding residents or visitors (meaning American marines and sailors) from obtaining *tuba* or *aguardiente* from the locals because fights broke out between marines and locals as a consequence, he noted, of "drunkenness." Despite official efforts, the prob-

lems of alcohol and of military-civilian relations would never be completely solved on Guam.

The new governor went on arbitrarily issuing civil orders, usually with Safford drafting the language in both English and Spanish. Order 3 halted all land sales until a new registry system was established by Safford. Order 4 prohibited celebrations and processions in villages on patron-saint feast days. Leary even halted the customary tolling of church bells in the morning and evening. With Order 5, Leary suppressed "the existing system of concubinage," and all couples "living together out of the bounds of wedlock are . . . to be married . . . in order that their children may become legitimate." Leary instructed Safford to perform divorces and ordered local justices of the peace (the *gobernadorcillos*) to perform civil marriages, regardless of church views. It was becoming evident to the Chamorros that the intent of many of these orders was to restrict the Catholic Church and to change local customs, not just to reform laws or governmental procedures.

Leary considered the remaining Spanish priests a problem because they condoned concubinage and themselves fathered illegitimate children. In August 1899, he ordered the Recollects expelled despite their pleas to Safford to remain. On 7 September, Father Resano and another Augustinian departed on the Japanese vessel *Jun-ho Maru* for Saipan, where Resano was assigned as provincial vicar. Later the same day, Fathers Ildefonso Cabanillas and Crisogono Ortín, the last Augustinian Recollects on Guam, departed on the collier *Nanshan* when it left for the Philippines. The priests' common-law wives and children remained on Guam with the mothers' families. Father Palomo was permitted to stay, probably at Safford's request and because he was a Chamorro.

In the meantime, the U.S. Marines were getting tired of pick-and-shovel work. Leary had them digging sewers, repairing roads, working on the governor's residence, and cleaning up the main Agana plaza for a parade ground. Trained for combat and unaccustomed to manual labor in the tropical climate, forty-seven resentful marines refused to report for work detail on 18 October. They asked that "natives" be hired for the work. Furious, Leary assembled all the marines the next morning and reprimanded them for their "mutinous, disgraceful conduct." According to one of the marines, Leary grimly threatened to shoot them, stating, "I have the law. I am supreme." The marines went back to work.

Owing to the "licentious and lawless conduct" of the marines, Leary issued Order 11, admonishing all Americans that "the natives of Guam are not 'damned dagoes,' nor 'niggers,'" as marines and sailors at times derisively called them. Nonetheless, the marines continued to cause serious problems (the next governor described some as "vicious and refractory characters"). A naval engineer on the island, Leonard M. Cox, wrote in 1904 of this early period of U.S. rule: "Colonies were a new thing to us. . . . As in every case of change in sovereignty, the interregnum brought forth its crop of abuses with which the American governor had at once to deal. Our troops, new to conquest and familiar with only one race other than their own . . . were in many cases lawless and turbulent."

While the Americans were getting established on Guam, the Germans replaced the Spaniards in the islands in Micronesia ceded by Spain to Germany. On 17 November 1899, the German "district captain" for the Marianas, Georg Fritz, arrived aboard the warship *Kudat* at Saipan, where he would serve energetically for eight years. Two weeks later, the last Spanish officials, along with the Macabebe troops, departed the Mariana Islands. German colonial administration in the Marianas was stricter than the American naval government of Guam but more sensitive to indigenous customs, such as maintaining Chamorro as the language of instruction in the schools. For the next forty-two years, Guam as an American colony would have a history separate from the rest of Micronesia under the Germans and then the Japanese. The artificial—in terms of culture and geography—separation of the Marianas into two political entities endures

today even though both are now American territories.

In the meantime on Guam, Governor Leary reported to the Navy Department with satisfaction that he had "disposed of the priests who were the ringleaders in encouraging vicious and demoralizing habits and customs." What Leary did not know was that the navy was releasing his reports to the American press. American Catholics all over the country angrily protested Leary's orders. The 6 January 1900 edition of the *Galveston Tribune,* for example, declared, FATHER KIRWAN PROTESTS. DENOUNCES THE ACTION OF GOVERNOR LEARY IN STOPPING RELIGIOUS PARADES.

The Catholic archbishop of New Orleans, who was also apostolic delegate to all the new U.S. territories, wrote Leary and asked to visit Guam on his way to the Philippines. Leary at first agreed and then reneged because of what he considered the "extraordinary egotism and officiousness displayed" in a second letter from the archbishop, which requested Leary "to revoke all orders issued . . . depriving the people of their legitimate religious liberty." As a result of the uproar, General Otis in the Philippines ordered an army major general, Joseph Wheeler, to inspect conditions on Guam en route back to the mainland. The elderly Wheeler, known as "Fighting Joe" from the Civil War, had been Teddy Roosevelt's divisional commanding officer in Cuba in 1898 and was highly respected. Despite Wheeler's reputation, Leary objected to the visit as an unwarranted army intrusion in a navy command. He was then instructed by his own superiors to receive Wheeler, but he was to "decline to recognize his instructions as official."

While Leary awaited Wheeler, the governor's residence was ready for occupancy near the end of November 1899. The building now had the first corrugated tin roof on Guam and was newly painted white with large green typhoon shutters hinged to all doors and windows. On 26 November, Leary moved in with pomp equal to any Spanish governor. Safford wrote of Leary's arrival in Agana, "He brought with him the band from the

Yosemite. . . . The Governor's steward and house servants are enlisted mess-Japanese. He has a pair of white stallions which he bought in Manila, and a Filipino coachman to drive them. He has a fine outfit of table-linen, silver, porcelain, and glassware."

The American newcomers wore different uniforms, spoke a different foreign language, and had more cash than the Spaniards, but, like the Spaniards, they also brought disease to Guam. By December 1899, typhoid fever was widespread. Six marines died the first year, including Captain Clarence L. A. Ingate on Christmas Eve from gangrene following an operation. He was buried on Safford's small *lancho* on San Ramón Hill behind the governor's residence.

In a proclamation on 1 January 1900, Governor Leary started the twentieth century off on Guam by abolishing peonage. This reform went into effect 22 February to eliminate the practice whereby the poor *manak'papa* paid debts to the *manak'kilo* by labor that sometimes lasted years. By February, after six months on Guam, Leary had issued fourteen executive general orders and three proclamations. These orders implemented agricultural and labor reforms, a revised land tax system (other Spanish taxes, however, continued), and a new tariff schedule for imports (later revised by Washington). Leary also instituted a much-needed public health program, with navy physicians and corpsmen from the *Yosemite* providing free treatment to Chamorros.

As Cottman had proposed originally in his report of 1899, Leary set up a public education system under naval control in place of the church school system, but, owing to the lack of teachers after the priests departed, only a few schools remained open initially. He prohibited religious instruction in schools, ordered all adult residents to learn to write their names, and urged everyone to learn English. Instruction in schools was to be in English, as soon as enough teachers were available.

On 6 February, Major General Wheeler arrived. Leary let Safford escort the unwanted guest, along with Wheeler's secretary and a *Harper's Weekly* correspondent, around the island for most of the four days the group was on Guam. A contingent of Chamorros, including Father Palomo, gave Wheeler a flowery petition in Spanish that requested Safford (who apparently knew nothing about it) be named governor if Leary was to be replaced.

While on Guam, Wheeler issued no instructions. He carried the Chamorro petition to Washington but did not mention it in his official report. The report was largely descriptive, and of social conditions Wheeler remarked only that "the orders with regard to religion are evidently considered as a hardship and are distasteful to a majority of the people." Like Spanish governors, Wheeler urged that a breakwater be erected in Apra Harbor. Later after a four-month survey of Guam from late 1900 into early 1901, an official "Guam Survey Board" under Captain John F. Merry also proposed a breakwater, but lack of appropriations by Congress prevented its construction.

As a consequence of Wheeler's mild assessment, no changes were made by Washington with regard to Guam, and Leary stayed on. Complaints by American Catholics subsided. In a brief but significant letter on 13 February, Leary requested that the official name for the island be "Isle of Guam, Pacific Ocean," in place of "Ladrone Islands." Washington eventually accepted the change in 1908, with the added designation "Mariana Islands."

Health conditions on Guam began to improve as drainage systems, a water distillation plant, and water storage tanks were constructed for the first time on the island. Leary instituted and enforced garbage collection and required outhouses as toilets in the main villages. Treatment by navy doctors started to reduce infection among the islanders of syphilis, tuberculosis, and a horribly disfiguring disease thought to be syphilis or leprosy but later diagnosed as gangosa, a form of tertiary yaws. On 10 March, Leary reported that Guam's first telephone system was installed and working between

Agana and Piti. He asked Washington to authorize a military commissary and a post exchange, and these would later be established permanently on Guam.

In an order reminiscent of Spanish galleon days, Washington instructed U.S. Army Transports (USATs) steaming to the Philippines from San Francisco via Hawai'i to stop at Guam on the westward leg with people, mail, money, and supplies. On the eastbound leg from Manila to San Francisco, the army transports followed the shorter great circle route directly across the north Pacific, just as had the Spanish galleons. One army transport stopped in Apra every one to three months. The transports were usually met a mile or two outside the harbor by Chamorro men and Micronesian crewmen (these were mostly from Palau and Yap) in small boats to sell fresh fruit and coconuts to the passengers and crews, just as the Chamorros had done with Spanish galleons.

One problem on Guam that surprised Safford was how local officials defrauded their own people. Two elderly women walked all the way from Merizo to Agana with an appeal against their *gobernadorcillo*. This official had altered the land title of one of the women to reduce the size of her property and dispose of the land gained. He had arrested the son of the other woman for stealing twenty-two coffee plants when in fact it was the *gobernadorcillo* himself who stole the valuable plants. Leary removed the *gobernadorcillo* from office, and Safford went on to grant over 1,000 land certificates to Chamorros under a new system of surveying and registration that he initiated on the basis of Spanish records. Nonetheless, land frauds would recur repeatedly on Guam.

Like other aspects of the American occupation that sowed the seeds of future problems on Guam, the local judicial system was initially left under Spanish laws and procedures. The Spanish legal system on Guam was replaced piecemeal by measures based at times on American laws but more often on immediate naval operational needs. In this early period, the Americans did not strictly enforce the Spanish real

estate tax of 1 percent of assessed value of property, which was left unchanged for the time being.

The most troublesome administrative problem for Leary and all later U.S. naval governors, just as under the Spanish governors, was inadequate funding for Guam's civil government and military installations. Eventually, the U.S. Congress began to appropriate funds for Guam through the navy budget, but it was invariably stingy. When funds were available, the navy gave priority in the Pacific to bases at Pearl Harbor, and at Cavite and Olongapo in the Philippines, not Guam. One historian later commented that Congress "showed a curious indifference to the affairs of Guam, while it succored the Philippines and Puerto Rico."

Leary requested another U.S. Marine battalion for Guam, but it was not sent. Frustrated and perhaps bored with Guam, Leary then asked for reassignment. In his last edict, Order 21, Leary prohibited public appearances in the nude by "males of the Caroline Islander's community." There were still ninety-six Carolinians at the village of María Cristina (today's Tamuning) living in their traditional style. Female Carolinians presumably could still appear nude in public. The same order also forbade cockfighting, the main sport on Guam and one dearly beloved by the men of the island. This order was as impossible to enforce as were earlier ones that attempted to discourage gambling and alcohol.

On 19 July 1900, Captain Leary was relieved as governor and as naval station commandant by Commander Seaton Schroeder. Safford was replaced by Ensign A. W. Pressey, who also spoke Spanish. Before departing, Safford gave away his furniture and household items and most of his land to his Chamorro servants and friends, selling only the San Ramón Hill property. When he and Captain Leary departed on the *Yosemite* for Cavite on 1 August 1900, Safford wrote in his diary, "As the ship weighed anchor and sailed away I felt real grief, as though leaving people of my own blood. I shall always look back upon the year spent on this lovely island as one of the happiest in my life."

Back in the United States, Leary—still a captain

and disappointed with his dull new assignment in command of a ship in the Philadelphia Navy Yard—died in 1901 of heart disease. Safford resigned from the navy in 1902 and became a curator at the National Herbarium in Washington, D.C. He earned a Ph.D. in 1920 and pursued a career as a botanist, ethnologist, and philologist. He wrote eighty published works, including the first English text on the Chamorro language (dedicated to Father Palomo) and two books about the plants and the history of Guam. Modest and intellectually inquisitive until the end, William Safford died in 1926 without returning to the island where he had served the local people and his own government with quiet distinction.

The Practice of Manifest Destiny

Governor Seaton Schroeder was more like Safford than Leary in his approach to the administration of Guam. He spoke French and Spanish, and within a month he allowed celebrations once more of saints' feast days in the villages. On 15 October 1900, he opened Guam's first ice plant. Cold storage of meat and other foods would eventually improve the diet and health of the local people, in addition to making life more pleasant for the Americans. In his first order on 29 November 1900, Schroeder abolished the Spanish ecclesiastical tribunals, which Leary, for all his anti-Catholicism, had neglected to eliminate. Within a year, the governor permitted the return of Catholic priests, three Spanish Capuchins initially (the Germans had given the Capuchin Order of Saint Francis responsibility for all Catholic missions in Micronesia, and the Americans followed suit). A fourth Capuchin arrived in 1907.

Schroeder was accompanied by his wife, Maria, and their children, the first American military family on Guam. American women soon established in Agana a military social circle that mirrored the protocol and traditions found on U.S. naval bases in that period. Some members of the upper-*manak-'kilo* Chamorro families of Agana were included in this small, elite society, but on the whole a cultural

and racial gulf remained between the Americans and the Chamorros.

Mrs. Schroeder raised funds from the mainland for a new hospital. She laid the cornerstone, and Father Palomo said the benediction in June 1901 for the two-story medical building near the old *colegio* ruins in Agana. Named the Maria Schroeder Hospital, with twenty beds and a dispensary, this facility and smaller clinics in Agat and Sumay provided free outpatient and surgical treatment for the first time to Chamorros.

Many Chamorros, however, initially feared the new medical procedures, and it was difficult to get the seriously ill to remain in the hospital, particularly women. The islanders still preferred home cures or folk remedies by the *suruhanus*. Nonetheless, the high Chamorro mortality rate began to decline. Outpatient treatment also began to reduce common afflictions such as "dhobie itch" (ringworms) and "lumbricoid worms" (mostly intestinal hookworms and also tapeworms). According to naval physician J. F. Leys, hookworms were a "veritable curse in this community."

The American doctors also found some Chamorros infected with the disease called locally *lytico-bodig*. The first death certificate under the U.S. naval government for this disease was in 1902. At first it was called "progressive muscular atrophy" by the Americans and later amyotrophic lateral sclerosis (ALS), known later in the United States as Lou Gehrig disease after the popular baseball player who died of it in 1941. The navy doctors were unable to prevent or cure the disease.

The new governor was rudely introduced to the hazards of the western Pacific when on 13 November 1900 a monstrous supertyphoon slammed into the island from out of the east. A marine in Agana gave an eyewitness account:

> The sea rose three feet in the streets, carrying buildings, trees and bridges away. Roads were torn up by falling trees, and only four stone buildings remained standing. The wind was very strong, blowing at the rate of 140 miles an hour, lifting the corrugated iron roof of the Governor's palace and carrying it out to sea. . . . It was

a pitiful sight to see men, women, and children out in the streets crying; mothers with babies in their arms looking for shelter.

At Apra Harbor, the *Yosemite* was at anchor with its engines disassembled for overhaul when the storm swept in. The ship's anchor lines parted, and the fierce winds drove the *Yosemite* over the Calalan Bank and out to sea, killing five sailors. The collier *Justin* put to sea the next day and found the *Yosemite* drifting helplessly northwest of Guam. The *Justin's* crew showed extraordinary heroism in the rescue of the sailors still on the *Yosemite* and in transferring $60,000 in Mexican gold coins to the collier. The *Yosemite* could not be towed, so the crews opened the sea valves, and the ship sank. It was the first American military vessel to join the many sunken Spanish ships in the deep blue waters off Guam. A replacement, the USS *Supply*, reached Guam in January 1903 and would remain until November 1917.

Thirty-four Chamorros died in the supertyphoon of 1900, with twenty-eight of these killed in Inarajan when enormous waves engulfed the village. Devastation was so widespread that Schroeder dispatched the *Justin* to Cavite for food and supplies. Schroeder wrenched his shoulder in a fall during the typhoon, and the stress may have made him touchy. In January 1901, he deported all ninety-six of the Carolinians living in María Cristina. They had stubbornly refused to clothe themselves as ordered by Leary. Unlike European visitors to Guam in the Spanish period, who viewed Carolinians as noble savages and disdained the Hispanicized Chamorros, the Americans held the opposite view. Schroeder wrote that the Carolinians were a "very low order of human animal . . . [who] contributed nothing to the welfare of the Island." So he sent them all to Saipan, where Georg Fritz welcomed them into the community of Carolinians still living there since Spanish times.

While the inhabitants of Guam were adjusting to U.S. military rule, the people of the Philippines had been waging war to get rid of the Americans. The U.S. Army captured the rebel leader Emilio Aguinaldo and other principal insurrectionists in February 1899. Aguinaldo subsequently took an oath of allegiance to the United States, was imprisoned for a time, and then freed. Other Filipino prisoners, however, refused to take the oath, notably the brilliant paralytic cripple Apolinario Mabini. The American commander, Major General Arthur MacArthur, Jr. (father of General Douglas A. MacArthur), sent these *irreconcilables* to Guam, just as the Spaniards had done with their Filipino rebels.

On 25 January 1901, thirty-four insurgent prisoners with fourteen servants arrived at Apra aboard the USAT *Rosecrans*. A week later, eleven more prisoners from Ilocos arrived on the USS *Solace*. Among the *Rosecrans* prisoners were Mabini, his brother Prudencio, and five generals. Governor Schroeder had his marines and the prisoners erect tents as a temporary prison at Asan in the vacant area where the last Spanish leprosarium had been wiped out by the typhoon of 1900. The camp was called the Presidio of Asan.

The exiles were allowed freedom to socialize with Americans and Chamorros, and Mabini wrote his memoirs. On 4 July 1902, the United States offered a pardon and amnesty to all Filipino insurgents who would take an oath of allegiance to the United States. Mabini and General Artemio Ricarte refused, but others accepted and departed Guam on 21 September 1902 for Manila on the USAT *Sheridan*. Three men opted to remain on Guam.

In February 1903, after two years of imprisonment, Mabini and Ricarte were finally allowed to return to Manila on the USAT *Thomas*. The Presidio of Asan was closed the same month. In Manila, before disembarking from the *Thomas*, Mabini took the oath of allegiance. Ricarte, however, again refused and was deported, eventually settling in Japan, recalcitrant to the end. Mabini, a tragic hero to his countrymen, who called him the "Sublime Paralytic," died of cholera on 13 May, three months after his arrival back in Manila. He was only thirty-eight years old.

The three former insurgents who chose not to return to the Philippines were the teacher-lawyer

Leon Flores (who founded a prominent local family), the lawyer Pancracio Palting (a future judge), and a young cook, Maximo Lorenzo Tolentino (who married Tomasa Crisostomo Lizama and raised a large family). Decades later, on 4 July 1961, the Filipino community erected on the Asan site a memorial to Filipino patriots held prisoner on Guam. The invocation at the ceremony was by Monsignor Felixberto Flores, son of Leon Flores. Proudly present was the last survivor of the Filipino exiles on Guam, the eighty-five-year-old former cook Maximo Lorenzo Tolentino.

Governor Schroeder had his staff conduct the first American census of Guam in August 1901. He reported the population as of 1 September as fourteen American citizens, 9,630 "citizens" of Guam, and thirty-two aliens (mostly Spaniards), for a total of 9,676 people on the island. There were actually more since he did not include U.S. military personnel in the report. These averaged about 158 in this period, mostly marines. Schroeder's census showed that the population of Guam had increased by almost 20 percent since Governor Olive's count of 8,199 inhabitants fifteen years earlier in 1886.

In late December 1901, the Chamorros of Guam presented another petition to the Americans. Thirty-two prominent island men requested Washington to send a commission to Guam to study ways to create a permanent civilian government on the island. The petition noted, "It is not an exaggeration to say that fewer permanent guarantees of liberty and property rights exist now than under Spanish domain."

Schroeder (who had already asked for a commission to study Guam's laws) endorsed the petition. The islanders described navy rule as "a military government of occupation," which should end since the war was over. By 1901, they feared that the naval government might become permanent. Their fears were justified; the Navy Department disapproved of any commissions to study civil issues.

Nevertheless, in 1903 the U.S. Senate passed a bill for a new government on Guam (but not necessarily a civilian one) in partial response to the petition. The House of Representatives let the matter die, mainly because of navy objections. The Chamorro petition of 1901 was the first in a long series of proposals that sought normal civil liberties and representative government for the people of Guam within the American federal system. The U.S. Navy consistently opposed every one of these proposals until 1950.

The navy's absolute authority on Guam was confirmed indirectly but definitively in 1901 by the U.S. Supreme Court in four cases that concerned the newly acquired insular territories. Collectively referred to as the *Insular Cases,* these arose over the Foracker Act of 1900, which established new tariff laws and a civil government in Puerto Rico. A major issue was whether constitutional restrictions (such as the Tenth Amendment) on congressional authority over the U.S. states also served to check federal power over the new island acquisitions, which were now called "flag territories" or "possessions."

The Supreme Court decided by a narrow five to four decision in the key case, *Downes v. Bidwell,* that the U.S. Constitution does not apply to the insular territories as it does to the states. This decision confirmed that the U.S. Congress has plenary power (i.e., unlimited authority) over all U.S. territories under Article IV, Section 3, paragraph 2 (called the Territorial Clause) of the Constitution. The reasoning of the majority was unabashedly Victorian in its racism, as expressed in the opinion of Justice Brown: "If these possessions are inhabited by alien races, differing from us in religion, customs, laws, methods of taxation and modes of thoughts, the administration of government and justice, according to Anglo-Saxon principles, may for a time be impossible."

In a concurring opinion, Justice White established a new territorial doctrine for the United States by making a distinction between "incorporated" and "unincorporated" territories. An incorporated territory is treated as part of the United States and may become a U.S. state. An unincorporated territory, on the other hand, is not "an integral part of the United States," according to Justice White, and thus not intended to become a U.S. state. The *Insular Cases* also clarified the distinction between "organized" and "unorganized" territories. Unorganized territories are those that have not received an "organic act" from the U.S. Congress to establish local self-government. Guam would be an unorganized territory until the 1950 Organic Act, but it remained an unincorporated territory.

It is worth noting a dissenting opinion in the *Insular Cases* by Justice Harlan:

> Whether a particular race will or will not assimilate with our people, and whether they can or cannot with safety to our institutions be brought within the operations of the Constitution, is a matter to be thought of when it is proposed to acquire their territory by treaty. A mistake in the acquisition of territory, although such acquisition seemed at the time to be necessary, cannot be the ground for violating the Constitution or refusing to give full effect to its provisions.

Unfortunately for the people of Guam, Justice Harlan's opinion did not become law. With considerable understatement, the U.S. attorney general informed the U.S. secretary of the navy in 1904 that, as a result of the *Insular Cases,* "the political status of these islands is anomalous. Neither the Constitution nor the laws of the United States have been extended to them." In other words, the navy could run the island as it wished.

Governor Schroeder in the meantime encouraged a back-to-the-farm movement with free grants of unclaimed land for agricultural use. Through this program, a number of ordinary Chamorro families obtained land for the first time. In June 1902, Schroeder established a leprosarium at Ypao on Tumon Bay, where twenty-five lepers and persons suffering from gangosa were isolated in a little camp of thatched huts. This camp lasted until 1912, when all remaining lepers were shipped involuntarily to a leprosarium on Culion Island south of Manila. Thereafter, until World War II, all lepers on Guam were sent to Culion for treatment. Most of these unfortunates died there.

Normal life on Guam was disrupted violently on 22 September 1902, when a tremendous earthquake struck the island at 11:24 A.M. The Agana church, Dulce Nombre de María, lost its bell tower once more, and one of the church walls collapsed. Bridges on the Agana-Piti road caved in, along with many coral masonry structures on the island. The Umatac church of San Dionisio was again left a pile of wooden rubble, just as in the great 1849 quake. The church would not be completely rebuilt until 1939 at a new location and this time of *mamposteria*. It still stands. One child was killed in the 1902 quake by falling debris. Tremors continued for an entire week, and public schools were closed for nearly two years. The extent of damage caused Schroeder to issue an order on 30 October to implement new construction standards to make buildings safer.

In the period 1901–1902, the first American topographical survey of Guam was accomplished under a young, energetic naval civil engineer, Leonard M. Cox, who was also chief of public works. Schroeder later had Cox write a description of Guam based on Cox's observations and Safford's writings. Schroeder persuaded the navy to publish the ninety-five-page study in 1904, and it became the standard guide in the pre–World War II era for Americans assigned to Guam. It was updated and republished in 1917 and 1926. In his original 1904 report, Cox noted that the people of Guam desired a civil government under a civilian governor and that they sought American citizenship as well as improvements in the island's infrastructure. This part of the original report was not included by the navy in later editions.

On 6 February 1903, Schroeder's two-and-a-half-year tenure as governor ended. By that date, the structure, the legal basis, and the military rationale for U.S. naval authority on Guam were firmly established. Until World War II, the island would be administered as if it were a ship, the "USS *Guam,*" with the governor as captain, U.S. military personnel as crew, and the Chamorros as mess attendants.

Ordered Tranquility
1903–1918

American Outpost

From 6 February 1903 until 10 December 1941, Seaton Schroeder was followed by over two dozen hardworking, sometimes capable, and sometimes obtuse American naval officers as governors and acting governors of Guam. These naval chief executives usually served short tours of duty, averaging only one year and five months each on Guam. Tours for American officers and enlisted men were deliberately kept short because of the unhealthy climate and poor living conditions on Guam in those days before air-conditioning. Officers received 10 percent additional salary and enlisted men 20 percent more as hardship pay for service on the island.

The short tours of American governors contrasted with the longer tenures of the sixty-three Spanish chief executives after Father San Vitores. The Spaniards had averaged three and a half years each on Guam. As a consequence of their short tenures, American governors rarely became knowledgeable about local conditions or the island people. These men all held midlevel ranks, and thus for most of them Guam was only a brief, somewhat exotic step on a career ladder to higher rank. For the people of the island, the naval and marine officers and their wives seemed mostly a blur of tall, red-faced men in starched white uniforms and delicately complected women in full-skirted dresses and wide-brimmed hats.

In the early 1900s, the daily life of the Chamorros still revolved around three basic institutions: the extended family, the church, and a subsistence economy based on farming family *lanchos* and some fishing. Every Monday morning there was a migration of whole families of Chamorros out of Agana and the villages to *lanchos,* some for a day or so, some for a week. There were as yet no metal plows; planting was done mostly by hand. Everyone returned at the weekend to their villages for church services, socializing, and cockfights. An American journalist visiting in 1905 called Guam "a lump of oriental loveliness" and described the average Chamorro as "less than a child, obstinately gentle, full of caprice . . . apparently wealthy, utterly poor." A German expatriate and longtime resident, Hermann Costenoble, wrote of the people of Guam, "As a matter of fact, everything that calls itself Chamorro has a wide and generous heart when approached by love." Neo-Chamorro traditional customs, called *i kustumbren Chamoru,* continued on, but a slow process of cultural erosion was under way as Americanization gathered momentum.

Political conditions, on the other hand, changed hardly at all on Guam. One of the most striking aspects of rule by the U.S. Navy on Guam was how little different it was for ordinary Chamorros from

Chamorro family hulling rice, early 1900s. Rice was cultivated on Guam from precontact times until the end of World War II, when large-scale cultivation ceased along with copra production. (From the collection of the Micronesian Area Research Center, Mangilao, Guam)

the previous Spanish military rule, other than the imposition of the English language and a more socially benevolent administration. The outside world, however, was changing rapidly in the early 1900s, linking Guam ever more tightly to the United States. Under Schroeder's successor, Commander William E. Sewell, Guam was connected by an undersea commercial telegraph cable to Manila on 1 June 1903 and with Midway, Honolulu, and San Francisco a month later on 4 July. This linkage completed the encirclement of the globe by cable, with a way station at Sumay village.

One of Governor Sewell's major acts was to formalize Guam's judicial system and procedures by General Order 69 issued on 30 November 1903. This system lasted with some changes until the 1930s, when Governor George A. Alexander established new laws based on California codes. Sewell also instituted new land tax rates in 1903 to replace the old Spanish tax of 1 percent of assessed value. The new tax varied with the type of property and location but was higher in any case than 1 percent. The Chamorros at that time were "land rich but dollar poor," and many did not have the cash to pay even this low property tax. The result was that, over the years, the naval government gradually acquired property through foreclosures for delinquent taxes, slowly alienating a number of Chamorros, mostly *manak'kilo,* from their land. Every year, "four to six titles, usually to poor land, reverted to the naval government," wrote one observer. Japanese migrants began to buy the choicest crop lands, which had the highest taxes, from the Chamorros.

The need to improve Apra Harbor's navigational buoys was dramatically demonstrated on 11 March 1904 when the cableship *Scotia* struck the Spanish Rocks of Calalan Bank. The acting governor, Lieutenant Raymond Stone, reported that the early morning sun blinded the captain and crew as the ship attempted to enter the harbor. The ship sank without loss of crew in shallow water not far from where the Spanish frigate *Infante Don Carlos* hit the same rocks and sank in 1814, giving them their name. New buoys and harbor lights were installed by the U.S. Navy, and the dangerous rocks were eventually covered after World War II by the huge breakwater constructed by the Americans over the Calalan Bank and the Luminao Reef. By the time of Governor George L. Dyer (May 1904–November 1905), governors were generally required to obtain approval of the Navy Department before issuing orders on new policies for Guam, and the navy became increasingly inflexible on political matters. In 1905, the navy approved a change of the old Spanish titles of village officials to English versions. The four appointed district *gobernadorcillos* became commissioners.

A positive step by the navy was the creation in 1905 of a local civil service, separate from the U.S. Civil Service, for islanders and Americans employed by the naval government. Under Dyer, the Maria Schroeder Hospital was enlarged on 5 October 1905. A new wing was named after Susana Dyer, the governor's wife, who obtained a $10,000 endowment for the hospital from the Russell Sage Foundation. The new wing served only women and children for modest fees. The enlarged facility became the Naval Hospital, serving military

and civilian patients (treatment was still free to Chamorros) in the area where today Guam's first skyscraper, the ten-story Pacific News Building stands. To help staff the medical complex, American naval nurses began to be assigned to Guam in 1910–1911.

In 1905, Governor Dyer disbanded the Insular Artillery and replaced it with the Insular Patrol, composed of a dozen marine enlisted men under a marine officer who also served as chief of police. The marines were assigned to the island's four districts, where they worked with the commissioners as police and also acted as foresters and game wardens and even taught English and served as principals in village schools, all new functions for American marines. By 1909, the superintendent of public education would be a discharged marine. A separate, small civilian police force of one sergeant and ten policemen, all Chamorros, served mainly in Agana under the chief of police.

Because of imprecise property boundaries on Guam, in 1905 Governor Dyer requested a detailed cadastral survey of the island and its waters by the U.S. Coast and Geodetic Survey Bureau. The U.S. Navy had acquired all Spanish crown lands when Guam came under American rule, but the precise sizes and locations of crown parcels were not clear. Crown property was initially estimated by the surveyor Cox to total about 105 square miles, or 67,200 acres (27,196 hectares), nearly half the total island and offshore islet land area of 214 square miles. Later estimates placed crown lands at about half Cox's figure, that is, about 36,000 acres (14,581 hectares), or about one-quarter of the island.

Most land was unsurveyed outside Agana and the main villages, so a major task for the U.S. Navy was to conduct an island-wide cadastral land survey. Dyer's request for a cadastral survey was approved, and piecemeal cadastral plots of Agana and other specific areas, and small-scale (mainly 1:20,000 and 1:62,500) topographic and hydrographic maps of the island, were made sporadically over the coming years. As incredible as it may seem, however, a comprehensive and thorough cadastral survey of the whole island has yet to be completed as of the early 1990s.

In consequence, transfers of land titles on Guam ever since 1899 have often been inaccurate and temptingly susceptible to fraud. By 1915, Governor William J. Maxwell complained that land ownership "was the source of many crimes and scandals, family feuds, and much protracted litigation." Poor land management, questionable tax assessments and condemnations, massive court litigation, and huge real estate swindles would occur in the decades ahead as consequences of inadequate cadastral information. Island-wide home mail delivery is still impossible as of the 1990s because many houses do not yet have numbered street addresses. The absence of a detailed cadastral survey of the entire island constitutes one of the major failures of American government on Guam in the twentieth century.

It was in the year 1907 that racial segregation was officially instituted on Guam. Segregation of races under Jim Crow laws for schools, housing, and so forth had been legal in the United States since the Supreme Court case of *Plessy v. Ferguson* in 1896. On Guam, Naval Station Order 47 in 1907 decreed that the Navy Department "opposed marriages between Marines and natives except in specially meritorious cases which must be referred to the [navy] Secretary." Later, the order was extended to cover navy enlisted men as well.

As might be expected, these efforts would fail to keep lonely marines and sailors on Guam from marrying Chamorritas in the coming years, even in cases that were not "specially meritorious," whatever that meant. One of the first Americans to marry a Chamorrita was Marcelo Sgambelluri, a young musician in the navy band who in 1905 organized an all-Chamorro band. He married Joaquina D. Camacho, and the Sgambelluri family is still prominent on Guam. A marine who was a village schoolteacher in 1903, Corporal James H. Underwood, was also one of the first Americans to marry a local woman—Ana Martinez. Another marine, First Sergeant John F. McDonald, married Dolores Mariano of Agana in 1908. These new

Chamorro-American families assumed increasing prominence in the decades ahead.

While American naval administration of Guam was settling into routine colonial patterns, the geopolitics of Oceania acquired new dimensions in the early years of the twentieth century. President McKinley won reelection in 1900, only to die from an assassin's bullets on 4 September 1901. Vice President Teddy Roosevelt succeeded to the presidency and was reelected in 1904. Under his big stick diplomacy, a new republic—Panama—was carved out of Colombia in 1903–1904 with American help to permit the U.S. Army Corps of Engineers to construct the Panama Canal. Started in 1906 and completed in 1914, the canal would enable the U.S. Navy, until then primarily an Atlantic fleet, to operate in either the Pacific or the Atlantic, or in both. These developments locked Guam permanently into a line of communications for American military and commercial interests across Oceania to the Philippines from the U.S. West Coast and Central America in almost a replica of the Spanish Pacific empire.

By this period, Japan was the dominant naval power in East Asia, but it lacked natural resources to continue its industrial growth. To obtain resources, Japan was expanding in two directions: one into North Asia to gain access to the iron, coal, and other assets of Manchuria, and the other southward through Micronesia to reach the tin, oil, and rubber of Southeast Asia. Japanese companies began to dominate the copra industry and other commerce on Guam and in the rest of Micronesia. The Germans in Micronesia, overextended and far from their European heartland, were not perceived by the Americans to be as much of a threat in the Pacific as the Japanese.

On 30 November 1908, U.S. Secretary of State Elihu Root and Japanese Ambassador Takahira-Kogorō exchanged diplomatic notes that created an agreement by which the two countries pledged mutual respect for the status quo and for each other's territories in the Pacific. Under the Root-Takahira agreement, the north-south line of communications of Japan into Micronesia and the east-west line of American communications to the Philippines crossed peacefully, for the time being, in the western Pacific Ocean. This situation created the potential for confrontation as the two nations' strategic interests became increasingly competitive. Guam was at the geographic center of this premonitory Japanese-American rivalry in the western Pacific.

As the new geopolitical scene unfolded in Oceania, the U.S. Navy began in 1904 to ask for funds from the U.S. Congress to fortify Guam. To back up these requests, in 1906 the navy started to formulate secret contingency war plans, each called "War Plan Orange," which cast Japan (designated by the color orange; the United States is always blue in American war plans) as the enemy in a future war. A premise of the Orange Plans was that the U.S. Army would defend the Philippines until the U.S. Navy could carry reinforcements and supplies across the Pacific. The navy's mission thus depended on holding Hawai'i and, if possible, Guam to secure the line of communications to the Philippines. The U.S. Army War College began to hold Blue-Orange war games in the 1907–1908 academic year. Simultaneously, Japanese naval planners were becoming aware of the strategic significance of Micronesia to Japan's national security. The first Japanese naval maneuvers against the U.S. Navy as the hypothetical enemy were held in 1908, and in 1910 the Japanese began to draft their own battle plans to defeat the United States in case of war.

The American Plan Orange was revised repeatedly, becoming joint army-navy plans, and in the 1911 version reasserted the "absolute necessity" of building heavily fortified bases at Hawai'i and Guam. The American Congress, however, assumed that war in the Pacific was unlikely and repeatedly refused to provide money for any large-scale fortifications on the American islands west of Hawai'i. A corollary of the American Orange Plans and of navy policies in general was that any interference in military authority on Guam by civilian concerns was to be opposed in the interests of U.S. national

security. The highly secret Orange Plans were not known, of course, to the people of Guam and would be kept secret until after World War II.

To placate the navy and enhance island security at minimal cost, President William H. Taft, a one-term Republican who succeeded Roosevelt in 1909–1913, issued an order on 23 September 1912 that Guam (along with Guantanamo Bay in Cuba, Pearl Harbor, and Subic Bay) be closed as a port to all "foreign vessels of commerce . . . except by special authority." This questionable order was the first of several such edicts that would keep Guam isolated from American and international commerce for the next fifty years, except for local trading ships, yet paradoxically would not prevent foreign spying on the island.

On Guam, naval governors routinely came and went. In 1908–1910, Governor Edward J. Dorn, who stressed the Americanization of Guam, instituted official observance of U.S. federal holidays. Also under Dorn, American currency became Guam's sole medium of financial exchange in July 1909, and in October the U.S. Congress authorized duty-free importation of Guam products into the United States and its territories. As an additional protective measure, Dorn prohibited aliens from purchasing or leasing Guam land for periods longer than five years. He wanted to curb the power of Japanese merchants, who, he reported, "still control the major part of the business of the Island." American citizens, on the other hand, were permitted to lease land on the island for up to fifty years.

Under Dorn, Guam's first newspaper, the *Guam News Letter,* was initiated in May 1909. A monthly in both English and Spanish, it was written by naval personnel. The Spanish language portions were dropped in 1911. Wire service news came daily by telegraphic cable from San Francisco and was censored before publication of any disastrous events or matters that threw a bad light on the United States. One of the paper's first local news scoops was of the 10 December 1909 earthquake on Guam that destroyed the Susana Hospital and damaged the old Agana church, still in disrepair from the 1902 quake. The hospital was immediately rebuilt, but not so the church. In 1910, the first commercial advertisement appeared in the *Guam News Letter,* that of Jacques Schnabel & Company, importers and wholesalers.

In July 1910, Governor Dorn also established the Island Court, with two judges to replace the Court of First Instance, which had only one judge. As since 1899, there were no trials by jury, and no decisions could be appealed beyond the island, even in capital cases. Maintaining law and order among the Chamorros was not a problem since all guns were strictly controlled, but by Dorn's tenure the heavy caseload of the trial court had backed up, owing to the tangle of Spanish laws and navy civil orders. As a remedy, Dorn created the island's first public prosecutor, called the "Island Attorney" at the time and later the attorney general. Despite the efforts of Dorn and later governors, the problem of inadequate police and judicial resources to cope with heavy legal caseloads would never be resolved on Guam.

It was also in 1910 that a schism threatened the Catholic hierarchy on Guam. Back in 1907, the Vatican removed the Marianas from the Diocese of Cebú, and the islands were made an apostolic prefecture under a German Capuchin order. A German, the Reverend Father Paul of Kirchhausen, was appointed apostolic prefect that year; he resided in Saipan. In 1910, he attempted to appoint another German Capuchin, Father Peter Callistus, to Agat. This provoked a local uproar. When Kirchhausen arrived at Apra Harbor with Callistus, Dorn refused to permit the two German Capuchins to stay, and they returned to Saipan. Callistus later wrote a Chamorro grammar in German. This intervention in church matters earned Dorn sardonic acclaim in a poem by an anonymous member of the Civilian Club of Guam in 1910:

> Salam! Salam!
> I'm the Governor of Guam,
> I'm glorious and great,
> I'm a pampered potentate,
> So I am,
> I run things as I please,

> Get down on your knees,
> I'm the ruler of the tightest
> little island in the seas,
> That's me!
> Those who do not like my way,
> I shut up or send away,
> I'm a wonder and I know it,—
> Of the thirty-third degree.

To quiet matters, in 1911 the Catholic church separated Guam from the other Marianas and made it an apostolic vicariate under a Spanish Franciscan Capuchin order from Catalonia. The Most Reverend Francis Xavier Vila y Mateu de Arenysele was named Guam's first apostolic vicar. He arrived in 1912 with four Catalonian Capuchins but died a year later. His place was eventually taken in 1915 by Monsignor (later bishop) Felipe Joaquin M. Olaiz y Zabalza, who served until 1934. Olaiz and all subsequent Spanish missionaries on Guam were ultraconservative Basques from the Capuchin Order of Navarre.

The acquisition of Guam had in the meantime attracted the attention of American Protestant missionaries. The American Board of Commissioners for Foreign Missions, a Boston-based interdenominational agency that had successfully established missions in the Hawaiian Islands, Kosrae, and Pohnpei, decided to send five American Congregational missionaries to Guam under the leadership of Reverend Francis M. Price and his wife. This dedicated little group founded the first Protestant mission and church on Guam in 1901 with the help, among others, of Major Kelton of the U.S. Marines, the Vicente M. Taitano family of Santa Rosa, and two brothers, José and Luis Castro (sometimes called Custino), and their families.

The Protestant community grew despite Catholic antipathy. Within a few years, about thirty local families were meeting regularly at the mission compound established by Reverend Price and his family at Adelup, which Price called Missionary Point. In 1905, the Prices were replaced by the Reverend H. B. Case and his wife, but funds from Boston ran out, and the mission closed in 1910. The Congregationalists were replaced in September 1911 by Baptist missionaries under Reverend Arthur U. Logan and his wife, who would remain for eleven years. Protestantism persevered on Guam during the coming decades, but it never made serious inroads among the overwhelmingly Catholic population on the island. In reaction to the Protestants, the Catholics organized a number of new religious societies on Guam to strengthen their solidarity.

By 1912, under Governor Robert E. Coontz, life on Guam for the Americans was fully settled into the placid colonial tedium of a small tropical outpost. Americans were beginning to find duty on the island rather pleasant, as Captain Coontz wrote: "The routine of a day at Guam . . . was to arise fairly early while it was cool. . . . I was in my office until one o'clock when we had lunch, after which we rested for a short time during the intense heat of the day, returning to work until four-thirty. From that time until six-thirty practically all the men and some of the ladies played tennis. . . . Socially there was some activity nearly every night."

Coontz, who had been on the *Charleston* when Captain Glass seized Guam, was a genial conservative who proposed few civil changes. He was, however, an energetic proponent of fortifying Guam. In this he was supported by the naval strategist Alfred Mahan, who declared, "Our every interest in the Pacific" could be secured by converting Guam into "a kind of Gibraltar." Coontz went on to become a four-star admiral and the chief of naval operations, but neither he nor Mahan, who led a "Guam lobby" in Washington, could persuade Congress to fortify Guam.

It was under Coontz in 1912 that the old Agana church was torn down. The historic Spanish-built church had huge pillars of unhewn *ifil* tree trunks as interior supports, but the structure was unsafe since the earthquakes of 1902 and 1909. Fierce typhoons on 15–17 December 1912 and 10 November 1913 delayed construction, and a handsome new domed cathedral, still named Dulce Nombre de María, was not completed until 1917

under the dedicated supervision of Father Luís de Leon.

Despite efforts at Americanization, by 1913 commerce on Guam was still dominated by hardworking Japanese firms and merchants, notably by the Nambō company regionally and by José Katsuji Ogawa (Kazug) Shimizu on Guam. To counter the Japanese, in 1913 the Navy Department invited a San Francisco trading firm—Atkins, Kroll & Company—to establish a branch on Guam to grow copra and import American goods. The invitation was accepted by the firm's head, Clifton H. Kroll, and the company set up an office in Agana and a warehouse in Piti in 1914. This resilient firm soon became the largest private business on Guam, and it would go on to diversify and survive both World Wars I and II. The company continues to serve the people of Guam in the 1990s, the oldest on the island.

The health of the island people was still a problem by the eve of World War I. In 1913, a measles epidemic with over 2,000 cases took more than three dozen lives, and, in 1915, whooping cough killed sixty Chamorro children. On the other hand, gangosa had been almost completely eradicated by this period, and a naval dentist was serving the population for the first time. A free sanitarium for tubercular patients was opened in 1916 on San Ramón Hill near the island's sole "high school" (actually a kind of vocational junior high until 1930, when Seaton Schroeder Junior High was built in Agana).

Regardless of persistent health problems among the Chamorros, the quality of life on the island was gradually improving. Since 1911 the navy had operated a small oil-fueled generator that supplied limited power for the radio station and electric lights in Agana, mostly in American installations and officers' quarters as well as to downtown streetlights and some businesses. Baseball was becoming a favorite sport of Chamorro youths, even though the navy forbade the use of the Chamorro language on the playing fields in order to encourage the use of English. A few Ford Model-Ts and motorcycles chugged up and down Agana's dusty streets, still paved only with crushed *cascajo*. One of the autos was owned by Frank Portusach, by then a well-off rancher.

There were also by this period six "saloons" in Agana and sixteen "public women," who depended "almost entirely on the enlisted force of the United States for their support," according to the governor's report of 1915. These local prostitutes were given navy medical checkups every Monday and came to be known as "Monday Ladies."

Public education on Guam was expanding but remained inadequate. Schools were perpetually overcrowded owing to shortages of classrooms, particularly in the southern villages. There was no coeducation; boys went to school in the morning, and girls used the same classrooms in the afternoon. All students were given free periodic medical examinations by naval doctors assisted by Chamorro practical nurses, a small number of whom were graduating each year from the Native Nurses Training School established in 1910 at Susana Hospital.

English had largely replaced Spanish in schools, government offices, courts, and most businesses by 1914, but Chamorro was still the dominant language in local homes and gatherings. Employment in the government bureaucracy was becoming a career for more and more Chamorro men, so in 1914 Governor William J. Maxwell, an innovative but unstable executive, created the first local retirement fund for the Guam civil service. Employees could obtain loans against their retirement accounts, a service that for the first time provided Chamorros some capital for major purchases and investments.

Two local civilian wage rates evolved: one rate for American citizens and a considerably lower one for Chamorros, even if they performed the same work. By 1912, a few Chamorro men had been permitted to enlist in the U.S. Navy, but only as mess attendants. Despite the racial inequity in navy hiring and the double standard in wage scales, and because the private sector paid even lower wages, government jobs with the prospect of retirement benefits became the mainstay of Guam's economy.

By this time, the Chamorros were no longer growing as much food on their *lanchos* as before. Governor Maxwell noted unhappily, "The whole population is now almost wholly maintained directly or indirectly by the allotments from Appropriations, Navy, for the maintenance of the Naval Establishment."

To reduce this dependency on government, Maxwell proposed that Guam be made an open port for normal commerce. His appeal was refused by higher authorities, who included by this period as assistant secretary of the navy a young, wealthy New Yorker named Franklin Delano Roosevelt. It was Roosevelt in 1914 who rebuffed a proposal by Maxwell that U.S. citizenship be considered for the people of Guam. As acting secretary of the navy, Roosevelt wrote, "The Department does not consider that the public interests make it desirable at this time to take up the general question of the citizenship of persons residing on Guam." Roosevelt's opposition "at this time" endured as navy policy for the next thirty-five years, until the Organic Act of 1950.

It was Governor Maxwell who one day at the end of June 1914 received the news from the Sumay cable station of the assassination of an Austro-Hungarian archduke in Europe. The governor was unaware that this distant event marked the beginning of another repetition of the parable of the tribes, this time on a gigantic scale called World War I. Maxwell also did not know that the consequences of that event would soon bring a German warship to its death on Guam and would drive him to a nervous breakdown.

The *Cormoran* and Preparations for War

The archduke's assassination alerted the Japanese more than it did the Americans, or even the Germans, to the potentialities of the oncoming war in the Pacific. Having laid the basis of their strategy by allying themselves with Great Britain since 1902, the Japanese quickly prepared in July and August 1914 to displace the Germans throughout Micronesia with British backing. The United States remained passive under the neutralist, nonprovocative foreign policy of the president who succeeded Taft, Woodrow Wilson, a two-term Democrat who served from 1913 to 1921.

Following the outbreak of war in Europe in early August 1914, Japan declared war on Germany on 23 August, and the Japanese navy swiftly seized the islands of German Micronesia. Japan claimed strategic control over all of what was formerly German Micronesia by 20 October 1914. New Zealand troops took German Western Samoa, and Australian forces occupied most of German Melanesia. With no significant ground garrisons in their Pacific colonies, the Germans mounted only token resistance.

The rapidity and breadth of the Japanese occupation of Micronesia stunned not only the Germans but also the Americans. Even the British were not pleased by their ally's audacity. The entire balance of power in Oceania was altered, leaving the United States and Japan to face each other uneasily north of the equator and Britain and France with their dominions and colonies dominant south of that line in the Pacific.

Little Guam was a neutral oasis in the midst of the swirl of war around it. It was not long, however, before Guam became involved when the American steamer *Rio Passig,* leased by the Germans to recoal their ships, entered Apra Harbor on 17 August in search of its lessors. Governor Maxwell, suspicious that the ship was violating U.S. neutrality in the war, interned it and forbade its crew the use of the Sumay cable station until the Navy Department ordered the ship released on 21 August. The *Rio Passig* departed on 15 September, only to be captured later by the British.

Next, a thirty-foot cutter in near-sinking condition sailed into Apra on 28 October with an exhausted crew of three German officers and four Papuan crewmen. They had voyaged against contrary winds and rough seas from Lamotrek Atoll in the Carolines. Their mission was to make arrangements for their mother ship, the German auxiliary cruiser SMS *Cormoran,* to recoal at Guam. The *Cormoran,* formerly the Russian ship *Riasan,* a

mail carrier out of Vladivostock before its capture by the Germans, was hiding at Lamotrek from the Japanese and desperately needed coal to escape from the Pacific. After dispatching the thirty-foot cutter to Guam to arrange for coal, Captain Adalbert Zuckschwerdt of the *Cormoran* kept his ship on radio silence at Lamotrek for the next two months as the allied noose tightened around the few German ships still in the Pacific. When the cutter failed to return, and after friendly Carolinian canoe voyagers warned that the Japanese were converting nearby Truk into a major base with many warships, Zuckschwerdt decided to make a run for Guam before the Japanese located him. On 12 December, with barely enough coal to reach the Marianas, the *Cormoran* steamed out of Lamotrek and headed north at top speed. On 14 December, the ship anchored in Apra Harbor with less than fifty tons of coal left.

Captain Zuckschwerdt promptly requested large amounts of provisions and 1,500 tons of coal from Maxwell in order to steam to German East Africa for safe haven. When Maxwell could only provide 200 tons of coal and limited provisions from Guam's small stocks, Zuckschwerdt resigned himself to internment. Maxwell went aboard the *Cormoran* on 15 December to impose the conditions of internment. Neutral nations normally removed interned crews from their ships, but in this case there were no readily available facilities to house the Germans on Guam, so they remained aboard the *Cormoran.* Firing pins were removed from the ships' eight 10.5-centimeter guns, but small arms were allowed to be retained on board by the crew. Radio use was restricted, but unarmed crew members were permitted ashore in the Agana-Piti area in uniform.

These were mild restrictions. Maxwell was well aware that the 373 men on the *Cormoran,* which included twenty-eight Papuans and four Chinese laundrymen, outnumbered the American marines on Guam. Berlin subsequently authorized the German ambassador in Washington to send substantial checks periodically to pay for provisions for the internees. Highly disciplined, the German officers and sailors avoided any disorderly conduct as they settled down in early 1915 for a long stay. Captain Zuckschwerdt proceeded to rent quarters in Agana and to buy a Ford from Atkins, Kroll. When in May 1915 the Russian government requested that the *Cormoran-Riasan* be returned to it, the U.S. State Department refused on technical grounds.

The outbreak of war in Europe and the Pacific had in the meantime stirred up considerable activity on Guam. In March–April 1914, a joint U.S. Army-Navy Board visited the island to assess defense needs. As a result, War Plan Orange was revised with an estimate that, in case of war, 8,500 marines would be needed to defend Guam. It was assumed at the time by military planners that the reefs around the island would deter a massive enemy invasion. As before, Congress did not authorize anything near what the military proposed. Instead, the marine battalion was increased in early 1914 by only 200 men.

Additionally, a new local military unit was formed, the Insular Force (not to be confused with the Insular Patrol, which was still functioning) to assist navy personnel at the port. Popular with the locals, the Insular Force numbered thirty-eight Chamorros by June 1915, and it would grow in the coming years to over 100 men. Chamorros jokingly called them *marinon mantiquilla* (butter sailors) because they enlisted to obtain navy commissary privileges. Access to military commissaries and post exchanges with their reduced prices has been a powerful inducement for Chamorros to have at least one family member work for the military ever since the Americans took over Guam.

Among the officers who arrived in 1914 with the joint U.S. Army-Navy Board was an exceptional marine officer who would become a legend, Captain Earl Hancock (Pete) Ellis. After the board departed in May, he stayed on as police chief, in which capacity he was also head of the Insular Patrol and intelligence officer for the military command on Guam. Bright and innovative, but at times bizarrely nonconformist owing to alcoholism, Ellis in 1915 demonstrated the practicality of amphibi-

ous assaults over reefs (a new concept at the time) by successfully landing a squad of marines by boat with a 4.7-inch gun and crossing the reef to Gab Gab Beach in Apra Harbor. These exercises revealed for the first time the vulnerability of Guam to seaborne invasion despite the encircling reefs, if the invaders were well supported by offshore naval gunfire.

Ellis actively engaged in intelligence gathering. At the time, the navy undertook intelligence missions through its Office of Naval Intelligence (ONI). Ellis, as Guam's ONI officer, posed as a businessman and reconnoitered Saipan, from which he theorized—correctly, as history would show—that a Japanese attack would be launched against Guam. Ellis also assigned one of his enlisted men in the Insular Patrol, a German-speaking corporal named Hans George Hornbostel, to determine if Hermann Costenoble was a German spy, as Ellis suspected. Costenoble, formerly of the German army, had settled on Saipan in 1903 and moved to Guam a year later. He became a prosperous farmer in the Atantano area with stores in Agana, Piti, and Sumay. At one time, he was director of agriculture for the U.S. naval government. Hans dutifully befriended the Costenoble family by dating one of the daughters, Gertrude. The young corporal confirmed that the father was indeed a German patriot and probably an agent for Berlin, but in the meantime Hornbostel fell in love with Gertrude. If the father were arrested, Hans would lose Gertrude.

He decided to ask the father for Gertrude's hand, but the old man, now suspicious of the young marine, refused. The two lovers then eloped and were married by the Reverend Arthur Logan at the Protestant church in Agana beneath an arbor of *cadena de amor* (chain of love, *Antigonon leptopus*), a pink and white flowered vine introduced to Guam by the Spaniards from Mexico. Hans turned in his reports on Costenoble, but the governor allowed the father to remain free for the time being.

Ellis in the meantime was transferred back to the mainland, where he wrote the seventy-seven-page "Report of a Military Reconnaissance of the Island of Guam, 1914–1915," in which he concluded that

Guam could be defended for a limited time and with great difficulty by a marine battalion if it retreated into strongholds on Orote Peninsula and in the Mount Tenjo area instead of trying to hold the beaches. He also suggested that a seaplane landing channel was feasible in Apra Harbor. Like many American military officers, Ellis did not believe that the Chamorros could manage self-government very well. He wrote, "The use of authority to favor friends and 'soak' enemies is the rule among native officials." Ellis would go on to become a combat hero in France after the United States entered the war, but this was not the last that Guam would see of him, or of Hans and Gertrude Hornbostel.

World War I increased demand in Japan for coconut oil, and Guam's copra production doubled from prewar sales of 1 million pounds annually. With the growth in the economy, Governor Maxwell established the Bank of Guam as a governmental entity in December 1915 (it opened on 3 January 1916) with an initial reserve of $15,000 in gold. The increased workload imposed by all the wartime developments began to affect Governor Maxwell. High-strung, with a short temper, he became autocratic. He prohibited whistling in public to stop Chamorro boys from mischievously whistling the wrong cadence when naval personnel were marching. At a baseball game, he chewed out an umpire (one of his own officers) in public, causing the game to be called. His relations with his staff and with Captain Zuckschwerdt also deteriorated.

In a dramatic incident, Governor Maxwell ordered the first execution of a man since the U.S. Navy took control of Guam. A Filipino, Pablo M. Corpus, found guilty of murder in December 1913, was hanged on 4 February 1916, after exhausting all appeals. Maxwell ordered the hanging despite a petition by a large number of local citizens to commute the sentence to life imprisonment.

The stress of these matters apparently pushed Maxwell to a nervous breakdown. On 29 April 1916, according to a terse statement in the *Annual*

Report of 1916, "Captain W. J. Maxwell was relieved from duty on account of illness, and on May 12th he sailed for the United States." He departed under a medical escort. After a brief interim of several acting governors, Captain Roy C. Smith became governor on 30 May.

Relations with the German internees immediately improved. The *Cormoran's* excellent thirty-five-piece band began playing regular performances in the Plaza de España and occasionally at the governor's residence. A typical morning at the plaza in 1916 was described by a resident:

> Guam was like the setting of a comic opera . . . there passed by, going about their business, American Naval officers in spotless white, Marine officers in white or khaki, German officers from the *Cormoran* in meticulous uniform, native men with their shirt tails always hanging out, lovely women of the island tightly swathed from waist down in their gaily colored trained skirts with sheer bouffant blouses of piña cloth, Marines in khaki, Franciscan monks in their brown cassocks and rope belts, American women carrying bright Japanese parasols, and German sailors on bicycles with ribbons dangling from their child-like straw hats.

Concerned about the defense of Guam in case of war with Germany, which had a respectable battle fleet based in China, the navy replaced the old six-inch guns at Orote with eight newer six-inch cannons and twelve three-inch guns. A tug, the USS *Piscataqua,* was assigned in 1916 as an auxiliary to the USS *Supply* at Apra and would remain until 1929.

On 15 January 1917, the General Board of the U.S. Navy made a secret study entitled "Strategic Problem, Pacific," which revised the 1914 Orange Plan and estimated that 185,000 troops would be needed to defend Hawai'i, Guam, and the Philippines. Later, Governor Smith recommended a defense force of 37,000 men on Guam alone, backed by 100 destroyers, fifty submarines, and six mine layers, to defend against a hypothetical invasion by 250,000 Japanese troops. The reefs were now acknowledged not to be a barrier to amphibious assaults. None of these fantastic estimates ever came close to being realized as demands in the Atlantic and in France took priority over the Pacific in the American war effort.

While naval strategists debated, Governor Smith, with Navy Department concurrence, took unprecedented initiatives on Guam. In early 1917, he established the First Guam Congress. It was a unicameral body made up of thirty-four "legislators" who were commissioners, deputy commissioners, and other prominent Chamorros, plus three American officers ex officio, all appointed by the governor. One of the officers was the new commanding officer of the marines, Major Edward B. Manwaring.

The first session of the Guam Congress opened on 3 February 1917 with a formal speech by the governor. He suggested that the congress focus on local economic matters. The Chamorro members, however, immediately began to debate political issues, as expressed boldly in a speech by member Tomás Calvo Anderson: "It is high time that there be granted to the people [of Guam], respectful, loyal, and devoted to the great American nation, the same rights that have been granted to the different States, territories and possessions...that we may know whether we are to be members of the American people or their servitors."

The Chamorros received a negative reply from the navy in a special session of the Congress on 17 March when Major Manwaring stated, "I am authorized to say that the Congress is intended as an advisory body to the Governor. Its recommendations should be limited to matters in the power of the Governor to regulate. Other matters cannot be even considered by the Governor....Hence any power not within the power of the Governor to regulate cannot be considered by him and is out of order in the Congress."

This circular but nonetheless clear message dampened the hopes of the Chamorros. The Guam Congress would continue to meet dutifully but unenthusiastically to discuss village affairs once a month or so over the next fourteen years until it was dissolved in 1931. Inevitably, public interest in the powerless Guam Congress waned, and in the coming years it became simply a rubber stamp for the governors, when it was not ignored by them.

Governor Smith also resurrected an island militia for the first time since the Spanish period. It grew out of a rifle club and an elite unit called the Guam Cadets organized in June 1912 of high school boys. In late 1916, Chamorro leaders petitioned the governor to establish military training for all the island's young men. The governor responded favorably and on 15 March 1917 decreed universal military training on Guam. All physically fit males between ages sixteen and twenty-three were to serve active duty in the Guam Militia.

By 30 June 1917, there were 920 enthusiastic Chamorros in the militia's three battalions of sixteen companies, with one or more companies from each village. The whole force was under the commanding officer of the marines, and, extraordinarily, the troops were unpaid. As under the Spanish, the Chamorro men responded with zeal to a purposeful cause that organized their otherwise unused energies. Smith requested Washington to send Springfield rifles and ammunition for the militia and planned to have it grow into a force of 2,000 "fully trained and efficient infantry." It never grew to that size, usually numbering around 900 men, but in 1919 the militia would be officially designated as part of the U.S. Naval Reserve.

Relations between the Americans and the interned Germans continued to be correct, and at times even more so. On 1 January 1917, an American naval nurse, Eleanore Blain, married Lieutenant Karl von Gebhard, an officer on the Cormoran. Major Manwaring performed the civil ceremony, followed by a religious wedding by Reverend Logan. One hundred American, German, and Chamorro guests danced at the reception in the Agana home of Doctor and Mrs. A. E. Peck, the head of the Naval Hospital, to music by the Cormoran's band.

The good feelings soured on 4 February 1917, when U.S. diplomatic relations with Germany were severed as a result of U-boat attacks on American ships. It was becoming clear that the United States might soon be at war with Germany. Governor Smith politely but firmly imposed tighter restrictions on the Germans and had the *Cormoran* inspected by his aide, Lieutenant Owen Bartlett, for explosive charges the Germans might use to scuttle the ship. None were found.

Captain Zuckschwerdt sold his Ford, and he and the other internees who lived ashore, including the newly wed von Gebhard, moved back aboard the *Cormoran*. On 2 April, when Zuckschwerdt learned that war would soon be declared against Germany by the United States, he secretly ordered that six drums of coal dust mixed with gasoline and armed with electrical blasting caps be hidden in the ship's forward starboard coal bunker next to the hull. He then waited to see what the Americans would do.

Guam and World War I

Captain Zuckschwerdt did not have long to wait. Early on the morning of 7 April 1917 (6 April by Washington, D.C., time, which is nine hours behind Guam time), Governor Smith received a coded flash cable that war had been declared. As previously planned, the governor immediately dispatched Lieutenants Bartlett and William F. Lafrenz (chief of the navy yard) to demand surrender of the *Cormoran*. While they were on their way from Agana in the official Ford sedan, U.S. Marine batteries on Orote and the slopes of Mount Tenjo were trained on the *Cormoran* to fire in case of German resistance. The station ship *Supply* moved to block the harbor entrance. At the Piti landing, the two lieutenants boarded the governor's "barge," actually a large, sleek mahogany speed boat, with an Insular Force crew and several armed marines under Lieutenant W. A. Hall to take over the German ship as a prize.

As the governor's barge set out, the prize party saw coming toward them the *Cormoran*'s daily supply launch under the command of von Gebhard, who was given the duty so that he could visit with his American bride at the dock. On seeing who was in the governor's barge, von Gebhard promptly turned back toward the *Cormoran*. The faster American boat pulled up parallel to the German launch, and Hall ordered Marine Corporal Michael B. Chockie to fire a shot across von Gebhard's bow to halt him.

Chockie stood up with his rifle and fired a shot. The Germans continued on until a second shot by another marine, apparently (this is a matter of controversy) Lieutenant Hall with his .45-caliber pistol, caused them to heave to. Hall and some marines then took the Germans to Piti in the *Cormoran*'s launch as prisoners of war while the barge went on. Only about two hours had elapsed since President Wilson had signed the declaration of war. Therefore, the shot by Chockie was the first one fired by an American in World War I. This action made the corporal something of a celebrity the rest of his life.

Meanwhile, Bartlett and Lafrenz proceeded to the *Cormoran*, where Bartlett alone went aboard just before eight o'clock. He presented a brief letter to Zuckschwerdt from Smith that demanded "the immediate and unconditional surrender of the ship and personnel." The German captain offered to turn over his officers and men but said that he could not surrender the ship. Shrewdly, he then asked Bartlett to submit that offer to Governor Smith.

Bartlett, put off by this unforeseen equivocation, replied, "When your answer is received, you will be treated as the enemy." He then saluted and left to deliver the offer to Smith. This was a mistake. While Bartlett was rejoining Lafrenz on the barge, Zuckschwerdt had all secret documents burned and gave the order to abandon ship over the stern. Most of the crew were on deck; they cheered the captain and began jumping overboard, lustily singing their national anthem, "Deutschland, Deutschland über alles." Zuckschwerdt then ordered the switch to be thrown to blow up the ship.

Bartlett and Lafrenz in the barge were moving away from the *Cormoran* as the cheering and singing occurred. Suddenly, Bartlett later wrote, they felt the "dull heavy shock of a muffled underwater explosion" against the bottom of the barge. Immediately, a mass of red flames, smoke, and debris shot with a roar up through the forward deck of the *Cormoran*, blowing away much of the bridge. Captain Zuckschwerdt and the last of his officers then calmly climbed over the stern rail and swam away as the *Cormoran* swiftly sank beneath the waters of Apra Harbor.

Boats from all over the harbor converged to pick up the survivors. Seven of the Germans died from injuries or drowning in the scuttling. Six of the bodies were found and buried with military honors in the small U.S. Naval Cemetery in Agana near the beach where Father San Vitores had landed over two centuries earlier. The Germans later erected next to the graves a cement obelisk with the inscription, "Den Toten von S.M.S. Cormoran, 7 IV 1917" (To the dead of the SMS *Cormoran,* 7 April 1917). The meter-high obelisk still stands among the rows of tombstones and crosses in the nearly forgotten little cemetery now flanked by a busy six-lane highway and a large car dealership.

The German officers were held at Camp Barnett and the enlisted crew at a camp at Asan, that favorite holding place on Guam. Corporal Hans Hornbostel was then given the unpleasant task of arresting his German father-in-law, Herr Costenoble, and the old man was interned with the *Cormoran* crew. On 29 April, all the German prisoners were sent back to the United States on the USAT *Thomas* under marine guard for confinement until their return to Germany after the war. Captain Zuckschwerdt eventually became a rear admiral in World War II. After its machinery and armament were salvaged by navy hard-hat divers, the *Cormoran* was left on the bottom of Apra Harbor at 120 feet, where it remains today.

The twenty-eight Papuans and the four Chinese stayed on Guam. The Papuans, housed in a camp at Piti dubbed "Cannibal City" by the locals, worked for the navy until all, except one who died, were repatriated on 2 January 1919 by the British (who had taken over Papua New Guinea) on a leased Japanese schooner. While on Guam, the Papuans were objects of much curiosity about their reputed cannibalism, but they held to their own view of reality. When asked what he thought on seeing for the first time the white man's marvel called a motorcycle, one Papuan replied, "He come, he stink, he go."

After the dramatic scuttling of the *Cormoran*, life on Guam settled down again to ordered tranquility. The first nonpolitical civic organization of Chamorro-speaking men, the Young Men's League of Guam (YMLG), was organized in April 1917. The YMLG would work quietly to support Chamorro culture and identity over the next seven decades. Eventually, a clubhouse was established, and the YMLG baseball team became a league leader. The purposes of the YMLG, however, were hampered by Naval Government Executive General Order 243 in 1917, which designated English as the only official language of Guam and ordered that "Chamorro must not be spoken except for official interpreting."

By this period, a regular baseball league with six teams, both military and civilian, was playing from November through April each year. Sales of Liberty bonds in support of the war boomed among Americans and Chamorros alike. From 4 through 7 July 1917, the naval government held the first Guam Industrial Fair. Patterned after American rural county fairs with a parade, exhibits, and amusements, the fair was a big success with the Chamorros. Proceeds were turned over to the Red Cross, which had established a chapter on Guam in 1916. Fairs continued to be held annually until World War II.

In the July Fourth ceremonies at the 1917 fair, Guam's flag was flown by the Guam Militia for the first time. Designed by Helen L. Paul, wife of a naval officer, and approved by Governor Roy Smith, the flag has a blue field with a central emblem bordered in red in the elliptical shape of a Chamorro sling-stone. Within the sling-stone are a proa and a coconut tree on the beach at Agana with the word *Guam* in the center. Naval authorities in Washington, D.C., ignored the flag for nearly ten years until Governor Lloyd S. Shapley asked for formal approval of it on 19 February 1929. Approval was granted, and in 1930 Governor Willis W. Bradley adopted the distinctive central emblem as the official seal of the island.

World War I had little effect on the social fabric of the Chamorros. A "back-to-the-soil" program to expand farming was mounted by Governor Smith in 1918, but, like most agricultural promotions by naval authorities, the effort produced little. After nearly two decades of U.S. naval government, local customs remained an ultraconservative mix of neo-Chamorro and Spanish traditions. The *Guam News Letter* of April 1917 complained that, after nineteen years of American rule, "very few inhabitants had learned to speak English." The main change was that the old *manak'kilo* families in Agana, whose ancestors were Chamorro *principales* and Spanish mestizos, now had competition from families into whom the new ruling class, the Americans, usually enlisted military men, were marrying. This new Chamorro-American elite was sometimes referred to as "American bamboo."

In most Chamorro families, the father was still the treasurer to whom all unmarried working children obediently gave their earnings. Marriages

Mouth of the Agana River, 1918. This scene shows typical thatched-roof and *mamposteria* masonry-wall houses of ordinary Chamorros in the early part of the twentieth century. The location is near where Father San Vitores landed in 1668 and where the Quipuha statue stands today next to the Paseo Park. The park was created with massive amounts of rubble from the buildings of old Agana destroyed by the American bombardment in World War II. (Guam Public Library, Agana, Guam)

Guam seal. The design is the central emblem of the Guam flag approved by the Navy Department in 1917. The seal itself was not approved until 1930. The elliptical shape is patterned after the form of the precontact Chamorro sling-stone. The lone palm tree at the mouth of the stream in the seal is based on the scene above of the old outlet of the Agana River after the massive typhoon of 1918 destroyed all but the tree on the left. A Chamorro proa was added, as was Urunao Point, in the background on the seal. (Guam Public Library, Agana, Guam)

were often arranged by the parents, and *suruhanu* herb doctors were routinely consulted for common ailments. Religious observances remained strict, with twenty-four-hour wakes. Many Chamorros still practiced *chenchule'* reciprocity and still disdained manual labor. Land and family lineage continued to be the basis of wealth and prestige, as described by a Chamorro historian, Reverend Joaquin Flores Sablan:

> The caste system was an unwritten code, but it determined the status of an individual in the society. The criteria by which a person was measured included wealth, family line, marriage with the ruling class, rental of church pews in the cathedral, the barrio of residence, and . . .

whether a person lived in a limestone-walled house or a wood-frame structure with sheet metal roofing. . . . Land ownership was the greatest security, particularly inherited properties which they treated as a sacred trust from their parents. To part with the land was the same as committing suicide.

While Guam had been coping with the *Cormoran,* in 1916 and 1917 the Japanese were restricting trade by foreign businesses to their islands in Micronesia, just as the U.S. Navy had done earlier for Guam. In November 1916, Atkins, Kroll complained to Governor Smith that its copra trade in Micronesia was being blocked by Japan. After State Department protests to Tokyo, the Japanese allowed the Atkins, Kroll schooner *Avarua* to trade at Saipan, Truk, and Jaluit under tight controls. The U.S. Navy suspected that the Japanese wanted to hide military bases from prying foreign eyes, so the director of ONI in Washington, Roger Welles, requested Governor Smith in September 1917 to "submit to ONI any information of interest in regard to activities of Japanese subjects . . . that may take place in adjacent islands." This request officially initiated American intelligence surveillance of the Japanese from Guam.

This surveillance improved on 20 November 1917, when the navy installed new facilities with two towers, each 400 feet high, at Libugon Hill for a high-powered radio station on Guam. The first small radio station had been set up at Agana Heights back in 1906, and by World War I radio almost eliminated cable as the means of official communications. Sensitive U.S. military messages began to be encrypted in 1918. Primarily a relay point between Pearl Harbor and Cavite for commercial and governmental messages, the Guam radio station would become an intercept facility in 1929 to eavesdrop clandestinely on Japanese radio messages throughout the Pacific.

In the meantime, Major Manwaring as ONI officer on Guam asked Clifton Kroll to have some employees of Atkins, Kroll report on Japanese activities and allow ONI agents to pose as crewmen on the *Avarua* to spy on the islands that the schooner visited. Clifton Kroll cooperated, and a number of intelligence reports resulted, although in this period Japan was not yet fortifying its newly acquired Micronesian islands and in fact was on the allied side with America in World War I.

Military matters became secondary on Guam in 1918 when several disasters struck the island. On 6 July 1918, a huge typhoon hit Guam dead on, killing two persons. "Telephone and electric light lines were a mass of tangled wire," according to the July 1918 *Guam News Letter*. Next, from late October to December, one of the worst epidemics in Guam's history swept across the island. This was influenza; it was raging worldwide and was brought to Guam by the USAT *Logan*. On Guam the disease killed 858 people, or nearly 6 percent of the population, according to navy records. Many older Chamorros were victims, and one historian estimated that 80 percent of the Chamorros who spoke Spanish died in the influenza epidemic.

Perhaps because it was wartime, the governor downplayed the epidemic's impact. The governor's *Annual Report* of 1919 devoted only two sentences to the influenza while blandly asserting, "The general sanitary conditions have perceptibly improved." Yet an American sailor wrote in December 1918, "We are carrying them [the dead] past the house at the rate of about fifty per day." The sailor's letter was intercepted by navy censors in Honolulu and never delivered. Later, President Wilson himself acknowledged the seriousness of the epidemic on Guam when he awarded a medal to Father Román María de Vera, one of the Spanish Capuchins, for his dedicated service in nursing hundreds of civilian and military victims of influenza on the island.

With the terrible influenza still rampaging on the island, it is understandable why the armistice that ended World War I on 11 November 1918 was not officially celebrated by the governor on Guam. By then, Smith was under severe personal stress as a result of wartime pressures. He was one of the more active and effective naval governors, but the navy did not appreciate his initiatives such as the Guam Congress or his handling of the *Cormoran*. Smith began to feel as if he had been unfairly exiled to Guam while his fellow officers were fighting gloriously in the Atlantic and in Europe. His messages to Washington were becoming close to incoherent when on 15 November 1918 the navy replaced him with Captain William W. Gilmer.

Early the next year, the Navy Department investigated Smith's tenure in a process reminiscent of the old Spanish *residencias*. The investigators concluded that Smith had been too innovative and too lenient in wartime conditions, mingling civil and military functions in a way that could have jeopardized the security of the island. In the history of the American naval governors of Guam, the Navy Department rewarded most those, such as Coontz, who changed things least.

The Quest for Identity
1918–1941

Racism, Arms Accords, and Political Frustrations

With the war over, the people of Guam and the American military personnel on the island hoped for a relaxation of wartime restrictions. This was not to be. Governor Smith's replacement turned out to be a humorless autocrat. Worse, he was a racist, not just personally, but in his official capacity as chief executive of the island.

In less than two years on Guam, Governor Gilmer issued over fifty stultifying general orders. He ordered, among other things, a halt to any whistling (Smith's earlier order against whistling had been ignored by Chamorro boys), a halt to smoking, institution of a preferential system by military rank for commissary purchases, and that all military personnel "be in their quarters by 11:00 P.M. and remain there until 5:00 A.M." Nearly all the orders prescribed fines for disobedience. For example, his EGO (Executive General Order) 312 of 13 May 1919 decreed that all males on Guam were liable to a tax of twenty-five cents if they did not deliver five dead rat heads to their district commissioner each month. All governors, including the Spaniards, repeatedly tried to eliminate the many rats on Guam, but without success; Gilmer had an obsessive fixation on the problem. The repressive social atmosphere under Gilmer was made worse when the manufacture or consumption of alcoholic beverages became illegal in July 1918 when the

Eighteenth Amendment (Prohibition) to the U.S. Constitution passed. Bootlegging of *aguardiente,* "aggie" to the sailors and marines, soon became common despite valiant efforts by the Insular Patrol to ferret out stills. Gilmer was also a hanging governor. On 19 September 1919, he had Juan Leon Guerrero Arriola hanged in the Agana jail yard for having committed murder.

It was during Gilmer's tenure that Padre Palomo died of a heart attack on 5 July 1919 at the age of eighty-three. This fine priest had been a pillar of spiritual strength for generations of islanders. A small park next to the U.S. Naval Cemetery on the Agana shoreline was later dedicated as the Padre Palomo Park.

What provoked a public backlash against Gilmer was EGO 326, which he issued on 29 September 1919. Back in 1907, the navy had tried to prevent military interracial marriages with Naval Station Order 47 but over the years had given up on the matter as a lost cause. By September 1919, according to a letter by former marine James H. Underwood, then the postmaster of Guam (he served as postmaster from 1915 to 1941 and then after World War II) and father of several children from his marriage with Ana Martinez, there had been sixty-three "white men who have married Natives of Guam." These included five men who deserted their families when transferred by the military. One of several notable Chamorro-American marriages that did endure was that of marine William G. Johnston and Agueda Iglesias in 1911. Johnston established the first movie house, the Gaiety Theatre, in Agana, and his wife became a prominent educator on Guam.

Governor Gilmer decided to remedy what he saw as a failure of navy resolve on the marriage issue; he would crack down on the mixing of races. His EGO 326 stated, "It is hereby ordered and decreed that on and after October 1, 1919, any white person residing on the Island of Guam, is forbidden to marry any person whole or part of Chamorro or Filipino extraction.... A white person who marries a person whole or part Chamorro or Filipino at any place other than Guam for the purpose of evading this order shall be denied admittance to Guam." Furthermore, common-law interracial marriages (which had been a routinely accepted practice on Guam for over two centuries) would be punishable as adultery under the same order.

Gilmer's decree immediately sparked howls of protest. Americans who were married to Chamorritas and Filipinas included, besides Underwood, McDonald, Johnston, and Sgambelluri, also Chester C. and W. H. Butler. These men fired off angry letters to the governor and to officials in Washington. On 14 November, a committee was formed to fight the order, and forty-two prominent Chamorros signed a letter to the governor with the demand "to have this discriminating law revoked." The Guam Congress followed with a similar request. Even Bishop Olaiz, who personally disapproved of American servicemen marrying Chamorro women, objected to the order.

Because of the backlash, Gilmer "temporarily suspended" the order on 9 October 1919 while he referred the matter to Assistant Secretary of the Navy Franklin Roosevelt. Gilmer wrote to Roosevelt that interracial marriages created a new clique of Chamorro-Americans that "wields a powerful influence" (presumably bad), that men were leaving the service to remain on Guam with their wives,

and that "the marriage of people of different religions is bad."

While awaiting a reply from the Navy Department, Gilmer continued to issue ludicrous orders: one prohibited any fandango, dance, play, or "any other nocturnal revelries" after a curfew of 10:00 P.M. On 4 March 1920, he decreed that all residents of Guam sixteen years old and older must be registered and obtain a *cédula personal,* or certificate of identification, to be used henceforth in all transactions to do with the government, such as tax payments, land transfers, birth registrations, court matters, etc. One of the purposes of this compulsory registration was to reduce the centuries-old Spanish custom whereby each child bore the father's family name first and the mother's maiden name second, as, for example, in Joaquin Torres y Martinez. Through the *cédula* process, and by dropping the *y,* the U.S. authorities were able gradually to reduce the practice of double names, with the result that some residents of Guam ended up with their mother's maiden name (the last in sequence) as the family name. World War II put a halt to the *cédula* registration process.

The marriage matter was resolved when Postmaster Underwood went to Washington in early 1920 and saw the chief of naval operations himself. This official was none other than Robert Coontz, the former governor of Guam and now an admiral. Embarrassed by Gilmer's orders, Coontz promised to remedy them. On 30 June 1920, Gilmer received a telegram from Franklin Roosevelt: "You will revoke EGO 326." And, on 7 July 1920, Gilmer was relieved by Captain Ivan C. Wettengel.

The new governor, an intelligent and fun-loving man, promptly rescinded the 10:00 P.M. curfew, the edict against whistling, and Gilmer's marriage and adultery law, thereby becoming instantly popular on the island. In an editorial, the *Guam News Letter* of July 1920 noted jubilantly, "Now is the time, friends, to restore to Guam the one-time 'happy family.'"

In 1920, the first regular ten-year U.S. census was taken on Guam. It showed a total population of 14,724, of whom 478 were military personnel, 548 "Non-Native residents," and 13,698 "Natives." These numbers reflected a boom of 70 percent in the Chamorro population in the first twenty years of American rule. Of all the changes brought about by the Americans, the improvement of sanitation and medical services, which in turn reduced infant mortality and prolonged lives, was proving to be the most beneficial to the local people.

The only military changes on Guam in this period came in 1920, when Governor Wettengel whimsically tried to create a squadron of "Guam Cavalry" with members of the Guam Militia mounted on bulls (a failure, the bulls proved untrainable) and in 1921 when a seaplane base was established at Sumay. On 26 February 1921, ten officers and ninety enlisted men of Flight L, Fourth Squadron (later called Scouting Squadron One), of the U.S. Marine Corps arrived in Apra Harbor aboard the USS *Jason* with six seaplanes. The water landing strip for the seaplanes was off Gab Gab Beach, as suggested years earlier by Pete Ellis, with a hanger, fuel tanks, and dock at Sumay.

Meanwhile, external forces were once more shaping Guam's destiny. In order to consolidate Japan's control of Micronesia, Tokyo concluded a secret treaty in 1917 with Britain, France, and Russia whereby in the peace agreement for World War I those countries would support Tokyo's claims in Micronesia in return for Japan's support of British, Australian, and New Zealand retention of German colonies south of the equator in the Pacific. When the Americans learned of this secret agreement in 1919 at the Paris Peace Conference, the U.S. Navy objected. The objection was based on the long-standing assumption of the Orange Plans that Guam would be isolated and the U.S. line of communications to the Philippines jeopardized by Japanese bases in the surrounding islands.

As a compromise, the British proposed that the former territories of Germany be divided into three kinds of mandates (A, B, and C, depending on state of development) and that these be administered by the occupying powers under the new international organization to be established—the League of Nations—by the peace treaty. President Wilson reluctantly agreed but demanded that the administering nations, such as Japan, agree to develop their mandates, to open them to free trade, and to refrain from fortifying them. Since Guam and the other U.S. territories were not mandates, they were exempt from these conditions. This formula was accepted in the Treaty of Versailles, signed on 22 June 1919.

The former German islands in Micronesia became a Class C Mandate, the least developed, under which technically they were wards of the League of Nations, but in effect they became integral possessions of Japan. A historian later aptly described this arrangement as "a fig leaf for the annexation of the territories coveted by Australia, New Zealand, and Japan, while it preserved the fiction of guardianship by the League of Nations."

President Wilson still attempted to limit the Japanese presence in Micronesia by demanding that Yap, a key international cable station, be exempted from the League of Nations mandate and be internationalized. The Japanese refused this unprecedented demand, and the "Yap crisis" provoked hysteria for a time in the U.S. press. American commentators indulged in an orgy of anti-Japanese books such as Frederick McCormick's *The Menace of Japan* and Walter Pitkin's *Must We Fight Japan.* One remarkable book in 1921, *Sea Power in the Pacific,* by British naval expert Hector C. Bywater, predicted that in a war Guam "would doubtless be the first Japanese objective." He also predicted a Japanese surprise attack on the American Pacific fleet in a prophetic book in 1925, *The Great Pacific War.* Bywater influenced U.S. naval strategists to alter War Plan Orange in 1926 and may also have inspired Admiral Isoroku Yamamoto (the Japanese naval attaché in Washington, D.C., in the late 1920s) to plan the Pearl Harbor attack that eventually took place in 1941. The Yap crisis faded in the early 1920s when the United States settled into "normalcy," as the new U.S. president, Warren G. Harding, a Republican who died in office in 1923, described the postwar era. Bywater's prophecies were forgotten by everyone—except the Japanese.

Japanese control of Micronesia became even more solidified when the U.S. Senate subsequently refused to ratify the Versailles treaty, thereby keeping the United States out of the League of Nations. In the end, the United States emerged as a loser in the postwar settlement in the Pacific, to the dismay of the U.S. Navy. To forestall a naval arms race in which Japan might emerge dominant in Asia, the Harding administration convened an international big-power conference that met in Washington, D.C., in 1921–1922.

The landmark Washington conference created a system to limit naval arms through a series of multilateral treaties, one of which—the Five-Power Naval Treaty—set limits on the numbers and tonnage of battleships and aircraft carriers that could be constructed by the major naval powers. Furthermore, in Article XIX of that treaty, which was signed on 6 February 1922, the United States agreed not to fortify any of its Pacific islands west of Hawai'i for ten years, at which time the treaty was to be renegotiated. In return, the old Anglo-Japanese alliance was abrogated. Ratification of the treaties by the U.S. Senate put a halt—again to the dismay of the U.S. Navy—to any fortification of Guam, including military airfields. A geopolitical calm then settled over the western Pacific for the next ten years.

The U.S. Navy nonetheless continued the secret game of intelligence gathering. In order to obtain more reliable reports than Atkins, Kroll and civilian travelers were supplying, in 1922 the U.S. Marine Corps sent Pete Ellis, now a lieutenant colonel after his famous war exploits, back to the region. Ellis traveled as a "copra trader" in Japan and throughout Micronesia, bouncing in and out of hospitals as a result of drinking bouts between spying efforts. He died in Palau on 12 May 1923 in an alcoholic haze. His mission was never clear and in the end was mostly futile. He found that the Japanese as of the early 1920s were not fortifying Micronesia as the U.S. Navy thought.

While on his strange last journey, Ellis was in contact with another ONI source, none other than Hans Hornbostel. Ellis' former assistant had been commissioned a marine lieutenant in the war and then returned to Guam while a marine to work as a forester. He left the Marine Corps in 1922. He and Gertrude then worked as archaeological-naturalist field investigators for the Bishop Museum of Honolulu. In this work, Hans traveled several times to the northern Marianas between 1924 and 1926. He also secretly provided information to the ONI on Japanese economic and political activities.

The Japanese grew suspicious of American visitors to Micronesia, so ONI switched its main surveillance to radio intercepts. In 1920, two new radio towers 600 feet high had been erected at Libugon on Guam, and, by 1929, regular intercepts of Japanese open and coded radio signals were under way. In that year, the navy moved a small cryptological team from Shanghai to Libugon. By 1935, U.S. intelligence services were breaking the Japanese military Red Code as well as the diplomatic Purple Code at secret facilities in Washington where messages collected on Guam and elsewhere were analyzed.

In internal island affairs, in 1922 under Governor Adelbert Althouse the navy reorganized the Guam public school system and patterned the courses of study after the California system. Coeducation was instituted because of the shortage of classrooms, and the navy continued to prescribe a detailed, rigid curriculum and all textbooks. Instructions to teachers in 1922 stated, "No teacher or principal is permitted to deviate from this course of study." Tougher steps were taken against use of the Chamorro language in schoolrooms and on school grounds. Incredibly, the naval authorities had Chamorro-English dictionaries collected and the books burned.

In March 1922, the last issue of the *Guam News Letter* appeared. The publication ended "on account of economic reasons." It was replaced in March 1924 by a new monthly, the *Guam Recorder,* which was privately owned by William W. Rowley, a blacksmith and former sailor on the *Yosemite.* Editor of the new monthly for years was Lieutenant Commander P. J. Searles. Associate editors were Hans Hornbostel and William G. Johnston. Searles was the mainstay of the *Guam Recorder* before World War II, writing numerous articles and the first history in English of Guam, which unfortunately was never published as a book.

By 1923, Guam's first golf course, the Sumay Golf Links, with eighteen holes was in place, and the Guam Golf Club was organized on 28 October 1923. By this period, America's favorite soft drink, Coca-Cola, was being sold on Guam by the Agana Bottling Works, owned by C. C. Butler and family. The year 1924 saw the establishment of the Guam Chamber of Commerce, which concentrated on promoting copra and agricultural production. Also active on Guam by then was Charleston Lodge 44 of the Free and Accepted Masons, established in Agana back in 1918 under the authority of the Grand Lodge in Manila. Agana and Sumay, but not the rural villages, were becoming more Americanized every year.

One event reported in the *Guam Recorder* was the establishment of the first official local holiday. Members of the Guam Teachers Association decided that it would be appropriate to commemorate Magellan's landing on its 400th anniversary. Chamorros had assumed through oral tradition that, since the Spanish galleons had normally halted at Umatac, Magellan must also have landed there, although after some sixteen generations since 1521 the tradition had no basis in fact. Funds were collected by public donations, and, on 6 March 1926, an obelisk was unveiled near the beach at Umatac. A plaque on the monument, which still stands, reads, "Magellan landed near here."

Thereafter, 6 March was celebrated annually on Guam until World War II as Magellan Day. It was revived as Discovery Day by the Eleventh Guam Legislature in 1971, complete with a lively village fiesta in Umatac and a reenactment of Magellan's landing. Research would later conclude that Magellan probably landed at either Tumon or Agana and that he came ashore on 6, not 7, March. Nonetheless, the Umatac landing is still celebrated each year, and, despite its Eurocentric connotation and

the wrong site, Discovery Day remains an official holiday on Guam.

In the 1920s, increasing numbers of high-ranking American federal officials and congressmen started visiting Guam by army transports on official junkets to the Philippines and Asia. The main U.S. Army Transport used throughout the 1920s and 1930s was the *President Grant,* a large, gleaming white, German-built steamer that could transport over 1,200 troops or passengers. Secretary of the Navy Charles Denby initiated the junkets in August 1923, and in July 1925 eleven members of the U.S. House of Representatives spent three days on the island. The U.S. congressmen attended a session of the Guam Congress, where Chamorros took the opportunity to ask politely for U.S. citizenship. The years 1926, 1927, and 1928 saw over two dozen more American congressional visitors, including the first U.S. senator, stop on Guam. Several of these visitors readily promised to submit bills in the U.S. Congress to give American citizenship to the people of Guam.

The Guam Congress was aroused by a different issue in September 1926, when a resolution was introduced in the Philippine House of Representatives to request the United States to cede Guam to the Philippines. The Guam Chamber of Commerce called it "ridiculous." On 12 October 1926, the Guam Congress adopted a resolution that not only rejected the Filipino initiative but again asked for "full" U.S. citizenship. Nothing came of the Filipino resolution.

The Chamorro request for American citizenship, on the other hand, was finally taken up when a bill was introduced in 1927 in the Sixty-Ninth Congress by two U.S. congressmen who had been on the 1925 visit to Guam. The bill was submitted in the context of efforts in 1926 and 1927 to grant American citizenship to the people of the U.S. Virgin Islands. Although acquired for defense purposes and under navy administration from 1917 to 1931, the Virgin Islands never assumed strategic military importance. Navy officials therefore endorsed U.S. citizenship for the Virgin Islands' inhabitants. The Guam bill, on the other hand, died owing to navy opposition, while citizenship for the Virgin Islanders was granted by the U.S. Congress in 1927.

In 1927, the Chamorros heard rumors that the U.S. Department of the Interior might take over administration of Guam and the Philippines. The Chamorros knew that the Interior had a reputation of treating American Indians shabbily, and—more important—that it received less money from the U.S. Congress for its wards than did the navy. Alarmed, the Guam Congress swiftly adopted a resolution, stating, "The people of Guam are perfectly satisfied with the present form of Government." The navy would use this and similar statements by Guam congress members to its advantage to block the Chamorros when they later asked again for more political rights. The switch of island administration to the Interior Department died, for the time being.

Bradley's Reforms and the Citizenship Drive

It was not until 1929 that local political conditions significantly changed, when on 11 June Commander Willis W. Bradley, Jr., replaced Captain Lloyd S. Shapley as governor. Bradley considered himself to be a "Progressive Republican" and a civil libertarian, a combination that made him more liberal than any other American naval governor on Guam. First in his class at Annapolis, he had won the Congressional Medal of Honor in World War I. Moreover, he knew the island well, having been in command in 1924–1926 of the USS *Gold Star,* known as the "Goldie Maru," a 4,500-ton cargo-passenger carrier, which was Guam's station ship from September 1924 until 10 December 1941.

Bradley immediately used the 1929 *Annual Report* (which covered the last year of the previous governor) to recommend that U.S. citizenship be granted Chamorros by federal legislation. This proposal was endorsed by a surprised Guam Congress in a resolution on 7 December 1929. The Guam Chamber of Commerce "emphatically" concurred. Pending federal action, Bradley issued a proclamation on 26 March 1930 that established "Guam cit-

izenship" for all residents and set up procedures for the naturalization of resident aliens as Guam citizens.

Then Bradley recommended to Washington that a bill of rights be granted Guam citizens by the U.S. president in order to protect the islanders from arbitrary decrees of naval governors. When Washington failed to respond for several months, Bradley went ahead on his own and proclaimed the Guam Bill of Rights on 4 December 1930. There were twelve provisions in the Bill, including for the first time the right of writ of habeas corpus and the privilege of voting in local elections regardless of race or sex. On 1 January 1931, the islanders held a large parade that ended in a public demonstration in the Plaza de España to thank Bradley. Former marine James Underwood, as the postmaster of Guam and the president of the Chamber of Commerce, led the speeches of appreciation.

The energetic Bradley followed up these startling measures with an even more dramatic reform, the reconstitution of the Guam Congress. By the time that Bradley arrived on Guam, the First Guam Congress was, in his words, "not functioning either as a representative body or in a manner to take full advantage of its possibilities." He accordingly dissolved the old Congress in March 1931 and issued another proclamation that established the Second Guam Congress. This body consisted of two houses: a House of Assembly, with twenty-seven members elected for two-year terms, and the House of Council, with fifteen members elected for four-year terms. The first election to the new Congress was held in March 1931, and Bradley opened the first session on 4 April.

Along with the establishment of the new Congress in 1931, Bradley implemented another political reform: the election of village commissioners for two-year terms. The next governor, however, resumed appointing the village officials in 1932 under the rationale that they were part of the executive branch.

Bradley embarked on an ambitious program to improve the island's inadequate roads and overcrowded schools, to establish a library, and to con-

Governor Willis W. Bradley, Jr., signing Bill of Rights, 1930. Beside him sits Monsignor Felipe Joaquin M. Olaiz y Zabalza, a Basque Capuchin and bishop of the Apostolic Vicariate of Guam from 1915 to 1936. The signing was in the garden of the governor's residence enclosed by old Spanish fence pillars (in background). (From the collection of the Micronesian Area Research Center, Mangilao, Guam)

struct new public buildings of concrete, such as chambers for the new Congress. The governor also extended commissary privileges to the Spanish priests because of their service to U.S. military personnel.

Unfortunately, the Great Depression was in full swing in the early 1930s. The navy, squeezed by congressional budget cuts, was not happy with Bradley's efforts and threatened to remove him in 1930. Bradley replied,

I have no particular desire to leave Guam this year, nor do I desire to ruin my naval career by argument with my superiors, and it seems that one or the other is in sight unless I am content to do as most of my predecessors have done, that is, simply let things drift along in the easiest channel without making any progress to speak of. Unfortunately, I am not built that way. When I see and understand the crying needs of Guam I shall fight for them as long as I am governor, even if it wrecks my future naval life. The result is that Guam has made more progress in the last year than in any previous two years—but that I seem to be constantly in hot water.

The navy backed down temporarily, but less than a year later, in April 1931, it was learned on Guam that Bradley would be recalled. The Guam

Portrait of Willis W. Bradley, Jr., as captain, U.S.N. Of all U.S. naval governors of Guam, Bradley, who served from June 1929 to May 1931, was the most helpful to the island's people. In addition to issuing Guam's first Bill of Rights, he sought U.S. citizenship for Chamorros, proclaimed them to be citizens of Guam, and reorganized the Guam Congress. (Painting by Robert H. Clark; courtesy of Anne Bradley Brucker)

Congress passed a resolution in praise of his "brilliant and vigorous" administration. Another resolution by the Chamorros asked the U.S. secretary of the navy to permit Bradley to act as "an agent to represent them in the United States." This appeal was ignored, and, after slightly less than two years of service on Guam, Bradley was replaced by Captain Edmund S. Root on 15 May 1931. Bradley was subsequently passed over by the navy for promotion to captain, but World War II revived his career. He retired as a captain in 1946 and went on to serve in 1948–1950 as representative of the Eighteenth District in Long Beach, California, to the U.S. Congress.

While Bradley left Guam in 1931 much more politicized than when he arrived, external events in the late 1920s and early 1930s caused even deeper changes in Guam's future. Plan Orange had been revised by the U.S. Navy once more in 1927–1928, and for the first time it assumed that Guam would fall in a war with Japan. In 1928, the U.S. Asiatic Fleet steamed to Guam for a mock invasion exercise. The fleet admiral found Apra Harbor too small for his ships and of "no value as a haven for vessels of war." In a somewhat feeble measure to prevent foreign surveillance, on 17 February 1930 President Herbert C. Hoover (Republican, 1929–1933) declared the airspace of Guam, as well as of Pearl Harbor, Guantanamo, and Subic Bay, prohibited to civil aircraft.

In accord with international treaties and budget cuts caused by the Depression, the U.S. Marine Corps seaplane squadron on Guam was withdrawn to San Diego in 1931, and all major ordnance pieces on the island were dismantled in 1932 despite the fact that conferences in Geneva in 1927 and in London in 1930 had failed to control the arms race. In 1935, the arms reduction system collapsed at another London conference. By then, Japan's government was dominated by militarists bent on expansion in the spirit of *bushidō,* the traditional code of honor and courage for Japanese *samurai* warriors of old. The Japanese Imperial Navy staged war maneuvers within sight of Guam and undertook surveys to construct military airfields, naval bases, and fortifications throughout Japanese Micronesia.

The United States in the meanwhile had elected a Democrat—Franklin Delano Roosevelt—as president in 1932. His platform of New Deal social and welfare programs to combat the Depression was welcomed by the new generation of Chamorro leaders who had grown up under American rule on Guam. These new Chamorro leaders included attorney Francisco Baza (Kiko Zoilo, and also called "F. B.") Leon Guerrero and businessmen Eduardo T. Calvo and Baltazar Jeronimo (called "B. J.") Bordallo, all members of the Second Guam Congress. The Second Guam Congress, like the First Congress, was purely advisory, and the governors after Bradley largely rejected its resolutions. As a consequence, public interest once more fell off rapidly, and at the second election in 1933 twelve seats were vacant for lack of candidates. The governors thereafter regularly appointed members to the vacant seats.

In this depressing political climate, Chamorro leaders tried once more to obtain American citizenship. In the January 1933 issue of the *Guam Recorder,* Congressmen Manuel F. Ulloa and Dr. Ramon M. Sablan made another appeal for U.S. citizenship, and the same issue printed a letter from Guam Postmaster James Underwood to a U.S. senator with yet another appeal. Encouragement came from President Roosevelt himself, according to a Chamorro who visited with the president in 1933 on a trip to the mainland. When the leaders on Guam learned of this encouragement, they organized a drive for another petition for citizenship. On 19 December 1933, the petition with nearly

2,000 signatures was endorsed by Governor George A. Alexander and sent to the White House and various federal officials.

In Washington, the petition was referred in 1934 to the Senate Committee on Immigration of the Seventy-third Congress by Senator Ernest W. Gibson, Republican of Vermont, with the intention that it become law. Gibson had been a visitor to Guam a few years earlier, and this conscientious New Englander took up the cause of the Chamorros out of sympathy with their plight. The secretary of the navy immediately opposed any bill based on the petition because, he wrote, Chamorros "are Orientals." President Roosevelt concurred, according to navy files, and the petition was filed and forgotten.

The Depression in the meantime had smothered economic activity on Guam. Copra exports declined from almost 6 million pounds in 1929 to less than 4 million pounds in 1932, and prices fell disastrously. Another victim of the Depression was the *Guam Recorder,* which Rowley had to sell on 2 October 1933. The buyer was none other than the U.S. Navy, which had not been happy with some of the monthly's editorials. The quality of the articles in the *Guam Recorder* remained high under the navy. Contributions of historical and other nonfiction pieces continued as under Rowley by writers such as the Hornbostels and Searles, including excellent translations by Margaret L. Higgins of San Vitores' history by García. Interest in Guam's history, long neglected, grew when the Guam Museum was established in 1933 under the custodianship of American Legion Mid-Pacific Post 1 until 1936, when the navy took over the small museum. Inexplicably, a modern museum adequate to preserve the island's rich history and cultural heritage has yet to be established.

In this period, Guam's first daily newspaper appeared in mimeographed format, the *Guam Eagle,* named in allusion to the great brown flying cockroaches on the island. The navy edited and distributed the paper, as it did the monthly *Guam Recorder.* Both publications would fall victims to World War II. The mid-1930s also saw for a few years Guam's first commercial radio, K6LG, owned by C. C. Butler's company. The station broadcast a local program on Wednesday nights for two hours.

A significant governmental change took place in December 1933 when Guam's judicial system was reorganized by Governor George A. Alexander. He abrogated previous laws and established new codes based on California codes. The last of the old Spanish laws, mostly to do with property matters, were eliminated. Nonetheless, as under the old codes set up by Governor Sewell in 1903, none of the justices on the Court of Appeals—the highest court in the system—had to be an attorney or otherwise qualified in law. The new codes still were a confusing mix of U.S. Navy and California procedures and laws.

Education on Guam was retarded by the Depression. Chamorro children in public schools numbered around 4,000 island-wide by the mid-1930s, but funds limited the number of teachers to 175, or a ratio of twenty-two students to one teacher. Navy policy had long been to provide schooling only to the sixth grade for Chamorros outside Agana. Agueda Johnston and others had to fight for the expansion of the education of village children through the high school level. Moreover, a large number of Chamorro children, predominantly girls, were still unable to attend school because of the shortage of classrooms. Many Chamorro teachers could still barely speak or write English and were not certified by stateside standards. On the other hand, the navy had been operating two elite schools on Guam since 1929, one in Agana and one at Sumay, for American children only, mostly military dependents. These two schools, with thirty students and six American teachers, had a student-to-teacher ratio of only five to one and charged a nominal tuition.

The end of the Depression brought one major commercial improvement and one minor social benefit to Guam. The minor benefit was the ending of Prohibition on 11 June 1934. The major improvement was the advent of civil aviation. In 1935, the dynamic Juan T. Trippe, president of Pan American

Airways, initiated regular trans-Pacific airmail service from San Francisco to Manila and back with a huge new seaplane, the Martin 130, named the *China Clipper.*

On Guam, Pan American seaplanes landed in Apra Harbor in a channel marked by lighted buoys. Shore facilities were built at Sumay on leased property of the former seaplane base. In 1936, Pan American constructed a twenty-room hotel, the Skyways Inn, at Sumay, and, on 14 October 1936, the first passenger flight landed in Apra Harbor. Those aboard were mostly newsmen on a free junket to provide publicity. Among them was Thomas H. Beck, the influential head of Crowell, Collier, and Macmillan publishers, who would later be of great help to Chamorros in their quest for U.S. citizenship. Regular flights with a crew of four or five and about fifteen passengers on the average took six days to cross the Pacific from San Francisco to Manila with overnight stops in Honolulu, Midway, Wake, and Guam.

By 1937, Chamorros were traveling on Pan American flights, and Governor James T. Alexander reported that postal receipts on Guam had trebled as a result of airmail service. Pan American added two more Martin 130s, called the *Hawaii Clipper* and the *Manila Clipper,* and extended passenger and cargo routes to Macao, Hong Kong, and Shanghai with weekly trans-Pacific flights out of San Francisco. The Pan American clippers made Guam the "Hub of the Pacific," according to publicity releases, with celebrities such as ex–world champion boxer Jack Dempsey and novelist Ernest Hemingway stopping for the one-night layover on Guam. Dempsey refereed a boxing match, and Hemingway went fishing for marlin.

The *Hawaii Clipper* disappeared mysteriously in March 1938 on the Guam-to-Manila leg. A two-week ocean search by the Guam station patrol ship, the USS *Penguin* (which had replaced the *Piscataqua* in 1929), failed to find any trace of the aircraft, crew, or passengers. A highjacking, or sabotage by Japanese saboteurs, was conjectured (Japan suspected that Pan American was spying for the ONI on flights near Rota and perhaps Palau), but

First Pan American passenger landing in Apra Harbor, 1936. The aircraft is the *China Clipper,* a Martin 130 seaplane, which landed on 14 October 1936 and was moored off Sumay. The Pan American clippers made Guam the "Hub of the Pacific," according to Pan American publicists, until World War II ended the flights. (From the collection of the Micronesian Area Research Center, Mangilao, Guam)

the plane most likely went down in a storm or as a result of systems failure. In 1939, Pan American added a new and bigger flying boat to their routes, the Boeing 18, each of forty-one tons with a 152-foot wingspan. The romantic Pan American clipper service would end, as did so many other things with the special style of the 1930s, when World War II began a new era in the Pacific.

The Depression years had brought about sharp changes in American relations with the Philippines, which in turn affected Guam. Philippine products, which were duty free in the United States, and Filipino immigrants, who worked for low wages, were now seen as unfair competition by depressed U.S. businesses and labor. With the spread of a militaristic imperial Japan, it was also becoming apparent that the United States might not be able to defend the Philippines in a Pacific war. As a consequence,

and pushed by the desire of Filipinos for independence, authorities in Washington decided on a divorce from Manila.

On 24 March 1934, President Roosevelt signed the Tydings-McDuffie Act, which made the Philippines a locally self-governing commonwealth for a ten-year period, after which would come independence and American withdrawal from military bases there. The Tydings-McDuffie Act alarmed Guam's leaders, so, when U.S. Secretary of War George H. Dorn stopped on Guam in late 1935, B. J. Bordallo, president of the House of Council of the Second Guam Congress, asked him to deliver another appeal to the U.S. president to clarify the civil status of Guam's people. Again, no action was taken by anyone in Washington.

In July 1936, the Second Guam Congress once more adopted a resolution that requested the U.S. Congress to grant American citizenship to Guam's people. This time the Guamanians planned to send two delegates—B. J. Bordallo and F. B. Leon Guerrero—to Washington to deliver the petition personally and to lobby for a bill to implement it. The Chamorros asked the governor, Captain Benjamin W. McCandlish, to match local donations with official funds to help pay for the expensive 16,000-mile trip, estimated to cost around $10,000. The governor refused the request with the specious excuse that official financial support of lobbyists for U.S. citizenship would be a breach of faith between the naval government and the federal government.

Undaunted, the Chamorros then launched a fund-raising campaign, and with the nickels and dimes of schoolchildren, as well as the dollars of their parents, the trip money was gathered. Even Governor McCandlish, perhaps embarrassed by the navy's lack of support, donated $20.00 of his own money. The money raised was not enough, so Bordallo and Leon Guerrero made up the difference with their own funds. On 7 November 1936, they embarked on the *Gold Star* for Japan. From there they took the Matson liner *President Lincoln* for San Francisco and traveled by train to Washington, D.C. The long route exemplified the problems in surface travel for civilians between Guam and the mainland in those days.

In Washington, the two men were taken under the wing of publisher Thomas Beck, who had stopped on Guam on Pan American flights and had empathy with the Chamorros. Consequently, the Chamorro delegates received good U.S. media coverage. The men also enlisted the help of Senator Gibson in drafting a bill for submission to the Seventy-fifth U.S. Congress to give American citizenship to the Chamorros of Guam. On 10 February 1937, Gibson and Senator Millard E. Tydings introduced the bill, S. 1450. Tydings, a Democrat from Maryland and chair of the Committee on Territories and Insular Affairs, had drafted the Philippines commonwealth legislation. On 15 February, a companion Guam bill, H.R. 4747, was submitted to the House of Representatives. Hearings in the Senate followed in April, and the two Chamorros

and their sponsors immediately ran into a high, hard wall erected by the U.S. Navy.

In an old-fashioned, straightforward colonialist statement, Secretary of the Navy Claude A. Swanson wrote to the committee,

> The complicated international situation in the Far East . . . and the fact that the United States is withdrawing from the Philippines all contribute to the undesirability of any change in the status of the people of Guam . . . these people have not yet reached a state of development commensurate with the personal independence, obligations, and responsibilities of United States citizenship . . . considerably increased Federal assistance in the form of relief funds would be required.
> The Navy Department recommends against the enactment of the bill S. 1450.

In their countertestimony, the two Chamorro delegates refuted every point by the navy and criticized naval rule of Guam as being "without any justification . . . a naval officer as Governor of Guam, has the power to make or break laws. . . . If any native official desires to hold his job he must not incur the displeasure of His Excellency [the governor] or he will find himself without a position as some . . . have found to their sorrow."

The argument of Bordallo and Leon Guerrero was based on the assumption that the 1899 Treaty of Paris between the United States and Spain placed a moral and a legal obligation under international law on the U.S. Congress to determine the status of the indigenous inhabitants of Guam. They noted that the inhabitants of Puerto Rico had been granted American citizenship by the Jones Act in 1917 in consequence of the 1899 Treaty of Paris and that the residents of the Virgin Islands were granted citizenship in 1927.

The navy trumped the Chamorro testimony by asking for a closed session with the committee to discuss classified defense information without the presence of Bordallo and Leon Guerrero. Behind closed doors, the navy presumably presented intelligence information and considerations based on the secret Orange Plans, about which, of course, the

Chamorros were unaware. Navy officials also cited earlier resolutions by the Guam congresses and statements by Chamorros of how satisfied they were with navy government.

Next, after its usual equivocations, the Department of State opposed the bill largely because it might provoke the Japanese, who were already suspicious of American purposes in Guam. By the final hearing on 9 June, it was clear the bill might not pass. Bordallo and Leon Guerrero then obtained, with Beck's help, a meeting with President Roosevelt. In the Oval Office, Roosevelt asked them, "Are the Navy people treating you right on Guam?"

Immediately both delegates respectfully replied, "Oh yes!" They apparently assumed that the president was asking about personal treatment of Chamorros by navy personnel (which was generally friendly), not about general political treatment (which was authoritarian). Their reply also reflected the typical Pacific islander's tendency to avoid confrontation in a personal exchange. The meeting turned to the presentation of gifts, and the president chatted about deep-sea fishing on Guam and elsewhere until the meeting ended. The two delegates, by being so ritually polite, lost a once-only opportunity to present the Chamorro case energetically to the president.

Short on money, Bordallo returned to Guam, flying between Honolulu and Guam on the *China Clipper* after writing a long report with recommendations to the Second Guam Congress. In his comments on the report, Governor McCandlish criticized Bordallo personally "because many of his statements were incorrect and many of his recommendations are in my judgement imprudent." McCandlish reflected the aging but stubborn navy argument that the Chamorros needed more time, in his words, "to develop the intelligence and managing ability for progress," before they could undertake the self-government that American citizenship would entail. He, like most naval officers, linked political rights to economic progress; that is, the Chamorros did not merit political rights because, he said, they "do not work hard to improve their economic conditions."

The U.S. Congress agreed with the navy view, and no action was taken by the Seventy-fifth Congress on the citizenship bill for Guam's people. Tydings and Gibson resubmitted the bill as S. 2962 in the Seventy-sixth Congress in August 1939, but by then everyone was preoccupied with the threat of world war, and Guam's appeal once more died. Subsequently, Guam's leaders obtained the help of the American Civil Liberties Union to attain rights for Chamorros, but nothing was accomplished before World War II suspended Guam's quest for citizenship. In the meantime, Leon Guerrero had remained in Washington and was low on money. He had to borrow against his land for cash. When he returned to Guam and was unable to repay all his travel debts, he lost some of the land.

End of an Era

While Guam's drive for American citizenship was dying in Washington, the "international situation," as Secretary of the Navy Swanson asserted, was deteriorating rapidly. At the end of 1936, Japan abrogated its obligations under all existing arms treaties and sealed off most of its Micronesian mandate to outsiders. The military-dominated government in Tokyo began serious fortification of its islands throughout Micronesia. Diplomatic maneuvering and its shadow, spying, heated up in the Pacific.

By the mid-1930s, a Japanese intelligence system was operating among patriotic Japanese nationals resident on Guam, including *nisei* (Japanese born and educated on Guam). Needing imports, the U.S. Navy for years had given permits to Japanese-owned commercial vessels with Japanese captains and crews to trade in and out of Apra Harbor. An example by the mid-1930s was K. Okano, the Chamorro-speaking captain of José Shimizu's seventy-five-ton copra schooner, the *Mariana Maru*, which had been authorized by the U.S. Navy since before World War I to trade out of Apra Harbor with Japan and the nearby Japanese islands in Micronesia. Okano presumably provided hydrographic, topographic, and navigational data about Guam to Japanese authorities.

Japanese loyalists on Guam included Takekuna (Samuel) Shinohara, owner of the Rooster Bar, Agana's only restaurant, and president of the Japanese Society of Guam; Jesus Sayama, a merchant; and Mrs. Kaneki Sawada, widow of a Japanese businessman. These Japanese patriots and others were under surveillance by the Guam police for the ONI by the late 1930s as possible informants working for Japanese intelligence agencies.

To assess whether Guam should be fortified as a defensive base with new airfields and naval facilities in the threatening new strategic situation, a board of naval officers under Rear Admiral Arthur J. Hepburn was formed in May 1938. Like the early Orange Plans, the Hepburn report recommended on 1 December 1938 that Guam be developed "as a major air and submarine base . . . and a fully equipped fleet base at a cost of $200 million." The Navy General Board, however, rejected large-scale fortification and narrowed the recommendations to harbor improvements at a cost of $5 million dollars to make Apra a "fortified air and submarine base." The improvements included once again the proposal to build a breakwater at Apra Harbor.

The Hepburn report was too late. Republican Congressman Hamilton Fish of New York objected that any military bases on Guam would constitute "a dagger at the throat of Japan." The Department of State wavered before also opposing the board's recommendations. Once more Congress did not authorize money for the fortification of Guam, or even for the breakwater. The only action taken was that Guam was closed in 1938 to all vessels of foreign registry, isolating the island even further.

Events in Europe took center stage in Washington's eyes when World War II erupted on 1 September 1939 with Germany's invasion of Poland. The American high command decided to make campaigns in the Atlantic and in Europe against Nazi Germany the number one priority, with war in the Pacific secondary. New U.S. global strategic plans, called "Rainbow War Plans," were drawn up in late 1939 and early 1940 to replace all previous U.S. strategic plans. Under Rainbow War Plan Five (which assumed war in Asia and in Europe and a

U.S.-U.K. alliance), the navy placed Guam in Category F, the lowest defense category, as U.S. territory that could not be defended.

As part of its preparations for war, the United States stepped up its efforts to decode Japanese encrypted communications after Japan joined the Axis Pact with Germany and Italy in September 1940. The cover name for the collection and cryptanalysis of Japanese signal intelligence was Operation Magic. The naval communication facilities on Guam played a valuable role in Operation Magic until 8 December 1941.

Meanwhile, in retaliation for new acts of Japanese aggression in China, in July 1940 the United States and Britain imposed a trade embargo against Japan on aviation gasoline and strategic metals. On 14 February 1941, in Executive Order 8683, President Roosevelt declared Guam to be a "defensive sea area and airspace reservation" off-limits to all foreign and domestic U.S. sea and air commercial carriers without permission of the U.S. Navy. A final drastic worsening of Japanese-American relations came in July 1941, when Roosevelt froze all Japanese assets in the United States in retaliation for Japanese aggression in French Indo-China. The Japanese promptly retaliated by freezing American assets in Japan. From then on, war between the two nations was inevitable.

On the eve of America's entry into World War II, social conditions on Guam were substantially different, and better in many respects from the navy's point of view, than they had been four decades earlier when Captain Glass steamed into Apra Harbor. Acculturation of the Chamorros into the American ethos was already deeper than their absorption into the Spanish culture in all social aspects except religion. The use of English on Guam was more widespread than had been the use of Spanish, and acceptance of the American lifestyle by Chamorros was already pronounced.

The 1940 census showed a total of 23,067 people on the island. Military personnel and dependents numbered 778, "non-native" residents (over half of whom were part Chamorro) numbered 787, and "natives" 21,502. The local population had increased by an incredible 128 percent over the 9,630 recorded in 1901. For years, officials of the U.S. Navy had been self-congratulatory about their accomplishments on Guam. The *Annual Reports* are full of compliments of governors to their predecessors and to themselves. Back in 1928, Secretary of the Navy Curtis D. Wilbur wrote, "During the period of Naval administration the population of Guam has doubled and the government has produced a happy, contented and patriotic people.... The needs and desires of the people of Guam, it is believed, are fully and sympathetically cared for by the present arrangement."

Beneath this assumption of benevolent progress by the navy, however, the reality of life by 1941 for ordinary Chamorros contradicted the official view. The island still had a subsistence "bull cart" economy; the port remained closed to normal commerce; de facto racial segregation between Chamorros and Americans still existed; and an unfavorable trade balance persisted, just as under the Spaniards. Rats and packs of boonie dogs still happily roamed the island, just as in Spanish times.

Navy efforts over the years to stimulate island agricultural production (primarily copra, corn, and rice but with kapok added by the 1930s as a money crop) and to foster local industry (such as the manufacture of tiles, plaited pandanus items, shell purses, salt, and salt soap) were only marginally successful. Although unemployment was low, the majority of the population depended on government support in some way. In a confidential intelligence assessment in June 1942, the Office of Strategic Services (the OSS, predecessor of the Central Intelligence Agency, or CIA) characterized prewar Guam as an island "with a basic tropical agricultural economy thrown seriously out of gear by the presence of the United States Naval Station . . . and by Naval Station work projects which have set wage standards out of proportion to return for labor in agricultural occupations."

The navy had brought electricity and many other amenities to Guam, but by late 1941 roads still amounted to only a meager eighty-five miles, all of crushed limestone *cascajo* except for the Sumay to Agana section, which was the island's first asphalt road. Improvements in island infrastructure were related mostly to naval needs. There was still no road the eighty miles around the island.

Moreover, the Americans had been gradually taking land away from the Chamorros. The two governments on Guam, the federal and the naval (the distinction was in practice inconsequential), owned a total of 19,431 hectares, or over one-third of the entire island by the eve of World War II. This was an increase of over 30 percent since 1899, and much of the expansion was at the expense of the Chamorros the naval government was supposedly protecting from outside exploitation. In the meantime, defense needs for land on Guam had actually shrunk in the 1920s and 1930s. The absence of an island-wide cadastral survey—still unfinished after numerous sporadic efforts—also hindered orderly economic development.

The lack of economic progress, however, had not inhibited the growth of the island's government. The executive branch, in 1941 under the still absolute authority of the governor, included fifteen municipalities, each with an appointed commissioner and all under a chief commissioner in Agana since 1931. Village civil officials wore uniforms and ties on duty, just like military personnel. The Marine Corps Insular Patrol rather than civil police still operated in each village. Chamorros still had no right to protection by grand jury, there were still no trials by jury or appeals to federal courts off-island, and all judges and attorneys served at the will of the governor. The first comprehensive printing of Guam's hodgepodge of naval and California-based laws was issued in 1937 as *The Codes of Guam*, but this compilation was incomplete because the navy never had a regular compiler of laws. The jumble of boards and administrative agencies created by the navy often operated by their own rules and regulations, which were rarely published.

In religious matters, the U.S. Navy was still not comfortable with the Catholic Church on Guam. Monsignor Olaiz was replaced in 1936 as titular bishop and apostolic vicar of Guam by Father

Miguel Angel de Olano y Urteaga, O.F.M. Capuchin, who had long been the parish priest at Sumay. The Spanish Capuchins from Navarre, all still ultraconservative Basques, opposed coeducation and other practices introduced by the Americans. Worst of all from the American view, the Spanish priests helped perpetuate the Chamorro language in their sermons and writings. In particular, Father Román María de Vera, who had received a medal from President Wilson for dedicated service in the 1918 influenza epidemic, for years helped preserve the Chamorro language in church rituals and daily life. A linguist, Father Román served from 1915 to 1941 on Guam and was a prolific writer of Chamorro-Spanish dictionaries, grammar texts, and hymnals, none of which were under navy purview.

As a result, the naval government began to replace the Spanish Capuchins, to the latters' dismay and anger, with American Capuchins in 1937. In 1939, the Guam diocese was placed under a Capuchin order based in Detroit, Michigan. By December 1941, of the fourteen priests on Guam, ten were Americans, two were Chamorros—Father Jesus Baza Duenas (ordained in Agana, 11 June 1938) and Father Oscar Lujan (Pale Scot) Calvo (ordained in Agana 5 April 1941)—and only two—Bishop Olano and his secretary, Father Jauregui Jesús de Begoña—were Spaniards. These fourteen men served nineteen churches and 22,000 or so Catholics on Guam.

The Baptists on Guam had also grown in numbers under the leadership of a Chamorro lay preacher, José Aguon Flores, during 1930–1935. After that, they were led by Reverend Joaquin Flores Sablan, who in 1935 graduated from Oakland City College in Indiana and was ordained as the first General Baptist minister of Chamorro descent. There were two Baptist churches on Guam in the late 1930s with approximately 400 members. Reverend Sablan, who was rector of the Agana General Baptist Mission Church, would also become one of Guam's most distinquished educators.

Education remained inadequate and an issue of contention on Guam right up to the war. The school system by late 1941 comprised twenty-four public primary schools, one private school (the Guam Institute), and George Washington High School. This high school was established in Agana in 1936 to replace the Seaton Schroeder Junior High School, which dated from 1930. Chamorro children in school numbered a little over 5,000 out of over 7,500 school-age children, or only 60 percent, and were taught only by Chamorros. All six American contract teachers on the island by 1941 taught in the two exclusive American schools.

A local board of education had finally been established in 1938, but it was only advisory to the governor and had no authority over personnel or the curriculum. An informed commentator would later write, "Not a single textbook adapted to the local customs and every day experiences of the Guamanian child had been developed." The Catholic Church, on the other hand, had prepared a number of such books, mostly by Father Román, for their schools on Guam, including some in the Chamorro language. The few Chamorros with college degrees included (in addition to the priests and Reverend Joaquin Sablan) Ramon Manalisay Sablan, who received his M.D. in 1938 from the University of Louisville, and José Roberto Palomo, the first Chamorro Ph.D. (in Spanish literature). Palomo graduated from Ohio State but remained on the mainland until after World War II. Ramon Sablan returned to practice medicine in Guam from 1940 to 1951. Not only was he the first local physician, he was also active intellectually as a teacher, the founder of the Guam Teachers Association, a linguist, a journalist, and a musician. In the early 1930s, he composed the music and wrote the lyrics for "The Guam Hymn," which is the island's anthem.

Use of the Chamorro language in public schools was still forbidden. The 1940 census reported that nearly 75 percent of all persons on Guam over age ten spoke English, yet Chamorro remained the main language in nongovernmental activities despite decades of American efforts to suppress it. The navy interpreted Chamorro insistence on speaking the indigenous language as a cognitive deficiency on the part of the local people. Chamorro children were thus being raised in a kind of schizophrenic half-English, half-Chamorro social environment that denigrated their Chamorro cultural heritage and made them feel inferior to Americans.

Navy expenditures for education per pupil on Guam in 1934 were $16.09, and by 1941 had dropped to $14.10, far lower than the poorest U.S. state. Illiteracy among Chamorros was actually increasing in 1940–1941, to nearly 17 percent over age ten. Despite the low wages of Chamorro teachers ($0.80 a day at entry versus $1.00 a day for laborers in navy jobs), their prestige was remarkably high, and many, such as Nieves M. Flores (owner of the Guam Institute private school), Superintendent Simon A. Sanchez, and Agueda Johnston (principal of the junior and the senior high schools), were leaders in civic affairs.

One knowledgeable person who was critical of the prewar Guam school system was Laura M. Thompson, a cultural anthropologist. In 1938–1939, she did ethnographic field research on the island as a consultant for the naval government. That fieldwork, mostly in Merizo, resulted in several scholarly articles and an outstanding book, *Guam and Its People*. Her book, published in 1941 and reprinted after the war, was the most comprehensive analysis of Chamorro culture since Louis de Freycinet's research in 1819.

In contrast to education, the American navy's record in public health on Guam was exemplary. The death rate fell dramatically from 27.8 per 1,000 persons in 1905 to 11.7 in 1940. Gangosa and leprosy were all but eliminated on the island, even though *lytico-bodig* persisted. Overall, Guam's population in 1941 in comparison with 1899 was more multiethnic, was better educated, enjoyed higher living standards, and was much healthier than when the Americans arrived. One difference since Spanish times was that Americanization and education had sown the seeds of discontent to a more profound extent among Chamorros in regard to political liberties, which had improved little since 1899. Chamorros resented most of all the pervasive racial discrimination practiced in the naval system. Americans were less class conscious but more racist than the Spaniards had been.

Over the sweep of Guam's long history, American military government prior to World War II can be judged to have been as much of a failure as that of the Spaniards, who made no pretense of trying to improve political and economic conditions on the island. Laura Thompson made the following judgment of the difference between the Spaniards and the Americans: "The Spanish Catholic regime, although involving great initial loss of physical life...introduced new channels of native self-expression and spiritual growth.... The American naval regime, on the other hand, while fostering population increase and physical development... suppressed many channels of native self-expression and creativity, apparently without providing adequate substitutes."

Prior to World War II, not only did the U.S. Navy on Guam fail to improve local civil liberties and governmental standards to anywhere near U.S. standards, it also fell short in its strategic defense mission of assuring the line of communications across the Pacific west of Hawai'i. The original compulsory Guam Militia was disbanded in 1937 owing to budget cuts. It was reinstituted as a small voluntary unit and in April 1941 was reorganized as the Insular Force Guard patterned after the California National Guard. It numbered 103 men by December 1941. Naval personnel on Guam by then numbered 274, U.S. Marines 153, and the Insular Force 168 for a total U.S. military presence of only 698 people, including five women nurses. Personnel in units that could be used in combat (i.e., sailors on armed vessels, U.S. Marines, and the Insular Force Guard) numbered only about 340 men.

Of the four naval vessels at Apra Harbor in late 1941, the most effective was the World War I–vintage minesweeper that served as a patrol ship, the 1,000-ton USS *Penguin*. It was armed with a few .50-caliber machine guns and manned by a crew of about fifty sailors and three officers. The other fair-sized vessel was an old decommissioned oiler, the USS *Robert L. Barnes,* affectionately known as the "Barney Maru," which had two .50-caliber machine guns. The other two vessels were small "YP" patrol boats. A fifth vessel, Guam's station ship, the USS *Gold Star,* was away on a trip to the Philippines when the war came.

The Barney Maru, immobile and tied to buoys in Apra Harbor, served as a training ship for navy mess attendants, among whom 358 Chamorros had graduated by the end of 1940 to earn $21.00 a month. This was the same pay as Filipino and American seamen received. The difference was that Chamorros and Filipinos usually stayed at base pay for years while white seamen "advanced quickly to higher rungs on the pay scale," according to one Chamorro former mess attendant. Dozens of these Chamorro mess attendants were serving off Guam in the navy when the war started.

The U.S. military forces for the defense of Guam on the eve of World War II were thus fewer than in World War I and were eerily similar in weakness to the Spanish forces on Guam in 1898. Other than two salute cannons, there was no artillery on the island, just as in 1898. Despite the many Orange Plans and all the efforts to fortify Guam, the U.S. Navy had failed to convince the U.S. Congress of the need to defend the island. Critics of the navy, such as Willard Price in his 1934 book *Japan's Islands of Mystery,* had long argued that, having allowed the surrounding Micronesian islands to fall into alien hands, the United States could no longer defend Guam. By late 1941, the navy itself accepted that Guam could not be defended. Rear Admiral Richmond Kelly Turner—who was head of the navy's war plans division—in a letter dated 6 October 1941 to the captain of the USS *Gold Star* wrote, "Guam is not really defendable no matter how many troops and fortifications you put there."

If the navy's judgment in all the Orange Plans on the defense of Guam was faulty, then all the authoritarian restrictions imposed on the Chamorros for over forty years by the navy in the name of U.S. national security were needless. It would have made little difference to the defense of the island in 1941 if Chamorros had been granted U.S. citizenship or

had been governing themselves from the very beginning of American rule.

The failure of American government in prewar Guam cannot, however, be attributed solely to the U.S. Navy. The main mission of the prewar naval governors, and their superiors in the Navy Department, was one of military defense, not civil development. The real culprit in Guam's needlessly constricted development from 1898 to 8 December 1941 was the U.S. Congress. It bears the authority and the responsibility under the Territorial Clause of the U.S. Constitution to ensure democratic government in all U.S. territorial dependencies. By allowing the archaic colonial doctrine of the Supreme Court's *Insular Cases* to stand instead of responding to the many appeals by the Chamorros and by a number of naval governors themselves for civil liberties, the U.S. Congress itself perpetuated military colonialism on Guam.

Judgments of naval rule were undoubtedly far from the mind of the last prewar naval governor on Guam, Captain George J. McMillin. In a spasm of war jitters in February–March 1941, the U.S. Congress appropriated some $4,700,000 for last-minute defense projects to improve Guam's harbor, including a seaplane patrol base. The island had been heavily damaged by a typhoon on 3 November 1940 and was still recovering when the new appropriation was made. With the additional funds, McMillin was hurriedly trying to dredge the harbor, build new water systems, bomb-proof key facilities, and construct new oil storage tanks at Cabras Island. Nearly seventy American contractors were hastily sent to Guam by December 1941, with bulldozers, dredges, trucks, and other equipment to do the work. The contractors hired Chamorro men for labor. Surveys and some preparations for airfields, notably on Orote Peninsula, were also under way, but all these activities would prove useless.

Earlier, on 17 October, the last American military dependents, 104 women and children, departed Guam on the USS *Henderson* except for one pregnant navy wife, Mrs. J. A. Hellmers. The last issue of the *Guam Recorder* in November 1941 did not say a word about the threat of war, but the cover showed the *Henderson* departing full of American families with the word *Aloha* alongside. Many Chamorros, alarmed by the evacuation and by blackout drills, began hoarding food, and some began to move to their *lanchos* for safety in anticipation of a Japanese attack.

Japanese military aircraft and ships from Saipan had begun reconnaissance of Guam as early as March 1941, and, during October and November, Japanese seaplanes were taking aerial photographs of the island with impunity. The U.S. State Department protested the overflights in vain to Tokyo. More ominous, formidable Japanese ground forces of over 5,500 soldiers in the South Seas Detachment from the 144th Infantry Regiment in China, plus a special naval guard force (similar to U.S. Marines) of over 400 men, the Fifth Keibitai under Commander Hiroshi Hayashi, were being assembled in the Bonin Islands. The commander of all these ground forces, which constituted a 6,000 man brigade-sized unit, was Major General Tomitara Horii. He received his orders on 29 November: "The detachment will seize Guam. The enemy situation on Guam is set forth in the special military map. Therefore the main force will seize and hold the Port Apra base (1), and a part of the force will seize and hold Agana City."

The American high command in Washington was well aware of Japanese war preparations through interceptions and decoding of Japanese communications. On 24 November, the acting chief of naval operations, Admiral R. R. Ingersoll, sent a secret message to all commands, warning, "Chances of favorable outcome of negotiations with Japan very doubtful. This situation coupled with statements of Japanese Government and movements of their naval and military forces indicate in our opinion that a surprise aggressive movement in any direction, including attack on Philippines or Guam is a possibility. . . . Guam will be informed separately."

On 4 December, McMillin received a coded telegram from Ingersoll to "destroy all secret and confidential publications and other classified matter. . . . Retain minimum cryptographic channels necessary for essential communication." The next day, in a memorandum, Ingersoll predicted that a Japanese attack would come after Christmas. Ingersoll planned to replace Governor McMillin by then with Captain Alexander R. Early and to give McMillin command of a battleship, but Early would never make it to Guam. On 6 December, the navy radio station at Libugon received a message from Washington to destroy all remaining classified materials.

Thus, the outbreak of war in the Pacific was expected by everyone on Guam—the Japanese, the Americans, and the Chamorros—except for the exact place, date, and time. Despite this expectation of war, however, the Chamorros and many Americans were confident that the United States would easily defeat the Japanese. This misplaced confidence was due to "childlike faith in the might and power of America," wrote Chamorro historian Pedro C. Sanchez.

In reality, the parable of the tribes was once more about to overwhelm Guam, this time in the form of twentieth-century warfare in a terrible sequence of two massive invasions within three years. These invasions would bring greater destruction to the environment of the island than all the previous alien intrusions, including even the original Spanish invasion of Guam two and a half centuries earlier.

10 The Way of the *Samurai* 1941–1944

The Bayonets of Omiya Jima

Dawn on Monday, 8 December 1941, on Guam, over 2,300 miles west of the international dateline, came four hours after the sunrise on Sunday, 7 December, at Pearl Harbor, about 1,400 miles east of the dateline. Nearly everyone on Guam was preparing for the celebration that day of the Feast of the Immaculate Conception. Bishop Olano described the preparations: "It was a beautiful morning. People, especially the younger men and women, thronged the door of the Cathedral to attend Solemn High Mass in honor of the Immaculate Concepcion. The Mass was to begin at eight. The Cathedral was bedecked in gala attire, for Agaña, Guam, was ready for the celebration."

A little after 8 A.M., eleven-year-old Paul Jerome Bordallo at his father's market in Agana was receiving a shipment of fish and lobsters from Merizo when he heard aircraft flying over Agana. He looked up to see nine planes, but they were flying so high he could not see that they were Japanese. At about the same time, in his office across the plaza from the cathedral, Governor McMillin was informing Paul's father, B. J. Bordallo, of a telegram received earlier that morning from the U.S. Asiatic Fleet headquarters in Manila with the news that Pearl Harbor was under attack. McMillin had alerted the military command and summoned Bordallo because he owned a small fleet of taxis that

McMillin wanted to use to evacuate people from the capital. Although McMillin had known of the Japanese attack on Pearl Harbor for over two hours, he had neglected to warn the civilian community thoroughly by the telephone system and other means of the very real danger of attack. As the two men talked, they heard the sound of aircraft overhead. McMillin remarked casually, "There they are!"

A few minutes later, and six miles away at Sumay, two Chamorros employed by the navy, Benito Wesley, the eighteen-year-old grandson of a New England whaler, and his friend Joaquin Sablan had just begun their daily chores in the Marine Corps officers' quarters when they heard the roar of aircraft. The young men rushed outside in time to see two warplanes with round red markings on their wings sweep by not more than a hundred feet over their heads. Bombs dropped from the planes over the nearby Pan American buildings and the big Standard Oil fuel tank. The tank was hit and burst into flames that sent up massive grayish-black billows of oil smoke to tarnish the clear sky over Guam for the first—but not the last—time in the island's history.

Another bomb from a following aircraft struck the Pan American hotel kitchen and killed workers Larry Lujan Pangelinan and Teddy Flores Cruz, the

163

first fatalities of the war on Guam. At the adjacent Pan American office building, Juan Wesley, Benito's father, fled outside just as another bomb struck. Stunned by the blast, Juan looked down to see his intestines oozing from a slash in his abdomen. He ripped off his T-shirt and plugged the wound as he staggered off to his Sumay home. There he fortunately caught a truck to the Naval Hospital in Agana. Juan Wesley survived the wound and the war.

Communion was ending in the Agana cathedral, and Bishop Olano asked a woman what was the cause of the commotion among the congregation. "Gerra, gerra, Señor Obispo," she replied in Chamorro. The bishop completed the mass and hurried across the plaza on foot to the governor's office, where he learned that war was indeed under way.

Olano then went to the hospital to attend the wounded while McMillin issued various orders. The governor closed all schools, stores, and offices, set up the evacuation of civilians from around military facilities, and mustered the island's military personnel. He also ordered the arrest of twenty Japanese citizens on the island, notably José Shimizu and Mrs. Sawada as well as Samuel Shinohara—who had showed his sympathies by proudly flying a Japanese flag at his Agana home that morning.

The Japanese planes turned to bombing military targets at the Piti navy yard, the Libugon radio towers, and vessels in and around Apra Harbor. Refugees from Sumay and Piti began to flee toward Agana, jamming the main road. In Apra, the *Robert Barnes* was repeatedly punctured by bullets but remained afloat while the crew swam to safety. The old ship would later be towed to Saipan after Guam was captured by the Japanese.

The *Penguin* was on patrol at sea the night of 7–8 December and had sprung a leak in a boiler. It also lost radio communication, so it was out of contact with the navy command radio station in Agana. The old converted minesweeper returned to Piti just before 8 A.M., and a third of the crew went home. The captain, Lieutenant James W. Haviland III, then received a handwritten note from Governor McMillin to put to sea immediately because of hostilities. Short of crew and at reduced speed, Guam's only warship of sorts then chugged out of Apra to meet its fate.

Three Japanese warplanes found the *Penguin* about a mile off Agat, and the pilots dove to the attack. Ensign Robert White, manning an antiaircraft gun, was killed by strafing. Lieutenant Haviland and two sailors were seriously wounded as the Japanese riddled the ship with machine-gun bullets and the shrapnel of near misses from exploding bombs. Leaving the *Penguin* dead in the water, the Japanese aircraft flew off to the north to refuel on Saipan.

Unknown to the Americans, some of the Japanese fighter and bomber aircraft had made an extraordinarily long flight in November from their base at Oppama near Yokosuka, Japan, to Saipan via the Bonins. These planes, plus naval aircraft and the Seventeenth Air Unit from the aircraft carrier *Seikawa* from the Japanese navy base at Truk, reinforced the seaplanes of the Eighteenth Air Unit at Tanapag, Saipan, in attacking Guam. The combat aircraft included the Mitsubishi A6M Zero-sen, which at the time was the best combat plane in the Pacific.

On the *Penguin*, Lieutenant Haviland, with part of his left arm blown off, ordered the crew to take off White's body and the wounded men in the ship's two life rafts (the one lifeboat was full of bullet holes) and then to scuttle the stricken ship before the Japanese returned. With insufficient room on the small rafts, uninjured men jumped into the water and swam safely to the Agat beaches after releasing the sea valves of the doomed *Penguin*. The little ship sank in the deep waters south of Orote Point. Once ashore, some of the uninjured sailors were armed to reinforce the Insular Force Guard in Agana.

Meanwhile, aliens, presumed to be Japanese, had been seen landing by canoes at daybreak; one group of five slipped ashore near Ritidian, and another group landed near Inarajan, where they scattered into the interior. The five at Ritidian were caught and interrogated. They turned out to be

Chamorros from Saipan sent ahead by the Japanese to cut telephone lines and act as scouts and interpreters for the invading forces. The men said that the invasion would come the next day at Agana Bay. The infiltrators were crowded into the same Agana jail cell as the twenty Japanese residents arrested earlier.

McMillin thought that the infiltrators' warning was, in his words, "a trick to have the Marines move from Sumay to the Beach during the night, in order that they [the Japanese] might make a landing in the Apra Harbor area without opposition." This would prove to be a costly misjudgment by McMillin.

McMillin also failed to give orders as planned previously for the thorough destruction of all military installations, stores, and facilities to deny their use by the Japanese. McMillin's aide for civil affairs, Commander D. T. Giles, the next day told one of the naval staff radiomen, George Ray Tweed, "We are going to offer only token resistance and surrender." Giles also gave Tweed permission to hide out in the countryside to avoid capture.

In the meantime, in the afternoon of 8 December, the Japanese began to bomb Agana. Houses were hit, including one below San Ramón Hill owned by the Reyes family where radioman Tweed rented the upstairs, but the bombing was not intensive. Nonetheless, civilians fled in terror into boonie areas until the air attacks stopped around five in the afternoon. Hardly anyone remained in Agana or the main villages. That night, during the long hours of blackout, thousands of Chamorros huddled in the jungles in what would become a vigil of courageous despair for the next thirty-one months.

About eight-thirty the next morning, Tuesday, 9 December, the Japanese leisurely resumed their bombing of Guam. They struck the Libugon radio towers and downtown Agana once more and strafed villages throughout the island during the day. McMillin had the U.S. Marines at Sumay take up defensive positions in the butts of the rifle range on Orote Peninsula. The marines shot down one Japanese twin-engined medium bomber by .30-caliber machine-gun fire. The 125 officers and men (minus the twenty-eight enlisted marines and one officer assigned elsewhere with the Insular Patrol) were under the command of Lieutenant Colonel William K. MacNulty. He and McMillin anticipated that the Japanese would land on the beaches near or inside Apra Harbor and come under the marines' guns.

To defend Agana, Governor McMillin assembled the three platoons of the Insular Force Guard. Each platoon numbered about twenty-eight Chamorros armed with small arms, submachine guns, and .30-caliber Lewis machine guns. The force was divided into two under the command of Chief Boatswain Mates Robert Bruce Lane and Robert O'Brien, the latter one of the *Penguin*'s crew. They were reinforced by about fifteen marines from the Insular Patrol and sailors from the *Barnes* and the *Penguin*. None of the Chamorros had fired a machine gun before, and some of the American staff personnel were not even qualified in small arms such as the .45-caliber pistol.

The platoons of the Insular Force Guard were deployed on the night of 9 December in a loose perimeter around the Plaza de España under Lane. Six of the *Penguin*'s sailors were stationed at the Agana power plant. There was no time for anyone to dig in; they did not even have sand bags as protection. At 2:00 A.M. on Wednesday, 10 December, nine Japanese troopships protected by warships began disembarking troops into landing boats at widely separate points off Guam. The landings took place at low tide, and in some places bamboo mats were laid on the coral so that the troops could walk over it. A battalion of army troops under Lieutenant Colonel Tsukamoto landed in Tumon Bay as the first wave on the northern beaches. Signal flares marked the landings. The units of the Fifth Keibitai with about 400 men followed as the second wave to the right of Tsukamoto at Tumon but became lost. Their boats turned right and moved westward around Hospital Point. They then crossed the reef in eastern Agana Bay and waded to Apurguan-Dungcas Beach.

Twelve miles to the south, units of the main

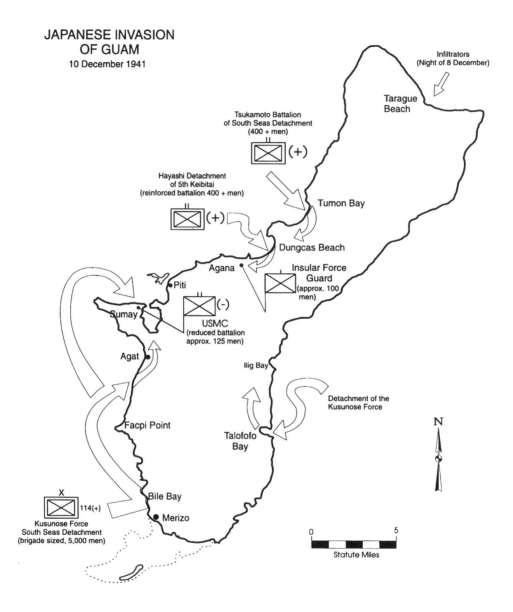

JAPANESE INVASION
OF GUAM
10 December 1941

Source: Iwano et al. (1946)

force of 5,000 army troops in the South Seas Detachment, mostly the 144th Infantry Regiment under Colonel Kusunose, began to land on the beaches of Bile Bay, just north of Merizo. Their mission was to attack northward to take Orote Peninsula and Apra Harbor from the U.S. Marines under the assumption that a road existed between Merizo and Agat. The remainder of the army units of the South Seas Detachment remained in transports offshore. Small elements of the Kusunose force were to land at Ylig Bay, but they landed by mistake at Talofofo Bay and marched throughout the night across the island toward Agana.

When the commanders of the main southern

force discovered that there was no Merizo-Agat road, the units deployed at Bile Bay reembarked on their landing boats and then moved north around Facpi Point to land at the Agat beaches. Prior to reembarking, the Japanese on shore temporarily occupied Merizo and lectured the frightened inhabitants.

While the southern attack was being delayed, the northern waves of Japanese troops landed unopposed at Tumon and at Agana Bay with bayonets fixed for close combat. Because the naval Keibitai landing at Apurguan-Dungcas Beach was closer to Agana than the Tsukamoto battalion landing at Tumon, the Keibitai forces would reach the capital first. As squads of the Keibitai fanned out on the Agana-Tamuning road along the beach, they encountered a jitney (a Filipino-style small bus made from a truck chassis) with seventeen Chamorros aboard who were fleeing Agana.

In the dark, the invaders opened fire on the vehicle and then charged under the assumption that the passengers must be hostile. The Japanese shot and bayoneted everyone inside, killing thirteen men and women and wounding three men. One young man, Gregorio San Nicholas, leaped from the back and escaped up the cliff behind the beach. Ben Limtiaco, one of the wounded, survived with partially paralyzed legs from stab wounds. Bishop Olano, who passed the jitney later that day, reported it "full of cadavers. All . . . killed by bayonets." The assault troops then moved on down the road toward Agana, attacking other Chamorro civilians they came across, including Luis P. Untalan, the principal of Padre Palomo School in Agana, and José C. Untalan. Luis survived, while José died.

At the Plaza de España, the Chamorro and American defenders waited with loaded guns in tense silence in the dim light. One of the Insular Force Guards, Pedro (Pedang) Guerrero Cruz, manned a machine gun at the northeast corner of the plaza closest to the Japanese line of march. He was assisted initially by fellow guard member Vicente Cruz (Ben) Chargualaf and then by Roman Eclavea Camacho, a teenager who was not even a member of the guard. Pete Cruz recalled that deadly morning: "I was frightened when I heard the

sound of metal hitting an object like a water canteen. Then I saw some figures moving and I opened fire. I ceased to be afraid. . . . I don't know exactly how long I fired that machine gun, but I know I kept firing until it got jammed and I couldn't reload it. Eventually, Lane told us to retreat, and we went to an area next to the Governor's Palace where we abandoned our weapons."

As the firefight erupted across the plaza, the Japanese were driven back twice, then flanked the perimeter, shooting and bayoneting some defenders. Ben Chargualaf was wounded (he would later die). Roman Camacho was one of those killed. The attackers then spread through the largely deserted town. The six American sailors from the *Penguin* who defended the power plant near Agana Beach were all killed in the initial assault. The Japanese mutilated the dead Americans.

By then, Governor McMillin, who was in his office that looked out on the plaza, was ready to give up. He later wrote, "The situation was simply hopeless, resistance had been carried to the limit." He had Chief Lane honk three blasts on the horn of an automobile in front of the building, and all fighting stopped.

After officers from both sides conferred in the plaza, Japanese troops entered the governor's residence and required McMillin, a heavy-set, six-foot-tall Annapolis graduate, to strip to his shorts. He was marched outside. There the Chamorro and American prisoners, about twenty men (the others had fled into hiding), were being assembled in their undershorts in the plaza and made to run a gauntlet. The Japanese laid a large U.S. flag on the grass and illuminated it with flashlights to show their aircraft that Agana had fallen. At McMillin's suggestion, the Japanese released their compatriots held in the jail across the plaza so that some could act as interpreters. McMillin then was taken back into the governor's residence, where around 7:00 A.M. on 10 December 1941, with Shinohara as interpreter, he signed a letter of surrender at the demand of Commander Hayashi of the Fifth Keibitai. The flag of the Rising Sun was then raised on the main flagpole as the real sun rose over Guam.

While the surrender was being arranged, two

last tragic deaths occurred among the American prisoners at the plaza. Marine Private First Class John Kauffman had a nerve defect that caused his face to twitch uncontrollably. A Japanese guard thought that Kauffman was making faces at him and plunged his bayonet into the marine's stomach. Another marine was slashed with a bayonet and bled to death. The plaza defenders were then all taken to the cathedral.

The marines at Orote learned by messenger of Mc-Millin's surrender before the Japanese forces made contact with them. When the Japanese Fifth Keibi-tai infantry arrived at Orote from Agana, Lieutenant Colonel MacNulty surrendered his marines in compliance with McMillin's official surrender. One U.S. officer described the surrender by the marines: "When they stood at attention while I lowered the colors, few could restrain their tears." These frustrated men would spend nearly four years as prisoners without promotions, honors, or even a citation from the Marine Corps.

Apra Harbor fell to the Japanese without a fight, and the entire island was captured virtually intact. The remaining elements of the South Seas Detachment landed from their transports in Apra Harbor. The radio station equipment in Agana and Libugon and some stores, trucks, and facilities had been destroyed by the Americans, but 4,000 gallons of gasoline, a number of vehicles, and several major facilities fell undamaged into Japanese hands. Even the Agana power plant, for which six American sailors died, escaped destruction. The bulldozers and other heavy equipment and trucks of the American contractors also fell to the Japanese and would be of great value to them later in the construction of airstrips and fortifications.

The capture of Guam had taken the Japanese less than six hours to accomplish once they landed. According to McMillin's report of the surrender (written in 1945 after he was released from a prisoner-of-war camp in Manchuria), those killed on the American side numbered between forty and fifty Chamorro civilians of all ages, one American civilian, four Chamorro Insular Force Guard members, nine American sailors, and four American marines. Perhaps over 100 persons were wounded; the exact figures are unknown. Japanese casualties are not known but reportedly included only ten men killed. The first days after the invasion, boonie dogs feasted on the dead bodies of Chamorros and Americans sprawled along the sides of roads until local men led by Father Calvo were permitted to bury the fifteen Chamorros killed along the Apurguan-Agana road and other bodies were interred. In a gesture of mercy, Commander Hayashi later allowed Father Calvo to conduct a religious service on 11 May for the dead at a small memorial erected by the Japanese across from the U.S. Naval Cemetery in East Agana.

The Japanese had expected the Americans to put up a tough battle for Guam, which is one reason the main Japanese force in the south was so much larger than the Marine Corps units they planned to fight at Orote. Nowhere in his report did Governor McMillin explain why the defense of Guam was so inept, why he did not promptly alert the civilian population or order evacuation of areas near military targets after he learned of the Pearl Harbor attack early on the morning of 8 December, why the main American fighting force—the U.S. Marine complement at Sumay—did not fight at all, or why the poorly trained Insular Force Guard bore the brunt of the combat. McMillin may have received orders that had expressly forbidden resistance. If so, he could have saved more lives by surrendering before the fighting commenced. On the other hand, if his orders were to delay the Japanese takeover, he should not have surrendered merely because the enemy had occupied the largely deserted capital but had not yet met the main U.S. force at Orote. Clearly, the American forces did not carry resistance "to the limit," as McMillin later asserted.

American accounts of World War II gloss over the fact that the American abandonment of Guam in 1941 was an inglorious footnote in the histories of the U.S. Navy and the U.S. Marine Corps. In the early days of World War II in other places, such as Wake Island and at Bataan, where the situations were also "simply hopeless," as McMillin claimed,

American forces fought much more tenaciously than they did on Guam. It was the valiant Chamorros of the Insular Force Guard and a handful of tough U.S. sailors who mainly upheld American military honor on Guam in those dark early days of World War II.

Among the legends of heroism by Chamorros of the Insular Force Guard that spread on Guam during the war years was the tale of Angel Leon Guerrero Flores and Vicente Cruz Chargualaf. When the plaza fell to the Japanese, Angel Flores, still at the plaza and with the badly wounded Chargualaf at his feet, supposedly refused to haul down the American flag in front of the governor's residence at the command of the Japanese. Infuriated, the Japanese allegedly bayoneted both men, then lowered and stomped on the American flag and raised the Japanese banner.

Pete Cruz, who saw Flores alive but wounded after sunrise the morning of the surrender, said flatly that the flag story did not happen. One fact, however, is undeniable: both Flores and Chargualaf died as a result of the fighting at the plaza. Years later, on 22 May 1978, the U.S. Navy Department confirmed their valor by awarding posthumous citations to the two fallen Chamorros in a ceremony at Sumay. Roman Camacho, the dead teenager, unfortunately was not honored since he was a civilian. Guam historian Pedro C. Sanchez, who was a boy in Agana in 1941, later wrote, "The Flag story, fact or fiction, was an important wartime event. . . . In the face of Japanese invasion and America's defeat on Guam with which they fully identified, the account lifted people's morale. . . . *Man-nina'i animo y Chamorro!* It inspired courage and hope among the Chamorros!"

Meanwhile, Major General Horii came ashore to assume command. A proclamation was issued in clumsy English that stressed the two main themes of Japan's imperial presence on Guam: a racist appeal to Asian solidarity and a threat of harsh punishment for any opposition:

We proclaim herewith that our Japanese Army has occupied this island of Guam by the order of the Great Emperor of Japan. It is for the purpose of restoring liberty and rescuing the Whole Asiatic people and creating the permanent peace in Asia. Thus our intention is to establish the New Order of the World. . . .

Those who conduct any defiance and who act spy [*sic*] against our enterprises, shall be courtmartialed and the Army shall take strict cause to execute said criminals by shooting!

Dated this 10th day of December 2601 in Japanese calendar or by this 10th day of December 1941.

By Order of the Japanese Commander-in-Chief.

Guam was not, as sometimes asserted, the only territory of the United States to be occupied by enemy forces in World War II. The U.S. islands of Attu and Kiska in the Aleutians were occupied in 1942 by the Japanese, but the indigenous Aleut inhabitants, except for an unfortunate handful left with some U.S. military weathermen, were evacuated prior to the Japanese invasion. Guam, therefore, still has the dubious distinction of being the only fully inhabited part of the United States to be occupied by an enemy in the war.

Under the assumption that Japan would permanently retain Guam in the New Order's "Coprosperity Sphere in Greater East Asia," the Japanese authorities renamed the island as well as Agana and all the villages. Guam became Omiya Jima (Great Shrine Island), while Agana was named Akashi (Red City). As the Chamorros would learn, the symbolism of the color red was ominously appropriate to life under the already bloody bayonets of their new conquerors.

New Aliens, Old Methods

The Japanese quickly rounded up all the Americans and foreigners that they could find. The military internees at first also included Insular Force Guards and five naval women nurses. The civilian prisoners included C. C. Butler, Marcelo Sgambelluri, James Underwood, William G. Johnston, and other Americans married to Chamorros, as well civilian contractors and Mrs. Hellmers and her newborn daughter. Bishop Olano and all the non-Chamorro priests were later rounded up and interned. The 492 prisoners were confined partly in the cathedral, in the building next door of the Knights of Christ the King (KCK), and some in the nearby Naval Hospital until all of the Americans were shipped to Japan as prisoners of war on 10 January 1942 on the *Argentine Maru.*

In Japan, they were joined by thirty Chamorro employees of Pan American captured when Wake Island fell on 23 December. The Japanese inexplicably treated these civilians as military prisoners of war. Ten unfortunate Chamorro employees on Wake had been killed, as were four Chamorro mess attendants on the battleship USS *Arizona* when it was sunk at Pearl Harbor. Many of the older Americans and Chamorros from Guam and Wake would die in the harsh conditions of Japan's internment camps.

Approximately 250 Chamorros of the Insular Force Guard and other local units were initially interned in the Dorn Hall Primary School on the side of the plaza opposite the cathedral. Twenty-six Chamorro nurses, unsung heroines of the war period, were also treated as prisoners and forced to work involuntarily throughout the occupation until July 1944. The Japanese immediately put the Chamorro men of the local military units to work as unpaid field-workers and as stevedores to unload ships in Apra Harbor. Subsequently, a work-release parole system was set up under which the Chamorro internees went home at night. Throughout the early period of the occupation, a number of Insular Force Guard members were beaten and tortured by the Japanese to obtain any military information they might have had. Many internees later worked as involuntary miners in an open-pit manganese mine that the Japanese attempted to operate in Libugon until the project was abandoned later in the war.

The nearly 6,000 Japanese troops constituted the largest military force to occupy Guam up until that time. To house all these men, the Japanese took over every public building in Agana, including the cathedral and the churches. The troops also looted many homes and stores. They bivouacked in tents in the plaza and other open spaces. Moving on the left side of roads, Japanese vehicles caused a number of accidents with the locals until all civilian cars, jitneys, and trucks were confiscated.

Guam historian Pedro C. Sanchez described the early days of the occupation: "Contributing to the crowded scene, there were hundreds of cavalry horses as well as horses used for carrying machine guns and other war equipment. With the horses came swarms of flies that were literally ten times as big as local flies. . . . There was the smell of pickled radish *(daicon),* dried seaweed, fish, sea-slugs and sea-cucumbers and the odor of soybean soup *(misu)* . . . from every corner of the city where hungry troops were preparing their meals in open fires."

Civil government under the Japanese was quickly placed under a civilian affairs section, called the Minseisho, of the Imperial Japanese Army. The Minseisho instituted an identification system; every resident had to obtain and wear a strip of cloth with Japanese characters identifying the bearer. This pass was issued only once. Called *lisiensan ga'lago* (dog tag) by the Chamorros, the pass was required until late 1942, when life became more routine.

The Minseisho also banned circulation of American money and the use of the English language. In the first days of occupation, American dollars could be turned in for Japanese yen, but at an extremely unfavorable rate of exchange. As a result, many Chamorros hid their American money. Rationing was implemented through coupons for purchases of all commodities. The Minseisho took over the Agana ice plant of Pedro P. Martinez and forced him to sell the best meat in his market to the Japanese before he sold to the Chamorros. The Japanese required weekly quotas of beef from the ranches of the Martinez family at Dandan, the Artero family at Upi, and the Bordallo family in Agat.

Monthly quotas were also imposed on villagers for crops and other food to be raised for the Japanese garrison. Food stocks and supplies of ordinary goods soon ran out, and locally owned stores gradually closed down. Only the stores of the new Japanese Kohatsu Company (which occupied the Atkins, Kroll store) and the J. K. Shimizu Company eventually remained open in Agana.

All bars were shut down, and the sale of alcoholic drinks was forbidden, even *sake*. This ban revived a lively bootleg business in *tuba* and *aguardiente,* just as in prohibition days back in the 1920s. A strict daily curfew was imposed from 10:00 P.M. to 4:00 A.M. As food dwindled, the majority of Chamorros reverted to living off the sea and the land in subsistence farming and fishing. Carabao carts once more became the primary means of civilian transportation, and federico nuts again became a food staple of the Chamorros, as in the old days. A barter system emerged among Chamorros and Japanese. Eggs were so popular as items of barter that the whole system came to be called *kōkan tamago,* the Japanese words for "exchange eggs."

The entire population of Sumay was swiftly evicted in the first few days to make way for a Japanese garrison, and five Chamorritas were raped by Japanese troops in the takeover. Schools reopened in April 1942 with Japanese sailors teaching the Japanese language, but, since much of the population was scattered into the countryside, school enrollment was low. Japanese civilian teachers, called *sensei,* and their families arrived by mid-1942 to replace the sailors, and Chamorro assistant teachers were trained. School programs and student enrollment on Guam slowly expanded, but the war years left a gap in the education of many of the island's children since the main subject was how to speak the Japanese language.

In November, two Japanese Catholic priests, Monsignor Fukahori and Father Peter Komatzu, arrived with Bishop Olano's permission. As citizens of non-belligerent Spain, Bishop Olano and his secretary had been freed after they arrived in Kobe with other prisoners from Guam and were staying with Jesuits in Tokyo until they could leave Japan. They were not, however, permitted to return to Guam.

Along with their troops, the Japanese also brought in forty-two prostitutes, mostly Korean "comfort women," and recruited about fifteen local "Monday Ladies" for five houses of prostitution. The house of prostitution for Japanese officers was in Anigua and housed Japanese "geishas," who were actually prostitutes. It was not long until a few local women became girlfriends of Japanese military personnel, just as they had with Spaniards and Americans.

Signs were quickly posted all over Guam in English, many handwritten, on the walls of offices, police stations, and the new sentry boxes called *kōbans,* with the words, "You must stop here and bow to us." Bowing was alien to the Chamorros, but they quickly learned that they must stop, turn, and bow to where the signs were posted, even if the place was unoccupied. Chamorros were also obliged to bow as a sign of respect to virtually all Japanese individuals. If the bow was too perfunctory or too obsequious, it brought a swift kick or some other punishment. One Chamorro, Juan Manibusan, the father of five children, had his spinal cord broken by Japanese and Saipanese policemen who beat him brutally when he failed to bow properly to the Dededo Police Station. Paralyzed, he died as a result of the beating.

More severe punishment was equally swift when two Chamorro youths were arrested for crimes. Alfred Leon Guerrero Flores of Agana was caught smuggling a note in December 1941 to an American prisoner about what was to be done with some dynamite hidden at the harbor. Francisco Borja Won Pat of Sumay was charged the same month with stealing from a warehouse of his former American employer in Sumay. The Japanese authorities apparently decided to make examples of these boys. On 6 January, a large group of people, including family members of the accused, was rounded up and marched to Pigo Cemetery.

There the two Chamorro youths were made to stand in front of freshly dug graves. A *taichō,* as Japanese officers were called, read the offenses in English. After a prayer by Father Oscar Calvo, the boys were blindfolded, and they waved goodbye. In anguish, Flores' mother cried out, "Adios y lahilo, ya si Yuus gachongmu" (Goodbye my son, God be with you). The two were then shot by a firing squad and fell back into their open graves.

While the people of Guam were uncomfortably settling down under the harsh Japanese administration, the war elsewhere was going extremely well for Japan. When Hong Kong fell to the Japanese a few days after Christmas 1941, massed troops held a military parade in Agana's Plaza de España. The Japanese held public celebrations again on 2 January 1942 when Manila fell, on 15 February when Singapore surrendered, and on 6 May when Lieutenant General Jonathan Wainwright surrendered at Corregidor. Chamorros were required to attend the victory parades and other gatherings to yell *banzai* on cue.

Japanese rule on Guam relaxed after 14 January 1942, when Horii and his army troops of the South Seas Detachment sailed away to take part in the battle for Rabaul in Melanesia. The administration of Guam was transferred to the Japanese naval guard force, renamed the Fifty-fourth Keibitai, with a garrison of approximately 300 men. Commander Hayashi remained in command of the Keibitai for the time being with his residence and offices in the American governor's palace. The civil affairs branch of the Keibitai, called the Minseibu, with a number of Japanese civilian administrators, took over day-to-day governance of the Chamorros. Lieutenant Commander Homura, an elderly retiree recalled to duty for the war, commanded the Minseibu for the duration of the Japanese occupation. Homura resided in a former U.S. military house in Adelup, and his offices were in the KCK building in Agana.

About fifty Chamorros from Saipan and Rota served as staff assistants, police investigators, and interpreters. The senior Saipanese was Juan Borja, known as Tun Juan Buko (*buchō* or *bukō* meant "boss"), who worked as liaison with Guam's village commissioners and Agana leaders through Vicente U. Zafra, the chief commissioner under the Americans at the time of surrender. Agana was organized into districts similar to the old Spanish

barrios, each under a Chamorro leader whom the Japanese called a *kuchō.* The village commissioners became *sonchōs.* Each district and village was headed by a Japanese *taichō,* usually a non-commissioned officer. Through the *kuchōs* and *sonchōs,* the Minseibu imposed communal work quotas, and assembled the people for propaganda sessions. In January 1943, the Minseibu organized three companies of unarmed paramilitary youth groups called *seinindan* among selected Chamorro students and *nisei* teenagers. The *seinindan* were gathered at times in camps for training and practiced marching until early 1944, when all Chamorro youths were conscripted into forced labor gangs.

Later, as the war swung back toward Guam and conditions deteriorated, the lot of the involuntary Chamorro *kuchōs* and *sonchōs* became extremely difficult. They had to endure considerable abuse from their own people who objected to the Japanese demands, yet the *kuchōs* and *sonchōs* had to carry out those demands without reporting malcontents, who would have been arrested by the Japanese police. Under the *kuchōs* and *sonchōs,* most able-bodied Chamorro men were mobilized in 1944 into labor gangs to construct airstrips as well as other military projects.

For police work, the Chamorros from the northern Marianas were led by Juan Castro and José P. Villagomez, the infiltrators of 8 December. The prewar Chamorro chief of police on Guam, Juan A. Roberto, as well as most other local policemen, continued to serve. Japanese policemen and Saipanese and Rotanese interpreter-assistants were assigned to police substations in all the villages. Under Japanese military law on Guam, suspects were presumed guilty until they proved their innocence. Beatings and sometimes torture were part of interrogations. An entire family could be punished with death for the wrongdoings of one of its members.

As a result of the imposition of strict social discipline and leveraged intimidation, and because firearms were forbidden to civilians, major acts of crime by civilians became rare on the island. For the Japanese, these were normal conditions for an occupied area in wartime. For the Chamorros, the discipline of the Japanese seemed harsh, but, until 1944, most civilians on Guam were not under extreme hardship. Even though martial law was in effect, the Japanese left most Chamorros and their property alone. Japanese discipline varied from village to village, depending on the personalities of the *taichōs* in charge. Some village *taichōs,* and the headquarters officers in Agana, treated Chamorros with respect, while others became little dictators.

The islanders called the most brutal of the Japanese officials *tek'cho na taichō* in Chamorro, a play on words that meant that the *taichōs* were so mean "they eat you up" (*tek'cho* describes carnivorous animals that prey on other animals). The islanders adopted an attitude of guarded, submissive neutrality toward the Japanese while hoping for the return of the Americans. A number of Chamorros secretly listened on shortwave radios to war news broadcast out of San Francisco by station KGEI. Among themselves, the Chamorros made up a secret little song to help keep up their morale with the refrain: "Oh, Mr. Sam, Sam, my dear Uncle Sam, Won't you please come back to Guam?"

With the Chamorros cowed, the Japanese police focused on searches for radios, firearms, American money, and other illegal items and on locating those few American servicemen who had eluded capture at the surrender of the island. By comparing American military duty rosters with prisoner-of-war rolls, the Japanese quickly determined that six American sailors were still loose on Guam. Two were from the *Penguin* crew and four from the Agana naval radio station staff. These six men, like many Chamorros at the time, believed that American forces would soon return, and they thought that they could hide out until then. The Americans first hid on the farms of Francisco Ogo and Manuel Aguon near Yona while the Japanese organized searches and offered a reward for the capture of the holdouts. The Japanese announced that the Americans would not be executed if they surrendered.

Rumors about the American holdouts grew to the point that the Japanese soon heard that the men were in the Yona area. The police concentrated their search there while they rounded up people for interrogation accompanied by savage beatings. The Americans split up and scattered to new locations with the assistance of Chamorros who gave them food, cigarettes, and firearms.

One of the holdouts was Radioman First Class George Tweed. He patched up a radio and clandestinely distributed for several months editions of the *Guam Eagle* that he typed with news of the war learned from San Francisco station KGEI. Despite misgivings by some Chamorros and at times the torture of others, no one informed on the Americans, and they all remained free for months. One stalwart Chamorro, Joaquin Limtiaco, was beaten viciously numerous times.

Nonetheless, on 12 September 1942, the Japanese caught three of the holdouts near Yona; they were A. W. Jones, M. L. Krump, and A. Yablonsky. They had split from Tweed, who was indiscreet; he sometimes attended Chamorro social functions in disguise. With the Japanese police was a Chamorro policeman, Adolpho Camacho Sgambelluri, the son of the American navy musician Marcelo who had married Joaquina D. Camacho before World War I and stayed on the island. Marcelo was interned at a prisoner-of-war camp in Japan. On Guam, his son Adolpho was playing a dangerous game of working for the Japanese while secretly warning Chamorros of impending searches and arrests whenever he could. This is how Sgambelluri described the execution of the three sailors:

> Before they sat down in the grave, they all looked around with a smile on their faces and one of them said, "so long boys." They sat down together with hands around their knees, and were made by Kimura (the Japanese officer) to bend their heads down.... Then the officer took out his sword and swung down on Krump's neck.... About this time Martin Borja (a Saipanese interpreter) said, "This will be a lesson to some of you." Then they (the Japanese and Saipanese) took turns thrusting their bayonets in the chests, backs, and sides (of the Americans).

Meanwhile, two other sailors, A. J. Tyson and C. B. Johnson, hid for six months on the ranch of Frank D. Perez at Oka, a few miles north of Agana in a cliffside area near the site of the present Guam Memorial Hospital. There they were often visited by Father Jesus Baza Duenas. The two Americans were guided by Perez to a safer location at the ranch of Tommy Torres at Mataguac in the Mount Machanao area in the north. The Japanese soon traced the two sailors, and the special unit of fifty Japanese troops assigned to capture the Americans arrested Tommy Torres at his ranch. They compelled him to lead them to the two holdouts on 22 October 1942. Both sailors were shot on the spot.

That left only Tweed. With the help of several Chamorros at great risk to themselves and their families, Tweed had moved several times. For about eight months he was hidden in Yona by the Manuel B. and Pedro R. Cruz family until he ended up in October 1942 in a cave-like crevasse on a densely forested, rocky cliff side at Toguac near Double Reef on the northwest coast of Guam. There he was safely sheltered in lonely isolation by the family of Antonio Cruz Artero for nearly twenty-one months until the American reinvasion. Prudently, Artero was careful to tell no one except a few members of his family about Tweed.

In the meantime, Chamorros continued to suffer because of Tweed. As more and more Chamorros were brutalized by the Japanese and Saipanese police for information about him, Agueda Johnston, who provided food to Tweed, asked him to give himself up. He refused and hinted to Johnston that, if any Chamorro turned him in, the Americans would seek revenge against the Chamorro after the war. Among those beaten were B. J. Bordallo and his sons Ricardo Jerome (Ricky) and Paul, none of whom knew where Tweed was. The older Bordallo was given thirty days to find Tweed or be executed. He walked all over the island but never seriously attempted to find the radioman. The Japanese did not execute Bordallo but instead put him in charge of garbage collection in Agana. Bordallo was reported as saying later, "Knowing that people were being killed or maimed, if Tweed had really been a hero, he would have turned himself in so that the wholesale brutalization of our people would cease."

Tweed became a secondary issue for the Japanese as Guam came under attack by American aircraft and submarines. These attacks began in January 1943, when a Japanese cargo carrier, the 8,360-ton *Tokai Maru* (Eastern Sea), was damaged inside Apra Harbor by a torpedo from the submarine USS *Flying Fish*. Two torpedos fired from outside the Calalan Bank traveled over the bank into the old *caldera grande*. One struck but did not sink the *Tokai Maru*. Seven months later, on 27 August, the submarine USS *Snapper* sent four torpedos across Apra, one of which hit the stern of the luckless *Tokai Maru*. In a quirk of fate, the *Tokai Maru* was anchored over the old *Cormoran*. The *Tokai* sank and came to rest nearly on top of the German raider. Years later, by the 1980s, these nautical victims of two wars would be popular sites for Japanese scuba divers, who would flock to Guam as tourists.

As the American threat grew, the Japanese increased the size of their Guam garrison and pushed the construction of airstrips. The strip on Orote Peninsula was started in October 1943 on the site of the Sumay golf course. By early 1944, the Keibitai, now under Captain Yutaka Sugimoto, numbered nearly 5,000 men, of whom about 700 were combat troops, 1,700 were in construction battalions and over 2,000 were aviation personnel for the aircraft at Orote airstrip and a new strip on the island's central plateau at Jalaguac-Tiyan (usually called Tiyan at that time, later the Naval Air Station).

On the other side of the world, the Anglo-American combined chiefs of staff met in Cairo in December 1943 and agreed on a Pacific strategy to defeat Japan by waging two major offensives simultaneously. One major thrust, led by General Douglas MacArthur, was to advance from New Guinea to the Philippines. The other offensive, similar to the old Orange Plans, would advance under Admiral Chester W. Nimitz's command from the Gilberts and Marshalls across the central Pacific to the Marianas, where a strategic bombing force was to be established to pound the home islands of Japan. With American successes from late 1943 into early 1944 in the invasions of the Gilbert and Marshall islands and the massive destruction of Japanese ships at Truk Lagoon in February 1944, the Japanese government realized that the Marianas would inevitably be invaded. The Japanese also realized that the newly developed B-29 superbomber of the Americans with a cruising radius of 1,500 miles could bomb the home islands of Japan from the Marianas. Guam is 1,350 flight miles from Tokyo. Therefore, the American drive across the central Pacific had to be repulsed on a final Japanese "home defense arc" that ran from the Bonins through the Marianas and the western Carolines.

Events overtook the Japanese defense plans. On 22 February 1944, twelve American carrier-based aircraft attacked the newly constructed Orote airstrip, damaging Zeros and killing four Japanese servicemen. Air raids became more frequent on the island, and the Japanese tightened security measures over the local people. The Chamorros were ordered to construct *bōkūgō* (air-raid shelters) and to stock them with food and supplies. Most *bōkūgō* were dugouts topped with coconut logs as well as tunnels dug into cliffs and hillsides.

The Japanese had not planned originally to construct large-scale fortifications on Guam and thus did not have much heavy construction equipment on the island. To build and repair defenses and airstrips, the Japanese had to rely on the Chamorro population and hundreds of Koreans and Okinawans brought in as laborers to back up the Japanese engineer battalions. The Japanese also put to use the American bulldozers and trucks captured when McMillin hastily surrendered.

For combat troops to reinforce the Marianas, the only reserves available were the divisions of the Japanese Kwantung Army that had been sitting largely unused in Manchuria to block any potential Soviet invasion of Japanese-occupied China. In February 1944, the Twenty-ninth Infantry Division of the Kwantung Army with nearly 10,000 soldiers

in three regiments—the Eighteenth, Thirty-eighth, and Fiftieth—under Lieutenant General Takeshi Takashina was ordered to the Marianas. The division was joined by units with 5,100 men from the Kwantung's First and Eleventh infantry divisions; this second group was designated the Sixth Expeditionary Force under Major General Toyashi Shigematsu.

The convoy of three destroyers and three troopships with the Twenty-ninth Division units aboard was attacked by the submarine USS *Trout* on 29 February near Saipan. One transport, the *Sakito Maru*, sank, with approximately 2,300 men of the Eighteenth Regiment lost along with eight tanks and equipment. The remaining ships then limped into Saipan. The Fiftieth Regiment was sent to Tinian, and the Thirty-eighth, with some of the remnants of the Eighteenth and two tank companies, went to Guam, where they arrived on 4 March. Meanwhile, the convoy with the Sixth Expeditionary Force escaped American submarines and arrived safely at Apra Harbor on 20 March. With the arrival of these army units, a new and by far the darkest chapter in Guam's occupation by Japan began.

Kempeitai and Kaikuntai: Militarism Amok

Lieutenant General Takashina assumed command of the entire island from the navy Keibitai and imposed harsh security measures through the Kempeitai military police of the Japanese army. With the army also came units of the Kaikuntai whose job was to provide the combat troops with food and supplies. Kaikuntai headquarters was in the center of the island between Ordot and Mangilao at a place called Tai, where the Japanese laid out a large agricultural plantation on which Chamorros were forced to work. The Kempeitai and Kaikuntai added more layers of administration over the Chamorros to the naval Minseibu of Homura, which continued to function.

Forced labor for all Chamorro males over twelve years old had been in effect since mid-1943, but under the Kaikuntai agricultural quotas and work requirements for all Chamorros, including women, girls, and old people, increased drastically. To augment the labor pool, the Japanese closed all schools and drafted everyone but children, even Japanese civilians of the Minseibu, to work. While men and boys worked mostly in labor battalions for heavy construction, females and older men worked primarily in the fields. New rice paddies were planted all over the island. In the paddies, the Kaikuntai used nicotine salt sulfur as an insecticide. Runoff from the paddies polluted some lagoons, killing considerable reef marine life, and permanently damaged patches of the Merizo lagoon.

For the most part, civilian laborers from mid-1943 on worked without compensation. Some workers received a bare subsistence ration of food, but most had to supply their own meals. They became slave laborers, working sometimes twenty-four hours at a stretch. Korean laborers and some Okinawans worked alongside the locals but were treated better than the Chamorros by the Japanese overseers. Many of the Koreans and Okinawans would die along with the Japanese when the Americans reinvaded the island, and the remainder would be deported to their homelands after the war.

Despite the increase in agricultural production spurred by the Kaikuntai, food was insufficient to support the new army units on Guam after March 1944. An extremely rainless dry season in the first six months of 1944 retarded local food production. The Japanese had earlier introduced to the Marianas (probably in the late 1930s) the giant African snail *Achatina fulica,* which grows to seven inches. It became a food source for the troops. Although edible, the snail also destroys crops, and it became a widespread pest on Guam after World War II.

Malnutrition began to affect everyone on the island. The Chamorros resorted to eating more of the plentiful cycad seeds of *fadang,* as they often had done in the past in times of food shortages. Few civilians had shoes—the Japanese requisitioned them, or they wore out—and most wore zories made with leather thongs and soles from old tires. People began to be infected by hookworms that

entered the body through bare feet as zories wore out and could not be replaced.

In early April 1944, American submarines and long-range PBY Catalina seaplanes were photographing the Marianas for targets in preparation for invasion. The U.S. operation to retake the Marianas was code-named FORAGER. It was to be the largest invasion of the war up until that time. A tight blockade was imposed around all the islands to choke off all supplies to the Japanese.

On 8 April, the submarine USS *Seahorse* torpedoed the 6,780-ton Japanese converted submarine tender *Aratama Maru* near the eastern coast of Guam. The burning ship made it into Talofofo Bay, where it sank three days later. The same day, 8 April, the *Seahorse* also damaged the 1,915-ton cargo ship *Kizugawa Maru,* which would be sunk in the middle of Apra Harbor two months later by air attacks.

U.S. Army Air Corps B-24 heavy bombers began to bomb Saipan and Guam for the first time in May when they accompanied navy PBY Catalinas. In a raid on 6 May, five U.S. planes were shot down by Japanese fighters, but American air power soon overwhelmed the Japanese air defenses. The B-24s began to bomb the Marianas regularly. On 11–12 June, Fast Carrier Task Force 58 of Vice Admiral Marc A. Mitscher unleashed a withering air assault against the Marianas that destroyed 150 Japanese planes in the air and on the ground.

From then on, the Americans ruled the seas and the skies of the Marianas. A Japanese officer on Guam wrote, "It is especially pitiful that we cannot control the air. We can only clench our fists with anger and watch." American dominance in the skies turned life on the ground into a hell as U.S. planes strafed and bombed Japanese, Koreans, Okinawans, and Chamorros alike. Antiaircraft fire, however, remained formidable, and falling shrapnel at times killed and wounded people on the ground. Falling shrapnel also triggered hundreds of delayed-action antipersonnel mines emplaced by the Japanese; the mines would pop up and explode unexpectedly after raids.

Despite the bombing, the Japanese continued to

construct ground defenses, mainly along the western side of the island. Reefs and lagoons were studded with underwater obstacles, barbed wire, and mines. Concrete strongpoints with machine guns, mortars, and light artillery provided mutually supporting enfilade and direct fire coverage of the beaches. Scores of dummy cannons made of coconut logs were mounted in lightly defended areas all around the coasts and on Cocos Island. Tunnel systems were embedded in the hills that overlooked potential landing sites, particularly in the ridges above Asan and in Mount Alifan behind Agat.

The seaward edge of the main ridge overlooking Asan, called Palasao by the Chamorros and the Japanese, would be named Bundschu Ridge by the Americans in the invasion in honor of a Marine company commander, Captain Geary R. Bundschu, who was given the task of taking it and who would die on it. Later the central portion of the ridge was named Nimitz Hill. Chorito Cliff, a steep spur of several sinuous hills, ran from Bundschu Ridge down to Asan Beach a few hundred yards west of Adelup Point. Chorito Cliff had long forced the Piti-Agana road to run along the water, and the Japanese fortified it heavily. Chorito for unknown reasons would be misspelled as Chonito by the Americans in their maps and all their postwar military histories.

Conditions on Guam worsened dramatically on 15 June, D-Day at Saipan, when U.S. forces began the invasion of the Marianas. While U.S. Marines fought their way onto Saipan's beaches, forty-six navy fighters and ninety-six dive-bombers blasted Guam. These intensive aerial attacks were followed the next day by a massive naval gunfire bombardment of Guam for three hours from the battleships USS *Pennsylvania* and USS *Idaho* and other ships of Admiral Raymond A. Spruance's Fifth Fleet. Later, naval fire sank the Japanese 6,870-ton auxiliary minelayer *Nichiya Maru,* which was tied up for repairs at a pier at Cabras Island. The wreck of the *Nichiya* still lies in over sixty feet of water next to the old GORCO pier in Guam's Commercial Port.

Because of the intensity of the 16 June bombard-

ment, the Japanese commanders thought that the Americans were about to invade the island. However, to their surprise and relief, dawn on 17 June revealed a clear horizon around Guam. The Americans had inexplicably sailed away.

What the Japanese did not know was that the U.S. landings on Guam had been scheduled for 18 June (called W-Day in U.S. war plans), three days after D-Day in Saipan. Because of the unexpected approach of the Japanese Combined Fleet from the Philippines toward the Marianas on 16 June, and also owing to the tenacious Japanese defense of Saipan, W-Day for Guam had to be postponed.

The American Fifth Fleet turned from the Marianas to meet the Japanese fleet on 18–20 June in the Battle of the Philippine Sea (called the "Great Marianas Turkey Shoot" by irreverent U.S. pilots). In that titanic battle to the west of the Marianas, the Japanese lost three aircraft carriers and 476 planes. By this time, both the Orote and the Tiyan airstrips had been bombed out. When some Japanese naval aircraft attempted to land on Orote airfield on 19 June, most crashed on the crater-pocked runway. The Battle of the Philippine Sea left Lieutenant General Takashina and his forces on Guam on their own to face the coming invasion.

Takashina knew that the respite from invasion was only temporary, and the 16 June bombardment had confirmed where the landings would likely come. He concentrated his main combat units along the coast from Adelup Point around through Agat, and he had them dig in for a stand to the death. The senior general on the island was Lieutenant General Hideyoshi Obata, commander of the Thirty-first Army for all the Marianas. Stranded on Guam en route to Saipan from Palau, he left the command of Guam in Takashina's hands but for unknown reasons approved a futile effort to reinforce his beleaguered men still fighting on Saipan.

This effort began on the night of 21–22 June, when a task force of two battalions with about 600 troops sailed in thirteen large boats from Guam to Rota, from which the force was to move on to Saipan. At Rota in rough seas in the dark, two boats overturned, and over 100 men drowned. One battalion then returned to Guam over the next few nights. This harebrained maneuver was symptomatic of the confused state of the Japanese command. The Americans would not occupy Rota until after Japan's surrender in 1945, so the Japanese troops left on the island never fought and in fact were starving by the war's end along with the local people on the island.

In the meantime, Admiral Nimitz, commander in chief of U.S. Forces Pacific and Pacific Ocean Areas (CINCPAC-CINCPOA), decided on 21 July as the new W-Day for Guam. The code name for the Guam portion of FORAGER was STEVEDORE. American photo missions and bombing strikes against the Marianas increased in tempo in late June and early July 1944. One pilot of a Grumman TBF Avenger torpedo-bomber in these combat raids on Guam was a young naval lieutenant, George Herbert W. Bush, flying from the light aircraft carrier USS *San Jacinto*. He was shot down close to Chichi Jima on 2 September. Rescued, he went on to become the president of the United States in 1988–1992.

In final preparation for the Guam invasion, American aircraft and ships constantly attacked the island day and night for thirteen straight days, beginning on 8 July. No one on Guam moved around by day. Under these conditions, the civilian population of Guam hindered Japanese troop movements. The Chamorros, being pro-American, also posed security problems. As a consequence, the Kempeitai cracked down ruthlessly on the local people to prevent espionage and sabotage, real or imagined. The Japanese believed that Tweed was transmitting by radio to the Americans intelligence information supplied to him by Chamorro spies. In reality, Tweed did not have a working radio.

Japanese discipline became brittle. When human will is driven to a pitch of extreme anxiety, it tends to snap suddenly when faced with overwhelming stress, even in seemingly well-disciplined military units. On Guam, the breakdown of Japanese military morale and discipline was manifested in numerous mindless atrocities against Chamorros.

Beheadings, rapes, and shootings of civilians occurred, mostly in the center and south of the island. On the other hand, in Yigo, the *taichō*, who was in love with a Chamorro girl, protected the local villagers against the harshest measures ordered by Agana.

A bizarre atrocity was the case of José Lizama Charfauros, who was foraging for food in the jungles of Fena when he encountered a Japanese patrol. The patrol leader made Charfauros kneel and then chopped at his back and neck with a sword. Left to die, Charfauros was found by friends days later, his wounds filled with maggots. The maggots helped save his life by cleaning out infection. Thirty-five years later, José Charfauros was still alive and happy, but with a large, half-inch-deep scar at the rear of his neck where the sword of the inept *samurai* had penetrated.

In a more deadly incident, on 8 July 1944 the Kempeitai arrested Father Duenas in Inarajan. The priest had often angered occupation authorities by opposing official directives and by denigrating the two Japanese priests on Guam as propagandists for Japan. He was also suspected by Japanese officers of making contact with American submarines and of spreading rumors of impending American victory in the Marianas. Most serious of all, the police believed that Duenas had knowledge of Tweed's whereabouts. The outcome was the arrest of the priest along with his nephew, former Island Attorney Eduardo Duenas. The police tortured the men at Inarajan and at Kempeitai headquarters in Agana Heights before turning them over to the Kaikuntai for execution. On 12 July, the two men were beheaded at Tai along with Vicente Baza. Juan (Mali) Pangelinan, who had helped Tweed, was also executed.

The irony of this tragedy is that, on 10 July at the time the priest, his nephew, and Mali Pangelinan were all being tortured to reveal information about Tweed, the American holdout was being rescued by the U.S. Navy on the coast at Toguac. Tweed signaled U.S. ships with a mirror and handmade semaphore flags. The destroyer USS *McCall* sent a boat to shore and took Tweed off.

The radioman became an instant, if transitory, war hero in the United States, with photographs and stories in *Life* magazine. Newspapers dubbed him "the ghost of Guam," and he was used in war bond drives. In September 1944, after Guam was retaken by the Americans, Tweed would return for a reunion with his Chamorro benefactors. Tweed's status as a hero, however, was tarnished in the eyes of many Chamorros when his memoirs, *Robinson Crusoe, USN,* written with journalist Blake Clark, were published in 1945.

Tweed-Clark wrote in the book that Mali Pangelinan had revealed to Duenas in confessional that he, Pangelinan, was helping the American. The book also said that Father Duenas violated the confessional by telling, under torture, the Japanese of Pangelinan's complicity. Pangelinan was then arrested and tortured by the Japanese, and he in turn betrayed Antonio Artero as the last protector of Tweed, according to the Tweed-Clark account. Regardless of who betrayed whom, by the time the Kempeitai closed in on the Artero ranch, Tweed had already been rescued, and the entire Artero family, alerted by friends, was hiding in Tweed's secret crevasse. Wisely, the Arteros did not come out until after the liberation.

Most Chamorros strongly resented Tweed's accusations against Father Duenas, whom they considered to be a martyr whose death may well have been caused by Tweed's remaining free. In March 1945, the priest's body was exhumed and reburied under the altar of the St. Joseph Church in Inarajan where he had served. A Catholic boys' high school was constructed at Tai in 1948 and named the Father Jesus Baza Duenas Memorial School.

Also in the future, General Motors would present a new Chevrolet sedan to Antonio Artero on behalf of the American people in recognition of Artero's bravery and loyalty. Tweed returned to Guam for the public presentation of the car in the Plaza de España in September 1946, but the occasion was marred by a demonstration of Chamorros against Tweed. Artero nonetheless accepted the car (he and Tweed remained firm friends) and also

accepted from Admiral Nimitz America's highest civilian award, the Medal of Freedom.

Tweed meanwhile retracted his accusations against Father Duenas, blaming coauthor Blake Clark for errors in the book, but Tweed never returned to Guam after 1946. A grade-B Hollywood movie, *No Man Is an Island,* of Tweed's war exploits appeared in 1962 but was filmed in the Philippines with supporting actors speaking in Tagalog, to the amusement of Chamorros who saw the film. After his retirement from the navy, Tweed became a farmer in Grant's Pass, Oregon, and died in an auto accident in 1989 at the ripe old age of eighty-nine, long forgotten as a war hero.

The postwar saga of Tweed was still in the future on 9 July 1944, the day before Tweed's rescue, when Saipan finally fell to the Americans after three weeks of some of the toughest fighting in the Pacific. The fall of Saipan, along with a major defeat of Japanese forces in Burma, caused a change of government in Japan. Army Lieutenant General Hideki Tojo, the hard-line prime minister who had led Japan into the war, resigned, and a cabinet under General Kaniaki Koiso assumed power as all Japanese commands braced for the next American assault.

As part of General Takashina's final preparations to meet the pending U.S. invasion on Guam, he issued orders on 10 July for all Chamorros throughout the island to be evacuated from their villages and to be marched to campsites in the southern interior of the island. This evacuation was apparently for security purposes to keep civilians from interfering with the defense of the island. Over the next few days and nights, long columns of hundreds of people poured out of the villages and marched inland on roads and trails, carrying whatever they could. Some rode carabao carts, but most were on foot, sometimes under air attack and always prodded by the bayonets and clubs of Japanese guards. There were stops at temporary sites en route to the main concentration camps. The largest number of refugees were herded into camps along the Manengon River inland from Ylig and Yona.

Southern villagers were collected mostly at camp-sites inland from Malojloj and Merizo.

The forced marches to the camps were especially hard on children. Forty years later in an interview, one marcher, Dolores Jones, recalled the ordeal of the 1944 evacuation when she was an orphaned eleven-year-old (her Filipina mother was executed by the Japanese; her Chamorro father was trapped in Manila) who had become the guardian of her small brothers and sisters: "Born in 1941 . . . Joey was three years old. I had him tied on my back, and Lulu, four years old, I was holding her with my right hand. And with my left I was holding my sister who was six years old. . . . We were walking day and night. I couldn't keep up with everybody. When I got tired, I would just lay down on the ground and sleep."

No buildings, latrines, food, or medicine were provided at the campsites. The Japanese troops themselves were short of supplies and could provide nothing for the Chamorros. The people built palm frond huts, used water from streams, and foraged for anything edible in the jungle. Approximately 18,000 persons huddled down in squalid conditions in the camps in the heavy daily rains of July to await their fate. Groups of boys and men were taken from the camps from time to time by Japanese guards to work sites and to carry supplies.

Of those Chamorros who remained near the beaches or who hid in coastal caves, dozens would be deliberately massacred by Japanese troops, while others were inadvertently slaughtered in the American bombardment. The circumstances of many wartime brutalities against Chamorros in this period are unknown as no eyewitnesses survived. One incomprehensible tragedy was the killing of young Mariquita Perez Howard, the Chamorro wife of an American sailor on the *Penguin*. While he was a prisoner of war in Japan, she was forced to be the personal servant of the head *taichō* of the Kaikun-tai camp at Tai. Beaten and abused, this vibrant mother of two little children was last seen being led into the jungle for execution by a Japanese soldier on 18 July, just three days before the Americans returned to Guam.

Her body was never found. Her husband, Edward Neal Howard, returned heartbroken for his little boy and girl after the war, and they were raised in the states. In 1982, the grown son, Chris Perez Howard, would publish a poignant book, *Mariquita: A Guam Story*, that concluded in both anger and sadness, "In the war between the United States of America and Japan, the peaceful and hospitable people of Guam were the losers."

Some of the most terrible mass executions of Chamorros by the Japanese took place near Merizo just prior to the invasion. On 15 July during a rainstorm, thirty bewildered villagers were herded by Japanese guards into a dugout cave at Tinta in the Geus Valley inland from Merizo. The Chamorros did not resist or run away because the Japanese would kill the families of anyone who did so. Inexplicably, the Japanese soldiers threw hand grenades into the cave and then bayoneted and beheaded a number of the Chamorros still alive. Fourteen Chamorros survived by playing dead as the Japanese departed to get out of the rain.

The next day, thirty young Chamorro men of Merizo were selected by the Japanese police *taichō* to dig a trench in the Geus Valley at a place called Faha near the Merizo cemetery. As the Chamorros were digging, Japanese guards tossed hand grenades and then machine-gunned the men, killing all thirty. A total of forty-six Chamorros are believed to have died in the Merizo preinvasion massacres. After the war, the victims were memorialized in April 1948 with their names on a bronze plaque on a monument that still stands beside the shore in Merizo.

In the meantime, the 800 or so people of Merizo were assembled and marched inland by the Japanese to campsites, first at Tingtinghanum for a night, then in the Atate area at Fineli (there were two Fineli camps; the other, now spelled Finile, was near Agat). Some village men among the evacuees learned of the massacres and decided to retaliate. On 20 July, with an old Springfield rifle that he had hidden, José (Tonko) Reyes led seven others and killed six Japanese guards at the camp, then attacked Japanese soldiers at a small supply depot, killing four more. The surviving Japanese fled into the jungle, leaving Merizo the first village on Guam to be liberated, and the only one liberated by the Chamorros themselves.

That night, fearing that the Japanese might return in force, Jesus Barcinas (who had been one of Laura Thompson's assistants in 1938) and five of the Merizo men paddled a canoe to Cocos to contact American ships. They found the little island deserted but covered with dummy cannons of logs. At daybreak, they paddled beyond the reef and were picked up by an American ship. These brave men assisted in the U.S. invasion as scouts and guides.

The American bombardment eroded Japanese discipline to a point where the behavior of many Japanese policemen and soldiers degenerated into a kind of destructive nihilism. In Agana on the night of 20 July, eleven Chamorro men, women, and young children—all accused of signaling U.S. aircraft—were bayoneted to death. Two teenagers—Juan (Bindan) Cabrera and Beatrice (Belok) Perez—escaped by faking death but bore lifelong scars from their wounds. At a cave near Fena, the *taichō* of the Agat police substation, Takebena, allowed his men to rape a dozen or so teenage Chamorro girls during 20–22 July, and the Japanese then killed a number of the helpless girls as the Americans advanced on the area, according to one survivor, Agnes Sucaldito of Agat. An unknown number of young Chamorro men were also killed in a massacre in another Fena cave at about the same time.

The American bombardment of Guam had gathered momentum from 18 July on to become by the morning of 21 July the most intense crescendo of conventional firepower ever inflicted on any locality in the Pacific war. On that date, W-Day, the island once more experienced an invasion by the Americans, this time in a shattering apocalypse of death and destruction that far surpassed the Japanese invasion of December 1941.

11 Return of the Americans 1944–1945

Liberation as Apocalypse

The American plan for the assault on Guam in 1944 resembled the Japanese invasion of the island in 1941 but differed in sheer massiveness and in the precise beaches where landings took place. One major U.S. force—the Third Marine Division under Major General Allen H. Turnage—would land northeast of Apra Harbor, but at Asan, not at Tumon and Agana bays as did the Japanese in 1941. The second major force—the First Provisional Marine Brigade led by Brigadier General Lemuel C. Shepherd and, as a reserve, the Seventy-seventh U.S. Army Infantry ("Statue of Liberty") Division under Major General Andrew D. Bruce—was to land south of Apra Harbor at Agat, just as the Japanese had done.

Together, the two U.S. forces made up the III Amphibious Corps, which once ashore would come under Major General Roy S. Geiger of the U.S. Marine Corps. A flyer and former commander of Marine Corps Aviation, Geiger—unlike some marine commanders—was a quiet man who worked smoothly with his army and navy compatriots. After the beachheads were established, the two forces were to converge to pinch off Apra Harbor behind a "Force Beachhead Line," or FBL (sometimes also called the Final Beachhead Line). With the FBL attained, and with the harbor and Orote airstrip in American hands, the combined army and

marine forces planned to push out to occupy the rest of the island.

The American commanders knew the Japanese order of battle and unit strengths on Guam from documents of the Thirty-first Japanese Army headquarters captured on Saipan. The Japanese commanders, on the other hand, did not know what they faced on the American side. The main opposing ground units were as outlined in Table 1, according to U.S. intelligence estimates in July 1944.

TABLE 1: ORDER OF BATTLE ON GUAM, 1944

Americans

Third Marine Division	20,328
Seventy-seventh Infantry Division	17,958
First Prov. Marine Brigade	9,886
III Amphib. Corps units	6,719
Total	54,891

Japanese

Army troops	11,500
Fifty-fourth Keibitai	2,300
Naval ground forces	2,700
Naval air units	2,000
Total	18,500

Sources: Crowl (1960, 329); Lodge (1954, 196–197).

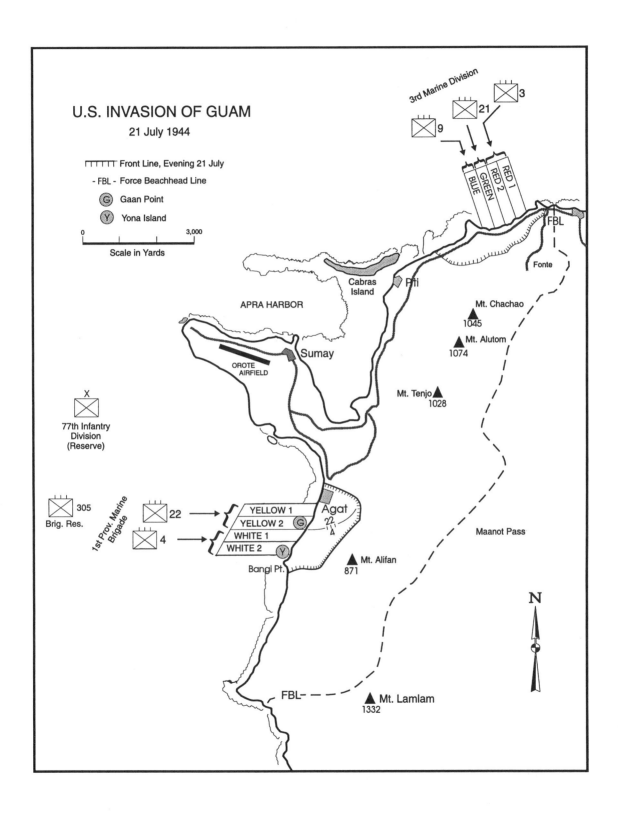

U.S. INVASION OF GUAM

21 July 1944

⊤⊤⊤⊤⊤⊤ Front Line, Evening 21 July

- FBL - Force Beachhead Line

Ⓖ Gaan Point

Ⓨ Yona Island

0   3,000

Scale in Yards

3rd Marine Division

⊠ 9

⊠ 21

⊠ 3

RED 1
RED 2
GREEN
BLUE

FBL

Fonte

Cabras
Island

Piti

APRA HARBOR

▲ Mt. Chachao
1045

▲ Mt. Alutom
1074

Sumay

OROTE
AIRFIELD

Mt. Tenjo ▲
1028

X
⊠

77th Infantry
Division
(Reserve)

⊠ 305

Brig. Res.

1st Prov. Marine Brigade

⊠ 22

⊠ 4

YELLOW 1

YELLOW 2 Ⓖ

WHITE 1

WHITE 2 Ⓨ

Agat

22
4

Maanot Pass

Bangi Pt.

▲ Mt. Alifan
871

FBL

▲ Mt. Lamlam
1332

N

The Americans thus had a three-to-one superiority in numbers. The Japanese forces actually numbered about 20,500, but over 3,000 of the 20,500 defenders were in support or construction battalions, not combat units. Furthermore, the total of effective Japanese troops declined significantly by W-Day as hundreds of men died or suffered wounds in the intensive preinvasion bombardment by the Americans since April. From April until the invasion, the Japanese cremated their dead every day, and the stench pervaded the island.

The W-Day landings were preceded on the nights of 17–19 July by three U.S. Navy underwater demolition teams (UDTs), who blew up reef and lagoon obstacles off the Agat and Asan beaches. On 20 July, the UDTs reported "the assault beaches cleared of obstructions." The next morning, the final preliminary bombardment of the beaches began before dawn at the military time of 0530 hours. This crescendo of firepower lasted for three deadly hours. A Japanese defender, machine-gunner Masashi Ito, described the effect: "The din robbed us totally of all sense of hearing. It wasn't the same as a boom or a roar that splits the ears: it was more like being imprisoned inside a huge metal drum that was incessantly and insufferably being beaten with a thousand iron hammers."

Pinned inside their caves and bunkers, the Japanese at first could not see the enormous U.S. fleet of eleven battleships, twenty-four aircraft carriers, and 390 other ships that massed off Guam's western shore. At 0806 hours, the first U.S. armored landing craft of the Third Marine Division crossed the line of departure 1,000 yards offshore of Asan. The landing craft were manned by men of the U.S. Coast Guard. At 0828, the first amphibious vehicle crunched up on Asan Beach, which was divided into four segments—Blue, Green, and Red 1 and 2—between Asan and Adelup points.

The Ninth Marine Regiment hit Blue Beach on the right flank nearest Asan Point, the Twenty-first Regiment splashed ashore on Green Beach in the center, and the Third landed at Red 1 and 2 near Adelup on the left flank. The air and ship bombardment shifted inland as the U.S. Marines charged over the beaches.

Five miles to the south, the Twenty-second Marine Regimental Combat Team (RCT) of the First Brigade landed at Agat on Yellow Beaches 1 and 2 north of Gaan Point at 0831 hours, as the Fourth RCT assaulted White Beaches 1 and 2 south of Gaan Point. The 305th Infantry Regiment of the army's Seventy-seventh Division followed after some delay (the U.S. Army did not have armored landing craft—as did the U.S. Marines) to occupy White Beach south of Gaan Point where the Agat cemetery stands.

Despite the bombardment, the Japanese emerged from their bunkers to fight. At Agat, a seventy-five-millimeter gun and a thirty-seven-millimeter gun mounted in a concrete blockhouse at Gaan Point killed seventy-five marines in the first wave before they even reached Yellow Beach 2. Subsequent waves of marines overran the blockhouse and killed all the defenders.

At the other beachhead in Asan, Second Lieutenant Yasuhiro Yamashita of the Eighteenth Regiment described the Asan landing from a hill above Piti: "All over, bodies were being blown up as the cannon shells fell. The earth and sand buried the soldiers. There was a lack of manpower, weapon power, and a weak first line defense unit. On the opposite side the Americans were landing on the beach and they were equipped to annihilate their opponents completely."

By nightfall on W-Day, the Americans had secured the beachheads up to 1,500 yards inland at Asan and over 2,000 yards deep at Agat. Over 25,000 U.S. troops were digging in and bracing for Japanese counterattacks. Thus, by the end of the first day, the Americans had a greater mass of men and more firepower ashore than the Japanese possessed to defend the entire island.

That night the Japanese counterattacked both beachheads, with the heaviest assaults at Agat, where Japanese infantry and four light tanks pierced the American left flank on the north of the beachhead. A bazooka man, Marine Private Bruno Oribiletti, who died fighting, destroyed two of the

Japanese tanks, and U.S. General Sherman tanks destroyed the other two in repulsing the attack. In the center at Agat, an infantry counterattack, led by the commander of the Thirty-eighth Regiment, Colonel Tsunetaro Suenaga, amounted to a futile suicide charge. The rash Suenaga died by rifle fire. Commander Asaichi Tamai, a naval aviator, took over Suenaga's command.

On the American right flank at the Agat beachhead, a small hill—called Hill 40 by the Americans—was the site of seesaw fighting as each side took and then lost the hill several times. The Americans finally secured it by the morning of 22 July. The counterattacks against the Americans at Agat were piecemeal and failed despite the brave but foolhardy charges by the Japanese. Wounded Japanese on the battlefield committed suicide rather than surrender.

On W-Day+1, 22 July, the Americans expanded their perimeters by attacking at dawn. At Asan, the Third Marine Regiment on the left flank of the beachhead seized Adelup Point and clawed its way up steep Chorito Cliff and Bundschu Ridge into the teeth of the Japanese defense. The Third finally secured edges of the high ground under heavy fire. In the center at Asan, the Twenty-first Marines fought their way up the slopes toward Mount Chachao, while on the right the Ninth Marines pushed toward Piti against light resistance. The men of the Twenty-first and Ninth regiments then settled into a relatively comfortable defense for the night. At Asan, however, the night of 22–23 July for the Third Marines on Chorito Cliff turned into a nightmare when they had to repel a ferocious Japanese bayonet charge at midnight.

At the Agat beachhead on W-Day+1, the Twenty-second Marine RCT swung north toward Orote Peninsula, while the Fourth Marine RCT and the 305th Infantry fought up the slopes of Maanot Pass in the area between Mount Alifan on the south and Mount Tenjo to the north. By 23 July, the fighting had assumed a pattern in which the Americans attacked in daylight hours behind massive artillery and air support and the Japanese counterattacked under the cover of night with weak artillery and no air support. On 24 July, General Takashina learned that the Americans were invading Tinian that morning. The battle for Tinian would last a week with over 8,000 Japanese deaths but only 328 marines killed, a ratio of more than twenty to one. In that battle, the Americans for the first time used a devastating new weapon, napalm bombs, that was soon used against Japanese troops on Guam.

From 23 to 25 July, the First Marine Brigade pressed northward from Agat toward Orote against stiffening resistance from the Japanese units forced back into the peninsula. On 25 July in broad daylight, Commander Tamai clumsily attempted to evacuate some of his troops from Orote by barge across Apra Harbor from Sumay to the Piti area, which was still in Japanese hands. U.S. artillery and air strikes sank the barges, killing many of the troops and leaving others to drown. While Tamai's barges were being sunk like sitting ducks, to the right of the First Marines the army's 305th Infantry, now with a sister regiment—the 306th Infantry—alongside, wheeled northeastward toward Mount Tenjo to link up by the end of the day on 25 July with the Ninth Marines, who were moving south from Asan. Apra Harbor was now cut off.

Meanwhile at Asan, on the left of the beachhead during 23–25 July, the Third Marines swept over what is now Nimitz Hill and fought to the edge of the Fonte Plateau, where General Takashina had his headquarters. Japanese maps and documents fell into American hands in the fighting and were translated by special U.S. Japanese-language translator teams, whose help proved indispensable. On a patrol at Fonte, Marine Corporal Robert P. Fowler found a Japanese officer's dispatch case with a map overlay that showed the locations of all Japanese units and headquarters. This information permitted the Americans to improve their night defenses and to prepare their daytime attacks for the maximum effectiveness, particularly for artillery fire.

Takashina planned major counterattacks for the night of 25–26 July to throw the Americans into the sea at both beachheads. One Japanese attack was to be mounted by the nearly 3,000 Japanese troops on Orote, the remnants of the Fifty-fourth Keibitai, the Thirty-eighth Infantry Regiment, the naval aviation personnel, and construction troops, all now bottled up in mangrove swamps at the neck of the peninsula and with cliffs and the ocean to their rear.

Sake, beer, and anything else alcoholic were all served liberally prior to the Orote counterattack, and just before midnight the drunken Japanese, led by officers waving swords, hurled themselves out of the mangrove swamps at the American lines without a preliminary artillery barrage. The Americans shot hundreds of white star shells and other flares into the cloudy night sky to illuminate the Japanese. Fire from American artillery, mortars, and automatic weapons slaughtered most of the attackers. The marines dragged their seventy-five-millimeter pack howitzers to within fifty yards of the lines to blast point-blank into the hordes of attackers. Those Japanese who reached the marine foxholes died in bloody man-to-man combat.

Marines under fire, Asan Beachhead, 1944. These are men of the Third Regiment, Third Marine Division, on Red Beach 2 the morning of the invasion, 21 July 1944. Asan Point in the background. (From the collection of the Micronesian Area Research Center, Mangilao, Guam)

Marines raising U.S. flag on Guam, 21 July 1944. In the background men and amtracks move toward the Asan Beachhead. (From the collection of the Micronesian Area Research Center, Mangilao Guam)

While the *banzai* massacre was taking place on Orote, the Japanese on the high ground above the Asan line rushed down against the marines behind an intense mortar and artillery barrage on the American positions. In the center-right of the perimeter, Japanese soldiers of the Eighteenth Regiment and the Tenth Independent Mixed Regiment smashed into the Twenty-first Marines down a hilly spur dubbed Banzai Ridge by the marines. As the Japanese charged, they screamed in English, "Wake up and die, marines!" Japanese suicide squads, with some men carrying TNT packs and mines strapped to themselves, penetrated as far as the division field hospital near the beach. A marine said of the hospital fight:

What a sight it was! The walking wounded, bandages and all, are banging away at the Japs. Some of the more seriously wounded men were firing from their beds.

After it was all over, they even found several dead Japs in the surgical tent. The Marines lost some men, of course, but we killed the Nips in bunches.

Over 3,500 Japanese men died in courageous but useless combat in the night attacks of 25–26 July on the two U.S. beachheads. In the close-in, murderous combat that took place on Guam, neither side was inclined to take prisoners. A few Japanese faked surrender and then opened fire or threw grenades as Americans approached. The Japanese also booby-trapped some of their own dead with live grenades in armpits and under bodies, causing the Americans to shoot all Japanese, even dead ones, as a precaution.

From 26 to 29 July, the Americans south of Apra overran Mount Alifan, took Sumay, then all Orote. The marines north of Apra pushed across the Fonte

Marines find plaque of prewar Marine Barracks at Sumay, 29 July 1944. These are men of the First Provisional Brigade who took Orote Peninsula. (From the collection of the Micronesian Area Research Center.)

Plateau to take the Libugon Hill area against entrenched pockets of Japanese, who launched one more company-sized *banzai* charge. Many Japanese soldiers, even those not wounded, committed suicide, usually by exploding a hand grenade against their stomachs while screaming, "Tennō Heika, Banzai" ("Long live the emperor"). The marines killed Major General Shigematsu at Fonte, probably on 26 July. They killed the Japanese island commander, Lieutenant General Takashina, on 28 July by tank machine-gun fire at Fonte shortly after he had issued orders for a Japanese withdrawal to a new defensive line between Dededo and Barrigada. Lieutenant General Obata then assumed direct command of the retreating Japanese units.

On the afternoon of 29 July, W-Day+8, Admiral Spruance and other high-ranking American officers came ashore for a solemn little ceremony to raise the American flag at the old Sumay Marine Barracks, now in ruins. By sundown of that day, American units had generally reached the Force Beachhead Line. This line stretched from Adelup to the heights of Libugon and then southward across the high ground of Mounts Chachao, Alutom, Tenjo, and Alifan down to the sea near Facpi Point. Apra Harbor and the Orote airstrip were safely in American hands behind this line. U.S. naval construction battalions (CBs, known popularly as "Seabees") swiftly repaired the Orote airstrip, and at 1650 hours on 30 July the first American aircraft landed, a Navy TBF-1 Grumman Avenger torpedo-bomber. Thereafter, much of the air support for the Americans operated from Orote while supplies began to pour in through Apra Harbor.

As supplies built up, the Americans paused on 30 July to regroup while General Obata moved his mangled Japanese forces to the north. The assault phase of the battle for Guam was over, and it had been won by the Americans.

The Will to Lose Hard

American bulldozers scooped out mass graves and buried thousands of Japanese dead behind the FBL. On their side of the line, the Japanese also buried their dead, many in unmarked locations now unknown. For decades after the war, the bones of these men would appear unexpectedly when new construction was undertaken on Guam. The Americans buried their own dead in temporary cemeteries, the largest at Pigo, and later disinterred and shipped the bodies to their final resting places in the United States.

Acts of heroism in combat had been numerous on both sides in the battles for the beachheads. In particular, Japanese army officers and soldiers in the attacks against Asan on the night of 25–26 July fought with honor and courage, but it was the Americans, as victors, who received the medals. Marines earned four Congressional Medals of Honor for extraordinary valor on Guam, two posthumously. One living recipient, Captain Louis H. Wilson, Jr., would go on to become commandant of the Marine Corps in the 1970s.

While the American forces paused to regroup behind the FBL, General Geiger sent out patrols from the Seventy-seventh Division on 27–30 July to reconnoiter the southern interior of Guam. He wanted to be sure that no large Japanese units might attack his southern flank. By this time, a number of Chamorros had filtered across the American lines, and some volunteered as scouts for the Americans. With Chamorros as guides, the army patrols to the south verified that no major Japanese forces lurked as far as Inarajan and Umatac, but the patrols did not penetrate all the way to Merizo.

Several hundred Chamorro refugees from Inarajan and Merizo were still camped inland from Merizo among the hills south of Fena and in Umafit inland from Inarajan. On 30 July, the U.S. Seventy-seventh Division sent a patrol into this area. Chamorro men in the camps contacted the Americans, and together they killed and chased away the Japanese guards. After the army patrol departed to report back, about 200 Chamorros from the camps marched toward Merizo in the hope of defending themselves better there until the Americans returned.

When the refugees reached Merizo, which was deserted, they gathered in the village schoolhouse. Soon, a platoon-sized force of Japanese soldiers appeared from Inarajan and attacked the refugees in the schoolhouse. In this final Chamorro versus Japanese skirmish, about seven Japanese soldiers died, and several Chamorros were killed and wounded, but the remaining Japanese fled.

While the incidents in the south were occurring, American shelling and air strikes against Japanese-held areas in the north continued unabated. Rear Admiral Robert L. Conolly, in charge of the U.S. bombardment and called "Close In" Conolly because of his belief in point-blank fire support, feared that the Japanese might still mount a costly house-to-house defense of Agana as they had done in Saipan's villages. So the last of the town was destroyed in order to liberate it with minimum American casualties. The devastation was vividly described by Don Pascual Artero: "So green in vegetation and so pretty a sight had Guam always been, now it was all burned. It had neither a tree, nor a coconut with leaves. All now was burned or destroyed by bullets and bombs. . . . From our cave in Toguac which looked towards Agana, we saw the destruction of the town where we had our property."

The need to raze Agana was questionable after 26 July, when the Americans knew from captured documents that no major Japanese units were in the town. On 29 July, to the astonishment of American forward observers on nearby hills, a small Japanese force staged a little parade in the open at Bradley Field parade ground near Anigua, perhaps to intimidate the Americans. But the Japanese withdrew before the Americans could call in artillery on them.

The Americans nevertheless continued to bombard Agana, destroying all major structures as well as many records and documents that they contained. The prewar Guam Museum was smashed, as were the governor's residence, the Naval Hospital, and the Tribunal y Cárcel. The Japanese had already carried off many of the museum artifacts to Japan (where they remain), and when American troops occupied the town they collected as souvenirs many of the remaining items strewn about in

the ruins. Of the Spanish edifices, only the Garden House (servants' quarters built in 1736 and to become the Guam Museum after the war) and the *azotea* (terrace) of the old *palacio,* parts of the *almacén* wall, and the Bridge of San Antonio survived. The Chocolate House, a picturesque small round structure in the *palacio* garden, was destroyed and would be rebuilt after World War II, as would the little bandstand in the plaza.

On the morning of 31 July, the American forces resumed the offensive. The Third Marine Division moved through the rubble of Agana with only a few casualties caused by land mines. By evening, the marines reached the plateau at Jalaguac just short of the Tiyan airfield. To the right of the marines on their southern flank, the Seventy-seventh Infantry Division swept across the island's narrowest part to reach the high bluff that overlooks Pago Bay north of Yona. By the night of 31 July, the Americans had cut the island in half.

As the American soldiers and marines moved forward, they came across more and more Chamorro refugees. The first small groups of Chamorros who escaped the concentration camps had crossed the American lines back on 24 July. They were taken in hand by the American civil affairs staff, who set up refugee camps with food, water, medicine, and support personnel at Asan (moved later to Anigua, where the camp grew and spilled into the Pigo Cemetery) and at Finile just south of the old village of Agat in and around the cemetery near what became New Agat village. For some unknown reason, tents had not been planned for, so the civil affairs men scrounged from military units to provide shelter for the refugees against the drenching cloudbursts and the scorching sun that alternate on Guam in the rainy season.

Late on the afternoon of 30 July, army patrols reached the edge of the concentration camps in the Manengon Valley. A group of Chamorros, including B. J. Bordallo and his family, followed a patrol back to the mountains above Agat, from where they moved behind the American lines the next day. On 31 July, troops of the Seventy-seventh Division overran the main camps. Some Japanese guards were killed, and the rest fled. The Americans handed out C-rations, candy, and cigarettes to the hungry refugees, many of whom promptly suffered diarrhea from gorging on chocolate candy. Thousands of Chamorros in the Manengon camps then trekked westward across the center of the island to the American refugee camps at Finile and Asan for food and help.

The Americans meanwhile set up a transit camp at Manengon for Chamorros from the camps in the far south. By mid-August, an estimated 18,000 Chamorros, the bulk of the island civilian population, were housed behind U.S. lines in three main refugee camps, which turned into muddy, sprawling shanty towns. Luckily, the civil affairs teams found caches of Japanese food and supplies, and some trucks abandoned by the Japanese, to feed and transport the Chamorros until the U.S. military logistical system was fully established.

In the drive northward from the FBL after 31 July, the Third Marine Division attacked on the left or western side of the island, and the Seventy-seventh Infantry Division was on the right with its flank on the windward coast. Where the island widened above Dededo, the First Provisional Marine Bri-

Bordallo family after fleeing concentration camp. This photograph was taken about 31 July 1944 at the Fineli refugee camp in Agat and shows B. J. Bordallo in center rear, Mrs. Josefina Pangilinan Bordallo in the center, and Paul and Ricky on the right. (Courtesy of Emilie G. Johnston)

gade moved up to the left of the Third Marine Division so that all three major U.S. combat units moved abreast to the north. The army's Seventy-seventh Infantry Division ran into the hardest fighting around Mount Barrigada on 2 August and at Mount Santa Rosa on 7 August, while the marines were held up briefly near Finegayan on 3–4 August. Small but bloody tank-infantry battles erupted at each of these locations.

In their advance, the Americans also came across gruesome scenes of Japanese atrocities inflicted earlier on Chamorros. On 8 August, a Marine patrol found thirty dead Chamorros, one a woman, in and around a Japanese army truck north of Yigo. On 9 August near the same area, another patrol stumbled onto twenty-one more bodies. Marine Private Joe Young described the dead Chamorros to a combat correspondent, Alvin Josephy, Jr., who wrote a dramatic account, *The Long, the Short, and the Tall,* of the Third Marine Division battles: "They lay in awkward positions—on their sides and their stomachs, and on their knees—like swollen, purple lumps. And none of them had heads, they had all been decapitated. The heads lay like bowling balls all over the place."

The dead were young people taken by the Japanese from the concentration camps for labor gangs to carry ammunition and supplies to the north. The Japanese killed the Chamorros to prevent them from providing information to the advancing Americans. The atrocities made the American soldiers and marines, and their Chamorro scouts, even less inclined to take any prisoners.

As the Japanese units retreated northward, they were accompanied by their own civilians—Japanese, Koreans, and Okinawans, including Minseibu and Kaikuntai personnel, with women and children and elderly men—all fleeing presumed death at the hands of the feared American marines and soldiers. These bewildered refugees included *nisei* and part-Chamorro, part-Japanese residents of prewar Guam such as members of the Takano, Onedera, Sawada, and Shimizu families.

According to Naoe Takano, she rarely walked more than fifty paces in Yigo without finding bodies of Japanese soldiers strewn along the path. Once, she recalled, "I felt a hand grab my leg. When I looked down, I saw and heard a dying soldier crying for water. But there was no water." She walked on.

When the group that included Naoe as well as Mrs. Kaneki Sawada and Mrs. Reji Dejima reached the high cliffs above Pati Point, they were informed that the next morning they must all jump off the cliffs in a mass suicide. This mass *hara-kiri* on Guam was to be a repetition of the hundreds of Japanese suicides on 9 July off the cliffs of Saipan when the Americans pushed to Marpi Point on the northern tip of that island. Fortunately, on Guam early the next morning, the Americans bombarded the Pati Point cliff line, and the refugees scattered, canceling the mass suicide.

Nonetheless, individual Japanese civilians on Guam did kill themselves out of fear of the Americans. Some Japanese civilians simply disappeared, presumably killed in the whirlpool of war that swirled around them. Among the old-time residents who died in the retreat to the north were Mrs. Kaneki Sawada and the elderly José Shimizu, a doyen of Japanese merchants on Guam since the early 1900s. José Shimizu's descendants would endure and make their family name one of the most respected on Guam in the long years of healing between Japanese and Chamorros after World War II.

Eventually, the Japanese civilian survivors, including Saipanese and Rotanese, fell into American hands in the Yigo area. Some civilians, including Chamorros married to Japanese, were interned with prisoners of war in a stockade at Agana Heights. Most were eventually deported or released, while a few had to face trials.

In the meantime, the U.S. forces pressed relentlessly northward. On 7 August, the Americans formally reactivated the Insular Patrol and then changed its name to the Local Security Patrol Force, or Combat Patrol, as it was popularly known, made up of Chamorro scouts. This new force performed valiantly in locating Japanese troops and equipment. A nineteen-year-old, Jesse Perez of Yigo, along with two friends, Jesus Aflleje and Joaquin Sablan, joined a U.S. Marine Corps unit, and each was given a carbine. Years later, Perez recalled combat and its sad aftermath for him: "We were confronted with a large group of Japanese. We fought it out in close combat, and Aflleje, Santos and a marine were killed. I was shot under my left armpit, the bullet piercing into my body and ripping my kidney. A second bullet is still lodged between my ribs. My arm muscle was smashed. The bullet in my ribs is enclosed in copper, and to this day I must avoid electric shocks." The Americans evacuated Jesse Perez to California for medical treatment, and a long, sinewy muscle of a snake was used to reinforce the bicep on his shattered left arm.

The U.S. forces also utilized K-9 dog platoons of German shepherds and Doberman pinschers. The dogs proved extremely effective as sentinals, scouts, and ammunition carriers. After the war, a grateful U.S. Department of Defense created near Yigo a "War Dog Cemetery," with the graves of twenty-four dogs killed in action. The cemetery is maintained by security units from Andersen Air Force Base, where sentry dogs are still used.

The last clashes between major units on Guam took place on 9–10 August along trails leading to the high ground above Tarague Beach. American patrols reached the cliffs above Tarague on 10 August, completing the drive to the north. When General Geiger learned of this action, he announced at 1131 hours on 10 August that all organized resistance by the Japanese was at an end on Guam. Late that afternoon, Admiral Nimitz landed on Orote airfield with his staff officers and with Lieutenant General Alexander A. Vandegrift, the commandant of the Marine Corps. The next day, they met with senior officers of III Amphibious Corps to plan the next phase of operations. Nimitz also held a press conference at which he read a letter to him from six prominent Chamorros who wrote, "We rejoice (at) the recapture of Guam and are extremely grateful for the timely relief we are now getting."

Geiger in the meantime had established an "enemy straggler line" across the north of the island between Fadian Point and Two Lovers Point. All stragglers were to be contained north of this line and mopped up. Geiger's action proved to be premature. Organized groups of Japanese remained stubbornly active in the north and south of the island despite the straggler line, and one more final little battle took place on Guam. On 10 August, soldiers of the 306th Infantry Regiment came across a large brush-covered hollow—actually a natural limestone sinkhole—at Mataguac Spring near Mount Mataguac just north of Yigo. Unknown to the American soldiers at the time, this depression concealed a fortified cave-bunker, the last command post of Lieutenant General Obata.

In the fight that followed on 10–11 August, it took many pole charges and hand grenades plus several 400-pound blocks of TNT to seal up the entrances to the cave-bunker. Eight Americans were killed and seventeen wounded in the action. When the Americans opened the entrances four days later, they found sixty Japanese bodies inside, among them Obata's. During the battle, Obata had sent out a last radio message on the night of 10 August to Imperial Headquarters in Japan: "We have only our bare hands to fight with. The holding of Guam has become hopeless. . . . I am overwhelmed with sorrow for the families of the many fallen officers and men. . . . I pray for the prosperity of the Empire."

On 11 August, Tokyo acknowledged the fall of Guam by designating the Japanese garrison there as a *gyokusai* (lit., a crushed jewel), meaning a hallowed death with great honor for all Japanese on the island who ended their lives in battle.

On 15 August, Guam was turned over to a U.S. Island Command, whose main mission was to provide support for the next operations in the Pacific war. So ended the Battle of Guam in 1944, but not the fighting on the island, for many defiant Japanese soldiers remained in the island's jungles.

The number of U.S. servicemen reported killed in action or who had died of wounds on Guam as of 11 August totaled 1,747. Of these, 1,520—or 87 percent—were U.S. Marines, men of steadfast courage who died mostly in the beachhead battles. American wounded totaled 6,053, again mostly U.S. Marines. An additional twenty-two men were missing in action and presumed dead. Thus, a total of 1,769 Americans died in the Battle of Guam.

The number of Chamorros and other civilians killed as a consequence of the war is not precisely known. Formal claims submitted to the U.S. Congress for Chamorro war deaths and injuries documented or witnessed from 8 December 1941 to 31 August 1944 came to 578, of which 320 were for deaths and 258 for injuries, but there were additional deaths and injuries unaccounted for and for which no claims were submitted. Geiger's headquarters reported 10,971 Japanese killed by American forces as of 11 August 1944. In the following weeks, the jungles of Guam became a killing ground as American-Chamorro hunter teams tracked down Japanese holdouts. Many of the holdouts depended on the munificence of American garbage dumps for food. By the end of September 1944, some 4,926 Japanese holdouts would be killed in spite of U.S. leaflets and broadcasts that induced a few to surrender.

One indomitable little group of eight Japanese soldiers decided to escape from the island entirely. They constructed a wooden raft, and one night in early December 1944 they launched it over the reef near Agat. They were carried by the trade winds westward into the Philippine Sea. By 30 December, a month at sea, the men were barely surviving on rainwater and occasional bonita that they shot. On that day, a monstrous dark form surfaced suddenly out of the sea almost beneath the raft. Stunned witless, the men saw the large white figures "I-47" on the side of the monster. It was a Japanese submarine.

The I-47 took them aboard and sailed safely back to its base at Kure, Japan. At first treated as deserters, the men eventually were accepted as honorable evaders. They were probably the only Japanese ground soldiers in all Micronesia to make it safely back to Japan before the war ended.

During the early months of 1945, a company-sized group of Japanese holdouts under Lieutenant Colonel Hideyuki Takeda near Tarague continued to evade capture. As the highest-ranking Japanese officer left alive, Takeda had ordered all Japanese holdouts to conduct guerrilla warfare against the Americans. By 31 August, American military records reported 18,377 Japanese dead on Guam, of whom about 200 were civilians. An unknown number of the dead were Okinawans and Koreans, whom the Americans counted as Japanese. Around 1,250 Japanese had surrendered by that date.

After the war ended, and in response to American propaganda to surrender, Takeda himself and sixty-seven of his men finally gave up on 4 September 1945. A week later, he persuaded another forty-six of his men to come in. These military prisoners were returned to Japan. From then on, about 130 Japanese, either as individuals or in small groups, held out, utterly convinced that American propaganda about the war's end was a lie. These hunted men led desperate lives, a few starving to death, and some resorting to cannibalism among themselves to survive. During the next three decades, 114 stragglers surrendered, and the remainder were killed, until Sergeant Shoichi Yokoi, the last straggler, surrendered in January 1972, an incredible twenty-six and a half years after the war ended. An American military assessment of the Japanese defense of Guam correctly characterized it as "suicidal bravery and inhuman tenacity—the will to lose hard."

Old Aliens, New Methods

The Americans did not slow the rapid tempo of their activities once large-unit combat ceased in the Marianas in August 1944. All commands immediately began preparations for the next major operations in the Pacific. Guam, Saipan, and Tinian had been seized by the United States for three strategic purposes: to lure out the Japanese fleet and defeat it in a decisive battle that would leave open the way to invade Palau, the Philippines, Formosa, Okinawa, and eventually Japan itself; to establish forward naval bases—principally at Apra Harbor—

that would support those invasions; and to construct air bases from which B-29s—nicknamed "Superfortresses" and called VHBs, or very heavy bombers, by the U.S. Army Air Corps—could bomb the Japanese home islands.

The first goal was fulfilled in June 1944 when the U.S. Fifth Fleet defeated the main Japanese Combined Fleet in the Battle of the Philippine Sea. That left the last two goals, over which the army and the navy would argue. For the navy, which had operational control of the central Pacific theater under Admiral Nimitz as CINCPAC-CINCPOA, the second goal had priority because the navy planned next to invade Peleliu and Angaur in Palau, Ulithi Atoll near Yap, and then the Philippines and Formosa.

The Army Air Corps, on the other hand, believed that the third objective should take priority. The Air Corps chief of staff, General Henry H. (Hap) Arnold, intended to make the Marianas into unsinkable aircraft carriers from which the Twenty-first Bomber Command of the Twentieth Air Force would mount massive air strikes against Japan. The Twenty-first Bomber Command was made up of five wings with over 500 B-29s under the command of Major General Curtis LeMay, who assumed command in September 1944. Air Corps strategists such as LeMay believed that the air assault might even make an invasion of the Japanese home islands unnecessary.

A preinvasion aerial survey of the Marianas in May 1944 by Air Corps Major General Walter H. Frank proposed five B-29 air bases on the islands: two on Guam, two on Tinian, and one on Saipan. Rota, small and mesa shaped, was not needed as an air base and therefore was not invaded. Each VHB base was to have two 8,500-foot asphalt runways and would house a wing of about 100 B-29s. Each bomber required eighty-five men as support personnel, of whom eleven were crew. Thus, the Air Corps planned to have over 45,000 men in the Marianas. One of the fields that the Air Corps planned to utilize on Guam was Tiyan, which by 1944 had a 6,000-foot runway constructed by the Japanese with the forced labor of Chamorros, Oki-

nawans, and Koreans. The Air Corps also planned to construct a support air base, called Depot Field, below the Jalaguac-Tiyan plateau in what was formerly the old Dededo-Finegayan area.

With regard to American strategic planning, Guam was not invaded just to "liberate" the island because it was a U.S. territory, despite much propaganda to that effect in the news media. Although political considerations played a role in the decision to retake Guam, the major factor was to fulfill U.S. strategic military objectives. The key to achievement of those objectives was the seizure of Saipan first in order to cut off Tinian and Guam from Japanese reinforcements and supplies and thus make the two latter islands more vulnerable to assault. From the strategic viewpoint, the Battle of Saipan, not the Battle of Guam, was the most decisive in the three invasions of the Marianas in 1944.

Civil matters nonetheless had to be taken into account. So, back in March 1944, Nimitz created a special headquarters called Forward Area Pacific Command headed by Vice Admiral John H. (Johnny) Hoover. This officer, a "dour and ill-humored" man according to a naval historian, was given responsibility for the islands of the central Pacific after they were conquered by U.S. forces. In March, Hoover assumed authority in the liberated Marshall-Gilbert islands, and, in July, his responsibility shifted to the Mariana Islands. Hoover's title then became Commander Marianas Area. In 1948, this title had changed to Commander U.S. Naval Forces Marianas (COMNAVMAR), directly under CINCPAC. Over the years following World War II, COMNAVMAR would become—and remains as of the early 1990s—the senior U.S. military post for all Micronesia.

To reestablish the navy's authority on Guam, Nimitz issued Proclamation 1 on invasion day, 21 July 1944, which was designated as Liberation Day. No Chamorros knew of Nimitz's edict until after he arrived on Guam on 10 August, but the proclamation established the nature of the island's government until 1950. In a style similar to that of Captain Richard Leary back in 1899 and of General Horii in 1941, Nimitz asserted, "All powers of government and jurisdiction in Guam and adjacent waters, and over the inhabitants thereof, and final administrative responsibility are vested in me as Admiral, United States Navy, commanding the forces of occupation and as Military Governor, and will be exercized through subordinate commanders by my direction. . . . No political activity will be permitted other than that authorized by me or under my authority."

As Nimitz's subordinate responsible for the Marianas, Hoover's authority on Guam was in turn delegated to Major General Henry (Hank) L. Larsen, U.S.M.C., who was named island commander by Nimitz on 15 August. Civilian administration was handled by Larsen's deputy chief for civil affairs, Marine Colonel Charles I. Murray. It was Murray's staff of 186 officers and men that administered the refugee camps for Chamorros. Chronologically, Colonel Murray replaced Lieutenant Commander

U.S. military commanders on Guam, December 1944. From left to right: Admiral Chester W. Nimitz, U.S.N. (in front seat), Commander in Chief Pacific and Commander in Chief Pacific Ocean Areas (CINCPAC-CINCPOA); Rear Admiral Forrest B. Sherman, U.S.N., of Nimitz's staff; Vice Admiral J. H. Hoover, U.S.N., Commander Marianas Area; and Major General Henry L. Larsen, U.S.M.C., Island Commander (in effect governor) of Guam, 1944–1946. (From the collection of the Micronesian Area Research Center, Mangilao, Guam)

Homura of the Minseibu. Homura had disappeared during the Japanese retreat to the north, presumably killed or a suicide.

As each island in the Marianas was occupied by the Americans, the first need of the navy was to acquire land, huge tracts of land, particularly around the harbors and at the sites of the planned airfields. Initially, the U.S. forces simply confiscated whatever land was needed and worried later about ownership and eminent domain procedures. Such expropriation posed no problems on Saipan and Tinian, both enemy islands. On Guam, a U.S. territory, formal legal acquisition of property by negotiated lease or purchase, or by condemnation, would eventually be required. In the meantime, and in some cases for several more years, the military paid nothing for much of the private land that it occupied on Guam, either as rent or in purchase.

Admiral Hoover first expropriated Orote Peninsula and all other property in and around Apra Harbor, including the village of Sumay, whose inhabitants remained in refugee camps for the time being. The navy also occupied much of the Libugon-Fonte area (including the old Palasao Ridge area, renamed Nimitz Hill by the U.S. Navy), most of the plateau between Agana Heights and Anigua (used eventually for a new naval hospital), and nearly all the Jalaguac-Tiyan plateau on which the partially completed Japanese airstrip stood. Some of the land was already owned by the federal and naval governments from prewar days.

Hoover and Larsen placed top priority on the construction of a permanent, multilane express highway, later named Marine Drive, from Apra Harbor to the sites for airfields and naval facilities. All major construction for the Air Corps and the navy on the island was under the Fifth Naval Construction Brigade commanded by Captain William O. Hiltabiddle, Jr., who was no stranger to Guam. He had served as a young naval officer on the island in 1925–1927. Under his command in 1944 was a force of nine Seabee battalions, three stevedore battalions, the Third Marine Division's engineer battalion, and four army engineer aviation battalions. This sizable construction force became

even larger by early 1945 and by the end of the war would swell to an incredible forty-seven battalions.

With the navy moving ahead on its own projects, Air Corps Lieutenant General Millard F. Harmon and a staff of officers arrived on Guam on 14 August to coordinate with the navy and prepare for construction of the B-29 bases. To the astonishment of the Air Corps officers, the navy had taken over Tiyan airfield to make it into the U.S. Naval Air Station (NAS), not a B-29 airfield. Construction on NAS by Seabees had started on 13 August, and the navy had already hired Chamorros as laborers. One of the first employed was Jesus D. Castro, who had been a forced laborer on the airstrip under the Japanese.

Since the navy had operational control of the Marianas, the Air Corps officers swallowed their anger over Tiyan and altered their plans. They decided first to construct the support base at Depot Field (later renamed in memory of General Harmon after he was lost at sea on a B-24 flight from Guam to Hawai'i in 1946). Depot Field was to be completed in November 1944 and was to be followed by completion of Northwest Field near Mount Machanao and then North Field (later named after Brigadier General James R. Andersen, who was lost on the same flight as Harmon) at Upi. General Harmon departed with the understanding that Seabees would be put to work promptly on the Air Corps bases to help the army engineer battalions.

The land for the B-29 bases was expropriated, but the Seabees remained assigned to the navy's projects as first priority. They cut through Chorito Cliff near the beach at Asan and bulldozed sections of Piti and Agana parallel to the beaches to make way for Marine Drive, regardless of private property lines. Supplies and equipment were initially transported by fleets of DUKWs, amphibious trucks that moved between cargo ships and DPs (disposition points) on shore. In Tumon Bay, the Seabees built a small island in the center of the reef as a DP to transship supplies. This island and the damage to the reefs caused by its construction remain today.

Simultaneously with the construction of new installations, the Seabees bulldozed the remnants of prewar buildings and Japanese structures. There did not appear to be any thought-out plan for rebuilding Guam by the military authorities at this stage in the island's reoccupation. Japanese fortifications of thick cement were left in place and remain today along Guam's beaches as subjects for endless photographs by Japanese tourists. The U.S. dozers also pushed tons of wrecked tanks, trucks, jeeps, weapons, and other junk as well as garbage from military camps into huge dumps and off cliffs into the ocean. One dumping spot for debris and garbage at Apuntua Point on Orote Peninsula became known as the Shark Pit, owing to the swarms of sharks attracted to the spills. Today, the ocean bottom below the cliff at Apuntua and in deeper waters off Orote is still covered with a jumble of old metal and empty fifty-five-gallon oil drums.

The frenetic U.S. military construction included a channel dredged into Apra's inner harbor, the old *caldera chica,* to establish a ship repair facility and submarine base. Old Fort Santa Cruz, on which Captain Glass had claimed Guam in 1898, was demolished to make way for the channel. The Seabees also completed large new buildings on Nimitz Hill for the advance headquarters of the Pacific Fleet plus a Flag Circle of handsome living quarters for high naval officers. Portions of this land were private property, but the navy did not pay rent at the time, which would result in considerable later criticism. Admiral Nimitz moved into this headquarters in February 1945.

Large cantonment areas for troop camps, supply warehouses, and ammunition and fuel depots began to materialize on Guam. Buildings were predominantly semicircular Quonset huts of corrugated tin sheeting. The Americans surfaced the main roads and airfield runways with asphalt made from bituminous materials mixed with limestone *cascajo.* Excavation of the limestone left numerous quarries, which remain today, great empty pits on some of the most expensive real estate on the island. Because limestone contains millions of tiny organic shell fragments of ancient mollusks, algae readily grows on asphalt in Guam's moist, humid climate. When wet, the algae becomes slick. Thus, for decades after World War II, Guam's blacktopped roads were treacherously slippery in the slightest rain, causing innumerable accidents.

The brown tree snake *(Boiga irregularis),* sometimes confused with the Philippine rat snake, may have been first introduced to Guam in this period as an accidental passenger in the thousands of U.S. military vehicles and tons of supplies shipped from storage depots on Manus in the Admiralty Islands north of Papua New Guinea, where the snakes are indigenous. Like most other introduced life forms, this snake would gradually become highly destructive of indigenous birds and animals, plus it would add to Guam's recurring electric power problems by climbing into transformers and shorting them out.

While Hoover, Larsen, and Hiltabiddle were busily transforming Guam into a military bastion with little thought to postwar civilian concerns, the combat commands that had captured the island were also being reshaped. The First Provisional Marine Brigade, still under Brigadier General Shepherd, departed by the end of August 1944 for Guadalcanal, where it would be beefed up to become the Sixth Marine Division and go on to invade Okinawa. The Seventy-seventh Infantry Division under General Bruce left Guam on 3 November for New Caledonia and would go on to fight in the Leyte and the Okinawa invasions. The Third Marine Division, which had taken the most casualties on Guam, camped along the east coast near Yona. Replenished with new marines and a new commander—the irascible Major General Graves Erskine—the division conducted sweeps of Guam's jungles to kill Japanese stragglers and trained for future operations.

Air Corps personnel began arriving in large numbers on the island, but to the dismay of the airmen they discovered that the navy had given low priority to the construction of B-29 bases. On Saipan and Tinian, where construction of airfields started promptly and earlier than on Guam, and where the chain of command was leaner, the B-29 air bases were operational in October and December, respectively. On 24 November 1944, 111 B-29s flew from Isley Field, Saipan, in the first high-altitude daylight raid against Tokyo.

From then on, the U.S. Joint Chiefs of Staff in Washington gave the VHB missions priority in the Pacific war. As a consequence, the navy's plan to invade Formosa was canceled, but the invasions of Peleliu and Anguar, which in retrospect should not have taken place, went ahead in September 1944 with severe and unnecessary toll in the lives of U.S. Marines. Admiral Nimitz and his commanders then focused on the assault against the Philippines, which began on 20 October 1944 when General MacArthur's forces invaded Leyte. The invasion provoked the last of the Japanese Combined Fleet into a confrontation on 22–25 October with the U.S. Third and Seventh fleets in the Battle of Leyte Gulf, the greatest naval clash in history. This gigantic encounter ended in disastrous defeat for the Japanese despite their use of *kamikaze* suicide air attacks in large numbers against the Americans for the first time.

Because of the navy's preoccupation with these massive naval operations, construction of the B-29 bases on Guam lagged. Depot Field, scheduled for November completion, was not available for use until 4 December and would not be completed until April 1945. Northwest Field, which also became a fighter base, was to have been operational by mid-December, but, when LeMay arrived on Guam in January 1945, he found the base unfinished. Not a shy man, LeMay commented caustically on Guam's navy commanders: "They had built tennis courts for the Island Commander; they had built fleet recreation centers, a Marine rehabilitation center, dockage facilities for inter-island surface craft, and every other damn thing in the world except subscribing to the original purpose in the occupation of those islands. . . . Thousands and thousands of young Americans died on those islands, in order to give us a base of operations against the Japanese. And here people were, piddling around with all this other stuff, and not giving us anything to fly or fight with."

On 25 February 1945, the first B-29 bombing mission from Guam finally took off from the still incomplete Northwest Field. The same month, Washington instructed Admiral Nimitz to have the Third Marine Division leave its camps at Yona to help the Fourth and Fifth Marine divisions seize the tiny island of Iwo Jima halfway between the Marianas and Japan. The U.S. Air Corps wanted to eliminate the Japanese fighter planes that used Iwo's airstrip to intercept B-29s en route to and from Japan, and the strip was needed as an emergency B-29 landing site to avoid ocean ditching by bombers crippled on their missions. From Iwo Jima, U.S. fighters could also escort B-29s to Japan as protection against Japanese home-based fighters.

After the Iwo Jima airstrip was in U.S. hands in early March (and 2,300 wounded marines from the battle were in Guam's Naval Hospital), LeMay switched to low-level firebombings of Japan's cities. On the night of 9 March, it took two hours for over 300 B-29s to take off from Guam, Tinian, and Saipan on the first mass incendiary bomb mission. Eight hours later, nearly 100,000 Japanese lay incinerated among mammoth fires that consumed sixteen square miles of Tokyo. The mission was judged a success, despite the loss of fourteen B-29s.

In the following weeks, waves of B-29s firebombed the great cities of Japan into ruins. It took a grueling fifteen hours for the trip to and from Tokyo by the bombers. The B-29s also seeded the Japanese coastal waters with thousands of mines to choke off all interisland maritime traffic. Each day, the roar of bombers filled the skies over Guam as the tempo of the strategic air war increased. Each night, giant searchlights shot fixed vertical shafts of light into the skies of the Marianas as beacons to guide the Superfortresses back to their island bases.

Under LeMay's prodding, North Field's first runway was completed in June 1945 and the second in July just before the war with Japan ended. LeMay's headquarters, barracks, mess halls, storage areas, and clubs spread along the bluff then called Harmon Cliffline, and now called Harmon and Tumon Heights, from Depot Field all the way to Two Lovers Point, where an officers' club was constructed.

An Air Corps recreational area was set up on Tumon Beach. The area was off-limits to Chamorros. The old San Vitores shrine was by then completely gone, along with several ancient *latte* stone sites bulldozed into oblivion. The entire north of the island from Pati Point to Ritidian Point became a gigantic military complex around North and Northwest Fields and navy communications facilities.

One long-term adverse effect (among several such) of the Air Corps construction was the widespread elimination of many ancient trees indigenous to the limestone forest of the northern plateau of Guam. Primeval forests were razed for military expediency. In particular, the tall, beautiful *ifil* and serianthes trees posed hazards to aircraft landings and takeoffs and so were cut down everywhere, along with other tall tree varieties. Military bulldozers piled brush into huge piles, which were burned, blanketing Guam with smoke for weeks from the great bonfires. *Ifil*'s hard, dense wood is fire resistant and not amenable to use as frame lumber, so great trunks of the trees lay in the jungles for years around the air bases. Because *ifil* and serianthes trees are so slow growing, they never made a full comeback on Guam. Today they are scarce.

Endings and Beginnings

While the air war against Japan gathered momentum, civil affairs on Guam moved slowly toward a more normal life for the Chamorros, but it was to be a new manner of living, not the old prewar ways. In October 1944, the civil affairs unit was upgraded to become the "Military Government of Guam" under General Larsen with ten departments responsible for executive functions (education, labor, public health, etc.) similar to the prewar naval government. Changes in governmental organization, laws, policies, and regulations were by proclamation, usually in CINCPAC's name. In May 1945, the military government was reorganized and personnel increased.

It was in the period 1944–1946 that the term *Guamanian* came into standard use, first by the Americans, then among the Chamorros themselves. Prior to World War II, the Americans referred to the indigenous people of Guam variously as Chamorros or natives. During the Marianas campaign, the U.S. media and military personnel had to differentiate between the Chamorros on Saipan and those on Guam. This was done by referring to them as *Saipanese* and *Guamanians*.

Food was provided free to all Chamorros by the military government through a rationing system until the war ended. One of the principal canned foods provided by the navy in this period was Spam. This processed meat became so extraordinarily popular with Chamorros that it was called "Chamorro steak" and is still immensely popular on Guam today. It was also in this period that Tabasco hot sauce from Louisiana became a favorite of Guamanians. Today, more Tabasco per capita is consumed on Guam than in any other place in the world. Since Apra Harbor remained a closed port, three civilian wholesalers were authorized by the navy to import goods by military transports through the navy supply depot: A. T. Bordallo, T. A. Calvo and sons, and J. M. Torres. Retail prices soon rose, so the navy imposed price controls. Higher prices in turn induced a thriving black market in the refugee camps.

Some Chamorros objected to being held in the refugee camps. Villagers from the south, where damage to housing was the least, were the first to return to their homes. Other Chamorros decided not to wait to be relocated. Led by Simon A. Sanchez, a small group of families left the Anigua refugee camp in late August 1944 and moved to land of the Lujan (Kapili) family just below the Jalaguac cliff in the old Dededo area. The military authorities tried to move them back, and the civil affairs commander cut off food rations to them. A Catholic naval chaplain, Commander Patrick Gerity, arranged to provide food to the Chamorros from nearby Seabee kitchens and stores. With Seabee help, the Chamorros constructed a wood and canvas community center and school. The stubborn little Chamorro community persevered and grew to become the center of the postwar municipality of Tamuning.

In 1944 and early 1945, the navy often moved groups of Chamorros from one location to another because of military needs, and civilian housing remained inadequate. Of the 3,286 dwelling places on Guam prior to the war, about 80 percent had been destroyed. From August 1944 through September 1945, the military government constructed over 1,400 dwellings in new communities in Agat, Asan, Santa Rita, Sinajana, Barrigada, new Dededo, Yona, and Talofofo. The Chamorros themselves built about 1,500 houses in the new communities and in prewar villages in the south.

By mid-1945, about 5,000 Chamorros still remained homeless in the refugee camps largely because the navy forbade resettlement of Agana and Sumay. General Larsen and his successors planned to make an Americanized "New Agana" with neat rectangular streets like Santa Monica, California, in place of the crooked lanes of prewar Agana. This plan would never be completed, and it would cause tremendous land tenure problems in the years ahead. In the meantime, rubble in the town was cleared slowly, and the former capital was scraped barren except for a few ruins and a temporary church on the cathedral site. Debris from Agana was piled out from shore near the former mouth of the Agana River. A prominent new peninsula was created called Baker Point. This area would be made into a park and renamed the Paseo de Susana in 1955. The little Agana River channel was once more moved, this time to flow into the sea on the east side of the Paseo de Susana, where it remains today.

The military government rebuilt or repaired seventeen churches (including two for the Baptists), but, as before the war, the navy was not happy with a Spanish bishop. So, when Bishop Olano returned to the island in March 1945, Admiral Nimitz arranged through the powerful archbishop of New York, Francis J. Spellman, to have Olano replaced. Spellman visited Guam in August 1945 with papers for Olano's resignation and apparently persuaded him to renounce his position on 21 August 1945.

The Vatican officially replaced Olano on 25 August with the Most Reverend Apollinaris William Baumgartner, O.F.M., an American Franciscan Capuchin, who arrived almost secretly on Admiral Nimitz's personal aircraft on 23 October. The new leader's title was Titular Bishop of Joppe, Vicariate of Guam, Vicar Apostolic of Guam. Olano was then pressured to leave, and on 26 October he sailed in sadness to Manila on the USS *Pastora*. Some Spanish priests would be assigned to Guam much later on, and Olano himself would later return to die on the island. But, with his departure as bishop in 1945, the Spanish mission on Guam came to an end 277 years after Father San Vitores first stepped ashore at Agana.

In contrast to the navy's heavy hand in land, housing, and religious matters, its efforts in public health were highly helpful. Eleven civil health stations, one in each village, were quickly established in 1944, and preventive immunization programs against typhoid, diphtheria, smallpox, and so forth were implemented. A 300-bed civilian general hospital was constructed of two sheet-metal Butler buildings between Oka and Saupon points (which thereafter became jointly known as Hospital Point) next to the huge Naval Hospital of Quonset huts. Medical treatment of local residents by the navy remained generally free, as before the war, between 1944 and 1950.

In education, the new military government proved much more responsive than the prewar one. The first three elementary schools opened on 1 October 1944 with Chamorro teachers and principals once more under Simon A. Sanchez as superintendent of schools. By the end of the war, twenty-one new schools were in operation with 167 Chamorro teachers and over 7,000 students. This student population was larger than the number in school in 1941 even though the total resident population was slightly smaller. George Washington High School reopened in early 1945 in Quonset huts in Agana under the prewar principal, Agueda Johnston. The high school would move to Sinajana in 1945, to Mongmong in 1952, and finally to its present location in Mangilao.

By the end of the war, 400 business licenses had been issued to Chamorros. Plants to bottle Coca-Cola and Pepsi-Cola began operations; the Johnston family set up their movie theater again, this time in a long Quonset hut in Agana; and the Martinez family reestablished their ice plant and meat market at a new location in Anigua. The Bank of Guam reopened on 15 March 1945 under navy management as the only financial institution permitted on the island. Fast growing in the coming boom years, the bank would open a branch on Saipan in January 1947. A navy report characterized the Bank of Guam as "a financial Gibraltar" but "an administrative peat-bog."

The navy encouraged Chamorros to return to farming; in particular, it wanted to revive copra production. Instead, the locals flocked to salaried jobs with the military and with civilian contractors, who were now being brought in on construction projects. Prior to the war, there had been about 1,200 Chamorro wage earners. By the end of 1946, approximately 6,000 Chamorros were wage earners, with about half of them working for the navy, even though the old prewar double wage standard between locals and stateside hires was reimposed for government positions. The Guam civil service was reinstituted with a forty-hour week, mostly for office positions, which were far more attractive than sweating in the sun for copra.

Along with the introduction of many more white-collar office jobs for locals on Guam, the military also for the first time installed air-conditioners in offices and living quarters. Longer tours of duty, in fact whole lifetimes of residence, became normal for Caucasians on Guam with air-conditioned work sites and homes.

The U.S. military buildup and reconstruction of the island infrastructure caused a heavy demand for workers, so for the first time Chamorro women found salaried jobs open to them as secretaries, clerks, and telephone operators. As a result, the old Chamorro custom of families moving out of the villages to their rural *lanchos* during weekdays to raise crops, returning for church and social affairs on the weekends, ceased in the postwar period.

While family and village fiestas continued to be held and many other neo-Chamorro customs persisted, most Guamanians now remained in the villages on weekends and went to work in offices or construction sites on weekdays and Saturday mornings. Only a minority of Chamorros, predominantly in the south, still practiced farming or fishing either as a livelihood or as a substantial source of supplementary income. Although some farming for row crops and fruit continued, copra and rice production for export or local commercial sale ceased after the war.

While the people of Guam were adapting to new patterns of life in early 1945, on 13 April they were saddened by the news that President Franklin Delano Roosevelt had died of a cerebral hemorrhage in Georgia. Roosevelt was considered a friend of the island since his days as assistant secretary of the navy in the World War I era. In reality, however, he had been a consistent supporter of naval policies that tended to restrict the civil liberties of the people of Guam. On the other hand, Roosevelt's successor—Harry S. Truman—would turn out to be the president most sympathetic in American history to the appeals of the Chamorros.

The war in the meantime ground on. Germany capitulated on 8 May, and on 22 June Okinawa was declared secure under American control. Preparations then began for the allied invasion of the home islands of Japan. It was feared by everyone that this last titanic assault would be the bloodiest in history. But it was not to be.

In February 1945, a naval commander, Frederic L. Ashworth, had unobtrusively visited Admiral Nimitz on Guam and then inspected the B-29 airfields in the Marianas. The commander was a member of the supersecret Manhattan Project, which had developed the atomic bomb. He informed Nimitz for the first time of "a new weapon . . . covered by the highest order of secrecy" that a special B-29 unit, the 509th Composite Group of the 393d Squadron, would deliver against Japan from the Marianas. Ashworth picked Tinian's North Field as the base for the 509th. At this point, even General LeMay himself did not know the 509th's mission.

LeMay learned of the mission on 27 June when Air Force Colonel Paul Tibbets, commanding officer of the 509th, visited LeMay at Depot Field to arrange for a special compound on Tinian for his unit. In early July, the 509th's fifteen B-29s flew into Tinian. They soon began practice bombing runs over Rota, dropping high explosive bombs on the hapless Japanese and Chamorros trapped and beginning to starve on the island. In mid-July, three special aircraft landed at the Naval Air Station on Guam with components for the new bombs, which were then assembled in secret and flown to Tinian. On 26 July, the cruiser USS *Indianapolis* delivered to Tinian the material for the warheads of the new weapons. The *Indianapolis* then halted briefly at Apra Harbor before heading to Leyte. En route on 30 July, the cruiser was sunk by a Japanese submarine, and some 800 men died by drowning and shark attacks. This event would have been cataclysmic, not just tragic, had it occurred a week earlier. The skipper of the *Indianapolis,* Captain Charles McVay, was returned to Guam for hearings in August on the disaster, and later he was court-martialed as a scapegoat by the navy even though he had not been negligent.

Meanwhile, the Twentieth Air Force commander, General Carl Spaatz, met with LeMay, Tibbets, and other officers on 29 July at LeMay's Twenty-first Bomber Command headquarters on the Harmon Cliffline to read a fateful order for the 509th "to deliver its first special bomb . . . after about 3 August 1945 on one of the targets: Hiroshima, Kokura, Niigata, and Nagasaki." On 6 August, at precisely 8:15:17 A.M., Colonel Tibbets, at the controls of a B-29 named the *Enola Gay* after Tibbets' mother, dropped the world's first atomic fission bomb, Little Boy, over the city of Hiroshima. Forty-three seconds later, at exactly 8:16, Little Boy exploded, and a new era began for all humankind.

The second atomic mission followed on 9 August with a plutonium fusion bomb called Fat Man that was dropped on Nagasaki by a 509th B-29 named *Bock's Car* piloted by Major Charles Sweeney. Over 78,000 people were killed instantly at Hiroshima and 35,000 at Nagasaki. Thousands more soon died from radiation, burns, and other effects. On the same day as the Nagasaki bombing, the Soviet Union entered the war against Japan by invading Manchuria.

On 15 August, in an unprecedented action, Emperor Hirohito personally broadcast to his war-weary subjects Japan's surrender. World War II ceased on 21 August, V-J Day, and, on 2 September 1945, the final terms of the Japanese surrender were signed in Tokyo Bay aboard the battleship USS *Missouri*. Thus, the B-29s from bases in the Marianas did end the war without the need to invade Japan, as LeMay had predicted, but only with a far more powerful weapon than his conventional high-explosive and incendiary bombs.

In the eyes of American military strategists, this one momentous operation—the atomic bombing of Japan—confirmed the immense strategic value of the Mariana Islands to U.S. national security, a value that far outweighed the relatively inexpensive costs of subsidizing the people of Guam for the use of their island. From the military viewpoint, this strategic value not only justified all past sacrifices to seize the Marianas but also impelled the permanent retention of the islands and the occupation of huge tracts of Guam's land by the United States to meet potential new threats. Fleet Admiral Ernest J. King, chief of naval operations during World War II, wrote that the Marianas were "the key to the Pacific War." And, he might have added, they would be an indispensable asset to the United States in future wars in the Asian rimlands.

12 Gibraltar of the American Lake 1945–1950

New Geopolitics, Old Realpolitik

After V-J Day, the rapid demobilization—called the Magic Carpet Program—of American forces drastically reduced the military presence on Guam. Admiral Nimitz and his CINCPAC staff, including Vice Admiral Hoover, departed Guam for Hawai'i in late August 1945, leaving Vice Admiral George D. Murray as the new COMNAVMAR and Marine Major General Larsen still island commander. As of 31 August 1945, the military population on the island was an enormous 201,718, and civilians numbered 21,838, for a total of 223,556. With a density of 1,045 persons per square mile, this was the largest number of people on Guam in the island's history before or since that date. Less than ten months later, by mid-June 1946, military personnel numbered only 36,923, a huge reduction of nearly 165,000, or 82 percent.

The Foreign Liquidation Commission started auctions of surplus military stocks on Guam in January 1946 and in August opened a Surplus Property Sales Store with bargains that provided the basis of several prosperous local businesses on postwar Guam. Hundreds of Quonset huts, barracks, jeeps, trucks, and assorted other vehicles plus huge amounts of surplus military equipment, weapons, fuels, canned foods, bottled beverages (including beer), and supplies were sold cheaply or left behind (with some stocks and munitions buried).

Military wives and children began to arrive on Guam by mid-1946. In June, the navy opened a regular large commissary store, and, by the end of 1946, the navy's Admiral Nimitz eighteen-hole golf course (for military only) was completed, with 150 acres of it on private land. On 20 September 1946, Pan American (renamed Pan Am after the war) reopened regular trans-Pacific commercial flights with military C-54s converted to airliners. Pan Am planes landed at the Naval Air Station, where a civilian terminal was set up on the opposite side of the runway from the navy's facilities.

All island activities, however, came to a jolting halt on 21–22 September 1946 when a typhoon smashed into the Marianas. Inappropriately called Typhoon Querida (Spanish for "darling"), the storm destroyed, among other things, the U.S. Naval Hospital of Quonset huts at Oka, but not the civilian hospital next door made of Butler buildings, as well as 4,000 feet of the breakwater under construction at Apra Harbor. Completion of the breakwater was delayed until June 1947; it was named the Glass Breakwater in honor of Captain Henry Glass, who seized Guam for the United States nearly a half-century earlier.

Magic Carpet nonetheless continued on, and, by the end of 1946, American forces had vacated vast military camps on Guam. Military personnel by then numbered fewer than 29,000. The downside of the hasty military evacuation in 1945–1946 was that much of the landscape of central and northern Guam was left cluttered with military debris. A journalist described postwar Guam: "From the air, it lies on the rim of the western sea like a lump of jade rimmed in silver and blue. . . . But Guam, from the air or a ship from the ocean sea, is a fantasy. . . . For Guam is a huge construction camp, rowdy, crude and jerry-built. It is also a vast junk yard and a onetime battlefield where the scars of combat still offend the eye everywhere."

This war-devastated image of Guam remained a lasting impression for journalists and for thousands of American servicemen who passed through the island. For years, Guam would be the butt of jokes in the United States as an uninviting place of military exile, where boredom led to "rock fever," a cranky longing to get off the island. One long-term effect of the military trashing of Guam was to accustom government officials to accept junk and old abandoned vehicles as normal parts of the island landscape. Over the next five decades, parts of Guam—particularly Cabras Island, Anigua, and Harmon—remained seedy junkyards. Despite the eventual establishment of a central landfill in Ordot for dumping garbage and trash, not one of the island administrations since World War II, whether naval or civilian, would prove capable of cleaning up junk and trash on Guam because of the high cost of disposing of it.

To stop soil erosion from areas where plants had been blasted away in the war, the Americans reforested the Marianas with a small tree native to tropical Latin America. Called *tangantangan* on Guam—originally named by botanists *Leucaena glauca* Benth and now *Leucaena leucocephala* (Lam.) de Wit—this quick-growing plant has good nitrogen-fixing ability, is food for cattle, makes good firewood, and provides straight poles for hut and fence supports. A similar but smaller plant, *talantayan (Leucaena insularum)*, is endemic to the Marianas but grows well only near the sea. The Spaniards introduced *tangantangan* to both Guam and the Philippines (in 1900, Safford noted that it was plentiful on Guam), but it was not widespread in the Marianas before 1947.

In October of that year, tens of thousands of *tangantangan* seeds were spread from military aircraft all over the Mariana Islands. On Guam, Boy Scouts and schoolchildren planted over a ton of the seeds in eroded areas and alongside roads. Soon, the reintroduced *tangantangan* was spreading merrily, shouldering out indigenous plants in some areas and halting erosion wherever it took hold. In the 1950s and 1960s, more *tangantangan* seeds were broadcast from aircraft over the mountain slopes along Marine Drive. Today, the trees are everywhere on Guam.

The military government also undertook the first island-wide repeated sprayings with pesticides, notably DDT, to reduce insects on Guam. The use of chemical insecticides substantially reduced mosquitos and other bugs, at least for a time, but also killed indigenous birds that depended on the insects for food.

One unpleasant matter left over from the war was the prosecution of Japanese and Chamorros accused of war crimes. A special navy court was set up at Nimitz Hill under John D. Murphy, director of war crimes, 1945–1949, for trials of 148 persons from throughout Micronesia as well as from Chichi Jima and Guam. Several Japanese servicemen committed *hara-kiri* rather than testify against former superiors. Of those arrested, 123 were military personnel. The civilians included women and some Saipanese and Rotanese Chamorros. The trials were open to the public, and the press published lurid accounts of cannibalism by Japanese officers and enlisted men who ate the cooked flesh of American prisoners, Okinawans, and even fellow Japanese during the war. The most heinous crime was by Captain Hiroshi Iwanami, the commmander of the Japanese naval hospital at Truk, charged with killing eight downed American naval pilots by torture through "inhumane experimental use of bacteria, dynamite, and bamboo spears." Of the 123 Japanese military tried, ten were acquitted, thirty received death sentences, and thirty-six life sentences. Only ten death sentences were carried out, all on Guam by hanging, among them three admirals and one lieutenant general. Captain Iwanami was one of those hanged. Of those charged with war crimes committed on Guam, twenty-four were convicted; eight were hanged, some for murders that involved cannibalism.

Japanese civilian residents of Guam, including Naoe Takano and Antonio Arriola Shimizu (the part-Chamorro son of José Shimizu), but not Reji Dejima, were deported to Saipan. Some deportees returned eventually to live on Guam. Among civilians convicted of crimes were the Saipanese police interpreters José P. Villagomez (ten years for murder of a Guam Chamorro, Vicente Sahagon Babauta) and Pedro Guerrero. Others found guilty were a Rotanese interpreter, Domingo S. Quintanilla (four and a half years for beating prisoners), and the former Agana restaurant owner Samuel Shinohara.

The navy accused Shinohara of assaulting Governor McMillin at the 1941 surrender. McMillin never confirmed the charge. The court found Shinohara guilty of treason against the United States even though he was not a U.S. citizen, and he was sentenced to be hanged. The sentence was commuted, and he served eight years in Sugamo Prison in Japan before returning to live out his life unobtrusively on Guam with his part-Japanese, part-Chamorro family. After all the trials were completed, the court and the stockade in Agana Heights were quietly closed in May 1949.

While local problems left over from World War II were being sorted out on Guam, the island began to feel the effects of the new world order that emerged from World War II. Delegates of forty-six nations had signed the United Nations Charter on 26 June 1945 in San Francisco. The U.N. Trusteeship Council was then created to oversee the promise of self-determination for eleven trusteeships worldwide. The former Japanese mandate islands of Micronesia were to constitute the eleventh trusteeship.

American military leaders, however, demanded the retention of Micronesia by the United States for national defense purposes. They and their congressional supporters argued that Micronesia's islands were too valuable strategically and had cost too much blood to be given up for idealistic reasons of decolonization. The U.S. Navy supported Bill H.R. 7044 in the Seventy-ninth Congress (1945–1946) for the United States to annex Micronesia and make Guam the capital of a new American territory with an organic act so that the area could eventually become a U.S. state. The bill died owing to State Department opposition. Instead of annexation, the United States asked for authorization to fortify the trusteeship islands in Micronesia and close them to outsiders. To calm proponents of decolonization, Truman promised to take steps to bring about self-determination by the Micronesians.

This compromise fit the new U.S. military strategy of creating an oceanic "base network" rather than depending on a string of bases across the Pacific as in the prewar Orange Plans. After visiting Guam and other islands in the region in July 1946, Secretary of the Navy James V. Forrestal described this strategy: "Single island positions cannot be considered strong bases. Selected islands can, however, together with Guam, form a far-reaching, mutually supporting base network, although alone would fall far short of being an impregnable bastion."

The network of oceanic bases was eventually to support a forward deployment of U.S. forces in allied nations around the Asian rimland as part of the containment of communism. U.S. control would also deny Micronesia to potential hostile powers such as the Soviet Union, China, and possibly Japan again in the distant future. Finally, the Americans wanted to use the isolated atolls of the Marshall Islands to test U.S. nuclear weapons. The United States had already begun atomic tests on 1 July 1946 with the first explosion at Bikini Atoll.

The Micronesian trusteeship was put under the U.N. Security Council, where the United States has veto power, rather than in the Trusteeship Council, where a majority vote decides issues. Soviet objections were overcome by a tacit understanding whereby the United States acquiesced to Soviet retention of four Japanese islands in the southern Kurils north of Japan, and occupied by the Soviet Union at the war's end, in return for Soviet agreement to American control of Micronesia. The U.N. Security Council unanimously approved the unique strategic trusteeship agreement with the United States on 2 April 1947, and the U.S. Congress ratified the agreement on 15 July 1947 by a joint House-Senate resolution. The title of the new dependency was the Trust Territory of the Pacific Islands (TTPI). Truman gave control of the trusteeship to the Department of the Navy and appointed CINCPAC, who administered the area from Hawai'i, as the first high commissioner. The trusteeship did not include Guam, which, as a U.S. flag territory, continued to be administered separately by the navy.

A year earlier, on 4 July 1946, the United States had granted the Philippines independence, and Manila signed a treaty by which the United States assumed responsibility for the strategic defense of the new Republic of the Philippines in return for American leases of bases at Subic Bay, Clark Field, and elsewhere in the islands. Japan in the meantime had come under the "MacArthur Constitution," which prohibited Japanese rearmament. The geopolitics of the Pacific were thus transformed from the prewar situation, in which Guam was a lonely American outpost surrounded by hostile Japanese islands, to one in which Guam was the center of an American-dominated lake that encompassed the entire western Pacific Ocean. From the American military viewpoint, the strategic error in 1898 of not claiming for the United States all Spanish Micronesia, or at least all the Mariana Islands, was at last rectified.

With the legal basis of American hegemony established in the area, the U.S. military began to build new, permanent facilities on key islands in Micronesia, primarily Kwajalein Atoll and Guam, as part of the new Pacific base network. COMNAVMAR's main mission in 1947–1950 was to complete those facilities on Guam, and for this purpose great

chunks of Guam's land were needed. In 1947, the National Security Act created the U.S. Air Force (USAF)—and the CIA as well as the National Security Council—in a massive reorganization of the armed forces into three branches in the new Department of Defense under James Forrestal. The USAF's Strategic Air Command (SAC) for heavy bombers was set up under General LeMay. North Field, soon to be a SAC base, was officially renamed Andersen Air Force Base (AAFB) on 15 April 1950, with Brigadier General James Roy Andersen's widow present at the ceremony. Northwest Field had been deactivated in late 1949, but the facilities were retained by the air force for munition storage and other uses.

The National Security Act was supposed to unify the U.S. armed forces but instead created quasi-independent military services in which the navy (because of Forrestal's association with it) emerged with augmented influence. With a free hand, the U.S. Navy implemented what critics called a "zoo policy" of keeping the TTPI isolated and undeveloped like an exotic anthropological park. This militarized Pax Americana would transform Guam into a small but highly valuable U.S. Gibraltar of the Pacific second only to Hawai'i, just as navy strategists had advocated ever since the first Orange Plans.

For the indigenous people of the region, however, it would be a different story. In the judgment of an analyst writing in 1975, American administration of Micronesia failed "dismally... to meet the diverse needs which exist among the islands." The militarized U.S. regional policy constricted Guam's development even though the island enjoyed an unprecedented economic boom the first five years after World War II.

Social Change and Economic Boom

While Washington was busy once more playing the old game of realpolitik in the new geopolitical setting of the postwar Pacific, Admiral Raymond A. Spruance, who had replaced Nimitz as CINCPAC (CINCPOA no longer existed), issued a directive on

12 December 1945 to reestablish peacetime naval government on Guam until such time as a permanent civil government was duly constituted. In accord with the directive, the wartime military government under Major General Larsen was replaced on 30 May 1946 by the "navy island government," with Rear Admiral Charles A. (Baldy) Pownall, formerly commander of naval air forces in the Pacific, as the appointed governor. Pownall had replaced Murray as COMNAVMAR in February 1946 and retained that command when he was made governor of Guam. The new governor therefore combined regional military authority and local civil power to a far greater degree than had any prewar American naval governor.

Because Pownall's military duties as COMNAVMAR took up most of his time, he delegated civilian affairs on Guam to a civil administrator—initially Navy Captain Milton A. Anderson—below the deputy governor. The civil executive branch was composed of twelve departments and agencies, each headed by a military officer. Rota, with fewer than a thousand residents, was administered from Guam until the TTPI took over all the northern Marianas in 1947.

For civil matters, Pownall reported back to the Pentagon to the office of the assistant chief of naval operations for island government. This office supervised the governments of Guam and American Samoa (Hawai'i, the third U.S. flag territory in the Pacific, had been under an organic act since 1900 with civil local self-government). Since Guam and American Samoa were not self-governing, the navy reported annually to the United Nations on the status of the islands. The first such report in July 1946 stated that navy policy was to "assist the natives toward achieving economic independence in a 'Guam for Guamanians' and a 'Samoa for Samoans,' . . . with the ultimate aim of fitting both races for United States citizenship."

Interestingly, the United Nations rejected the navy's first report and criticized navy rule on Guam as "colonial" and "departing from the principles of a democratic nation." As a result, in late 1946, in a rare editorial devoted to Guam, the *New York Times* asked "what has been done . . . to institute the necessary reforms on Guam?" The Seventh Guam Congress, which was the last prewar Congress, had reconvened in March 1946, and also sent a message to President Truman, asking his assistance in providing civil liberties. Truman sent off a letter to Pownall for public release in which the president expressed sympathy for the people of Guam, but no other action was taken.

On Guam as of June 1946, nearly two years after liberation, the makeshift refugee camps for Chamorros were at last empty, but an estimated 10,000 people still lived in temporary government-provided houses in the new communities. The navy had ambitious plans for five major civilian rehabilitation projects for construction of new villages and a general hospital, all at an estimated cost of $20 million. The Seventy-ninth U.S. Congress, however, appropriated only $6 million on 1 August 1946, and this money was to be expended by January 1949. That amount proved inadequate.

Larsen used nearly all the $6 million on "New Agana" alone for paved roads, curbs, and streetlights along the neat new rectangular blocks of the capital. A large section of eighty-two lots between the Plaza de España and the beach was condemned in 1947 and made into a rather featureless park, later named Skinner Plaza. The new town layout, however, chopped up old lots in a tangle of property lines that resulted in numerous lawsuits and endless delays over eminent domain that prevented the return of most former residents to Agana. The new blocks in Agana remained largely empty except for a few major buildings, notably the jail, the new legislative hall (dedicated by Pownall in July 1948) for the Guam Congress, and the temporary church on the site of the prewar Dulce Nombre de María.

As a consequence of limited funds and various delays in resettlement, at the navy's request the Seventy-ninth U.S. Congress passed P.L. 225, the Land Transfer Act, in November 1945 to make federal land available to Guam residents in replacement of land acquired for military use. After much delay, in

1948 and 1949 the navy offered Guamanians in the temporary communities the opportunity of buying their new government-provided lots at bargain prices instead of waiting to rebuild on their old prewar properties. Hundreds of Guamanians accepted the navy's offer. The prewar village patterns were thus massively rearranged in the central and northern villages, where the majority of Chamorros resided.

In education, the first postwar class of George Washington High graduated on 30 June 1946 on the outdoor stage of Johnston's Gaiety Theatre, located in Sinajana by then, with Governor Pownall as speaker. Children of American personnel now attended public schools, or the private Catholic schools that Bishop Baumgartner was reestablishing, together with Chamorro children. The bishop also took the lead in obtaining scholarships for Chamorros to Catholic seminaries, colleges, and universities on the mainland. A number of upper-class families of Agana sent their children at family expense to mainland universities and colleges.

In June, a public referendum requested the governor to call a general election under a reapportioned municipal system that reflected population shifts caused by the war. Governor Pownall promptly agreed. In the election on 13 July 1946, the first woman to be elected to the Guam Congress, Rosa T. Aguigui, a teacher at the Merizo Elementary School (and assistant to Laura Thompson before the war), won a seat in the House of Assembly.

There were as yet no formal political parties, and legislators served without salary. The Eighth Guam Congress convened on 10 August in a Quonset hut in Agana. About this time the U.S. Navy and locals adopted the name *Guamanian* for all permanent inhabitants of the island. This ethnically neutral designation was the result of informal polls and school contests in which the public chose *Guamanian* over the traditional term *Chamorro* and such other names as *Guamese, Guamians,* or *Guamericans.* After the war, people from the forty-eight states were usually referred to as *mainlanders* or *statesiders.* By the 1970s, Caucasians were sometimes called *haoles,* a Hawaiian word.

As a result of the numerous military athletic leagues on Guam, American football and basketball joined cockfights, boxing, and baseball as popular sports among Guamanians. Armed Forces Radio Station WXLI GUAM, established in October 1944, broadcast from 8:00 A.M. to midnight daily. This station, which became WVTG GUAM in 1947, introduced disk jockeys with programs of American popular music and regular news broadcasts. Programs were in English but included a "Guamanian Hour" of Chamorro music and community news.

A daily military newspaper, the Guam edition of the *Navy News,* started in late 1945. In 1946, the Catholic vicarate began to publish an English-language weekly (with some articles in Chamorro), *Umatuna Si Yuus,* which has continued to serve the community ever since, now under the title *Pacific Voice.* The *Navy News,* which published little local news even though its masthead called Guam "the Crossroads of the Pacific," turned into the *Guam News* in 1947 and in 1950 would be sold to Joseph Flores, who renamed it the *Guam Daily News* (with the Sunday edition called the *Territorial Sun*), which became the island's main newspaper.

While the navy encouraged social change on Guam in the late 1940s, it was far more conservative in economic matters. The navy's policy was expressed in the official monthly navy report to Washington in April 1946: "The economic development [of Guam] must be geared to meet the demands of these service and service connected personnel and cannot be geared to the financial, technical, or business ability of the Guamanian entrepreneur." By insisting on a command economy for Guam that restricted private investment, the navy believed it could limit postwar inflation and civilian demands that might place limits on military priorities. Inflation was curbed, but Guamanian demands for civil liberties would prove impossible to contain.

Publicly, the navy based its curtailment of free enterprise on the need to protect the Guamanians from foreign and American merchants. The navy even argued that "any policy to guard the Guamanians against foreign exploitation must consider the need to guard the Guamanians against exploitation by Guamanians." Those Guamanians whom the navy considered to be exploiters of their fellow Guamanians were mostly from the old *manak'kilo* families. As might be expected, the navy's attitude provoked opposition to naval government among those families.

The means that the navy used to control commerce was the requirement of a security clearance for anyone traveling to and from the region. The legal basis was President Roosevelt's 1941 Executive Order 8683, which remained in effect even though the war had ended. The navy permitted no civilian tourists or businessmen, foreign or American, to visit Guam unless affiliated with a military purpose. The airfields and Apra Harbor remained closed to civilian commerce except for Pan Am flights, which carried airmail as well as passengers, and for military charters of civilian ships and aircraft, on which authorized local businesses could transport goods. Local firms could not employ alien workers, as could the military and off-island contractors. To protect Guamanians from outside exploiters, local businesses had to be at least 51 percent owned by Guamanians, and only Guamanians could purchase property on Guam or lease it for more than five years.

Despite the restrictions on outside investment, Guam's economy boomed from late 1945 into the early 1950s, owing initially to war surplus sales, then to the extraordinary volume of military construction on the island. To get around prohibitions on outside investment, a number of U.S. servicemen and civilians stationed on Guam teamed up as minority partners with Guamanians to form successful businesses. These partnerships included one between Kenneth T. (Ken) Jones, Jr., and Segundo (Sai Pakito) P. Leon Guerrero, who formed Jones and Guerrero (J & G) Enterprises. Other businesses were kept in local hands, such as the Ada family enterprises under Pedro Ada, who became Guam's first millionaire, and the Calvo Enterprises led by Eduardo T. Calvo.

Politics and the Renewed Drive for Citizenship

Local politics began to emerge on Guam after the war with a vague general split between Guamanians who tended to support navy policies and those who did not. This political division began in 1946 when a group of fifteen prominent Chamorro men set about to create a nonprofit association called the Friends of Guam. Led by Francisco B. Leon Guerrero, the group included Judge José C. Manibusan, Father Oscar Calvo, Simon A. Sanchez, B. J. Bordallo and his brothers, Carlos and Tomás, and other members of families whose roots and outlook went back to the old mestizo *manak'kilo* families. Throughout the postwar period until the Organic Act, B. J. Bordallo, now silver haired, served as president of the House of Council. The speaker of the House of Assembly, Eduardo T. Calvo, was also associated with the group.

These same men had led the struggle for Chamorro civil rights prior to the war. They still opposed military restrictions and now sought civil government. Naval officers called them the "opposition group" and believed that the association was instigated by members of the "Big Five" families (a reference the navy apparently borrowed from Hawai'i) of C. C. Butler, José M. Torres, the Gollo-Perez family, Pedro P. Martinez, and the Bordallos.

All associations had to be registered with the naval government before they could function, but the civil administrator, Captain Anderson, refused to register the Friends of Guam. An American journalist, Lloyd Norman of the *Chicago Tribune*, reported that "the Navy is quietly trying to break the grip of the 'Big Five' families upon Guam's economy." He also noted that Captain Anderson kept a blacklist of "commies" in the opposition group.

To counter the opposition group, the naval government encouraged "have-not" local families to invest in a new retail trade company, the Guam Commercial Corporation, under the leadership of Antonio Borja Won Pat. This shrewd former schoolteacher of Chinese-Chamorro ancestry (his father was a Chinese cook who was brought to Guam from Hong Kong by a naval officer in 1905 and who married Soriano Borja) had been a well-known representative of Sumay village to the House of Assembly prior to the war. After the war, he became an entrepreneur as owner of the Hollywood Cafe in 1946–1947 (which, along with B. J. Bordallo's Coconut Grove Restaurant, was one of the first two civilian places to serve beer) and other commercial enterprises and as president of the Guam Junior Chamber of Commerce.

Chamorros who invested in the Guam Commercial Corporation tended to support the navy view that "Guam has to achieve a self-supporting economy before it can be ready for American citizenship," as Won Pat said to Lloyd Norman in May 1947. Navy officials said that they supported these men in order to encourage entrepreneurship, but a navy analysis in December 1946 (restricted to official Washington readers at the time) frankly described Guam as a "regulated, non-competitive economy supervised by a paternalistic government."

The Guam Commercial Corporation was successful in the boom on Guam from 1946 into the early 1950s, but it would go bankrupt in 1954. Its members nevertheless used the corporation and tacit navy support as a base to dominate local politics for the next twenty years after establishing the Commercial party in late 1946. Won Pat became speaker of the House of Assembly in July 1948 and would go on to be the first speaker of the new Guam Legislature in 1951 and Guam's first delegate to the U.S. Congress in the 1960s. He was the island's most influential politician until the early 1980s.

The Friends of Guam dissolved as an organization in 1947, but the members, notably F. B. Leon Guerrero and B. J. Bordallo, went on to lead the fight to end naval government and bring about the Organic Act of 1950. They formed the Welfare party in 1949 but were not successful in electoral politics largely because they represented the vestiges of the old prewar *manak'kilo* elite and were therefore not particularly popular with ordinary Chamorros. In any case, those Guamanians who took strong public stands on political issues, whether pro- or antinavy, were a minority. The majority of Guamanians avoided offending their military rulers.

These quiet Guamanians nevertheless generally agreed on one issue: they wanted to be U.S. citizens. The first mass naturalization of Guamanians as U.S. citizens took place on 12 July 1946, when 113 uniformed Guamanian men in the U.S. Navy were sworn in on the Plaza de España as Americans. By then, Guamanian and Filipino men eighteen years old or older who knew English could join the regular U.S. armed forces for four-year hitches. Those men who served a minimum of three years could be naturalized under the Nationality Act of 1940, and about 600 Guamanian veterans of World War II (who also came under the GI Bill of Rights) were naturalized in the postwar period.

While Guamanian servicemen could obtain citizenship, Guamanian civilians could not be naturalized because they were neither born in the United States (since Guam was an unincorporated territory) nor foreign citizens, who can be made U.S. citizens by congressional legislation. In May 1946, the Seventh Guam Congress asked the navy once more to seek citizenship for all Guamanians, but nothing came of the effort. Subsequently, the Eighth Guam Congress debated the citizenship issue and on 4 January 1947 unanimously requested in Joint Resolution 1 that Governor Pownall ask the U.S. Congress to grant American citizenship to Guamanians and to pass an organic act for the island. For technical reasons (failure to provide "official copies" to the governor), Pownall delayed transmittal of the request to Washington until April. It was then held up by the debate building up in Washington over Guam's governance.

The debate had begun in 1946 but was amplified by a one-day visit to Guam in February 1947 by Secretary of the Interior Harold S. Krug along with California Congressmen Norris Poulson and Clair Engle and Hawai'i's delegate to Congress, Joseph B. Farrington. Krug supported civilian government for

Guam and endorsed the old proposal that Guam should come under the Department of the Interior, as were the Virgin Islands by then.

In the meantime, a second joint resolution at the session of the Guam Congress on 4 January 1947 asked the governor to refer all "local laws," including the civil budget of the naval government, to the Guam Congress for review and approval before enactment. Unlike the delay over the citizenship–organic act resolution, Pownall recommended to Washington that the second resolution be approved. As with the first resolution, the Department of the Navy delayed action because it was by now also waiting for a report by a three-man civilian fact-finding committee headed by Dr. Ernest M. Hopkins, president of Dartmouth College. The committee was visiting Guam and American Samoa in February and March 1947.

The Hopkins committee had been charged in January by Defense Secretary Forrestal with inspecting and recommending changes in the governments of Guam and American Samoa because of the criticism of navy rule by liberals and the media in the United States. After visiting the islands and holding public meetings, the committee submitted a report on 25 March 1947 to Forrestal that recommended Guamanians be given U.S. citizenship, an organic act, local legislative powers, a new trial court, and a special court for land matters. The report criticized navy administration, but in a constructive manner, and recommended that the navy continue to govern Guam until an organic act was enacted.

Following the Hopkins report, a cabinet-level U.S. secretarial committee created by Truman back in 1945 finally released its report on 18 June 1947. It, too, recommended that "separate organic legislation for Guam to provide civil government and to grant citizenship, a bill of rights, and legislative power to Guamanians should be enacted this session." Although some liberals criticized the Hopkins report as a whitewash of navy rule, several bills that incorporated the Hopkins proposals were promptly introduced in the Eightieth Congress.

Reforms of Guam's government were vigorously supported on the mainland in 1947 by liberals such as Harold L. Ickes (former secretary of the interior), Congressman Poulson, and Delegate Farrington. Ickes' antinavy blasts were countered by the well-known novelist John P. Marquand in a *Harper's* magazine article in August 1947 that argued that navy rule on Guam was benevolent and necessary for national defense.

Public and congressional knowledge of Guam was also greatly increased by the appearance in 1947 of the third edition of Laura Thompson's 1941 book, *Guam and Its People.* This revised postwar edition sharply criticized Guam's naval administration. As of 1947, Thompson's book was the only comprehensive analysis of Guam since Safford's turn-of-the-century publications. Another source of antinavy sentiment was the small Institute of Ethnic Affairs in Washington, D.C. The president of the institute, John Collier, was Laura Thompson's husband, and she was a founding member. He had been commissioner of Indian affairs in the Interior Department under Harold Ickes, where he had been sensitized to the plight of indigenous peoples. The institute distributed a mimeographed antinavy newsletter, the *Guam Echo,* from 1947 to 1950 supported by subscriptions from Guamanians and statesiders. *Guam Echo* editor Dolores Coulter, along with John Collier, bombarded newspapers with letters critical of naval rule in Guam, the TTPI, and American Samoa.

Laura Thompson also wrote several journal articles that criticized the naval government, and she appeared before congressional committees in support of reforms for Guam, notably to endorse H.R. 2753, which reflected the Hopkins committee's recommendations. This reform bill was introduced in the Eightieth Congress by Poulson and reintroduced in the Eighty-first (1949–1950) as H.R. 3799. Despite her testimony and the lobbying by the Institute of Ethnic Affairs, these and other bills to provide Guamanians civil rights failed. Nevertheless, the selective (i.e., targeting only relevant congressional committee members) but intense lobbying—which was done without paid lawyers or public relations firms—by Collier, Thompson, and other statesider advocates of native rights was of great value to the Guamanian cause in eventually bringing about the 1950 Organic Act.

While the debate over Guam's affairs heated up in Washington, back on Guam Governor Pownall, angry at Guamanian opponents of navy rule who supported the *Guam Echo,* ordered security investigations and special ONI surveillance of F. B. Leon Guerrero and his associates. Pownall released the findings, which alleged that F. B. was a communist subversive. The people of Guam ignored the ridiculous allegations.

Meanwhile, former Guam Governor Willis W. Bradley, Jr., now a U.S. congressman from California, also sponsored a citizenship bill (H.R. 874) early in the Eightieth Congress, but it too failed. Bradley believed that the navy should continue to administer Guam because navy budgets were larger than the Interior's and the latter's oversight of the Virgin Islands was proving dismal. In June 1947, Bradley wrote an eloquent letter to Guam's legislators that influenced them to pass a resolution in July 1947 (revised and voted on again in September) that endorsed navy rule. Only F. B. Leon Guerrero opposed the pro-navy resolution, and he voiced his opposition in Chamorro, which the ste-

nographer for the Guam Congress did not translate or record, presumably to confuse ONI eavesdroppers. Bradley changed his mind and in early 1948 sponsored another bill, H.R. 3563, in the Eightieth Congress for civil government on Guam, but it failed to clear committee. Bradley, a Republican, also lost his reelection bid that year.

Under mounting pressure by all the bills, reports, and critics to liberalize Guam's government, the navy decided that it was time to compromise. On 7 August 1947, Secretary of the Navy John L. Sullivan issued a proclamation that gave the Guam Congress authority to legislate, including budgets, and to override a veto by the governor by a two-thirds majority in both houses. The bill in question would then be referred to the secretary of the navy for resolution. This step toward American-style democracy received much praise at the time and was later dubbed the Interim Organic Act. It relieved the political pressure on the navy and deflected enactment of reform bills that would have curbed navy authority on Guam.

After the Interim Organic Act, measures passed by the Guam Congress and signed by the governor were henceforth called acts with the force of local law. Relations between Pownall and the Guam Congress returned to normal in 1948. That year saw passage of a local act that instituted elections of

Bishop Baumgartner and Governor Pownall, 1948. Charles A. Pownall was Commander Naval Forces Marianas (COMNAVMAR) and Governor of Guam, 1946–1949. The Most Reverend Apollinaris W. Baumgartner, an American Capuchin, was bishop of Guam from 1945 to 1970. These two men were the most influential officials on Guam in the immediate post–World War II years. (From the collection of the Micronesian Area Research Center, Mangilao, Guam)

village commissioners for four-year terms, later changed to two-year terms; the governor still appointed the chief commissioner. Guamanians soon learned, however, that the governor's powers over the Guam Congresses remained largely intact. The Interim Organic Act allowed the governor the authority to change laws and to initiate legislation by executive order when the Guam Congress was not in session. The Congress usually met on Saturdays for regular sessions and one other day a week for committee work or special sessions. This amounted to about fifty days per fiscal year, so the governor was not seriously limited in his day-to-day power. He also, of course, usually had the support of the secretary of the navy when he vetoed bills. So there was no real separation of powers; it was still a military executive government as before the war.

War Claims and Land Alienation

Nowhere was the governor's power more manifest than in his control of compensation for Guamanian war claims and in the acquisition of land for military purposes. Much of his power derived from public laws passed by the Seventy-ninth Congress in 1945–1946 that were well meaning but often proved contrary to Guamanian interests when implemented. In addition to P.L. 225, the Land Transfer Act, which allowed Guamanian refugees to buy government land, another measure was P.L. 224, the Guam Meritorious Claims Act, passed on 15 November 1945, authorizing payment for war-connected claims. A third law, and the most counterproductive for Guamanians, was P.L. 594, the Land Acquisition Act, passed on 2 August 1946, which authorized the Navy Department to acquire private land needed for permanent military installations on the island.

A Land and Claims Commission to administer these and previous laws had begun to operate in April 1945, and it became the focus of Guamanian discontent. In order to hold down expenditures, the Navy Department placed ceilings of $5,000 on each property loss claim and $4,000 on each death or injury claim. Overall, 795 war claims by over 4,000 claimants (often with several family members per claim) were submitted to the commission by the deadline of 1 December 1946 for deaths (320 claims), injuries (258 claims), and property damage (217 claims). The navy accepted only a portion of the claims and paid a total of $8.3 million in compensation to 4,429 recipients by the time the last claim was settled in 1957. Only one maximum death claim of $4,000 was paid, that of Maria Mafnas Cruz for the execution of her husband in 1942 by the Japanese for assisting American holdouts. All other death payments were less, including precisely $3,327.38 for Father Duenas, who had been executed for assisting the American holdout George Tweed.

The largest amounts for property losses went to the biggest landowners, such as the Catholic Church, Atkins, Kroll, and the Torres, Butler, Martinez, and Bordallo families. The claims and the payments to Chamorros were compensation for deaths, injuries, and damages caused mostly by the Americans in the reinvasion of Guam in 1944, not by the Japanese, from whom many Guamanians also expected compensation.

Most Guamanians accepted the claims settlements, but dissatisfaction grew in the early 1950s when they learned that the United States had waived Guamanian war claims against the Japanese in the peace treaty with Japan. Later, under locally elected governors, the government of Guam began appeals to obtain war reparations when it was learned that Micronesians in the TTPI were authorized reparations from the United States and Japan through the 1971 Micronesian Claims Act (P.L. 92–39), which provided a fund of $20 million for war claims. This was a larger amount for compensation to former enemies than the United States provided to its own loyal Guamanians. Guamanian appeals, however, fell on deaf ears in Washington; as of the early 1990s, war reparations have yet to be authorized for the people of Guam.

Inadequate compensation for war claims was not, however, as frustrating for the Guamanians in the period 1944–1950 as was the acquisition of their land by the military. By late 1944, in addition to land taken for U.S. military bases, 1,500 acres of the best farmland on Guam were appropriated to grow produce and raise livestock and poultry for military consumption. In a quirk of history, much of this land was on the former infamous Kaikuntai plantation at Tai. Management of the U.S. military farm was initially under the Foreign Economic Administration and then under the United States Commercial Company (USCC), an entity of the U.S. federal government. Guamanians, already barred from military installations unless employees, were blocked from their *lanchos* on or near the USCC "Restricted" areas in Tai and elsewhere until the USCC was liquidated and it turned over its responsibilities to the island Department of Agriculture in June 1947.

Although the number of military personnel fell drastically in the demobilization after the war, military need for property on Guam did not decrease in the Cold War that followed. On 11 August 1945, Admiral Nimitz wrote the U.S. chief of naval operations that U.S. objectives after the war would require 75,700 acres, or 55 percent of the island. This acreage, he wrote, included not only "those lands directly employed by the military forces, but additional land adjacent to the used areas to insure control of the total areas for defense and security reasons and to provide for future needs, installations and possible expansion."

Of the 75,700 acres needed to make Guam into a Gibraltar of the Pacific, 28,345 were already owned by the United States from prewar purchases and tax confiscations, and 29,460 more acres were to be purchased (or condemned if the owner would not sell) at an average price of $54.00 per acre (officials at the time said the price was $62.50 per acre, but they overestimated). The remainder of 17,895 acres was to be leased from Guamanian owners at about $0.60 an acre. These modest amounts were based on 1941 appraisals even though prices on Guam by May 1947 had risen over 100 percent above the 1941 levels. The navy defended the low amounts paid as proper to avoid "ruinous and inflated land values . . . which could wreck the island economy."

One major problem was that 40 percent of the needed land was unsurveyed because the navy had never completed an island-wide cadastral survey. The navy resumed cadastral work in 1944, including translations and abstractions of old Spanish land records, but halted it in 1945 under the press of more immediate priorities. The Land and Claims Commission used imprecise records to the navy's advantage to lease private land in large parcels at reduced collective rates instead of by individual lots at higher rents. The navy argued that the "lack of title information and survey data made it impractical to attempt to lease private land with standard leases."

By June 1947, only 190 out of 1,519 Guamanian claims for rent due were being paid. The Land and Claims Commission was condemning land but soon bogged down in the legal complexities of hundreds of property transactions. The commission was understaffed as well as inexperienced in real estate matters. Higher commands nonetheless pressured the staff to meet tight deadlines for land transfers in order for construction of new military projects to proceed.

American military strategists planned to make Guam not only a logistical and operational base but also a secure link for command, control, communications, and intelligence functions (C^3I in military terminology) throughout the Asian rimland and the western Pacific under CINCPAC headquarters in Hawai'i. For this purpose, major projects included a 4,800-acre naval communications master station in Finegayan and a 2,922-acre area for arrays of high-frequency radio antennas in Barrigada. Among other postwar projects was an enormous naval magazine of nearly 7,000 acres in the Fena area in south-central Guam. This area was for storage of conventional and nuclear warheads, chemical warfare agents, and munitions. To link the Fena Naval Magazine with the harbor, the navy completed the Atate Road in mid-1947 and in 1950 finished the all-weather Cross Island Road (now Route 17) between Agat and Talofofo. A dam completed on the Maagas River in 1951 created the 2,185-acre Fena Reservoir inside the naval magazine area to ensure a water supply to the navy's Apra Harbor and Nimitz Hill facilities and to the civilian communities in the southern half of the island.

To acquire land for the military's needs, the Land and Claims Commission cut corners in appraisals and in legal technicalities. Some Guamanians willingly sold or leased land to the military out of patriotism and with the understanding that they could eventually buy it back or redeem leases. Others, however, began to object, and some took their cases to court. It was in this unhappy atmosphere that navy officials received the Hopkins committee report. In addition to recommending political changes to curb navy authority, the report criticized the navy's handling of war claims and land matters. The committee concluded, "No additional land, not presently occupied by the military forces, should be taken if it can possibly be avoided. Only if such land is actually essential to national defense should the ousting of the local residents even be considered."

Naval authorities were concerned that the report might cause Washington to delay land acquisitions and thereby jeopardize strategic military objectives, although in reality much of the acquired land was for future contingency use and consequently lay unused for decades. In reaction to the Hopkins report, Pownall accelerated land condemnations instead of slowing them, and in October 1947 he created by executive order the "Superior Court" of Guam that had been recommended by the Hopkins Committee. The navy hired a statesider, John C. Fischer, as judge and gave him jurisdiction over civil actions and land condemnation cases. Pownall, however, did not assign two Guamanians to the court as the Hopkins committee proposed. A naval staff officer at the time, Roy E. James, wrote in 1949, "The new Superior Court is in reality a device by which all land condemnation proceedings are taken from the regular courts of Guam and placed in a court in which Guamanian judges have no role."

The Superior Court did speed up the processing of land transfers through condemnations: of some 6,000 cases on the court's docket, nearly 3,000 were cleared by the end of 1949. Abuses, on the other hand, did not end. Judge Fischer regularly rejected Guamanian claims for higher compensation, which he called "puffing," and transactions were not always properly registered. When his rulings were appealed, they were invariably upheld since the navy had also made him the presiding judge of the Court of Appeals.

In a Guam *Navy News* article in December 1947, United Press reporter Miles Vaughan argued that local cries of "oppression" over navy land policies were due to "a very few isolated cases" where large Guamanian landholders tried to obtain excessive prices for their properties. Later investigations and court claims, however, concluded that "threats, coercion, appeals to patriotism, and fear of military reprisal" pressured hundreds of Guamanians to sell or lease land for inadequate compensation. These coercive tactics, which were unnecessary (the navy had more than enough funds to pay fair prices for the land condemned) embittered many Guamanians toward the navy for years to come.

Increasingly frustrated by the navy's insensitivity, the Ninth Guam Congress passed resolutions in 1948 to have Guamanians represented in land decisions and to halt military plans to condemn Tumon Bay. The U.S. Air Force wanted to make the entire bay into a segregated military recreational area off-limits to local fishermen and to local use of the beach. To the outrage of Guamanians, nine families were evicted from their Tumon properties, and military police proceeded repeatedly to arrest locals fishing in the lagoon and bay while the condemnation was still under review.

The governor rejected the other resolutions but compromised on Tumon, making only half the bay off-limits to Guamanians. Fed up with Judge Fischer, who upheld the governor, the Guam Congress passed a bill in April 1949 that requested the governor to abolish the Superior Court. Pownall emphatically vetoed the unwelcome measure, and his veto was upheld by the secretary of the navy in June.

One U.S. congressman, William Lemke, who visited Guam with a subcommittee in November 1949, commented in a congressional hearing on the navy's handling of land matters: "There were plenty of signs of abuse. . . . For instance on Guam the military took the lands of the people and forgot to even ask them how much they wanted, or to pay for it. Where the Governor now lives and Admiral Nimitz had his headquarters—they finally offered, after they heard our committee was coming, $14.10 for rental of 15 acres of one of the most beautiful spots anywhere."

The site was Flag Circle on Nimitz Hill, and the $14.10 in rent was for the entire year. Despite complaints, the Land and Claims Commission went right on acquiring land, and the navy's Superior Court kept operating until the Organic Act was enacted. By the beginning of 1950, just before the Organic Act altered federal land policies on Guam, the property controlled by the federal government through ownership or by leases was 58 percent of the island, or 3 percent more than planned by Nimitz back in 1945. Most of the permanent military projects were moving toward completion, and old unneeded installations—but not always the land on which they stood—were abandoned. Orote airfield, for example, was deactivated in February 1949, but the navy retained the entire peninsula. For the next four decades, land on Guam would be held hostage to the Cold War.

By early 1949, Guamanians were faced with another major problem: the influx of thousands of off-island American contractors and Filipino construction workers with salaries and allowances differentiated largely on the basis of race, not on equality of work. Guamanian anger over the privileges of American employees, on top of other frustrations, would lead to a dramatic confrontation between the Ninth Guam Congress and Governor Pownall and then to the removal of naval government itself from Guam.

The End of Naval Government

After the postwar military demobilization, the navy began bidding out construction of new military projects to American civilian contractors. The largest contracts were for construction of the Apra Harbor breakwater for over $8 million in 1945–1948 with the J. H. Pomeroy Company of San Fran-

cisco; for the dredging of the harbor by the Guam Dredging Contractors, 1946–1950, for $13.7 million; and for general construction island-wide by the Brown-Pacific-Matson (BPM) consortium over the period 1946–1956.

Hundreds of technicians and white-collar American employees of these and other contractors, as well as naval government hires, poured into Guam. By the end of 1947, there were nearly 7,000 American nonresident contract workers on the island. American reporter Harold Martin described many of these men in a November 1947 article in the *Saturday Evening Post:* "Some arrived drunk and stayed drunk as soon as they came ashore. . . . Bail jumpers, alimony dodgers, car thieves, artists in the forging of checks, armed robbery and the rolling of drunks—they descended on Guam. . . . I never saw such people, said a contractor . . . we are getting scum I never had to work with before. But we need men so badly we don't try to screen them."

Not all the newcomers, of course, were "scum." Many reliable, hardworking men came as foremen, technicians, and engineers. Some of these, along with discharged servicemen, remained on the island and married Guamanian women, just as had the Spaniards and U.S. sailors and marines before the war. Also like the Spaniards, the Americans turned to the Philippines for skilled and manual workers owing to the labor shortage on Guam. In May 1947, the governments of the United States and the Philippines exchanged notes that constituted an agreement for "the recruitment and employment of Philippine citizens by the U.S. military forces and its contractors in the Pacific, including Guam."

Technically, immigration to Guam came under the U.S. Immigration Act of 1917, but that act was tacitly ignored, and the U.S. Navy, not the U.S. Immigration and Naturalization Service (INS), processed and controlled immigrants and nonimmigrants in Guam and the TTPI until June 1952, when dual administration was established between the navy and the INS. In fact, the U.S.-Philippines exchange of notes was not in compliance with U.S. immigration laws but was expedient to allow the military to obtain Filipino laborers. BPM and the

Marianas Stevedoring and Development Company (referred to as MASDELCO) were authorized to import as many alien laborers as needed on Guam, usually on one- or two-year contracts without need for Philippine passports or U.S. visas. The U.S.-Philippines exchange of notes specified that Filipino workers were to be paid the current Philippine wage, with a 25 percent overseas differential, and were to receive room, board, medical care, and round-trip transportation from the point of hire. These requirements would be repeatedly violated by contractors in the years ahead.

Filipino workers, predominantly Visayans, soon flooded into Guam by military and chartered civilian transportation at a rate of up to 500 per month. A lively financial industry grew to handle thousands of dollars in currency exchanges and in remittances by workers to their families in the Philippines. Huge camps, towns in fact, were constructed to house these men and the few Filipinas among them. The largest, Camp Roxas north of Agat–Santa Rita (on former Bordallo land), with mess halls, movie houses, a beach, and miles of dreary barracks, held 7,000 men, mostly Visayans. Camps Edusa near Dededo, and Marbo (named after the air force's Marianas-Bonin command area and also called Magsaysay City) in Yigo housed mostly Ilocanos and Tagalogs. Camp Quezon was in Mangilao near the present site of the University of Guam. Camp Asan, located on the site of the old Asan *presidio* that held Filipino rebels in 1902–1903, housed American civilian employees of the military. Camp Asan, unlike the other camps, contained a bowling alley and other amenities. It would become an annex to the Naval Hospital in 1968 and then close in 1972, only to be reopened temporarily in 1975 to house Vietnamese refugees.

A major problem for Guamanians with the labor system from the 1940s into the 1970s was the differential pay scales established by the navy. There were four civilian pay scales on Guam: an A scale for Americans hired on the mainland at the highest wages and brought to Guam with the most benefits and with commissary-PX privileges; a B "local hire" scale for Americans hired on Guam at lower pay and benefits than mainland hires; another "local hire" scale for Guamanians at a still lower rate, even if they did the same work as the higher-paid Americans; and a fourth, and lowest, scale for Filipino contract workers at about one-third of the American A scale. The Filipinos, who numbered around 28,000 in 1948, usually did most of the labor. This system saved the U.S. military money and provided high profits to contractors. The system also constituted outright exploitation of local and alien laborers.

The navy's rationale for segregated wages was to prevent inflation on Guam. Inflation was curbed, but the result was to make the aliens' low wages, which were artificially set by the government, the prevailing wages for Guam's small, struggling private sector. Guamanians of Chamorro descent understandably shunned these low salaries and flocked into higher-paying and more comfortable government jobs, swelling the island bureaucracy enormously.

The composition of the labor force and employment by sector thus shifted dramatically by 1950 in comparison with 1940. Before the war, the island workforce was 92 percent Chamorro, of whom 53 percent were in agriculture. By 1950, 65 percent of the workforce was non-Chamorro (mostly Filipino contract workers), and only 6 percent was in agriculture. The cultivation of rice, a staple food on Guam since precontact times, practically ceased (most rice since World War II has been imported to Guam from California, as are other foods). Chamorros now worked primarily for the government. The overloading of the public sector on Guam left the private sector depressed by the mid-1950s and perennially short of labor thereafter.

By the end of 1948, relations between Pownall and the Guam Congress had deteriorated over wage policies, temporary alien workers, land issues, and local civil rights. In January 1949, after much debate, the House of Council passed another resolution to petition for U.S. citizenship. Simultaneously, the council approved for the first time a controversial bill for a special committee to draft an organic act to be submitted to the U.S. Congress.

While these two measures were being considered, the House of Assembly was also investigating violations of the prohibition against Americans owning local businesses through Guamanian "front men." Antinavy sentiment was most pronounced in the Guam House of Assembly. The assembly subcommittee on trade and commerce chaired by Jesus C. Okiyama subpoenaed an American civilian employee of the navy, Abraham (Abe) Goldstein, who had financed the Guam Style Center, a women's clothing store. The power of the Guam Congress to subpoena Americans had already been vetoed by Pownall back in October 1948, so, when Goldstein appeared before the subcommittee in early February 1949, he refused to answer questions on the basis that the Guam Congress was exceeding its authority.

The Guamanians were aware that Abe Goldstein might decline to answer, and they intended to provoke a confrontation with Pownall in order to stir up media attention in support of the bill for an organic act and the petition for citizenship. One assemblyman, Carlos P. Taitano, had recently been a captain in the U.S. Army and knew the power of the American press when aroused. In early 1949, he met two visiting newsmen from the United Press International (UPI) and Associated Press (AP) bureaus in Honolulu. They agreed to file stories about Guam from Honolulu in return for exclusive reports from Taitano.

On 12 February, the Okiyama committee declared Goldstein guilty of contempt and issued a warrant for his arrest. Governor Pownall promptly intervened and halted execution of the warrant by the police. Speaker of the House of Assembly Won Pat then met with Pownall, who advised him to refer the matter to the executive branch for resolution. Won Pat, angered at Pownall's stiff-necked reaction, relayed this advice to the House of Assembly on 5 March, the day the assembly was debating the controversial organic act bill and the latest petition for citizenship.

Infuriated by Pownall's actions, the assembly passed the bill and the petition. They then voted unanimously on a motion to adjourn until "this body receives a reply on the action of the Congress of the United States relative to the Organic Act for Guam as passed by both Houses of the Guam Congress." This was the first time the Guam Congress ever defied U.S. authority on the island. Carlos Taitano rushed, without telling his colleagues, to report to his press contacts in Honolulu by telegram. Both UPI and AP swiftly desseminated the news. The *New York Times* reported "GUAM ASSEMBLY QUITS" on 6 March and "CONGRESS WALKOUT" on 7 March.

On 8 March, Pownall called for a special joint session of the Guam Congress for 12 March. On 11 March, the members of the assembly met informally and decided not to attend. The same day, through Taitano's reports, the *Honolulu Advertiser* headlined "GUAM CONGRESS REVOLT GROWS." On 12 March, only one assemblyman, Joaquin Aguon, showed up at the joint session to hear Pownall defend his actions. Five days later, after getting legal advice from his attorney general (exceedingly poor advice, it would turn out), Pownall announced that thirty-four of the thirty-six assemblymen (two had voted to attend the 12 March session) had willfully violated the law and that their seats were vacated.

Moreover, and here Pownall made an error fatal to his and the naval government's future on Guam, he announced, like the old *Yo, el Rey* edicts of the Spanish kings, that he would appoint replacements to the vacant seats instead of holding elections. Public reaction was immediately hostile. Meetings in twelve of Guam's nineteen villages declared that the people would not recognize any appointees. This was a sound legal stance since the governor had approved an act the year before that vacant seats could be filled only with the "prior concurrence of the Guam Congress."

Guamanian defiance of the military government was gleefully reported by the wire services and mainland news media, just as Carlos Taitano wanted. "GUAM REBELS AT NEW NAVY" proclaimed a *Washington Post* article on 3 April. In the article, Taitano was reported as saying that the political revolt grew out of three major long-standing grievances: "(1) Arbitrary rule by naval government; (2) lack of a constitution or documents anywhere guaranteeing civil rights; (3) lack of a court of appeal beyond the Secretary of the Navy." Letters caustic of navy rule hit the mainland newspapers, one of the most critical written to the *New York Times* by Dolores Coulter, editor of the *Guam Echo*. Members of the U.S. Congress queried the White House for explanations. Pownall had unwittingly done exactly what the reformers had hoped for.

White House reaction was swift and unsympathetic to the navy. Truman, a moderately liberal Democrat, had been reelected president in 1948, and he was thereafter one of the most decisive presidents in U.S. history. He was also well informed about Guam. In view of Guam's status under United Nations (UN) criteria as a non-self-governing colony, the first thing Truman did in March 1949 when he learned of the walkout in Agana was to ask the State Department for an assessment. State replied by the end of March that the Guamanians were loyal and not a security risk to the United States but that, unless a change was made in Guam's government, they could become radicalized. State urged that the Department of the Interior take over in one year.

The White House instructed the Interior Department to draft an organic act for civilian government of Guam. On 14 May, Truman approved the draft and notified the navy and the Interior Department by letter that the act would be introduced as an administration bill into the Eighty-first Congress and that the navy was to turn over administration of Guam to the Department of the Interior within twelve months. The draft organic act was then submitted to the U.S. Congress as Bill H.R. 4499. Truman also ordered the transfer of American Samoa and the TTPI to the Interior within two to three years.

Interior met with the Navy Department to plan the transition, which involved replacement of Pownall with an appointed civilian governor. An interagency agreement was quickly worked out and approved by Truman, but with the provisos that the navy would retain a voice for an interim period in the administration of the island and also that the security clearance would remain in force under navy control. The navy would later justify continuation of these provisos on the grounds that Guam was a U.S. support base for the Korean War, which broke out on 27 June 1950.

Pownall, now feeling the heat from Washington, issued a proclamation on 2 April 1949 that returned Guam's elected assemblymen to their seats. On 7 May, they jubilantly returned to the Guam Congress hall.

The incident over the ownership of a women's dress shop was a turning point in the political history of Guam. If the walkout had not happened, the Korean War would in all probability have been justification for the navy to perpetuate its rule on Guam into the 1950s. As it turned out, the walkout set in motion the end of military government on Guam after an incredible duration of 277 years since the death of Father San Vitores in 1672.

At a special joint session on 21 May, the Ninth Guam Congress passed a resolution thanking President Truman for his "momentous decision in calling for transfer of the administration for Guam to a civilian agency." A week earlier, the Guam Congress had created a special two-man committee to proceed to Washington to appeal for passage of an organic act as a follow-up to the transfer of administration. The men selected were F. B. Leon Guerrero and Antonio Won Pat.

Unlike the similar trip undertaken by Leon Guererro and B. J. Bordallo in the 1930s, this time the Guam Congress authorized $10,000 for expenses, and this time the outcome of the visit would be successful. Other Guamanians also lobbied for the organic act in Washington in this period, including Agueda Johnston, Concepcion Barrett, and B. J. Bordallo (who took along his teenage children Barbara, Paul, and Ricardo). Meanwhile, the issue of Abe Goldstein's subpoena was dropped. He left Guam unobtrusively.

Governor Pownall retired on 1 September 1949 and grandly departed Apra Harbor on the USAT *General Butner* beneath a farewell flyover by B-29s and navy aircraft. Pownall, a respected naval aviator and commander of an aircraft carrier task force in World War II, was somewhat a victim of circumstances as the last naval governor of Guam. From the military viewpoint, he fulfilled his mission as COMNAVMAR. During his fateful three and a half years on Guam, he ably supervised construction of vast installations that turned the island into a key link in the worldwide U.S. defense system. Unfortunately, the same trait of assertiveness that made him a fine naval officer prevented him from being flexible in civil matters, where patience and subtlety were needed.

On 7 September 1949, Truman issued Executive Order 10077, which formally transferred administration of Guam to the Department of the Interior effective 1 July 1950. The same order revoked President McKinley's Executive Order 108-A of 23 December 1898, which had given Guam to the U.S. Navy. At Interior Secretary Krug's recommendation, Truman appointed Carlton S. Skinner as Guam's first civilian governor (other than the Sisto-Pérez-Coe "acting governorships" in 1898–1899). Skinner was a tall, thirty-six-year-old journalist from Connecticut who was the public relations director for the Department of the Interior. He had visited Guam with Krug in February 1947.

Skinner took the formal oath of office on 27 September 1949 in the newly rebuilt bandstand in the center of the Plaza de España. Seven weeks later, he was baptized rudely by the Pacific Ocean when Typhoon Allyn swept over Guam on 17 November, smashing Inarajan and destroying 124 houses, some bridges, and most of the crops on the island.

Meanwhile, before proceeding with Bill H.R. 4499, the Eighty-first Congress sent a specially formed House subcommittee on public lands, known as the Miles committee for its chairman John E. Miles, to visit Guam, American Samoa, and the TTPI. The Miles committee held three days of hearings on Guam in late November 1949. All the hundred or so Guamanians who testified favored the draft organic act in H.R. 4499 but suggested a number of changes. Much pent-up frustration over land condemnations also burst forth at the hearings. The subcommittee, and later the full standing committee on public lands, replaced H.R. 4499 with H.R. 7273, which incorporated twenty-three changes. Democratic Congressman J. Hardin Peterson introduced H.R. 7273 on 13 February 1950 with the intent, he said, "to put an end to our neglect of the rights of the Guamanian people over the last 50 years."

Naval officials did not agree with those words but by 1950 believed that they could safely turn the island over to a civilian government without jeopardizing strategic military missions in the western Pacific. In the hearings, the navy representative accepted the inevitable on a slightly defensive note of prudential forgetting: "The Department of the Navy desires to endorse most strongly the proposal now before the Congress. . . . The Department of the Navy, in reviewing the 50 years of its administration on Guam and American Samoa, feels a pride which is believed justifiable in the progress made on these islands."

In his testimony, Governor Skinner diplomatically lauded the navy for its long administration of Guam. He also noted, on the other hand, that "the people of Guam have had enough paternalistic protection. They want emancipation."

A similar view was expressed by Tun Kiko Zoilo—F. B. Leon Guerrero—the pudgy, self-taught lawyer and tenacious Chamorro-rights advocate who had first appealed to American justice thirteen years earlier. All other testimony, mainly by liberal Democrats, also favored the bill. On 17 April, Leon Guerrero and Won Pat met Truman to present a petition signed by 1,700 Guamanians in favor of the draft organic act. On 23 May, the U.S. House, controlled by a Democrat majority, passed the measure, and, on 26 July, the U.S. Senate, also controlled by the Democrats, approved it, with one major change: it made the new Guam Legislature unicameral. Also, the Senate report on the bill noted that, despite the change in government, Guam remained under the doctrine of the 1901 *Insular Cases* without any possibility of statehood: "As an unincorporated Territory, Guam like Puerto Rico and the Virgin Islands is appurtenant to the United States and belongs to the United States, but is not a part of the United States, as distinguished from Alaska and Hawaii, which are incorporated territories. Unincorporated areas are not integral parts of the United States and no promise of statehood or a status approaching statehood is held out to them."

President Truman signed H.R. 7273 into law on 1 August 1950 as the Organic Act of Guam, but it was made effective as of 21 July, the sixth anniversary of Liberation Day in 1944. The only Guamanian invited to be present at the signing in the

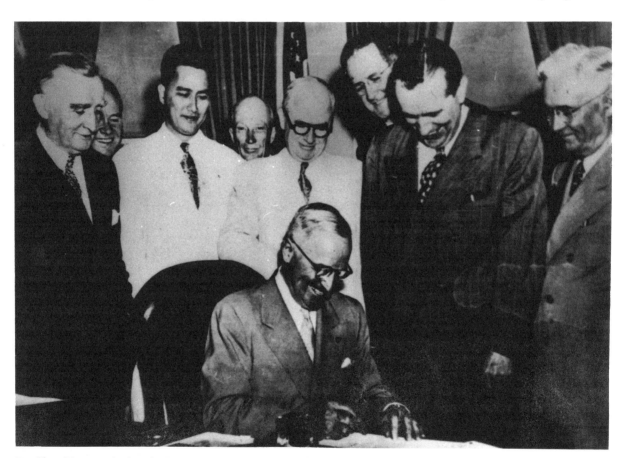

President Truman signing the Guam Organic Act, 1950. The ceremony took place in the White House on 1 August 1950. Truman's signature made the act a federal law codified as 48 U.S.C. § 1421, et seq. The only Guamanian present at the ceremony was Carlos P. Taitano, later speaker of the Eighth Guam Legislature (behind the president in a white suit). The Organic Act, passed by the U.S. Congress without a vote on it by the people of Guam, made Guamanians U.S. citizens, established civilian government, and remains the basic law of the island until the local people approve a constitution of their own. (From the collection of the Micronesian Area Research Center, Mangilao, Guam)

White House was Carlos Taitano, who by then was a student at the Georgetown University Law School in Washington, D.C.

The eight years and eight months from 8 December 1941 to 1 August 1950 had been a period of the most traumatic involuntary changes for the island's people and environment since the Spanish-Cha- morro wars. Although Guam was still bound by the old colonial dogma of the *Insular Cases,* the year 1950 marked the beginning of a new era for the island, an era of gradual decolonization, rising material standards of living, and peaceful social transformation for the people of Guam.

13 Under the Organic Act 1950–1970

Partial Decolonization

The first few years after passage of the Organic Act produced an intense but progressive governmental transformation on Guam. Prior to the act, the navy administered Guam as a military base with the island's civil government of minor priority within the military chain of command in the Pacific under CINCPAC, who reported to the Pentagon. After the act, the island government's responsibilities expanded to correspond approximately to those of a tiny U.S. state with direct civilian links to the Congress and the executive branch, even though in size, people, and resources Guam is equivalent (albeit with some unique differences) to a small, semirural county in the U.S. system.

Governor Skinner, who worked under the navy until the Organic Act passed Congress, found himself reappointed all over again in 1950 under the Interior Department. He replaced all military personnel in the government with civilians, predominantly Guamanians, under new wage scales and a merit system for the 1,728 classified civil service positions. The navy removed itself from banking by selling the Bank of Guam to the Bank of America in 1950. The U.S. selective service system was applied to Guam in 1951, and young Guamanians enlisted eagerly in the armed forces, easily filling Guam's annual quotas for the Korean War. Civilian police and firemen, now nearly all Guamanians, ensured

law and order without any further involvement of the U.S. Marines.

In 1950, Skinner separated the civilian hospital at Oka, still in its two rusty Butler buildings, from the Naval Hospital and named it the Guam Memorial Hospital (GMH). For civilian medical personnel, Skinner sent recruiters to the Philippines to hire physicians and nurses on contract. Those hired were accorded American credentials after examinations but received salaries considerably lower than U.S. standards. After fulfilling their contracts, many of these Filipino professionals remained on Guam, becoming U.S. citizens and forming the nucleus of the island's private medical community for many years.

Research started on the local disease *lytico-bodig* after naval pathologists found a high incidence of deaths among Chamorros from what the Americans still thought, as before the war, to be ALS (Lou Gehrig's disease), which is fairly rare (about two new cases per 100,000 people) in the United States. The doctors discovered, however, that *lytico-bodig* was not rare on Guam and that in some aspects it differs from ALS.

The naval physicians renamed the *bodig* aspect, in which the spinal cord and brain are attacked, *parkinsonism-dementia complex*. In the *lytico*, or ALS, aspect, a sound brain is imprisoned in a paralyzed body. The relation between the two aspects is unclear. Umatac was long the center of the illness, as it had been in Spanish times, so it seemed that it might be hereditary, but it turned out not to be. Some researchers suspected consumption of *fadang*, the cycad federico seeds, which had increased among Chamorros in the war years, to be the cause of the disease, as Spanish governor Felipe de la Corte had warned in 1865. Other researchers thought that the high content of aluminum in Guam's soil and water might be a cause.

In 1956, a research office funded by the federal government opened in GMH under Leonard T. Kurland and Donald Mulder, doctors from the Mayo Clinic, to study the disease. Research on this "Guam riddle" has continued ever since, primarily on-island by neurologists K-M. Cheng and John Steele. As of the 1990s, the causes and the cure of *lytico-bodig* have yet to be established, to the despair of Chamorros who still suffer from this deadly malady.

Meanwhile, Governor Skinner expanded the Guam public school system and revised the curriculum to reflect stateside standards. Classes continued to be in English as before the war, but the Chamorro language was no longer forbidden in schools. Chamorro technically remained illegal in government offices until 1972, when the Twelfth Guam Legislature made both English and Chamorro the two official languages of Guam. In practice, however, people spoke Chamorro freely anywhere on the island after 1950. On 30 June 1952, the Territorial College of Guam with a two-year curriculum was established in a cluster of elephant Quonset huts on the George Washington High School campus in Mongmong as Micronesia's first institution of higher education. This little junior college for elementary school teachers, with an initial faculty of five and an enrollment of 123 students, was set up under the DOE (Department of Education) by Dr. José R. Palomo, the first Guamanian Ph.D. and the director of the DOE 1950–1951. Palomo created the school with the assistance of his alma mater, Ohio State University, which accepted transfer

credits until 1956, by which time the College of Guam was accredited on its own.

Despite the civil transformation of local government, COMNAVMAR still ruled more than one-third of Guam's land area and all the surrounding air- and water space except submerged inshore areas, which interior claimed. Rivalry lingered for years between naval and civilian officials, owing to problems unresolved by the Organic Act. For all its welcome reforms, the act contained significant anomalies in American law with respect to Guamanian civil rights, local autonomy, the structure of the new civilian government, and the role of the military. The major provisions of the Guam Organic Act were as follows.

American Citizenship: Section 4 of the Organic Act conferred congressional—not constitutional—U.S. citizenship on those inhabitants of Guam born on the island after 11 April 1899, their children, and all those of Spanish and other nationalities resident on the island as of 11 April 1899. This provision excluded nonresident Filipinos (mostly contract workers) and other foreign nationals on Guam in 1950 not born on the island. The first sentence of Article XIV (the Fourteenth Amendment) of the federal Constitution—by which constitutional citizenship is automatic for persons born in the United States—did not apply to Guamanians because they were born in a territory. Authority for Guamanians to be U.S. citizens was later assumed under the Immigration and Naturalization Act (INA) of 1952 (8 U.S.C. 1407).

As U.S. citizens after 1950, Guamanians could travel more easily with U.S. passports. Entire Guamanian families, not just men, began to move to the mainland even though the navy still controlled travel clearances until 1962. Gradually over the next decades, particularly after 1962, thousands of Guamanians, some of them the best educated, departed to live permanently in the states, where higher wages and living standards offered more opportunities than Guam.

The Organic Act did not confer on Guamanians who remained on the island all the traditional functions of American citizenship, such as full political participation in the national government (e.g., permanent residents of Guam cannot vote for the U.S. president or vice president), protection from federal power, and access to all federal economic and social benefits. It took a while for Guamanians to understand these anomalies, and many now consider themselves "second-class" Americans.

Bill of Rights: Section 5 of the Organic Act provided a Bill of Rights under Guam law similar to that of the U.S. Constitution, but it did not unequivocally confer on Guamanians all the constitutional protections of U.S. law, notably the privilege of habeas corpus and the prohibition against bills of attainder (Article I, Section 9, clauses 2 and 3). Not until 1968, as part of the Guam Elective Governor Act (implemented in 1970), would the Congress amend the Organic Act to apply to Guamanians the Article I guarantees and the first nine U.S. constitutional amendments. However, the Tenth Amendment and the first sentence of the Fourteenth Amendment, which would limit congressional power over Guam, still do not apply to the island as of the early 1990s.

Political Status: Prior to the Organic Act, U.S. officials usually called Guam a *possession* (with a small *p*). Section 3 of the Organic Act for the first time specifically declared Guam to be an unincorporated organized *Territory* (with a capital *T*) of the United States, but in practice the federal government still treated the island as an unorganized territory in accord with the *Insular Cases* doctrine. Thus, despite the elimination of military government, the Organic Act granted only limited self-rule to Guamanians. The Ninth Circuit Court confirmed the neocolonial nature of the island's status in several cases, most recently in 1985 in *Sakamoto v. Duty Free Shoppers, Ltd.:* "The Government of Guam is in essence an instrumentality of the federal government." As a consequence, the United States still had to report annually to the United Nations about Guam's progress toward self-determination. Responsibility for the preparation of these rather meaningless, bland reports shifted from the navy to the State Department, with the Interior's assistance.

The reports ended in the late 1970s after the people of Guam were electing their governors.

The Organic Act functions as a constitution for Guam, but it does not derive its powers from the people of the island. They never voted on it. The U.S. Congress retains plenary power (i.e., full authority) to amend the act or to enact any legislation it wishes for Guam without the consent of the Guamanians, a power that the Congress does not possess when dealing with the citizens of a U.S. state. In other words, the Organic Act did not apply to Guam the normal statutory and judicial presumptions that favor local democratic government in the American system. Most Guamanian leaders were nonetheless satisfied for the next twenty years after 1950 for Guam to remain an unincorporated, organized territory of the United States. They concentrated on piecemeal reforms in the Organic Act, not on a basic redefinition of the island's status.

Civilian Administration: Section 3 of the act organized a civilian government for Guam under "the general administrative supervision of the Secretary of Interior." Guam was placed, along with other U.S. territories at the time (but not Puerto Rico), under the director of the Office of Territories within the Bureau of Land Management in the Interior Department. The Interior functioned in the twentieth century as the federal clean-up crew for the neocolonialist residue of American Manifest Destiny of the nineteenth century.

In the bloated bureaucratic maze of Interior, the insular territories are among the least important concerns. Although there have been fine civil servants in territorial affairs, such as Ruth G. Van Cleve (director, 1964–1969), these dedicated few could not overcome the glacial inertia of the layered federal bureaucracy. Therefore, Guam slipped to an even lower federal priority under the Interior than under the navy. In the 1970s, after several reorganizations, the Office of Territories became the Office of Territorial and International Affairs (OTIA), and, in 1979, the director became an assistant secretary appointed by the White House. From 1979 into the 1990s, these assistant secretaries of

OTIA have all been political appointees, the majority have been women (resented politely by the male-dominated leaderships of the islands), and none have had extensive knowledge of the Pacific territories, to the recurring consternation of Guamanians.

Another problem—one yet to be resolved—for Guam with the Interior's supervision lay in the contradictory nature of the department's missions. In Washington, the Interior is charged with representing and protecting Guam's interests. On Guam, the Interior represents Washington and protects federal interests. When the two roles conflict, which is often the case, the Interior naturally protects federal interests first even though its officials have exercised considerable restraint in policy matters ("suggesting" policy to governors rather than "instructing" them). Therefore, the relationship between Guamanians and the Interior Department became adversarial, as was the relationship between Guamanians and the Navy Department.

Local Government: Section 3 of the Organic Act specified for the first time on Guam a local government of "three branches, executive, legislative, and judicial." The commissioner system in the nineteen villages was not addressed in the act and continued as before. The government of Guam as a whole came to be called GovGuam for short by people on the island, by the media, and by federal authorities in Washington.

In the federal and in state constitutions of the United States, the legislative branch of government, which is the one most representative of the people, is first in sequence and shares power equally with the other branches. The Organic Act reversed this traditional pattern by placing Guam's executive branch (Section 6) ahead of the legislature (Section 10), both in sequence and in power. What the act did was to carry over much of the old naval governor's powers to the appointed civilian governor. The effect was to perpetuate U.S. control of Guam through the executive branch.

Under the Organic Act until amended in 1968, the governor of Guam was appointed by the U.S. president for a four-year term. The original act also provided for an appointed "Secretary of Guam" who functioned as a lieutenant governor until 1970, after which time the Elective Governor Act of 1968 made the position a formal lieutenant governor elected jointly with the governor. The act gave the governor of Guam direct responsibility under Sections 29(a) and (b) for public health and education, which in the states are partially protected from direct executive control by independent boards and commissions.

The Organic Act authorized the governor to pass on to the U.S. president for resolution any legislation the governor vetoed but that was overridden by a two-thirds majority of the legislature. Three such controversial bills were forwarded to President Dwight D. Eisenhower in the 1950s and one in 1966 to President Lyndon B. Johnson; all four vetos were upheld. This anomaly, whereby a federally appointed governor could circumvent a locally elected legislature, was removed by the 1968 Elective Governor Act. The 1968 act, however, did not substantially reduce the governor's other powers. Once Guamanians took over as elected chief executives after 1970, they used the broad powers granted Guam's governor to administer (and to politicize) education, medicine, law enforcement, and other public services on the island more directly than is the normal practice in American state governments.

While the Organic Act provided for a strong executive, it placed limits on the powers of Guam's legislative branch. The Organic Act created a single house, named the Legislature of Guam, of not more than twenty-one senators. The only other unicameral legislature in the United States is that of Nebraska. A single house instead of an unnecessary bicameral legislature for the small territory has saved Guam money. In the beginning, Guam's senators considered their work to be part-time public service, but gradually they came to view it as a full-time occupation (and sometimes as a lifetime career).

The senators are elected biennially in even-numbered years. After the first election under the Organic Act took place on 7 November 1950 and the new body convened in January 1951, it designated itself to be the First Guam Legislature (1951–1952) in place of the Eleventh, and last, Guam Congress. An amendment of the Organic Act in 1966 (P.L. 89–552) allowed the legislature to decide if elections were at large or by district. Elections remained at large until the 1978 and 1980 elections (Fifteenth and Sixteenth Legislatures), which were by districts, and then—to assure Chamorro political control in face of a rising Filipino population—switched back in 1982 to at large, making electoral districting a controversial issue.

Only the U.S. Congress may alter the Organic Act, and in the years since 1950 the act has been amended many times, usually at the request of the Guam Legislature. Section 11 explicitly restricts Guam's legislative power to local matters "not inconsistent with the provisions of this Act and the laws of the United States applicable to Guam." What is or is not inconsistent (called *inorganic* with respect to the act) and what is applicable have been matters of litigation. In short, under the Organic Act, Guam lacks the local legislative autonomy possessed not only by the U.S. states but also by the U.S. Commonwealths of Puerto Rico (since 1952) and the Northern Mariana Islands (since 1976).

Law and the Judiciary: Section 22 of the Organic Act initiated the creation of a civil legal system on Guam. At the top of the system, the act established the District Court of Guam, which had jurisdiction for all cases arising from local as well as federal laws until 1974. Section 22 also authorized the new government of Guam to establish local courts. Appeals went to the U.S. Ninth Circuit Court in San Francisco and on to the Supreme Court.

The District Court absorbed the cases of the old Superior Court, which dissolved when the Organic Act went into effect. To support the new federal court, the act created positions for a U.S. district attorney and a U.S. marshal on Guam under the U.S. Department of Justice. The Navy's ONI (which later changed its name to the Naval Intelligence Service) continued to be the only federal investigative agency on Guam until 1974, when the

Federal Bureau of Investigation set up an office in Agana. Contrary to rumors, the CIA never established an office on Guam.

To accomplish the reorganization of Guam's judiciary, and to recompile the island's laws after the Organic Act, the First Guam Legislature hired attorney John A. Bohn as legislative counsel. Bohn, along with Albert B. Maris, a former judge on the Guam Court of Appeals, wrote the Judiciary Act of Guam, which was passed in 1951 as P.L. 1–17. This act set up a supervisory Judicial Council for Guam and three local courts: the Island Court for trials of criminal and civil cases; the Police Court for traffic cases; and the Commissioners Court for justice-of-the-peace matters. A quarter of a century later, under the authority of Section 22 of the Organic Act, the Twelfth Guam Legislature passed the Court Reorganization Act (P.L. 12–85), which was implemented on 16 January 1974. This important law abolished the Police and Commissioners courts and renamed the Island Court the Superior Court (with Joaquin C. Perez the first presiding judge) with jurisdiction over all cases arising from Guam law. Income tax cases, however, are still tried in the District Court. Appeals from the Superior Court go to the District Court and then up the federal appellate chain.

In the meantime, Bohn recodified the laws of Guam from all the old statutes, acts, executive orders, and so forth that had made up the confusing accretion of laws under the naval governments. This much-needed local codification culminated in 1953 in P.L. 2–26 (the penal code), P.L. 2–27 (the civil code), P.L. 2–28 (the probate code), and P.L. 2–29 (the civil procedures code), which combined made up the new Code of Guam. Bohn also published the Guam Codes until 1974, when an office of the compiler of laws was established by the legislature to keep track of changes in Guam's laws and to publish them. The new organization and new code finally gave Guam a sound judiciary responsive to local needs, but the reforms were incomplete. The Organic Act omitted mention of trials by jury and rights to grand jury indictment, which did not exist under the navy. It took a few years to establish jury trials and grand jury indictments in both federal and local courts on Guam.

Another anomaly was that the act created only half the standard judicial branch, the trial half, found in U.S. states. Each state also has a local appellate court system under its own constitution. As of 1994, Guam still had neither since appeals from the island's Superior Court were made to the federal appellate structure. Thus, in reality, the 1950 Organic Act established only two and a half branches of local government on Guam, not three as the act proclaimed.

Taxes and Duties: Under naval rule, the residents of Guam—Chamorros and Americans alike except for military personnel—did not pay income taxes. With the transfer to civilian government, funds were needed in place of the navy subsidies to support the island government. In order to avoid having Congress appropriate annual subsidies to Guam, as it did for the navy, Section 31 of the Organic Act simply imposed federal income taxes on all residents and businesses on the island. This shocked everyone on Guam. Screams of protest rose, and court suits challenged the taxation, but lost.

Since 1951, all island residents have paid their income taxes on standard U.S. Internal Revenue Service forms, just as Americans do in the states, but that money is not sent to the IRS in Washington. Federal taxes collected on the island remain in the Treasury of Guam. This form of taxation is called a mirror tax since it duplicates the federal tax but in actuality is a local tax. Originally, the mirror tax was supposed to be temporary until Guam was in better financial shape, but it continued of its own momentum.

Real estate taxes, which had been suspended since the war, were reinstituted in 1953 at rates of 1 percent of 50 percent of assessed market value for land and 0.5 percent for buildings, regardless of zoning or use. This low—and popular—rate helped stop the loss of land by Guamanians, owing to tax debts, as occurred before the war. The Organic Act also empowered Guam to sell general obligation bonds within certain limits. Such bonds would be of great assistance to finance expansion of utilities, but Guam's weak economy and poor financial management would at times limit the island's bond ratings and ability to float issues.

Revenue for Guam is also gained by keeping the federal income taxes paid by all nonresident U.S. federal and military personnel on active duty or retired on the island as well as fees from customs, passports, immigration, etc. This revenue, called Section 30 money from the Organic Act provision, is "covered" over to the Treasury of Guam instead of going to the IRS. Since the military population on Guam has been substantial over the years, this Section 30 money has provided millions of dollars annually to GovGuam.

Guam's economy is also assisted by the island's status under Section 27 of the Organic Act as a duty-free port; that is, like a number of other U.S. free ports, Guam is not part of the customs area of the United States. The First Guam Legislature abolished all customs taxes for the island, and businesses import goods free of U.S. tariffs. This benefit was of limited impact as long as the military security clearance curbed commerce until 1962. Thereafter, duty-free status boosted tourism.

Guam temporarily benefited to a limited degree in the 1970s and 1980s from two U.S. trade programs extended by a 1954 amendment of Section 27 of the Organic Act: Headnote 3(a) of the U.S. Tariff Code and the Generalized System of Preferences. These programs initially facilitated access to the U.S. market through a quota system for products assembled on Guam (mainly watches and textile apparel) from foreign goods that total no more than 50 percent of the final value. Under pressure from domestic special interests, however, the U.S. Congress changed U.S. protective quotas on such products from time to time, eventually killing Guam's small watch and apparel businesses by the early 1990s.

The Military Role and Land: Even though GovGuam assumed civil jurisdiction over the island in 1950, the U.S. military presence on the island remained overwhelming, and much of the local postwar history of the island revolved around attempts by civilians to obtain what the military was supposed to give them under the Organic Act. As noted earlier, the navy retained the security clearance. The military did not want to open up Apra Harbor to more commercial shipping, handled at the time by the navy, which would place burdens on military facilities. The navy also feared espionage by the Soviet Union in the fervidly anti-communist atmosphere of the Cold War years. An American scholar on U.S. territorial law described the adverse impact of the security clearance: "By limiting the availability of skilled personnel, especially in the civilian construction market, just when Guam was attempting to rebuild from the destruction of World War II, the Executive Order [for the security clearance] effectively prevented economic development on Guam. Once the controls were removed in 1962, a booming tourist industry arose in relation to Guam, an embarrassing indication to the Federal government of their short-sighted vision of Guam's potential."

While the military security curtain around Guam hindered commercial development, military retention of land and utilities on the island caused the most severe long-term problems for the private sector on Guam. Section 28 of the Organic Act required all property, including utilities, used by the naval government for "civil affairs" to be transferred to the new civilian government within ninety days of 1 August 1950. However, Section 33 of the act gave the U.S. president the extraordinary authority to designate any part of Guam a military reservation, even if privately owned. The president also retained the power to close Guam to vessels and aircraft of foreign nations.

The navy and air force feared that transfer of all the island's utilities to local control under Section 28, particularly the generation of electric power, could jeopardize military operations because local civilian management might not be dependable at all times. Moreover, just before passage of the Organic Act, the U.S. Congress authorized by P.L. 80–564 on 17 June 1950 a massive $45 million construction program for Guam on properties under military control at the time of the act. The navy, backed

by the Interior Department, persuaded President Truman to use Section 33 to make a major exception to Section 28 and retain in military hands the property of installations earmarked by P.L. 80–564. The properties that the military wished to retain totaled an enormous 42,380 acres. They included all the major bases built since the war, the island's one power plant at Piti, the Fena Naval Magazine and Reservoir, and much of the sewer, water, power, and telephone systems usually considered part of "civil affairs."

To make retention of Guam's land by the military legal, Skinner was instructed to sign a quit-claim deed on 31 July 1950—the day before the Organic Act went into effect—whereby GovGuam transferred all condemned properties to the United States of America "for its own use." Truman issued Executive Order 10178 on 31 October 1950, returning all the property in the quitclaim deed to the navy to be divided among the military services by need. These steps were taken without consulting Guamanian officials or owners of leased properties. Interior then entered into agreement with the navy whereby the latter provided logistical support to GovGuam but retained control over all of Apra Harbor except the new Commercial Port at Cabras Island. This left the navy and air force in direct control of about 49,600 acres, or over 36 percent of the island. Nearly 22 percent of the island under the military prior to the Organic Act was turned over to GovGuam in 1950–1951, leaving about 42 percent in private hands. In short, Guamanians believed that they were fleeced of huge portions of their island.

Overall, then, navy and air force officers had little to be unhappy about with the Organic Act. On Guam, the military still retained a massive presence and broad authority to accomplish its missions. The geopolitics of national defense remained paramount in U.S. policy toward Guam, as in the surrounding TTPI, and the federal government was still in firm control of the island government to ensure order and stability. The priority on military matters whenever Washington looked at Guam and the western Pacific would endure for the next

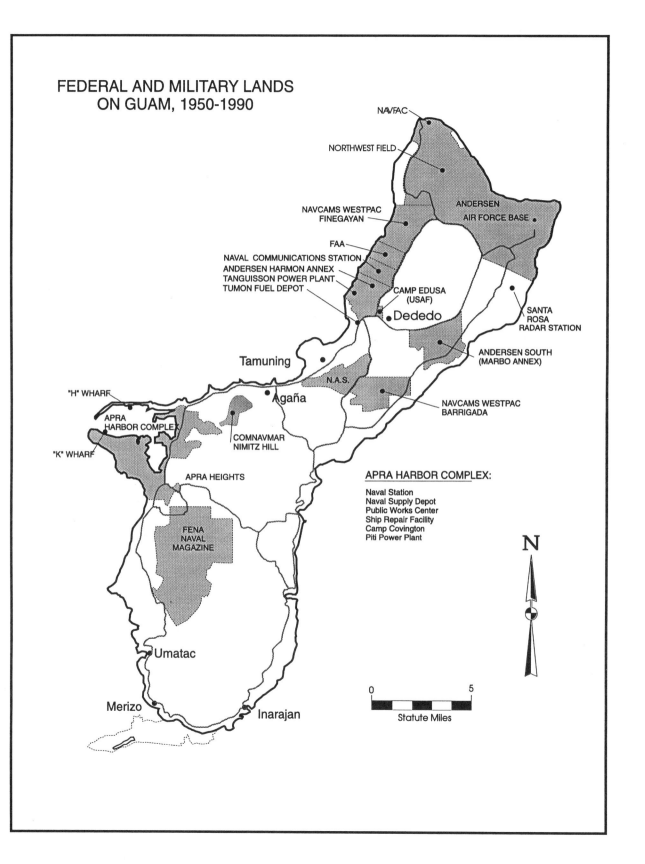

FEDERAL AND MILITARY LANDS
ON GUAM, 1950-1990

NAVFAC

NORTHWEST FIELD

ANDERSEN
AIR FORCE BASE

NAVCAMS WESTPAC
FINEGAYAN

FAA

NAVAL COMMUNICATIONS STATION
ANDERSEN HARMON ANNEX
TANGUISSON POWER PLANT
TUMON FUEL DEPOT

CAMP EDUSA
(USAF)

Dededo

SANTA
ROSA
RADAR STATION

ANDERSEN SOUTH
(MARBO ANNEX)

Tamuning

N.A.S.

Agaña

NAVCAMS WESTPAC
BARRIGADA

"H" WHARF

APRA
HARBOR COMPLEX

"K" WHARF

COMNAVMAR
NIMITZ HILL

APRA HEIGHTS

FENA
NAVAL
MAGAZINE

APRA HARBOR COMPLEX:

Naval Station
Naval Supply Depot
Public Works Center
Ship Repair Facility
Camp Covington
Piti Power Plant

N

Umatac

Merizo

Inarajan

0   5

Statute Miles

forty years until the end of the Cold War in the 1990s.

Most Guamanians were also pleased with the Organic Act regardless of its anomalies. The islanders were Americans at last, they were participating in their own government, and military authority was curbed even though still present. Guamanians tend not to measure progress by stateside standards, as mainland Americans often do. Rather, islanders compare new conditions against what existed on the island in the past, and in that respect the quality of life for Guamanians from 1950 on was clearly better than before the Organic Act.

Civilian Governors, Military Priorities

During Skinner's tenure as governor, Guam served as a busy support base for the Korean War (25 June 1950–27 July 1953). In July 1950, within two weeks of the outbreak of the war, the U.S. Air Force reactivated the Far East Bomber Command with B-29 bombers operating from Andersen Air Force Base and Northwest Field to bases in Japan and Okinawa. At that time, air force headquarters was still at Marbo, south of Andersen. The conclusion in September 1951 of the U.S.-Japan Mutual Security Treaty formalized U.S. responsibility for the strategic defense of Japan. This treaty and its later amendments increased Guam's importance as a support and operational base for CINCPAC's missions in the northwestern as well as the western Pacific with long-term forward deployment of the U.S. Seventh Fleet in those regions. By the end of 1951, SAC had allocated fifteen nuclear bombs to its wing on Guam for potential use against Soviet targets from Vladivostok to Irkutsk. In 1952, the Department of Defense was authorized for the first time to store nuclear warheads in depots outside the United States. Soon thereafter, presumably, nuclear weapons for the air force and the navy began to be stored at Andersen and the Fena Naval Magazine, guarded by marines.

The military in this period still depended on large numbers of Filipino alien workers to complete military construction projects in the western Pacific. Control of contract workers on Guam changed as a result of the Immigration and Naturalization Act of 1952, when the INS assumed joint administration (and later full administration) with the U.S. Navy. This act contained a provision, Section 101(a)(15)(H), that established three "H" worker categories, the second of which, called H-2, allowed aliens to perform "temporary services or labor, if unemployed persons capable of performing such service or labor cannot be found in the United States."

This provision allowed the military to continue to use Filipino contract workers. To assist these men, the Philippines established a consulate on Guam in 1950, but it was run by an honorary consul, an American. As of late 1952, there were still approximately 17,000 Filipino H-2 workers on Guam, of which 3,000 worked in local (i.e., Guamanian) defense-related businesses, so Filipino Foreign Service Officers took over the consulate. The number of Filipino workers dropped in the late 1950s as military projects were completed and the large labor camps closed. In 1959, responding to resolutions by the Guam Legislature to reduce the number of Filipino workers, the INS ordered a three-year phaseout of all alien contract laborers to begin in 1960. The Guam Chamber of Commerce, the navy, and the Interior Department all opposed this order, but the highly independent INS went ahead, and by 1962 most H-2s would be gone from Guam. As will be seen, however, this action only temporarily interrupted the flow of H-2 workers to the island.

While these developments were unfolding on Guam, Republican Dwight Eisenhower had been elected president in the November 1952 elections. The president-elect promptly visited American troops in South Korea in early December to fulfill a campaign promise. On the way back, he landed on Guam to board the cruiser *Helena* for the leg to Pearl Harbor by sea. During his short stay on the island, Eisenhower was told by the COMNAV-MAR, Rear Admiral Ernest W. Litch, that Skinner was interfering with navy operations. Litch had clashed with Skinner over the need for more electricity for the civilian sector from the navy-controlled Piti power plant. Because of the Korean War, Litch believed that military needs should take priority over civilian needs.

Neither Skinner (who happened to be off-island) nor his deputy, Randall S. (Pat) Herman, were invited by Litch to meet Eisenhower; the trip was kept secret until the president-elect reached Guam. As a consequence of hearing only one side of the story from Litch, Eisenhower, according to a newspaper account, "angrily ordered that Gov. Carlton Skinner...be fired after the Republican Administration takes over January 20." Skinner's problems were compounded when Typhoon Hester struck southern Guam on New Year's Day, 1953, and he had to ask Litch for assistance. On 12 January 1953, a *Guam Daily News* headline asked, "WHO RULES GUAM?" That question was answered on 20 January, when Skinner resigned. He departed Guam in February, leaving Pat Herman as acting governor until Eisenhower's new appointee arrived on 23 April.

The new governor, Ford Q. Elvidge, was a Seattle attorney and contributor to Eisenhower's campaign fund and a friend of Interior Secretary Douglas McKay. Elvidge was business-like, stressing the need for economy and self-sufficiency (two durable chimeras, as under the navy). Later, after leaving Guam, he wrote that he was dismayed when he arrived on the island to find trash, toads, giant snails, and "Hundreds of wild, abandoned dogs [that] roamed the boondocks." He launched island-wide cleanup campaigns and initiated a GovGuam program to purchase stocks of surplus military supplies and equipment still stored in large amounts on the island.

The new governor was also a conservative moralist who prohibited gambling at the Liberation Day Festival and tried to outlaw taxi dancers. He failed to get rid of prostitutes or the boonie dogs. Stuffy and overbearing, he also argued repeatedly with Guam's senators, vetoing nine bills in 1953 alone. On the other hand, he got along well with COMNAVMAR and his staff, with whom he played golf regularly. Unlike Skinner, he was able to obtain a larger allotment of electricity from the navy for civilian consumers.

Elvidge was also the first governor to move into the new governor's residence, called Government House, completed in 1954 on the hill above Agana. Under his administration, the commercial radio station KUAM opened in March 1954, and the Guam Museum reopened the same year in Agana in the Garden House, the Spanish *palacio* servants' quarters that had survived World War II. This small museum—like a number of other historical preservation efforts related to the precontact Chamorro and Spanish eras—was neglected by the legislature and governors over the next four decades.

The Korean War ended during Elvidge's term, but the geopolitical value of Guam did not lessen. In fact, the Department of Defense expanded Guam's role in the new U.S. strategy of deterrence based on the threat of nuclear retaliation by long-range bombers in case of communist aggression against the United States or its allies after the U.S.-Japan Mutual Security Treaty went into effect on 28 April 1952. That role was visibly manifested in August–September 1953 when SAC flew giant new six-engine turbo-prop B-36 bombers to Guam, Okinawa, and Japan in a month-long exercise called Operation Big Stick. This was the first of innumerable large-scale military exercises that utilized Guam in the decades ahead.

The Third Air Division took over Andersen in 1954, and the whole base was put under SAC control in 1955. Thereafter, SAC began to rotate B-36s from their home bases in the states to Guam on three-month tours. In July 1956, the air force's first jet bombers, sleek swept-wing B-47s, replaced the B-36s. Along with the B-47s came KC-97 tankers for midair refueling. By this time, Andersen was SAC's chief base in the Pacific, one of thirty-eight overseas bases that encircled the Sino-Soviet Bloc.

It was also during Elvidge's administration that TTPI headquarters was transferred from Hawai'i to Guam on 29 September 1954. The Interior Department had assumed administration of the trusteeship from the navy in 1951, but the TTPI staffs remained in Hawai'i until Delmas H. Nucker was appointed acting high commissioner (and later high commissioner) in 1954. That year, he moved TTPI headquarters to Guam to a compound in Maite of sturdy wooden cottages with tar-paper roofs and called the Hotel Tropics.

TTPI headquarters came to Guam instead of Saipan because the main northern Mariana Islands (and later all the Marianas north of Saipan) were mysteriously removed from Interior's jurisdiction on 1 January 1953 and placed back under the navy. Not until years later did the public learn that the CIA, under the cover of a Naval Technical Training Unit, or NTTU, was secretly using Saipan to train foreign agents, mostly Chinese Nationalists in the early years. The CIA constructed a huge base at a cost of $28 million for the NTTU in the central mountains of Saipan. The existence of this major secret installation was one reason that the navy perpetuated the stringent security clearance for the TTPI and Guam after the Korean War ended.

The NTTU supported Nationalist China's preparations to invade mainland China from Taiwan. When the invasion never took place, Washington quietly closed the NTTU operation in May 1962. Interior resumed jurisdiction over Saipan and the other northern Mariana islands on 1 July and moved TTPI headquarters from Guam into the fine concrete offices and residences on Saipan formerly occupied by the CIA. Guam was thus capital of two Pacific political entities from 1954 into 1962.

In the meantime, now that it exercised real power under the Organic Act, the Guam legislature had become the focus of lively local electoral politics. Some 65 percent of Guam's eligible voters cast ballots in the first legislative election (there were no primaries in this period) under the Organic Act on 7 November 1950. High voter participation would be characteristic of Guam's regular elections from then on. Politics became one of the most popular activities on the island, with Guamanians tending to vote in family blocs through the Chamorro *pare* system for favorite personalities who functioned as *patrones* rather than on issues.

In the 1950 election, the new Popular party under Antonio Won Pat's leadership handily defeated the candidates of the Welfare party. The defeat caused the frustrated Welfare party to disband in early 1952, and some of its leaders joined the Popular party, but they remained unhappy. In the 1952 and 1954 elections, the Popular party again won most of the seats, except for a few lost to independents, and Won Pat was elected speaker each time.

A revolt erupted within the Popular party in early 1955 when eight incumbent members in the legislature broke away to establish a separate voting bloc with three independents. The dissidents included some disgruntled former Welfare party members and were led by prominent *manak'kilo* family heads such as Eduardo T. Calvo, Frank D. Perez, and B. J. Bordallo. With a narrow majority of eleven votes, they elected F. B. Leon Guerrero as speaker of the Third Guam Legislature, deposing Won Pat from that position. The rebels then formed the Territorial party a few months before the 1956 election. In the meantime, two statesiders—Bert Pugh and Edgar R. Crain—formed the Guam party in the hope that statesiders on the island would unite behind them. While local politics preoccupied the Guamanians, Governor Elvidge resigned a year early on 19 May 1956.

As a result of the Territorial party's formation, the 1956 election for the Fourth Guam Legislature turned into a wide-open political contest on Guam. Popular party Senator James T. Sablan led the assault on the Territorials nightly at fiesta-like political rallies called *gupot* in Chamorro. According to Guam historian Pedro Sanchez, Sablan's harangues "ranged from the hilarious use of the Chamorro and English languages to malicious attacks on his opponents." He and other Popular party candidates criticized the Territorials as the "party of the rich" who represented the old privileged *manak'kilo* class. The tiny statesider Guam party was simply ignored by most voters.

The Popular party won all twenty-one seats in 1956 in what was called a Blackjack victory (for the card game). One of the new senators was Ricky Bordallo, a son of elder statesman B. J. Bordallo, who retired that year. The devastated Guam Party dissolved, and the Popular party went on to dominate the 1958, 1960 (another Blackjack victory), and 1962 elections, with Antonio Won Pat again elected speaker each time. In effect, Guam had a one-party legislature under the Popular party in the 1950s. In 1960, the party changed its name to the Democratic party of Guam and formally affiliated with the national U.S. Democratic party.

While local politics bubbled along in the legislative and village commissioner elections, Governor Elvidge's successor, Richard Barratt Lowe, arrived on 29 October 1956. The new governor had served on Tinian in World War II as a naval officer and was governor of American Samoa from 1953 until his appointment to Guam. Conservative in outlook, he compared the U.S.-Guam relationship to that of father and child. He upheld navy control of utilities but did not get along with the Interior Department. One of his first actions was to establish the position of assistant secretary of Guam, to which he named a popular senator, Manuel Flores (Carson) Leon Guerrero.

In the mid-1950s, the economy of Guam settled down to routine but respectable development after the postwar boom ended. In August 1956, radio station KUAM brought the first television broadcasts to Guam on tapes, usually a week or more old, of Los Angeles programs. Because lots in Agana were still tied up in controversies, commercial development was spreading northward along Marine Drive, gradually making Tamuning the island's business center. On 18 August 1957, the new, multistory Guam Memorial Hospital (GMH) building was dedicated by Governor Lowe at Oka a mile east of the old site. The new GMH had taken nearly six years to construct at a cost of $5.6 million, but it would prove to be poorly designed and inadequate as the island population grew. The year 1957 was also when the Soviet Union launched Sputnik, the first man-made object to orbit the globe. Sputnik jolted the world into the space age and catapulted the Soviet Union and the United States into a missile race that would magnify Guam's role in U.S. national defense as a station for tracking missiles and satellites.

Lowe's relationship with the navy was cordial from 1956 to 1958 while Rear Admiral W. B. Ammon was COMNAVMAR. Ammon's replacement, on the other hand, was "six feet four inches of red-faced belligerent pomposity," according to Lowe. The new COMNAVMAR, Rear Admiral W. L. (Skee) Erdmann, quickly attempted to reassert naval authority over the civilian government. He criticized GovGuam officials, requested a special school for military dependents, snubbed Lowe, and prohibited navy personnel from attending some local public events, such as the Chamber of Commerce's annual fund-raising rodeo. Lowe asked that Erdmann be recalled, but the navy refused, and the irascible admiral outlasted the governor, who resigned in frustration a year early on 14 November 1959.

Lowe had the last laugh, however, when Erdmann subsequently left Guam in 1960 to retire. The admiral exercised military RHIP (rank hath its privileges) by smuggling forty-two cases of duty-free whiskey—purchased at the Guam naval PX—into California with his household effects. Caught and indicted, he pleaded guilty with tears in his eyes. He was fined $15,000 but did not lose his navy retirement benefits.

In 1959, when Lowe was preparing to resign the governorship, he recommended that Joseph Flores, the publisher of the *Guam Daily News,* be appointed to replace him. After a delay due to Flores' reluctance to take the job, he was appointed and sworn in on the Plaza de España on 9 July 1960. He was the first Guamanian to govern the island since the interregnum in 1898–1899.

Richard Lowe's legacy included the only book written by an American governor about his administration on the island. Titled *Problems in Paradise,* the book covered Lowe's tenure on American Samoa as well as on Guam. In his recommendations, he wrote, "I think the time has come to give consideration to the granting of limited commonwealth status to both Guam and the Virgin Islands by providing for an elected delegate and an elected governor in both territories." This was the first mention of commonwealth for Guam.

Guam's new governor, Joseph Flores, had been one of a handful of Chamorro men allowed to enlist in the regular navy on Guam in 1917 during World War I. He served in the navy five years, becoming an American citizen, and then prospered in publishing in California for the next thirty years before returning to Guam in 1947 and buying the *Navy News* in 1950. Successful in business, active in civic, veteran, and church affairs, he had the reliable, conservative qualities sought by the Republican administration in Washington.

Under Flores in 1960, Pan Am inaugurated east-west jet airline service across the Pacific via Guam in Boeing 707 airliners. Also in 1960, the U.S. Congress extended the Social Security system to Guam by P.L. 86–778. With the gradual expansion of island commerce, the Bank of Hawaii was licensed in February 1961 to operate on Guam in competition with the Bank of America.

In 1961, land transportation improved when the Department of Public Works asphalted the Agat-Umatac road for the first time. Back in 1945, the Seabees had cut a dirt road through the steep hills south of Agat to Umatac (there had never been a real road, only paths, over these hills under the Spaniards). Rain, however, repeatedly washed away parts of the Seabee track. The asphalting of this segment finally completed an all-weather highway the mere eighty miles around the island after sixty-three years of American administration.

The alien labor situation was altered in 1960 when the "Aquino Ruling" (based on a Board of Immigration Appeals case) permitted certain categories of nonimmigrant alien workers admitted to Guam prior to December 1952, and still on the island owing to continuing contract employment, to remain as permanent U.S. residents under the 1917 Immigration Act. By February 1962, about 1,700 Filipino nonimmigrant aliens were able to obtain permanent residence on Guam. Along with other Filipino contract workers who had married American citizens, these H-2 workers admitted as residents eventually became American citizens by applying for a "green card." Once U.S. citizens, Filipinos who remained on Guam (many departed for Hawai'i or the mainland) in turn petitioned for immediate family members in the Philippines to enter Guam and apply to become U.S. citizens. Over the years, this flow of immigrants to Guam outside the regular U.S. immigrant quota for the Philippines gathered momentum to the point where Americans of Filipino origin became the largest ethnic minority on Guam, with about one-quarter of the island's population. They comprised the majority of residents of Dededo, the largest village on Guam.

Despite the phaseout of the H-2 program, workers were still needed for military construction as Guamanians continued to shun such work. As a result, H-2 workers were replaced by a new category, the Defense Parolee Program under the provisions of the 1952 Immigration and Naturalization Act. Unlike H-2 workers, parolees had to work under the old discriminatory low wage scales, thus providing military contractors the same source of cheap alien labor for U.S. defense purposes as before.

In education, Governor Flores supported the appointment in 1957 of the first Guamanian to be dean of the Territorial College of Guam (there was no president at the time). This was Pedro C. Sanchez, a Ph.D. in educational administration from Stanford University and son of the respected Chamorro educator Simon A. Sanchez. At the time, Dr. Sanchez and Paul Carano were researching a book, *A Complete History of Guam*, subsequently published in 1964, that was the first comprehensive history of the island. It would serve as a valuable text for high school and college classes for the next twenty years. The college moved in 1960 from Mongmong to its present magnificent cliffside site in Mangilao overlooking Pago Bay. In 1961, the school was upgraded to become a four-year undergraduate institution.

Meanwhile, Democrat John Fitzgerald Kennedy had won the 1960 presidential election against

Republican Richard M. Nixon, so Flores, a Republican, submitted his resignation. The next governor, Texan William P. (Bill) Daniel, was appointed through the influence of fellow Texan Lyndon B. Johnson, the powerful former Democratic majority leader of the U.S. Senate and by then Kennedy's vice president, and Price Daniel, Bill's brother and former Democratic governor of Texas. Bill Daniel was inaugurated on 20 May 1961, with Manuel Guerrero as secretary of Guam.

Guamanians knew they were in trouble when the new governor requested that he be introduced at public occasions as a movie actor. He was inordinately proud of his role as a bit player in John Wayne's 1960 epic movie *The Alamo*. Daniel renamed the governor's residence "the Governor's Palace." He wore gaudy country-western clothes at public functions and rode a big white horse named Alamo, unwittingly reminding elderly Guamanians of the haughty Spanish governors in the old Juan Malo stories. In a well-publicized effort to improve island agriculture, he launched Operation Guam Friendship whereby he persuaded stateside friends and Texas farmers to donate animals to Guam's Department of Agriculture. Bulls, stallions, milk goats, boars, and even Texas armadillos arrived (the latter soon disappeared). He arranged the purchase by GovGuam of two bulldozers and a big Caterpillar tractor from a Texas firm; then he pocketed the $3,800 commission for the transaction.

The natural courtesy of Guamanians kept them at first from publicly criticizing this Texan bull in their island china shop, but eventually voices were raised. Karl R. Anderson wrote on 7 January 1962 in the *Guam Daily News*, "Your attempt to better Guam would fare much better if, somehow, you could lose the idea that you are dealing with an inferior breed of people." Complaints did not faze Daniel. In a last escapade in 1962, he sought to obtain three fur pieces for his wife from Chinese furrier Peter Chang in Agana. The governor offered to pay for one piece and keep the other two as "gifts." When Chang requested full payment, the burly Daniel choked the furrier by his tie. Chang then lodged a complaint with the police. Faced with this embarrassment, and perhaps bored after seventeen months on the job, Daniel resigned on 13 September 1962, to the great relief of Guamanians, but President Kennedy did not accept the resignation until January 1963. Daniel meanwhile embarked on a round-the-world tour as a self-proclaimed "goodwill ambassador" for Guam while he continued to draw his governor's salary for four more months.

A major accomplishment of Bill Daniel on Guam—in addition to comic relief—was to help get rid of the navy security clearance. He requested Secretary of the Navy John Connally—a personal friend and fellow Texan—to lift the clearance. With the Korean War long over and the NTTU base on Saipan closed, there was no further need for the clearance. On 21 August 1962, President Kennedy issued Executive Order 11045, which discontinued the security clearance for Guam. Finally free of this military shackle, Guam could begin normal development of its private sector.

Guamanian Governors, Civilian Priorities

After Daniel departed, Manuel Guerrero was left in charge until a new governor was selected. Guerrero had first made his mark when he served as the chair of the rules committee in the First Guam Legislature in 1951–1952. He subsequently served in several executive branch positions before surviving seventeen months as secretary of Guam under Daniel. The island was fortunate to have the experienced, patient Guerrero as its leader when on the night of 11–12 November 1962 Supertyphoon Karen smashed into the island.

At her peak, Karen's sustained winds rose to an estimated 173 miles per hour (the navy's anemometer broke at 144 miles per hours), punctuated by gusts up to 207 miles per hour. The atmospheric pressure fell so fast (to 27.05 inches from the normal 29.92 inches on the barometer) that doors and windows, and some entire rickety buildings, exploded outward. The eye of this awesome storm swept swiftly across Guam from east to west right over Umatac, with the strongest winds on the northern arc over Agana and Apra Harbor.

Amazingly, only nine people were killed by Karen, thanks to early warnings by the Joint Typhoon Warning Center (the JTWC had been established in 1959 by combining navy and air force weather efforts) and to the fact that the storm struck at night, when nearly everyone was inside. Guerrero declared martial law and asked for federal assistance while he organized relief efforts. In his report to the secretary of the interior, Guerrero wrote, "Over 90 percent of the island's buildings were destroyed or badly damaged.... Following the storm the island defied description as every tree, every blade of grass had been beaten to brown, shriveled masses.... Damage from the storm ran well over $100 million." The navy's report said that Karen's impact was equivalent to a "near-miss by a nuclear bomb, less its heat and fall-out contamination." One of the storm's victims was Guam's only outdoor drive-in movie theater; located in Tamuning, it was destroyed, never to be rebuilt.

Within hours after the storm ended, President Kennedy (who was still coping with the October Cuban missile crisis at the time) declared Guam a major disaster area. He authorized $16 million for immediate relief. GovGuam and the military erected tent cities for the hundreds of people whose homes were wiped out. Acting Governor Guerrero's leadership impressed federal officials and led to his nomination by Interior Secretary Stewart Udall to replace Daniel (who tried to return to Guam when he learned of Karen but was dissuaded for fear that he might prolong the disaster). Guerrero was sworn in as governor on 9 March 1963.

No sooner had Guerrero moved into the governor's residence (the name of which he changed back to Government House) when another typhoon—Olive—lashed Guam on 29 April 1963, undoing much of the reconstruction accomplished in the five months since Karen. Kennedy once more declared the island a disaster area and sent more help. These two natural disasters turned out to be the means for over a decade of massive capital improvements on Guam. Guerrero flew to Washington, where,

assisted by fellow Chamorro Richard F. (Dick) Taitano, who was then director of territories in interior, he obtained a huge financial package from the Congress under the Guam Rehabilitation Act (P.L. 88–170) of 4 November 1963, which provided $45 million in federal funds, partly as a grant and with about 60 percent as a loan.

This act was the last signed by President Kennedy to assist Guam. The island's people, along with the rest of the nation, were stunned at the news of Kennedy's assassination on 22 November 1963 while the president was driving through Dallas with John Connally, by then governor of Texas, and their wives. Kennedy's successor, Lyndon Johnson, continued the generous federal financial support of Guam.

To provide labor needed for rehabilitation, the INS permitted Filipino workers (and several hundred Micronesians for the first time) into Guam under a second parolee program, the Reconstruction and Rehabilitation Program, on six-month contracts, which were extended until May 1970. The number of alien workers on Guam began to rise again, to nearly 4,500 by the end of 1967. These workers continued to be exploited by being given poor food and forced to suffer "filth and squalor...in living quarters," according to one report.

The abuses resulted in the formation in December 1964 of the first labor union on Guam, the Operating Engineers Union Local 3 of the AFL-CIO, with 1,500 (mostly Filipino) members. Local 3 was soon followed in April 1965 by the creation of an American Federation of Teachers unit on Guam, the Guam Federation of Teachers (GFT) Local 1581, which within a few years became the island's largest union. The Guam Department of Labor was assigned to investigate contract labor problems but proved incapable of preventing abuses then or when such exploitation occurred repeatedly in the future. The abuses prompted the Philippine government under President Ferdinand Marcos to complain. "MARCOS THREATENS LEGAL ACTION AGAINST LABOR CONTRACTORS HERE," blared the headline in the *Pacific Journal* on 20

February 1968. The Philippine consulate was upgraded to a consulate general, and the problems were patched over, but only temporarily.

Because of economic growth in the mid-1960s as a result of federal rehabilitation funds as well as the surge in Vietnam-related military projects, the need for outside labor grew beyond the parolee programs. Consequently, the INS reinstituted the H-2 program on Guam in early 1969. Parolee workers were phased out in 1970, with many converting to H-2 status under which they were paid higher wages when in the late 1960s the U.S. Fair Labor Standards Act applied the U.S. minimum wage ($2.03 per hour in 1969) to nonimmigrant alien contract laborers.

The reinstated H-2 system opened up Guam to the fourth wave of Filipinos (and later other nationalities) in the island's history. The first influx had been Filipino soldiers with the Spanish invasion in 1668–1698, many of whom were absorbed into Chamorro society. The second wave was the *deportados* and convicts in the 1860s–1890s. The third wave came in the late 1940s into the 1950s as military contract workers. The fourth influx, mostly H-2 workers, gathered momentum in the 1970s and 1980s and had not yet ended as of 1990.

With the infusion of federal money into Guam in the 1960s, Guerrero launched extensive urban renewal and housing programs beyond what existed before Karen. New homes and other buildings were constructed mostly of reinforced concrete block walls on concrete foundations under flat concrete slab roofs with wide overhangs. This square pillbox style, still prevalent everywhere on Guam, is not particularly attractive but provides good protection from typhoons. Government land was provided at nominal cost to private developers to build low-cost concrete houses in new village sections called Kaiser subdivisions for the Kaiser Company, which constructed them along with the Black Construction Company. The largest was Liguan Terrace in Dededo where 1,500 two- and three-bedroom houses with lots sold for $14,000–15,000 in the mid-1960s. In 1965, the Office of Land Management completed a master island-wide land-use plan, published in 1966. This effort was the first of several such plans, none of which would be implemented fully over the next twenty-five years owing to inaction by the legislature, which wished to control land matters itself.

While post-Karen reconstruction was under way, the Seventh Guam Legislature passed a law introduced by Senator Ricky Bordallo for a Washington representative to act as liaison between the Guam Legislature and the U.S. Congress. Back in 1953, the legislature had transmitted the first of several petitions to the Congress to authorize a delegate, but the Interior Department repeatedly shot down the requests. Interior argued that approval of an official, nonvoting Guam delegate would make the island an incorporated territory, which implied eventual statehood, contrary to the understanding behind the Organic Act. Frustrated, the Guam legislature finally created on its own an unofficial delegate with four-year terms by P.L. 7–173 in 1964. It would prove to be a wise step.

In a close special election on 15 March 1965, for the $22,500-a-year delegate's job, Democratic leader Antonio Won Pat beat Territorial candidate Felix Lujan (Bejong) Crisostomo. Won Pat would be reelected to the Washington position again in 1968. He was just a lobbyist, but he shrewdly acted as if, in his words, "the incumbent was in fact a Member of Congress in everything but the name—and the power."

In the meantime, legislative politics took a twist when the Democratic party lost the majority in the November 1964 election for the Eighth Legislature. Among the new Territorial senators were Carlos Garcia Camacho and Paul McDonald Calvo (son of Eduardo T. Calvo), both future governors, and Kurt S. Moylan, a future lieutenant governor. Former island leader F. B. Leon Guerrero was no longer running for public office; he suffered a stroke in 1962 and passed away in 1974.

The Territorials—with a thirteen to eight margin in seats—blocked the Democrat-supported urban renewal program of Governor Guerrero. The Territorials preferred to promote private investment. In

November 1965, they passed P.L. 8–80, which established the Guam Economic Development Authority (GEDA) to provide up to $1.5 million business loans and to issue "QCs" (qualifying certificates) that provide tax rebates to investors of up to 75 percent on corporate income tax for up to twenty years, plus abatement of other taxes. GEDA was authorized to issue bonds for the financing of businesses. The interest on these "project revenue bonds" is tax exempt and thus can be issued at interest rates below commercial rates. The tax-exempt bonds, QCs, and other benefits became strong incentives for Japanese investors to set up hotels on Guam.

In the 1966 elections, however, urban renewal was the big issue, not GEDA, with the Democrats blasting the Territorials for blocking the popular renewal program. To the shock of the Territorials, the Democratic party won all twenty-one seats in another Blackjack landslide. Crushed, the Territorial party soon dissolved, and some of its members, led by Carlos Camacho, Joseph Flores, and Kurt Moylan, formed the Republican party on 21 November 1966. With a Democratic majority, the Ninth Legislature reinstated Guerrero's urban renewal program.

The surge of construction that resulted from the infusion after Karen of federal rehabilitation money in the 1960s and 1970s invigorated business activity throughout the island. In 1963, Governor Guerrero formed a tourist commission and with commendable foresight launched a determined effort to attract visitors to Guam. In 1965, when some 5,000 tourists—mostly stateside Americans on their way elsewhere—were stopping on the island, there were only about seventy hotel rooms, mostly in the Cliff Hotel on the hill above Agana. In April 1966, QC-supported construction began on the first of Tumon's luxury hotels, the $5 million Guam Hilton with 200 rooms. The driving force behind the Hilton was Ken Jones and J and G Enterprises. The Hilton would not be completed until 1972 after the smaller Tokyu, Continental, and Fujita hotels, all with QCs, had opened on Tumon Beach.

To accommodate increased tourism, the new Guam International Air Terminal was dedicated on 5 March 1966 at the Naval Air Station on the opposite side of the runway from the navy's Brewer Field. The federal government, prompted by the military (the Vietnam War was under way), had opposed the expansion of the international airport but had to bow to the inevitable as civilian use increased. In 1967, the Federal Aviation Authority recognized a new airline that appeared when the United Micronesian Development Association and Aloha Airlines entered into partnership with Continental Airlines in 1966 to establish Continental–Air Micronesia. Known as "Air Mike," it became the main regional carrier when tourists were permitted into the TTPI in 1968 and the Japanese rediscovered Guam. In 1969, nearly 58,000 Japanese arrived, filling to capacity the 1,000 hotel rooms that existed by then. On 1 October 1970, Japanese Airlines (JAL) initiated regular flights between Tokyo and Guam on DC-8 jets. From then on, development of Guam's private sector was tied to tourism.

Guam received a worldwide publicity boost in this period when the international press reported that Gregorio D. Perez caught a world-record Pacific blue marlin of 1,153 pounds while fishing three miles off Ritidian Point on 21 August 1969. This all-tackle record stood until 1983 with the International Game Fish Association and symbolized the return of Chamorros to the sea centuries after the Spaniards had forced them to be island bound.

In spite of symbolic strides by Chamorros, by the late 1960s the Americanization of Guam was becoming irreversible in cultural as well as in political matters. Although *i kustumbren Chamoru* continued in village saint-day fiestas and in many other traditional activities, and the *pare* system was still important, island young people were becoming more American with every graduating class from the high schools and the college. In 1970, Joseph Flores sold the *Guam Daily News* to Hawaiian millionaire Chin Ho for $1.2 million. The new owner changed the paper's name to the *Pacific Daily News* and upgraded the printing plant. Chin Ho hired a witty skeptic, Robert Udick, as publisher and retained as editor Joseph Murphy, who in addition to editing the paper since 9 December 1965 also wrote a daily column, "Pipe Dreams." In the early 1970s Chin Ho sold the paper to Gannett, a huge mainland newspaper chain, which retained the paper's staff. Insightful, humorous, and reliable, Joe Murphy and Bob Udick together made the *PDN* the most popular news source in the western Pacific.

Local Guam matters, however, were overshadowed by dramatic regional and world developments in the turbulent years of the mid- and late 1960s. By this period, the worldwide U.S. military strategy against the Soviet Union and its allies was governed by the Single Integrated Operational Plan, SIOP for short. This top-secret plan coordinated the three strategic U.S. nuclear weapons systems, each capable of delivering megatons of thermonuclear destruction: long-range bombers under SAC control; submarine-launched ballistic missiles (SLBMs) under the navy; and intercontinental ballistic missiles (ICBMs) also under SAC. Guam was the only place where two of these deadly strategic weapons systems—bombers and SLBMs—out of the three were located together. This unique concentration of nuclear weapons presumably made Guam a target for Soviet missiles, against which there were no defenses.

In March 1964, SAC replaced the B-47s on Guam with B-52 bombers accompanied by KC-135 tankers for air refueling. Beginning the same year, Polaris SLBMs were deployed to Apra Harbor aboard submarines serviced by the tender USS *Proteus,* which arrived 29 November 1964. Up to twelve Polaris submarines, and later the larger Poseidon missile versions, along with the smaller nuclear-powered and -armed attack submarines, operated for the next twenty years out of Apra.

When the *Proteus* tender arrived at Guam, a Soviet "fishing" trawler took up station in international waters beyond the three-mile limit off Ritidian Point. This electronic intelligence-gathering ship apparently monitored American submarine patrols and B-52 takeoffs. The Soviet ship was relieved by another out of Vladivostok every six weeks or so until the surveillance ended in the 1980s. At times, the crews of the spy ships exchanged Russian vodka for American cigarettes with Guamanians fishing in small boats.

In addition to the strategic weapons systems on Guam in the 1950s and 1960s, both the navy and the air force maintained aviation squadrons on the island for medical evacuations, communications with submarines, weather reconnaissance, airborne early warning, and joint search and rescue (SAR) missions in conjunction with the two ships of the U.S. Coast Guard based on Guam. By the 1970s, the navy was using the reliable P-3 Orion aircraft (with a distinctive tail projection like a stinger that is a magnetic anomaly detector to locate subs) for SAR and weather duties, signal intelligence gathering, reconnaissance, and antisubmarine missions. Other military facilities that appeared on the island in the 1960s included the Pacific barrier radar network, dishes for tracking and telemetric control of satellites, a NASA (National Aeronautics and Space Agency) station at Dandan, a sound surveillance system (SOSUS) of underwater hydrophones arrayed across the western Pacific out of a top-secret building called NavFac (for Naval Facility) at Ritidian Point, and signal and electronic intelligence-gathering installations at the Finagayan master communications station, where a huge circular "elephant cage" antenna occupies several acres of ground.

While Guam was fulfilling its geopolitical role, a regional political metamorphosis was occurring in the surrounding TTPI. The Congress of Micronesia, a bicameral legislature of elected representatives from all the TTPI districts, was established in late 1964. By 1966, the Micronesians were pressing the United States for a change in their political status to end the UN trusteeship. This transformation—the decolonization of the TTPI—would eventually have a powerful effect on Guam's political development, but of more immediate impact on Guam was the cancer-like growth of the Vietnam conflict into a full-scale war in the 1960s.

Guam served first as a support base for the American advisers dispatched to South Vietnam by President Kennedy, beginning in 1962. This role was broadened in mid-1965 to include direct combat operations by B-52Fs from Andersen after U.S. ground combat units were deployed in South Vietnam. On 18 June 1965, twenty-seven bombers of the Third Air Division at AAFB launched the first of thousands of conventional "iron bomb" strikes against Viet Cong targets in Vietnam. Andersen turned into a hornet's nest of intense activity as the numbers of air force personnel and aircraft rapidly expanded over the next few years. The B-52s at Andersen also maintained their SIOP ready-alert status with Mark 28 thermonuclear hydrogen bombs in case of war with the Soviet Union.

While the Vietnam War ground on with mounting bloodshed, politics went on as usual on Guam. Back in 1962, the Sixth Guam Legislature started sending pleas to the Congress to authorize a locally elected governor. Various bills for the same purpose were introduced but died in committee. Instead of hiring public relations firms, lobbyists, or attorneys, the Guamanians placed full-page ads in the *New York Times* and the *Washington Post* (the two newspapers read by most congressmen) in support of an elected governor. Won Pat also lobbied ardently for the measure.

These efforts culminated in P.L. 90–497, the Guam Elective Governor Act, which Congress passed on 1 September 1968. This law amended the Guam Organic Act to permit elections by the people of Guam, beginning in 1970, of a governor and lieutenant governor every four years with a limit of two successive terms. One welcome provision in the act specifically applied the due process and equal protection clauses of the Fourteenth Amendment of the U.S. Constitution to the people of Guam.

Guamanian elation over the Elective Governor Act was tempered by one provision, Section 9-A, that gave authority to the Interior Department's comptroller to audit all accounts, including taxes, of GovGuam. This federal audit was in addition to the requirement for the governor's annual financial report to the Interior Department. Most Guamanians view these "watchdog" audits as unwarranted federal intrusions into local affairs. Interior has no such authority in the U.S. states or in Puerto Rico. Island leaders were so upset with Section 9-A that the Ninth Guam Legislature took out a critical full-page ad in the *Washington Post* and recessed one week in protest. Nevertheless, GovGuam has not been able to eliminate the federal audits, which are now conducted out of the Inspector General's office in the Interior Department.

While the Elective Governor Act was being legislated, the Ninth Guam Legislature approved a bill in August 1968 introduced by Democratic Senator Dick Taitano to create Guam's first constitutional convention. With Antonio (Tony) Palomo as president, forty-three elected delegates met from 1 June 1969 to 29 June 1970. The convention did not draft a full constitution. Instead, it proposed thirty-four changes to the Guam Organic Act. The proposals were transmitted to the U.S. Congress, but it was the wrong time for such initiatives. Washington was obsessed with Vietnam, and the Guamanian people were preoccupied with the elections for governor in 1970. As a result, and owing mostly to Won Pat's persistence, only one major convention proposal would eventually be approved: the authorization of a nonvoting official Guam delegate to the Congress in 1972.

National U.S. elections had taken place in the meantime in November 1968, and Republican Richard Nixon was elected president. Governor Guerrero, a Democrat, submitted his courtesy resignation, which was accepted in July 1969. The modest but efficient Guerrero had served Guam steadfastly as governor for six years and four months, the longest tenure of any governor until then since the Spanish era.

Nixon's appointee as replacement for Guerrero was local Republican leader Carlos Garcia Camacho. He was forty-four years old and had served as a dentist with the rank of captain in the U.S. Army. Nixon appointed thirty-one-year-old Kurt Moylan,

Governor and Mrs. Manuel Guerrero. A Democrat, Manuel Flores (Carson) Leon Guerrero was appointed governor of Guam by President John F. Kennedy in March 1963 and served the people of Guam ably and effectively for over six years until July 1969. (Micronesian Area Research Center, Mangilao Guam)

originally from Hawai'i, to be secretary of Guam. The appointments were confirmed by the U.S. Senate on 20 June 1969.

After appointing Camacho, Nixon flew to Guam on an around-the-world trip that included watching the splashdown in the Pacific of Apollo XI, the first moon vehicle. At a 25 July 1969 news conference at the Top-of-the-Mar officers' club on Nimitz Hill, the president announced a new U.S. foreign policy, the Guam Doctrine, also called the Nixon Doctrine. He said that American troops would no longer be sent abroad to fight for nations threatened by aggression; those nations would have to assume their own defense with American help other than ground troops. The immediate result was that

B-52 missions from Guam increased in tempo and ferocity. The air force built three tent cities on Andersen to accommodate enlisted crews of additional B-52s, while officers filled the new Tumon hotels. On 31 March 1970, the Third Air Division at AAFB was elevated to become the Eighth Air Force with the Forty-third Strategic Wing of B-52s the main operational unit in place of the 3960th Strategic Wing.

By then, Guam was one of the few communities in the United States where the majority of Americans still loyally supported the war. In December 1969, Governor Camacho flew to Vietnam for a five-day visit over Christmas with some 6,000 pounds of gifts for Guamanian servicemen. Johnny

G. Sablan, a popular Chamorro singer, was part of the governor's entourage. The war was going badly since the Viet Cong's Tet Offensive in early 1968, and Camacho's visit was a tangible gesture of home support for Guamanians fighting in Vietnam. They welcomed their governor warmly with minifiestas, complete with Chamorro songs and food of red rice, roast pork, and *kelaguen* (marinated raw meat or fish in grated coconut) with spicy *finadene* sauce. His 1969 visit to Vietnam boosted Camacho's popularity, which he carried into the fall 1970 elections.

The 1970 elections included September primaries for the first time, and nearly every adult on Guam was emotionally absorbed in the first-ever local gubernatorial race. Camacho initially picked Senator G. Ricardo Salas, a prominent Chamorro politician, as running mate, but they soon squabbled, and Salas was dumped in favor of Kurt Moylan. The Camacho-Moylan ticket ran unopposed in the primary, which turned out to be a smart move on the part of the Republicans.

The Democrats in the meantime were splitting into three factions. Former governor Manuel Guerrero led one ticket with running mate Dr. Antonio C. (Tony) Yamashita, who resigned from his position as president of the University of Guam (the College of Guam had been elevated by the legislature by P.L. 9–233 to university status on 12 August 1968). The second Democratic ticket in the primary was that of Senators Ricky Bordallo and Dick Taitano. Bordallo was a loquacious, energetic populist, while Taitano was a respected former director of the Office of Territories and deputy high commissioner of the TTPI. The third Democratic ticket was headed by Joaquin Camacho Arriola, an outgoing lawyer and speaker of the Ninth Guam Legislature, who ran with Vicente Bamba, a newly retired judge and popular former senator.

In the lively campaigning for the primary, Dick Taitano created Guam's first island-wide grassroots political organization throughout the villages, working with family networks through the *pare* system to socialize voters into Democratic party politics. The Bordallo-Taitano campaign also bene-

fited from the zeal, talents, and blonde charm of Madeleine Zeien Bordallo, Ricky's statesider wife, who turned out to be a tireless campaigner. Arriola took the boldest position on issues. He proclaimed the heretofore unspoken opposition of Guamanians of Chamorro descent against the flow of Filipino workers (he called them "transient aliens") into Guam. Arriola promised to stop the inflow, which many Chamorros perceived to be a threat to Chamorro culture and control of their island.

The Arriola initiative boomeranged, costing his ticket Filipino and statesider votes without swinging Chamorro voters away from the other tickets. To the surprise of many residents, Bordallo-Taitano came in first in the Democratic primary by a close margin over Guerrero-Yamashita, but neither ticket won a majority. After a contentious campaign of two weeks, Bordallo-Taitano won the runoff, but the infighting left the Democratic party badly divided. As a consequence, Camacho-Moylan won the general election in November 1970 by a big margin (for Guam) of 11.6 percent, or 2,368 votes out of 20,424 cast. Meanwhile, the elections for the Eleventh Guam Legislature (1970–1972) resulted in the Democrats winning fifteen of the twenty-one seats.

The year 1970 also marked a major change in the Catholic community on Guam when Bishop Baumgartner had a stroke and was incapacitated. His work was assumed by Monsignor Felixberto Camacho Flores. On 18 December 1970, the Most Reverend Apollinaris William Baumgartner, O.F.M. Cap., died, and, on 16 May 1971, Monsignor Flores was ordained the first Guamanian bishop. Bishop Baumgartner had served the people of Guam with distinction and love for twenty-five years, the longest tenure of a bishop in Guam's history. During that time, he built many schools and churches, reconstructed the Agana Cathedral, and in 1965 saw his vicariate raised to the Diocese of Agana. He was buried in his cathedral. As the decade of the 1970s began, Guam's government and main religion were both again in local hands for the first time in over 300 years.

14 Ocean Chrysalis 1970–1980

Chamorro Politics, American Acculturation

The election of Carlos Camacho in 1970 was the first occasion in Guam's postcontact history wherein the people of the island chose their own chief executive of government. Yet this positive step in Guam's political development came at a time when much of what remained of traditional neo-Chamorro culture—the language, family ties, and retention of land—was being threatened by Americanization, by development, and by tourism. A cultural watershed was passed sometime in the late 1960s when English began to replace Chamorro as the main language in a majority of island homes.

The American presence permeated every nook and cranny on the island with music, words, and images. Additional Protestant denominations, including Episcopalians, Seventh-Day Adventists, Lutherans, and Mormons, established churches and schools on Guam in the postwar decades, reducing Catholicism's predominance somewhat. Large-scale shortwave radio transmitters erected in the south of Guam broadcast multilingual Protestant missionary messages to the Asian mainland. In 1970, KGTF, a member of the Public Broadcast System, joined KUAM as Guam's second local television station, and, in 1971, ex-marine Lee Holmes brought the second cable television company to the Marianas (the first one was blown away in a typhoon). With several radio and three television stations broadcasting daily, the American cultural embrace of Guam tightened irreversibly. The outcome—the gradual disappearance of the indigenous identity—began to be of serious concern to thoughtful Guamanians of Chamorro descent. This period witnessed the cultural transformation of the Chamorros into their third identity, symbolized by the way the local people have counted. The precontact Chamorros said *hacha, hugua, tulo;* the partially Hispanicized Chamorros said *uno, dos, tres;* the Americanized Guamanians say one, two, three.

It was in the early 1970s that a surrealistic last event of World War II took place on Guam when Sergeant Shoichi Yokoi, the final Japanese straggler, was found on 24 January 1972, over a quarter of a century after the war. Two hunters, Manuel de Garcia and Jesus M. Duenas, captured Yokoi in the jungle about five miles inland from Talofofo. He had lived in a concealed, deep and roomy hole he had dug and had survived largely on boiled federico nuts and on fish and shrimp that he trapped in streams. He made his own clothes and traps from palm fibers. A real-life Rip Van Winkle and Robinson Crusoe combined, Yokoi returned to Japan a celebrity. He wrote a book, married, and revisited Guam several times as a man respected for his incredible fortitude.

While Yokoi was still in hiding, and unknown to him, his countrymen had returned to Guam to construct the South Pacific Memorial Park at General Obata's last command post near Mataguac Hill, Yigo, with the help of Monsignor Oscar Calvo. Dedicated in May 1970, the park honors those of all nationalities who died in World War II and includes a small chapel and a tall white monument that symbolizes hands held in prayer. Beneath the hands is an ossuary with the bones collected on Guam of hundreds of fallen Japanese soldiers. Nearby, entrances to Obata's cave-bunker still lie open, like healed-over wounds, on the edge of the quiet sunken glade at Mataguac Spring. The glade is ringed by dense clumps of tall bamboo trees that rustle restlessly, a death-haunted place beneath the now peaceful blue skies of Guam.

While these final footnotes to World War II were taking place on Guam, in Washington Antonio Won Pat (called "Pat" there but "Tony" on Guam) had become a close associate of Congressman Philip Burton, an energetic California Democrat on the powerful House Interior and Insular Affairs Committee. Burton later became chair of the committee and a benevolent despot in territorial affairs; Republican opponents called him the "Godfather of the Pacific." He pushed through P.L. 92–271 on 10 April 1972—over Interior Department objections—which established official delegates for Guam and the Virgin Islands in the Congress with two-year terms. The unofficial Virgin Islands delegate at the time, and an ally of Won Pat, was fellow Democrat Ron de Lugo. Both Won Pat and de Lugo won the November 1972 elections for the official positions and took seats in the House of Representatives on 3 January 1973.

Although sweet for the islanders, this victory for the two territories in gaining official representation did not significantly alter the neocolonial political status of the islands since neither of the new insular delegates had voting rights on the floor. They could, however, vote in committees, a power both men used to the hilt to help their constituents in the years ahead as they built up seniority in the Con-

gress. Won Pat was reelected every two years, often without challengers, until 1984.

On Guam in the meantime, the Camacho-Moylan administration was focusing on the new scope of local political and economic authority opened up by Guamanian control of the island's executive branch after 1970. The island was still dependent on the navy for electric power. The problem was that power generation was barely adequate to meet both the military demand and the needs of the ever-growing private sector. To assure its own supply of electricity, the navy held on to the old power plant at Piti and to its new 26.5-megawatt plant at Tanguisson (constructed by the navy in the 1960s) as well as its emergency generators. To manage civilian power needs, Camacho and the Ninth Guam Legislature created the GPA (Guam Power Authority) in 1968. In 1969, GPA issued revenue bonds for $8.1 million to finance new power lines and another 26.5-megawatt generator for the Tanguisson plant (GPA later took over management of the Tanguisson plant).

Electricity nonetheless remained inadequate, and a power crisis occurred in 1970–1971. GPA brought in a thirty-megawatt power barge from Okinawa and later built smaller diesel power generators as temporary solutions. Frustrated, Governor Camacho pushed the navy to agree in 1972 to hand over all power generation to GPA in June 1975. In the interim, the navy accepted a Power Pool Agreement to share electricity with the civilian sector. In the agreement, the navy insisted on a single island-wide power system to assure that the military would get electricity. On the basis of the agreement, GPA issued new multimillion dollar bond issues in 1972 and again in 1974 to finance four big base-load, steam-powered General Electric generators at Cabras Island in a new plant next to the navy's old one. Two of the new generators, each with sixty-six-megawatt capacity, would come on line in August 1974 and June 1975, respectively, but the other two were never built because the 1973 Arab oil embargo caused a recession on Guam and reduced revenues to the point where two more generators could not be funded. By the mid-1970s,

GPA found itself deeply in debt, still dependent on the navy's generators and lines, and unable to provide sufficient electricity to the private sector with reserve capacity to meet emergencies. This tenuous power situation would worsen in the future.

Despite problems with utilities, local control of executive departments opened up more jobs for Guamanians, both on merit and as political patronage. Between 1970 and 1974, GovGuam employment increased from 5,486 jobs to 8,570, a 56 percent increase, and, by November 1974, jumped to over 9,000 jobs, including many temporary and limited-term hires, most of whom were taken aboard just before the 1974 elections, and many of whom became permanent. The Guam Commercial Port and the Department of Public Works (DPW) became havens for "featherbedding" employment of supporters of politicians. Many new positions in government, however, served valid public service needs, such as in the Guam Telephone Authority (GTA), which separated out of the Public Utility Agency of Guam (PUAG) on 1 April 1974 as an autonomous agency. The navy at the time was still operating its own telephone system. Free of military-civilian entanglement, GTA service remained on a Third World level for years but eventually improved, unlike GPA, when a new switch plant was constructed and trunk lines were installed.

While GovGuam executive agencies and departments expanded, the Camacho-Moylan administration completed the low-rent, low-cost housing projects initiated under Governor Guerrero through the federally supported Guam Housing and Urban Renewal Authority (GHURA). Camacho then initiated a new 501-unit low-cost GHURA development of single-family homes in Dededo in the early 1970s. With more jobs open to them, many Guamanians could afford by then to purchase homes through mortgages for the first time. Per capita income for local residents was estimated at just over $2,000 in 1970, well below the mainland U.S. figure, but a huge jump locally in comparison with prewar income. By 1976, per capita income on Guam was just over $3,000 in constant dollars when it leveled off in the recession of the mid-1970s. As a consequence of higher local incomes, private housing projects blossomed with medium-priced ($25,000 and up, such as Ypaopao Estates) to high-priced (over $50,000, such as Barrigada Heights) homes that quickly sold out.

Overall, Guam was becoming suburban in the American style of single-family homes in contrast to the old Chamorro style of married children living for years with parents in multifamily dwellings in village centers. New homes usually had to be all concrete and typhoon-proof to be insured and financed by mortgages. To take advantage of the economic growth, Jesus Sablan Leon Guerrero and José Leon Guerrero Untalan, both formerly with the Bank of America branch in Agana, founded the Bank of Guam in 1972. Unconnected to the old naval Bank of Guam, and capitalized initially with the Calvo family holding the largest block of stocks, this new local bank grew phenomenally.

Tourist infrastructure, with GEDA help through QCs, was also expanding. Governor Camacho restructured the old Guam tourist commission and made it into the Guam Visitors Bureau (GVB) in 1970 by executive order. The GVB was designated as a "quasi-autonomous instrumentality of the government," an appellation that would later cause wrangling between private and governmental tourist interests. New high-rise hotels popped up on Tumon Beach in the 1970s. The Guam Dai-Ichi, Okura, and Reef hotels joined the Hilton, Tokyu, Continental, and Fujita. The source of investment capital shifted from American investors to Japanese corporations that bound together airlines, travel agents, and hotels on Guam to roots in Japan.

By the end of 1972, hotel rooms on Guam totaled 1,270, and they were filled to overflowing in 1973 with over a quarter of a million tourists, of whom 70 percent were Japanese. Japanese travel wholesalers packaged group tours to Guam, usually for five days, that catered to middle-class clients at lower cost than to Hawai'i, and the island became a favored destination for Japanese honeymooners. The Guam legislature tapped into the stream of tourist yen when it levied a hotel occupancy tax in the early 1970s, pumping millions of dollars into Guam's treasury in the following years despite the fact that much of the profit from packaged tours stays in Japan.

U.S. military expenditures, personnel, and Section 30 payments on Guam continued to rise in 1970–1973 because of the Vietnam War, which provided additional GovGuam and commercial revenues. Guam's role as a support and operational base for the Vietnam War also brought about the first open clash between military priorities and civil needs since the 1949 Guam Congress walkout. The navy's ammunition wharf was at H (Hotel) Pier on the Glass Breakwater in Apra Harbor within two miles of the busy Commercial Port. Military truck convoys loaded with bombs took priority on the crowded two-lane highway from the breakwater through the port area to Marine Drive and then to Andersen or to the naval magazine at Fena. Department of Defense regulations require ammo wharfs to be beyond a two-mile blast radius from civilian facilities in case of accidental explosions. Ordnance could be unloaded at Hotel Pier only through waivers. Faced with these constrictions, in 1967–1968 the navy conducted a survey to locate a new site for an ammo wharf on Guam.

In November 1969, the navy formally announced—without consulting either the public or GovGuam officials—that it planned to build a new ammo wharf at Sella Bay, an uninhabited, pristine little enclave on the coast between Agat and Umatac, at an estimated cost of over $100 million. Local reaction was initially ambivalent since the navy promised "numerous job opportunities will be created" by the project. Soon, however, opposition surfaced among senators in the Eleventh Guam Legislature (1971–1972), which was controlled by a majority of fifteen Democrats.

Opposition to the Sella project was led by Democratic Senators Paul J. Bordallo and Frank G. Lujan. Paul Bordallo—Harvard educated, successful in business, and a younger brother of Democratic leader Ricky Bordallo—was an outspoken defender of Chamorro rights, and he owned substantial land at Sella Bay. Lujan, a lawyer who authored one of Guam's most important laws, the 1974 Court Reorganization Act, was also a staunch advocate of indigenous rights. While the two senators launched legislative resolutions against the Sella plan, a new local group, the Guam Environmental Council, petitioned the Department of Interior to establish a seashore park in the Sella area to stop the new wharf.

The COMNAVMAR at the time, Rear Admiral Paul E. Pugh, was negotiating with Governor Camacho to swap military land for the Sella property owned by GovGuam. Camacho wanted the entire Naval Air Station in exchange for Sella. The admiral refused that swap but agreed to allow unrestricted access to the civil air terminal (still screened by marine guards at the time) and to give GovGuam the last one-third of Cabras Island, plus some other land, in return for public land at Sella. The two signed an agreement to that effect. The matter stalled when several environmental organizations, along with Paul Bordallo (who was reelected in 1972 to the Twelfth Legislature with thirteen other Democrats), promptly sued Governor Camacho in the District Court to halt the land swap. They lost, then appealed to the Ninth Circuit Court of Appeals, one of the most liberal of federal appellate courts at the time.

There they won. In March 1973, the Ninth Circuit unanimously reversed the District Court ruling, stating that land exchanges of Guam's public property must have the concurrence of the local legislature. In May 1973, a new COMNAVMAR, Rear Admiral G. Steve Morrison, finally briefed the legislature on the Sella Bay project to obtain concurrence, but it was too late. Senator Paul Bordallo lobbied vociferously against legislative approval of the swap, and another petition was circulated, eventually signed by approximately 15,000 residents and sent to the Interior Department, to "Save Sella Bay." The navy compounded its difficulties when it refused to show Won Pat the study on the ammo wharf because he did not have the necessary security clearance. He then criticized the plan, and the Twelfth Legislature did not approve the land swap.

In an amazing demonstration of arrogance, naval officials in Washington decided to go ahead with the Sella project anyway. To get around the appellate court's decision and the legislature, they planned to obtain the Sella land by invoking eminent domain. Rear Admiral Morrison immediately saw the folly in that path; he consulted with local civilian groups such as the Chamber of Commerce and persuaded them to agree to an alternative wharf site on Orote Peninsula on navy property just inside the harbor entrance in place of Sella. With the Vietnam War winding down, the Pentagon reluctantly agreed in 1974 to the Orote site, named K (Kilo) Wharf. A brief campaign by a group called SOB (Save Orote's Beauty) in turn tried to block Kilo Wharf, but it fizzled out.

On 19 July 1974, Morrison went ahead and granted unrestricted civilian access to the international air terminal at the Naval Air Station under a forty-year joint-use agreement with GovGuam even though the land swap was moot. The new ammo wharf was not completed at Orote until the late 1980s, long after the Vietnam War had ended and the B-52s had been withdrawn from Guam. Hotel Wharf was turned over to GovGuam and is now used for tour ships. Sella Bay and a huge surrounding area of 12,500 acres from Agat to Merizo were designated in April 1978 as the Territorial Seashore Park, within which development was restricted. Sella Bay remains uninhabited and pristine as of the early 1990s.

Another outcome of the Sella Bay fight was the emergence of Chamorro-rights advocacy in the context of land taking by the military. A Chamorro group called the July 7th Committee appeared in 1970 but soon faded. Of more potential benefit to the local people, the Twelfth Guam Legislature passed P.L. 12–226 in 1974, the Chamorro Land Trust Act. Sponsored by Senator Paul Bordallo, it authorized a Chamorro Land Trust Commission to lease "Chamorro homelands" (GovGuam land) to "native Chamorros." The act was patterned after the Hawaiian Homes Commission Act, which the U.S. Congress recognized in 1975 as granting limited landholdings such as homesteads to indige-nous peoples. The Guam law, however, was not implemented for the next eighteen years because of legal questions and difficulties in defining who were native Chamorros. The matter would not be tested in court until 1992 by a Chamorro-rights group, the Chamoru Nation. They won, and the court ordered the governor at the time, Joseph F. (Joe) Ada, to form the commission and implement the law.

Elsewhere, a political tidal change was occurring in the 1970s all around Guam in the Trust Territory of the Pacific Islands as the various districts initiated negotiations with Washington to change their political status. The TTPI broke into four entities: the Marshalls, Palau, the Northern Marianas, and a group of four—Kosrae, Pohnpei, Truk, and Yap—that would become the Federated States of Micronesia (FSM). All except the Northern Marianas sought a new status of free association with the United States. In the Northern Marianas, a series of four polls from 1958 to 1969 showed that a strong majority of the inhabitants favored unification with Guam to form a new U.S. Territory of the Marianas in which everyone would be American citizens. Unification, however, was foreclosed for the time being by a special referendum on Guam in November 1969 when Guamanians voted on the issue for the first time. In a low voter turnout of only 32 percent, a majority of 58 percent of Guamanians voted against reunification of the Marianas.

Among the reasons for the rejection was that many Guamanians had not forgotten, or forgiven, the brutality of some Rotanese and Saipanese on Guam in World War II. Others reasons were that the Northern Marianas were less developed than Guam at the time (and thus might be an economic burden for Guam), and that the November 1969 election for the first local governor of Guam overshadowed and complicated the reunification issue. The leaders of the Northern Marianas, rebuffed by their fellow Chamorros on Guam, then appealed to Washington for "membership in the United States political family." Guamanians did not realize that World War II had convinced American strategists to retain Rota, Tinian, and Saipan, or at the minimum to deny them (as in the case of free association for the rest of the TTPI) to any potentially hostile power, in order to assure the security of Guam's defense installations. Washington responded to the appeal of the Northern Marianas, and by December 1972 negotiations were under way.

Guamanians were therefore surprised when they learned that Washington was prepared to provide more money and to grant greater local autonomy to the Northern Marianas than Guam enjoyed. Guam's leaders then established a status commission of their own in 1973. Chaired by Senator Frank Lujan and limited to senators, the commission issued a report in September 1974 that listed nine complaints against the United States. The report also called for a constitution for Guam and the creation of a U.S.-Guam committee to review the military presence on the island, and suggested that a good "interim status position would be similar to the commonwealth status granted Puerto Rico and that which is being discussed for the Marianas." This conclusion was similar to one in favor of commonwealth made by Won Pat in his annual report in 1972.

To focus attention on the status issue, in October 1974 the Guam legislature invited the UN special committee on decolonization to visit Guam and affirmed that Guam was "not self-governing," as Washington had claimed since 1970. A two-page ad was placed in the *Pacific Daily News* on 23 October 1974 that reprinted the UN General Assembly's Resolution 1514 on "the right to complete independence" for colonial areas as the ultimate political status. The U.S. government did not permit the UN committee to visit Guam. Over the years to come, unofficial Chamorro and sometimes even official GovGuam delegations would appear before UN committees to ask for help. Since Guam already belonged to the United States, unlike the Northern Marianas (which the United States held only in trust), there was no imperative for Washington to address Guam's complaints or to involve the United Nations in the status issue, so no action was taken.

Guam's appeals to the United Nations were in effect counterproductive in that they merely angered officials in Washington.

Recession, Refugees, and Pamela

The political controversies in the early 1970s combined to chip away the popularity of the Camacho-Moylan administration. To compound Governor Camacho's problems further, Guam's ten-year, post-Karen economic boom came to a crunching halt in 1974 when the impact of the 1973 Arab oil embargo hit the island. Oil and gasoline prices soared worldwide, the economies of both the United States and Japan dipped, and the flow of tourists to Guam dwindled.

With a recession under way, all elected incumbents on Guam found themselves in trouble in the 1974 elections. By this time, Governor Camacho was in poor health owing to the stress of the many problems that his administration had faced. Sensing the vulnerability of the Camacho-Moylan ticket, a faction in the Republican party challenged the incumbents with a rival ticket of Senators Paul Calvo and Tony Palomo.

For their part, the Democrats presented four tickets for the primary election: Ricky Bordallo and Rudolph G. (Rudy) Sablan, the latter a former executive assistant to Governor Guerrero and executive director of the Island Court; Manuel Guerrero, but this time with David D.L. Flores, his former director of agriculture, as a running mate; Pedro C. Sanchez, ex-president of the University of Guam, with Esteban U. Torres, a retired naval officer; and Joaquin Arriola again, this time with Theodore S. (Ted) Nelson, a school principal turned politician.

The Democrats, who as usual received fewer campaign contributions than the Republicans, relied on village "pocket" meetings. In these fiesta-like gatherings, Ricky Bordallo's emphasis on Chamorro rights, expressed fluently and emotionally in English and in Chamorro, attracted the biggest crowds. The Calvo-Palomo ticket attacked the

Camacho-Moylan administration for alleged favoritism, abuses of public office, and corruption. (In April 1975, Camacho, Moylan, and other former administration officials, including Frank F. Blas and John D. Gilliam, would be charged by a grand jury with "misuse of funds" and other crimes that involved kickbacks at the Commercial Port, but the charges appeared to be politically motivated and were dropped.)

Dick Taitano, manager of the Bordallo-Sablan campaign, broadened the patronage-based Bordallo-Democratic organization that he had set up in the 1970 elections. This grassroots political infrastructure proved decisive: Bordallo-Sablan swamped the other Democrats with a plurality of nearly 50 percent of the Democratic votes (the legislature had amended the election law to permit a plurality rather than a majority for the primary nomination). Democrats then rallied behind Bordallo-Sablan for the general election.

It was a different story with the Republicans. The Camacho-Moylan ticket barely beat Calvo-Palomo by 261 votes in the primary. Because the count was so close, Calvo and Palomo decided on a write-in campaign in the general election. As a result, none of the three tickets won a majority in November, but Calvo-Palomo came in third and were eliminated. With the Republicans divided by the write-in, Bordallo-Sablan squeaked by Camacho-Moylan with 51.3 percent, or less than 600 votes of 22,255 cast in the runoff election on 19 November. Carlos Camacho, worn out (he would die in 1979 of diabetes and liver failure), relinquished Republican leadership to Paul Calvo and went back to his dentistry practice. Ricky Bordallo in turn consolidated his dominance of the Democratic party, a control that would last twelve years until the fateful elections of 1986.

Won Pat was reelected without a challenger, but the Republicans won twelve seats in the Thirteenth Guam Legislature. Joe Ada, only thirty-one years old and only in his second term, was elected speaker. Republican control of the legislature would last six years until the elections for the Sev-

enteenth Legislature in 1981. Paul Bordallo and Frank Lujan, who had stood up to the navy, lost their seats in the 1974 election. Both were attacked by opponents as being too antimilitary.

With Guam in a recession, Governor Bordallo imposed austerity measures in the government after his inauguration on 6 January 1975, including a 25 percent cut in all departmental budgets and a freeze on GovGuam hiring. Nevertheless, the new administration watched helplessly as outside factors battered Guam's little economy. Pan Am charter flights between Japan and Guam ceased in April 1975, and the flow of tourists slumped by 16 percent to a total of only about 105,000 in 1976. Even worse, the U.S. Navy reneged on the agreement to turn over its power generators and lines in 1975. The navy claimed that the GPA could not meet the performance standards needed to assure electricity for the island's single power grid.

New investments evaporated on Guam, and over 2,000 H-2 workers returned to the Philippines. The recession also swelled emigration of Guamanians (mostly Chamorros) to the mainland. Chamorros resident on Guam in 1975 were only 55.5 percent of the island's population, while Filipinos had grown to over 19 percent. By 1980, there would be 17,662 Guamanians resident in California, mostly in the Los Angeles and San Diego areas. By 1990, Guamanians living permanently in California would number over 25,000.

Guam's consumer price index (always high in comparison with the states) vaulted over 20 percent per year between 1973 and 1976. Unemployment jumped from 8.3 percent in May 1975 (the first time unemployment was measured on the island) to 13.3 percent in May 1976. By this period, Guam's poor were receiving federal welfare entitlements initiated by Washington under the Johnson administration in the 1960s. From the end of 1974 to May 1976, the number of Guamanian recipients of food stamps skyrocketed from fewer than 300 to nearly 4,500 people. By 1980, food stamp recipients on Guam would total 22,462 in more than

4,000 families, over 20 percent of the civilian population. Guam, like the mainland, was moving into a welfare economy, a process politically impossible to stop once under way. Food stamps and other federal welfare support became a permanent feature on the island, even though the number of food stamp recipients later dropped in the boom of the late 1980s.

Federal subsidies kept Guam afloat financially in the mid- and late 1970s. Direct federal rebates and grants-in-aid provided about twenty-five cents of every GovGuam budget dollar. Massive indirect federal funds subsidized Guam in everything from the crippled childrens' service to spinoffs from construction contracts for military projects. By 1978–1979, these funds totaled, in the words of *Pacific Daily News* editor Joe Murphy, "an incredible $424.3 million, or $4,000 for every man, woman, and child on Guam."

About the only island business that benefited from the 1973 Arab embargo was GORCO, the Guam Oil and Refining Company. Founded in 1970 with GEDA approval of a QC with a maximum 75 percent tax rebate on dividends for the company's ten stockholders, GORCO built a lucrative refinery in the Atantano Valley to supply aviation jet fuel to the military as well as oil to GPA and the navy for power plant fuel. GORCO also prospered in the early 1970s because of the Vietnam War. Operations by B-52s intensified with the "Christmas bombing" in 1972 against the cities of Hanoi and Haiphong in Operation Linebacker II. These strikes were intended to force the North Vietnamese back to the stalled Paris peace talks. At the peak of the operation, about 165 B-52s were based at Andersen. The bombing worked, and on 28 January 1973 a ceasefire was signed at Paris. The United States then rapidly withdrew its combat forces from Vietnam and the extra B-52s from Guam. Eventually, only fourteen B-52s remained at Andersen.

Deserted by the Americans, the South Vietnamese were unable to withstand the renewed North Vietnamese assaults. By April 1975, communist forces were at the gates of Saigon, and a massive, panic-stricken exodus of tens of thousands of non-communist refugees began by aircraft and ships out of the country. Saigon fell on 30 April, and the first part of America to bear the brunt of the defeat was Guam, "Where America's Day Begins," according to the *Pacific Daily News* masthead and GVB tourist slogan for the island. Once more, Guam became an oasis of refuge as the first planeload of Vietnamese refugees on a Flying Tigers Airline jet from Vietnam landed unexpectedly at the civilian international terminal in mid-April. The aircraft was promptly impounded on the order of Governor Bordallo. After a week of bureaucratic confusion, Washington authorized the evacuation of refugees from Vietnam through Guam. Refugees began to arrive at Andersen early on the morning of 23 April 1975 in an unprecedented human torrent called Operation New Life. As CINCPAC representative in Guam and the TTPI, Rear Admiral Morrison assumed control of the operation. Within two days, over 14,000 more bewildered Vietnamese, Filipinos, and other nationals from South Vietnam arrived on Guam by aircraft.

These initial arrivals were the well-off refugees, mostly pro-American government officials and officers with their families. The flood of refugees quickly saturated the local lodging capacity, despite the prompt dispatch of hundreds of Vietnamese on to the states daily by aircraft after each person was processed for identity and given a quick medical examination. To house the transients, Seabees bulldozed the *tangantangan* off the old runway at Orote airfield and erected a tent city for 40,000 people.

The refugees still poured in, with over 13,000 arriving on one day alone, 7 May. COMNAVMAR opened a second major camp at the old Asan shore site where Filipino insurrectionists had been interned some seventy years earlier and buildings still stood from the former Naval Hospital annex used for Vietnam casualties. Up to thirteen smaller camps were also set up, ranging from the Tokyu Hotel in Tumon and United Service Organization at Piti to the old Camp Roxas sport field near Santa Rita. The U.S. Army flew in nearly 2,000 soldiers to administer Orote's tent city. The U.S. Marines managed Asan, while the air force coped with the flood through Andersen. Governor Bordallo provided full assistance by GovGuam agencies for water, power, and other needs.

On 11 May, the carrier USS *Midway* sailed into Apra Harbor and off-loaded not only people but 101 former Vietnamese military and Air America (the CIA airline) aircraft. Civilian ships and boats of all sizes with yet more refugees began to arrive on 15 May, when the on-island population of evacuees peaked at 50,430, or about half the number of Guam's residents. Most refugees in this seaborne steerage wave were poor, and many had decided that they wanted to return home. Security problems arose in June when the latter vociferously demanded to be repatriated to Vietnam. Their return was held up as U.S. officials waited for the United Nations to make the arrangements. Dengue fever erupted among the refugees, and the military quickly sprayed over a third of Guam with the pesticide Malathion to kill the mosquitos that transmitted the disease. The fever subsided but the spraying also caused fish kills and perhaps destruction of other wildlife on the island.

In the middle of this tense situation, a new COMNAVMAR, Rear Admiral Kent J. Carroll, relieved Morrison. In late August and early September, the repatriates rioted over the delay in their return to Vietnam; they burned buildings and vehicles at the Asan camp. Admiral Carroll ordered U.S. Marshals to quell the violence with heavy doses of tear gas, the first ever employed on Guam. Strikes by the repatriates followed before the Vietnamese freighter *Thuong Tin One* (arranged at Ricky Bordallo's suggestion) finally departed 16 October with 1,600 of them bound for South Vietnam, where many were promptly clapped into communist "reeducation camps" for years.

On 1 November 1975, the last refugee camp on Guam—Asan—was closed. A total of 111,789 men, women, and children from South Vietnam had passed through Guam. Overall, Operation New Life was a remarkable success, given the short notice, the lack of preparation, and the massive number of refugees. The positive response of the government and people of Guam to the unprecedented evacuation of so many aliens through their island was a solid demonstration of Guamanian tolerance and of their loyalty to the United States.

Earlier in 1975, Guamanians learned that a covenant had been signed on 15 February in Washington, D.C., to establish the Commonwealth of the Northern Mariana Islands (the CNMI) as an American territory in "political union" with the United States. The new commonwealth status promised the CNMI people U.S. citizenship and local self-government over land, immigration, labor, and taxes. The United States also pledged a generous financial assistance package to the CNMI for seven years with renewal to be negotiated (between fiscal years 1978 and 1992, the CNMI would receive $420 million in direct federal subsidies, or nearly $2,000 per resident per year, mostly for infrastructure, in addition to indirect federal funding of food stamps, welfare benefits, etc.).

It had taken less than three years of negotiations once they began in December 1972 for the people of the CNMI to be accepted for American citizenship (the CNMI Constitution and the first local government would be installed 9 January 1978, with citizenship granted formally on 30 September 1986, when the U.N. trusteeship ended for the CNMI). In contrast, it had taken the people of Guam nearly fifty years to accomplish the same goal. For Guamanians, as one observed, "It seemed ironic and unfair to many that they, who had obediently and patriotically served the United States for seventy-five years, should have less self-government than their neighbors." By being united but flexible in negotiations with the United States, the Northern Marianas moved ahead of Guam in political development.

In reaction to the CNMI Covenant, the Republican majority in the Thirteenth Guam Legislature created the second Guam political status commission in early 1975. Republican Senator Frank F. Blas was elected chair, but this time membership was not restricted to senators, and fifteen people were appointed from both parties. The commission's chief task was to prepare legislation for a plebiscite on status by the people of Guam in 1976. The legislature designated the commission to be the sole body to represent Guam in status negotiations with Washington. The commission members promptly requested President Gerald Ford (who had replaced Nixon in August 1974 after the Watergate scandal) to send a representative to confer with them.

These steps antagonized Democrat Won Pat in Washington, who was not officially consulted or included in the commission. His response was to undercut the Republican legislative initiative by introducing two resolutions in the U.S. Congress, one in February 1975 that called for Congress to consider a constitution for Guam, and another in June to establish a joint U.S.-Guam status commission separate from the one on Guam. Belatedly, the Guam senators removed their exclusive negotiating authority, but this change did little good. Faced with Guam's divided and contradictory efforts, the White House delayed naming a presidential representative, and the Congress took no immediate action on Won Pat's resolutions.

All political activity, however, as well as all routine matters, came to a halt in mid-May 1976 when the Joint Typhoon Warning Center (JTWC) issued a tropical cyclone formation alert. One of the most enormous typhoons of the century was spiraling out of its spawning ground in southeast Micronesia and heading directly for Guam. On 19 May, the air force evacuated its Guam-based B-52s to Kadena Airbase on Okinawa. On 20 May, Governor Bordallo declared Guam to be in Typhoon Condition I (typhoon imminent), with winds already ripping away some tin roofs.

The storm was Pamela, the century's third supertyphoon to strike Guam dead on. A supertyphoon was then considered to be a cyclone with sustained winds higher than 148 miles per hour (a new classification for supertyphoons, Category V with 155 miles per hour winds or higher, was instituted by meteorologists in the 1980s). The century's first

supertyphoon, unnamed, to hit Guam was the one on 13 November 1900; the second was Karen on 11–12 November 1962. Pamela, with sustained winds from 140 to 150 miles per hour for hour-long periods and bursts to 190 miles per hour, moved leisurely across Guam at eight miles per hour. The eye started passing over the island at 4:00 P.M. on 21 May, with the center passing over Yona and Piti. The immense size of Pamela can be judged by her eye: it was a crater-like twenty miles across, and, instead of being clear like the eyes of most typhoons, it was cloudy and ominously foggy even though winds dropped inside. Because the eye took over an hour to pass over the island, some eyewitnesses believed that Pamela reversed direction and crossed the island twice.

Since Pamela moved more slowly than Karen (lingering forty-eight hours over the island, with six hours of winds higher than 120 miles per hour), it caused more damage than Karen's higher winds. On the other hand, only one death was attributed directly to Pamela, compared to nine for Karen and thirty-four in the 1900 supertyphoon. Fewer lives were lost to Pamela because of the improved forecasting methods and accurate warnings by the JTWC and because more buildings on Guam were all concrete by 1976.

Nevertheless, most power poles were down, crops were gone, farm animals were killed or scattered, hundreds of coconut trees lost their crowns, and nearly all other trees, bushes, and shrubs were left naked of leaves. Pamela also poured twenty-seven inches of rain on Guam in twenty-four hours, ten inches more than Karen. Sustained sprays of water through even the tiniest cracks around windows and doors ruined interiors of homes and offices. In Apra Harbor, eighteen small boats and a dozen large vessels up to freighter size sank or were swept onto reefs, where some remained for years. Oil spills spread around Commercial Port and Dry Dock Island in the harbor. The spills were not cleaned up in those days before environmental protection was of much concern.

Governor Bordallo declared martial law, and a curfew was enforced for several days. Schools did not reopen until the fall semester, giving students a nearly four-month vacation. Damage to military bases was estimated at $200 million, split almost evenly between navy and air force installations, and damage to private and public civilian property was roughly estimated at $300 million, or about a half billion dollars total for the island.

As with Karen, Washington immediately came to Guam's assistance after Pamela. The island was declared a major disaster area, and the Federal Disaster Assistance Administration (FDAA) swiftly sent out people and money. Victims could submit claims to FDAA offices within a few days of the storm and promptly received compensation for damages. Private insurance compensation came to over $25 million. The American Red Cross, reliable as ever, sent workers and mounted fund drives in the states for Guam, eventually providing over $10 million worth of assistance.

Federal funds for Pamela-related rehabilitation of the civilian community on Guam totaled about $115 million by 1978, of which $38 million was provided by the U.S. Small Business Administration, and $21 million went directly to individuals for relief. The total was more than the relief funds provided after supertyphoon Karen in the 1960s, even with adjustments for inflation. Although the United States has often been politically insensitive in its treatment of Guam over the years, the American people, charity groups, military services, and government have generously provided money, food, and other aid to the island in times of natural disasters.

Like Governor Guerrero after Karen in 1963, Ricky Bordallo in 1976 after Pamela saw federal assistance not only as an opportunity to reconstruct storm-damaged facilities but also as a means to improve Guam's infrastructure and economy. Bordallo, however, went beyond the proposals of Guerrero. In January 1977, Bordallo requested that Washington fund an enormous new development program of nearly $289 million for Guam. Among the projects he proposed was a grandiose capitol complex on East Agana Bay with modern, glass-sheathed buildings of over 200,000 square feet to house all three branches of GovGuam.

This glittering fantasy was not supported by the Republican majority in the Thirteenth Guam Legislature, which endorsed a more realistic program for improvement of roads, housing, and so forth. In Washington, Congressman Won Pat sided with the Guam legislature. Consequently, the U.S. Congress did not approve Bordallo's proposal.

Unfazed, the governor quickly revised his proposal and requested it again, this time as a "Marshall Plan for Guam" that included new projects. Not only did Bordallo intend to repair Pamela's damages and improve the island's infrastructure, he also wanted to fulfill all the projects promised but not completed by the naval government after World War II, notably the rebuilding of Agana. The governor lobbied vigorously for his plan in Washington, but the reaction was again unreceptive.

Bordallo's political opponents, both Democratic and Republican, derided him as a quixotic dreamer. But his extravagant requests were surprisingly successful. In addition to the $115 million for typhoon-related rehabilitation, Washington gave Guam $120 million in federal grants and loans for non-typhoon-related specific capital improvement projects and another $132 million for GovGuam operations and services. Overall, Bordallo obtained approximately $367 million in 1975–1978, the highest amount of federal funding for civil development in Guam's history for a four-year period.

At times, however, Bordallo's proposals were too costly and too impractical for even his most ardent supporters. An example was his dream of building a giant tower in the shape of a *latte* stone 200 feet high near Two Lovers Point above Tumon Bay. This Latte of Freedom was to be a civic center with an auditorium on the top and was proposed as Guam's contribution to the U.S. bicentennial celebration in 1976. Cost for the tower was estimated at $20–$25 million and was to be met by fund drives among private citizens, not by government money. By the time Bordallo left office in 1978, over a half million dollars had been raised. This money was put into a trust that rose to over a million dollars, but the tower was never built.

On the other hand, Bordallo initiated and completed more public construction in his first term than any other governor of Guam since Admiral Pownall. One long-term project was the commencement of a new terminal for the international airport (the Guam Airport Authority [GAA] had been initiated by Republican senators and began operations in January 1976). Other projects were the Agana marina and sewer treatment plant; the Guam Public Market, opened in 1977 at the Paseo Park in Agana (and burned to the ground in 1982); the first monument to a traditional Chamorro leader, a handsome eleven-foot bronze statue of Quipuha dedicated in July 1977 at a small park next to the Paseo; residences for the elderly—Guma Trankilidad—initiated in 1977 on a beautiful beach site at Tumon; and the first Chamorro-style public meeting hall—the Sagan Dinaña—completed in 1978 near the statue of Quipuha.

A Bordallo initiative that provoked an uproar was the addition of a second floor and a red-tiled roof to expand Government House into a Spanish-style mansion. A tunnel was dug to connect the residence to a federally funded underground Civil Defense Center next door (called "Disaster Dugout" by the *Pacific Daily News*). When the governor tried to build a long, high wall at a cost of $350,000 to enclose the residence, he was halted by public outcry and a federal turndown of funds. Later, when numerous large public functions were held free every week in the enlarged residence (Guam had no civic center for large social gatherings), Bordallo's foresight was applauded.

Another project realized in Bordallo's first administration was the acquisition of a new building for the Guam Memorial Hospital. The old GMH at Oka had gradually deteriorated since its post-Karen renovation. In 1973, a GMH patient died by electrocution when he touched an air conditioner, another was later scalded to death in a bath, and one frustrated GMH administrator admitted to the press that "a patient's life is in danger" at the hospital. In 1974, the facility lost its accreditation once more. By the mid-1970s, GovGuam was considering sites for a new facility.

Meanwhile, Catholic leaders planned to create their own hospital to replace the small Catholic medical center in Agana opened in 1955. The Diocese of Agana under the energetic leadership of Bishop Felixberto Flores obtained large loans and launched donation drives for construction in 1973–1975 of the 221-bed Medical Center of the Marianas (MCM). It was built at Oka on the site of the Mercy Convent only a mile from the old GMH. Bishop Flores hoped that the two hospitals would complement each other. As it turned out, the two competed for patients.

Opened in January 1976, the MCM facility quickly became too heavy a financial burden for the diocese to sustain since most of the public still went to GMH, where treatment was not only cheaper but often free. By Guam law, GMH had to provide care to the indigent and to Medicare and Medicaid patients, but, also by law, it could not compel payment for that care. With MCM going bankrupt, Flores offered to sell the new hospital to GovGuam. Governor Bordallo readily agreed to the bishop's offer.

For financing, Bordallo turned to Washington. In a concerted effort, Won Pat and Phil Burton then obtained a federal grant-in-aid from the U.S. Congress of $25.5 million for GovGuam to purchase MCM and another $10 million for public health and other projects. This money, however, was held up by Interior Department officials, who thought that the MCM price was too high. To save the diocese from bankruptcy, Bordallo went ahead and had GMH move into the MCM building in January 1978. Parts of old GMH were turned over later to the Department of Mental Health and Substance Abuse, whose patients vegetated in the coming years in the shabby old facilities.

The Diocese of Agana ended up taking a loss when GMH replaced MCM, but the new facility was no bargain for Guam's taxpayers. The new GMH promptly slid toward bankruptcy when it could not make the $100,000-a-month lease payments to the major MCM creditor, Aetna Insurance. By September 1978, GPA was threatening to cut off power to the hospital for its failure to pay over $100,000 in overdue electricity bills. GMH managed to survive on local appropriations until the federal money bailed it out when the funds were finally released in May 1979. Ever since then, however, the hospital has experienced grave problems in administration (politicized by appointees of the governors), in finances (owing to its inability to collect bills), and in providing quality medical services (low staff salaries caused personnel problems, and budget shortfalls caused equipment shortages). Although the need for a public hospital was unquestioned, inept management of GMH made possible one of the slickest scams in the history of the island.

The GMHP Scam and a Failed Constitution

The scam came about through health maintenance organizations (HMOs), which in this period were beginning to provide medical services to groups of people on Guam under prepayment plans, either through public facilities like GMH or through private clinics. GovGuam had initiated a voluntary hospital insurance plan for its employees back in 1966, and, by the mid-1970s, the private Family Health Plan (FHP), founded on Guam in 1973 by Dr. Robert Gumbiner at the request of Bishop Flores, was the only HMO on Guam for GovGuam employees. FHP was profitable and effective, but it was owned and run mostly by statesiders.

A number of local doctors led by Dr. Ernesto M. Espaldon—a Republican senator and leader of the Filipino community—and Dr. Eduardo Ortiz—chair of the GMH Board of Trustees—proposed to set up a GovGuam-owned HMO through GMH in order to provide GovGuam employees less expensive quality medical care. After considerable debate, the Republican-controlled Fourteenth Guam Legislature (1977–1978) unanimously passed the Guam Health Act on 11 May 1977, which created the Guam Memorial Health Plan, or GMHP, effective 27 July. The same law made GMH "autonomous" so that its board of trustees (all, however, still appointed by the governor) could oversee GMHP.

To organize and manage GMHP, the hospital trustees gave a three-year contract for the period May 1977–May 1980 to the California-based Medical Services Association (MSA), affiliated with Hyatt Medical Management Services. In 1980, MSA reorganized into Health Management International (HMI), which received another three-year contract from the GMH trustees. MSA/HMI were owned in part and run by H. Ted Levenson as president and Jacquie C. Wilkinson as vice president.

Over the years 1977–1981 the Levenson/Wilkinson team would fail to pay Guam taxes, bilk GMH of tens of thousands of dollars (the exact amount has never been determined), and drive GMHP into bankruptcy with a deficit of $2.8 million. Of that deficit, about $2 million was owed by GMHP to GMH. By 1979, GMHP was accused of foisting "inaccurate financial statements" on GovGuam. As a result, GMH once more tottered on the brink of bankruptcy by 1980. In September 1981, the GMH trustees belatedly terminated HMI's contract, and Levenson and Wilkinson departed Guam in a smokescreen of legal obfuscations. The befuddled Guam legislature then took another nine months to separate the hospital from GMHP and initiate liquidation of the latter. Finally, on 8 September 1982, the GMH trustees filed their first suit against HMI for recovery of money lost owing to "mismanagement."

That was the wrong charge. Wilkinson and Levenson were skilled managers—of a massive con game. First, they energetically signed up members in GMHP by an enticing advertising campaign, expanding membership from fifty-three in 1978 to over 5,400 by January 1980. They then skimmed off the monthly payments made by GMHP members for insurance premiums while ignoring GMH bills and notices to GMHP to pay for the medical services provided those members. To forestall exposure, Levenson and Wilkinson entertained GMH trustees, favored certain physicians with referrals, made hefty political contributions to Democratic and Republican candidates for public offices, and promised repeatedly that GMHP intended to pay off its debts to GMH. Wilkinson claimed that the payment problem was due to a communication "mix-up." Wilkinson and Levenson retained local lawyers with connections to GMH and politicians to fend off attempts to have MSA/HMI accounts audited.

GMH never did recover its money. No MSA/HMI accounts were found to audit. When the GovGuam Department of Revenue and Taxation seized MSA/HMI's assets in 1982 for a tax liability of nearly $300,000, only $256 was found in the bank account. By then, Levenson and Wilkerson had long since departed Guam. Action to bring them to trial was not pushed; it might have embarrassed or even compromised some prominent politicians, doctors, and lawyers on Guam.

GMHP eventually reorganized and resumed operations as a private provider of health care. As for GMH, it has yet to attain financial or operational health. In fiscal year 1990, unrecovered bills totaled $4.4 million, and the hospital's operating deficit was $9.2 million. The facility (which had regained accreditation in 1980–1982) again lost its accreditation by the Joint Commission on Accreditation of Hospitals in June 1983 for "an accumulation of problems" and remained unaccredited into the 1990s.

Another ambiguous accomplishment under Bordallo's first administration was the establishment of the Guam Community College (GCC) in 1977. Back on 22 June 1972, the U.S. Congress had accorded land grant status to the University of Guam. Won Pat, again relying on the help of Phil Burton, obtained congressional approval of a $3 million endowment for the University of Guam (UOG) and annual grants of approximately $450,000. In June 1976, the Thirteenth Guam Legislature made UOG an "autonomous" nonprofit public corporation under an appointed board of regents through the Guam Higher Education Act. This act was prompted by an accreditation visit of the Western Association of Schools and Colleges (WASC), which warned that UOG needed to be shielded from political interference.

With all this help, by the fall semester of 1977 UOG reached an enrollment of over 3,500 full-time-equivalent students with a faculty of about 190, predominantly statesider academicians, in four colleges: liberal arts, agriculture, education, and business. The university also assumed a regional outreach educational mission, and Micronesians from throughout the TTPI (where the Interior Department had since the 1960s improved the TTPI's long-neglected public education) began to attend. Enrollment was open; that is, all applicants had to be accepted, regardless of academic qualifications, which means that a large proportion of UOG courses were (and remain) actually high school–level classes called "developmental" mathematics and English for students who do not meet minimal U.S. undergraduate college standards.

Governor Bordallo, however, did not believe that UOG was providing adequate practical, job-oriented education for Guam's youths. In 1976, he proposed a technical college that, in his eyes, would grow into a Guam version of the Massachusetts Institute of Technology. After a fair amount of political skirmishing in the Republican-controlled legislature, GCC was established in 1977 near George Washington High School in Mangilao within a mile of UOG.

As with the establishment of the two hospitals within sight of each other at Oka, the creation of two college-level institutions close to each other in Mangilao resulted in competition and duplication of effort between them. Consequently, UOG's enrollment plummeted by nearly half over the years after 1977 as numerous freshmen and sophomores signed up at GCC, where tuition was lower and where some classes replicated first- and second-year classes at UOG. By the early 1980s, UOG had to reduce its master's degree programs and began to suffer budget shortfalls.

GCC also duplicated the politicization of administration that exists at UOG. The governor appoints the boards for both schools. The trustees of GCC and UOG, the heads and vice presidents of both institutions, and even deans have been selected by Guam's governors on the basis of political affiliation, even though search committees go through the appearance of selection on merit.

The support of two overlapping higher educational institutions by the small island community of Guam is a heavy financial burden that few U.S. counties undertake with populations comparable in size to Guam's. Academic competition between GCC and UOG and the recurring political influence in their administration by GovGuam leaders would inevitably lead to serious difficulties in the financing and accreditation of both schools in the 1980s, just as occurred with Guam's two hospitals in the 1970s.

The Bordallo-Sablan administration of 1974–1978 was also plagued by problems not unique to Guam. Drug traffic ballooned on Guam in the late 1970s as marijuana from Palau and the CNMI and heroin from Asia flowed into and through the island. The crime rate on the island "escalated spectacularly," according to authorities. When Washington pumped money into Guam to combat narcotics, the tempting flow of dollars led to corruption in the Guam police (then part of the Department of Public Safety along with firemen). Director Pedro A. E. Manibusan and three other high-ranking police officers were indicted in July 1977 for stealing money from an antidrug operation called Cihik (Tiny Bird). Manibusan's first case ended comically in a mistrial when the recently hired court stenographer turned out to be incompetent and fled the island, notes and all. Manibusan and the others were retried and found guilty.

A number of other GovGuam officials were indicted and found guilty (often by federal prosecution) of embezzlement and other crimes in the same period. In February 1977, the acting corrections chief and eight penitentiary guards (all poorly paid) were indicted for various crimes and eventually jailed. But imprisonment did not solve much. The creaky, overcrowded Guam penitentiary was a laughingstock. Prisoners casually escaped, some repeatedly, and usually spent a few days with family or friends before being picked up or turning themselves in. The attorneys general of Guam, all

political appointees since 1970, acquired a reputation for following orders from the governor's office and at times avoiding politically sensitive cases. This politicization of local justice, and the growth of island crime, led federal authorities to expand the staffs of the U.S. district attorney's and the Drug Enforcement Agency (DEA) and FBI offices on Guam.

In the meantime, GPA was slip-sliding toward bankruptcy because of increased oil prices and mounting debts. In 1976, GPA defaulted on its bond anticipation notes, but the Department of the Interior came to GPA's rescue by guaranteeing a loan in early 1977 by the Federal Finance Bank (FFB) for $36 million for post-Pamela repairs and to pay off GPA's defaulted notes and loans. Even with this assistance, GPA, short of sufficient cash flow, soon asked that repayment of the FFB loan be canceled. The federal authorities refused the request, and the loan would not by repaid until the early 1990s. A congressional Government Accounting Office audit in 1977 concluded that "Gov-Guam's financial situation is a mess" but said that the Interior Department shared the blame. One audit in this period showed that, out of 2,000 or so government vehicles, 400 were unaccounted for owing to "sloppy accounting practices." GovGuam as a whole barely avoided a payless payday in February 1978, a threat repeated several times thereafter.

One of the reasons that the Bordallo-Sablan administration was having financial difficulties was the federal requirement that Guam provide matching funds to obtain federal grants-in-aid for Medicaid, food stamps, aid to dependent children, education, and the other social programs on which the island had come to depend. GovGuam tended to divert funds from capital improvements in order to match federal grants-in-aid. To assist the territories, Phil Burton initiated the Omnibus Territories Act of 1977 (P.L. 95–134, signed by President Jimmy Carter on 15 October), which allowed federal authorities to waive requirements for the insular territories to match funds for some of the programs.

These waivers allowed Guam to save a great deal of money in the coming years, but capital infrastructure on the island still did not improve tangibly despite the creation of the Bureau of Planning in 1977. That year, a consulting firm completed an island-wide land-use plan for the Bordallo administration as a consequence of P.L. 12–200, the Comprehensive Planning Act of 1974. The act mandated an island-wide development plan on the basis of the 1966 master plan, which was outdated by 1974 because of unexpected population growth. The legislature failed to implement fully the 1977 plan, just as with the 1966 plan.

Another helpful provision in the 1977 Omnibus Territories Act amended the Organic Act to permit the U.S. District Court on Guam to review claims for compensation for private property condemned by the navy after World War II. A month later, José Herrero Torres filed the first of what would become hundreds of such claims. The bitter legacy of military land condemnations was complicated by Guam's tangled land records. By the late 1970s, less than 22 percent of GovGuam land had been properly surveyed and registered. This situation left much of the remaining 28,211 acres of unregistered public land exposed to encroachment by owners of adjacent private parcels.

To remove this threat, in 1974 the Twelfth Guam Legislature included a provision in the Chamorro Land Trust Act that restricted transfers of public land to those between owners of contiguous fractional lots and to exchanges for land of equal value. Unfortunately, the law was not enforced. By the early 1990s, a number of big-time land swindles resulted that involved huge encroachments on unsurveyed public land by crooked surveyors, real estate brokers, attorneys, and senior GovGuam land management officials.

Even when federal officials sought to improve land use on Guam, there were sometimes hidden penalties for the people of the island. In August 1978, the U.S. National Park Service established the War in the Pacific National Historical Park on Guam. The park was made up of seven separate large areas where World War II battles took place,

notably the Asan and Agat invasion beaches. Although a welcome addition to the island, the park blocked a long-planned Agat small boat harbor that was on the verge of construction at Gaan Point. Despite protests by the angry people of Agat, the Department of the Interior compelled the U.S. Corps of Engineers and GovGuam to move the harbor to a new site several miles away near Nimitz Beach, a less favorable location. Interior forced the move by declaring a rusty old World War II sewer pipe at Gaan Point to be a "historic landmark," the only sewer so distinguished in the history of the United States. Costs for the harbor at the new site jumped, and construction was delayed for eight years.

Creation of the war park also halted nearly all development along the lovely Agat shoreline, but for years Congress did not appropriate enough money for the National Park Service to purchase the private property within the park boundary along the shore. Landowners were stuck in limbo throughout the 1980s into the 1990s, unable to develop their property while uncompensated for the unfinished park. In another case, the U.S. Congress transferred 927 acres of federal land and submerged areas in the Commercial Port area to GovGuam in 1979 for port expansion. The law included an amendment—the Brooks Amendment—that limited any sale or lease of the land by GovGuam to a market value determined by the U.S. General Services Administration, and money from such transfers goes back to the U.S. Treasury, not to the people of Guam.

Another land case that provoked local protests for years involved large tracts of former copra plantations along the undeveloped beaches of Urunao and Falcona (owned mostly by the Artero family) and Jinapsan (owned by the Castro and other families). These beautiful beaches lie on each side of Ritidian Point, where the navy operated the top-secret NavFac installation, and are surrounded by military land. (The beaches themselves, like all Guam ocean-front property, are public lands up to the mean high-water mark.) Normal recreational, developmental, or any other use was denied the owners and the public for military security reasons throughout the 1970s and 1980s and on into the 1990s, even after NavFac was closed.

Congressman Burton, prompted by Won Pat, followed up the first Omnibus Act in 1977 by annual omnibus territories acts. With "Christmas tree" appropriations for the island, these annual pork barrel bills would bail out GovGuam repeatedly over the coming years but did not reduce the deficit. The bills originated in a subcommittee that Burton created in 1978, the Subcommittee on Pacific Affairs (formerly the Subcommittee on National Parks and Insular Affairs, later changed to the Subcommittee on Insular and International Affairs) under the House Committee on Interior and Insular Affairs. In early 1979, Won Pat was made chair of this subcommittee, which became the focus of federal-territorial relations in the Congress. As the subcommittee chair, as well as being a member of the House Armed Services Committee, Won Pat was able to make sure that Guam received a good share of federal funds each year.

Despite financial headaches in the public sector, the private sector perked up in February 1977 when the Greyhound Racing Track opened in Tamuning with betting permitted on the dog races. Until then, gambling had been limited to cockfights and church-run bingo sessions, and to games of chance at the annual Liberation Day carnival, where—astoundingly—even minors may gamble for cash prizes. In this period, off-island promoters were trying to have slot machines and casino gambling approved. Bishop Flores, however, mounted an anticasino campaign, fanning fears that Japanese Yakuza and American Mafia crime syndicates might come to Guam if casinos were permitted. On 16 April 1977, in an island-wide referendum, the public turned down casinos and slot machines. The

Antonio Borja Won Pat. Photograph taken in the early 1970s. He was Guam's most prominent political leader for nearly forty years after World War II. He served as speaker of the House of Assembly of the Guam Congress from 1948 to 1951 and as speaker six times of the Guam Legislature from 1951 through 1965. He was a founder of the Guam Democratic party in 1960 and was unofficial Guam delegate to the U.S. Congress, 1965–1973. He served as official Guam delegate to the U.S. Congress from 1974 through 1984. (From the collection of the Micronesian Area Research Center, Mangilao, Guam)

legislature subsequently permitted electronic poker machines on the island (with a hefty but unenforceable tax), but it outlawed them in the mid-1980s under pressure from church and civic groups after the machines proved addictive and spread everywhere, even to small "mom and pop" grocery stores.

While public attention focused on gambling issues, the Guam political status commission held a referendum on status options on 4 September 1976. A majority of 58 percent of Guamanians voted for "improved status quo" out of five options on the ballot. Statehood garnered 24 percent, status quo received 9 percent, independence only 6 percent, and "other" 3 percent. Oddly, "commonwealth" was not an option on the ballot.

While concern with political status gathered momentum on Guam, in Washington Delegate Won Pat lobbied on his own for authority for Guamanians to write a constitution. On 21 October 1976, Congress passed P.L. 94–584, which gave the legislatures of Guam and the Virgin Islands authority to create constitutional conventions. In December 1976, the Thirteenth Guam Legislature responded with a law to create a constitutional convention by a nonpartisan election of delegates on 16 April 1977. The thirty-two delegates included Senator Carl T. C. Gutierrez, an energetic Democrat elected president of the convention. For legal advice, the convention retained Washington attorney Arnold H. Leibowitz, an expert on federal-territorial law. He had previously served as adviser to the first Guam political status commission. From July to December 1977, the convention wrote an excellent, locally responsive constitution based on the latest models in the U.S. states.

The final draft called for establishment of a Guam Supreme Court, protection of Chamorro traditions, and elected boards for DOE and UOG, along with standard provisions found in the most recent state constitutions. The document was sent off for review in early 1978 to the White House, then occupied by Democrat Jimmy Carter, and to the U.S. Congress. The plebiscite on the draft act was to coincide with the 1978 gubernatorial elec-

tions on Guam, but the constitution became a partisan issue when Carl Gutierrez declared his candidacy for governor based largely on his presidency of the convention. The Republican-controlled Fourteenth Legislature promptly put off the constitutional plebiscite until April 1979 and then again to August 1979. Local partisan politics, as so often happens on Guam, took precedence over statesmanship in the decisions of Guamanian leaders.

On the eve of the 1978 elections, Governor Bordallo found himself in trouble. On the personal side, Bordallo, once the owner of one of the island's largest automobile dealerships, was nearly bankrupt owing to land investments that turned sour. On the political side, he had bickered with the Republican-controlled legislatures and was accused of having the police spy on senators. He had reduced the roll of GovGuam employees from some 13,000 to 8,300, thereby angering a sizable block of Chamorro voters. His troubles worsened when he quarreled openly with his popular lieutenant governor, Rudy Sablan. As a result, Sablan ran against Bordallo in the 1978 primary, with attorney José I. (Joe) Leon Guerrero as a running mate. Bordallo picked Dr. Pedro C. Sanchez to run as lieutenant governor on his ticket.

With the Democrats split, the Republicans united around the single slate of Senators Paul Calvo and Joe Ada. Calvo projected the assured personality of a business executive, which was attractive after four years of Bordallo's busy extravagance. Calvo-Ada ran on a "balance-the-budget" theme to reduce Guam's reliance on federal funds. They blamed Bordallo for the huge jump in GovGuam's deficit during his administration. A complication arose for both tickets when Carl Gutierrez chose Dr. Joseph S. (Joe) Dizon, a Filipino Republican, former political science professor at UOG, and staff director of the constitutional convention, as his running mate on an independent ticket.

In the September 1978 primary, the Gutierrez-Dizon team received only 757 votes, far short of the 20 percent of the total needed to carry them into the general election. Bordallo-Sanchez beat Sablan–

Leon Guerrero, but the divisions between the Democratic candidates weakened their support among the independent voters who decide Guam's close elections. These independents went mostly for Calvo-Ada, who won the general election with 52 percent of the votes. Delegate Won Pat, unopposed, was once more reelected. In the legislature—elected by districts for the first time—the Republicans won a majority of fourteen seats. Thomas V. C. (Tommy) Tanaka, Jr., a genial businessman, was elected speaker of the Fifteenth Guam Legislature (1979–1980) after considerable infighting among the Republicans.

The new governor promptly canceled twenty-six last-minute contracts that Bordallo had signed. Calvo, an experienced and capable manager, lowered GovGuam's deficit by a respectable $27 million in 1979, but thereafter it began to climb once more to the highest point in history by 1982. One reason for the deficit was the inability (or reluctance) of GovGuam to collect taxes, a problem about which federal auditors repeatedly complained throughout the 1970s and 1980s and into the 1990s. The delinquency rate of Guam's real estate taxes in 1977 was nearly 28 percent, higher than in any comparable community in the United States. Poor administration and political influence in the Department of Revenue and Taxation made it possible for some taxpayers to avoid payment of taxes. Foreclosures on real estate for delinquent taxes were virtually impossible. Despite later improvement of tax administration by computerization, efficient tax collection is still a problem for GovGuam as of the early 1990s.

Another reason that Guam's debt grew was that GPA was again near bankruptcy owing to defaults on repaying the $36 million FFB loan of 1977 and other debts. GPA received a new lease on life when Won Pat persuaded Congress in November 1979 to extend the FFB loan at a lower interest rate and to provide some $10 million in federal grants for other GPA projects, including replacement of wooden power poles with concrete poles. Although typhoon proof, the new poles—graceless pillars festooned with electric wires and television cables—

were ugly additions to Guam's scenery. The alternative—underground power lines—was judged too expensive. The Guam Telephone Authority (GTA) received a financial shot in the arm at this time with a $20.8 million loan from the U.S. Rural Electrification Administration (REA) for a major reconstruction program in 1979–1980. Ironically, REA would not extend a loan to Guam's electric utility, which needed money more than the telephone agency, because of GPA's low bond rating.

While Guam's economy began to regain health under the Calvo-Ada administration, entertainment improved visibly on the island when on 16 January 1978 KUAM-TV under Jon Anderson broadcast Guam's first live television program from the mainland. It was Super Bowl XII between the Dallas Cowboys and the Denver Broncos (Dallas won, 27 to 10). Tourism received a boost when the new international airport terminal began operations in August 1979. Duty Free Shoppers, along with JAL, Pan Am, Continental, and Braniff, underwrote $43 million in revenue bonds to finance construction of the terminal. The Guam Airport Authority then accepted Duty Free Shoppers' bid of $140 million for an exclusive concession for the lucrative duty-free shops in the terminal. GAA thereafter became one of the few GovGuam agencies to earn more than it spent.

The first major political event in the Calvo-Ada administration was the vote on the draft Guam constitution on 4 August 1979. President Carter and the U.S. Congress had earlier approved the draft without any changes, but on Guam opposition had grown among Chamorro-rights activists, who viewed the constitution as a Washington-mandated revised Organic Act that did not halt Filipino immigration or rectify inequities imposed on Chamorros by military and Interior Department authorities. By 1978, the most active Chamorro group was a coalition called Para Pada y Chamorros (*para* means "stop," and *pada'* is "slap"; the name is a play on words meaning "stop slapping Chamorros").

For its part in the 1979 referendum, the Guam legislature funded a public education campaign on the constitution. Curiously, the contract for the campaign was given to the UOG College of Agriculture and Life Sciences because it employed extension agents throughout the island. As should have been expected, these agricultural specialists proved inexpert at explaining the complexities of the constitution. According to the *Pacific Daily News,* the public remained "uninformed and confused about the 14-article constitution." Opponents of the constitution also included many of Guam's teachers, statesiders, and attorneys (the latter disliked the provision for a Guam Supreme Court). Even the *Pacific Daily News* came out against the constitution in an editorial just before the vote.

Faced with this opposition, Guam's political leaders shied away from actively endorsing the draft constitution, thereby leaving the document unprotected from its opponents. Won Pat favored it, but he remained in Washington most of the time. As a consequence, in a low voter turnout of only 47 percent, the people of Guam turned down the island's first—and so far only—constitution by a huge majority of nearly 82 percent of the 13,154 votes cast. A UN delegation observed the 1979 referendum and noted in its report that the negative vote seemed due mostly to local dissatisfaction with the status quo. Carl Gutierrez (who himself had politicized the plebiscite) attributed the rejection to the desire of Guamanians to settle the "status question" first, with the constitution to follow later. The constitutional exercise was "an expensive lesson in democracy—and futility," wrote Joe Murphy in the *Pacific Daily News.* He had predicted that the draft would fail because of the lack of unity in support of it by Guam's leaders.

The drafting of constitutions in the islands prompted a review by the Carter administration in late 1979 of federal territorial policy. The review, called the "White House Inter-Agency Task Force Report," included hasty inputs from the territories. President Carter issued a policy statement based on the review on 20 February 1980, which for the first time in U.S. history accepted "all options," including presumably independence, as open to the territories, so long as national security interests were

protected. Carter's initiative died, however, when Republican Ronald Reagan was elected in 1980 to the White House and froze territorial policy.

In light of the rejection of the draft Guam constitution, in early 1980 Senator Tony Palomo commissioned the first comprehensive study of the feasibility and benefits of various political status options for the island. In a thorough analysis of all options, the study pointed out that integration of Guam with Hawai'i as a county was impractical. Statehood was judged to be politically infeasible as long as the Marianas remained divided. Free association or independence would result in the loss of American citizenship for island residents, an undesirable prospect for most Guamanians. A public opinion poll was part of the study; it confirmed that a majority of island residents was dissatisfied with the status quo and desired closer ties with the United States. The study concluded that commonwealth status along the lines of the CNMI model would be the most feasible and beneficial option for Guam, both politically and economically.

In May 1980, the legislature created Guam's third political status commission, called this time the Commission on Self-Determination, along with five task forces, one for each major status option, including commonwealth. Each task force was to prepare a study of its option and explain it in an island-wide education campaign to culminate in a September 1981 referendum in which the people would decide the status that they desired for Guam. The commission was also to draft a Territorial-Federal Relations Act to be voted on at the same time. This task was undertaken by Attorney Charles H. Troutman of the Guam Law Revision Commission.

With these steps, the people and government of the island launched a formal quest for a new political status. Over the next ten years, the pursuit of the phantom of political self-determination would be a major priority of the island's governments. Other events, however, would intervene to make economic issues, particularly Japanese economics, not political issues, the main determinants of the island's development in the 1980s.

15 Unfinished Quests 1980–1990

Land Claims, the Papal Visit, and a Strike

For many Guamanians, the decade of the 1980s started off with the happy possibility of obtaining monetary redress in court for the massive acquisition of their property by the navy after World War II. About 600 land claims reached the courts in 1980 after the 1977 Omnibus Territories Act reopened the issue of post–World War II land condemnations by the navy. Won Pat aroused appetites enormously on the island when he estimated that retroactive compensation for land claims could be $500 million, which with interest since World War II might ultimately reach $3.5 *billion.*

Guamanian hopes dimmed when District Court Judge Cristobal C. Duenas dismissed the first major case, *Stanley Castro Limtiaco v. United States of America,* in 1981. But on appeal on 29 April 1982 the U.S. Ninth Circuit Court reversed and remanded Duenas' judgment. The appellate judges reasoned that the condemnations before the old navy courts were not "contested cases" in that persons whose land was condemned had not appeared to contest the condemnations because to do so was largely useless. With this victory for Guamanians, more of them filed claims, reaching a total of 1,377 claims for 3,525 parcels of condemned land. In March 1983, all the cases were merged into a class action with seventy-three-year-old John Bohn—who had worked on the cases for

years—as chief counsel along with twenty-one other attorneys.

On 25 May 1983, the U.S. Justice Department offered to settle all the claims out of court for a total payment of $39.5 million. Since the earlier overblown estimates had raised exaggerated expectations, $39.5 million outraged the claimants, now organized into the Guam Landowners Association with Bohn as executive director. Bohn accepted the offer without consulting the association, which then fired him (he still, however, represented litigants in the class action suit). The issue of fairness was reviewed by District Court Judge Robert Peckham, who decided in June 1984 the offer was fair even though he disregarded the undue influence that the navy had exercised in setting the postwar land values. A majority of the claimants then accepted the settlement, and money was eventually prorated among the 5,200 former owners and heirs on the basis of ex post facto evaluations of their former properties as of the 1940s. Some 200 disgruntled claimants, mostly those with the largest claims, refused the settlement; they or their heirs continued legal action, which was still going on in the 1990s with about $6 million yet to be prorated of the accrued total award of over $42 million for all claimants.

The class action litigation over private land

265

claims did not affect military retention of the parcels for which compensation was sought. GovGuam itself sued the federal government in 1984 under the U.S. Quiet Title Act to recover excess land still held by the navy, but the case was dismissed in 1986 as beyond the statute of limitations by a mere twelve days. By then, the navy had begun to release more parcels of excess military land, initially over 900 acres in 1983 near the Commercial Port.

In spite of such transfers, land held by the government (military-federal and GovGuam) in 1984 was still over 50 percent of the island's total area of 136,960 acres, only slightly lower than the 51 percent held in 1946. The military-federal proportion was 42,478 acres, or about 32 percent in 1984, of which most was military land, according to the 1984 Guam Land Use Plan. That plan reported GovGuam holdings as 26,036 acres, or 18 percent, and the remaining 68,446 acres were in private hands. Return of more military land moved closer in 1986 after the Arny report—named after then–Deputy Assistant Secretary of the Navy L. Wayne Arny III—recommended that 3,546 acres of excess military property be returned to civilian hands. Later, with the downsizing of military bases in the early 1990s, a whopping 28,389 acres of military land would become potentially excess to defense needs. Transfers to GovGuam of such acreage, however, were delayed by red tape, involving congressional approval and the processing of transfers through the U.S. General Services Administration, and by plans of the Defense and Interior departments to establish wildlife refuges on much of the property. Consequently, by the early 1990s, the amounts of Guam's land held, respectively, by the military and federal agencies, by GovGuam, and by private owners would be little changed since 1984, or even since 1946.

While unresolved land issues smoldered on in the 1980s, the Calvo-Ada administration faced more immediate problems when GovGuam employees sought a wage increase. In 1980, full-time Gov-Guam workers numbered 9,056. With 27 percent of all jobs, public and private, government still constituted the largest employer on Guam. In turn, the main union in GovGuam was the Guam Federation of Teachers (GFT), with nearly 2,400 members, most of whom were DOE statesider teachers. About half of all DOE teachers were statesiders, many of whom were hired on contract for a few years at the same salaries as local hires. Chamorros and Filipinos made up the other 50 percent of DOE teachers and most of the large DOE central administrative staff; they were nearly all local hires, and most did not belong to the GFT.

Teachers' salaries, which are on a different scale than GovGuam civil service positions, consistently lagged behind the national average. Moreover, inflation had diminished purchasing power on Guam, while income stagnated from the 1960s into the early 1980s, particularly for professionals in education, law, and medicine. Low salaries, inflation, and Guam's high cost of living provoked the GFT to launch a petition to place a referendum question on the ballot for the November 1980 election: whether GovGuam employees should receive a 30 percent cost-of-living salary adjustment. The petition drive failed, but, since it was an election year, the legislature responded with a bill of modest GovGuam pay increases. Governor Calvo signed the pay bill in August 1980 as financially reasonable. The bill, however, did not satisfy the three unions on the island (the GFT, the Operating Engineers Local 3, and the small new Chamorro Employees Labor Union, CHELU).

This situation became explosive when the senators of the lame-duck Fifteenth Guam Legislature gave themselves, their staffs, and GovGuam directors and judges—but not ordinary GovGuam workers—munificent raises in December 1980 without a hearing or a floor debate. Senatorial salaries jumped $7,020, or 27 percent, to $26,000 a year, one of the highest incomes of all U.S. state legislators even though Guam is smaller than any state.

Outraged, union leaders screamed, "Double-cross!" On 19 December, the GFT held a rally at the Paseo basketball court in Agana of "350 to

1,000" people (depending on who counted, the police or GFT). By a show of hands, they overwhelmingly voted for a strike action if not given a 30 percent raise. The same day, Governor Calvo—caught in the middle between the legislature and the GFT—vetoed the senatorial raise.

Apprehensive of GFT's confrontational mood, on 23 December CHELU (the word *chelu* also means "brother/sister" in Chamorro) withdrew its support of any strike action. The senators then overrode the governor's veto on 31 December, the last day of the Fifteenth Guam Legislature, by a fifteen to zero vote. The governor called the override an insult but sternly warned that he would dismiss any employees who went out since strike actions by government employees are illegal under Guam law. The GFT then held a hasty vote by written ballot on 7 January on the strike question; of the 75 percent of the membership who voted, 70 percent wanted to strike. Calvo swiftly sought an injunction to block the strike, and Superior Court Judge Janet Weeks granted it on 10 January 1981.

The GFT leaders ignored the court order. On 12 January, they launched the island's first mass strike (a small GFT strike action had occurred in 1975 over class sizes). The union estimated that 1,500 GovGuam employees were out the first day, including nonteachers, but that total was inflated. The *Pacific Daily News* reported that, of 1,464 classroom teachers, 758 did not report to work, mainly statesiders. Of these, 749 were suspended by DOE Director Dr. Katherine Bordallo Aguon.

Picket lines appeared at schools. Of the 27,000 or so public school students, over half stayed home the first day of the strike. School bus drivers, nearly all Chamorros, joined the strike, as did some school aides and several dozen faculty at GCC and UOG. Some members of the Operating Engineers Local 3 went out, mostly port employees, but they soon returned to their jobs. The strike then became a GFT versus GovGuam action.

By the end of January, strikers totaled about 900 people. Since this number was only about 10 percent of all GovGuam workers, the strike was doomed. This lack of support, however, was not apparent at first to the GFT leadership owing to the passionate feelings aroused in the first few weeks of hectic confrontations. Dr. Katherine Aguon appealed to the public not to allow the strike to harm the island's children. This appeal was effective. As of February, Guam's public school system was still functioning with double class sessions in high schools taught by nonstriking and substitute teachers. Absent students in the meantime began to drift back to school.

On 3 February, twenty days into the strike, DOE Director Aguon fired 649 of the suspended teachers. She also announced the hiring of 224 "qualified" replacements, many of whom were not certified by U.S. teaching standards. They were heckled as scabs by strikers on the picket lines. On 4 February, Judge Weeks levied a fine on the GFT of $2,000 for each workday missed by not complying with her injunction.

Instances of petty violence—fights, spitting, slashing of tires—erupted at picket lines. On 7 February, the GFT staged a sit-in at the legislature. Police arrested sixty-one protesters, mostly statesiders. The *Pacific Daily News* ran a photograph of several Guamanian policemen carrying GFT Executive Director Marcia Hartsock out of the legislative hall.

Discussions began between Governor Calvo and GFT President Conrad Stinson. The GFT proposed that Bishop Flores act as mediator. Flores declined, and, in a 16 February letter to Stinson, Calvo reiterated, "There is no money for a pay raise." Discussions with the GFT were halted by the governor when pickets appeared at residences of GovGuam officials. At Government House, fifteen UOG professors dressed in formal academic caps and gowns circled the entrance in a lighthearted gesture. The president of the university, Dr. Rosa Roberto Carter, fired all fifteen, regardless of tenure.

The situation turned into a clash of values between statesiders (the majority of strikers) on one side and Chamorros and Filipinos (most of whom stayed on the job) on the other side. The statesiders tended to be non-Catholic, liberal in outlook, and individualistic in behavior. At work, many dressed (unlike most Chamorro and Filipino teachers) in shorts, T-shirts, and zories. The casual attitude of statesiders was perceived by many Guamanians as a lack of respect *(tai respetu)* for the teaching profession and for students. Chamorros and Filipinos have always held teaching in high esteem.

When Governor Calvo, joined by Bishop Flores, appealed for the support of the government, they often spoke in Chamorro. They noted that the cultural traditions of the island rested on interdependence and cooperation—*ina'fa'maolek* in Chamorro—not on confrontations with authority. Leaders of a new Chamorro group, the Organization of People for Indigenous Rights, or OPI-R (like CHELU and other local titles, the name was a play on Chamorro words: *oppe* means "to speak out," in this case for rights), which had replaced Para Pada, agreed with the governor and declared themselves against the strike.

A Chamorro core value is the avoidance of *mamahlao,* the shame or embarrassment of a family when one of its members acts in a self-serving or confrontational way. Linked to *mamahlao* is the local tradition of respect for a *patrón*—a person of authority, a protector, or a benefactor—who assists a family by providing jobs or other benefits to its members. For Chamorros, the most authoritative benefactors on Guam are the governor and the bishop. Furthermore, Chamorros were reluctant to strike against their kinsmen or their *kumpaile, kumaile,* and *mangga'chong*—godparents and close friends in *pare* networks—employed by GovGuam. Thus, many Guamanians perceived the 1981 strike as an assault by outsiders against local authority and traditions.

Politically, the strike tended to pit Democrats against the Republican administration and the Sixteenth Guam Legislature, where Republicans held a majority. Democratic leader Ricky Bordallo, who was already campaigning to take the governorship in the 1982 election, came to GFT rallies with Madeleine Bordallo—then a new senator—to show support and counsel compromise.

In the midst of the strike, His Holiness Pope John Paul II visited Guam in February 1981. The papal visit grew out of efforts begun back in the 1950s by Father Oscar Calvo and Father Juan M. H. Ledesma—a Filipino Jesuit scholar—to seek beatification of Father Diego Luís de San Vitores. They undertook research in Spain and the Philippines in the 1960s and translated into English a Spanish biography of San Vitores, *The Apostle of the Marianas,* by the Jesuit historian Alberto Risco. In 1968, the Guam Vicariate completed an imposing new open-air shrine at the site of San Vitores' martyrdom at the east end of Tumon at Naton Beach, then still largely empty of hotels and other buildings.

Father Calvo's gradual loss of eyesight halted his active participation in research, but the beatification effort was carried on by Bishop Flores with Father Ledesma in the 1970s. In the late 1970s, when Flores learned that Pope John Paul II planned to visit the Philippines and Japan, the Guamanian prelate invited him to Guam. The pope accepted, and, on 22 February 1981, he stepped off a Philippines Airlines jet to kneel and kiss the ground of Guam. He concluded the arrival ceremony with the gentle Chamorro words, "Hu guiya todos hamyu!" (I love all of you!).

The next day he celebrated an open-air mass at the Plaza de España with a crowd of 15,000–25,000 people. He also unveiled a sign to change Agana's Saylor Street to Chalan Santo Papa Juan Pablo Dos. Guamanians later erected a monument to John Paul II, a life-size bronze statue that rotates 360 degrees, to the delight of Japanese tourists, on a traffic island in the middle of Chalan Santo Papa, where he celebrated the mass. The pope ignored the teachers' strike during his twenty-four-hour stay on the island.

With the departure of the pope, all eyes on Guam turned once more to the strike. The Sixteenth Guam Legislature, still with a Republican majority and with sixteen incumbent carryovers, did nothing to resolve the massive problem created by the Fifteenth Legislature. The American Federation of Teachers (AFT) provided interest-free loans to Guam's strikers. The AFT also sent experts to the island to help the GFT in negotiations. When negotiations resumed, the head of the GovGuam team, now Calvo's executive assistant, Matt Lonac, the former manager of Calvo's hardware business, outmaneuvered the GFT team led by Conrad Stinson by playing on the need to compromise.

A problem for the union was that the GFT leadership did not have a real negotiating strategy since the strike had been a spontaneous reaction to the legislature's unexpected pay raise for its own members. The strikers, in Stinson's words, would simply hold out "as long as it takes" for the 30 percent raise. The GFT also demanded that DOE rehire all teachers on strike and return the high schools to a single session. All this time Dr. Aguon succeeded in keeping the schools open. With the GFT negotiators conveniently uncompromising, Lonac went on talking but made no concessions while he waited for the dwindling bank accounts of the payless strikers to decide the issue.

Lonac proved correct. Strikers began to drift back to work as the negotiations droned on. Finally, on 11 March, the *Pacific Daily News* headlined, "GFT CALLS IT QUITS." Stinson had lamely announced the previous day, "We declared unilateral peace." Some 500 strikers, their money and patience running out, had voted on 10 March to end the fifty-eight-day walkout. Governor Calvo appeared on television to offer 200 jobs in DOE with no reprisals to strikers who applied for those specific jobs. By then, 303 substitute teachers had been hired and were kept on the rolls. Many strikers accepted the governor's offer, but over 200 others—some of them the most qualified teachers, including UOG professors—departed Guam with their families. Bus drivers returned to work and on 8 June reached agreement with DOE for back pay. The GFT paid a $35,000 fine to the Superior Court for breaking the injunction.

By 1982, the school system was generally back to normal operations, but settlements of individual striker cases dragged on through the Guam Civil Service Commission and the courts for years. The courts decided the initial twenty-day suspensions of strikers by DOE Director Aguon were illegal. In February 1984, the second Bordallo administration resolved most of the last legal matters for those who had returned to work.

The futile strike of 1981 damaged Guam's educational system and the GFT. The union never regained the influence that it possessed in late 1980. In 1984, the GFT claimed a membership of about 800, but an economic directory that year reported that it was a mere 535. Eight years later, membership reached about 1,400, far less than in 1981 and still largely statesiders. Uncertified teachers hired temporarily in the strike were grandfathered into DOE with provisional certifications and became permanent hires. Striker versus nonstriker antipathy persisted for years, and the quality of public education on Guam suffered. This deterioration was evident when Guam's public high school students repeatedly scored lower than most students elsewhere in the nation on Scholastic Aptitude Tests for years following the strike.

Every new DOE director in the 1980s and early 1990s (all were political appointees, some without doctorates; one was a lawyer) announced plans to improve education on Guam, yet management of DOE was lethargic—at times incompetent—and much classroom teaching remained mediocre. As on the U.S. mainland, administrators (mostly school principals and central staff) were rewarded with more money and power than classroom teachers, drawing many of the latter into graduate studies in educational administration and other nonsubstantive degrees that led them away from the classrooms to the detriment of quality instruction. Uncertified teachers continued to be hired, and school facilities failed to keep pace with population growth. Military parents complained that their children came home speaking English with strange accents and broken syntax learned at school. In the late 1980s, the military services considered establishing a Department of Defense (DOD) school system for their dependents on Guam because of the poor quality of Guam's schools. The DOE would thereby lose the large annual DOD subsidy. A separate military system was averted by a DOE-navy agreement negotiated by a sympathetic COMNAVMAR, Rear Admiral T. J. Johnson (1987–1990), that requires English-language testing of DOE teachers and remedial training of those who fail. In the meantime, private schools—St.

John's Episcopal School and other religious academies—where standards remained high, saw their enrollments surge as many island parents removed their children from public schools.

The root cause of Guam's many problems with public education was the Organic Act, which gave excessive appointive power over DOE to the governor and budgetary control to the legislature, resulting in politicization and bureaucratization of the system. Yet no serious effort was undertaken by Guam's leaders to have the Organic Act amended to provide for an elected school board with independent authority over the DOE budget (i.e., power to raise school funds through real estate taxes), as in most American school districts. The other solution is implementation of a constitution for Guam that accomplishes the same aim of depoliticization, but after the defeat of the draft constitution in 1979 a new constitution became contingent on a change in Guam's political status. The teachers' strike of 1981 also had a political impact, but of a paradoxically divided nature: many senators who had provoked the strike by their pay raise were reelected over and over again in the years ahead by Guam's forgiving electorate, who viewed them as defenders of local traditions and authority during the strike. On the other hand, Governor Calvo, who was perhaps least responsible for the strike and who led the opposition to it, would not be treated so kindly by the voters in the 1982 elections.

By 1982, Calvo's economic policies had disappointed his supporters, particularly the business community, which was now becoming sizable. The GovGuam payroll, which in 1978 Calvo had promised to trim, instead swelled by 22 percent. The deficit had ballooned to $83.3 million in 1982, $10.7 million above the deficit that Calvo had inherited in 1978.

To increase electric power production, Calvo proposed a $100–$150 million ocean thermal energy conversion plant off Cabras Island. Such plants had proved practical in Japan and Nauru, but the financing of Guam's plant fell through, and little was done to provide for the inevitable increase

in future power demand. In 1982, once-prosperous GORCO was in trouble because of tax problems and the drop in the military's need for fuel. In 1984, the GORCO refinery, Guam's only significant industrial entity, closed.

In addition to Calvo's economic and strike headaches, he—like Bordallo—compounded his problems by quarreling with his lieutenant governor. The result was that he dropped Joe Ada from his ticket in the 1982 gubernatorial race, replacing him with a personable young attorney, Peter F. (Pete) Perez, Jr., from one of Guam's most prominent families, the Gollo-Perez clan. Calvo's problems mounted when another Republican ticket challenged him in the primary: the team of Senators Kurt Moylan and Frank F. Blas.

The Democrats also offered two tickets in the 1982 primary. To avoid another split with his number two, Ricky Bordallo picked a political newcomer as his running mate: fifty-two-year-old Colonel Edward Diego Reyes of the U.S. Air Force. A decorated Vietnam War veteran, Eddie Reyes promptly retired from the air force (after twenty-eight years of service) and returned to Guam to run with Bordallo. The other Democratic ticket was headed by Rudy Sablan, who ran again with Joe Leon Guerrero.

In the primaries, Bordallo-Reyes swamped Sablan–Leon Guerrero by a 35 percent margin. Calvo-Perez easily beat Moylan-Blas by 12 percent. In the campaign for the general election, the main tactic of the Calvo-Perez team, using the incumbent governor's authority, was to mount a massive program to asphalt miles of the island's unpaved roads, including the private driveways of constituents. Bordallo-Reyes launched a lively multimedia campaign under the classical Democratic slogan "People First."

The race for Guam's delegate in Washington took on special interest in 1982 when Won Pat was challenged by a political outsider who, like Eddie Reyes, was a retired military officer. This was Vicente Garrido (Ben) Blaz, a former brigadier general in the U.S. Marine Corps. When he retired in 1981, Blaz was the highest-ranking Guamanian in the armed forces. Won Pat had weathered a strong challenge in the 1980 election by Republican Tony Palomo, but in Blaz in 1982 he faced an opponent who not only called for new blood in Washington but also demonstrated ties with the Reagan White House.

In the meantime, Calvo ran into more problems when his hasty road-paving project turned sticky. The federal comptroller's office, that annoying thorn in the side of GovGuam, revealed that money used for driveways was from the federal highway fund; such use was improper. Some private contractors doing the paving overcharged GovGuam through questionable or nonexistent contracts, while others who performed the work were not paid.

The charges hurt Calvo's image, and the aggressive, unpredictable Bordallo put the moderate, reserved Calvo on the defensive. Bordallo had political talents that other candidates on Guam lacked: a keen awareness of public opinion and the ability to attract—and manipulate—the media. He also had the capacity to surprise, which drew large crowds to hear him. For example, as a dramatic campaign climax, the Bordallo-Reyes ticket rented the entire amusement park of entrepreneur Mark V. Pangilinan in Yigo with free rides and fireworks, attracting a huge and happy crowd.

On his part, Calvo resorted to hiring temporary GovGuam workers—1,427 of them—to garner votes. These "Ninety-day wonders" cost taxpayers about $4 million but did not quite tip the electoral balance. Bordallo-Reyes won by 1,402 votes, slightly less than a 5 percent edge out of the 28,996 total votes. Won Pat squeaked by Ben Blaz with only 718 votes, a thin victory that assured a Won Pat versus Blaz rematch in the next election. The 1982 election also ended the eight-year Republican control of the legislature. A majority of fourteen Democrats swept into the Seventeenth Guam Legislature on the coattails of Bordallo-Reyes.

Following his reelection in 1982, Bordallo mounted the most extravagantly flamboyant inaugural in Guam's history in the Plaza de España on 3 January 1983, despite the recession that was under way. In the dense rhetoric of his long inaugural speech, he called for an "economic rearmament" of Guam and attainment of commonwealth status for the island.

The Status Search and Another Boom

Guam's quest for a new political status stumbled off to a hesitant start in January 1982 when the first official referendum was held to determine which status the people of Guam desired. Originally scheduled for September 1981, the referendum had to be postponed when the Commission on Self-Determination was unable to complete its preparatory work in time. But the public was not really interested: only 37 percent of Guam's normally conscientious electorate voted on 12 January on the seven options presented. Commonwealth—defined in the ballot along the lines of the 1975 CNMI covenant—was picked as the preferred option, but by a plurality, not a majority, of 49 percent over second-place statehood at 26 percent. Ten percent chose the status quo, and each of the other options received less than 10 percent.

Because no option received a majority, the legislature scheduled a second referendum, with commonwealth and statehood as the only choices, to coincide with the regular primary on 4 September 1982, when voter interest would be higher. Eighty-two percent of the registered voters turned out and chose commonwealth again over statehood by 73 to 27 percent. Guam finally had a definite status goal.

With Bordallo's election in November 1982, the old Republican-controlled Commission on Self-Determination dissolved while the new Democratic administration and legislature considered how to attain commonwealth status. Bordallo decided on a strategy that went beyond commonwealth. His ultimate goals were reunification of the Chamorro people and then statehood for the Marianas once they were united. The sequence that he saw to attain these ends was as follows. First, make Guam a commonwealth equal in status to the CNMI. Second, draft and implement a constitution compatible with commonwealth status (the constitution could also reform GovGuam, such as curbing the governor's appointive powers and halting legislative use of riders to sneak through bills). Third, reunify the Marianas under one constitution; unification is the only way either Guam or the CNMI has a chance of becoming a state (the precedent is Hawai'i, which would never have become a state if it had been divided as are the Marianas). Finally, seek statehood as a united Commonwealth of the Marianas.

Bordallo knew that this long-range strategy on political status faced formidable obstacles. Therefore, he revealed his vision only to a few advisers while he undertook the process one step at a time. As a beginning, he convened a working group to expand an informal draft version of the commonwealth act written by Charles Troutman. While that draft was being rewritten, he decided to initiate talks with Interior to lead to formal negotiations as had taken place with the Northern Marianas. In June 1983, Bordallo wrote a letter to the head of OTIA, Pedro Sanjuan, with a list of issues as the basis of talks. Sanjuan politely acknowledged the letter and then did nothing.

As a result of OTIA's tepid response to Bordallo, Won Pat introduced a resolution in Congress that called on President Reagan to designate an executive official to negotiate a status change with Guam. This effort failed when neither OTIA nor the White House endorsed the resolution. The picture brightened in July 1983 when Won Pat led a five-man congressional delegation to visit Guam. Won Pat's staunch ally, Phil Burton, had died, leaving Guam in need of new congressional supporters. One such supporter was with the July delegation, a Republican from New Mexico, Manuel Lujan, Jr., who was vice chair of the House Interior and Insular Affairs Committee (he would later become the secretary of the interior under President George Bush). Lujan and the other congressmen suggested that Guam submit a commonwealth act directly to Congress, thereby bypassing footdragging by the Reagan-Bush administration.

This suggestion was followed by a letter in October 1983 to Governor Bordallo and Carl Gutierrez

(speaker of the legislature at the time) from Lujan and Morris K. Udall, Democrat of Arizona and chair of the House Interior and Insular Affairs Committee. They invited Guam to follow the legislative route rather than negotiating with the executive branch. Bordallo and Gutierrez responded positively, and Won Pat then invited them to meet him and Lujan in Albuquerque (Lujan's home office) in December to discuss procedures to bring about the change.

At Albuquerque on 7 December, a large bipartisan delegation of Guam's leaders committed themselves to submitting a commonwealth act as a working draft, not as a final unchangeable document, to Congress by June 1984, a mere six months. Lujan told the Guamanians to throw everything they wanted into the draft to expand local autonomy, including "the kitchen sink," but they must be prepared to compromise and to negotiate substantive changes in the bill. The commonwealth act was to replace the 1950 Organic Act, but this time the people of Guam would vote on the version Congress passed.

In January 1984, the Eighteenth Guam Legislature established a new bipartisan Commission on Self-Determination with representatives from the three branches of government, the public, and the village Commissioner's Council. Governor Bordallo was chair. For legal counsel, the commission retained Washington attorney Arnold H. Leibowitz, the respected federal-territorial law expert who had assisted earlier Guam political status commissions and the constitutional convention. Charles Troutman, by then compiler of laws for the legislature, also continued to serve as an on-island legal adviser to the commission. By early 1985, well past the Albuquerque target date, the commission produced a semifinal synthesis, called Working Draft 4, crafted by Leibowitz from various versions.

The heart of the act in terms of federal-territorial relations was that Guam would remain under U.S. sovereignty but that the Congress would allow the island's citizens corporate control of their own government under their own constitution. Guam's people sought protection from federal authority in a manner similar to that enjoyed by citizens of the U.S. states. Of more direct impact, the Department of the Interior's oversight of Guam would cease, as would other colonialist federal controls such as the Jones Act, which limited shipping between Guam and other U.S. ports to American flag carriers only, a restriction that did not apply to the Virgin Islands.

Guam's version of commonwealth, unlike those of Puerto Rico or the CNMI, aimed at eliminating unincorporated status under the old *Insular Cases* by making the island an integral part of the United States even if Guam is never fully incorporated as a state. Guam would thus move closer to the United States and no longer be a mere "possession" of the federal government. The result, it was hoped, would be greater certainty in Guam's relationship with the United States without precluding an alternative status—either statehood or independence—in the future. Commonwealth status, however, cannot make Guam a member of the U.S. Electoral College (which is gained only by statehood or a constitutional amendment), so the act did not call for Guam's citizens to be given the privilege of voting in U.S. presidential elections.

The Guam commission explored congressional reactions to the act on visits to Washington in late 1984 and 1985. Reactions were favorable, but Udall recommended that the people of Guam not vote on the draft prior to its submission. He noted that Congress would inevitably alter the act, thereby disappointing the people of Guam if they had already voted on the text.

Udall's suggestion was not followed because of concern on Guam with two issues—actually different sides of the same coin—that from the Chamorro point of view were not sufficiently addressed in the draft: Chamorro self-determination and the protection of the indigenous people and their culture from being submerged by outsiders. The 1980 census revealed that Guamanians of Chamorro descent had slipped from a majority to a plurality of the island's inhabitants. The decline of the indigenous people on Guam as a proportion of the island's population since 1940 is shown in Table 2.

TABLE 2: POPULATION OF GUAM, 1940–1990

	Chamorros	Non-Chamorros*	Total
1940	20,177 (91%)	2,113 (9%)	22,290
1960	34,762 (52%)	32,282 (48%)	67,044
1980	47,845 (45%)	58,134 (55%)	105,979
1990	57,648 (43%)	75,504 (57%)	133,152

*Includes U.S. military personnel and dependents.
Sources: 1940–1980: *Guam's People*, (1988, Table 8.3, 138, from U.S. Bureau of Census reports). 1990: *Census '90: 1990 Census of Population and Housing . . . Guam*, (Washington, D.C.: U.S. Department of Commerce, U.S. Government Printing Office, 1992), Tables 11, 21. (Note: The 1990 census on Guam was bungled, and it is generally assumed that the population was several thousand higher than the official figure.)

Despite being only a plurality of residents on Guam after 1980, Guamanians of Chamorro descent still were the majority of voters throughout the 1980s since many newcomers—Micronesians, military personnel, and temporary residents not U.S. citizens—were ineligible or not registered to vote. Nonetheless, unchecked immigration by aliens and emigration by statesiders and U.S. nationals will diminish Chamorro political control of the island. Thus, defenders of Chamorro rights fear that American pluralism perpetuates what they perceive as the cultural and political victimization of Chamorros on Guam.

OPI-R members and many average Guamanians in the 1980s saw commonwealth as a transition status that could pry loose the federal American stranglehold on Guam while expanding local (i.e., Chamorro) control. They pressed for provisions in the act that would promote Chamorro self-determination and give GovGuam control of immigration and authority to determine what federal laws would apply to the island. Many OPI-R suggestions were adopted through the work of commission members Paul Bordallo and Rudy Sablan, who moderated OPI-R language for inclusion in the act. The commission did not agree to OPI-R's most radical demand, that only Chamorros be permitted to vote on the act. The issue of who would vote on a constitution (Chamorros only or all registered voters) once the act was approved was left to be decided in the future. In a political definition, the act stated that the indigenous Chamorro people are "all those born on Guam before August 1, 1950, and their descendants."

Apprehensive that the act might infringe on sovereign federal powers, in early 1985 Congressman Udall recommended substantive revisions in the draft, the most significant being a request to remove wording that required Guam's approval of major changes in military bases and a provision that gave Guam's congressional delegate near veto power over the applicability of federal law to Guam. Udall stated that, if these changes were made, the commonwealth act would be approved in the fall of 1985 by the House of Representatives. Udall's proposals appeared reasonable to Bordallo—who well understood the political reality that Guam must compromise to get the act through Congress—and the governor knew that Udall had the clout to assure the act's passage.

Bordallo also intended to write into Guam's future constitution those provisions—notably protection of Chamorro rights—that Congress might reject in the draft commonwealth act. Guam's quest would thus not depend solely on the commonwealth bill but would follow a two-step negotiating scenario to seek by local Guam law that which Congress objected to as federal law. So, at the 16 April 1985 session of the commission, Bordallo recommended that Udall's suggestions be accepted at the next meeting.

Immediately, the OPI-R and Republican leaders objected to Bordallo's proposal. At the next meeting on 18 April, Senator Joe Ada appeared and threatened to withdraw Republican support of the act if Bordallo gave in to Udall. Ada believed that Guam had to stand firm against any watering-down of Chamorro aspirations; he would rely only on the commonwealth act in an all-or-nothing-at-all strategy. Governor Bordallo and other commission members, mindful of the need for unified support of the act, then rejected Udall's suggestions. Wording was instead toughened to give GovGuam

mutual consent on any changes to the act and on any federal laws applicable to Guam and greater control over land and over the 200-mile oceanic Exclusive Economic Zone (EEZ), immigration, and trade. Overall, Guam's act asked for more autonomy than the CNMI had obtained, notably in mutual consent powers.

After the rebuff of Udall, attitudes toward the act split into ethnic lines on Guam and into a Guam versus Washington dichotomy overall. A quick study issued in May 1986 by the Congressional Research Service questioned the constitutionality of many of the act's provisions. Congressional committee and staff members in Washington shifted from being allies to being passive adversaries of the act as it became pro-Chamorro in content. Statesider residents of Guam disliked Section 102, which promoted Chamorro self-determination. Guamanians of Filipino origin opposed Article 7, which would place Guam outside the United States for immigration and thereby reduce opportunities for Filipino-Americans on the island to bring in relatives for naturalization.

An event that slowed the quest for commonwealth was the defeat of Won Pat in the November 1984 election for Washington delegate by Republican Ben Blaz. Won Pat challenged the election results, but he lost, and Blaz was seated in 1985. So ended the outstanding political career of Antonio Borja Won Pat, a career that began prior to World War II and that included the speakership of the Guam legislature a record six times. His public service to the people of Guam was the most helpful of any Guamanian political leader in the postwar era. He died on 2 May 1987 of a heart attack in a hospital near his Washington, D.C., home at the age of seventy-eight. After a state funeral in the Agana Cathedral-Basilica, he was buried in the Piti Cemetery.

Because Won Pat had chaired the House Subcommittee on Insular and International Affairs, he had been in a powerful position to push Guam's quest for commonwealth, which he firmly supported as an interim status necessary to attain statehood. Ben Blaz, on the other hand, while serving with poise in Congress, was a minority Republican in Democratic congresses. Therefore, despite his energetic efforts, Blaz faced greater political obstacles than Won Pat in bringing about compromises and in obtaining majority party support in Washington for passage of legislation favorable to Guam, including the commonwealth act.

By the time the revisions of the draft commonwealth act were completed, it had become emotionally as well as legally controversial, both on Guam and in Washington. This had not been the case with the CNMI covenant. The next step was to hold a plebiscite—contrary to Udall's counsel—on the final draft. This also had not been the case with the CNMI. Guam's political leaders believed that a vote prior to submission to the Congress would demonstrate Guamanian solidarity and thus reduce the chances of revisions in Washington. Guam's senators, however, undercut this goal by their opposition to a possibly divisive status vote at their own regular election in 1986 at which they would have to take stands on commonwealth, so they delayed the plebiscite until August 1987. This loss of momentum slowed Guam's quest for commonwealth to a snail's pace in the following years.

All the while the drafting of the commonwealth act was under way, Ricky Bordallo was launching initiatives in his second administration that were as controversial as those in his first term. In a standard reshuffle, he replaced Republicans in unclassified—and even in some classified civil service—GovGuam positions with loyal Democrats, and he resumed political infighting with the legislature, even though it was now controlled by Democrats. By the 1980s, Guam's political operators were adept at a phenomenon of American politics called "burrowing." Burrowers are political appointees who convert from appointive jobs to civil service positions, avoiding competitive reviews or examinations and remaining on government rolls despite changes in administrations. On Guam burrowers used the *pare* and *patrón* systems to ensure permanent GovGuam employment with its retirement benefits, among the most munificent in the world. The politicization of education in particular intensi-

fied. Later investigations revealed that DOE Director Gloria B. Nelson illegally promoted over 400 DOE personnel, presumably loyal Bordallo Democrats, from 1983 through 1986.

One of Bordallo's first policy initiatives was a bold but bizarre plan to solve the island's power shortage. In March 1983, he signed an agreement with energy entrepreneur Stanley Z. Siegel to explore the use of windmills to generate electricity. The $400 million project called for an initial emplacement of 500 tall propeller-type turbines to be driven by the northeast trade winds. If successful, they would be followed by 4,500 more of the spindly machines all across the mountains of Guam. The legislature's reaction was predictable: "WINDMILLS BLOW SENATORS' MINDS," proclaimed the *Pacific Daily News*. The project died for lack of legislative support.

After the failure of Bordallo's tilt at windmills, no one in GovGuam during the next decade seriously planned for additional big base-load power generators despite the creation of the Public Utilities Commission in October 1984 to comply with Federal Finance Bank regulations to coordinate and improve utility services. Paradoxically, while GPA's politically appointed board and management turned over with each new administration and were thus usually inexpert, the work crews stayed in their jobs and became increasingly skilled. These crews performed valiantly in typhoons and other emergencies. Poor management of GPA and the lack of foresight by Guam's elected leaders to meet rising power needs caused (along with typhoons) the island to suffer recurring electrical outages in the late 1980s and early 1990s when demand outstripped the capacity of Guam's decrepit power system.

One successful Bordallo undertaking in the mid-1980s was construction of a new executive branch office complex in renovated buildings on Adelup Point in an old elementary school condemned because of structural faults. The result was a grandiose jumble of buildings in Spanish style with red-tiled roofs and white walls next to a parade ground (the former school playground). Bordallo was criticized for the project, but later governors happily occupied the premises. Visitors and residents of the island in general now consider the complex a worthwhile addition to Guam's public buildings.

An educational problem that the Bordallo-Reyes administration inherited was the shaky accreditation status of the University of Guam. UOG President Dr. Rosa Carter had been appointed in 1977 during Bordallo's first administration. In June 1978, UOG received the equivalent of an A grade on an accreditation visit by the Western Association of Schools and Colleges (WASC). By 1980, however, UOG was in trouble. GCC was draining away students, and UOG faculty morale dropped after 1978 when Dr. Carter approved only two of twenty-seven faculty members recommended for promotion. Serious accounting and management problems also surfaced. As in primary and secondary public education, administration at UOG, accompanied by politicization, took priority over teaching. After another WASC inspection in June 1981, Dr. Carter received a "warning" for ten deficiencies. Little was done to correct the problems, and UOG lost its off-campus classes on Guam's military bases to the University of Maryland overseas program because of navy and air force dissatisfaction with UOG standards.

After Bordallo was sworn in as governor in January 1983, he appointed new members to the UOG Board of Regents. In May, three UOG professors asked the regents to remove Dr. Carter for reasons of mismanagement and misuse of university funds. The board, chaired by the highly respected attorney J. U. Torres, fired Dr. Carter for these causes on 15 June. She promptly sued the board for $2 million, charging that the regents fired her for political reasons. She was replaced as UOG president in July by Dr. José Q. Cruz, who had been on Bordallo's campaign staff.

Following another WASC inspection in November 1983, UOG was notified in January 1984 that it had slipped to a "show cause" status. The university had to show within a year why accreditation should not be withdrawn. The main deficiency was political interference. The next WASC step—withdrawal of accreditation—means that other educational institutions may not accept UOG credits of students who transfer or who seek graduate degrees elsewhere. Loss of accreditation would also eliminate UOG's popular ROTC program.

The UOG faculty and the new administration of Dr. Cruz worked hard to solve the school's management and academic deficiencies while the legislature passed a law for six-year staggered terms for UOG regents to prevent the governor from packing the board with his appointees and thereby controlling the institution. These reforms did not eliminate political influence at UOG but were sufficient to move the university back to "probation" after a WASC inspection in 1985. Subsequently, the university was taken off probation and began to climb back to acceptable standards under a new president, Dr. Wilfred P. Leon Guerrero, who was appointed in 1987. Dr. Carter lost her suit against the UOG regents, but—in a typically Guamanian act of gracious tolerance—they offered a substantial financial settlement, which she accepted.

Religious leadership in the meantime changed on Guam after the papal visit in 1981. The visit had been a high point in Bishop Flores' stewardship of the Catholic community. Subsequently, Pope John Paul II elevated the Diocese of Agana to an archdiocese as part of a church reorganization throughout the world. On 20 May 1984, Bishop Flores was installed as the first metropolitan archbishop of Agana, and the Vatican also honored Guam by elevating Agana's Dulce Nombre de María to a cathedral-basilica.

In November 1984, the pope announced the beatification of San Vitores, and the Jesuit martyr was formally beatified as the Blessed Diego of the Marianas at an elaborate ceremony attended by many Guamanians in Saint Peter's Basilica in Rome on 6 October 1985. A mass followed at the San Vitores memorial on Naton Beach at Tumon. This shrine, now overshadowed by the high-rise Reef Hotel next to it and blocked from Naton Beach by noisy jet-ski and other tourist concessions and restaurants, is rarely visited. Archbishop Flores, a much beloved man, died during a kidney transplant operation on 25 October 1987 at age sixty-four. Catholic leadership of Guam passed to Anthony Sablan Apuron, O.F.M., D.D., a Guamanian Capuchin, who had been named bishop in February 1984.

While the people of Guam coped in the mid-1980s with the old familiar problems of inadequate electric power, educational and medical deficiencies, and poor roads, an upturn in Guam's economy was gaining momentum. The upturn was due primarily to a massive buildup in Japanese tourism and investments on Guam. Tourism grew primarily because of the Marianas' location; the islands are the nearest and least expensive foreign tropical destinations for Japanese travelers. By 1984, private-sector employment on Guam had jumped nearly 28 percent over 1982. Fourteen commercial banks, two savings-and-loan associations, and three credit unions jostled for the money on Guam. Northwest Airlines joined Continental–Air Micronesia, JAL, and All Nippon Airways (which first began its worldwide expansion with its Guam route) in providing regular flights in and out of Guam. Braniff, however, withdrew from Guam as the airline sank into bankruptcy. Of sadder note was the decline of Pan Am, which ceased flights to the island on 1 April 1984.

By 1985, tourism was adding about $200 million a year to Guam's economy, and property values in the Tumon hotel area and then all over the island began to rise dramatically. The old cottages of the Continental Hotel were bulldozed and replaced with the large, modern Pacific Islands Hotel and Club. The wealthy little island of Nauru initiated construction in 1985 of the luxurious high-rise Pacific Star Hotel under All Nippon Airways management. Another welcome development in 1985 was the advent of regular live television broadcasts by satellite transmissions from the U.S. mainland.

By 1986, hotel rooms on Guam numbered over 3,000, and the number continued to rise. They were needed: in 1988, over 585,000 visitors, predominantly Japanese tourists, came to the island, a 55 percent rise over 1985. Unemployment rates fell. Not even the dramatic stock market crash of October 1987 on Wall Street slowed Guam's boom. The island was becoming more sensitive to Japan's economic health than it was to the U.S. economy. The tourist flow was greatly facilitated when visas were no longer required after 1 October 1988 for citizens of Japan to visit Guam for up to fourteen days (visas, however, were still required for visitors from the Philippines, Taiwan, China, and Korea).

The surge in tourism sparked a boom in construction. H-2 workers again flooded into Guam, this time including Chinese, Koreans, and even Malaysians in addition to Filipinos. Many of these workers encountered the same sly complicity of exploitation between contractors and labor recruiters as had their predecessors, and the Guam Department of Labor would be just as ineffective as in the past in preventing the exploitation.

To finance infrastructure to support economic growth, the Bordallo-Reyes administration turned to bond issues. These alluring bond initiatives, along with the growth of corruption from tolerable small-time bribery of officials for favors—a longestablished practice on Guam—to metapolitical big-time venality at the highest GovGuam levels, would lead to a tragic end for Ricky Bordallo.

Scoundrels, Scandals, and a Suicide

Rumors, speculation, and finally news reports surfaced by mid-1986 that the governor and other officials were being investigated by a federal grand jury. The U.S. attorney in charge of the case was K. William (Bill) O'Connor, a tough and experienced federal prosecutor. The FBI beefed up its Guam office to support the investigation. Both political parties on Guam were preparing for the 1986 gubernatorial elections, so an investigation of the Democratic administration could not have come at a worse time for Bordallo.

Ricky Bordallo and Eddie Reyes had worked together in harmony despite Bordallo's retention of most decisions in his own hands. As a result, they ran again as a team. They mounted a massive

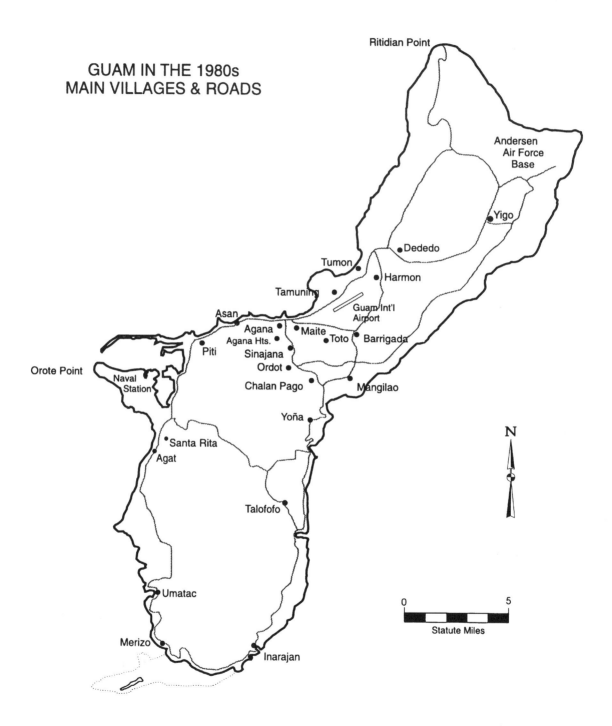

GUAM IN THE 1980s
MAIN VILLAGES & ROADS

Ritidian Point

Andersen
Air Force
Base

Yigo

Dededo

Tumon

Harmon

Tamuning

Guam Int'l
Airport

Asan

Agana
Agana Hts.
Sinajana
Ordot
Chalan Pago

Maite
Toto
Barrigada

Piti

Mangilao

Orote Point

Naval
Station

Yoña

Santa Rita

Agat

Talofofo

Umatac

Merizo

Inarajan

N

0   5
Statute Miles

media campaign, but the themes and platform lacked cohesion. Bordallo was promoted as "the Builder," while Reyes—ironically, as it turned out—chaired a White-Collar Crime Task Force. Their main campaign theme was expressed in the gimmicky slogan "I ♥ Guam," in bright red against a white background.

In the primary, the incumbent team was challenged by Carl Gutierrez, running this time with Senator John Perez Aguon on the "Sunshine" ticket. The Republicans also offered two tickets in the primary: Senators Tommy Tanaka and Antonio R. (Tony) Unpingco against Senators Joe Ada and Frank F. Blas. The Ada-Blas team campaigned under the attractive slogan *"Mauleg"* ("good" in Chamorro) displayed in a benign blue color, notably on television, which was becoming the main means of political compaigning. A lighthearted statesider tandem of Jeff Pleadwell and Bill Roth, owners of Jeff's Pirate Cove Restaurant in Ypan-Talofofo, ran as an independent ticket.

Politics veered into uncharted waters on 3 September, just three days before the primary, when a federal grand jury, like Spanish inquisitions of old, summoned the governor before it. Bordallo read the jury a statement that stigmatized the federal investigation as "a Republican conspiracy to oust him from power." He refused to answer questions and stalked out. Later that day, he was indicted on eleven counts, including extortion, bribery, obstruction of justice, witness tampering, and various conspiracy and wire fraud charges.

These bombshell indictments came too close to the primary on 6 September to change the outcome. Bordallo-Reyes easily defeated Gutierrez-Aguon by over 27 percent of the 16,000 or so Democratic votes. For the Republicans, Ada-Blas beat Tanaka-Unpingco by a 15 percent margin of the 14,000-plus Republican votes. The Pleadwell-Roth team garnered only 760 votes, eliminating them from the general election. The larger Democratic vote in the primary and Bordallo-Reyes' polls as of the first week after the primary showed that the incumbents would easily beat the Ada-Blas challengers in the general election. The Bordallo-Reyes lead, however,

evaporated in the following weeks as reports of new accusations, plea bargaining, and more indictments spewed out in the media like an avalanche of dirty laundry.

On 12 September, Bordallo pleaded not guilty to all charges, and his attorneys asked that the trial be delayed until after the general election. The request was refused by District Court Judge Cristobal Duenas when prosecutor O'Connor revealed that threats had been made on a witness's life because he had agreed to provide evidence and testify against Bordallo. Trial was set for 22 October, thirteen days before the 4 November general election, but was postponed to January 1987 when the FBI uncovered other alleged bribes to Bordallo in connection with a $300 million municipal bond issue on Guam.

By the time of Bordallo's indictment, the taint of corruption had already enveloped GovGuam. This taint was due to investigations, arrests, and trials of lesser GovGuam officials as well as Bordallo family members and business associates, even though some of the offenses predated his administration. Among such trials was the October 1985 conviction on extortion charges of former DOE Director Dr. Katherine Aguon. Five DOE officials were indicted with her, and six vendors were implicated, but only Dr. Aguon ended up serving eighteen months in a federal prison in California. While she was in prison, her conviction was overturned on appeal and remanded. She was never retried after her release from prison and resumed her work on Guam as an educator.

In the Aguon and other cases, the prosecutors employed an investigative method used on the mainland in which the FBI first nailed lower officials, go-betweens, and vendors with evidence of wrong-doing, then pressed them into gathering evidence against unsuspecting higher officials in conversations by wearing hidden tape recorders and using bugged telephones. In return for informing on each other and on higher-ups, suspects were not indicted, or they plea bargained for reduced sentences in their own cases (one exception, Bordallo business associate Danny Leon Guerrero, steadfastly refused to compromise himself or the governor and went to federal prison as a result).

In late October, Bordallo's situation worsened when he blurted out at a UOG lecture and again at a Chamber of Commerce luncheon that he had received $10,000 as a "gift," a kind of *chenchule'* in the governor's words, from businessman Kenneth T. Jones. Jones was later fined $20,050 after pleading nolo contendere to a misdemeanor for exceeding campaign donation limits.

In all these and subsequent proceedings, Lieutenant Governor Reyes was never implicated. Eddie Reyes emerged from all the scandals of the second Bordallo administration with his reputation for integrity unblemished and his support for Bordallo unwavering.

In light of the adverse publicity from the federal indictments and subsequent revelations, it was no surprise when the Bordallo-Reyes ticket lost the general election to the Ada-Blas "Mauleg" team on 4 November. The margin of victory was 2,581 votes, or 7.6 percent. Political scientist Dr. Joe Dizon, the pollster for the Ada-Blas campaign, admitted, "Only one thing did him [Bordallo] in— the *indictment*." Despite losing the gubernatorial race, the Democrats retained their majority in the Nineteenth Guam Legislature with thirteen seats. Delegate Ben Blaz easily triumphed by a 29 percent margin over his Democratic challenger, retired army colonel and former brigadier general in the Guam National Guard Frank C. Torres, Jr.

Bordallo's troubles escalated on 20 November when the federal grand jury handed down a superceding indictment against him on seventeen counts. New charges stemmed from the Ken Jones $10,000 "gift" and for bribes related to the $300 million municipal bond project as well as a new extortion charge that involved government contracts. On 24 November, Bordallo entered a not guilty plea to the new charges, which he still maintained were politically inspired and prompted by overzealousness on the part of U.S. Attorney O'Connor. The bond project turned out to be a gigantic scam, involving not only Guam but also frauds on the mainland by the same bond brokers, a collection of audacious flimflam hustlers who made Levenson and Wilkinson of the GMHP scam look like amateurs.

In March 1985, a short, balding man was shown into Governor Bordallo's office. He had been referred to Bordallo by a prominent Washington attorney. The visitor was introduced as Dr. Frederick L. (Fred) Mann, a banker from Toronto with a Ph.D. from the London School of Economics. Mann had established a bank on Saipan in 1984, and in partnership with a Wall Street investment banking firm, Matthews & Wright Inc., he was trying to package a multimillion dollar bond issue for the Northern Marianas Housing Authority. Fred Mann was charming, sincere, and utterly plausible as a banker.

Mann proposed to Bordallo a $300 million tax-exempt GovGuam mortgage bond issue to finance construction of housing units on Guam through GEDA. A quick survey by Matthews & Wright showed Guam in need of over 4,000 such housing units in 1985. Money from the bond sales could be invested immediately in escrow (in high-yield U.S. Treasury bonds or trust funds, for example) under an arbitrage process whereby GovGuam could earn profits estimated by Mann as $25 million from dividends until the bond money was shifted to finance construction of the housing. Arbitraged bonds, Mann argued, would allow GovGuam to get around a provision in the Organic Act that limits Guam's public obligation bond debt to 10 percent of the assessed value of all land on the island, a limit estimated as $200–$250 million in the mid-1980s.

The arbitrage bond process was due to end by federal law on 1 September 1986. Thus, Guam had to accept Mann's deal quickly. Bordallo was already well aware of arbitrage bonds as a means to finance infrastructure. He had attempted to float GovGuam bonds in the overly ambitious amount of $850 million in 1983 for development projects but was blocked by U.S. Treasury officials skeptical of Guam's ability to repay the bonds.

In October 1985, at Bordallo's request, the Eighteenth Guam Legislature passed Bill 628 to authorize a nonrated municipal bond issue worth $300 million through GEDA for the construction of nearly 5,000 low- and medium-cost, multifamily housing units on Guam. The governor signed the bill into law as P.L. 18–20. He and other GovGuam officials met in New York on Halloween, 31 October, to sign the deal with Matthews & Wright executive Arthur Abba Goldberg (known in banking circles as "Abba Dabba Do" and "Abba Cadabra" for his flashy ways of bond financing) and Edward K. Strauss, a bond counselor. A consortium of twenty-four housing developers was formed on Guam to construct the houses with money to be generated from the bond sales. Several of these developers invested (and some dropped out) in preparation for construction, and some even went to closing on land for their projects. Matthews & Wright also agreed to underwrite another bond issue through GEDA for $1.85 million to construct a computer factory on Guam.

Goldberg arranged financing of the bonds through a New Jersey credit union. Financing for the developers was through the Pittsburg National Bank, and the mortgages for land were escrowed through the Puller Mortgage Company on the mainland. All these entities and persons charged large—very large—up-front fees, which were paid by the developers.

In the meantime, Matthews & Wright was underwriting other huge tax-exempt bond deals in about thirty U.S. municipalities. These bond issues amounted to a fantastic $2.3 *billion*. The deals were primarily in poor communities on the mainland that, like Guam, were in great need of housing and financial assistance. Mann and Matthews & Wright were able to get away with such razzle-dazzle because municipal bonds, unlike corporate securities, were not reviewed by the U.S. Securities and Exchange Commission prior to sale under the freewheeling financial policies of the Reagan-Bush administration. Municipal bonds were floated primarily on the word of bond counselors, such as Edward K. Strauss, under the old adage, "Let the buyer beware."

Bordallo was alerted in July 1985 by OTIA head Richard Montoya, and again by a *Guam Business News* article in February 1986, that Mann and the bond scheme were questionable. The governor went ahead with the deal because Guam needed low-cost housing and because there was no clear evidence that the venture was not sound. Meanwhile, Mann and Matthews & Wright had secretly wired payments for a "campaign contribution" of $70,000 through a Hong Kong front to pay vendors in Hong Kong for posters, brochures, and other campaign paraphernalia for the committee to reelect Bordallo-Reyes. These transactions were arranged by Bordallo's economic adviser, John D. Gilliam, who was also in charge of Bordallo's media campaign in the 1986 election.

The FBI stumbled across the Hong Kong payments while gathering evidence on the earlier bribery case against Bordallo. Prosecutor O'Connor then confronted Gilliam, who agreed to provide evidence of the transactions in return for leniency on a charge of extortion of money from Fred Mann and on other charges of moral turpitude that involved failure to pay returns on stocks that he and his wife sold to GEDA and failure to repay GEDA loans for a communications company they owned.

The whole flimsy house of bonds came crashing down on 19 November 1986, when, in return for providing evidence, Gilliam pleaded guilty in Guam's District Court to one count of wire fraud in the $70,000 "contribution" to the Bordallo-Reyes campaign by Mann and Matthews & Wright. Gilliam's plea agreement in turn led to Bordallo's superceding indictment on 20 November.

It turned out that Fred Mann was really Manfred Lother Mann, born in Leipzig, Germany, before World War II. He had been convicted of defrauding a dying Toronto widow in 1984 of her savings of $64,000. His "Ph.D." was nothing more than an honorary degree bought from a Canadian Bible college. His Saipan bank had been an unlicensed shell with no assets. The credit union in New Jersey through which Mann, Goldberg, and Strauss "financed" bonds for Matthews & Wright was a mere front through which they floated fake checks. In short, Fred Mann was a flimflam man whom even a casual check of his background would have exposed as a complete fraud.

Mann and his conspirators, as well as financial participants such as the Pittsburg National Bank and the Puller Mortgage Company, all made money from the bond issue through the up-front fees. The conspirators put up no money themselves, and the brokers sold no bonds, merely making it appear that they were selling them by fast shuffles of complicated documents. They siphoned off millions in fees from all the deals throughout the United States. Of that amount, an estimated $14–$20 million was fleeced from the taxpayers and developers on Guam, money that was never recovered. No housing units were constructed, nor was the computer factory. The whole swindle was incredible in its boldness and cleverness.

At Bordallo's trial in January–February 1987, charges against members of Bordallo's staff and businessmen who paid bribes were dropped in exchange for testimony against the ex-governor. Prosecutor O'Connor presented over 200 pieces of evidence. On 13 February, the jury acquitted Bordallo of charges in the bond deal but convicted him on ten counts of the original charges of extortion, bribery, and conspiracy. On 3 April, Ricky Bordallo was sentenced to nine years' imprisonment and had to pay a $35,000 fine and $79,600 in restitution. He appealed his conviction and settled down to write his memoirs while awaiting the appellate court decisions.

Elected Governors of Guam

(Guam Public Library, Agana, Guam)

Carlos Garcia Camacho (R, 1971–1974).

Ricardo Jerome Bordallo (D, 1975–1978, 1983–1986).

Matthews & Wright executive Arthur Goldberg pleaded guilty in federal court on the mainland in 1989 to three counts of mail fraud; he paid $125,000 in restitution to GovGuam and served time in a federal prison. Counselor Edward Strauss pleaded guilty to misprision of a felony and was disbarred. Matthews & Wright as a company was sued by many of the firm's victims but got off in its Guam trial because of clumsy prosecution by GovGuam attorneys. Matthews & Wright is still in business.

Under his plea agreement with O'Connor, John Gilliam was given five years probation plus fines and restitution. He paid these off through community service. Only one of the Guam developers fleeced in the bond issue, the Donicker Corporation, pursued litigation against the Pittsburg National Bank to recover costs and damages. Donicker won in the Superior Court of Guam, but appeal of that decision was still undecided as of 1993 in the Ninth Circuit Court.

As for Fred Mann, he fled to Canada, where he fought extradition for years after being indicted on fifty-two counts. He was extradicted to New York in 1993, where in exchange for a guilty plea to one count of racketeering for bribery he was ordered to

Paul McDonald Calvo (R, 1979–1982).

Joseph F. Ada (R, 1987–1990, 1991–1994).

pay a mere $62,500 in restitution and a $30,000 fine and was sentenced to a five-month jail term. This sentence confirms the opinion of many who believe that crime pays, and pays well, in the United States because of the contorted and excessive legalism in the nation's judicial system.

After the dramatic ups and downs of the Bordallo-Reyes years, many Guamanians welcomed the passive conventionality of the Ada-Blas administration. Prior to the 1986 general election, Ada announced that the Commonwealth Act "is the agenda for 1987 and 1988." He reconstituted the Commission on Self-Determination under his chairmanship, and a vote on the Commonwealth Act was held on 3 August 1987. Only 39 percent of Guam's electorate turned out to vote yes or no on each of the twelve articles. The voters rejected by narrow margins Article 1 on the U.S.-Guam political relationship and Chamorro rights and Article 7 on immigration.

The commission then did a minimal rewrite of the rejected articles and scheduled a new plebiscite on the two for 7 November at a special election to fill a seat in the Guam legislature vacated by the sudden death of Senator-elect Marilyn Won Pat, the daughter of the late Tony Won Pat. Concerned that the act's provisions on Chamorro rights might again be rejected, the OPI-R mounted an energetic campaign among Chamorros for a *hunggan* ("yes" in Chamorro) vote. Nearly all incumbent and former political leaders of Guam except Filipinos urged a yes vote. More Chamorros turned out this time, and 58 percent of all registered voters approved both articles by big majorities. Democrat Madeleine Bordallo won the empty Senate seat.

The act was submitted to Congress as H.R. 4100 in February 1988 by Congressman Ben Blaz. Congress referred the bill for study to an unwieldy Federal Interagency Task Force created in June 1988 with representatives from the Department of Interior, Defense, and—incredibly—twenty-one other federal agencies. After George Bush became president in January 1989, he appointed Stella Guerra head of OTIA and chair of the task force (dubbed

by Guam's media as BATFOG—the Bush Administration Task Force on Guam). In August 1989, a leisurely seventeen months after the act had been submitted to Congress, the task force released a long, detailed report critical of most of the act's provisions.

Four and a half months later, in December 1989, the House Subcommittee on Insular and International Affairs—Won Pat's old committee, by then chaired by Ron de Lugo—held a hearing in Honolulu on the draft act. Guam's leaders, OPI-R activists, and many ordinary Guamanians traveled to Honolulu to present emotional pleas in support of the act. De Lugo asked if the Guamanian side was prepared to negotiate compromises in the text. Governor Ada answered that the commission would not negotiate any changes. Ada stated (exactly as Udall had predicted) that the commission could not change the text since it had been approved by the people of Guam in a plebiscite. To Ada's uncompromising stance, Ron de Lugo replied, "That road map . . . is designed for disaster, designed for failure . . . we have to be able to confer and compromise."

De Lugo then directed the federal task force (Stella Guerra had up to then stonewalled status discussions with Guam) to confer with the Guam Commission on Self-Determination to resolve the differences over the act. The two sides proceeded to meet over a dozen times from December 1990 until mid-1992.

In the meanwhile, Governor Ada and the Guam commission discarded the understanding at Albuquerque that commonwealth was intended to move Guam closer to the United States. Instead of Guam becoming a part of the federal system "in union" with the United States, Ada presented a new aim: commonwealth was to be, he said, a "partnership that respects our [Guam's] will." This unyielding stance was applauded by many Chamorros and would help Ada-Blas to win reelection in 1990. Partnership, however, implies equality of sovereignty between Guam and the United States. De Lugo warned that if Guam's new purpose was "really free association with a commonwealth label slapped on it . . . the whole process ends up, no matter what you do, as a bitter, sour process."

That is what occurred. While Ada and the Guam commmission altered Guam's status goal and discarded Bordallo's negotiating scenario, they did not come up with a viable alternative strategy to attain their new goal. Some revisions in the act were agreed to in the BATFOG talks, but lack of agreement to some degree remained on nearly three-quarters of the act, and flat-out disagreement continued on over a third of the issues, including mutual consent, the EEZ, immigration, and the provision on the Chamorro Land Trust. By the end of the Bush-Quayle administration in 1993, and after ten years of effort and great expense (by 1993 Guam was paying a largely unneeded Washington legal counsel an overweening $20,000 per month), Guam's quest for commonwealth was in serious doubt of ever being realized.

While Guam's Commonwealth Act bogged down owing to lack of compromise between Washington and the Ada-Blas administration, the worldwide geopolitics of the Cold War had been undergoing a tremendous transformation. By the late 1980s, Mikhail Gorbachev's policies of *glasnost* (openness) and *perestroika* (restructuring) in Moscow were leading to the breakup of the Soviet Union as an empire and to the death of communism as an ideology. For Guam, the impact of geopolitical changes began back in 1980–1981 when the seven Poseidon missile submarines based at Apra Harbor were withdrawn. That left only attack submarines still operating out of Apra with the *Proteus* as tender.

In the mid-1980s, several pre-positioned ships of the Military Sealift Command began to cruise out of Apra Harbor. Crammed with vehicles, provisions, and munitions, these cargo ships were ready for immediate logistical backup of military interventions by the United States in conventional conflicts such as the 1991 Persian Gulf War. A major change in the air force presence on Guam came in October 1988 when SAC's Forty-third Strategic Wing at Andersen traded its nuclear deterrent role

for a conventional mission. In September 1990, the wing with its last fourteen B-52Gs was phased out of Andersen, which was left largely empty except for the headquarters staff of the Thirteenth Air Force. The B-52s, along with the navy's missile submarines, had been among the most durable and effective weapons of deterrence in the successful containment of the Soviet Union throughout the post–World War II era. As an operational base for those systems, Guam played an incalculably valuable role for the United States in the containment strategy.

Despite the pulldown of U.S. strategic operational forces, Guam continued to be a key communications and support base into the 1990s for CINCPAC resources in the Pacific and Asia. In fiscal year 1990, military expenditures on Guam reached an all-time high of $895 million before declining thereafter. By then, GovGuam officials and Chamorro-rights activists were pressing for the shift of the Naval Air Station to Andersen Air Force Base and transfer of all Brewer Field to civilian control. These goals would be approved in 1993 as U.S. military forces were reduced worldwide. In the meantime, large military expenditures and expanded Japanese tourism and investments produced the most hectic economic boom in Guam's history during the late 1980s and into 1990–1991, despite inadequate infrastructure and the complacently inept management of Guam's public services by the administration of Governor Joe Ada in that period.

By then Japan's *ohte* (lit., its "big hand") dominated Guam's development. The Japan Travel Bureau was the largest tour wholesaler for Guam and helped keep the island's over 4,000 hotel rooms at about an 80 percent occupancy rate. Japanese-financed high-rise luxury condominiums sprang up by the dozens. In Tumon Bay in particular, the exploitation of public property for private profit was carried out heedlessly with the beach and bay invaded by jet-skis, a large ugly dinner boat, and other tourist concessions owned by, catering to, and employing mostly nonlocals. The parable of the tribes was manifesting itself once more on Guam,

People of Guam, 1990

(*Legacy of Guam* by Manny Crisostomo. Guam:
Legacy Publications, 1991)

Ben Meno

Jesus Guerrero Cruz, 79, and sister
Maria Cruz Mafnas, 81.

but this time by alien geo-economic penetration
rather than by predatory military colonialism.

The boom in the late 1980s transformed Tamuning and Tumon into ill-planned part-American,
part-Japanese transcultural clutter. Harmon,
already chaotic through lack of planning, became
an ever more trashy maze of warehouses, garages,
and a teeming weekend flea market. Prostitution in
the form of "massage parlors" proliferated in
Tamuning, and the first HIV cases appeared on
the island. There were also, of course, benefits
from the tourist boom. Guam's first large-scale,

fully enclosed shopping center—the Micronesian
Mall—opened in October 1988 between Harmon
and Dededo. In 1989, a big, glitzy dinner theater,
the Sand Castle, with excellent Las Vegas–style
shows, opened in Tumon. Huge golf course–condo-
minium developments for Japanese tourists rose
along the Mangilao-Marbo coast and in the
Manengon area where fifty years earlier Chamorros had huddled in concentration camps under
Japanese bayonets.

The Department of Public Works struggled constantly to upgrade Guam's highways, but never suf-

Juan Cruz and 1-year-old granddaughter Kailani Cruz.

ing became an impossible dream from Agana through Dededo.

In 1986, the transformation of the TTPI districts other than the CNMI into the FSM and the Republics of the Marshalls and Palau opened the gates for Micronesian emigration to Guam. Under the compacts of free association between Washington and the new states, the latters' citizens are treated as U.S. nationals and may travel without visas to U.S. areas. Enticed by Guam's boom, thousands of Micronesians—mostly from Chuuk (formerly Truk) in the FSM—poured into the island in the late 1980s. Additionally, the numbers of Koreans, Japanese, and Chinese as well as the continued inflow of Filipinos, both as legal and—increasingly—illegal resident aliens, swelled the non-Chamorro population. The new migrants to Guam included a high proportion of women and families, and thus these newcomers did not tend to marry into local families and be absorbed into Chamorro culture as did the predominantly male immigrants in earlier times.

While these expatriates filled many labor needs, thousands also qualified for welfare assistance once on Guam. They added heavily to social pressures on the island's already overloaded educational, health, and criminal justice systems. They often had to crowd into inadequate housing since the Ada-Blas administration, unlike every previous administration since Governor Guerrero, failed to initiate large-scale public housing projects. The result was a severe shortage in low- and medium-priced housing by the 1990s alongside a glut of high-priced luxury condominiums built mostly for Japanese.

Human population pressure began to overstress police capabilities and to jam court calendars on Guam. The quality and responsiveness of island law enforcement and the judicial processes deteriorated. A new prison in Mangilao turned out to be too small and nearly as easy to escape from as its predecessor. Firearms and ammunition of all kinds were easily obtained on Guam, legally or illegally. As a result, from 1986 through 1990, the island's crime index rose by 39 percent, or nearly 10 percent per year. The increase in crime was over three times faster than the population growth of 2.3 per-

ficiently to cope with the enormous growth of vehicular traffic. Low shipping costs from Japan and a steady exchange rate favorable to the yen against the dollar resulted in sales of tens of thousands of Japanese-made trucks and cars on Guam in the 1980s. By 1990, an inordinate 100,796 vehicles were registered for the island population of 133,152. With no reliable public bus system on tiny Guam, automobiles became a superfluous necessity for everyone and a necessary superfluity for all. Traffic jams at peak hours became the norm on the main roads, at times approaching gridlock in the not infrequent power outages, and adequate park-

cent per year on Guam in the same period. Guam was beginning to demonstrate, in the words of ecologist Garrett Hardin, the Malthusian demostat, whereby the human carrying capacity (the number of people multiplied by the physical quality of life) of the central part of the island was being overloaded. Demographic stress causes diseconomies of scale manifested in the ineptitude of public services, creeping political malfunction, and growing social destabilization as traditional values erode.

By 1990, population growth and development had transformed the island into a multiethnic, nontraditional community. On the positive side, unemployment practically disappeared and local incomes soared to the highest levels in Guam's history. On the negative side, the price of profit brought pollution and destroyed the habitat of indigenous flora and fauna. Trash and junk vehicles littered the edges of Guam's roads, quite impervious to the futile cleanup efforts mounted spasmodically by GovGuam agencies and volunteer groups. Evergrowing garbage dumps and the use of pesticides on golf courses began to contaminate the water lens and wells. Many of Guam's reefs were dying from silt runoffs from construction sites. The progeny of brown tree snakes introduced to Guam back in World War II now crawled everywhere, killing off native birds and even attacking small children. Only about 500 *fanihi,* the Marianas fruit bat, survived on Guam by 1990. *Koko,* Guam's unique flightless rail, numbered a mere fifty birds, and overfishing was reducing offshore fish populations. In an irony of nature, the annual red tide of "San Vitores' blood" in Tumon Bay, formerly considered miraculous manifestations of God's concern, ceased to appear. The high-rise hotels along the beach disrupted the flows of fresh water from the plateau above and diluted the dinoflagellates that formerly caused the red tides.

Much construction under the Ada-Blas administration had a detrimental effect on the natural environment since the Territorial Land Use Commission and the Department of Public Works nearly always granted zoning variances and building permits to large projects in the absence of long-range plans for island development. The permit process and its integrity bogged down under the load of requests, so senators regularly passed laws to rezone the property of individuals who wished to bypass the slow regular permit process of land management. Hundreds of these questionable spot-zoning laws were passed. The legislature itself by the 1990s had swelled into an oversized bureaucracy with one of the largest staffs and budgets proportional to constituents in the entire United States. With no real controls on spending by the legislatures and administration officials, GovGuam's deficit continued to grow. The specious accounting of the Ada-Blas administration and Guam's senators was as routine as their smiling sophism that reflected the profligacy of America in the Reagan-Bush decade.

GovGuam's inadequacies were manifold, yet compared with other U.S. territories—notably the CNMI, where frenzied development severely overstressed local governmental capabilities—Guam looked good from Washington's viewpoint. The June 1992 Interior Department report on the "State of the Islands" (all U.S. territories except Puerto Rico) concluded, "The Government of Guam is perhaps the best administered of the United States insular area governments." In fact, by the 1990s, Guam for the first time had surpassed a U.S. state in per capita income. The 1990 U.S. census (with 1989 figures) showed Guam at $9,929, Mississippi at $9,648, and the U.S. national per capita income at $14,420. In the forty-five years since World War II, Guam had moved from a Third World to a First World economic status, except for reliable electric power. The boom would burst like a punctured balloon in the worldwide recession that began in 1991–1992, but until then Guam wore the happy face of excess.

As the decade of the 1990s began, one resident no longer involved in the hectic development of Guam was former Governor Ricky Bordallo. On Wednesday, 31 January 1990, after lunch and an interview for a local magazine, he drove off alone in his jeep. He was dressed as usual like a farmer in a T-shirt, faded blue denim jeans and jacket, and a widebrimmed straw hat.

His court appeals had been only partially successful. In 1988, the Ninth Circuit Court overturned eight of his convictions (prosecutor O'Connor, it turned out, had been overly zealous after all) but upheld the convictions on conspiracy to obstruct justice and witness tampering. Bordallo then appealed to the U.S. Supreme Court, but it refused to hear the case. In December 1989, he was resentenced by District Court Judge Duenas to serve four years on the remaining convictions. He then resolved on one last dramatic act to symbolize his own plight and the cause of the Chamorro people.

The last day of January was the day he was to depart to report to a federal minimum security facility in California. That afternoon, he drove his jeep to the Paseo Loop, where the great bronze statue of Quipuha gazes toward the horizon beyond the streams of traffic that flow along Marine Drive. Bordallo parked his jeep near the Agana River outfall and walked to the foot of Quipuha. Repairs had recently been done to the statue, and a length of chain still lay on the rear of the stone apron of the monument.

There was no one close by except some road repair workers on Marine Drive. Bordallo had not told anyone of his intentions. Overhead, the northeast trade winds swept clumps of sunlit clouds across a typically bright blue sky, and pairs of white fairy terns darted in flight over the nearby beach where Father San Vitores had stepped ashore on Guam long ago.

With his back to the rear of the statue and to the Americanized postmodern world beyond, Bordallo placed about him hand-lettered placards that he had made. The signs called for justice and a halt to the deculturation of the Chamorro people. He draped a Guam flag around his shoulders in a final symbolic gesture. Then he removed a loaded .38-caliber pistol from his jacket pocket.

Bordallo placed the end of the gun barrel against his right temple and squeezed the trigger. He fell on the flag, by then splattered with his blood, and his right ankle became entangled in the chain on the apron as his legs jerked spasmodically. By the time the police responded to a road worker's emergency call, they found the former governor still breathing but beyond help. An ambulance took him to the U.S. Naval Hospital, where he died about four-thirty. He was sixty-three years old.

Like Quipuha, Ricky Bordallo was overcome by a tragic destiny imposed from without and abetted from within. This destiny challenges the belief that history's movement is linear or that there is a difference between past and present. Both men failed their people, but the people themselves go on with a sovereignty of spirit and a sturdy sense of community that have always redeemed them despite the failures of their leaders and of the island's governments during three centuries of colonial rule.

Colonialism imposed the Western concept, firmly held from Aristotle to well after Clausewitz, of the sovereignty of politics, the implacable conquering impulse of the parable of the tribes, over culture in human affairs. By enduring as a cultural identity against overwhelming outside forces, the people of Guam demonstrate a deeper truth: that politics should be the perpetuation of culture by its own means. For in the centuries since Magellan, the people of the island have learned to combine the rich lifeblood of their traditions with the one great gift of Europeans to traditional peoples: the understanding that creative life springs from the insights, thought, and vision of the individual, loyal to his or her experience of value in the local community, not to the dicta of outside authority.

Now, at the end of the twentieth century, the islanders for the first time in their postcontact history hold their destiny in their own hands. What path will they choose in the twenty-first century—economic growth, political sovereignty, or indigenous cultural continuity? And these paths, regardless of what advocates of each may say, are not necessarily compatible.

And will the island itself, with all the changes for better or for worse throughout its history, remain what it was to its first human inhabitants and to residents and visitors ever since, a small green oasis, like earth herself, a bright beckoning landfall in the vast unknown ocean that surrounds us all?

Appendix
Chief Executives of Guam
1668–1990

By date of accession

Sources: *Hojas de Servicio, Capitulo XXXII, Simancas, Badajoz* 1894; AHPA E-I-C5 (g) 1894; Official U.S. Navy Reports, 1899–1950; contemporary newspapers, 1950–1990.

Note: There were several kinds of acting and interim governors. Some acting governors are not listed because their tenures were very brief. Spanish interim governors were often assigned by Manila, at times as *sargento mayor,* until Madrid appointed a regular governor. Spellings of Spanish names sometimes varied.

Spanish Period, 16 June 1668–20 June 1898 (230 years)

Father Diego Luís de San Vitores, S.J.	16 June 1668
Father Francisco Solano, S.J.	2 April 1672
Father Francisco Ezquerra, S.J.	13 June 1672
Father Peter de Coomans, S.J.	2 February 1674
Captain Damián de Esplana (first *sargento mayor*)	16 June 1674
Captain Francisco de Irisarri y Vivar (unofficial governor)	10 June 1676
Captain Juan Antonio de Salas (unofficial governor)	21 June 1678
Captain Joseph de Quiroga y Losada (acting unofficial governor)	5 June 1680
Captain Antonio Saravia (1st official governor)	15 June 1681
Sargento Mayor Damián de Esplana	3 November 1683
Captain Joseph de Quiroga y Losada (acting)	? February 1686
Lt. General Damián de Esplana	? September 1689
Sargento Mayor Joseph de Quiroga y Losada	16 August 1694
General José Madrazo (interim)	26 July 1696
Sargento Mayor Francisco Medrano y Asiain (interim)	15 September 1700
Sargento Mayor Antonio Villamor y Vadillo (interim)	1 September 1704

Sargento Mayor Manuel Argüelles y Valdés (interim)	? 1705
Lt. General Juan Antonio Pimentel	1 September 1709
Captain Luís Antonio Sánchez de Tagle	21 November 1720
Captain Juan de Ojeda (acting)	4 April 1725
General Manuel Argüelles y Valdés	28 September 1725
Sargento Mayor Pedro Laso de la Vega y Bustamente	12 February 1730
Captain (Navy) Diego Félix de Balboa (interim)	1 November 1730
General (Navy) Francisco Cárdenas Pacheco	25 August 1734
Sargento Mayor Miguel Fernández de Cárdenas	2 April 1740
Captain Domingo Gómez de la Sierra	21 September 1746
Lieutenant (Navy) Henrique de Olavide y Michelena	8 September 1749
General Andrés del Barrio y Rábago	6 November 1756
Lieutenant (Navy) José de Soroa	20 November 1759
Lieutenant (Navy) Henrique de Olavide y Michelena	9 June 1768
Sargento Mayor Mariano Tobías	15 September 1771
Sargento Mayor Antonio Apodaca (interim)	15 June 1774
Captain Phelipe de Ceraín	6 June 1776
Lt. Colonel Joseph Arleguí y Leóz	21 August 1786
Lt. Colonel Manuel Muro	2 September 1794
Captain Vicente Blanco	12 January 1802
Captain Alexandro Parreño	18 October 1806
Lieutenant José de Medinilla y Pineda	26 July 1812
Captain José Montilla (interim)	15 August 1822
Captain José Ganga Herrero	15 May 1823
Lt. Colonel José de Medinilla y Pineda	1 August 1826
Captain Francisco Ramón de Villalobos	26 September 1831
Lt. Colonel José Casillas Salazar	1 October 1837
Sargento Mayor Gregorio Santa María	1 October 1843
Félix Calvo y Noriega (interim)	7 April 1848
Lt. Colonel Pablo Pérez	8 September 1848
Lt. Colonel Felipe María de la Corte y Ruano Calderón	16 May 1855
Lt. Colonel Francisco Moscoso y Lara	28 January 1866
Colonel Luís de Ibáñez y García	17 August 1871
Lt. Colonel Eduardo Beaumont y Calafat	24 March 1873
Lt. Colonel Manuel Brabo y Barrera	14 January 1875
Lt. Colonel Francisco Brochero y Parreño	15 August 1880
Colonel Angel de Pazos y Vela-Hidalgo	18 March 1884
Captain Antonio Borredá y Alares (acting)	3 August 1884
Lt. Colonel Francisco Olive y García	1 November 1884
Lt. Colonel Enrique Solano Llanderal	22 July 1885
Lt. Colonel Joaquín Vara de Rey y Rubio	21 April 1890
Lt. Colonel Luís Santos Fontordera	14 August 1891
Lt. Colonel Vicente Gómez Hernández	23 August 1892
Lt. Juan Godoy del Castillo (interim)	1 September 1893
Lt. Colonel Emilio Galisteo y Brumenque	31 October 1893
Lt. Colonel Jacobo Marina	24 December 1895
Lieutenant Ángel Nieto (interim)	15 February 1897
Lt. Colonel Juan Marina	17 April 1897

Interregnum, 21 June 1898–7 August 1899 (1 year, 1 month, and 2 weeks)

Captain Henry Glass, U.S.N.	21 June 1898
José Sixto (acting unofficial governor)	23 June 1898
Joaquín Pérez y Cruz (acting governor)	1 February 1899
William P. Coe (acting unofficial governor)	11 July 1899

**First U.S. Naval Period, 7 August 1899–10 December 1941
(42 years, 4 months)**

Captain Richard Phillips Leary, U.S.N.	7 August 1899
Commander Seaton Schroeder, U.S.N.	19 July 1900
Commander William E. Sewell, U.S.N.	6 February 1903
Lieutenant Frank H. Schofield, U.S.N., (acting)	11 January 1904
Lieutenant Raymond Stone, U.S.N., (acting)	28 January 1904
Commander George L. Dyer, U.S.N.	16 May 1904
Lieutenant Luke McNamee, U.S.N., (acting)	2 November 1905
Commander Templin M. Potts, U.S.N.	2 March 1906
Lt. Commander Luke McNamee, U.S.N., (acting)	3 October 1907
Captain Edward J. Dorn, U.S.N.	28 December 1907
Lieutenant F. B. Freyer, U.S.N., (acting)	5 November 1910
Captain George R. Salisbury, U.S.N.	12 January 1911
Captain Robert E. Coontz, U.S.N.	30 April 1912
Commander Alfred W. Hinds, U.S.N., (acting)	23 September 1913
Captain William J. Maxwell, U.S.N.	28 March 1914
Captain Roy C. Smith, U.S.N.	30 May 1916
Captain William W. Gilmer, U.S.N.	15 November 1918
Captain Ivan C. Wettengel, U.S.N.	7 July 1920
Lt. Commander James S. Spore, U.S.N., (acting)	28 October 1921
Captain Adelbert Althouse, U.S.N., (acting)	7 February 1922
Captain Henry B. Price, U.S.N.	4 August 1923
Captain L. S. Shapley, U.S.N.	7 April 1926
Commander Willis W. Bradley, Jr., U.S.N.	11 June 1929
Captain Edmund S. Root, U.S.N.	15 May 1931
Captain George A. Alexander, U.S.N.	21 June 1933
Commander Benjamin W. McCandlish, U.S.N.	27 March 1936
Commander James T. Alexander, U.S.N.	8 February 1938
Captain George J. McMillin, U.S.N.	20 April 1940

**Japanese Occupation, 10 December 1941–10 August 1944
(2 years, 8 months)**

Major General Tomitara Horii	10 December 1941
Commander (Navy) Hiroshi Hayashi	14 January 1942
Captain (Navy) Yutaka Sugimoto	? 1944
Lt. General Takeshi Takashina	20 March 1944
Lt. General Hideyoshi Obata	28 July 1944

**Second U.S. Naval Period, 15 August 1944–21 July 1950
(5 years, 11 months, and 1 week)**

Major General Henry L. Larsen, U.S.M.C. (island commander)	15 August 1944

Vice Admiral Charles A. Pownall, U.S.N.
    (COMNAVMAR and governor)   30 May 1946
Carlton S. Skinner (governor)   27 September 1949

U.S. Department of Interior Period, 21 July 1950–4 January 1971
(20 years, 5 months, and 2 weeks)

Carlton S. Skinner (reappointed governor)	21 July 1950
Randall S. Herman (acting)	20 February 1953
Ford Q. Elvidge	23 April 1953
William T. Corbett (acting)	19 May 1956
Richard Barrett Lowe	14 October 1956
Marcellus G. Boss (acting)	16 November 1959
Joseph Flores	9 July 1960
William P. Daniel	20 May 1961
Manuel F. L. Guerrero (acting)	20 September 1962
Manuel F. L. Guerrero	9 March 1963
Carlos G. Camacho	20 July 1969

Elected Governor Period, 4 January 1971–1990

Carlos G. Camacho	4 January 1971
Ricardo J. Bordallo	6 January 1975
Paul M. Calvo	1 January 1979
Ricardo J. Bordallo	3 January 1983
Joseph F. Ada	5 January 1987

Abbreviations

AAFB	Andersen Air Force Base
AFT	American Federation of Teachers
AP	Associated Press
BATFOG	Bush Administration Task Force on Guam
BPM	Brown-Pacific-Matson
CB	Naval construction battalion (a.k.a. Seabees)
CHELU	Chamorro Employees Labor Union
CIA	Central Intelligence Agency
CINCPAC	Commander in Chief U.S. Forces Pacific
CINCPOA	Commander in Chief Pacific Ocean Area
CNMI	Commonwealth of the Northern Mariana Islands
COMNAVMAR	Commander United States Naval Forces Marianas
DOD	Department of Defense
DOE	Department of Education
DP	disposition point
DPW	Department of Public Works
EEZ	Exclusive Economic Zone
EGO	Executive General Order
FDAA	Federal Disaster Assistance Administration
FBL	Force (or Final) Beachhead Line
FHP	Family Health Program
FFB	Federal Finance Bank

FSM	Federated States of Micronesia
GAA	Guam Airport Authority
GCC	Guam Community College
GEDA	Guam Economic Development Authority
GFT	Guam Federation of Teachers
GHURA	Guam Housing and Urban Renewal Authority
GMH	Guam Memorial Hospital
GMHP	Guam Memorial Health Plan
GORCO	Guam Oil Refining Company
GPA	Guam Power Authority
GTA	Guam Telephone Authority
GVB	Guam Visitors Bureau
HMI	Health Management International
ICBM	intercontinental ballistic missile
JTWC	Joint Typhoon Warning Center
KCK	Knights of Christ the King
MARC	Micronesian Area Research Center
MASDELCO	Marianas Stevedoring and Development Company
MCM	Medical Center of the Marianas
MSA	Medical Services Association
NA	National Archives (Washington, D.C.)
NAS	Naval Air Station (Agana)
NTTU	Naval Technical Training Unit
OFM Cap.	Order of Friars Minor, Capuchin (Franciscan)
ONI	Office of Naval Intelligence
OPI-R	Organization of People for Indigenous Rights
OSA	Order of Saint Augustine
OSS	Office of Strategic Services
OTIA	Office of Territorial and International Affairs
PDN	*Pacific Daily News*
PUAG	Public Utility Agency of Guam
PX	Post Exchange (military)
QC	qualifying certificate
RCT	regimental combat team
REA	Rural Electrification Administration
RG	Record Group (National Archives)

SAC	Strategic Air Command
SAR	search and rescue
SIOP	Single Integrated Operational Plan
SJ	Society of Jesus (Jesuits)
SLBM	submarine-launched ballistic missile
SMS	Seine Majestät Schiff (His Majesty's Ship)
TTPI	Trust Territory of the Pacific Islands
UDT	underwater demolition team
UOG	University of Guam
UPI	United Press International
USA	United States Army
USAF	United States Air Force
USAT	United States Army Transport
USCC	United States Commercial Company
USMC	United States Marine Corps
USN	United States Navy
USS	United States Ship
VHB	very heavy bomber
WASC	Western Association of Schools and Colleges
YMLG	Young Men's League of Guam

Notes

Prologue

1   Kotzebue quote: Kotzebue (1967b, 3:92).

2   Magellan's voyage: See Pigafetta (1969); Lévesque (1992, 1:231–248); and Wallis (1954). See Lévesque (1992) for a comprehensive documentation translated into English and for analysis of early European explorations in Micronesia.

Chapter 1: Aliens 1521–1638

5   Magellan's sighting of Rota and Guam: See Rogers and Ballendorf (1989) and the account in Blair and Robertson (1903–1909, 1:196–197), where Ginés de Mafra, a pilot on the *Trinidad,* describes the sighting. Magellan was lame from a wound received fighting Moors in North Africa.

6   Albo's log: See Albo (1971); Lévesque (1992, 1:221–229) (Lévesque, who spells Albo as Alvo, also provides translations of Pigafetta and the Genoese pilot on the Guam landfall); Navarette (1971, 340). A fake "diary" of Magellan was printed in the *Guam Recorder,* Vol. 3, No. 10, January 1927, 265–267.

Pigafetta's quotes: See Pigafetta (1969). The original manuscript by Pigafetta was in Italian with some dialogue in Spanish; it was being edited for the pope when it disappeared in the sack of Rome in 1527 by—of all people—Spanish soldiers.

Chamorro derivation: Driver (1985, 5); see also Plaza (1971). A log by pilot Esteban Rodríguez with Legazpi in 1565 translated *chamurre* as "friend"; English translation in Lévesque (1992, 2:91). In 1602, Juan Pobre used the word *chamuri* as the indigenous term for an *hombre principale* in Spanish, meaning a headman, not a chief. In the 1990s, some indigenous rights activists began to use *Chamoru* in place of *Chamorro,* and in 1994 the Chamorro Language Commission of Guam adopted *Chamoru* in place of *Chamorro* in the indigenous language.

7   Grass on Guam's mountains: The accounts of Legazpi by friars Juan de Grijalva (1624) and Gaspar de San Agustín (1975) describe the grassy summits.

Landfall on Guam's northwest coast: See Albo (1971); Ginés de Mafra (1921); Rogers and Ballendorf (1989); and Quirino (1988, 18). See Lévesque (1992, 1:196–197) for the view that the landing was at Agat or Umatac.

Enrique: For a refutation that he was a Cebuan, see Lévesque (1992, 1:292–293).

10   *Guahan* for Guam: Information on the Portuguese map of 1545 was apparently obtained from the Spaniards after the *Trinidad* was captured in the Moluccas (see Lévesque 1992, 1:332–333).

Gonzalo de Vigo in the Marianas: Colín and Pastells (1900–1902, 2:598); Driver (1985, 2–5).

11   Loaysa and two charts: Lévesque (1992, 1:422); Wallis (1954, 92). Loaysa is sometimes spelled Loaisa.

Loaysa's *Victoria:* This was not Magellan's *Victoria.* The Spaniards used a name, usually of a saint, repeatedly for different ships.

Gonzalo de Vigo and Baham: Driver (1985, 11); Driver (1987, x–xi).

Alonso de Salazar on Guam and kidnapping of Chamorros: Lévesque (1992, 1:438–441); Blair and Robertson (1903–1909, 2:35); Uncilla (1907, 348); Oviedo (1855, Chap. 16).

12   Bernal Díaz quote: Elliot (1970, 65).

Quote from Vitoria: Vitoria (1557, App. C, xc). Vitoria did not refute the secular legality of sovereignty established by offensive war over a territory; he only condemned such conquest as theologically a sin in the eyes of God, not among nations.

Villalobos expedition and naming of the Philippines: Lévesque (1992, 1:567–624); Spate (1979, 97–100); and *Collección de documentos inéditos . . . de Ultramar* (1886, 2, Pt. 1:1–94).

13   Legazpi's crews and instructions: Lévesque (1992, 2:23–77); Blair and Robertson (1903–1909, 34:1280–1605, 249–255). See Gschaedler (1954) for history.

San Lucas's desertion: Hezel (1983, 22–29).

13– Legazpi at Guam: Legazpi's *Relation* in *Collección de documentos inédi-*
14   *tos . . . de Ultramar* (1886, 2, Pt. 1:119–138); and in Navarrete (1971, Vol. 17, Document 5). Guam landing and Hernando de Riquel's account in *Collección de documentos inéditos . . . de Ultramar* (1887, Vol. 3, Document 38, 76–81, 89–90); Morga (1971, 319); Blair and Robertson (1903–1909, 2:105–113). Major accounts and documents translated in Lévesque (1992, 2:79–409).

14   *Goaam, Goam,* etc. as early names of Guam: Driver (1985, 6, 9, 42). The Portuguese map of 1545 showed the southernmost island as *gua-han* (see note above on p. 000). Purchas (1905, 198) quoted the chief

pilot of Dutch ships under Oliver van der Noort as stating in 1600, "The Island was called Guana." The name could have derived from the Chamorro phrase *guaha hanom,* "a place where there is water."

15   Urdaneta's map: Grijalva (1624, fol. 121v); Wallis (1954, 200). Urdaneta's map was found in 1935 in the National Library of Peru; it is reproduced in Cuevas' (1943) biography of Urdaneta and is called the Portocarrero map. See also Noone (1986, 282, n. 513).

      San Pablo wreck at Guam: Lévesque (1992, 2:383–393); San Augustín (1975, 298–299); Guzman-Rivas (1960, 32); Blair and Robertson (1903–1909, 3:29–44).

16   Manila galleons: See Schurz (1959) and Guzman-Rivas (1960). The galleons out of Manila were also called *Naos de la China* and *Naos de la seda* (silk galleons). When two galleons sailed together, the flagship (not always the largest) was the *Capitana,* the consort the *Almiranta* (Schurz 1959, 193).

      La Sarpana etc. for Rota: Driver (1983, 199–200).

17   Cavendish at Guam: Burney (1803–1817, 2:90); Lévesque (1992, 2:568–571). The English accounts of Cavendish call the island *Guana.*

18   Antonio de los Angeles: Driver (1977) translation of Ribadeneira.

19   Francisco García: This Jesuit wrote the first history of Father San Vitores' mission in the Marianas in 1681 (published in Spain in 1683). References to García are to the Nieves M. Flores Memorial Library English language edition of 1985, which gathers into one volume the partial translation of García by Margaret Higgens in the *Guam Recorder,* September 1936–July 1939.

      Juan Pobre's account of 1602: This account, translated by MARC's Marjorie G. Driver (1983), is the most detailed eyewitness description of Chamorros prior to Spanish rule.

20   Wreck of the *Concepción:* Blair and Robertson (1903–1909, Document 35, Vol. 29, 170). This wreck was excavated by marine archaeologists near Agingan Point, Saipan, in 1987–1988 (see Mathers et al. 1990).

      Concepción survivors: Blair and Robertson (1903–1909, Vol. 29, Document 35, 168–169). For Esteban Ramos, see Mathers et al. (1990, 59–60), citing Casimiro Díaz, *Conquista de las Islas Filipinas* (Valladolid, 1890), 402.

      Chamorro headman Taga and the Virgin Mary: García (1683, 53).

      Release of cats and dogs: García (1683, 39).

      Flies and mosquitos: García (1683, 49).

Chapter 2: The Place of Before Time Ancestors 1638–1662

21   Submerged mountain range: The northeastern edge of the range follows the Andesite Line.

      Geology of Guam: Tracey et al. (1964); Engebretson et al. (1985).

22   Long-distance dispersal of life forms: Analogous models are the Gal-

apagos, analyzed in Perry (1984), and the Hawaiian Islands, analyzed in Fosberg (1948). For a study of wild bean dispersal to the Marianas from Australia by migratory birds, see Hymowitz et al. (1990).

Geckos: *Achiak* or *gualiig* in Chamorro. Six varieties exist in the Marianas, with *Sepidodactylis lugubris* the most common.

Proto-Austronesian origins of western Micronesians: Howells (1973, 243); Bellwood (1978, 284). See also Pietrusewsky and Turner, essay in Hunter-Anderson (1990).

Voyages out of Indonesia and the Philippines: Alkire (1977, 10–13).

Origins of western Micronesian languages: Howells (1973, 245); Bellwood (1978, 131–132). See also Dyen (1962, 1965).

23   Separate cultures in Micronesia: In the 1970s, Micronesians argued that a "Kachau empire," a "voluntary association" of Carolinians with perhaps Nan Madol in Ponape or Lelu in Kosrae as a capital, existed in the twelfth and thirteenth centuries (see Nakayama and Ramp 1974).

Span of 3,500 years: Reinman (1977, 89, 90); Kurashina and Clayshulte (1983, 11–13); and Moore (1983, 214). Butler (1988, 450) states that the oldest site on Rota dates from 2,000 years B.C., or 4,000 years ago.

Quote, Chamorros not mixture of Caucasoid-Mongoloids: Howells (1973, 249).

Micronesia not stepping stone to Polynesia: Bellwood (1978, 282).

Chamorro inbreeding: That fewer genes lower resistance to introduced diseases (by reduction of haplotypes in genetic inheritance) has been noted in Polynesia (see Searjeantson et al. 1982). Islander inbreeding did not mean that their genes were inferior, only that they had fewer different genes.

Eastern Micronesia and dispersion westward: See Goodenough (1957); Howells (1973, 254–255); Gibbons and Clunie (1986); and Solheim, Pietrusewsky, and Turner's essay in Hunter-Anderson (1990).

24   Swift microevolution: Laysan finches introduced in the 1960s to northern reefs of Hawai'i developed different beaks in just two decades (see the report by Jan Ten Bruggencate, *Honolulu Star-Bulletin and Advertiser,* 27 March 1988, D-1.

Mariana fruit bats: *Pteropus mariannus* (*Fanihi* in Chamorro) and *Pteropus tokudae.* The latter, smaller bat is presumed to be now extinct.

Marianas red ware: See Spoehr (1957), Kurashina et al. (1981, 6); Bellwood (1978, 282–283).

Rice cultivation on Guam: Reported by Pigafetta in 1521, Legazpi in 1565, Antonio de los Angeles in 1596, Van Noort in 1600, and Juan Pobre in 1602. Also see Pollock (1983).

25   Original Chamorro myths: Christianized variations of Chamorro legends evolved under the Spanish; see Van Peenen (1974) for examples.

26   Importance of breadfruit: Juan Pobre in Driver (1983, 209, 213). Juan

Pobre wrote that seedless breadfruit *(Artocarpus altilis)* was then called *orimayes* (now *lamae, lemai,* or *lemmai*) in Chamorro; it was called *rima* by the Spaniards and other Europeans. Wild breadfruit with seeds is *dukduk* (also spelled *dugdug* or *dokdok*) in Chamorro *(Artocarpus mariannenesis).*

26–27   Introduction of plants: Guzman-Rivas (1960, 118) states that the Spaniards introduced 115 tropical American plant species into Guam. There was also transmittal from other directions; an example is, in Chamorro, the *alangilang* tree *(Cananga odorata),* which is *ilangilang* in Tagalog. This tree's flowers emit a sweet-smelling perfume in the evening. The "official flower" of Guam is *Bougainvillea spectablis, nobiu* in Chamorro, from Melanesia.

27   Betel use by Chamorros: García (1683, 44).

Tuba, *agi,* and *arak:* Guzman-Rivas (1960, 100); Thompson (1945, 34).

28   Captain Melis's quote: Cited in Purchas (1905, 198).

28–29   Sunama's marlin and flying fish: Juan Pobre in Driver (1983, 208–209).

29   García quote: García (1683, 43).

Giants: Mendoza in Blair and Robertson (1903–1909, 6:138).

Quote of Gómez Pérez Dasmariñas: Driver (1991a, 105; translation from the Boxer Codex); also translated in Lévesque (1992, 2:619).

Massage as remedy: Juan Pobre in Driver (1983, 216).

"Fabulous poetry": García (1683, 217).

Chamorro nakedness: Precontact nakedness poses problems for artists in prudish contemporary Guam; modern illustrations usually show precontact Chamorro men in loincloths and women in Polynesian-style grass skirts or aprons, none of which were ever worn habitually on Guam.

Cavendish quote on hair style: Quoted in Burney (1803–1817, Vol. 2).

Bleached hair: Driver (1983, 207); Thompson (1969, 10).

29–30   Character of Chamorros: Antonio de los Angeles in Blair and Robertson (1903–1909, 10:262); and in Driver (1977, 19). Juan Pobre in Driver (1983, 207); García (1693, 45, 46); Morga (1971, 320); Purchas (1905, 198).

30   Juan Pobre's quotes: Driver (1983, 210–211).

31   Derivation of the word *proa:* The *Compact Edition of the Oxford English Dictionary* (1971, 2309). Other spellings are *prao* (French form, also used by Carano and Sanchez), *prau* (Legazpi), *prahu* (Malay), *parão* (Portuguese), and *prow* (Dampier).

Quote on proa: Dampier (1937, 300–301).

Esteban Rodríguez quote on proa's woven sails: *Colección de documentos inéditos . . . de Ultramar* (1886, 2, Pt. 2:387–388). Sails, like Chamorro mats, were woven from two kinds of screw pine (pandanus): *pahong (Pandanus dubius)* and *akgok (Pandanus fragrans).*

Proa dimensions: Dampier in 1696; Walter on Anson's voyage (1928, 321–324) in 1742; and Rochon on Crozet's voyage in 1772 (copied mostly from Dampier's description). Modern analyses are Whitney (1955); Haddon and Hornell (1975, 414); Doran (1981); and most accurately in Shell and Neyret (1987).

Woodes Rogers quote: Rogers (1969, 268); Leslie (1889, 113). Rogers so admired the proas that he carried one back to England.

Large interisland proas: Blair and Robertson (1903–1909, 2:113); Burney (1803–1817, 1:238); Dampier (1937, 300–301); and Walter (1928, 339).

33   Filipino designs by 1780s: Haddon and Hornell (1975, citing Duperrey).

Pre-*latte* and *latte* periods: Moore (1983, 216–217); Alkire (1977, 22).

Quote on fish for inland produce: Juan Pobre in Driver (1983, 213).

33–   Descriptions of *latte:* Thompson (1940, 447–464); Graves (1986, 139,
34   152); and Hunter-Anderson (1989).

34   Legazpi descriptions of *latte* dwellings: *Colección de documentos inéditos...de Ultramar* (1886, 2, Pt. 2:250–251); Blair and Robertson (1903–1909, 2:113).

Juan Pobre quote on *latte:* Driver (1983, 211).

Family autonomy: Cunningham (1984, 92–94); Cunningham (1992, 157–196). Cunningham's 1992 book, a fine secondary school text, is the most comprehensive ethnohistory to date of precontact Chamorro culture.

34–   Property ownership over reefs and ocean and obligations for use: Frey-
36   cinet (1839, 157). Ownership of the reef and ocean is still normal in parts of Micronesia; see Johannes (1981, 65) for an example of Palauan tenure.

36   Juan Pobre's quote on questioning: Driver (1983, 215).

Managed commons distinct from primitive communism: Hardin (1985, 95–101).

Chamorro castes and classes: Cunningham (1992, 165–170). Some writers divide precontact Chamorro society only by classes, not by castes.

Juan Pobre quote on Chamorro castes: Driver (1983, 213).

37   Quote on women: García (1683, 48).

Juan Pobre on women: Driver (1983, 213).

Austrian visitor's quote: Fernberger von Egenberg (1972, 189) described how Chamorros used European nails as penis pins to prevent sexual intercourse until marriage, a custom found in Burma, Borneo, the Philippines, and Kiribati. Pigafetta (1969, 85–86) mentions the practice, as does Morga (1971, 278).

38   Ancestor veneration with skulls etc.: Driver (1977, 19–21); García (1683, 50); Driver (1983, 214); Freycinet (1839, 193). Butler (1988,

404, 433) concludes that skulls, mostly of adult males, were removed sometime after burial.

Juan Pobre's quote on ancestor skulls: Driver (1983, 214).

Juan Pobre's quote on *makahnas:* Driver (1983, 214).

Aniti and *taotaomo'na:* Thompson (1945, 13–22) states that *taotaomo'na* is a postcontact superstition that evolved from belief in *aniti.*

Forms of *chenchule':* Juan Pobre in Driver (1983, 209, 210).

"Subsistence affluence" and gift giving: See Sahlins (1972).

39 Chamorro warfare mainly for vengeance: Cunningham (1984, 50); Thompson (1945, 18–20).

Quote of Martín Ignacio de Loyola: Translation of RAH *Colección,* Muñoz No. A-70 (Sig. no. 9/4807), fols. 110v–163, in Lévesque (1992, 2:518).

García on headmen authority limited to villages: García (1683, 48). Early Spanish writers never used the word *chief (Cacique)* for Chamorro headmen. Knudson (in Hunter-Anderson 1990, 121) concludes that Chamorros were organized only into "estate groups" and villages.

40 Parable of the tribes: Schmookler (1984, 21–22).

"Resilient" versus "power-based" societies: Butler (1988, 470–471).

Chapter 3: Father San Vitores 1662–1672

41 Visit to Ladrones in 1662: García (1683, 10, 11); the day and exact island are not reported. García's history, based on Jesuit letters and reports from the missions, is the main source for later works on San Vitores, including Andrés de Ledesma (1672), Morales (1737), Le Gobien (1700), Murillo Velarde (1749), Castro (1723), Colín and Pastells (1904), Risco (1935, 1970), and Juan Ledesma (l981). These books are hagiographic to glorify religious aspects of San Vitores' life. Some writers spell San Vitores as Sanvitores.

Description of San Vitores: García (1683, 159); Murillo Velarde (1749, nn. 724–731).

42 No mission in the Ladrones: Blair and Robinson (1903–1909, 9:226); Colín and Pastells (1900–1902, Vol. 1, n. 178); Beardsley (1964, 123). The earliest request for a mission was in 1596 (see Hezel 1970, 1982).

Esteban of the *Concepción:* Risco (1970, 195); García (1683, 152); Ledesma (1981, 429). Burrus (1954, 936) quotes a San Vitores letter that Esteban was a "Tagalan," while other accounts call him a Visayan.

Early life of San Vitores: García (1683, 4–6); Ledesma (1981, 27–132). See Risco (1970) for popular account.

San Vitores in the Philippines: Costa (1967, 470–472); García (1683, 11, 12). San Vitores' letter is quoted in Ledesma (1981, 220–222).

43 Biblical phrase: García (1683, 13).

Obsession of San Vitores: García (1683, 12); Ledesma (1981, 213).

Letter to father and *Memorial:* García (1683, 18–21); Ledesma (1981, 260–264).

Poblete's letter and enclosures: Risco (1970, 93); Ledesma (1981, 273–276).

44   Letter to Nithard and quote: García (1683, 21–23); Ledesma (1981, 264–267).

Quote on Spain "a shattered Monarchy": Elliot (1970, 360).

Philip IV's Ladrones *cédulas:* García (1683, 24). Ledesma (1981, 279–282) gives the texts. The *cédula* to San Vitores authorized him to go to Japan but was interpreted to mean the Ladrones, considered at the time to be extensions of the Japanese Islands.

San Diego to Peru: Higgens' note in García (1683, 26) quotes San Vitores' friend Brother Lorenzo Bustillo as saying that the ship rolled over on its side at Cavite when the order to go to Peru was given but miraculously rolled back up once the order was rescinded. This was one of numerous miracles that García and other Catholic writers describe as occurring during San Vitores' life and after his death because of his religious devotion.

Mexico City earthquake and funds: García (1683, 30); Ansaldo (1669, 15).

45   First grammar and catechism of Chamorro language: Burrus (1954) provides the text. An original copy, now in ARSI, Opp. NN. 352, was sent on 18 June 1668 by San Vitores to Pope Clement IX along with his first report on the Marianas. The title of the grammar was *Grammaticae Institutiones Marianae Linquae.*

Arrival at Agaña: Ansaldo (1669) gives an eyewitness account but mixes up the dates. "Tierra, Tierra" quote, García (1683, 36).

Quote on gold exchanged for iron: Ansaldo (1669, 16).

Hagatña: The town's name from 1668 until 1899 was Agaña for the Spaniards and Chamorros. It was Agana (without the diacritic) after 1899. In 1992, in order to re-Chamorrize place names, Hagatña was restored, but Agana (pronounced Agaña) remains standard.

Quote on landing: Ansaldo (1669, 16).

45–   Medina's reception: García (1683, 53).
46

46   Baptism of Mariana and naming of Marianas: García (1683, 37).

47   Use of Marianos: Higgens' translation often used *Chamorros,* but García's Spanish text of 1683 used Marianos, *indios,* or *nativos.*

Pueblo de los Martíres: García (1683, 54). San Vitores bestowed religious names on every island, with Guam called San Juan, but none survived except for Asunción in the northern Marianas.

Quote on animals: Ansaldo (1669, 17).

Members of San Vitores' mission: Ledesma (1981, 323–324).

Chamorro population: An issue of much debate. In 1602, Juan Pobre estimated "more than 60,000" on Guam and 12,000 on Rota, but he

did not visit Guam. In his *Papel de motivos* of 1665, San Vitores estimated 20,000 on one unnamed island (presumably Guam) based on
Admiral Esteban Ramos' eyewitness estimate after the *Concepción*
wreck (in Ledesma 1981, 268, 275). The Flemish Jesuit Gerardo Bouwens, who served on Guam 1672–1673 and 1675–1712, wrote in 1673
that there were 12,000 Chamorros on Guam. In 1683, García gives
50,000 on Guam based on San Vitores' reports. Pimentel, writing in
1709, estimated that the population of all the Marianas was only
24,000 in 1668. Demographer Underwood (1973) makes a conservative estimate of 30,000 on Guam in 1668, using all sources except Juan
Pobre and Bouwens. Hezel and Driver (1988) lowered the estimate to
20,000–30,000 for Guam and 50,000–70,000 for all the Marianas in
1668, using all sources except Bouwens. The figures of 12,000 for
Guam by Bouwens and 24,000 for all the Marianas by Pimentel based
on firsthand observations are probably the most accurate estimates of
Chamorros as of 1668.

48   Location of San Vitores' first mission buildings: See Degaldillo et al.
(1979, 6–8).

Salgado quote: Maggs (1923, 70) gives translation of letter of 29 June
1683 by Salgado to the Duquesa de Aveiro.

Quote on no Chamorro laws: García (1683, 48).

49   Quote on Choco: García (1683, 69).

Quote on description of San Vitores: García (1683, 84).

50   San Vitores' cilice and *disciplina*: García (1683, 60).

Trances and "outside himself": García (1683, 99).

Coral masonry *mampostería*: A combination of timber rafters and
frames with masonry walls of coral rocks cemented together with a
mortar of coral and slaked lime made from burned coral.

Burial of Quipuha: Ledesma (1981, 340).

Salcedo arrested: Murillo Velarde (1749), Plaza translation (1987, 42–
43).

13,000 Chamorro baptisms: Ledesma (1981, 303), citing San Vitores'
reports in AGI, *Filipinas,* 58, 4–12.

June 1668 *cédula* on galleon stops at Guam: Schurz (1959, 248).

51   San Vitores' quote on use of force: García (1683, 115, 116).

52   Three Chamorro ambassadors: García (1683, 124–130).

Hurao's speech: Le Gobien (1700), Daly's MARC translation (1949,
17). García (1683) makes no mention of Hurao's speech, and Brosses
(1967, 2:498) in 1756 flatly states that Le Gobien put words "in the
mouth of" Hurao. The speech was nonetheless used prominently on
memorials and in government publications in the twentieth century as
an expression of Chamorro victimization, even though it is fictitious.

53   Quote on impact of battles in 1671: García (1683, 143).

Father López's map: Published in Le Gobien (1700) with mostly
Chamorro names for fourteen of the Mariana Islands. In 1752, Jacob

Bellin redrew the López map for a new edition of Le Gobien, and this version of Guam remained standard until Louis I. Duperrey drew new maps on the 1819 expedition of Louis de Freycinet (see Driver 1987).

53– Queen Mariana's *cédulas:* See Driver (1968) for lists and translations of
54   principal decrees. Quote of *Cédula* 88 in Driver (1968, 282).

54   Quote on Chamorro women becoming Christians: Le Gobien (1700), Daly MARC translation (1949, 124).

Quote on second Quipuha: García (1683, 143).

Barzan's death and quote on chopping up the Chamorro: García (1683, 148, 150, 151).

55   Accounts of San Vitores in Tumon: García (1683, 152–157); Ledesma (1981, 428–439, 444–450 [which quotes the report of Father Francisco Solano, who took over the mission after San Vitores' death], 463–465 [which quotes the report of Manila Governor de Leon]); Maggs (1923, 104, 105 [quoting letter by Father Francisco Ezquerra on 3 May 1672]).

Mata'pang: In the Spanish period, Mata'pang was treated as a villain. In the late twentieth century, he began to be treated as a Chamorro patriot, and a public park on Tumon Beach is named after him.

55– Details and sources on the deaths of Calonsor and San Vitores:
56   Ledesma (1981, 440–501). There were three formal depositions by Chamorros on Guam, one of whom, named Bayug, said that he was an eyewitness to the murder.

57   San Vitores' last words: Chamorro *Yu'us,* pronounced "dzuus," is a transliteration of the Spanish word *Dios* for God.

Modern Chamorros equivocal over San Vitores' role: Palomo (1985, 4–5).

Chapter 4: The Spanish Conquest 1672–1698

58   Quote on Chamorro factions: García (1683, 160).

59   Fight at Hospital Point: Some later accounts than García (1683) erroneously have the Spanish force march around the ocean side of the point; that side is a narrow ledge pounded by surf and impassable except briefly at very low tides.

First horse and quote: García (1683, 184).

60   Quartering of Tumon Chamorro: García (1683, 198).

Chapel and miracles at Tumon: García (1683, 157). For a refutation of the miracles (water in Tumon turning red as San Vitores' blood and barrenness of the chapel site), see Arago (1839, 288–290). For a scientific explanation of red tide caused by dinoflagellates in the water, see Matson (1991).

Basilio quote on bones: García (1683, 225).

First Spanish-Chamorro church marriage: Maggs (1923, 208) quotes a 1686 letter by Father Antonio Xaramillo to the Duquesa de Aveiro.

61   Quote on formation of political republic: García (1683, 229).

Quote on "Let the dog die": García (1683, 234).

García and Aguarin quotes: García (1683, Spanish original, Bk. 5, Chap. 17, 537). Aguarin's speech contains phrases and words similar to the Hurao speech in Le Gobien (1700, 183). Le Gobien may have based his Hurao "quote" on García's account of Aguarin's speech.

62   Quote on head of Monroy's killer: García (1683, 273).

63   Quote on "gentle yoke of Christ": García (1683, 275).

Orders to Quiroga: Hurtado (1680, 18–20); Ibáñez y García (1990, 180).

64   Aguarin's capture: García (1683, 295). Maggs (1923, 135, 136) provides Solórzano's report of 23 July 1684 on the Rota raid.

65   Quote on 1680 typhoon: García (1683, 299).

Quote on martyrs' blood: García (1683, 305).

Saravia's titles: Maggs (1923, 148–149) on Solórzano's report of 30 May 1682.

Cédula of 1679: AGN, *Reales Cédulas,* Vol. 17, 1679, MARC Collection.

66   Chamorro oath: Repetti (1946, 433–437) quotes Solórzano's report of 30 May 1682; also in Maggs (1923, 149).

Quote from Saravia's letter of June 1682: Maggs (1923, 157).

Churlish Chamorros on Saipan: Maggs (1923, 164).

67   Saravia's troop request and Charles II's *cédula:* Affidavit of Father Gerardo Bouwens (spelled Bouvens and Bonwens in some accounts) of 23 April 1706 in Ibáñez y García (1990, App. 7, 191).

Esplana and Quiroga appointed after Saravia's death: Maggs (1923, 182) quotes 30 May 1683 letter by Bouwens (Bonwens in Maggs).

Quote on Punni's death: Repetti (1941, 495).

Salvage of *Concepción* cannons: Bouwens' letter to the queen of Spain, 1 May 1685, AGI, *Filipinas,* 3 (for the 1684 salvage by Quiroga); report of Governor Antonio Villamor de Vadillo of 9 January 1709, AGI, *Ultramar,* 561, 204 (for 1704–1705 salvage).

1684 Chamorro uprising: Maggs (1923, 182) quotes letter of 30 May 1683 by Bouwens, who was wounded in the uprising; also see Father Luís de Morales report, 1689–1690, translated by Abella (1973).

Death of Yura: Morales (1689–1690, 14).

Friendly Chamorros' help: Morales (1689–1690, 23, 24).

68   Morales quote of 19 August attack: Morales (1689–1690, 20).

69   Quote on "large groups . . . left . . . Guahan": Morales (1689–1690, 38).

Eaton on Guam: Burney (1803–1817, 3:305, 306).

Swan and Dampier on Guam: Dampier (1937, 201–208); Maggs (1923, 200).

69–   *Santa Rosa* galleon and La Carolina: Blair and Robinson (1903–1909,
70   41:48, 38:264) (they twice mistake the name of the galleon).

70   Esplana by proa to Cavite and trial: Driver (1988a, 34), citing AGI, *Filipinas* 12, 194, and 212–214.

      1688 epidemic: Le Gobien (1700), Daly MARC translation (1949, 166).

      1689 epidemic: Driver (1988b, 140), citing Father Bustillo, 23 May 1690, ARSI, *Filipinas* 14, 76–77.

      1690 Guam population of 1,800: Hernandez (1690, 44, 45).

      1690 population other than Guam: Hernandez (1690, 45).

71   Chamorro women sterilizing selves and killing babies: Delgado (1892/1751, 115) was the first printed source of this statement; repeated (usually without attribution) down the years by Rochon (1891/1783, 83); Concepción (1789, 7:347–348); Chamisso (1817) in Kotzebue (1967b, 3:78–79); Louis de Freycinet (1839/1820, 330); Ibáñez y García (1990/1886, 83); and Beardsley (1964, 135).

      Agia quote: Agia (1604, 56).

      Spaniards killed in Spanish-Chamorro wars: Ibáñez y García (1990, 183–186).

72   *Pilar* wreck: Driver (1988a, 37); AGI, *Ultramar,* 562, Vol. 2, 275, 357.

      Esplana's titles at death and theft of *situado*: Driver (1988a, 34, 41), citing AGI, *Filipinas,* 16, 48, 99, 136–143, and 208–210.

      Quiroga's expeditions: Quiroga (1696).

73   Quiroga's reputation: Later writers emphasized Quiroga's ruthlessness, calling him a "tyrant" (Carano and Sanchez 1964, 77–79; Sanchez 1989, 43) and an "arrogant soul" (Freycinet 1839, 37). Quiroga was a good soldier and no more ferocious than other Spanish commanders in the Marianas, just the most effective.

      Chamorro last stand on Aguijan: Le Gobien (1700), Daly MARC translation (1949, 174, 175); Quiroga (1696); Hezel (1989, 8–10).

      Madrazo's resettlement of northern Chamorros: Murillo Velarde (1749, Bk. 4, Chap. 22, 373); Corte (1970, 32); Safford (1901, 35); Hezel (1989, 12, 13); Pimentel (1709, 214–215); Quiroga (1696).

Chapter 5: Oasis in the Ocean 1698–1800

74–   Evolution of *principalía* class and family names; See Ramirez (1983)
75   for genealogies.

76   Filipino-style houses in Agaña: Pineda (1792, 9–10).

      Epidemic of 1700 and unburied corpses: Corte (1970, 61).

      Medrano proposal to relocate Chamorros: Hezel and Driver (1988, 151), citing Bustillo's letter of 10 April 1702 in ARSI, *Filipinas* 13, 324–325, and 326–332.

      Jesuit figures 1698–1702: Hezel and Driver (1988, 140).

      Poor quality of troops: Quiroga (1720, 18); Hezel and Driver (1988, 143), citing 20 May 1681 letter of Father Solórzano in Maggs (1927).

      Dampier on Rota in 1705: Funnel (1969, 229–230).

Argüelles as governor: Argüelles is not listed as governor in the history by Ibáñez y García (1990) or by Carano and Sanchez (1964) but is so identified by Governor Pimentel in his 1709 letter and in AGI, *Filipinas,* 528 C-45, B-3; and in LCM 1, 1–102b.

76–   Census and 1709 epidemic: Pimentel (1709, 214–215).
77

77   Pimentel's request for Quiroga *encomienda*: Pimentel (1709, 211).

Woodes Rogers on Guam: AGI, *Filipinas,* 129, 64; Rogers (1969, 264, 267–268).

Inundation of Fort Guadalupe: AGI, *Filipinas,* 94, 11, 14.

Residencias of Pimentel: AGI, *Filipinas,* 94, 14, 17; AGI, *Ultramar,* 561, Pt. 1, 15; AGI, *Filipinas,* 129, 11, 13, and 168, 4–6, and 526, 1, and 527, Pts. A–B, and 528, Pts. A–B.

Exploitation by governors: Hezel and Driver (1988, 144).

78   Chamorros required to work for Spanish governors: Quiroga (1720, 21); AGI, *Ultramar,* 561, 232–241.

Banishment of Jesuits Ibargüen and Cantova: Quiroga, 8 June 1719 letter in AGI, *Ultramar,* 561, 1529–1533.

Barbinais: Brosses (1967, 219–225); Cheng (1984) gives excerpts from Barbinais' *Nouveau Voyage Autour de Monde* (Paris, 1724).

Clipperton on Guam: Burney (1803–1817, 4:544–546). Some later accounts confuse the battle site, erroneously placing it in Apra Harbor.

78–   1722 petition by *indios*: AGI, *Filipinas,* 562, 1, 1–48; Driver (1968, 26).
79

79   Quiroga's accusation against Pimentel: See Quiroga (1720).

Quiroga's retirement and death: AGI, *Filipinas,* 418, 1:57.

Sánchez de Tagle's flight and death: Hezel and Driver (1988, 148), citing AGI, *Ultramar,* 561, 2, 232–241, and 241–597; AGI, *Filipinas,* 530, 1–22.

Population 1710–1742: Freycinet (1839, 331–333, 354).

Cédula exempting Chamorro women: Freycinet (1839, 499).

Plan for Filipino immigrants: Hezel and Driver (1988, 155), citing Coro Barrutio, 30 March 1722, AGI, *Ultramar,* 562, 910, and 2, 313–321. Also noted in AGI, *Filipinas,* 562, 1–48; and AGI, *Ultramar,* 561, 2, 692–697 (1754).

1727 census: AGI, *Ultramar,* 561, 814–910.

Argüelles' 1726 proposal: Hezel and Driver (1988, 152), citing Argüelles' letter of 24 April 1726, AGI, in *Ultramar,* 561, 3, 745–809, and 810–914.

Council of the Indies rejection of proposals: Letter of 13 July 1728, AGI, *Filipinas,* 95, 34–36.

79–   Mexican silver and cost of Spanish Pacific: Chaunu (1960, 268).
80

80   French ships in the Pacific: Dunmore (1965–1969, 1:193).

Apra Harbor opened and Fort San Luís constructed: AGI, *Filipinas,* 371, 1; Delgadillo et al. (1979, 32).

Naval officers as governor: For Balboa, see Cadarso y Rey (1894, 6).

Anson at Tinian: See Heaps (1974) and Barratt (1988b) for English literature on Anson. In French, see Brosses (1967) and Prévost d'Exiles (1746–1760, Vols. 10, 11).

81   Noble savage literature and the Pacific: Spate (1988, 237–263).

Barbinais on 1700 *palacio:* See Cheng (1984); Brosses (1967, 220).

Agaña *palacio* of 1744: Driver (1989b, 6).

Descriptions and quotes on 1747 celebrations: McClurkan (1987, 7–45), translating from AHPA E-I-c-5,6.

81–   Gómez's *residencia:* Safford (1899, 47).
82

82   Mobilization of men in 1762: LCM 25.

Few Cavite ships: Safford (1899, 54), citing Pages (1791).

Charles III's *cédula* on Jesuits: Costa (1967, 582); Campbell (1921, 514).

82–   Arrival of *Guadalupe* 1769: AHN, 242, 9j.
83

83   Jesuit expulsion: Safford (1899, 65); Costa (1967, 592–593).

Jesuits in Marianas and thirty-seven deaths: Hezel (1989, 89–90).

Jesuit and catechist martyrs: Risco (1970, 221–222).

Quote, "most dangerous mission": Costa (1967, 456).

Quote of 1829 on Jesuits: *Memoria Sobre las Yslas Marianas* (1829, 2).

Tobías as governor: AGI, *Ultramar,* 562, 3, 743–783; Rochon (1891, 92–94; and Raynal (1778, 94–95).

Deer imported from Philippines: Rochon (1891, 86).

84   Crozet's voyage: See descriptions by Rochon (1891), Raynal (1778), and Dunmore (1965–1969, 2:166–199).

Tobías punished by Spaniards: La Perouse (1968, 1:510).

1783–1816 population trends: Underwood (1976, 203–209).

85   Spain's claim and British-French reaction: Frost (1988, 90, 91).

1788 quote by viceroy of Mexico: Frost (1988, 98).

Malaspina expedition: See Malaspina's diary (1984); Higueras (1988, 147–163); and Cerezo Martínez (1987, 135–175).

1787 *cédula:* PNA, Marianas Bundle, 1–7, Exp. 1, 31 January 1791.

1787–1788 Lamotrekese voyages to Guam: Barratt (1988a, 23, 24); Kotzebue (1967b, 2:240–241); Hezel (1983, 103–104).

86   Pineda quote on lack of roads: Pineda (1792, 3).

Malaspina's conviction: Cerezo Martínez (1987, 97, 98).

Records of Malaspina: Higueras (1988, 158–162). Most manuscripts are at the Naval Museum, and drawings are at the Botanical Garden, Madrid.

87   Fire and typhoon 1793: AHN, *Ultramar,* 5854, 36, 75.

      Muro arrival and epidemic in 1794: Haswell (1917, 201–202).

      Muro's administration: LCM 35, 7b.

      1798 Te Deum mass: LCM 9, 63–64.

      Chapter 6: Twilight of Pax Hispanica 1800–1898

88   Muro's resignation: LCM 34, 1.

      Blanco's charter of the *Lydia:* Haswell (1917, 201).

      Spanish Pacific money: Foreman (1980, 259); Basso (1968, 6–9).

      Muro a "Tyrant:" Haswell (1917, 208).

      Muro's *residencia:* Reports in LCM 34, 1 (1801); LCM 35, 7b (1802); and PNA, *Marianas,* 1–3, Exp. 61, 1–19.

88– Quote on Chamorros: Haswell (1917, 211). "Venereal" was probably
89   syphilis, often confused with leprosy, and often inherited.

89   Trepang: Echinoderms, mostly *Holothuroidea,* of which *H. aculeata* or *Microthele nobilis* (teat fish or mammy fish), fat and whitish, is the most edible.

      Guam governor's monopoly over trepang: Chamisso (1986, 205).

      Pearls on Guam: Haswell (1917, 206–207).

      Pearl diving ceases: Chacon Lara (1885, 47).

      Torres and Carolinian trade with Waghal: Kotzebue (1967b, 2:240–241); Chamisso (1986, 272–273); Hezel (1983, 103–104).

      Torres family on Guam: Joseph Miguel de Torres in LCM 25, 5b, 14a (1762), and LCM 2, 39b (1768); Juan Francisco Regis de Torres in AHN, *Ultramar,* 5169, 28, and LCM 1, 117b and LCM 34, 4b; Luís de Torres is named in numerous Spanish records, including AHN, *Ultramar,* 5169, 28, and LCM 1, 35b through LCM 34, 4b. For genealogies, see Souder (1978, 1981) and Ramirez (1983).

90   Kotzebue quotes on Parreño: Kotzebue (1967b, 2:249).

      Fort Soledad completed: AHN, *Ultramar,* 5853, 2a; Delgadillo et al. (1979, 48).

      Medinilla as governor: See LCM 14 for *bandos,* and LCM 9 and 18.

      Ferdinand VII's decree ends galleons: AGI, *Filipinas,* 381.

      Wreck of the *Santiago:* LCM 97, 47a; Driver (1987, 33); Driver (1990b, 23); Kotzebue (1967b, 2:247).

      Chamisso quote on Marianos no longer swimmers: Kotzebue (1967b, 3:83); also *Guam Recorder,* Vol. 2, No. 22, January 1926, 299 (translation by H. G. Hornbostel).

90– Ferdinand VII's reduction of *situado:* AHN, *Filipinas,* 5853.
91

91   Kotzebue quote on last Chamorro couple: Kotzebue (1967b, 2:247).

      Chamisso quote on Chamorro couple: Barratt (1984, 31).

      Population figures 1816: Kotzebue (1967b, 3:91).

Freycinet quote on Rota Chamorros: Freycinet (1839, 277).

Corte quote on pure Chamorros: Corte (1970, 62).

Marche quote on pure Chamorros: Marche (1982, 6).

Wheeler quote on pure Chamorros: Wheeler (1900, 16).

Chamorros thought to be extinguished: For example, Griffith (1978, 30) wrote, "The original Chamorros disappeared utterly and completely." This and similar statements by other writers are erroneous.

92   Golovnin's quote: Barratt (1984, 42).

Freycinet visit: LCM 97; Freycinet (1839, 276–515).

Quote on poor people of Ypao: Freycinet (1927, 94).

Quote on music: Arago (1971, Pt. 2, 49).

Quote on religion: Arago (1971, Pt. 1, 248, 250).

Friar Ciriaco and six illegitimate children: Safford (1899, 219–220); Sullivan (1957, 88–89) (Sullivan spells the name Cyriaco). For biographies of Augustinians in the Marianas, see Sádaba del Carmen (1906).

Chamorro sniffing of hand: Freycinet (1839, 377).

92–   Legends of Two Lovers Point: Freycinet (1839, 368).
93

93   Freycinet on Guam's depression: See numerous tables in Freycinet (1839, 416–515); quote on stagnating economy (p. 466).

Guam's semiwild dogs: Freycinet (1839, 414).

93–   Hydrographic survey and subsequent publications: See Driver (1987)
94   for translation of the 1863 Spanish publication.

94   Earliest American whaleships: See indices in Langdon (1984).

95   Novales revolt in Manila: Foreman (1980, 104–105).

Naval mutiny at Umatac: Duro (1973, 328–337); PNA, Marianas Bundle 3–1, Exps. 22, 5–7b, and 23, 8–10; Safford (1901, 115–119) writing from uncited Spanish records.

Passivity of Chamorros: Driver (1991b, 10), translation of report by Captain Manuel Sanz, 1827.

Lütke on Guam: See Lütke (1971); Barratt (1984, 1988a).

95–   Dumont d'Urville on Guam: See Dumont d'Urville (1987) for 1828
96   visit (pp. 255–258) and for 1839 visit (pp. 375–376). Dumont d'Urville attributed first use of the word *Micronesia* to Domeny de Rienzi, a French geographer, in 1831 at a Paris meeting of the Société de Géographie.

96   Expatriates on Guam: Safford (1899, 175).

Ganga's plan: *Año de 1829* (1829, 1–27, 48–67); see also del Valle (1991, Chap. 3).

Ricafort's orders of 1828: AHN, *Filipinas,* 5853; Driver (1991c).

Memoria sobre las Yslas Marianos: AHN, *Filipinas,* 5853.

97   Villalobos' mission: *Año de 1829* (1829, 218–231, 269–279); Driver (1991c); see also del Valle (19931).

Villalobos proposals: Villalobos (1833, 40–43).

Land grants to locals: See examples in LCM 40.

Avoidance of tithes/taxes: Corte (1970, 257–258); Olive y García (1984, 22); LCM, *Memorias y Documentos de las Islas Marianas,* Vol. 3, No. 9, Document 16, 6 (*Descripción de las Yslas Marianas,* Santa María, 1844).

98   Dumont D'Urville 1839 quote: Dumont d'Urville (1987, 375).

Jurien de la Gravière visit and quote: Jurien de la Gravière (1854, 7).

Governor and treasurer collusion: Corte (1970, 66, 309).

Sixty whalers per year and revenue: Corte (1970, 69).

Quote from *Emily Morgan* log: *Emily Morgan* (1925, 103). See McGrath (1986) for excerpts from other whaler logs.

99   Governor Pérez and Manila's aid: Ibáñez del Carmen and Resano (1976, 3); Safford (1899, 241–263, 267, 269–271).

Masters on Guam: LCM 3, 31–35; 78b–79b; 144b–145b. See Ballendorf and Wuerch (1991) for full history; and Despatches from the U.S. Consul in Guam, 22 November 1855.

Sarah Mooers wreck: Ballendorf and Wuerch (1991, 319–321).

USS *Vandalia* at Guam: Safford (1899, 393); Despatches from the U.S. Consul in Guam, 22 November 1855.

100   Cessation of Guam *situado* in 1855: Corte (1970, 67).

Quote on permanent deficit: Corte (1970, 262).

Quote on 1856 epidemic: Ibáñez del Carmen and Resano (1976, 6). The diaries of the Augustin Recollect Fathers Aniceto Ibáñez del Carmen and Francisco Resano del Sagrado Corazón that make up the *Chronicle of the Mariana Islands* (1976) give detailed accounts of life on Guam from 1847 until 1899.

Population before and after 1856 epidemic: Corte (1970, 312).

Palomo family: Safford (1899, 399). See also Souder (1981).

Royal order of 1857: PNA Carolines Bundle 11, Exp. 7, F 1–1 1857, and AHN, *Ultramar, 5854, Madrid 31 Agosto* 1857.

Chinese convicts 1858: Safford (1899, 46).

100– Corte's proposals: See Corte (1970, 391–495).
101

101   Quote of Corte on *fadang:* Corte (1970, 512).

Lytico-bodig and *fadang:* See Monmaney (1990) for history.

Cavite Mutiny 1872 and *deportados* to the Marianas: Foreman (1980, 106–108, 362–364); Ibáñez del Carmen and Resano (1976, 38).

Bully Hayes arrested on Guam: Lubbock (1931, 297–301).

Quote on Filipino secret agitation: Foreman (1980, 108).

101– Assassination of Pazos and quotes: Ibáñez del Carmen and Resano
102   (1976, 57); LCM 82 (1885–1899, Criminal investigation following the assassination of the governor of the Islands, Angel de Pazos); and García de la Purisima Concepción (1964, 64[14]–65[15]).

102   Reorganization of military: LCM, *Memorias y Documentos de las Islas Marianas, Parte 3*, 45–74; Olive y García (1984, 48).

Father Palomo's quote: Corte (1970), Hornbostel translation with Palomo continuation (p. 3).

On guard against Chamorros: Cadarso y Rey (1894, 15).

Quote on Chamorro grammar: Topping (1973, 7).

Maternal dominance of neo-Chamorro families: Thompson (1969, 52, 53, 248, 285); Nelson and Nelson (1992, 109).

103   Family in neo-Chamorro society: See App. D in Haverlandt et al. (1975).

104   Chamorros absorbed newcomers: Spoehr (1954, 57, 62–67).

Neo-Chamorros closer to Filipino culture: Spoehr (1978, 259).

Neo-Chamorros distinct from Filipinos: Thompson (1969, 292) Domingo Abella believed that neo-Chamorros and Filipinos were the same people by the early twentieth century (see Abella 1973).

Juan Malo stories: See Van Peenen (1974, 49–62) for examples.

Madrid 1887 exhibition: The Exposición de Filipinas opened in June 1887 in the Crystal Palace of the Madrid El Retiro. Two Chamorros— José Aflague Flores and Antonia de los Santos Leon Guerrero (later Antonia Ada)—represented the Marianas at the exhibition. José Portusach donated two large golden cowry shells, *Cypraea aurantium*, from Guam's reefs. See description in Miyagi (1975).

104–   Olive y García quotes: Olive y García (1984, 66).
105

105   Communal labor: Corte (1970, 128). Corte complained that communal labor *(polo)* on Guam was ineffective, which is one reason that convicts were sent to the island.

Hacienda system: *Haciendas* (ranches) should not be confused with the *Hacienda Publica* (Treasury/Department of Public Finance).

Quotes on Chamorro workers: Olive y García (1984, 24, 8).

Local democracy: PNA, Marianas Bundle 18, Exp. 23, F 1–7.

Our Lady of Camarin: Ibáñez del Carmen and Resano (1976, 68); *Guam Recorder*, Vol. 3, No. 10, January 1927, 286–287; see Jorgensen (1984) for most complete discussion. An iron plate on the bottom of the statue indicates that the *Pilar* wreck at Cocos in 1690 may have been its origin. The statue was also known as "Mary of the Crabs" (María de Cangrejos). It became the patroness of the *dotación* company and was placed in a niche or small tabernacle (*camarín* in Spanish) behind the altar in the Agana *presidio* barracks chapel constructed in 1736, but it was moved to the cathedral in 1884 after the Pazos assassination.

105–   Massacre of *deportados*: Ibáñez del Carmen and Resano (1976, 70);
106   Safford (1899, 473–474) also provides an eyewitness account by his cook.

106   Resiliency of Chamorro identity: Thompson (1969, 287–291); Spoehr (1978, 254). For example, Father Palomo, from a *manak'kilo* family,

was still using *indios* as the ethnic designation for *manak'papa* Chamorros in baptismal records in the 1890s.

Chapter 7: The Anglo-Saxon Way 1898–1903

108 McKinley quote on manifest destiny: Olcott (1916, 379).

109 Roosevelt quote on *Maine:* Roosevelt letter to Diblee, 16 February 1898, in Roosevelt Papers.

Glass's orders: Naval Board's recommendations to Long in *Bureau of Navigation* Appendix, 68, 151, in NA, RG 45, 9345; copy also provided in Walker (1945, 3).

Charleston's seizure of Guam: Eyewitness accounts include Gutiérrez (1899), Portusach (1917), Glass (1898), Coontz (1930), Sixto (1899), Cabanillas and Ortín (1899), Ralli (1899), Myers (1931, 1933), and White (1900). Detailed secondary accounts include García de la Purísima Concepción (1964), Beers (1914), Walker (1945), Griffith (1978), and Pozuelo Mascaraque (1989). Cox (1917, Apps., 87–93) provides Glass' reports and surrender documents; originals are in NA, RG 45, Subject File 1776–1911, Class 2, VI, Guam Affairs.

Quote on *Charleston's* entry into Apra: Coontz (1930, 205).

110 Quote on prices of fruit and monkeys: Ralli (1899, 162).

Marina's surrender: NA, RG 80, 9351. Translated in Cox (1917, 89).

111 Quote on native soldiers' joy: White (1900, 10–11).

Quote on population's distress: Cabanillas and Ortin (1899, 27).

111– Portusach quotes: Portusach (1917, 710–711). Glass never mentioned
112 Portusach in his reports. Portusach wrote his article nineteen years after the event from memory.

112 Quotes in 1898 protocol: *Foreign Relations* (1898, 829).

Naval War Board recommendations: Message of 24 August 1898, NA, RG 45, 9345; Braisted (1958, 52).

Poll on bases: *Literary Digest,* Vol. 17, 10 September 1898, 307–308.

McKinley quote: *Christian Advocate* (New York), 22 January 1903.

113 Commentator on Micronesia's strategic value: See Robinson (1898) and Pomeroy (1951, 11) on Robinson's contacts with the U.S. Paris Peace Commission.

Quote on U.S. control of the Carolines: Captain R. B. Bradford (naval attaché to the U.S. Paris Peace Commission), in U.S. Senate (1899, Pt. 1, 474).

Treaty of Paris: *U.S. Statutes-at-Large,* Vol. 30, 1754–1762; specifically 10 December 1898, 30 Stat. 1754, and 1759 (1899); full hearings in U.S. Senate (1899).

114 Executive Order 108-A: U.S. Senate (1950); NA, RG 80, 9351. This order is sometimes cited as No. 5 of the McKinley administration.

Leary's instructions: NA, RG 45, 9345, letter from McKinley and Long to Leary, 12 January 1899, in General Correspondence File.

Sixto's assumption of command and quotes: See Sixto (1899).

Pennsylvania whooping cough: Ibáñez del Carmen and Resano (1976, 71).

115 Cottman's report: Cottman in NA, RG 80, 9351.

Taussig's orders issued on Guam: NA, RG 80, 9351.

116 Kaiser quotes: Kaiser (1899, 4, 7).

Elcano and poliomyelitis: Safford (1905, 122).

117 Kaiser on July Fourth: Kaiser (1899, 12).

Yosemite: Leary's supplies included the first billiard table, baseball and tennis gear, and printing press on Guam (see NA, RG 19, Ship's History of the USS *Yosemite* [SS-121]).

Leary's 10 August proclamation: NA, RG 80, 9351.

118 Safford quote on Spanish archives: Safford (1901, 18).

119 Chamorro petition to deport Filipinos: Leary letter of 26 August 1899, No. 18-G, in NA, RG 80, 9351.

Expulsion of priests: Beers (1914, 26); Cabanillas and Ortín (1899, 35, 36).

119– Marines' insubordination and quotes: Letter by Major Allen C. Kelton,
120 26 October 1899, to commandant of Marines, in U.S. Marine Corps Historical files concerning Guam, Navy Yard, Washington, D.C. See Clifford's (1904) account for marine enlisted view.

120 Cox quote: Cox (1917, 43)

Chamorro retained by Germans in schools: Costenoble (1905–1910, 49).

Leary quote: Leary letter of 11 October 1899, NA, RG 80, 9351.

Archbishop and Leary quotes: NA, RG 80, 9351.

Quote to receive Wheeler: NA, RG 80, 9351.

120– Safford quote on Leary's move to Agana: Safford (1901, 141).
121

121 Wheeler on Guam: Safford (1901, 191–210).

Petition for Safford as governor: NA, RG 80, 9351.

Wheeler quote: Wheeler (1900, 36).

Change of name to Guam: Leary letter of 13 February 1900, No. 10-G, in NA, RG 80, 9351. Schroeder also asked for the name change in his Second *Annual Report of the Governor of Guam* (cited as *Annual Report* hereafter), 16 July 1902, No. 265, 13, 4. The official change was by Navy Department Special Order 6, 28 October 1908.

122 Defrauding of Merizo women: Safford (1901, 33, 43).

Spanish laws in effect: These included the Penal Code, the Law of Civil Procedure, and a 1893 Mortgage Law (Ley Hipotecaria) for real estate procedures, which Safford partly modified and which should have been totally replaced to avoid much litigation in the future.

Quote on Congressional indifference: Beers (1914, 45).

Safford quote on departure: Safford (1901, 254).

123 Safford's career: See Nelson (1952).

Capuchins to Guam: Sullivan (1957, 100–101).

Ley quote: *Annual Report,* Dyer, 21 June 1904, 8g–9g.

Lytico-Bodig death 1902: Monmaney (1990, 88).

Quote on 1900 typhoon: See Clifford (1904).

Justin rescue of *Yosemite:* Beers (1914, 57–58); Schroeder (1926, 37).

123–   Quote on Carolinians: NA, RG 80, 9351, Report of Schroeder to secre-
124   tary of the navy, 31 January 1901, No. 75-G.

124 Carolinian population in German Marianas: Fritz (1986, 9).

Mabini and Filipino insurrectionists on Guam: Beers (1914, 67); Mabini (1965, 322).

125 Asan ceremony 1961: *Guam Daily News,* 5 July 1961.

1901 census: *Annual Report,* Schroeder, 16 July 1902, 264–265.

Average military complement of 158 on Guam: Beers (1914, 66).

Chamorro petition of 1901: U.S. House (1902, 2).

Senate bill in 1903: U.S. Senate (1903); Beers (1914, 51).

Insular Cases (all 1901): For an analysis, see Leibowitz (1989).

Brown's opinion: *Insular Cases, Downes v. Bidwell,* 286.

125–   White's opinion: *Insular Cases, Downes v. Bidwell,* 311–312.
126

126 Harlan's opinion: *Insular Cases, Downes v. Bidwell,* 384–385.

Attorney General's quote: *Annual Report,* Maxwell, 20 August 1914, 26.

1902 earthquake: Schroeder (1926, 52).

USS *Guam:* Thompson (1969, 65) described Guam's naval government as "a military regime similar to that on a battleship." James (1949, 79–80) described it as "the United States Naval Vessel *The Island of Guam* with some 20,000 civilian members of the crew." James was a naval officer in the Guam military government in 1944–1946.

Chapter 8: Ordered Tranquility 1903–1918

127 Events and orders under naval governors, 1903–1941: Sources other than those cited are in the *Annual Report of the Governor of Guam,* 1901–1941, MARC copies. Each *Annual Report* was for a fiscal year, July 1–June 30, and was usually submitted in August or September. Naval governor orders are also in MARC copies of *Guam: Brief Extracts 1905–;* and in General Orders.

Hardship pay for Americans: Beers (1914, 64).

Naval ranks of governors: Ranks ranged from lieutenant (as acting governors) through captain; an admiral was not assigned until after World War II; see the Appendix.

No metal plows: Costenoble (1905–1910, 57).

Quote on Guam and Chamorros: French (1905, 376).

Quote of Costenoble: Costenoble (1905–1910, 47).

129   Quote on Chamorro loss of lands: Souder (1987, 214).

Susana Hospital: *Annual Report* 1909, 16, and 1910, 5; Cox (1917, 58).

Request for cadastral survey: *Annual report* 1905, 52g.

Size of Guam: As of 1990, the Guam Bureau of Planning uses 135,680 acres, or 212 square miles, which does not include coastal islets. Karolle (1988) uses 136,960 acres, or 214 square miles (55,427 hectares), which include Cocos and all other coastal islets. Karolle's figure is used in this history. In comparison, Oahu in the Hawaiian Islands is 593 square miles in area, or over twice the size of Guam.

Public lands reduced by half: Cox (1917, 84) overestimated crown lands as 67,200 acres with half leased and 515 acres owned by the naval government by purchases around 1904. Coote (1950, 23) uses 36,000 acres. Thompson (1969, 115) states (without sources) that crown lands in 1899 were 36,030 acres.

130   Maxwell quote on land scandals: *Annual Report* 1915, 10.

Naval Station Order 47: NA, RG 80, 9351, Box 482 (1818:6).

130–   Root-Takahira agreement and Orange Plans: Braisted (1958, 6–8, 32–
131   35). U.S. plans for war with Japan arose out of the 1906–1907 crisis.

131   Orange War Plans: See Miller (1991) for detailed analysis.

"Absolute necessity" of fortifying Guam: See Mahan (1912, 1970).

Taft order: Executive Order 1613; *Annual Report* 1914, 3–4.

Guam duty free: *Guam News Letter,* Vol. 1, No. 6, 15 October 1909, 2.

Dorn order on alien land sales and leases: *Annual Report* 1909, 1.

132   German Capuchin incident: *Annual Report* 1910, 7; *Guam News Letter,* Vol. 2, No. 2, 25 June 1910, 3–4; Sullivan (1957, 104–105).

Dorn Poem: Anonymous, reported in Dorn's private diary, 1910, 3, Box 1, Dorn Papers. Dorn took the poem with good humor, noting in his diary, "They [the authors] proved that Governor a horse's ass."

Spanish Capuchins to Guam: *Guam Recorder,* Vol. 14, No. 8, November 1937, 8; Sullivan (1957, 105–108).

Protestants: Sablan (1990, 118–128); Beers (1914, 41); Thompson (1969, 183).

Luís Castro-Custino: *Guam Recorder,* Vol. 3, No. 6, October 1926, 203.

133   Coontz quote: Coontz (1930, 338).

Mahan quote: Cited in Seager (1977, 485).

Nambō: This was the Nan'yō Bōeki Kabushikigaisha (South Seas Trading Company); Peattie (1988, 24–26).

Shimizu firm: Cox (1917, 69).

Atkins, Kroll: *Annual Report* 1916, 27; Ballendorf (1983).

1913 measles and 1915 whooping cough victims: *Annual Report* 1916, 27.

134   "Six saloons" and sixteen "public women": *Annual Report* 1915, 11–12.

Retirement fund: *Annual Report* 1915, 15; 1917, 10–11.

Two wages: Thompson (1969, 148).

Maxwell quote: *Annual Report* 1915, 18.

Roosevelt quote: Letter to Governor Maxwell, 30 October 1914, in NA, RG 80, 9351 (1374).

135   Altered balance of power: Braisted (1971, 162–164); Peattie (1988, 48–49).

SMS *Cormoran*: Descriptions in Ward (1970) and in Burdick (1979).

Cormoran internment: *Annual Report* 1915, 3; Ward (1970, 64–73).

136   Insular Force: *Annual Report* 1915, 6.

Marinon mantiquilla: Sablan (1990, 304).

Ellis on Guam 1914–1915: Ballendorf (1983, 80).

Ellis' reef crossings and proposals: Ellis (1915, 67, 75).

Hornbostel and Costenobles: U.S. Marine Corps (1958, 23–24). A son of Hermann Costenoble, H. Costenoble wrote a grammar in German of the Chamorro language, *Die Chamorro Sprache*. 'S-Gravenhage'. M. Nijhoff, 1940.

137   Ellis quote: Ellis (1915, 16).

Copra in World War I: *Annual Report* 1920, 42.

Bank of Guam: *Guam News Letter*, Vol. 7, No. 6, December 1915, 18.

Maxwell's behavior: Ward (1970, 74–76).

First execution under U.S. Navy: *Annual Report* 1916, 28; *Guam News Letter*, Vol. 7, No. 8, February 1916, 5, 8, 9. Executions were rare under navy rule.

Maxwell relieved: *Annual Report* 1916, 1.

Description of Guam in 1916: Quoted in Ward (1970, 79).

General Board study 1917: Braisted (1971, 206–208).

138   Anderson quote: "First Session of Guam Congress," *Guam News Letter*, Vol. 8, No. 8, February 1917, 2.

Manwaring quote: "Guam Congress: Animated Extra Session March 17th," *Guam News Letter*, Vol. 8, No. 9, March 1917, 27.

Guam Militia: Established by Executive General Order 225, 8 February 1917; *Annual Report* 1917, 36; documentation in NA, RG 80, 9351.

See also "Brief History of the Guam Militia," by Colonel Joaquin Torres, militia commander, in *Guam Recorder,* Vol. 9, No. 11, February 1933, 185.

Blain–von Gebhard marriage: Ward (1970, 41, 81).

139   First shot in World War I: The U.S. Navy disputed Chockie's claim, saying that a sailor on the USS *Mongolia* fired the first shot against a U-boat in the Atlantic on 19 April 1917; see accounts in the *United States Naval Proceedings,* Vol. 43, No. 172, June 1917, 1328. Another account states that Lt. Hall fired the first shot with his pistol; see letter of Brig. Gen. H. K. Pickett, U.S.M.C., in *Chevron,* 24 October 1942, 7.

139–   Sinking of the *Cormoran: Guam News Letter,* Vol. 8, No. 10, April
140   1917, 1, 2; see also Ward (1970), Burdick (1979), and Bartlett (1972).

140   Salvage of the *Cormoran:* See Ward (1970, 105–106). In 1960–1965, Phillip Soliday and, in 1965–1975, Herbert Ward made hundreds of scuba dives on the *Cormoran;* they retrieved much of the ship's furnishings and the personal belongings of the crew. Ward wrote a history of the ship and drowned deep in one of the cabins on 24 June 1975, perhaps a suicide.

Papuans on Guam: "New Guinea Prisoners of War Leave," *Guam News Letter,* Vol. 10, No. 7, January 1919, 2.

Flag: *Annual Report* 1918, 31; NA, RG 45, EG54, Box 2047.

141   Guam seal adopted: *Annual Report* 1930, 123. The scene with the proa and palm may have been based on a painting by Francisco Feja Feja (*PDN,* 25 February 1992, 3).

141–   American bamboo and quote on caste system: Sablan (1990, 23, 25,
142   28).

142   Atkins, Kroll complaint: See Ballendorf (1983) for letter by Clifton Kroll to Smith, 25 November 1916.

Roger Welles quote: Cited by Ballendorf (1984, 85).

New radio station: *Annual Report* 1918, 10.

142–   Atkins, Kroll and ONI: See Ballendorf (1984) for ONI reports, NA, RG
143   38.

Influenza deaths in 1918: *Annual Report* 1919, 13. Sullivan (1957, 118) states that the death total was 950.

Sailor's quote on influenza: Letter from E. D. Perry to F. Wisner, 16 December 1918, in NA, RG 45, Box 457, PS Guam.

Wilson medal to Father Román de Vera: Sullivan (1957, 119).

Investigation of Smith: NA, RG 45, Box 457, PS Guam.

Chapter 9: The Quest for Identity 1918–1941

144   EGOs and quotes: Documentation in NA, RG 80, 9351, Box 484; also *Guam News Letter,* Vol. 11, No. 4, October 1919, 10.

145   Johnston-Iglesias marriage: See Johnston (1974).

1920 census figures: *Annual Report* 1921.

146 Marine seaplane squadron on Guam: *Annual Report* 1922, 49; U.S. Marine Corps (1958, 34–40); see Johnson (1977) for history.

Quote on League mandates as fig leaf: Peattie (1988, 55).

Quote by Bywater: Bywater (1921, 262).

Yamamoto inspired by Bywater: See Honan (1991).

147 Ellis and Hornbostel in Micronesia: Peattie (1988, 237–240); see also Ballendorf (1984). The Marine Corps suspected that Ellis was poisoned; Ballendorf (1990, 84) concludes that he died from effects of alcoholism.

Hornbostels: Hans was commissioned an army major in 1940, and he and Gertrude were captured by the Japanese in Manila in 1941. Held as prisoners in Santo Tomás Prison, Gertrude was infected there with leprosy. After the war, both lived in a Louisiana leprosarium for years until she recovered.

Quote on teaching: Memorandum of Superintendent of Public Instruction Thomas Collins, 12 December 1922, in NA, RG 80, 9351, Box 486 (1983–2070).

Navy burns books: Thompson (1969, 218).

Guam Recorder established: NA, RG 80, 9351, Box 459, (2161–2203); see history in *Guam Recorder,* 2d Ser., Vol. 1, No. 1, October 1971, 3.

148 Umatac not where Magellan landed: See Rogers and Ballendorf (1989).

President Grant: Guam Recorder, Vol. 16, No. 3, June 1939, 112.

Chamorro pleas for citizenship 1920s: *Guam Recorder,* Vol. 2, No. 17, July 1925, 131–133, and Vol. 4, No. 1, April 1927, 1.

Filipino resolution for United States to cede Guam: *Guam Recorder,* Vol. 3, No. 7, October 1926, 181; Vol. 3, No. 8, November 1926, 209–210.

Bill on Chamorro citizenship: U.S. House (1927); *Guam Recorder,* Vol. 4, No. 1, April 1927, 1; Vol. 4, No. 2, May 1927, 29.

149 Guam Congress rejection of Interior: NA, RG 80, EG54/A18-2 (271028).

Bradley's political views: NA, RG 80, Hooper File, letter to Captain S. C. Hooper, 16 April 1930; Maga (1988, 117–118); and Farrell (1991b).

Guam Congress endorsement of Bradley: NA, RG 80, EG54/A18-2 (261028-2).

Bradley proclamations: *Annual Report* 1930, 4, 124; *Guam Recorder,* Vol. 7, No. 1, April 1930, 1; Vol. 7, No. 12, March 1931, 233, 235–236, 243–253; also see Bradley.

Bill of Rights: *Guam Recorder,* Vol. 7, No. 10, January 1931, 191.

Chamorro parade and demonstration 1931: *Guam Recorder,* Vol. 7, No. 11, February 1931, 213; also see Bradley.

Bradley quote on Guam Congress: *Annual Report* 1931, 7.

Second Congress and election: *Annual Report* 1931, 7, 8; Zenor (1949, 60).

150 Navy unhappiness with Bradley: Letter from Captain W. R. Furlong, 11 June 1930, in NA, RG 80, EG 54/A9-10.

Bradley quote: Letter to Captain W. R. Furlong, 2 May 1930, in NA, RG 80, EG54/A9-10 (300502).

151 Guam Congress resolutions on Bradley: Guam Congress, Concurrent Resolution No. 2, 4 April 1931, and No. 4, 6 April 1931, in NA, RG 80, EG 54/A9-10 (310410 and 310414).

1927–1928 Plan Orange: Maga (1988, 101–104); Miller (1991, 207).

Quote on Apra: Cited by Miller (1991, 207).

Hoover order to close airspace: Executive Order 5281, quoted in *Guam Recorder,* Vol. 7, No. 8, November 1930, 164.

152 F. B. Leon Guerrero: Nelson (1965, 9–11).

B. J. Bordallo: The Bordallo family on Guam was founded by Baltazar Bordallo, a Spaniard who came from Ponape (Pohnpei) to Guam in the 1890s and married Josephina Borja Pangelinan from Sumay. See The Awakening (1965), Pt. 2, 35, and Pt. 3, 12.

Voter apathy and empty seats: *Annual Report* 1933, 2.

Ulloa, Sablan, Underwood appeals for citizenship: *Guam Recorder,* Vol. 8, No. 10, January 1932, 436–437.

Chamorro visitor and Roosevelt: The Awakening (1965, Pt. 3, 36, 39); Griffith (1978, 312), citing papers of Senator Ernest Gibson, file on "Guam Citizenship," University of Vermont Reference Library, Burlington, Vermont. See also Bordallo (1982, 117–121). No name was given for the Chamorro visitor.

1933 petition for citizenship: U.S. Senate (1937, 51–52).

Chamorros "Orientals" and Roosevelt concurrence: Navy memorandum to White House, 6 September 1933, in NA, RG 80, EG54/P1-4 (330906).

Fall in copra exports: Thompson (1969, 155).

153 School statistics mid-1930s: Thompson (1969, 220–221, 359).

Pan American Martin 130 clippers: Gandt (1985, 33–40).

154 Pan American Boeing No. 18 clippers: *Guam Recorder,* Vol. 16, No. 1, April 1939, 91; also see Higgens (1938).

1935 appeal via Dorn: U.S. Senate (1937, 53).

154– 1936 Resolution: U.S. Senate (1937, 40); original in NA, RG 80, EG54/
155 A18 (360710).

155 McCandlish donates $20.00: The Awakening (1965, Pt. 3, 36).

Media coverage: *Washington Post,* 12 March 1937.

Swanson's quote: U.S. Senate (1937, 2).

Quote critical of navy: U.S. Senate (1937, 9).

155– Closed hearings: Testimony by Cmdr. R. O. Davis, 16 April, in U.S.
156 Senate (1937, 76).

156 Meeting with Roosevelt: Bordallo (1982, 142–143); The Awakening (1965, Pt. 3, 36).

B. J. Bordallo's report: Original dated 15 June 1937 in MARC collection of Guam Congress documents. Leon Guerrero's transmittal on 14 July 1937, in NA, RG 80, EG54/A18 (370710).

McCandlish quote on Bordallo: Letter of 26 July 1937, in NA, RG 80, EG54/A18 (370726).

McCandlish quote on Chamorros not working: Letter of 13 July 1937 to Collier Publishing Co., in NA, RG 80, EG54/P1-4.

ACLU represents Guam: Documents in NA, RG 80, EG54/P1.

F. B. Leon Guerrero debt for trip: Palomo (1984, 73).

Japanese informants on Guam: Palomo (1984, 10, 11, 48, 50).

157 Hepburn report: Pomeroy (1951, 124–143).

Guam in Category F: Memorandum of Admiral R. E. Ingersoll, 20 December 1940, in NA, RG 80, EG54/A16-3, Box 91.

Operation Magic: NA, RG 457, MAGIC intercepts SRDJ Series; see also Dorwart (1983).

Executive Order 8683: 3CFR 894 (1938–1943).

1940 census: Thompson (1969, 37).

158 Wilbur quote: Letter of 28 March 1928 to Congressman J. Maas, in NA, RG 45, EG54/ONI, Box 2047 (390522).

Quote from OSS assessment: OSS R & A 744, 20.

Government land figures: Souder (1987, 213–214); Thompson (1969, 118).

No jury trials: Dorr v. United States, 105 U.S. 138.

Navy judiciary on prewar Guam: Stevens (1956, 86–87).

158– Bishop Olano and Capuchins: Olano (1949, iv); Thompson (1969,
159 186–187).

159 Father Román: Umatuna Si Yuus, 13 December 1959, 4.

Baptists and Reverend Sablan: Sablan (1990, 78–96, 131); Thompson (1969, 185).

School system 1941: Thompson (969, 358–359). See also Annual Report 1941.

Quote on no local text books: James (1946, 276).

Dr. Ramon Sablan: See obituary by Senator Manuel U. Lujan, P.D.N., 11 April 1970, 23.

160 Chamorro illiteracy under navy: Griffith (1978, 230–233).

Teachers' and laborers' pay: Griffith (1978, 230–233); Thompson (1969, 147).

Mortality rates: Griffith (1978, 244–245).

Failure of naval government: Thompson (1969, 292–306).

Thompson quote: Thompson (1969, 300).

Defense forces on Guam 1941: McMillin (1945, 16–25) listed 153 marines to include the Insular Patrol.

160–   Guam military vessels: The heavy cruiser USS *Guam* served in World
161   War II. It replaced the river gunboat USS *Guam*, built in Shanghai in 1927. The gunboat was changed to the USS *Wake*, and it was captured by the Japanese in 1941. In 1965 an amphibious assault ship was named the USS *Guam*.

161   Barney Maru and mess attendants: *Guam Recorder*, Vol. 16, No. 7, October 1939, 280–281; Sanchez (1990, 14).

       Quote by Turner: Lademan (1969, 52–53).

       February–March 1941 appropriation for Guam: U.S. Senate (1941, 44).

162   Quote on Horii's orders: NA, RG 33, entry 319, original in File 6, Serial 24, File (case) No. 7, 1 January 1946, Report by L. H. Barnard, RE: Japanese Plan to Attack Guam (1941), ATIS Captured Document No. 1541. See also Iwano et al (1946).

       Ingersoll warning: MAGIC intercepts, Summaries, Vol. 4, Sec. 76, 72: telegram 24 November 1941, OPNAV to CINCAF, COMS 11–13, 15.

       Quote to destroy classified materials, 4 December: MAGIC intercepts, Summaries, Vol. 4, Sec. 92, 86: telegram 4 December 1941b, OPNAV to NAVSTA Guam.

       Quote on Chamorro faith in America: Sanchez (1983, 8).

       Chapter 10: The Way of the *Samurai* 1941–1944

163   Quote on Agana mass: Olano (1949, 1).

       Descriptions of 1941 invasion: American and Chamorro eyewitness accounts include Olano (1949), McMillin (1945), O'Leary (1941), Sablan (1990), Owings (1981), and Palomo (1984) (the latter two accounts are based on numerous interviews with participants). Japanese accounts include ATIS Captured Document No. 1541; and Iwano et al (1946).

       Wesley and Sablan witness bombing: Palomo (1984, 3, 4).

163–   First fatalities: Palomo (1984, 4).
164

164   Quote, "Gerra, Gerra": Olano (1949, 2).

       Infiltrators: See Calvo (1992b, 7) for names.

165   Quote on trick information on landing: McMillin (1945, 11).

       Quote by Giles: Tweed (1945, 5).

       Japanese bomber shot down: Spicer (1946, 2).

165–   Japanese units: Lodge (1954, 8); Crowl (1960, 23); see also Iwano et al
166   (1946).

167   Olano quote on cadavers: Olano (1949, 13).

       Quote by Cruz on fighting: Palomo (1984, 27, 28). Cruz also recounts the plaza fight in Owings (1981, 219–224).

168   Quote on marines' surrender: Spicer (1946, 3).

Dead and wounded figures: McMillin (1945, 14).

Burial and memorial: Calvo (1992a, 15); Calvo (1992b, 20).

Orders to McMillin not to resist: No such orders have been located, but one report (Spicer 1946, 2), stated that orders were received by McMillin.

169   Cruz refutation of flag story: Owings (1981, 233–237, 244).

Quote on flag story: Sanchez (1983, 23).

10 December Japanese proclamation: Sanchez (1983, 25).

170   492 Guam prisoners to Japan: The *New York Times,* 16 January 1942, reported the total as 432, citing Japanese sources. Other sources reported the total as 476 (42 U.S. officers, 5 nurses, 297 U.S. enlisted men, 119 civilians, 13 clergy).

Chamorro internees and mine: Apple (1980, 30); Sanchez (1983, 36).

Quote on Japanese occupation: Sanchez (1983, 26, 27).

170–   Occupation measures: Sanchez (1983, 39, 56–57).
171

171   Japanese priests with Olano's permission: As Spanish nationals (Spain was neutral in the war), Olana and his secretary were released in January 1942 in Tokyo (see Olano 1949).

172   Quote of Mrs. Flores: Sanchez (1983, 34).

Seinindan and Japanese administration: See Lowe (1967, 281–295) for translations of Japanese officials' notes, 1942–1943.

173–   Sgambelluri's quote on beheading: Palomo (1984, 112).
174

174   Antonio Artero: Antonio was the son of a former Spanish soldier, Don Pascual Artero y Saez, who married a Chamorrita on Yap and immigrated to Guam in 1901, where he was hired by Balthazar Bordallo as a *vaquero* and became a prosperous landowner. Antonio married a U.S. naval officer's daughter (see Artero y Saez 1948).

Bordallo given thirty days to find Tweed: Author's interview with Paul Bordallo, 25 August 1992.

Bordallo quote on Tweed: Palomo (1984, 161).

Submarine attacks: See records in Roscoe (1949).

175   Sinking of *Sakito Maru:* Satoh (1978, 46).

176   Nicotine salt sulfur as insecticide: Owings (1981, 57), quoting José Barcinas.

Giant African snail: See Lange (1950).

Chamorros infected by hookworms: Monmaney (1990, 85).

Quote on U.S. control of air: Quoted in Crowl (1960, 323–324), from CINCPAC-CINCPOA Translation 10634, extracts from the diary of 2d Lt. Imanishi, 38th Regt.

177   Chorito misspelled as Chonito: Apple (1980, 83).

177– Futile Rota event: Japanese account in Satoh (1978, 79–84).
178

178   George Bush in raids against Guam: Stinnett (1991, 86).

      Charfauros attempted beheading: Palomo (1984, 170).

      Father Duenas suspected: Horie (1967, 209); Critchfield (1988, [5]–
      146, citing *Riku shi dai yonjū san kisei* [Records of the 43d class, Japan
      Military Academy], 375–376).

      Execution of Father Duenas and others: Sanchez (1983, 77–81); Pal-
      omo (1984, 179–181); Olano (1949, 143–147).

179   Concentration camps: About 10,000 Chamorros were in camps in the
      Manengon Valley; other camps were at Pajesjes, Atate, and Talofofo;
      see eyewitness accounts in Owings (1981).

180   Quote of Dolores Jones: Owings (1981, 308).

      Quote by Chris Howard: Howard (1982, 124).

      Merizo massacres and uprising: See eyewitness accounts in Owings
      (1981); secondary accounts in Sanchez (1983, 82–83); Palomo (1984,
      185–187). A postwar Japanese account blamed the Merizo massacres
      on a Chamorro girlfriend, named Obera, of the village *taichō;* she had
      the villagers arrested as spies in order to get rid of a rival girlfriend of
      the *taichō.* The Japanese account reported that the villagers killed
      Obera after the Japanese fled (see Satoh 1978, 55–75).

181   Atrocities in Agana and Fena in July 1944: Sanchez (1983, 82–84); Far-
      rell (1984, 39–44); Olano (1949, 136–147); Whaley (1992, 36).

Chapter 11: Return of the Americans 1944–1945

182   U.S. invasion of Guam: Detailed American military histories include
      Crowl (1960), Lodge (1954), Shaw et al. (1966), Meyers (1947), Far-
      rell (1984), and Gailey (1988). For the Japanese view, see Takeda
      (1946, 1952) and Satoh (1978). For a vivid eyewitness account, see
      Josephy (1946).

182– Troop strengths: Crowl (1960, 329), Lodge (1954, 196–197), and
184   Shaw et al. (1966, 444) all give 18,500 for Japanese strength. Satoh
      (1978), quoting Japanese officers, gives 20,800.

184   UDT quote: Crowl (1960, 339), citing Task Force 53 Report, Guam,
      Incl. A, 11.

      Ito quote: Ito (1967, 20).

      Gaan Point guns: Lodge (1954, 48). The Japanese at the Gaan Point
      blockhouse fought bravely to the death. The blockhouse was never
      demolished, and the last of the defenders' bones were found in the
      1980s in the rubble inside.

      Yamashita quote: Satoh (1978, 108).

185   Colonel Suenaga's suicide charge: Satoh (1978, 108).

      Capture of Japanese documents: Francis (1944, 18).

187   Quote on "Wake up and die, marines!": Francis (1944, 26).

      Quote on hospital battle: Berry (1983, 186).

Japanese casualties 25–26 July: Lodge (1954, 87).

Japanese booby traps: Military Reports, No. 25, 41.

189 Suicides and cry of "Long live the Emperor:" Satoh (1978, 114).

Army patrols to south: Lodge (1954, 103–105); Crowl (1960, 374–376).

Chamorro guides: Palomo (1984, 222–224).

189– Merizo school battle: Accounts by Jesus Crisostomo in Owings (1981,
190   197) and by Francisco G. Lujan in Palomo (1984, 220–222) and in
"Inarajan Uprising," *Pacific Profile,* Vol. 3, No. 6, July 1965, 54.

190 Artero quotes on destruction of Guam: Artero y Saez (1948, 101, 110).

U.S. civil affairs staff and camps: Souder (1965, 24).

Bordallo leads group from camp: Author's interview with participant
Paul Bordallo, 25 August 1992.

192 Atrocities in north: Lodge (1954, 153). Satoh (1978, 3) gives an eyewitness account by Mrs. Takano of the beheadings.

Quote on decapitated Chamorros: Josephy (1946, 91).

Japanese civilian refugees: Palomo (1984, 190–192); see also Satoh (1978).

Naoe Takano quote: Palomo (1984, 191).

Local Security Patrol Force: CINCPAC telegram, 15 August 1944,
NCWR 79–81, Reel No. 10, Folder I-A.

193 Jesse Perez quote: Palomo (1984, 223–224).

Quote from Chamorros' letter to Nimitz: Letter in Farrell (1984, 181).

Obata's last message and death: Quoted in Shaw et al. (1966, 567),
citing a Japanese Self-Defense Force Study of Guam written in 1962;
see also Takeda (1946, 1952).

Gyokusai: Satoh (1978, 165).

193– U.S. casualties on Guam: Lodge (1954, 178–180).
194

194 Chamorro casualties: Bamba, Exhibit C, 2.

Japanese casualties and holdouts: Shaw et al. (1966, 572), citing U.S.
military reports.

Japanese escape by submarine: Satoh (1978, 165–172).

Cannibalism among Japanese: See "Death Notes" in Satoh (1978) for
cases of the horror to which Japanese holdouts were driven by despair
and by fidelity to the military fatalism (not fanaticism, as the U.S.
media often mistakenly reported) of *bushido.*

Quote on "will to lose hard": Military Reports, No. 25, 41.

195 Frank survey and B-29 airfields: Hubbell (1945, 10); Lodge (1954, 9, n.
24), citing ONI-99, Strategic Study of Guam, 1 February 1944; Gailey
(1988, 20).

195– Nimitz Proclamation No. 1: NCWR 79–81, Reel No. 8, Folder II. For a
196   detailed but uncritical explication of Guam's wartime and post–World
War II military government, see Griffith (1978, 273–302).

197 Transformation of Guam 1944–1946: See Souder (1983b) series.

Harmon visit and Navy takeover of Tiyan: See Hubbell (1945).

Hire of Castro: Selby (n.d., 8).

198 Brown tree snake: See McCoid (1991); and Jaffe (1994).

199 LeMay quote: LeMay and Kantor (1965, 340).

200 Sanchez-led settlement in Tamuning: Sanchez (1983, 121); Sanchez (1989, 255).

201 Olano replaced: Olano (1949, 132–134); Sullivan (1957, 176–178).

Postwar conditions: NCWR 79–81, Reel No. 3, Folder IV-A, "Information on Guam," 15 June 1946, unpublished report by the Island Government, no author given. See also Carano and Sanchez (1964, 417–418, 423–424); and Souder (1983b).

202 400 business licenses: Souder (1983b [*Panorama,* 6 May, 6A]).

Figures on wage earners: Lovelace (1946, C1).

Reduction of farming: Coote (1950, 12) estimated that, in 1941, about 2,400 Chamorro families derived their living from farming on between 15,000 and 17,000 cultivated acres. By 1949, there were only about 600 full-time and 700 part-time farmers on 1,700 acres under cultivation.

Ashworth quote: Thomas and Witts (1978, 89, 97).

203 Spaatz's order on atomic bombs: Thomas and Witts (1978, 244–245).

Quote by King: King (1952, 557).

Chapter 12: Gibraltar of the American Lake 1945–1950

204 Population 1945: Lodge (1954, 164), citing Island Command War Diary, 15–31 August 45, Enclosures B and F.

Population 1946: NCWR No. 79–81, Reel 3, Folder IV-A, "Information on Guam," Island Government, no author given, 15 June 1946, 5.

205 Quote on Guam: See Martin (1947).

Tangantangan and *talantayan:* See Fosberg (1960); Moore and Krizman (1981, 76). Planting on Guam in *U.S. Naval Administration Guam, Monthly Reports,* 31 March 1947, 25, and 30 September 1947, 25; Apple (1980, 74); and *Navy News* (Guam), 10 October 1947, 2.

Insecticides and killing of birds: Sablan (1990, 238).

205– Japanese war trials: See *Final Report of Navy* (1949, Vol. 1); Piccigallo
206 (1979); NCWR 79–81, Reel 33, Folder I, 17 May 1949, "Historical Narrative of Special War Crimes duties performed by personnel of Marine Barracks, Guam"; and *Navy News* (Guam), series of articles in September 1946 and June 1947.

206 Deportees and Villagomez and Shinohara trials: Palomo (1984, 231–232).

All Micronesia to be U.S. territory: The Hopkins committee also recommended that Guam and the other Mariana Islands be administered as one entity, but this sensible proposal was rejected owing to archaic State Department views that clung to the artificial division created by the 1899 Paris treaty and the League mandates.

Forrestal quote: *New York Times,* 24 September 1946, 28.

206– U.S.–Soviet Union tacit deal: *New York Times,* 13 January 1947, 8.
207

207 TTPI Agreement: Trusteeship Agreement for the Former Japanese Mandated Islands, Approved by the Security Council on 2 April 1947, entered into force 18 July 1947, 61 Stat. 397, T.I.A.S. No. 1665, 8 U.N.T.S. 189.

Quote on U.S. failure in TTPI: McHenry (1975, 226).

208 Quote from first navy report to the United Nations: See U.S. Navy Department (1946–1949).

Quote from UN critique: Maga (1988, 196), citing NA, RG 59, Box 5009.

New York Times editorial and U.S. reaction: Maga (1988, 195–197).

Civilian rehabilitation projects: See U.S. Senate (1945); *Navy News* (Guam), 17 September 1946, 1.

209 Election of the Eighth Guam Congress: Sanchez (1989, 298). The bicameral Guam Congresses were as follows: the First, 1917–1931; the Second, 1931–1933; the Third through the Seventh followed every two years, 1933–1941, with the Seventh carried over to June–July 1946; the Eighth, 1946–1948; the Ninth, 1948–1950; the Tenth, 1950–January 1951. The unicameral Eleventh was the first legislature under the Organic Act and formally changed its name in January 1951 to the First Guam Legislature.

Designation as Guamanians: Sanchez (1989, 264).

April 1946 quote on Guam economy: Report for Island Command War Diary, April 1946, 14, in *U.S. Naval Administration Guam, Monthly Report,* 30 April 1946.

209– Quote on need to guard Guamanians from Guamanians: Report for
210 Island Command War Diary, 1 May 1946, 1, in *U.S. Naval Administration Guam, Monthly Report,* 31 May 1946.

210 Quote on Big Five: Souder (1983b [*Panorama,* 20 May, 12-A]).

211 Quote of Won Pat: Sanchez (1989, 297).

December 1946 Navy analysis quote: *U.S. Naval Administration Guam, Monthly Report,* 31 December 1946, Enclosure G, 67.

Majority quiet and in favor of citizenship: Sanchez (1989, 297).

Civilians excluded from citizenship: See *U.S. Statutes-at-Large,* Vol. 54, 1137, 1149.

Joint Resolution 1: *U.S. Naval Administration Guam, Monthly Report,* 31 December 1946, 20–28.

212 Second Joint resolution: U.S. Senate (1947, 4421).

Hopkins committee recommendations: Hopkins (1947, Pt. 2, 2). Other members of the committee were Dr. Knowles A. Ryerson of the University of California and Maurice J. Tobin.

Quote of 18 June 1947 secretarial report: *Guam Echo,* 1 July 1947, 1.

Ickes' criticisms: *Evening Star* (Washington, D.C.), 9 April 1947, A13. Ickes went public against the navy in a *Collier's* magazine article on 31 August 1946 and wrote several vehement antinavy letters to newspapers, including to the *New York Times,* 21 October 1946, saying that the navy's "whole policy is one of repression."

Thompson support of Guam reforms: *Congressional Record,* 1947, A2715–A2716. For a description of Thompson's efforts on behalf of the Guamanians, see Thompson (1991, 80–87).

213   ONI investigation of Leon Guerrero: Maga (1988, 198).

Bradley letter: Text in Guam Congress, *Congressional Record,* 5 July 1947, 36–37.

Proclamation on Interim Organic Act: *U.S. Naval Administration Guam, Monthly Report,* 31 August 1947, Enclosure E and App. to Session of Congress, 15.

214   War Claims figures: Bamba, Exhibit C, 1, 2; Sanchez (1984, 267); Hopkins (1947, Pt. 3, 11); NCWR No. 79–81, Reel 1, Folder II (NA RGs 38–127), Memorandum of 22 September 1948.

215   Nimitz quote and 1945 land figures: NCWR 78–91, Reel 32, Folder IV, 11 August 1945, Memorandum from CINCPAC to CNO, Endorsement 1, par. 4.

Land prices: NCWR 78–91, Reel 32, Folder VII, 31 May 1945, Report No. 1 of Land and Claims Commission for Guam, by L. J. Wilson to CNO, 10. In the report, the navy used a figure of 134,900 total acres on Guam. In 1946 congressional hearings, the navy used a total figure of 144,000 acres, an error of over 9,000 acres that illustrates the sloppy land management practices of the U.S. Navy on Guam.

Quote on ruinous land values: Bohn (1982, 57).

Quote on leases: Cited by Bohn (1982, 42) from unpublished COMNAVMAR report, Real Estate Appraisals for Loss of Use, undated [1947], 13.

Chemical warfare agents stored at Fena: *PDN,* 23 April 1977, 1.

216   Hopkins committee quote: Hopkins (1947, Pt. 3, 15).

Roy James quote: James (1949, 87). James was fired from his government job in Washington after returning from Guam and criticizing the navy in articles (see *Guam Echo,* 14 May 1949, 4).

"Oppression" cases: *Navy News* (Guam), 7 December 1947, 5.

Quote on land abuses: See *Report on Post-war Land Takings on Guam* (1972); Bohn (1982).

216–   Lemke quote: U.S. Senate (1950, 36–37).
217

217   Construction contracts: Campbell (1987, 26), citing COMNAVMARIANAS NOTE 5750, serial 4506, 6 July 1959, 22–25, which reported total postwar military construction costs on Guam as $379.2 million.

7,000 American workers in 1947: *Guam's People* (1988, 191).

Quote on drunk Americans: See Martin (1947).

U.S.-Philippine May 1947 labor agreement: U.S. House (1979, 4).

218 Requirements for contract laborers violated: *Historical Overview* (1980, 16).

Filipino worker camps: See Campbell (1987); *Historical Overview* (1980).

28,000 alien workers 1948: *Guam Echo,* 31 August 1948, 4.

Employment by sectors: *Guam's People* (1988, 191).

219 Goldstein subpoena: See *U.S. Naval Administration Guam, Monthly Report,* 31 March 1949; Bordallo (1982, 212–221).

Taitano and walkout: Taitano (1983, 136); Palomo (1984, 254–255).

Quote on adjournment: Guam Congress, *Congressional Record,* House of Assembly, 5 March 1949, 5.

Meetings in villages: Tansill (1951, 72).

219– Taitano quote: *Washington Post,* 3 April 1949, 3B.
220

220 Coulter letter: *New York Times,* 23 May 1949.

State Department assessment: NA, RG 59, Box 5009, Memorandum for the Undersecretary of State, 30 March 1949. See also Maga (1988, 204–205).

Interior-navy agreement: Bohn (1982, 63–71).

Quote from 21 May resolution: Guam Congress, *Congressional Record,* Special Joint Session, 21 May 1949, 5.

Lobbying by Guamanians: *Guam Echo,* 30 July 1949, 2, and 31 October 1949, 4.

221 Miles committee: Like the Hopkins committee, Miles recommended that Washington "explore the possibilities of common administration for Saipan, Tinian, Rota, and Guam." This logical idea was not followed up. See report in the *Guam Echo,* 30 January 1950, 2.

Peterson quote: *Guam Echo,* 31 March 1950, 4–5.

Quote of navy testimony: U.S. Senate (1950, 9–10). For a self-laudatory view of navy postwar rule, see *U.S. Navy Report* (1951); see also Zenor (1949).

Skinner quote: *Guam Echo,* 15 May 1950, 2.

222 Quote on Guam still an unincorporated territory: U.S. Senate (1950, 13).

Organic Act of Guam: Act of 1 August 1950, Chap. 512, 64 Stat. 384 (codified as 48 U.S.C. § 1421, et seq.).

Chapter 13: Under the Organic Act 1950–1970

224 1,728 classified positions: *Annual Report* 1951, 9.

225 Postwar *lytico-bodig* research: See history in Monmaney (1990).

226 Guamanians "second-class" Americans: See Guam Legislature Resolution 256, U.S. House (1968, 18); Taitano (1983, 133).

Guam a U.S. "possession": Van Cleve (1974, 14–22).

Quote on Guam's status: *Sakamoto v. Duty Free Shoppers, Ltd.,* 40, 764 F.2d 1285 (9th Cir. 1985); see discussion in Leibowitz (1989, 363–365).

227 Contradictory Interior missions: Leibowitz (1989, 336, 399).

Eisenhower and Johnson uphold vetos: Lowe (1967, 337–346).

228 No CIA office on Guam: In the 1980s, the CIA reportedly established a trust company on Guam as an offshore tax haven that was a subsidiary of BBRDW, Inc., in Hawai'i, which was a conduit for CIA funds. See Hayes et al. (1986, 179–180).

P.L. 12-85: This Guam law also established a Guam Supreme Court and resulted in the first U.S. Supreme Court case in regard to Guam, *Guam v. Olson,* 444 U.S. 1016 (1978). On a technicality, the court blocked the establishment of the Guam Supreme Court; see the analysis in Leibowitz (1989, 373–374).

228– Jury trials: Local juries came through *Hatchett v. Guam,* 212 F.2d 767
229 (9th Cir. 1954), cert. dismissed, 348 U.S. 801 (1954); followed by P.L. 3-42, which formally established juries for island courts.

229 Tax challenges 1950–1952: Listed in *Annual Report* 1952, 8–9.

Guam a free port: Originally Sec. 27 of the Organic Act; now under 19 U.S.C.A. Sec. 1202, Headnote 3.

230 Quote on security clearance: Leibowitz (1989, 350–355).

Executive Order 10178: 3 CFR 361 (Comp. 1949–1953), 48 U.S.C. Sec. 1421f n. (1970).

49,600 acres retained by navy in 1950: Executive Order 10178; Sanchez (1989, 306–307).

232 Fifteen nuclear bombs to Guam: Hayes et al. (1986, 67), citing L. Rumbaugh et al., *Tactical Employment of Atomic Weapons,* Report ORO-R-2 (FEC), Tokyo, 1 March 1951, declassified 1983, available at the Army War College, Carlisle Barracks, Pennsylvania.

1952 Immigration and Nationality Act: 8 U.S.C. 1101.

17,000 Filipino workers in 1953: *Historical Overview* (1980, 6).

233 Eisenhower's quote on Skinner: Souder (1983b [*Panorama,* 3 June, 12A]), quoting Lloyd Norman of the *Chicago Tribune.*

Quote on dogs: Elvidge (1956, 80). Elvidge's derogatory remarks about Guamanians in a *Saturday Evening Post* article after he left Guam caused resentment on the island (Lowe 1967, 309–314).

Third Air Division and B-36s: Strategic Air Command (1982, 47, 49).

234 Nucker and TTPI policy: Lowe (1967, 417–418); see also Price (1966).

CIA base on Saipan: The purpose of the base remained secret until exposed in 1972 by the *Pentagon Papers* in the *New York Times* excerpts and the book by Beacon Press, Boston. Confirmation followed in 1974 by Victor Marchetti and John Marks in *The CIA and the Cult of Intelligence* (New York: Knopf). The CIA attempted, unsuccessfully, to suppress or censor both books.

Elections 1950–1962: Dizon (1982, 1–4); (Sanchez 1989, 326, 328–330).

Quote on James Sablan: Sanchez (1989, 330).

235 Quote on Erdmann: Lowe (1967, 426).

Erdmann incidents and trial: Lowe (1967, 426–437).

235– Quote on limited commonwealth for Guam: Lowe (1967, 450).
236

236 Agat-Umatac road never completed by Spaniards: Sánchez y Zayas (1865–1866, 645). Umatac was reached by a road opened in World War I through Inarajan and Merizo.

Aquino Ruling and 1,700 Filipinos as residents: *Historical Overview* (1980, 12).

237 Daniel as governor: Sanchez (1989, 340–341); Souder (1983b [*Panorama,* 24 June, 4A–6A]).

Wang incident: Souder (1983b, [*Panorama,* 24 June, 6A]).

Executive Order 11045: 3 CFR 629 (Comp. 1958–1963).

Karen wind speeds: Kotsch (1962, 6).

Barometric pressure: The world-record low of 25.91 inches was recorded for a 1958 typhoon in the western Pacific.

238 Guerrero quote on destruction: *Annual Report* 1963, 1.

Quote on equivalent to nuclear bomb: Kotsch (1962, 1).

Guam Rehabilitation Act: P.L. 88–170, *Annual Report* 1965, 3.

Quote on "filth and squalor": Quoted by Campbell (1987, 66) from the *Weekly Graphic,* 1968, 30; see also *Historical Overview* (1980, 18).

First labor union: *Guam Times Weekly,* 12 December 1964, 1.

Repeated exploitation: For similar abuses twenty years later, see "Alien Workers Allege More Abuse," *PDN,* 2 June 1986, 1.

239 First master plan: Souder (1983b, [*Panorama,* 24 June, 6A]).

Quote on Guam representative's role: Won Pat (1972, 5).

1964 election: Sanchez (1989, 347).

240 Tourists and hotel rooms 1965–1969: Van Cleve (1974, 91).

241 Guam's role in SIOP: See Hayes et al. (1986).

Guam a probable nuclear target: Webb (1974, 75).

Military installations on Guam in 1960s: See Hayes et al. (1986, Apps., 439–447); Fieldhouse (1985, App. A, 221).

242 Guam Elective Governor Act: P.L. 97–497, 82 Stat. 842, 11 September 1968, 48 U.S.C.A. § 1422.

Ninth Legislature protest: *PDN,* 14 June 1968, 1; Van Cleve (1974, 100).

Proposals of First Guam Constitutional Convention: See *Congressional Record* (1972); *Guam Constitutional Convention* (1969–1970).

243 Camacho 1969 visit to Vietnam: *Guam Daily News,* 1 January 1970, 19–22; Sanchez (1989, 352–354).

244 Arriola opposition to aliens: *PDN,* 19 August 1970, 1.

1970 election: See Dizon (1982); Sanchez (1989, 355–360).

Chapter 14: Ocean Chrysalis 1970–1980

245 Yokoi found: *PDN,* 26 January 1972, 1, 16–17.

246 Burton "Godfather": *PDN,* 29 March 1980, 1.

247 GovGuam employment and unemployment figures: *Guam Annual Economic Review* (1975, 50); Sanchez (1989, 373). Statistics on Guam's employment, finances, etc. vary among sources.

Per capita income: *Overall Economic Development Plan* (1977, 32); Kruger (1981, Table 7, 86).

1,270 hotel rooms 1972: *Guam Visitor* (Tamuning), Vol. 1, No. 9, November 1972, 16, 34.

247– Tourism and hotel tax: *PDN,* Advertising Supplement, 1 May 1980,
248 10A.

248 Camacho suit: *Bordallo v. Camacho,* 475 F.2d 712 (9th Cir. 1973).

Navy angers Won Pat: *PDN,* 20 May 1973, 1.

249 Navy to use eminent domain to obtain Sella: Interview, 27 March 1992, with Richard Wyttenbach, civil-military liaison officer on Morrison's staff in 1973–1974.

Chamorro Land Trust Act: 21G CA Chap. 75, 1989, 580–605.

Polls on unification: Farrell (1991a, 536–537).

Quote on Northern Marianas' appeal: Text in Farrell (1991a, 582).

250 1973 Political Status Commission: Guam Status Report (1974, 22).

Quote on commonwealth as interim status: Guam Status Report (1974, 19).

Won Pat support of commonwealth: Won Pat (1972, 23).

Ad with UN Resolution 1514: Indigenous rights advocates sometimes confuse this resolution, passed 14 December 1960, which focused on independence as a final political status, with UN Resolution 1541, passed 21 December 1960, which addressed free association as well as either independence or integration with an independent state as fulfilling self-determination (see United Nations 1960).

251 Camacho and others charged with misuse of funds: *Honolulu Star-Bulletin,* 8 April 1975, 1.

1974 slates and election figures: Dizon (1982, 51).

Tourist slump: *Statistical Abstract, Guam 1977.*

Chamorro emigration to mainland: See Munoz (1979) (whose figures are too high); and *PDN,* 16 May 1991, 1, citing U.S. censuses.

Chamorros 55.5 percent in 1975: *Overall Economic Development Plan* (1977, 23).

Consumer price indices 1973–1976: *Guam Annual Economic Review* (1976, 42).

Unemployment 1975–1976: *Guam Annual Economic Review* (1976, Fig. 9, 43).

251– Food stamp recipients: Bordallo (1978, 29); Souder (1983a [*Panorama*,
252   9 September, 6B]).

252   Joe Murphy quote: *PDN*, 8 August 1979, 23, citing 1979 U.S. Government Printing Office booklet "Geographic Distribution of Federal Funding in Territories and Other Areas Administered by the U.S."

First refugees: Souder (1983a [*Panorama*, 6 September, 14B]).

Refugee figures: *Operation Newlife* (1976, 20–22, 72).

253   Pesticide Malathion: The military continued to use Malathion and the herbicide Diuron 80 on Guam installations into the 1970s, killing many indigenous birds. Jaffe (1994, 26–27).

Federal funding of CNMI fiscal year 1978–fiscal year 1992: *PDN*, 20 March 1993, 1.

Quote, Guamanians and CNMI: Bordallo (1982, 253).

254   Presidential representative on status: In 1976 OTIA Director Fred M. Zeder II drafted a "Covenant" to create a Guam Commonwealth, but it came to nothing when the Carter administration took office in 1977.

Data on Pamela: See *Super Typhoon Pamela* (1976), *Environmental Impact Assessment* (1976). The strongest storm recorded in the Pacific was Supertyphoon Tip in October 1979 (with 190 miles per hour sustained winds and gusts to 250 miles per hour), which missed Guam (see interview with Lt. Col. C. P. Guard, *PDN*, Advertising Supplement, 3 June 1991). A typhoon in the eastern hemisphere is the same as a hurricane (from Spanish *huracán*) in the western hemisphere.

255   Military damage: *PDN*, 26 May 1976, 1.

Civilian damage: *Honolulu Advertiser*, 27 May 1976, B-5.

Rehabilitation, SBA, and insurance claims paid: *PDN*, Supplement, Territorial, Pamela Anniversary Edition, 21 May 1977, 4A, 9A.

Bordallo $289 million proposal: *PDN*, 16 February 1977, 1.

Guam Marshall Plan: *PDN*, 15 March 1977, 3.

Federal funding to Guam 1975–1978: Sanchez (1989, 388).

Latte tower: "Latte Project Mushrooms," *PDN*, 20 April 1977, 1.

256   "Disaster Dugout": *PDN*, 10 August 1977, 1.

GMH patient electrocuted: *PDN*, 1 January 1973, 1.

Quote of GMH administrator: *PDN*, 31 July 1973, 4.

MCM-GMH competition: "Guam Memorial, New Hospital to Compete," *PDN*, 22 June 1977, 1.

Free care of indigents: Statement by GMH administrator T. P. Skouros, *PDN*, 2 January 1977, 6.

GMH debt to Aetna: "GMH Faces Foreclosure," *PDN*, 22 August 1978, 1.

257   Drs. Espaldon and Ortiz vs. statesider physicians: *PDN*, 29 September 1977, 1.

GMHP, Levenson/Wilkinson, and MSA/HMI: See Shapiro (1983).

GMHP $2.8 million deficit: Shapiro (1983, 6, 20).

Quote on GMHP statements: *PDN*, 24 December 1979, 1.

GMH suit against HMI: Shapiro (1983, 6, 176).

258   Wilkinson claim of communication "mix-up": *PDN*, 23 April 1981, 1.

Tax liability: *PDN*, 22 April 1981, 1–4.

Prominent people perhaps embarrassed: For the names of those involved in the GMHP scandal, see Shapiro (1983, 81, 183–189, 199).

GMH deficits 1990: "Audit: GMH Lost Millions," *PDN*, 10 April 1992, 1.

GMH loss of accreditation: *PDN*, 23 June 1983, 1.

Bordallo's views on GCC: *PDN*, 4 July 1977, 1, 5; Sanchez (1989, 389).

UOG enrollment down by nearly half: Enrollment in fall 1977 was 3,501 full-time-equivalent students; in fall 1988 it was 2,032, or 47 percent less than 1977 (Carriveau 1985, 72).

259   Drug traffic: "Police Crack Down on Saipan Pot Trade," *PDN*, 28 January 1977, 1; and "12 Arrested in Weekend Heroin Raids," *PDN*, 31 May 1977, 1.

Quote on crime: *PDN*, 30 November 1978, 1.

DPS corruption and Cihik: See articles in the *PDN*, 28 April 1977, 1; 22 April 1981, 3; and 23 April 1981, 1.

Prisoner escapes: For one example, see "Convict Returns, Easy Go, Easy Come," *PDN*, 10 February 1977, 1.

FFB loan to GPA: *PDN*, 4 February 1977, 1.

GAO quote on Guam a "mess": *PDN*, 21 April 1977, 1; and 18 September 1977, 1.

400 vehicles unaccounted for: *Hawaii Business* (1979, 48).

260   P.L. 12–200: This law was the basis for island-wide planning since the 1960s. Subsequent plans included the first Guam Historic Preservation Plan in 1978. For a listing of these plans, see *Guam Inventory of Planning Information* (1989, 1990).

1977 Amendment of Organic Act: 48 U.S.C. § 1424. See *Franquez v. United States*, 604 F.2d 1239, 1241–1242 (9th Cir. 1979).

Unregistered public acreage: Souder (1983b [*Panorama*, 9 September, 5B]).

Land swindles: See summary of 1990–1991 cases in *Guam Business News*, August 1991, 17.

Agat boat harbor issue: See "Villagers Blast Feds for Harbor Denial," *PDN*, 21 July 1979, 1.

261   1977 referendum on gambling: *PDN*, 14 January 1977, 1.

262   1976 political status referendum: Guam Election Commission (1977); for discussion of the vote, see Rogers (1984, 6–7).

Draft Guam Constitution: See *Guam Constitutional Convention 1977* (1979).

Reduction of GovGuam: Souder (1983a [*Panorama*, 16 September, 5B]).

262–   1978 elections: See Dizon (1982); Guam Election Commission (1978).
263

263   Deficit reduced $27 million: *PDN*, 30 January 1980, 1.

Tax problems and delinquency: Souder (1983b [*Panorama*, 9 September, 4B]).

264   Quote on public "uninformed": *PDN*, 18 October 1978, 8.

Editorial against constitution: *PDN*, 5 August 1979.

1979 constitutional plebiscite: See Guam Election Commission (1979); United Nations (1979). The death penalty was also turned down in this plebiscite.

Carl Gutierrez quote: *PDN*, 5 August 1979, 1.

Joe Murphy quote: *PDN*, Editorial, 19 March 1979, 15.

Carter quote on status options: *PDN*, 17 February 1980, 22.

1980 study of political status options: See Rogers, Warner, and Sablan (1980).

Chapter 15: Unfinished Quests 1980–1990

265   Won Pat estimate: Gault and Nygard (1984, 12).

Land case to Ninth Circuit: *Stanley Castro Limtiaco v. United States of America*, C.A. Nos. 81–4148–81–4150, 675 F.2d 1069–1071 (9th Cir. 1982). For the argument of the Guamanians, see Bohn (1982).

200 claimants refuse settlement: *PDN*, 31 July 1983, 1.

266   GovGuam suit: *Guam v. United States of America*, 744 F.2d 699 (1984).

28,389 acres potentially excess early 1990s: *PDN*, 1 October 1993, 4.

GovGuam employees 1980: *Guam's People* (1988, Table 11.17, 228).

Ethnicity of teachers: *Guam's People* (1988, Table 11.6, 216).

GFT petition: *PDN*, 29 April 1980, 1.

266–   Union quote and threat to strike: *PDN*, 16 December 1980, 1; and
267   17 December 1980, 4.

267   Calvo vetoes Bill 535: *PDN*, 20 December 1980, 1.

CHELU withdraws: *PDN*, 24 December 1980, 4. Both CHELU and Operating Engineers Local 3 soon dissolved.

GFT 7 January strike vote: *PDN*, 8 January 1981, 1.

Injunction: *PDN*, 11 January 1981, 1. Guam Code 4 GCA Chap. 9 prohibits strikes against the government; 4 GCA Chap. 10–the Public Employees-Management Relations Act (PEMRA)–allows certain GovGuam employees to organize unions for exclusive bargaining, but also prohibits strikes by those employees.

Numbers of teachers on strike: *PDN*, 16 January 1981, 1. Estimates on numbers and ethnicity of strikers vary. DOE unofficial figures show that of 1,337 teachers when the strike started, 695 went on strike along with 99 DOE nonteacher employees. Of the 794 strikers, DOE listed 515, or 65 percent, statesiders, 19 percent Chamorros, and 16 percent Filipinos.

Aguon fires 649 and hires 224: *PDN*, 4 February 1981, 1.

Calvo letter to Stinson: Office of the Governor, 17 February 1981.

268   Statesiders versus locals: *PDN*, 6 February 1981, 1.

Join Paul II's visit to Guam: Sanchez (1989, 407–417).

269   500 vote to end strike: *PDN*, 11 March 1981, 1.

Settlement February 1984: See text of Governor Bordallo's memorandum in the *Guam Tribune*, 14 February 1984.

GFT membership 535 in 1984: *Community/Business Profile* (1984, V-5).

Guam public education damaged: "Schools still Hurting from Strike," *PDN*, 16 January 1984, 3; *PDN*, 12 December 1984, 1; and "Teachers Failing Proficiency Tests," *PDN*, 2 October 1986 (in 1986, 40 percent of new DOE teachers failed the English test).

270   Calvo disappoints supporters: See "Pessimism, Optimism, a Plan for the Future," *Hawaii Business News*, April 1982, 45–55.

271   1,427 temporary hires: Souder (1983a [*Panorama*, 16 September, 5B]).

1982 election: See Guam Election Commission (1983).

Political status votes: For summary histories of the Guam political status process in the 1980s, see Rogers (1984, 1986, 1988a, 1988b); see also the sample ballot insert in the *PDN*, 29 August 1981, 4A.

271–   Bordallo's status strategy: From discussions between the author and the
272   governor in 1982–1983. The author was a voluntary adviser to Governor Bordallo in 1982–1983 and was executive director of the Guam Commission on Self-Determination under a consultant's contract from January 1984 to December 1986, when the Commonwealth Act was drafted.

272   Bordallo letter to Sanjuan: *PDN*, 6 July 1983, 5.

Lujan quote on "kitchen sink": The author was present at the Albuquerque meetings as one of the many advisers and heard the statement.

Working Draft 4: See Rogers (1984) for full text.

273   Jones Act: Act of 2 March 1917, 39 Stat. 353; part of U.S. coastwise shipping laws (46 U.S.C. 13, etc.) applied to Guam by the Merchant Marine Act of 1920 (41 Stat. 996). U.S. airline cabotage laws also apply to Guam (see Leibowitz 1989, 395–396).

Udall suggestion on vote: Text of Udall letter of 16 October 1986 in *PDN*, 8 November 1986, 1.

Only Chamorros to vote on commonwealth: Some Chamorro activists argued that Guam should seek rights similar to some Native American tribal governments on reservations where federal U.S. law is restricted but the Indians retain full U.S. citizenship and some have received compensation for land taken by the U.S. government in accord with the U.S. Supreme Court decisions in *Morton v. Mancari*, 417 U.S. 535 (1974), and the Alaskan Native Claims Settlement Act, 43 U.S.C. 1601–1627 (Supp. V 1975) (see Leibowitz 1989, 433–434).

274 1984 delegate election: Guam Election Commission (1987, 45).

Won Pat's career: See *Guam Tribune*, Special Supplement, 1 August 1986.

275 Illegal DOE promotions: *PDN*, 23 April 1992, 3.

Quote on windmills: *PDN*, 3 June 1983, 1.

276 Low UOG faculty morale: *PDN*, 10 February 1978, 1.

WASC and UOG problems: See *PDN* articles by Paul Wiseman, 19 September 1983, 6–8; and 17 November 1983, 3.

Dr. Carter fired: *PDN*, 18 June 1983, 1.

Show cause status of UOG: *PDN*, 11 January 1984, 3.

277 Private sector 28 percent jump: *Community/Business Profile* (1984, 11).

$200 million from tourism: *Guam Business News*, November 1984, 13.

585,000 visitors 1988: GVB figures, *Guam Business News*, June 1989, 76.

279 Quote by Bordallo to grand jury: *PDN*, 6 September 1986, 1, 3.

Bordallo indictment: Text of charges in *PDN*, 5 September 1986, 7–16.

Katherine Aguon indictment: See Aguon (1988). She claims that she was implicated falsely by DOE subordinates, principally Frank Granich, who admitted taking bribes but plea bargained to freedom.

280 Ken Jones case: *PDN*, 30 October 1986, 1; *PDN*, 13 November 1986, 1.

Impact of trials on 1986 elections: *PDN*, 4 November 1986, 5; and *Guam Tribune*, Extra Edition, 3 April 1987, 1–2.

1986 election results: See Guam Election Commission (1987). The November 1986 election also saw the defeat of an initiative to require a balanced budget; defeat was caused by the unpopular Santos Amendment, authored by Senator Frank R. Santos, which counts blank ballots as negative votes on public initiatives.

Dizon quote: Dizon (1987, 115).

Superceding Bordallo indictment: *PDN*, 21 November 1986, 1.

Bordallo second plea of not guilty: *PDN*, 25 November 1986, 1.

Mann and bond scam: See Goodman (1988) for a report on the whole scam.

1983 arbitrage bonds: *PDN,* 1 December 1983, 3; 15 December 1983, 1; and *Guam Business News,* February 1986, 10–11; March 1988, 18.

281   Moral turpitude by Gilliam: *Guam Tribune,* Extra Edition, 3 April 1987, 2.

Gilliam pleads guilty: *PDN,* 20 November 1986, 1.

282   Bordallo sentence: *Guam Tribune,* Extra Edition, 13 April 1987, 1.

283   Gilliam sentence: *PDN,* 13 February 1990, 1, 4.

283– Mann extradition and sentence: *PDN,* 7 October 1993, 9.
284

284   Ada quote: *PDN,* 28 October 1986, 3.

Task force report: Federal Interagency Task Force (BATFOG) report released 1 August 1989; the Guam Commission on Self-Determination released a point-by-point refutation on 3 January 1990.

De Lugo quote: "De Lugo: CSD Making Passage Impossible," *Guam Tribune,* 13 December 1989, 7. For full report of the Honolulu hearing, see U.S. House (1989).

Commonwealth as partnership: *Guam Commission on Self-Determination Newsletter,* Vol. 2, Nos. 3–4, Fall–Winter 1991 (*PDN* reprint, 23 March 1992, 42).

284– De Lugo 1991 quote: "Commonwealth Snagged," *PDN,* 11 March
285   1991, 1.

285   BATFOG talks: See *Guam Commission on Self-Determination Newsletter,* Vol. 2, Nos. 3–4, Fall–Winter 1991 (*PDN* reprint, 23 March 1992). For critique of BATFOG talks, see Rogers (1992).

Over 4,000 hotel rooms 1990: *PDN,* Islander, 24 June 1990, 11.

287   Registered vehicles 1990: *Guam Business News,* September 1993, 41.

Micronesians to Guam: *PDN,* 15 May 1992, 3–4, 8; see Hezel and McGrath (1989).

Deterioration of justice: In 1992, a majority of ninety-three Guam attorneys polled rated the Superior Court "poor" (*PDN,* 28 November 1992, 3).

Crime growth: *Guam Tribune,* 7 October 1992, 8, citing DPS statistics.

287– Population growth 2.3 percent: *Guam Business News,* June 1992, 61.
288

288   Malthusian demostat: Hardin 1993, 303–311. Hardin's wise reflections on the detrimental impact of uncontrolled economic development and human over-population apply particularly to small islands such as Guam.

500 fanihi: Islander Magazine, Pacific Sunday News, 4 October 1992, 9.

50 koko: Islander Magazine, Pacific Sunday News, 25 October 1992, 6.

289   Bordallo appeals: *PDN,* 4 October 1989, 1.

Bordallo suicide: *PDN,* 3 February 1990, 5.

Glossary

The orthography of the indigenous Chamorro language of the Mariana Islands has been changed several times. The *Chamorro-English Dictionary* by Donald M. Topping, Pedro M. Ogo, and Bernadita C. Dungca used principles adopted by the Marianas Orthography Committee in 1971 and is used in this book as the standard reference for spelling Chamorro words. In 1983 a new system of spelling was adopted by the Chamorro Language Commission of Guam, but a new dictionary with that orthography has not been published. As a result, and as noted throughout this book, there are variations in the spelling of many Chamorro words. In 1994 the word *Chamorro* was changed to *Chamoru* in the indigenous language on Guam by the commission, but the spelling "Chamorro" remains standard usage in the English language.

Acha'ot (Chamorro): Second-ranked class of *chamorri* high-caste people in precontact Chamorro society. Also *achoti* and *atcha'ot*.

Alcalde (Spanish): Appointed mayor/justice of the peace, always a Spaniard or mestizo military officer, of a municipality such as a district or village on Guam from the 1690s until early 1800s.

Alcalde administrador (Spanish): Title that replaced *alcalde* in the early 1800s until replaced by elected *gobernadorcillos* in 1885.

Almacén (Spanish): Government warehouse/storehouse/military depot/armory. Several existed on Guam under Spanish rule, with the largest in Agana and Umatac.

Aniti (Chamorro): Spirit of an ancestor other than one's own in precontact Chamorro culture, and not necessarily hostile or evil. In modern Chamorro *aniti* is an evil spirit/demon and is sometimes synonymous with *taotaomo'na*, "people of before," who are manifestations of ancestral spirits. Similar to *anito* in Pilipino, meaning animism/fetish.

Anti (Chamorro): Benign spirit of one's own ancestor in precontact culture. Soul in contemporary Chamorro. Also *ante*.

Audiencia (Spanish): Highest judicial council in the Spanish colonial empire. The Manila *audiencias* had jurisdiction over the Mariana Islands from 1668 until 1898.

Augustinian Recollect: Friar (*fray* in Spanish) who is a member of the Roman Catholic religious Order of Saint Augustine (O.S.A.) that replaced the Jesuits on Guam from 1769, when the Jesuits were expelled, to 1899, when the Augustinians were expelled.

Austronesian: Language family of the indigenous peoples of Southeast Asia and much of Oceania, including Chamorros; formerly called Malayo-Polynesian.

Bando (Spanish): Edict/decree/order issued by Spanish executive officials.

Barangay (Tagalog): Socio-political neighborhood unit of municipal government, composed mostly of related families within a *barrio* in a town or village in the Philippines and Marianas under Spanish rule.

Barrio (Spanish): Precinct/quarter/district of municipal government in a town or village in the Spanish empire.

Beatification: Act of the pope by which a deceased Roman Catholic of exemplary moral and spiritual character is declared "Blessed," as was Father Diego Luís de San Vitores, for having brought about two miracles; may lead to sainthood in the Roman Catholic Church.

Bodig (Chamorro): Fatal and incurable disease, Parkinsonism-dementia complex, that attacks the human spinal chord and brain; occurs on Guam in association with *lytico*. Also *boddek*.

Caldera grande (Spanish): Big Crater; large outer area of Apra Harbor that was the main ship anchorage after 1734 with Piti and Sumay as ports.

Caldera chica (Spanish): Little Crater; the shallow inner portion of Apra Harbor dredged after 1944 to become part of the U.S. Naval Station.

Capuchin: Friar in the Roman Catholic Franciscan religious Order of Friars Minor, Capuchin (O.F.M. Cap.) that replaced the Augustinians on Guam in 1901 after the Augustinians were expelled by the U.S. naval governor.

Caste: Traditional social group with ascribed status into which a person is born and remains for life. Two castes existed in precontact Chamorro society: *chamorri*, high-ranking, and *manachang*, commoners; both castes were eliminated by the Spaniards.

Cédula (Spanish): Decree/permit issued by executive governmental authority. *Real cédula* was a Spanish royal order; *cédulas personales* were identification papers that continued on Guam under U.S. Navy rule.

Chamorri (Chamorro): In precontact Chamorro society the highest caste, composed of two classes, *matua* and *acha'ot*. The Spaniards replaced the *chamorri* with the *principalía* class.

Chamorro: Name of the people, language, and culture indigenous to the Mariana Islands; *chamurre* to early Spaniards, and *Chamoru* in the Chamorro language on contemporary Guam.

Chenchule' (Chamorro): A gift or service in precontact Chamorro culture that obligated the recipient to reciprocate to the giver. In contemporary neo-Chamorro culture *chenchule'* is a system of reciprocity based on needs and obligations, usually familial. Also *chinchule'*.

CINCPAC: Commander in Chief of U.S. Forces Pacific. Four-star admiral with headquarters in Hawai'i in command of all U.S. military forces in Asia, the Indian Ocean, and the Pacific Ocean, including nuclear weapons.

Clan: A group of families of one class and often the main social unit in traditional societies; descended from a common ancestor and share a common territory. Clans remain in contemporary Guam society as loose groupings of families with common neo-Chamorro origins.

Class: Category of people of similar prestige/rank within a society; a person may change class, unlike caste, by behavior and circumstance.

Collier: Ship needed at the end of the nineteenth century to resupply steamships with coal for long voyages. The Americans seized Guam to make it a coaling station and reduce U.S. Navy dependency on colliers.

Comare (Chamorro from Spanish *comadre*): Godmother/ godsister. Also *komadre/komaire/komalie/comari*.

Commonwealth: Generic term for various political statuses of unincorporated territories in the U.S. system as defined by agreement between the federal government and the territory. The agreements are voluntary, cannot be unilaterally abrogated, and expand self-government of the territory. U.S. territorial commonwealths have been the Philippines (1935–1946); Puerto Rico (1952–); and the Northern Mariana Islands (1976–). Guam seeks a commonwealth status with greater self-government than any other U.S. territory.

COMNAVMAR: Commander U.S. Naval Forces Marianas. Two-star admiral with headquarters on Guam who represents CINCPAC in Micronesia.

Compare (Chamorro from Spanish *compadre*): Godfather/ godbrother. Basis, along with *comare*, of the *pare* extended family system in postcontact neo-Chamorro culture. Also *kompaile/kompaire/compare/pare/pari*.

Confinado (Spanish): Civilian convict, local or nonlocal, usually distinct from *presidiarios* and *deportados*, under Spanish rule; worked on public work projects and private farms.

Deportado (Spanish): Nonlocal civilian prisoner exiled to penal colonies such as Guam for anti-Spanish or, after 1898, anti-American activities. Some remained after release to become part of the neo-Chamorro culture.

EEZ: Exclusive Economic Zone established internationally by the U.N. Convention on the Law of the Sea, but not fully agreed to by the United States. A 200-nautical mile belt of sea and seabed adjacent to a nation-state's 12-nautical mile territorial sea where the nation-state has control of all natural resources.

Eminent domain: Legal process whereby a government may acquire private property for public use with payment of compensation to the owner. The U.S. military acquired enormous tracts of land on Guam through eminent domain after World War II for defense purposes.

Franciscan: Member of one of three Roman Catholic religious orders of friars: Friars Minor (O.F.M.); Friars Minor, Capuchin (O.F.M. Cap.); and Friars Conventual (O.M.C.). Spanish and American Capuchins have been the main priests of the Roman Catholic Church on Guam under American rule.

Free association: Voluntary relationship between sovereign nation-states by agreement in which one nation-state delegates to another responsibility for its defense. The relationship may be terminated unilaterally.

Geopolitics: Combination of geography and national interests that makes a place (examples are Panama,

Gibraltar, Hawai'i, and Guam) of heightened strategic importance to major nation-states for foreign policy, military, or commercial reasons.

Gobernadorcillo (Spanish): Mayor/justice of the peace of a village on Guam; appointed from the Chamorro *principalía* class from 1791 to 1885 as assistant to an *alcalde* and thereafter elected until 1898 in place of *alcaldes*. Appointed thereafter by U.S. naval governors. In 1905 the title was changed to commissioner; in 1948 it became an elected position; and in 1989 the title was changed to mayor.

Gobernador politico-militar (Spanish): Chief executive of an insecure province such as Guam in the Spanish empire; reported to a governor-general and was delegated full political and military powers in local matters; always an appointed Spanish military officer.

Guahan (Chamorro): Guam. The name appeared in reports of Espinosa's attempt to return to Panama in 1522, and of the Legazpi expedition in 1565.

Guajan (Spanish): Guam, pronounced exactly as *Guahan* above. First appeared in 1668 in reports by the San Vitores mission.

Guamanian: Permanent resident of Guam, regardless of ethnicity, but usually refers to those of Chamorro ancestry. The term appeared under U.S. naval rule and was adopted in 1946. All Guamanians are U.S. citizens since 1950.

Haole (Hawaiian): A white person.

I kustumbren Chamoru (Chamorro): Customs of the Chamorros; a mixture of precontact indigenous culture with postcontact Spanish, Filipino, American, and other influences that formed the contemporary neo-Chamorro identity.

Ina'fa'maolek (Chamorro): Concept of communal interdependence and cooperation with established authority, "getting along" rather than confrontation in order to deflect or resolve serious threats to the family or community. Also *in'afa'mauleg*.

Incorporated U.S. territory: An area that is integral to the United States and is intended by the U.S. Congress to become a U.S. state as defined by the Supreme Court in the *Insular Cases,* 1901. The last two incorporated territories to become U.S. states were Alaska and Hawai'i, both in 1959. Guam is not an incorporated territory.

Indigenous: Anything that originated in a particular place; native/endemic.

Indio (Spanish): Indian; generic name applied in the fifteenth and sixteenth centuries by Spanish explorers searching for India and the Indies to all peoples in the Americas, Oceania, and parts of Asia. Chamorros were *indios* to the Spaniards.

Jesuit: Member of the Roman Catholic religious order, the Society of Jesus (SJ), loyal primarily to the pope rather than to a national Catholic ruler. The Jesuit mission established by Father San Vitores on Guam in 1668 lasted until the Jesuits were expelled in 1769 by King Charles III of Spain. Jesuits returned to Guam, mostly as teachers, in the 1960s.

Kaikuntai (Japanese): Military logistical support unit of the Imperial Japanese Army in World War II; responsible for many atrocities against the Chamorros on Guam in 1944.

Keibitai (Japanese): Imperial Japanese Naval Guard Force with missions similar to U.S. Marines. The Fifth Keibitai, a battalion-sized unit, invaded Guam in 1941 and, with a title change to the Fifty-fourth Keibitai, was the main occupation force until 1944.

Kempeitai (Japanese): Imperial Japanese Army military police. Part of the occupation force on Guam in 1944.

Lancho (Chamorro from Spanish *rancho*): Family ranch/farm on Guam after the Spanish conquest when all Chamorros were required to farm in place of fishing or other traditional occupations. Many contemporary Guamanians still farm *lanchos*.

Latte (Chamorro): Distinctive stone pillars with hemispheric capstones that supported important buildings in precontact Chamorro culture. Abandoned after the Spanish conquest ended in 1698.

Lytico (Chamorro from Spanish *paralytico*): Fatal and incurable disease, similar to amyotrophic lateral sclerosis (ALS), that paralyzes the human body; occurs on Guam in association with *bodig*. Also *litiku*.

Maga'haga (Chamorro): "First daughter"; highest-ranking woman in precontact Chamorro clans; mother, sister, or wife of a *chamorri* village headman.

Maga'lahi (Chamorro): "First son"; village headman, highest-ranking male member of the *matua* high class in precontact Chamorro society. Also *maga'hagen*.

Makahna (Chamorro): Shaman-sorcerers in precontact Chamorro culture who violently opposed conversion to Christianity and were eliminated by the Spaniards.

Mamahlao (Chamorro): Sense of proper individual and group behavior based on community mores. Also shame or embarrassment caused a family by self-serving unsanctioned behavior of a member; avoided by deference to established norms and authority. Also *mamalao*.

Manachang (Chamorro): Lowest caste of precontact Chamorro families/clans.

Manak'kilo (Chamorro): "High people"; elite of *principalía* class that replaced precontact *matua* as the highest-ranking local families on Guam after the Spanish conquest; lived mostly in central *barrios* of Agana and married Spaniards to become mestizos and most Hispanicized of Chamorros; disappearing as a class since World War II through Americanization. Also *mannakhilo'* and (before World War II) *manggi Hagatña*.

Manak'papa (Chamorro): "Low people"; lowest class of postcontact Chamorros; replaced the *manachang*; intermarried more with Filipinos than with Spaniards and resided in Agana outer *barrios* and in rural areas with little Hispanicization. Disappearing as a class under Americanization. Also *mannakpapa* and (before World War II) *manggi sengsong*.

Mariano (Spanish): Name of an inhabitant of the Mariana Islands under Spanish rule from 1668 to 1898; synonymous with Chamorro/*nativo*/*indio*.

Matua (Chamorro): Highest-ranked class of *chamorri* high-caste people in precontact Chamorro society. Also *matao*.

Memoria (Spanish): Report/account.

Mestizo: From Spanish: Person of mixed Spanish and non-Spanish ancestry; ranked socially below pure Spaniards and above pure *indios* in the Spanish empire; *mestisu* in the Chamorro language.

Minseibu (Japanese): Civil affairs branch of the Keibitai that governed Guam under the occupation by the Imperial Japanese Navy, 1942–1944.

Minseisho (Japanese): Civil affairs section of the Imperial Japanese Army that occupied Guam from the invasion in December 1941 to mid-January 1942 when administration was transferred to the Minseibu.

Monsoon: Wind that changes direction with change of season; the southwest monsoon out of Southeast Asia from about June through August brings the rainy season to Guam, often with typhoons, and was the primary natural phenomenon that brought initial life forms, including humans, to western Micronesia and the Mariana Islands in prehistoric times.

Nativo (Spanish): Native; used synonymously with *indio*/Mariano/Chamorro.

Neo-Chamorro: Term to distinguish postcontact from precontact Chamorro people and culture; represents a mixture of ethnicities and customs, mostly Spanish, Filipino, and North American, but still distinctively Chamorro in identity.

Obra pía (Spanish): A "pious work"; a cash endowment by wealthy Spanish sponsors of a religious mission or activity. The most famous *obra pía* for Guam was the 3,000 peso annual subsidy by Queen Regent Mariana for the Colegio de San Juan de Letrán that lasted for over two hundred years from 1672 until the 1880s.

Oceania: The insular area of the Pacific Ocean, as distinguished from the rimlands, that lies on both sides of the equator and the international dateline; includes all the islands of Melanesia, Micronesia, and Polynesia, but not Southeast Asia, Taiwan, or the main islands of Japan. Oceania was formerly called the "South Seas" or the "South Pacific."

Organized U.S. territory: An area under U.S. sovereignty which has limited self-government usually granted by an "organic act" of the U.S. Congress; may be either unincorporated (not to become a U.S. state) or incorporated (to become a U.S. state). Guam is an organized unincorporated U.S. territory under the 1950 Organic Act.

Pare system (Chamorro): Extended family ties among godparents, godbrothers, godsisters—and sometimes close friends/cronies—and their families established through the rite of baptism. Also *pari* system.

Patrón system (Spanish): Loyalty and respect for a patron or boss in a position of authority or power who is expected to protect and help the families under his patronage.

Patronato real (Spanish): Royal patronage with exclusive rights granted by papal bulls to the Spanish crown to control all activities of the Catholic Church within the Spanish empire. These rights enabled the Spanish crown to mesh religious, political, and commercial means to expand the Spanish empire by providing military garrisons *(presidios)*, state subsidies *(situados)*, and supplies *(socorros)* to Catholic missions, such as that of Father San Vitores in the Mariana Islands.

Peninsular (Spanish): Spaniard born in Spain; Iberian; always ranked higher in the Spanish empire than anyone born outside Spain. Also *gachupin*.

Peonage: Forced servitude under Spanish rule whereby all Chamorro men other than *principales* were required to work (called *polo*) forty days a year on public projects or on Spanish crown land in lieu of taxes. Cashless families of the *manak'papa* lower class also fell into peonage in order to repay, through long-term labor, debts owed to wealthier *principales*. The first U.S. naval governor abolished peonage on Guam in 1900.

Plenary power: Sovereign jurisdiction with full authority to make law. The U.S. Congress has plenary power under the territorial clause of the U.S. Constitution over all U.S. territories, but not over U.S. states.

Presidiario (Spanish): Convict imprisoned in a *presidio,* usually for a criminal offense. On Guam these were mostly nonlocal ex-soldiers. Many remained on Guam after release, married Chamorro women, and raised neo-Chamorro families.

Presidio (Spanish): A military garrison, both its personnel and its buildings; may include a fort. The Agana *presidio* protected the Guam mission and personnel in the seventeenth and eighteenth centuries by forts near the beach. In the nineteenth century the *presidio* was a cluster of barracks, stables, and penitentiary across the street from the *palacio* and where the Agana jail now stands. In English, presidio refers only to the buildings of a Spanish military facility.

Principalía (Spanish): Highest class of postcontact Chamorros, called *principales,* under Spanish rule in the Marianas; replaced the *chamorri* and served as village *gobernadorcillos* and heads of *barangays.* Agana mestizo *principales* formed the *manak'kilo* elite. These classes continued under American rule but are now considerably blurred by Americanization.

Realpolitik: From German: Policy based on coldly realistic analyses of national interests and the implementation of that policy through the use of power, including all political, economic, and military means from diplomacy to warfare.

Reducción (Spanish): Conversion and collection of pagans into Christian congregations by the Spaniards; involved cooperation between missionaries of the church and soldiers of the state through the *patronato real.* The *reducción* of all Chamorros in the Marianas was accomplished by the Spanish-Chamorro Wars, 1672–1698.

Residencia (Spanish): Court of inquiry in the Spanish empire at the central level (Havana, Mexico City, Lima, and Manila) that reviewed the conduct and performance of Spanish governors of provinces such as Guam; many governors of Guam were found guilty of malfeasance in office and punished, usually by fines.

Sargento mayor (Spanish): An officer's title, not a rank, as the commander of a garrison at a *presidio.* On Guam he was the second highest official and often served as interim governor appointed by Manila until the Madrid-appointed governor arrived.

SIOP: Single Integrated Operational Plan; the top secret U.S. war plan that synchronizes the targets and launch trajectories worldwide of the triad of strategic nuclear weapons systems (bombers, intercontinental ballistic missiles, and submarine-launched ballistic missiles) against potential enemies. Guam has been a key base in SIOP.

Situado (Spanish): Cash payroll and subsidy from the Royal Spanish Treasury in New Spain (Mexico) for the Guam mission and *presidio;* usually silver coins carried annually by the galleon from Acapulco from the 1670s until 1810, then by the Cavite supply ship until 1898. Also *subsidio real* (royal subsidy).

Socorro (Spanish): Supplies for the Guam mission and *presidio* that were carried by galleons from Acapulco along with the *situado* from the 1670s until 1684, then by the Cavite supply ship until 1898.

Suruhana/Suruhanu (Chamorro): Female/male folk-herb healer who appeared after the Spanish conquest, probably from the precontact *makahna* tradition; the word may have derived from the Spanish, *cirujano* (surgeon). On contemporary Guam the Office of the Suruhanu is an ombudsman for public complaints.

Taichō (Japanese): Officer, commissioned or non-commissioned, notably one in charge of a village on Guam during the Japanese occupation, 1941–1944.

Tano' (Chamorro): Land. In Guam's history the ownership and use of land has been a central issue of absorbing local concern, particularly since World War II because of the deprivation caused Guamanians by military and federal retention of enormous tracts of island land.

Tasi (Chamorro): Ocean/sea.

Trade winds: Seasonal steady winds out of the northeast and the east in a band between about the 23° and the 12° north latitudes of the Pacific Ocean from January to around June annually. These winds carried Magellan, then Spanish galleons and all other sailing vessels from east to west across the central Pacific Ocean until steamships appeared in the 1870s.

Unincorporated U.S. territory: An area under U.S. sovereignty that is not intended by the U.S. Congress to become a U.S. state as defined by the Supreme Court in the *Insular Cases,* 1901. Guam, Puerto Rico, the Virgin Islands, American Samoa, and the Northern Mariana Islands are all unincorporated territories, despite differing political statuses such as commonwealth.

Unorganized U.S. territory: An area that is a possession/colony of the United States without self-government. Guam was an unorganized territory from 1898 until 1950 under U.S. naval government.

Uritao (Chamorro): Young, unmarried Chamorro males of a clan in precontact times; also their bachelor houses. *Uritaos* furnished the main warriors against the Spaniards in the Spanish-Chamorro Wars. Also *urritao*.

Yu'us (Chamorro from Spanish *Dios*): God. *Si Yu'us ma'ase'* (lit., "May God have mercy on you") has come to mean "Thank you." Also *Yu'os*.

Bibliography

Only those sources cited in the chapter notes or referred to in the text are listed. Primary and secondary sources are listed together alphabetically by author or source, with repositories noted in the cases of manuscripts or rare materials. The largest collection of documents about Guam is held in the Micronesian Area Research Center (MARC) at the University of Guam, Mangilao, Guam 96923. Unless otherwise noted, citations of primary Spanish and American naval period documents are to copies in the MARC collection.

Abella, Domingo
  1973 Guamanians and Filipinos: Are they the same people? An introduction to the study of Philippines-Marianas relations. *Guam Recorder,* 2d Ser., Vol. 3, No. 4, December, 9–12.
(AGI) Archivo General de Indias, Sevilla. Colección de Documentos Relativos a la Micronesia.
  1611–1778 *Copias a máquina cuyos originales para el MARC.* 79 Vols. (Includes *legajos* from *Contratación, Guadalajara, Indiferente General, México, Filipinas* and *Ultramar.*)
Agia, Miguel
  1604 *Servidumbres personales de indios. Tratado . . . sobre una cédula reale . . . que trata del servicio personal y repartimientos de indios* (Lima). Edited by F. Javier de Ayala. Seville, 1946.
(AGN) Archivo General de la Nación, México, D.F. *Reales Cédulas.*
Aguon, Katherine B.
  1988 *Me versus the World.* New York: Carlton Press.
(AHN) Archivo Histórico Nacional, Madrid. Colección de Documentos Relativos a la Micronesia. *Ultramar, Filipinas.*
(AHPA) Archivo Histórico de la Provincia de Aragón, San Cugat del Vallés, Barcelona. *Marianas.* 7 Vols.
Albo, Francisco
  1971 *Derrotero del Viage de Fernando de Magallanes en demanda del Estrecho . . . .* In Navarrete (1971), Vol. 16.

Alkire, William H.
  1977 *An Introduction to the Peoples and Cultures of Micronesia.* 2d ed. Menlo Park, Calif.: Cummings Publishing Co.
Annual Report of the Governor of Guam
  1901–1941 Original typed reports to the secretary of the navy. Washington, D.C.: NA Microfilm, 3 Rolls, No. 10-37-5. Also in RG 80, Records of the Department of the Navy, and in copies in the MARC Collection. (References are to the MARC copies.)
  1951– *To the Secretary of the Interior.* Washington, D.C.: U.S. Government Printing Office.
Año de 1829, Testimonio de Expedientes sobre dotación y defensa de Islas Marianas. . . .
  1829 AHN, *Filipinas,* 5853, 132–165.
Ansaldo, Marcelo, SJ
  1669 *Carta del Jesuíta Marcelo Ansaldo a la reina, Doña Mariana de Austria, sobre el estado de las islas del Japon, Filipinos y Marianas, y obra realizada por el PS Vitores.* AHN, *Diversos,* 389, 2, Mayo 30, Manila. Copy in the MARC Collection. Translated by Felicia Plaza, *Guam Recorder,* 2d Ser., Vol. 1, October–December 1971, 13–17. Also translated by Juan Ledesma (1981, 333–337).
Anson, George
  1748 *A Voyage round the World in the Years MDCCXL, I, II, III, IV.* London: John & Paul Knapton of Lugate Street.

Apple, Russell A.
  1980 *Guam: Two Invasions and Three Military Occu-
       pations.* Miscellaneous Publication No. 3.
       Mangilao, Guam: MARC.

Arago, Jacques Étienne Victor
  1822 *Promenade Autour du Monde pendant des
       anneés 1817 . . . 1820, Sur les Corvettes du Roi
       l'Uranie et la Physicienne Commandées par M.
       Freycinet.* 2 Vols. Paris: Leblanc.
  1839 *Souvenirs d'un Aveugle, Voyage autour du
       Monde.* 2 Vols. Paris: Hortet & Ozanne.
       (Republished in 2 Vols. with notes by François
       Arago and many illustrations. Paris: Lebrun
       1868.)
  1971 *Narrative of a Voyage round the World in the
       Uranie and Physicienne Corvettes.* Biblioteca
       Australiana No. 45. Amsterdam: N. Israel; New
       York: Da Capo Press. (Facsimile reprint of
       2 Vols. [London: Treuttel & Wurtz, 1823].)

(ARSI) Archivum Romanum Sociatatis Iesu, Rome.
       Filipinas, 13–14, 20.

Artero y Saez, Pascual
  1948 El Maestro Artero: An Autobiography. Unpub-
       lished manuscript, translated from the Spanish
       by students under the direction of Sister Felicia
       Plaza, Agana, Guam, 1970. Mangilao, Guam:
       MARC.

ATIS Captured Document No. 1541
  1946 Embarcation Instructions Issued to Troops Par-
       ticipating in the Greater East Asia War. NA, RG
       331, Entry 319, File 6, Serial 24, Case No. 1, 1
       January 1946. (Original Japanese order, part of
       intelligence report by L. H. Barnard re Japanese
       Plan to Attack Guam, 1941.)

Awakening, The
  1965 *Pacific Profile,* Pt. 1, Vol. 3, No. 8, October; Pt.
       2, Vol. 3, No. 9, November; Pt. 3, Vol. 3, No.
       10, December. (No author given; based on
       accounts and memoirs of Baltazar J. Bordallo.)

Ballendorf, Dirk Anthony
  1983 Seventy Years of Atkins, Kroll on Guam.
       Unpublished manuscript. Mangilao, Guam:
       MARC.
  1984 Secrets without Substance: U.S. Intelligence in
       the Japanese Mandates, 1915–1935. *Journal of
       Pacific History,* Vol. 19, No. 2, 83–99.
  1990 Earl Hancock Ellis: A Final Assessment. *Marine
       Corps Gazette,* Vol. 74, No. 11, November, 78–
       87.

Ballendorf, Dirk Anthony, and William L. Wuerch
  1991 Samuel J. Masters, U.S. Consul to Guam, 1854–
       56: Harbinger of American Pacific Expansion.
       Diplomacy and Statecraft, Vol. 2, No. 3,
       November, 306–326.

Bamba, Cecilia
  1982 *Report of the Guam War Reparations Commis-
       sion.* Agana: Fourteenth Guam Legislature.

Barratt, Glynn, ed. and trans.
  1984 *Russian Exploration in the Mariana Islands
       1817–1828.* Micronesian Archaeological Sur-
       vey Report No. 17. Saipan: Division of Historic
       Preservation.
  1988a *Carolinean Contacts with the Islands of the
       Marianas: The European Record.* Micronesian
       Archaeological Survey Report No. 25. Saipan:
       Division of Historic Preservation.
  1988b *H.M.S. Centurion at Tinian, 1742: The Ethno-
       graphic and Historic Records.* Micronesian
       Archaeological Survey Report No. 26. Saipan:
       Division of Historic Preservation.

Bartlett, Owen, Commander, U.S.N. (ret.)
  1972 Destruction of S.M.S. "Cormoran." *Guam
       Recorder,* 2d Ser., Vol. 2, No. 4, October–
       December. (Reprinted from *U.S. Naval Institute
       Proceedings,* August 1931, 1044–1051.)

Basso, Aldo P.
  1968 *Coins, Medals and Tokens of the Philippines.*
       Menlo Park, Calif.: Chenby Publishers.

Beardsley, Charles
  1964 *Guam Past and Present.* Tokyo: Charles E. Tut-
       tle Co.

Beers, Henry P.
  1914 *American Naval Occupation and Government
       of Guam, 1898–1902.* Administrative Reference
       Service Report No. 6. Washington, D.C.: Office
       of Records Administration, Navy Department.

Bellwood, Peter S.
  1978 *Man's Conquest of the Pacific.* Auckland:
       Collins.

Berry, Henry
  1983 *Semper Fi, Mac.* New York: Berkley Books.

Blair, Emma H., and James A. Robertson, eds.
  1903–1909 *The Philippine Islands, 1493–1898.*
       55 Vols. Cleveland: Arthur H. Clark Co.

Bohn, John A.
  1982 Memorandum of Remedial Proceedings in
       Guam Land Acquisition Case Filed Pursuant to
       the Omnibus Territories Act of 1977 (P.L. 95–

134, 48 U.S.C. § 1424c). Filed, District Court of Guam, Agana, Guam Civil Case, 26 January 1982, No. 77–00072 MF.

Bordallo, Penelope C.
1982 A Campaign for Political Rights on Guam, Mariana Islands, 1899–1950. M.A. thesis, University of Hawai'i.

Bordallo, Ricardo J.
1978 *Guam, a New Era of Growth: Governor's Report to the People of Guam on the State of the Territory.* Agana, Guam: Governor's Office, 6 February.

Bouwens, Gerardo, SJ
1673 Letter, 8 October, to Fathers M. Schweitzer and A. van Horenbeeck (unpublished original in Latin). Vol. 2, Fol. 232–232v, No. 872–915, Archives Générales du Royaume, Archives Jésuitiques, Province Flandro-Belgique, Antwerp.

Boxer, Charles Ralph
1950 A Late Sixteenth Century Manila MS (Boxer Codex). *Royal Asiatic Society Journal,* April, 37–49.
1958 The Manila Galleon: 1565–1815. *History Today,* Vol. 8, No. 8, 544–545.

Bradley, Willis W., Jr., Commander, U.S.N.
1931 Notes for My Relief as Governor of Guam 1931. Unpublished typescript in Bradley papers at MARC; see Wuerch, William L., Working Paper No. 60, Governor Willis Bradley, Jr., Inventory of Papers. Mangilao, Guam: MARC.

Braisted, William R.
1958 *The United States Navy in the Pacific, 1897–1909.* Austin: University of Texas Press.
1971 *The United States Navy in the Pacific, 1909–1922.* Austin: University of Texas Press.

Brosses, Charles de
1967 *Histoire des navigations aux terres australes.* Vol. 2. Biblioteca Australiana No. 1. Amsterdam: N. Israel; New York: Da Capo Press. (Facsimile reprint of 1756 original by Durand, Paris.)

Burdick, Charles B.
1979 *The Frustrated Raider.* Carbondale and Edwardsville: Southern Illinois University Press.

Burney, James F. R. S.
1803–1817 *Chronological History of the discoveries in the South Sea or Pacific Ocean.* 5 Vols. London: Luke Hansard & Sons.

Burrus, Ernest J., SJ
1954 Sanvitores grammar and catechism in the Mariana (or Chamorro) language (1668). *Anthropos,* Vol. 49, 934–960. Posieux, Schweiz: Herausgegeban vom Anthropos-Institut.

Butler, Brian M., ed.
1988 *Archaeological Investigations on the North Coast of Rota, Mariana Islands.* Micronesian Archaeological Survey Report No. 23. Carbondale: Southern Illinois University, Center for Archaeological Investigations.

Bywater, Hector C.
1921 *Sea-Power in the Pacific: A Study of the American-Japanese Naval Problem.* London: Constable.
1925 *The Great Pacific War: A History of the Japanese-American Campaign of 1931–33.* London: Constable.

Cabanillas, Ildefonso, O.S.A., and Crisogono Ortín, O.S.A.
1899 *Memoria.* Manila, 25 September. Mangilao, Guam: MARC. Translated from the Spanish by Marjorie G. Driver. Yankees Capture Guam. *Guam Recorder,* 2d Ser., Vol. 1, No. 1, January–March, 25–36.

Cadarso y Rey, Luís
1894 Islas Marianas: Informe dado por el Capitán de Fragata a la Commandancia General del Apostadero de FILIPINAS. Typescript copy. Mangilao, Guam: MARC.

Calvo, Oscar Lujan
1992a Commander's kindness touches priest's heart. *Guam Tribune,* 21 March, 20.
1992b *Guam 1941* (brochure for commemorative exhibition, Bank of Guam, on the fiftieth anniversary of the invasion of Guam). Agana, Guam: Island Type and Art.

Campbell, Bruce L.
1987 The Filipino Community of Guam (1945–1975). M.A. thesis, University of Hawai'i, Pacific Islands Studies.

Campbell, Thomas
1921 *The Jesuits, 1534–1921.* New York: Encyclopedia Press.

Carano, Paul, and Pedro C. Sanchez
1964 *A Complete History of Guam.* Rutland, Vt.: Charles E. Tuttle.

Carriveau, Kenneth L., ed.
  1985 *University of Guam, Facts and Figures, 1952–1982.* Mangilao: University of Guam.
Castro, Francisco Antonio de
  1723 *Laureola Sacra de la Vida y martirio del Venerable Padre Diego Luís de San Vitores.* Madrid: Gabriel del Barrio.
Cerezo Martínez, Ricardo
  1987 *La Expedición Malaspina 1798–1794.* Madrid: Ministerio de Defensa, Museo Naval; Lunwerg Editores.
Chacón Lara, Francisco
  1885 *Memoria, Proyecto y Estatutos de Colonización de las Islas Españolas. Marianas, Carolinas y Palaos.* Sevilla: Salvador Acuña.
Chamisso, Adelbert von
  1986 *A Voyage Around the World with the Romanzov Exploring Expedition in the Years 1815–1818 in the Brig Rurik.* (Translated by Henry Kratz from the German. *Reise um die Welt. . . .* Leipzig, 1836). Honolulu: University of Hawai'i Press.
Chaunu, Pierre
  1960 *Le Philippines et le Pacifique des Iberiques.* Paris: SEVPEN.
Cheng, Silvia E., trans.
  1984 A Relation of Explorers of the Pacific in Guam and Micronesia from the 17th to the 19th Centuries. Working Paper. Mangilao, Guam: MARC.
Clifford, John H.
  1904 *History of the Pioneer Marine Battalion at Guam, Ladrone Islands, 1899, and the Campaign in Samar, Philippine Islands, 1901.* Portsmouth, N.H.: Chronicle Job Print.
(CNH) Center for Naval History.
  1912–1947 Records of the Strategic Plans Division and Predecessor Organizations. Naval History Division. Operational Archives. Vol. 1, Ser. 1–16, Boxes 4, 35, 48, 49, 91, 103, 147B, 193, 255. (Declassified original Navy records.) Washington, D.C.: Navy Yard.
Colección de documentos inéditos relativos al descubrimiento, conquista y organización de las antiguas posesiones españolas de Ultramar
  1886 2d Ser., Vol. 2, I, *De las Filipinas.* Madrid: Sucesores de Rivadeneyra. Reprinted by Kraus Reprint, Nendeln, Liechtenstein, 1967.
  1887 2d Ser., Vol. 3, II, *De las Filipinas.* Madrid: Sucesores de Rivadeneyra. Reprinted by Kraus Reprint, Nendeln, Liechtenstein, 1967.

Colín, Francisco, and Pablo Pastells, SJ
  1900–1902 *Labor evangélica* (1663). 2 Vols. Barcelona: Henrich y Compañía.
  1904 *Labor evangélica de los obreros de la Compañia de Jesús en las Islas Filipinas: Nueva Ed. de Pablo Pastells.* 3 Vols. Barcelona: Henrich y Compañía.
Community/Business Profile.
  1984 4th ed. Agana, Guam: The Paladin Group, October.
Concepción, Juan de la, O.S.A.
  1789 *Historia General de Filipinas, Tomo VII.* Manila.
Congressional Record
  1947 29 May. Extension of Remarks of Norris Poulson. 80th Cong., 1st Sess., Vol. 93, A2568–A2570. Washington, D.C.: U.S. Government Printing Office.
  1972 10 April. Communication from the Government of Guam Relative to the First Constitutional Convention. 92d Cong., 2d Sess., Vol. 118, 11885. Washington, D.C.: U.S. Government Printing Office.
Coontz, Robert E.
  1930 *From the Mississippi to the Sea.* Philadelphia: Dorrance & Co.
Coote, Robert
  1950 A Report on the Land-Use Conditions and Land Problems on Guam. Unpublished manuscript, Pacific Division of Territories, Department of the Interior, Washington, D.C. Mangilao, Guam: MARC.
Corte y Ruano Calderón, Felipe de la
  1970 *Descriptive and Historical Report on the Mariana Islands.* Translation of *Memoria descriptiva é histórica de las Islas Marianas.* (Original written in 1865 and published in Madrid in 1875 in *Boletín del Ministerio de Ultramar,* National Printing Office.) Translated by Helen L. Paul. (Part 2 of the report was translated separately in 1937 by Gertrude C. Hornbostel with the title *A History of the Mariana Islands, November 1520 to May 1870, with a Continuation by the Reverend Father José Palomo y Torres.*) Mangilao, Guam: MARC.
Costa, Horacio de la, SJ
  1967 *The Jesuits in the Philippines, 1581–1768.* Cambridge, Mass.: Harvard University Press.
Costenoble, Hermann H. L. W.
  1905–1910 *The Marianas.* Selection of articles published in *Globus* magazine, Germany, Vols. 88–

98, translated from the German by Susanne de C. Wilkins. Working Paper No. 33. Mangilao, Guam: MARC, 1981.

Cottman, Vincendon L., Lt., U.S.N.
1899 Report on Guam to the Secretary of the Navy, 20 February. Handwritten letter, 28 pages, with 3 enclosures: Report by Asst. Surgeon M. V. Stone, U.S.N., on diseases; Translation of Spanish pamphlet on Guam by Padre Aniceto Ibáñez; and a weather report for January 1899 on Guam. Originals in NA, RG 80 General Records of the Department of the Navy, General Correspondence, 1897–1915, File 9351 (11–38).

Cox, Leonard M.
1917 *The Island of Guam*. Washington, D.C.: U.S. Government Printing Office. Partially rewritten by Capt. E. J. Dorn, U.S.N., 1910; revised by Passed Asst. Paymaster K. C. McIntosh, U.S.N., 1911; revised and enlarged by Lt. Cmdr. M. G. Cook, U.S.N., 1916. Reprinted in 1926.

Critchfield, Theodore M.
1988 The Story Behind the Story. *Journal of the Pacific Society,* No. 38 (Vol. 11, No. 1), (1)–150–(7)–144, April.

Crowl, Philip A.
1960 *United States Army in World War II: The War in the Pacific: Campaign in the Marianas*. Washington, D.C.: Office of the Chief of Military History, Department of the Army.

Cuevas, Mariano
1943 *Monje y Marino: La Vida y los Tiempos de Fray Andrés de Urdaneta*. México: Editorial Galatea.

Cunningham, Lawrence J.
1984 *Ancient Chamorro Kinship Organization*. Agat, Guam: L. Joseph Press.
1992 *Ancient Chamorro Society*. Honolulu: The Bess Press.

Dampier, William
1937 *A New Voyage Round the World*. London: Adam & Charles Black. (Reprint of the 1927 ed. of Dampier's original 1697 and subsequent versions.)

Delgadillo, Yolanda, M.M.B., Thomas B. McGrath, SJ, and Felicia Plaza, M.M.B.
1979 *Spanish Forts of Guam*. Publication Series No. 7. Mangilao, Guam: MARC.

Delgado, Juan J., SJ
1892 *Historia General Sacro-Profana, Política y Natural de las Islas Del Poniente llamadas Filipinas:* Biblioteca Histórica Filipina (originally published in 1751). Manila: El Eco de Filipinas.

del Valle, María Teresa
1991 *The Importance of the Mariana Islands to Spain at the Beginning of the Nineteenth Century*. Educational Series No. 11. Mangilao, Guam: MARC.

Despatches from the U.S. Consul in Guam, Ladrone Islands
1854–1856 Original handwritten despatches by Consul Samuel Masters. Washington, D.C.: NA, RG 59, General Records of the Department of State, Microfilm, Roll 1, No. 10-10-5.

Dizon, Joe S.
1982 *Political Parties and Elections in Guam*. Agana: Guam Research Associates.
1987 *Winning Ways*. Agana: Guam Research Associates.

Doran, E. B.
1981 *Wangka: Austronesian Canoe Origins*. College Station: Texas A&M Press.

Dorn, Edward John
1868–1936 Papers. 5 Containers. Boxes 1, 4. Manuscript Division, Library of Congress, Washington, D.C.

Dorwart, Jeffery M.
1983 *Conflict of Duty: The U.S. Navy's Intelligence Dilemma, 1919–1945*. Annapolis, Md.: Naval Institute Press.

Driver, Marjorie G.
1968 Documents Relating to Micronesia in the Archivo General de la Nación, México. Working Paper No. 13. Mangilao, Guam: MARC.
1977 The Account of a discalced friar's stay in the Islands of the Ladrones. *Guam Recorder,* 2d Ser., Vol. 7, 19–21. Translation from Spanish of Marcelo de Ribadeneira. *Historia de las islas del Archipelago Filipino y reinos de la Gran China, Tartaria, Cochinchina, Maluca, Siam, Cambodge y Japon*. Edited by P. Juan R. de Legísima, O.F.M., Capitulo XIX. Madrid: Editorial Católica, 1947.
1983 Fray Juan Pobre de Zamora and His Account of the Mariana Islands. *Journal of Pacific History,* Vol. 18, No. 3, 198–216. Translation from Spanish of the *Relación Sobre la pérdida del galeón San Felipe (1598–1603)*. MSS II, Bloomington, Indiana University, Lilly Library. In MARC Microfilm Collection.

1985   *Guam: A Nomenclatural Chronology.* Educational Series No. 5. Mangilao, Guam: MARC.

1987   *Navigational Data for the Mariana Islands.* Translation of a publication by the Spanish Hydrographic Office, Madrid, 1863. Mangilao, Guam: MARC.

1988a   Cross, Sword, and Silver: The Nascent Spanish Colony in the Mariana Islands. *Pacific Studies,* Vol. 11, No. 3, 21–51, July.

1988b   *Fray* Juan Pobre de Zamora: Hitherto Unpublished Accounts of His Residence in the Mariana Islands. *Journal of Pacific History,* Vol. 23, No. 1, 86–94, April.

1989   The Spanish Palacio in Agana. *Islander, Pacific Daily News,* 12 November, 5–7.

1990a   *The History of the Marianas, with Navigational Data, and of the Caroline and Palau Islands.* (Translation from the Spanish of Luís de Ibáñez y García. *Historia de las Islas Marianas.* Granada: Paulino V. Sabatel, 1886.) Mangilao, Guam: MARC. New, expanded edition published in 1992 as Educational Series No. 12. Mangilao, Guam: MARC.

1990b   Maritime Activities in the Mariana Islands 1521–1898. In *Submerged Cultural Resources Study of Micronesia,* ed. Toni Carrell. Washington, D.C.: National Park Service.

1991a   An Account of the Islands of the Ladrones. (Translation from Spanish of the Ayer Manuscript 1409a, Boxer Codex, Newberry Library, Chicago, *Relación de las Yslas de los Ladrones,* original by unknown author, 1590, aboard the *Santiago.*) *Journal of Pacific History,* Vol. 26, No. 1, 103–106, April.

1991b   *Description of the Mariana Islands* by Manuel Sanz. (Translation from the Spanish of the unpublished manuscript C-19-11, No. 2, Servicio Geográfico del Ejército, Madrid.) Educational Series No. 10. Mangilao, Guam: MARC.

1991c   A Report on the Mariana Islands. (Translation from the Spanish of the unpublished manuscript *Expediente formado a raíz de la Real Orden de 14 de diciembre de 1828. Cartas y correspondencia de Don Alexandro Parreño,* in AHN, Ultramar Legajo 5854.) *Journal of the Pacific Society,* No. 51 (Vol. 14, No. 2), (27)–132–(39)–120, July, 27–39.

Dumont d'Urville, Jules Sébastien César
1987   *Two Voyages to the South Seas.* Vol. 1, *Astrolabe 1826–1829.* Vol. 2, *Astrolabe and Zélée 1837–1840.* Translated and edited by Helen Rosenman. Honolulu: University of Hawai'i Press.

Dunmore, John
1965–1969 *French Explorers in the Pacific.* 2 Vols. Oxford: Clarendon Press.

Dyen, I.
1962   The Lexicostatistical Classification of the Malayopolynesian Languages. *Language,* Vol. 38, 38–46.

1965   A lexicostatistical classification of the Austronesian languages. *International Journal of American Linguistics,* Memoir 19.

Elliot, J. H.
1970   *Imperial Spain 1469–1716.* Harmondsworth: Viking Penguin.

Ellis, Earl Hancock
1915   *Report of a Military Reconnaissance of the Island of Guam 1914–1915.* Confidential report transmitted by the governor of Guam, 25 September. NA, RG 38, Ellis File in CNH. Copy in MARC Collection.

Elvidge, Ford Q.
1956   I Ruled Uncle Sam's Problem Child. *Saturday Evening Post,* 1 December, 49, 75–76, 80.

Emily Morgan Log
1925   "Whalers in Guam in 1850." *Guam Recorder,* June–September. Mangilao, Guam: MARC.

Engebretson, David C., Allan Cox, and Richard G. Gordon
1985   Relative Motions Between Oceanic and Continental Plates in the Pacific Basin. Special Paper No. 206. Boulder, Colo.: Geological Society of America.

Environmental Impact Assessment of Typhoon Pamela
1976   Agana, Guam: Environmental Protection Agency, June.

Farrell, Don A.
1984   *The Pictorial History of Guam: Liberation–1944.* Tamuning, Guam: Micronesian Productions.

1986   *The Pictorial History of Guam: The Americanization 1898–1918.* Tamuning, Guam: Micronesian Productions.

1991a   *History of the Northern Mariana Islands.* Saipan: Public School System, Commonwealth of the Northern Mariana Islands.

1991b *The Pictorial History of Guam: The Sacrifice 1919–1943.* San Jose, Tinian: Micronesian Productions.

Federal Interagency Task Force (BATFOG)
1989 Section-by-Section Report on S.317 (H.R. 98). A Bill to Establish the Commonwealth of Guam. Unpublished report from OTIA released by the Office of Guam Delegate Ben Blaz, 1 August 1989.

Fernández Duro, Cesáreo
1973 *Armada Española desde la unión de los reinos de Castilla y de Aragón.* 9 Vols. Madrid: Museo Naval.

Fernberger von Egenberg, Christoph Carl
1972 A Pre-Missionary Manuscript Record of the Chamorro, Micronesia. Translated from the German by Karl R. Wernhart. *Journal of Pacific History,* Vol. 7, 189–193.

Fieldhouse, R.
1985 *Nuclear Battlefields, Global Links in the Arms Race.* Cambridge, Mass.: Ballinger.

Final Report of Navy War Crimes Program in the Pacific.
1949 5 vols. Submitted by the director of war crimes, U.S. Pacific Fleet, to the secretary of the navy. Washington, D.C.: Department of the Navy, Navy Historical Center. (Microfilm copy in MARC Collection.)

Foreign Relations
1898– *Papers Relating to the Foreign Relations of the United States.* Washington, D.C.: U.S. Government Printing Office.

Foreman, John
1980 *The Philippine Islands.* Manila: Filipiniana Book Guild. (Reprint of 1906 [3d] ed. New York: Charles Scribner's Sons.)

Fosberg, F. R.
1948 Derivation of the Flora of the Hawaiian Islands. In *Insects of Hawaii,* Vol. 1, *Introduction,* ed. E. C. Zimmerman. Honolulu: University of Hawai'i Press.
1960 The Vegetation of Micronesia: 1. General Descriptions, the Vegetation of the Mariana Islands and a Detailed Consideration of the Vegetation of Guam. *American Museum of Natural History Bulletin,* Vol. 64, No. 1, 1–76.

Francis, Anthony A., 1st Lt., U.S.M.C.
1944 "Wake Up and Die": The Battle of Banzai Ridge, Guam, M.I. Original manuscript, U.S. Marine Corps Archives, Guam file. Later pub- lished in *Marine Corps Gazette,* Vol. 29, June 1945, 13–18.

French, Willard
1905 An Isolated American Island: How We Are Neglecting Our Duty to Guam. *Booklover's Magazine,* March, 369–379.

Freycinet, Louis Claude Desaulces de
1839 *Voyage autour du monde executé sur les cor- vettes de S.M. l'Uranie et la Physicienne pen- dant les années 1817–1820.* Vol. 1, *Histoire du Voyage.* Bk. 3, *Iles Mariannes.* Paris: Pillet Aine.

Freycinet, Rose de
1927 *Journal du voyage autour du monde a bord de l' Uranie 1817–1820.* Paris: Societé d' Editions Geographics, Maritimes et Coloniales. (Reprint of the original *Journal de Madame Rose Desaulces de Freycinet.* Paris, 1825.)

Fritz, Georg
1986 *The Chamorro: A History and Ethnography of the Marianas.* Translated from the German by Elfriede Craddock from *Eine Geschicte und Ethnographie der Marianen, Ethnologisches Notizblatt,* (Berlin), Vol. 3, No. 3, 1904, 25– 110. Saipan: Division of Historic Preservation, Commonwealth of the Marianas.

Frost, Alan
1988 Science for Political Purposes: The European Nations' Explorations of the Pacific Ocean, 1764–1806. In *Spanish Pacific from Magellan to Malaspina.* Madrid: Ministerio de Asuntos Exteriores; Lunwerg Editores.

Funnel, William
1969 *A Voyage Round the World Containing an Account of Captain Dampier's Expedition in the Years 1703 and 1704.* Biblioteca Austra- liana No. 57. Amsterdam: N. Israel; New York: Da Capo Press. (Facsimile reprint of original 1707 ed. by W. Botham for James Knapton, London.)

Gailey, Harry A.
1988 *The Liberation of Guam, 21 July–10 August 1944.* Novato, Calif.: Presidio Press.

Gandt, Robert L.
1985 The China Clipper, Transpacific Pioneer. *Pan Am* (Pan Am Airlines magazine), November, 33–40.

García, Francisco, SJ
1683 *Vida y martyrio de el Venerable Padre Luís de Sanvitores, de la Compañia de Jesús, primer*

apóstol de las Islas Marianas, etc. Madrid: Ivan García Infanzón. Partially translated by Margaret M. Higgins, *Guam Recorder,* September 1936–July 1939. The Higgins translation was edited into a single unpublished volume by the Nieves M. Flores Memorial Library in Agana, Guam, 1985. References in the present book are to the Flores edition. Books 1, 2, and Chaps. 1–4 of Bk. 3 of Garcia's history were also translated by Sister Felicia Plaza for MARC, 1980, with the unpublished manuscript in the MARC Collection.

García de la Purísima Concepción, Rafael, O.R.S.A.
1964   *Estela de una estrella.* Marcilla (Navarra): Boletín de la Província de San Nicolás de Tolentino.

Gault, Cathy Sablan, and Stephen V. Nygard
1984   Atoning for Deeds. *Guam Business News,* October, 10–17.

General Orders
1899–1941   *General Orders, Naval Government of Guam.* In *Government of Guam Code.* Agana, Guam: Compiler of Laws.

Gibbons, J. R. H., and F. G. A. U. Clunie
1986   Sea Level Changes and Pacific Prehistory: New Insight into Early Human Settlement of Oceania. *Journal of Pacific History,* Vol. 21, No. 2, 58–82.

Glass, Henry
1898   Report to Secretary of Navy John D. Long, 24 June. NA, RG 45. Washington, D.C.: Bureau of Navigation, Office of Naval Records and Library.

Goodenough, W.
1957   Oceania and the Problem of Controls in the Study of Cultural and Human Evolution. *Journal of the Polynesian Society,* Vol. 66, 146–155.

Goodman, Howard
1988   Anatomy of a Scandal. *Guam Business News,* March, 8–15.

Graves, Michael W.
1986   Organizations and Differentiation within Late Prehistoric Ranked Social Units in the Mariana Islands of the Western Pacific. *Journal of Field Archaeology,* Vol. 13, No. 2, Summer, 139–154.

Griffith, Richard Roy
1978   From Island Colony to Strategic Territory: The Development of American Administration on the Island of Guam: 1898–1950. Ph.D. diss.,

University of Denver. Facsimile No. 7823794, University Microfilms International, Ann Arbor, Mich.

Grijalva, Juan de, O.S.A.
1624   *Crónica de la Orden de N.P.S. Agustín en las provincias de la Nueva España.* Mexico: Imprenta de Ioan Ruyz.

Gschaedler, Andre
1954   Mexico and the Pacific, 1540–1565. Ph.D. diss., Columbia University. MARC Collection.

Guam: Brief Extracts . . . and Annual Reports . . .
1905–   Washington, D.C.: U.S. Government Printing Office.

Guam Annual Economic Review
1975–   Agana: Department of Commerce, Government of Guam.

Guam Business News
1983–   (Monthly.) Agana: Glimpses of Guam.

Guam Commission on Self-Determination
1990   *Our Quest for Commonwealth* (Quarterly Newsletters). Agana, Guam: Commission on Self-Determination.

Guam Congress, *Congressional Record*
1947–   Agana, Guam: MARC Collection.

Guam Constitutional Convention
1969–1970   *Proceedings of the First Constitutional Convention of Guam, 1969–1970.* Hong Kong: Green Pagoda Press.

Guam Constitutional Convention, 1977
1979   Agana, Guam: Government of Guam.

Guam Daily News and *Sunday Territorial Sun* (1952–1964)
1950–   Agana, Guam: Published by Joseph Flores.

Guam Eagle
1936–1941   Agana: U.S. Naval Government of Guam.

Guam Echo
1947–1950   (Mimeographed newsheet.) Washington, D.C.: Institute of Ethnic Affairs.

Guam Election Commission
1977–1990   *Election Comparative Analysis Report.* (Annual.) Agana: Guam Election Commission.

Guam Inventory of Planning Information
1989   Vol. 1, *Social and Economic Planning.* Agana: Government of Guam, Bureau of Planning.
1990   Vol. 2, *Environmental and Physical Planning.* Agana: Government of Guam, Bureau of Planning.

Guam News (formerly *Navy News*)
1947–1950 Agana: U.S. Military Government of Guam.

Guam News Letter
1909–1922 Agana: U.S. Naval Government of Guam.

Guam Recorder
1924–1941 1st Ser., Vols. 1–18. Agana, Guam: Published by W. W. Rowley, 1924–1933; and the U.S. Naval Government of Guam, 1933–1941. Mangilao, Guam: MARC.

1971–1979 2d Ser., Vols. 1–9, October 1971–September 1979. Mangilao, Guam: MARC.

Guam's People: "Continuing Heritage": A Statistical Profile of the Territory of Guam, 1920–1980.
1988 Prepared by selected members of the Interagency Committee on Population. Agana: Government of Guam.

Guam Status Report
1974 Report on the Status of Guam. Agana: Legislative Political Commission of the Twelfth Guam Legislature. Unpublished. Copy in Nieves M. Flores Library, Agana, Guam.

Guam Times Weekly
1964– Agana, Guam. Published by Manuel L. José.

Guam Tribune and *Sunday Panorama*
1970–1992 Agana, Guam. Published by Mark V. Pangilinan.

Gutiérrez, Francisco García
1899 *Año de 1898–99*. Report, *Referente á la evacuación de las Islas Marianas*. Legajo 1532, 37–80. Madrid: Museo Naval.

Guzman-Rivas, Pablo
1960 *Reciprocal Geographic Influences of the Trans-Pacific Galleon Trade*. P.h.D. diss., University of Texas. Facsimile No. 60-4543, University Microfilms International, Ann Arbor, Mich.

Haddon, A. C., and James Hornell
1975 *Canoes of Oceania*. Bernice P. Bishop Museum Special Publications 27, 28, 29 (reprint of 1936–1938 papers). Honolulu: Bishop Museum Press.

Hardin, Garrett
1985 *Filters Against Folly*. Harrisonburg, Va: Penguin Books.

1993 *Living Within Limits: Ecology, Economics and Population Taboos*. New York: Oxford University Press.

Haswell, William
1917 Remarks on a Voyage in 1801 to the Island of Guam. *Historical Collections of the Essex Institute* (Salem, Mass.), Vol. 53, July, 193–214.

Haverlandt, Otto Ronald, et al.
1975 *The Social-Economic Impact of Modern Technology upon a Developing Insular Region: Guam*. 4 Vols. Mangilao: University of Guam Press. Unpublished, typed copy in MARC Collection.

Hawaii Business
1979 Special Report, Guam and Micronesia. Vol. 24, No. 9, March. Honolulu: Hawaii Business Publishing Corp.

Hayes, Peter, Lyuba Zarsky, and Walden Bello
1986 *American Lake: Nuclear Peril in the Pacific*. Harmondsworth: Penguin Books.

Heaps, Leo
1974 *Log of the Centurion*. (Based on the original papers of Capt. Philip Saumarez on board HMS *Centurion*, Lord Anson's flagship during his circumnavigation 1740–1744.) New York: Macmillan Publishing Co.

Hernández, José, SJ
1690 Letter: Conditions in Guam in 1690. Translated by W. C. Repetti, SJ, *Guam Recorder*, Vol. 18, 1941, 230–231. Also in *Vignettes of Philippines-Marianas Colonial History*, ed. Domingo Abella. Manila: IAHA, 1962.

Hezel, Francis X., SJ
1970 Catholic Missions in the Caroline and Marshall Islands: A Survey of Historical Materials. *Journal of Pacific History*, Vol. 5, 213–227.

1982 From Conversion to Conquest: The Early-Spanish Mission in the Marianas. *Journal of Pacific History*, Vol. 17, Nos. 3–4, 115–137.

1983 *The First Taint of Civilization: A History of the Caroline and Marshall Islands in the Pre-colonial Days, 1521–1885*. Honolulu: University of Hawai'i Press.

1989 *From Conquest to Colonization: Spain in the Mariana Islands 1690 to 1740*. Saipan: Division of Historic Preservation.

Hezel, Francis X., SJ, and Marjorie G. Driver
1988 From Conquest to Colonization: Spain in the Mariana Islands 1690–1740. *Journal of Pacific History*, Vol. 23, No. 2, October, 137–155.

Hezel, Francis X., SJ, and Thomas B. McGrath, SJ
1989 The Great Flight Northward: FSM Migration to Guam and the Northern Mariana Islands.

Pacific Studies, Vol. 13, No. 1, November, 47–64.

Higgins, Margaret M.
1938 Guam—Perch of the China Clippers. *National Geographic,* Vol. 74, No. 1, July, 99–122.

Higueras, Dolores
1988 The Malaspina Expedition (1789–1794). In *Spanish Pacific from Magellan to Malaspina.* Madrid: Ministerio de Asuntos Exteriores; Lunwerg Editores.

Historical Overview of Guam's Temporary Non-immigrant Alien Labor Policies, 1947–1980
1980 Unpublished Government of Guam Study. Agana, Guam: Bureau of Planning, December. MARC Collection.

Honan, William H.
1991 *Visions of Infamy: The Untold Story of How Journalist Hector C. Bywater Devised the Plans That Led to Pearl Harbor.* New York: St. Martin's Press.

Hopkins, Ernest M., Maurice J. Tobin, and Knowles A. Ryerson
1947 *Hopkins Committee Report for the Secretary on the Civil Governments of Guam and American Samoa.* Unpublished. Washington, D.C.: U.S. Department of Navy, 25 March. (Library of Congress ref. JG 6003 1947 V 53.)

Horie, Yoshitaka
1967 *Higeki no Saipan* (Tragedy of Saipan). Tokyo: Hara Shobō.

Howard, Chris Perez
1982 *Mariquita: A Guam Story.* Agana, Guam: PPh & Co.

Howells, William White
1973 *The Pacific Islanders.* New York: Scribners'; London: Weidenfeld & Nicolson, Ltd.

Hubbell, James H., Captain, U.S.A., ed.
1945 Monograph IV, History of VHB Construction in the Marianas and Iwo Jima. Unpublished manuscript. Harmon Field, Guam: Headquarters, 20th Air Force, September 1945. Copy in library, War in the Pacific National Historical Park, Air Force Reel No. 7, Asan, Guam.

Hunter-Anderson, Rosalind L., ed.
1990 Recent Advances in Micronesian Archaeology. *Micronesica,* Supplement No. 2, October. Mangilao: University of Guam Press.

Hurtado, Don Juan de Vargas y
1680 *Instruction* (to the governor of the Marianas, Don José de Quiroga, 7 September 1680). Translation by Father S. P. Staudt, O.F.M., published in the *Guam Recorder,* No. 5, September 1938, 180–187; October 1938, 14–15, 38.

Hymowitz, T., R. J. Singh, and R. P. Larkin
1990 Long-Distance Dispersal: The Case for the Allopolyploid *Glycine tabacina* (Lubill.) Benth and *G. tomentella* Hayata in the Western Central Pacific. *Micronesica,* Vol. 23, No. 1, 5–13.

Ibáñez del Carmen, Aniceto, O.S.A., and Francisco Resano del Sagrado Corazón, O.S.A.
1976 *Chronicle of the Mariana Islands.* Translated from the Spanish by Marjorie G. Driver. Mangilao, Guam: MARC.

Ibáñez y García, Luís de
1990 *The History of the Marianas with Navigational Data, and of the Caroline and Palau Islands.* Translated and annotated by Marjorie G. Driver from *Historia de las Islas Marianas.* . . . (Granada: Paulino V. Sabatel, 1886.) Mangilao, Guam: MARC. New, expanded edition published in 1992 as Educational Series No. 12. Mangilao, Guam: MARC.

Insular Cases
1901 *Downes v. Bidwell,* 182 U.S. 244 (1901); *Armstrong v. United States,* 182 U.S. 243 (1901); *Dooley v. United States,* 182 U.S. 222 (1901); *DeLima v. Bidwell,* 182 U.S. 1 (1901).

Ito, Masashi
1967 *The Emperors' Last Soldiers.* Translated from the Japanese by Roger Clifton. New York: Coward-McCann. (Ito's diary was translated by Craig B. Smith as *The Diary of Sergeant Ito.* Los Angeles: Whirlwind Press, 1986.)

Iwano, Masataka, et al.
1946 The Central Pacific Operation Record. (History of the Japanese invasion of Guam, 1941.) Japanese Monograph No. 48, Vol. 1, November 1946. Washington, D.C.: Office of the Chief of U.S. Army History. In Charles W. Snell, Data on the Order of Battle and Tactics of Japanese Forces on Guam in 1944, unpublished manuscript, Department of the Interior, National Park Service, November 1983. Copy in library, War in the Pacific National Historical Park, Asan, Guam.

Jaffe, Mark
1994 *And No Birds Sing.* New York: Simon & Schuster.

James, Roy E.
1946 Military Government: Guam. *Far Eastern Survey,* Vol. 15, No. 18, 11 September, 273–277.
1949 The Island Possession of Guam. In *America's Pacific Dependencies . . . : A Symposium.* New York: American Institute of Pacific Relations.

Johannes, R. E.
1981 *Words of the Lagoon: Fishing and Marine Lore in the Palau District of Micronesia.* Los Angeles: University of California Press.

Johnson, Edward C., Lt. Col., U.S.M.C.
1977 *Marine Corps Aviation: The Early Years 1912–1940.* History and Museums Division, Headquarters, U.S. Marine Corps. Washington, D.C.: U.S. Government Printing Office.

Johnston, Emilie G.
1974 *A Saga of Agueda.* Agana, Guam: Johnston Enterprises.

Jorgensen, Marilyn Anne
1984 Expressive Manifestations of Santa Marian Camalin as Key Symbol in Guamanian Culture. Ph.D. diss., University of Texas at Austin. MARC Collection.

Josephy, Alvin M., Jr.
1946 *The Long and the Short and the Tall.* New York: Alfred A. Knopf & Co.

Jurien de la Gravière, Jean Paul Edmond
1854 *Voyage en chine et dans les mers et archipels de cet empire pendant les années 1847–50.* 2 Vols. Paris: Charpentier. (The Guam portion, pp. 184–211, was translated by Douglas Haynes in the *Islander, Pacific Daily News* [Guam], 3 June 1990, 4–7.)

Kaiser, Louis A.
1899 Diary of Lieutenant Louis A. Kaiser, U.S.N. Unpublished manuscript. Typed copies in Library of Congress.

Karolle, Bruce G.
1988 *Atlas of Micronesia.* Mangilao, Guam: MARC.

King, Ernest J., and Walter M. Whitehill
1952 *Fleet Admiral King—a Naval Record.* New York: W. W. Norton & Co.

Kotsch, William J.
1962 Report on Supertyphoon Karen. Memorandum from commanding officer, U.S. Fleet Weather/Joint Typhoon Warning Center, COMNAV-MARIANAS, 23 November. MARC Collection.

Kotzebue, Otto von
1967a *A New Voyage round the World . . . 1823–26.* Biblioteca Australiana No. 21. Amsterdam: N. Israel; New York: Da Capo Press. (Facsimile reprint of original, 2 Vols., 1830, by Henry Colburn and Richard Bentley, London.)
1967b *A Voyage of Discovery into the South Sea . . . 1815–1818.* Biblioteca Australiana No. 17. Amsterdam: N. Israel; New York: Da Capo Press. (Facsimile reprint of original, 3 Vols., 1821, translation from the Russian by H. E. Lloyd, Longman, Hurst, et al., London.)

Kruger, Russell Carl
1981 Guam: Development of a Service-Oriented Economy. Ph.D. diss., American University. Facsimile No. 8118323, University Microfilms International, Ann Arbor, Mich.

Kurashina, Hiro, and Russell N. Clayshulte
1983 Site Formation Processes and Cultural Sequence at Tarague, Guam. Paper presented at the Fifteenth Pacific Science Congress, Dunedin, New Zealand. MARC Collection.

Kurashina, Hiro, Darlene Moore, Osamu Kataoka, Russell N. Clayshulte, and Erwin Ray
1981 *Pre- and Proto-historic Cultural Occurrences at Tarague, Guam.* Mangilao, Guam: MARC.

Lademan, Joseph U., Jr.
1969 The Gold Star and Guam: War in the Western Pacific 1941–42, A Personal History. Unpublished manuscript. Laguna Beach, Calif. MARC Collection.

Langdon, Robert A.
1984 *Where the Whalers Went.* Canberra: Pacific Manuscripts Bureau, Research School of Pacific Studies, Australian National University.

Lange, W. Harry, Jr.
1950 Life History and Feeding Habits of the Giant African Snail on Guam. *Pacific Science,* Vol. 9, No. 4, October, 323–335.

La Perouse, Jean F. G. de
1968 *A Voyage round the World.* Biblioteca Australiana No. 27. Amsterdam: N. Israel; New York: Da Capo Press. (Facsimile reprint of translation from the French of 1799 edition, 2 Vols., by A. Hamilton, London.)

(LCM) Library of Congress, Washington, D.C.
1678–1899 The Records of the Spanish Colonial Government in the Marianas Islands. 30 Vols.

Original documents and microfilm. Manuscript Division. Items 1–157. LC 78–55319.

Ledesma, Andrés de, SJ
1975 *Mission in the Marianas: An Account of Father Luis de Sanvitores and His Companions, 1669–1670 (Noticia de los Progressos de Nuestra Santa Fe en las Islas Marianas, Ilamadas antes de los Ladrones, written in 1672).* Translated by Ward Barrett. Minneapolis: University of Minnesota Press.

Ledesma, Juan M. H., SJ
1981 *The Cause of Beatification of Ven. Diego Luís de San Vitores, Apostle of the Marianas.* Manila and Agana: Sacred Congregation for the Causes of Saints Historical Section 94. Deposition *(Positio Historica)* on the life and martyrdom officially presented. Rome. Translated from the Spanish by Juan M. H. Ledesma, SJ. Tamuning: Guam Atlas Publications.

Le Gobien, Charles, SJ
1700 *Histoire des Isles Marianes, nouvellement converties à la Religion Chrétienne, et du martyre des premiers Apostres qui y ont prêché la foy.* Paris: Pepie. Translated in 1949 by Paul V. Daly, SJ, MARC, Guam; and published in the Guam Catholic weekly *Umatuna Si Yuus* (Agana), 26 July–20 December, 1964.

Leibowitz, Arnold H.
1989 *Defining Status: A Comprehensive Analysis of United States Territorial Relations.* Dordrecht: Martinus Nijhoff.

LeMay, Curtis, and MacKinlay Kantor
1965 *Mission with LeMay.* Garden City, N.Y.: Doubleday & Co.

Leslie, Robert C.
1889 *Life Aboard a British Privateer in the Time of Queen Anne, Being a Journal of Woodes Rogers, Master Mariner.* London: Chapman & Hull.

Lévesque, Rodrigue, ed.
1992 *History of Micronesia: A Collection of Documents.* Vols. 1, 2. Gatineau, Canada: Lévesque Publications.

Lodge, O. Robert, Major, U.S.M.C.
1954 *The Recapture of Guam.* U.S. Marine Corps Monograph Series, Historical Branch G-3 Division Headquarters, U.S. Marine Corps. 1984 ed. Fredericksburg, Tex.: Awani Press.

Lovelace, Doug
1946 War Aftermath Upsets Economy of Guamanians; Navy Food and Wages Replace Farm Pursuits of the Native. *Evening Star* (Washington, D.C.), 10 November, C1.

Lowe, Richard Barrett
1967 *Problems in Paradise: The View from Government House.* New York: Pageant Press.

Lubbock, Basil
1931 *Bully Hayes, South Sea Pirate.* Boston: Charles E. Lauriat Co.

Lütke, Frédéric
1971 *Voyage Autour du Monde 1826–1829.* Biblioteca Australiana Nos. 58, 59, 60. Amsterdam: N. Israel; New York: Da Capo Press. (Facsimile reprints of translation into the French from Russian by F. Boyé of 1835–1836 eds. 3 Vols., by Firmin Didot Frères, Paris.)

Mabini, Apolinario
1965 *The Letters of Apolinario Mabini.* Manila: National Heroes Commission, Office of the President, Republic of the Philippines.

Mafra, Ginés de
1921 Log on the *Trinidad,* 1521. Manuscript in National Museum, Madrid.) In *Descripción de los reinos, costas puertos y islas que hay desde el Cabo de Buena Esperanza hasta los Leguios, por Fernando de Magallanes,* ed. Antonio Blásquez y Delgado-Aquilera. Madrid: La Real Sociedad Geográfica.

Maga, Timothy
1988 *Defending Paradise: The United States and Guam, 1898–1950.* New York: Garland Publishing.

Maggs Bros., trans.
1923 *Bibliotheca Americana et Philippina.* Pt. 3, Catalogue No. 442. London: Maggs Bros.
1927 *Australia and the South Seas,* Catalogue No. 491. London: Maggs Bros.

MAGIC intercepts, Summaries, NA, RG 457, 459.
1978 *The Magic Background of Pearl Harbor* (A-126). 8 Vols. U.S. Department of Defense. Washington, D.C.: U.S. Government Printing Office.

Mahan, Alfred Thayer
1912 Memorandum on the Fortification of Guam, October 15. General Board, Navy Department, Subject File, Studies 422, MARC Files, Naval Operational Archives AR 146–79.

1970 *Lessons of the War with Spain, and Other Arti-cles.* Freeport, N.Y.: Books for Libraries Press.

Malaspina, Alejandro, and José F. Bustamante
1984 *Viaje científico y político a la América Meridi-onal, a las Costas del Mar Pacífico y a las Islas Marianas y Filipinas, verificado en los años de 1789, 90, 91, 92, 93 y 94 a bordo de las corbe-tas Descubierta y Atrevida de la Marina Real . . . Diario de viaje de Alejandro Malaspina.* Madrid: El Museo Universal.

Marche, Antoine-Alfred
1982 *The Mariana Islands.* Translated from the French by Sylvia E. Cheng from *Nouvelles archives des missions scientifiques et littéraires.* Vol. 1, *Nouvelle Série.* Paris, 1889. Mangilao, Guam: MARC.

Martin, Harold
1947 Heart Trouble in Paradise. *Saturday Evening Post,* 1, November, 30, 100–102, 105–106.

Mathers, William M., Henry S. Parker III, and Kathleen A. Copus, eds.
1990 *Archaeological Report, the Recovery of the Manila Galleon, Nuestra Señora de la Con-cepción.* Sutton, Vt.: Pacific Sea Resources.

Matson, E. A.
1991 Water Chemistry and Hydrology of the "Blood of Sanvitores," a Micronesian Red Tide. *Micro-nesica,* Vol. 24, No. 1, June, 95–108.

McClurkan, Carolyn
1987 Dossier Compiled upon the Occasion of the Royal Funeral Rites for Felipe V and the Proclamation of the Coronation of Fernando VI in the City of Agana, 1747. Working Paper No. 49. Mangilao, Guam: MARC. Translated from the Spanish from AHPA E-1-C-6; E-1-C-5b; E-1-C-5r.

McCoid, M. J.
1991 Brown Tree Snake *(Boiga irregularis)* on Guam: A Worst Case Scenario of an Introduced Preda-tor. *Micronesica,* Supplement No. 3, June, 63–69.

McGrath, Thomas B., SJ
1986 Whalers in the Marianas. *Journal of Pacific History,* Vol. 21, No. 2, January, 104–109.

McHenry, Donald F.
1975 *Micronesia: Trust Betrayed.* Washington, D.C.: Carnegie Endowment for International Peace.

McMillin, George J.
1945 Memorandum, 11 September 1945, Surrender of Guam to Japanese, to Secretary of the Navy.

In NA, RG 38, copy in NCWR 79–81, Reel No. 10, Folder I-A. MARC Working Paper No. 44. Also in *Guam Recorder,* 2d Ser., Vol. 2, Nos. 2–3, April–September 1972, 9–25 (with missing pages in appendix).

Memoria sobre las Yslas Marianas formada en el Ministe-rio de Hacienda por Real Order de 14 de Diciembre de 1828.
1829 AHN, *Filipinas,* 5853. Copy of July 1859 in the Biblioteca de la Real Academia de la Historia, Madrid. Portions translated by Marjorie G. Driver. A Report on the Mariana Islands by Alexandro Parreño, Madrid, 1828. *Journal of the Pacific Society,* No. 51 (Vol. 14, No. 2), July 1991 (27)–132–(39)–120.

Meyers, Max, Lt. Col., U.S.M.C., ed.
1947 *Ours to Hold High: The History of the 77th Division in World War II.* Washington, D.C.: Infantry Journal Press.

Military Reports, No. 25
1945 The Defense of Guam: The Will to Lose Hard. (No author given.) January, File 228.03 HRC, Geor O Guam. Washington, D.C.: Office of the Chief of the U.S. Army, History. Copy in library, War in the Pacific National Historical Park, Asan, Guam.

Miller, Edward S.
1991 *War Plan Orange.* Annapolis, Md.: Naval Insti-tute Press.

Miyagi, Dale S.
1975 Spanish Micronesia and the Philippine Exposi-tion of 1887. *Guam Recorder,* 2d Ser., Vol. 5, No. 2, 31–43.

Monmaney, Terence
1990 Annals of Science: This Obscure Malady. *New Yorker,* 29 October, 85–113.

Moore, Darlene
1983 Measuring Change in Marianas Pottery: The Sequence of Pottery Production at Tarague. M.A. thesis, University of Guam.

Moore, Philip H., and Richard D. Krizman
1981 *Field and Garden Plants of Guam.* Cooperative Extension Service, College of Agriculture and Life Sciences, University of Guam. Mangilao, Guam: University of Guam.

Morales, Luís de, SJ
1689–1690 An Account of Events That Took Place in the Marianas during the Year Covering the Early Part of 1684 to the First Part of May

1685. Translated by Domingo Abella. *Vignettes of Philippines-Marianas Colonial History.* Manila: IAHA, 1962.

1737 *Historia de las Islas Marianas.* Archivo Histórico de la Provincia de Aragón, fol. 13, E-I-C 5(c). MARC Collection.

Morga, Antonio de
1971 *Sucesos de las Islas Filipinas* (1609). Hakluyt Society Works, 2d Ser. Translated by J. S. Cummins. Cambridge: Hakluyt Society. Also in W. E. Retana, ed., *Sucesos de las Islas Filipinas.* Madrid, 1909.

Morgan, William N.
1988 *Prehistoric Architecture in Micronesia.* Austin: University of Texas Press.

Morris, Roger
1987 *Pacific Sail: Four Centuries of Western Ships in the Pacific.* Southampton: Ashford Press.

Munoz, Faye Untalan
1979 An Exploratory Study of Island Migration: Chamorros of Guam. Ph.D. diss., University of California, Los Angeles. Facsimile No. 7915672, University Microfilms International, Ann Arbor, Mich.

Murillo Velarde, Pedro, SJ
1749 *Historia de la província de Philipinas de la Compañía de Jesús: Segunda Parte.* Manila: Imprenta de la Compañía de Jesús por Nicolas de la Cruz Bagay. Bk. 4, pp. 288–298, translated by Sister Felicia E Plaza. Working Paper No. 51. Mangilao, Guam: MARC, 1987.

Myers, John T.
1931 Capture of Guam Recalled by Brigadier General John T. Myers, U.S.M.C. *Guam Recorder,* Vol. 8, No. 7, September, 366.
1933 Extract from Journal Kept on Board U.S.S. Charleston, June 19–22, 1898. *Guam Recorder,* Vol. 9, No. 11, February, 187.

(NA, RG) National Archives, Record Groups, Washington, D.C. U.S. Navy, General Records of the Navy Department, General Correspondence.
1897–1915 RG 80, 9351, and Boxes 383, 384, 400, 401, 482, 484, 486, 489.
1926–1940 RG 45, 9345, and EG54/p1 to EG55/L, Box 2047. RG 59, Box 5009.

Nakayama, Masao, and Frederick L. Ramp
1974 Micronesian Navigation, Island Empires and Traditional Concepts of Ownership of the Sea.

Study for the Joint Committee on the Law of the Sea Conference, Fifth Congress of Micronesia, Saipan, Mariana Islands, 14 January 1974. MARC Collection.

Navarette, Martín Fernández de, ed.
1971 *Colección de Documentos y manuscriptos compilados por Fernández de Navarrete.* Vols. 3, 16. Museo Naval de Madrid. Reprint by Kraus-Thomson Organization, Nendeln, Liechtenstein.

Navy News (became *Guam News* in 1947)
1945–1947 Agana: U.S. Military Government of Guam.

NCWR 79–81, NA, RGs 38 and 127, excerpts from General Correspondence of the secretary of the navy and other documents.
1898–1950 Indexed in Working Paper No. 44. Mangilao, Guam: MARC.

Nelson, Evelyn Gibson, and Frederick J. Nelson
1992 *The Island of Guam: Description and History from a 1934 Perspective.* Edited by Mary S. McCutcheon from 1940 manuscript. Washington, D.C.: Ana Publications.

Nelson, Frederick J., Captain, U.S.N.
1952 Lieutenant William E. Safford—Guam's First Lieutenant Governor. *U.S. Naval Institute Proceedings,* Vol. 78, No. 8, 550–561.

Nelson, Joan
1965 F. B. Leon Guerrero, Machete Scientist, Alias Lawyer without Portfolio. *Guam Times Weekly,* 17 April, 9–11.

Noone, Martin J., S.S.C.
1986 *General History of the Philippines. Pt. 1, Vol. 1, The Discovery and Conquest of the Philippines (1521–1581).* Manila: Historical Conservation Society.

Olano y Urteaga, Miguel Angel de
1949 *Diary of a Bishop.* Manila: University of Santo Tomas Press.

Olcott, Charles Sumner
1916 *The Life of William McKinley.* Vol. 1, Boston: Houghton Mifflin.

O'Leary, James B.
1941 Diary. Personal Papers Collection, PC102, Marine Corps Historical Center, Washington, D.C.

Olive y García, Francisco
1984 *The Mariana Islands 1884–1887: Random Notes of Governor Francisco Olive y Garcia.*

Translated from the Spanish by Marjorie G. Driver. Mangilao, Guam: MARC.

Operation Newlife, After Action Report, Guam, 1975
   1976 Guam: Commander in Chief Pacific Representative, Guam and the Trust Territory of the Pacific Islands (Rear Admiral K. V. Carroll). 003100 Ser. 487, 3 March.

OSS R & A 744
   1942 Guam: A Social-Political-Economic Survey. (Declassified from Confidential.) Washington, D.C.: Office of Strategic Services, National Archives, Microfiche M1221 MF-1-1, 17 June.

Overall Economic Development Plan, Guam, U.S.A., 1977
   1977 Agana, Guam: Bureau of Planning, June.

Oviedo y Valdés, Gonzalo Fernández de
   1855 *Historia general y natural de las Indias, islas y tierra firme del Mar Océano* (1557 in manuscript). 4 Vols. Madrid: RAH.

Owings, Kathleen R. W., ed.
   1981 *The War Years on Guam: Narratives of the Chamorro Experience*. 2 Vols. Miscellaneous Publication No. 5. Mangilao, Guam: MARC.

Pages, Pierre Marie François de
   1791 *Travels round the World in the Years 1767–71*. London.

Palomo, Tony [Antonio M.]
   1984 *An Island in Agony*. Agana, Guam: privately published.
   1985 Tragic Legacy of Westernization. *Islander, Pacific Daily News* (Agana, Guam), 10 March.

(PDN) *Pacific Daily News*
   1970– Agana, Guam.

Peattie, Mark R.
   1988 *Nan'yō: The Rise and Fall of the Japanese in Micronesia, 1885–1945*. Honolulu: University of Hawai'i Press.

Perry, R., ed.
   1984 *Key Environments, Galapagos*. Exeter: Pergamon Press.

Piccigallo, Philip R.
   1979 *The Japanese on Trial: Allied War Crimes Operations in the East 1945–1951*. Austin: University of Texas Press.

Pigafetta, Antonio
   1969 *Magellan's Voyage: A Narrative Account of the First Circumnavigation*. Translated and edited by R. A. Skelton. 2 Vols. New Haven, Conn.: Yale University Press.

Pimental, Juan Antonio
   1709 *Carta No. 9 en la que da cuenta de haber tomado posesión de aquel gobierno.* . . . Agana, Guam, 24 November. Documentos Relativos a la Micronesia, AGI, Ultramar, 561, Vol. 2, 210–220. MARC typescript.

Pineda y Ramírez, Antonio de
   1792 *The Guam Diary of Antonio de Pineda y Ramírez, February 1792*. Translated by Víctor F. Mallada; edited by Marjorie G. Driver. Mangilao, Guam: MARC, 1990.

Plaza, Felicia, M.M.B.
   1971 Origin of the Word Chamorro. *Guam Recorder,* 2d Ser., Vol. 1, No. 1, 4–5. Guam: MARC.

(PNA) Philippine National Archives
   1718–1899 Marianas Collection of Documents 1718–1898 (in Spanish), from the Ateneo de Manila University, 1973, in 29 bundles collected in 58 volumes. MARC Collection.

Pollock, N. J.
   1983 The Early Use of Rice in Guam: The Evidence from the Historical Records. *Journal of the Polynesian Society,* Vol. 92, 509–520.

Pomeroy, Earl S.
   1951 *Pacific Outpost: American Strategy in Guam and Micronesia*. Stanford, Calif.: Stanford University Press.

Portusach, Frank
   1917 History of the Capture of Guam by the United States Man-of-War *Charleston* and Its Transport. *United States Naval Institute Proceedings,* Vol. 43, April, 707–718.

Pozuelo Mascaraque, Belén
   1989 El Final de la presencia Española en las islas Marianas (1898–1899). In *España y el Pacífico,* ed. Florentino Rodao. Madrid: Agencia Española de Cooperación Internacional & Asociación Española de Estudios del Pacifico.

Prévost d'Exiles, Abbé Antoine François, et al.
   1746–1760 *Histoire generale des voyages*, etc. 20 Vols. Paris & The Hague.

Purchas, Samuel
   1905 *Hakluytus Posthumus, or Purchas His Pilgrimes* (1625). Vols. 2, 3. Glasgow: James MacLehose & Sons.

Quirino, Carlos
   1988 *Philippine Cartography (1320–1899)*. Reprint of 1959 ed. with introduction by R. A. Skelton. Amsterdam: N. Israel/New York: Da Capo Press.

Quiroga y Losada, Joseph de
   1696 (Anonymous, attributed to Quiroga.) *Relación de la conquista y restauración de las Islas Marianas,* 1 April, ARSI, Filipinas, 12, 306–307, 308–311.
   1720 Letter of May 26, AGI, *Filipinas 95,* 18–33. Also in Documentos Relativos a la Micronesia, AGI, *Ultramar, 562,* 18–33, and 561, Vol. 5, *Expediente* 17. Translated by Marjorie Driver in the *Journal of Pacific History,* Vol. 27, No. 1, June 1992, 98–106.

Ralli, Pandia
   1899 Campaigning in the Philippines with Co. I of the First California Volunteers. *Overland Monthly,* 30, February.

Ramirez, Anthony J. H.
   1983 *La Sangri Yama* (The Blood Calls): A Family Portrait. *Guam Tribune Weekender Panorama* (Agana), 24 December 1982–19 October 1984. Series of forty articles on genealogies of Guamanian families.

Raynal, Abbé Guillaume
   1778 *Histoire philosophique et politique des establissements et du commerce des Européens dans les deux Indes.* 7 Vols. Paris: Lacombe. Translated by J. O. Justamond, F.R.S., as *A Philosophical and Political History of the Settlements and Trades of the Europeans in the East and West Indies.* London: A. Strahan and T. Cadell, 1788. Portion on the Marianas published in the *Guam Recorder,* Vol. 7, No. 5, August 1930, 88–90, 94–95.

Reinman, Fred M.
   1977 *An Archeological Survey and Preliminary Test Excavations on the Island of Guam, Mariana Islands, 1965–66.* Mangilao, Guam: MARC.

Repetti, William Charles, SJ
   1940 A Supplementary Note to the First History of Guam. *Guam Recorder,* Vol. 17, No. 3, June, 99.
   1941 A Letter from Saipan in 1684. *Guam Recorder,* Vol. 17, No. 12, March, 494–496, 520–521.
   1946 The Beginnings of Catholicity in the Mariana Islands. *Catholic Historical Review,* Vol. 31, No. 4, January, 431–437.

Report on Post-war Land Takings on Guam.
   1972 Special Committee on Federal Problems, Eleventh Guam Legislature, Agana, September.

Riquel, Hernando
   1565 Notarial Attestation of the Taking of Possession of the Ladrones Island (26 January). Translated by Domingo Abella. Pacific Profile, No. 1, January 1965, 18–20, 34–36. Original in *Colección de documentos inéditos . . . de Ultramar (1886),* Vol. 3, 79–81.

Risco, Alberto, SJ
   1935 *Heroes of the Catholic Apostolate: The Apostle of the Mariana Islands, Diego Luis de San Vitores, of the Company of Jesus.* Bilbao: College of Berriz, Cultura Misional. (References to this book are to an unpublished 1970 English translation by MARC, translator unnamed.)
   1970 *The Apostle of the Marianas: the Life, Labors and Martyrdom of Ven. Diego Luís de Sanvitores, 1627–1672 (1935).* Translated by Juan M. H. Ledesma, SJ; edited by Msg. Oscar L. Calvo. Agana, Guam: Diocese of Agana.

Robinson, Edward Van Dyke
   1898 The Caroline Islands and the Terms of Peace. *Independent,* Vol. 50, 13 October, 1046–1048.

Rochon, Abbé Alexis Marie de, ed.
   1891 *Crozet's Voyage to Tasmania, New Zealand, the Ladrone Islands, and the Philippines in the Years 1771–1772.* Translated by H. Ling Roth. London: Truslove & Shirley. (From *Nouveau Voyage á la Mer du Sud Commencé sous les Ordres de M. Marion.* Paris, 1783.)

Rogers, Captain Woodes
   1969 *A Cruising Voyage Round the World.* Biblioteca Australiana No. 63. Amsterdam: N. Israel; New York: Da Capo Press. (Facsimile reprint of original 1712 ed. by A. Bell & B. Lintot, London.)

Rogers, Robert F.
   1984 *Guam's Search for Commonwealth Status.* Educational Series No. 4. Mangilao, Guam: MARC.
   1986 *The Guam Commission on Self-Determination.* Educational Series No. 5. Mangilao, Guam: MARC.
   1988a *Guam's Commonwealth Effort.* Educational Series No. 8. Mangilao, Guam: MARC.
   1988b Guam's Quest for Political Identity. *Pacific Studies,* Vol. 12, No. 1, November, 49–69.
   1992 Commonwealth: Will It Float? *Perspective, Pacific Sunday News,* 17 May, 20.

Rogers, Robert F., and Dirk Anthony Ballendorf
   1989 Magellan's Landfall in the Marianas. *Journal of Pacific History,* Vol. 24, No. 2, October,

193–208. Spanish translation by José Luis Porras in *Revista Española del Pacifico, Asociación de Estudios del Pacifico*, No. 2, Año II–1992.

Rogers, Robert F., Don C. Warner, and H. D. Sablan
1980 *A Reassessment of Guam's Political Relationship with the United States.* Prepared for the Fifteenth Guam Legislature. Agana, Guam: Venture Development Management Resources.

Roosevelt, Theodore
n.d. Papers. Library of Congress, Washington, D.C.

Roscoe, Theodore
1949 *United States Submarine Operations in World War II.* Annapolis, Md.: U.S. Naval Institute.

Sablan, Joaquin Flores
1990 *My Mental Odyssey.* Poplar Bluff, Mo.: Stinson Press.

Sádaba del Carmen, Francisco, M.R.P.
1906 *Catálogo de los Religiosos Agustinos . . . de Filipinas.* Madrid: Imprenta del Asilo de Huérfanos del Sagrado Corazón de Jesus.

Safford, William Edwin
1899 *The Marianas Islands, Notes Compiled. . . .* Copied from original handwritten notes at Tanglewood, Chillicothe, Ohio. Copies at MARC and Library of Congress, Manuscript Division. Published in *Guam Recorder,* Vol. 18, November 1940–November 1941. (References in this book are to the 1899 MARC copy.)
1901 A Year on the Island of Guam. (Extracts from the notebook of a naturalist on the island of Guam.) Unpublished. MARC typescript copy. Published in *Guam Recorder,* Vol. 9, October 1932–Vol. 12, January 1936; and in 1910 by H. L. McQueen, Washington, D.C. (References in this book are to the MARC typescript.)
1905 *The Useful Plants of the Island of Guam.* Contributions from the U.S. National Herbarium, Vol. 9. Washington, D.C.: U.S. Government Printing Office.

Sahlins, Marshall D.
1972 *Stone Age Economics.* Chicago: Aldine Atherton.

San Augustín, Gaspar de, O.S.A.
1975 *Conquista de las Islas del Poniente llamadas Filipinas (1565–1615).* Biblioteca "Missionalia Hispánica," Vol. 18. Madrid: C.S.I.C. (Edition of 1698 original.)

Sanchez, Adrian C.
1990 *The Chamorro Brown Steward.* Tamuning, Guam: Star Press.

Sanchez, Pedro C.
1983 *Guam 1941–1945: Wartime Occupation and Liberation.* Tamuning, Guam: Sanchez Publishing House.
1989 *Guahan: Guam: The History of Our Island.* Agana, Guam: Sanchez Publishing House.

Sánchez y Zayas, Eugenio
1865–1866 Voyage of the Spanish Corvette "Narvaez" from Manila to the Mariana Islands. Translated from the Spanish. *Nautical Magazine and Naval Chronicle* (London), Vols. 34, 35.

San Vitores, Diego Luís de, SJ
1660–1672 Writings (letters, reports, memorials, etc.). The most complete compilation is Ledesma (1981).

Satoh, Kazumasa
1978 *Guamu no chi to suna* (Blood and sands of Guam). Translated from the Japanese by Iris K. Tanimoto-Spade. Unpublished manuscript. MARC Collection.

Schmookler, Andrew Bard
1984 *The Parable of the Tribes.* Berkeley and Los Angeles: University of California Press.

Schroeder, Seaton
1926 Admiral Seaton Schroeder's Reminiscences of His Tour of Duty as Governor of Guam. *Guam Recorder,* Vol. 3, No. 1, April, 7–21; Vol. 3, No. 2, May, 36–37.

Schurz, William Lytle
1959 *The Manila Galleon.* New York: E. P. Dutton & Co.

Seager, Robert, II
1977 *Alfred Thayer Mahan: The Man and His Letters.* Annapolis, Md.: Naval Institute Press.

Searjeantson, S. W., D. P. Ryan, and A. R. Thompson
1982 The Colonization of the Pacific: The Story according to Human Leukocyte Antigens. *American Journal of Human Genetics,* No. 34, 904–918.

Selby, E. C., Lt. J.G., U.S.N.
n.d. From an Acorn . . . The Twenty-Five Year History of the Naval Air Station, Agana, Guam (1942–1969). Unpublished manuscript. MARC Collection.

Shapiro, Mark R.
    1983 *The House That Jacquie Built.* Agana, Guam:
         Mark Shapiro.
Shaw, Henry, Bernard Nalty, and Edwin Turnbladh
    1966 *History of U.S. Marine Corps Operations in
         World War II.* Vol. 3, *Central Pacific Drive.*
         Washington, D.C.: Marine Corps Historical
         Center.
Shell, Richard, and J. B. Neyret, SM
    1987 Early Accounts of the Chamorro Flying Proa.
         Mariner's Mirror (National Maritime Museum,
         London), Vol. 73, No. 1, February, 45–49.
Sixto Rodríguez, José
    1899 Asunto: Events Which Occurred on the Mariana
         Islands on the 21st and 22nd Days of June,
         1898, upon the Arrival of the North American
         War Cruiser Charleston. AHN *Filipinas,* 5359,
         1–18. Translated from the Spanish by Caroline
         McClurkan, 1985. Unpublished document.
         MARC Collection.
Souder, Paul B.
    1965 The Problem of Feeding, Clothing and Housing
         18,000 War Refugees. *Pacific Profile,* Vol. 3,
         No. 6, July, 24–27.
    1978 Heritage: A Genealogy of the Souder-Torres and
         Affiliated Families throughout the Nineteenth
         and Twentieth Centuries. Unpublished manu-
         script. MARC Collection.
    1981 Familian Chamorro: A Genealogy of Resident
         Families on Guam during the Nineteenth and
         Twentieth Centuries. Unpublished manuscript.
         MARC Collection.
    1983a The Boom and the Bust Years 1971–1982.
         Guam Tribune Weekender Panorama (Agana),
         Vol. 1, No. 50, 9 September; No. 51, 16
         September.
    1983b Fortress—Guam? Guam's Postwar Military
         Government, Naval Government and Civilian
         Government. *Guam Tribune Weekender Pan-
         orama* (Agana). Vol. 1, No. 32, 6 May; No. 33,
         13 May; No. 34, 20 May; No. 35, 27 May; No.
         36, 3 June; No. 38, 17 June; No. 39, 24 June.
    1987 Guam: Land Tenure in a Fortress. In *Land Ten-
         ure in the Pacific.* 3d ed. Suva: University of the
         South Pacific.
Spate, O. H. K.
    1979 *The Spanish Lake.* Vol. 1 of *The Pacific since
         Magellan.* Canberra: Australian National Uni-
         versity Press.

    1988 *Paradise Found and Lost.* Vol. 3 of *The Pacific
         since Magellan.* Minneapolis: University of
         Minnesota Press.
Spicer, Donald, Colonel, U.S.M.C.
    1946 Memorandum for MG A. H. Turnage, U.S.M.C.,
         11 July. Subj: Recognition of the Action at
         Guam, December 8–10, 1941. CNH.
Spoehr, Alexander
    1954 *Saipan: The Ethnology of a War-Devastated
         Island. Fieldiana: Anthropology,* Vol. 41. Chi-
         cago: Chicago Natural History Museum.
    1957 *Marianas Prehistory: Archaeological Survey and
         Excavations on Saipan, Tinian, and Rota. Field-
         iana: Anthropology,* Vol. 48. Chicago: Natural
         History Museum.
    1978 Conquest Culture and Colonial Culture in the
         Marianas during the Spanish Period. In *The
         Changing Pacific: Essays in Honour of H. E.
         Maude,* ed. Niel Gunson. Melbourne: Oxford
         University Press.
Statistical Abstract Guam
    1976– (Annual.) Agana: Department of Commerce,
         Government of Guam.
Stevens, Russell L.
    1956 *Guam, U.S.A.: Birth of a Territory.* 2d rev. ed.
         Honolulu: Tongg Publishing Co.
Stinnett, Robert B.
    1991 *George Bush: His World War II Years.* Mis-
         soula, Mont.: Pictoral Histories Publishing Co.
Strategic Air Command
    1982 *The Development of the Strategic Air Com-
         mand, 1946–1980.* Omaha: Office of the Histo-
         rian, Strategic Air Command.
Sullivan, Julius, O.F.M. Cap.
    1957 *The Phoenix Rises: A Mission History of Guam.*
         New York: Seraphic Mass Association.
Super Typhoon Pamela After-Action Report.
    1976 Commander, U.S. Naval Forces Marianas. Guam.
Taitano, Carlos P.
    1983 Guam: The Struggle for Civil and Political
         Rights. In *Politics in Micronesia.* Suva: Univer-
         sity of the South Pacific.
Takeda, Lt. Col. Hideyuki
    1946 The outline of the Japanese Defense Plan and
         Battles of Guam Island. Accession No. 65A-
         4556, Box 73, File Folder E1-2, Marine Corps
         Historical Center, Washington, D.C.
    1952 Letter of January 24 to BG J. C. McQueen,
         Guam, Monograph and Comment. Accession

No. 65A-4556, Box 73, File Folder C7-1, Marine Corps Historical Center, Washington, D.C. Also in MARC, NCWR 79–81, Reel 32, Folder I, from NA, RG 127.

Tansill, William R.
1951 *Guam and Its Administration.* Legislative Reference Service, Public Affairs Bulletin No. 95. Washington, D.C.: Library of Congress.

Thomas, Gordon, and Max Morgan Witts
1978 *Enola Gay.* New York: Pocket Books.

Thompson, Laura Maud
1940 The Function of Latte in the Marianas. *Journal of the Polynesian Society,* Vol. 49, 447–465.

1945 *The Native Culture of the Marianas Islands.* Bulletin No. 185. Honolulu: Bernice P. Bishop Museum.

1969 *Guam and Its People: A Study of Cultural Change and Colonial Education.* Facsimile by University Microfilms, Ann Arbor, Mich., of 1947 Princeton ed. (1st ed. Honolulu: American Council Institute of Pacific Relations, 1941; 2d ed., rev. Princeton, N.J.: Princeton University Press, 1947; 3d ed. New York: Greenwood Press, 1969).

1991 *Beyond the Dream: A Search for Meaning.* Monograph Series No. 2. Mangilao, Guam: MARC.

Topping, Donald M., Pedro M. Ogo, and Bernadita C. Dungca
1975 *Chamorro-English Dictionary.* Honolulu: The University Press of Hawai'i.

Topping, Donald M., with the assistance of Bernadita C. Dungca
1973 *Chamorro Reference Grammar.* Honolulu: The University Press of Hawai'i.

Tracey, Joshua I., et al.
1964 *General Geology of Guam.* Washington, D.C.: U.S. Government Printing Office.

Tweed, George R., and Blake Clark
1945 *Robinson Crusoe, USN: The Adventures of George Tweed, RM 1/C, U.S.N. on Jap-Held Guam.* New York: Whittlesey House, McGraw-Hill Book Co.

Umatuna Si Yuus
1946– Agana, Guam: Diocese of Guam (Weekly newspaper, later the *Pacific Voice.*)

Uncilla y Arroita Jáuregui, Fermín de, O.S.A.
1907 *Urdaneta y la conquista de Filipinas.* San Sebastián, Impr. de la Província.

Underwood, Jane H.
1976 The Native Origins of the Neo-Chamorros of the Mariana Islands. *Micronesica* (University of Guam), Vol. 12, No. 2, 203–209.

United Nations
1960 General Assembly Resolution 1541. 15 UN GAOR, Supp. (No. 16), UN Doc. A/4684.

1979 General Assembly. *Report of the United Nations Visiting Mission to Guam.* 5 October. UN Doc. A/AC. 109/L. 1345.

U.S. Department of the Interior
1992 *A Report on the State of the Islands.* Washington, D.C.: Office of Territorial and International Affairs, June.

U.S. House of Representatives
1902 *Petition Relating to Permanent Government of the Island of Guam.* Document No. 419. 57th Cong., 1st Sess. H. Doc. 419. Washington, D.C.: U.S. Government Printing Office.

1968 90th Cong., 2d Sess. H. Rep. 1521. Washington, D.C.: U.S. Government Printing Office.

1979 *Report on the Use of Temporary Alien Labor in Guam.* Committee on the Judiciary. 95th Cong., 2d Sess. Washington, D.C.: U.S. Government Printing Office.

1989 *Guam Commonwealth: Hearing before the Subcommittee on Insular and International Affairs, etc.* One Hundred First Congress, First Session, on H.R. 98. Guam Commonwealth Act Hearing held in Honolulu, HI., December 12, 1989. Washington D.C.: U.S. Government Printing Office.

U.S. Marine Corps, Historical Files
1899–1941 Various original documents concerning Guam, unnumbered folders, Marine Corps Museum, Navy Yard, Washington, D.C.

1958 The U.S. Marine Corps on Guam, 1898–1941. MS AO 3D-mrs, 2 Jul. (no author given), in the Marine Historical Files on Guam, Center for Naval History, Naval Yard, Washington, D.C.

U.S. Naval Administration Guam. *Monthly Reports* and *Quarterly Reports*
1946–1950 Agana: Naval Government of Guam. MARC Collection.

U.S. Navy Department
1946–1949 Information on Guam Transmitted by the United States to the Secretary-General of the United Nations Pursuant to Article 73(e) of the Charter. Washington, D.C.: Department of the

Navy. Unpublished reports, July 1946, June
  1947, 1948, 1949 (OpNav-P22-100 A, C, G).
U.S. Navy Report on Guam, 1948–1950
  1951 Washington, D.C.: U.S. Government Printing
         Office.
U.S. Senate
  1899 55th Cong., 3d Sess. S. Doc. 62. Washington,
         D.C.: U.S. Government Printing Office.
  1903 Joseph B. Foraker Introducing S. 6599, a Bill to
         Provide a Government for the Island of Guam.
         Congressional Record, Vol. 36. 57th Cong., 2d
         Sess., 15 December 1902. Washington, D.C.:
         U.S. Government Printing Office.
  1941 *Hearings . . . Fourth Supplemental National
         Defense Appropriation Bill for 1941.* Senate
         Committee on Appropriations, Subcommittee,
         3–4 March 1941. Washington, D.C.: U.S.
         Government Printing Office.
  1945 *Hearing on S. 1466, A Bill Authorizing Rehabil-
         itation on the Island of Guam.* Committee on
         Naval Affairs. 79th Cong., 1st Sess., 9, 11
         October 1945. Washington, D.C.: U.S. Govern-
         ment Printing Office.
  1947 Memorial of Guam Legislature Relative to
         Political Status of Guam. *Congressional
         Record,* Vol. 93. 80th Cong., 1st Sess., 2 May
         1947. Washington, D.C.: U.S. Government
         Printing Office.
  1950 *Hearings . . . on Legislation "Providing Civil
         Government for Guam," April 19, 1950.* S.
         Rep. 2109, to accompany H.R. 7273. 81st
         Cong., 2d Sess., 20 July. Washington, D.C.: U.S.
         Government Printing Office.
U.S. Statutes-at-Large . . .
  1875– Washington, D.C.: U.S. Government Printing
         Office.
Van Cleve, Ruth
  1974 *The Office of Territorial Affairs.* New York:
         Praeger Publishers.
Van Peenen, Mavis Warner
  1974 *Chamorro Legends on the Island of Guam.*
         Publication No. 4. Mangilao, Guam: MARC.
Villalobos, Francisco Ramón
  1833 *Geographic, Military and Political Descrip-
         tion of the Island of Guam.* Translated from
         the Spanish by Sister Felicia Plaza. Working
         Paper No. 8. Mangilao, Guam: MARC,
         1979.

Vitoria, Francisco de
  1557 *De potestate civili.* Lyon: Jacobo Boyero y luego.
         (Excerpts in Gerhard von Glahn. *Law among
         Nations.* 4th ed. New York: Macmillan Publish-
         ing Co., 1981.)
Walker, Leslie W.
  1945 Guam's Seizure by the United States in 1898.
         Pacific Historical Review, Vol. 14, March,
         1–12.
Wallis, Helen M.
  1954 *The Exploration of the South Sea, 1519 to
         1644.* Ph.D. diss., Oxford University. MARC
         Collection.
Walter, Richard
  1928 *Anson's Voyage Round the World.* London:
         Martin Hopkinson.
Ward, Herbert T.
  1970 *Flight of the Cormoran.* New York: Vantage
         Press.
Webb, James H., Jr.
  1974 *Micronesia and U.S. Pacific Strategy: A
         Blueprint for the 1980s.* New York: Praeger
         Publishers.
Whaley, Floyd
  1992 Survivors Recall Massacre. *Pacific Sunday
         News,* 22 March.
Wheeler, Brigadier General Joseph, U.S.A.
  1900 Report on the Island of Guam. No. 28, Docu-
         ment No. 123, War Department, Adjutant
         General's Office, June 1900. Washington, D.C.:
         U.S. Government Printing Office.
White, Douglas
  1900 The Capture of the Island of Guam: The True
         Story. *Overland Monthly,* Vol. 35, March, 225–
         233.
Whitney, Harry Payne
  1955 An Analysis of the Design of the Major Sea-
         Going Craft of Oceania. M.A. thesis, University
         of Pennsylvania. MARC Collection.
Won Pat, Antonio B.
  1972 *Annual Report of Guam's Representative in
         Washington to the People of Guam and the
         Guam Legislature.* Washington, D.C., June.
         MARC Collection.
Zenor, M. Dean
  1949 United States Naval Government and Adminis-
         tration of Guam. Ph.D. diss., University of
         Iowa. MARC Collection.

Index